THE WILEY SERIES ON
NET-ENHANCED ORGANIZATIONS
Transforming the Organization
Through Internet Technologies

RICHARD T. WATSON

Series Editor

E-BUSINESS TECHNOLOGIES
Supporting the Net-Enhanced Organization

CRAIG VAN SLYKE
University of Central Florida

FRANCE BÉLANGER
Virginia Polytechnic Institute and State University

JOHN WILEY & SONS, INC.

Acquisitions Editor   *Beth Lang Golub*
Assistant Editor   *Lorraina Raccuia*
Marketing Manager   *Gitti Lindner*
Managing Editor   *Lari Bishop*
Associate Production Manager   *Kelly Tavares*
Production Editor   *Sarah Wolfman-Robichaud*
Photo Researcher   *Sara Wight*
Illustration Editor   *Jennifer Fisher*
Cover Design   *Jennifer Fisher*
Cover Image   *G. Retherford / Photo Researchers*

This book was set in *Times* and printed by *R.R. Donnelley & Sons*. The cover was printed by *Lehigh Press Lithographers*.

ISBN: 0471-393924

Printed in the United States of America

10 9 8 7 6 5 4 3 2 1

To my wonderful and very patient wife, Debbie,
for her support and encouragement,
and to my parents, Mary and Chet,
for instilling in their children a love of learning.
CVS

To my best friend and husband, Pierre,
for his patience and encouragement;
and to my family and friends, for believing in me.
FB

BRIEF CONTENTS

CONTENTS

FOREWORD

Dear Reader,

We live in a world of ubiquitous high bandwidth networks and mobile Internet connections. New technologies, new strategies, and new terminologies are rapidly developing in the field of e-business.

NEO, Wiley's Series on Net-Enhanced Organizations: Transforming the Organization through Internet Technologies, will provide you with the resources you need to respond to the latest changes and trends in the field. The books in this series will help you to develop a comprehensive understanding of e-business and its technological underpinnings, essential knowledge in the Internet age of the neo-modern business.

As the series editor, I will be working closely with Wiley's editorial staff and authors to bring you textbooks specifically designed to meet your need to understand how Internet technology supports the net-enhanced organization.

We are proud to present you with the first book in this groundbreaking series: E-business Technologies: Supporting the Net-Enhanced Organization by Craig Van Slyke and France Bélanger.

I am sure you will enjoy reading about the net-enhanced organization and learning how it is changing the nature of business. Because this form of organization is so new and in its formative stages, this book (and the series) will position you at the forefront of business knowledge.

And keep an eye out for upcoming texts in this exciting new NEO series.

Best regards,
Richard T. Watson, Series Editor
J. Rex Fuqua Distinguished Chair for
   Internet Strategy
Director of the Center for
   Information Systems Leadership (CISL)
University of Georgia

PREFACE

In 1996, a guest speaker for a management-oriented MIS class told the student to "keep an eye on this Web thing." Two short years later, the dot-com boom was underway, which was quickly followed by the dot-com bomb. In the span of just a few years, electronic business over the Internet and Web went from a fuzzy concept, to a craze, to being deeply integrated into the fabric of many businesses. It is difficult to fully appreciate the speed with which network-enabled applications became a part of everyday life. In the mid-1990s, few people had heard of the Internet. Today it is difficult to find an ad in a magazine that does not include a Web address. Understanding electronic business has become a requirement for anyone entering the business world of the twenty-first century.

Which brings us to this book. In the last few years, a number of electronic commerce/business texts have come onto the market. This book is unique in its focus on the technologies underlying e-business. This is not a book focused solely on e-business strategies; it is a book about technology. The goal of this book is to give the reader an understanding of the important technologies that enable e-business. We believe that a solid understanding of the underlying technologies is crucial to an understanding of what is happening today and in the future in the world of e-business.

Writing a book on e-business technologies is a formidable task. There are dozens of technologies that make e-business possible. Simply choosing which of these to cover is difficult. Then the question of depth must be addressed. For many of these technologies, a complete treatment requires one or more books devoted to a single technology. Our goal for this book is to provide sufficient depth for you to have a basic understanding of each technology and where each fits on the e-business landscape. We are not trying to make you an expert on any single technology. (However, we do try to point you to resources that will help you gain more in-depth knowledge.)

Before you can put the technology pieces together, you must have a basic understanding of e-business in general. Because of this, we devote the first three chapters of the book to helping you see the "big picture" of e-business. The remaining chapters are each devoted to a set of e-business technologies.

There are several features of this book of which you should be aware. First, each chapter includes a list of key terms introduced in the chapter. Being involved in e-business requires speaking the language. Even if you are not pursuing a career that is directly technology-related, knowing the basic e-business terminology helps you communicate with the technology folks. Second, we provide Review Questions for each chapter. These questions will help you check your understanding of the various topics covered in the chapter. Each chapter also includes Exercises that require you to actively apply the knowledge gained from the chapter. The Review Questions require you to know the concepts; the Exercises require you to use the concepts. Discussion Points included in each chapter are intended to help you think through issues and concepts presented in the chapter. For example, you may be asked to debate an issue with one of your fellow students, or you may be asked to take a position on a controversial topic and to then justify your position. The Discussion Points help you gain an appreciation for the complexity of issues related to e-business technologies. Finally, selected chapters include Hands-On Projects. These require you to interact with the technologies discussed in the chapter. By completing the projects, you learn by doing. Sometimes, understanding must come from doing, rather than simply reading and talking about a technology. In cases where we feel this is particularly applicable, we try to give you projects to guide you.

We also encourage you to visit the Web site that accompanies this textbook. As you will learn, the e-business world is one that changes quickly and frequently. The Web site provides you with important information, such as technology updates and resources for additional exploration. Also, we use the Web site to inform you of any changes to Web addresses mentioned in the book.

A student completing this book will:

- Have a broad understanding of the impacts of and barriers to e-business
- Have an appreciation for the vast variety of technologies that enable e-business
- Gain broad knowledge of the importance of critical e-business technologies
- Have more in-depth knowledge in a number of key e-business technologies
- Understand how the various technologies fit together to enable e-business

SUPPLEMENTS

An instructor's manual and test bank are available to accompany this text. In addition, adopters have access to a Web site that provides:

- PowerPoint slides to accompany each chapter
- Links to Web sites that offer additional information
- Links to software tools discussed in the book
- Content updates
- Updates to Web site addresses mentioned in the book
- Additional material from the instructor's manual

ACKNOWLEDGEMENTS

In preparing this book, we received tremendous help from a number of individuals whom we would like to thank. First, we want to acknowledge the reviewers who have been through previous drafts of the material contained in this book and provided insightful comments that have helped bring it to its current form:

David Anderson

Deborato Chatterjee

Kai Koong

Jean-Pierre Kuilboer

Fred Niederman

Alan Graham Peace

John Story

William J. Tastle

Some people also helped with examples used in the book. In particular we would like to thank Kelly McNamara-Hilmer for her help in providing some examples in chapter six, and Jeremy Maddrey for his help in providing some examples in Appendix A. Our thanks also goes to Dr. Jim Courtney for his insightful comments on early versions of this text.

We are also extremely grateful for the work of a great team at John Wiley & Sons and Leyh Publishing. In particular, we would like to thank Beth Golub, Editor, and Lorraina Raccucia, Editorial Assistant, at John Wiley & Sons, and Lari Bishop, Managing Editor, at Leyh Publishing. Their efforts at guiding and supporting us have made the process of writing this book less daunting than it might have been otherwise.

Finally, but not least, we want to give our thanks to our families and friends who have supported us throughout this process.

Craig Van Slyke
France Bélanger

ABOUT THE AUTHORS

Craig Van Slyke is an Assistant Professor of Management Information Systems at the University of Central Florida. He was formerly a member of the Management Information Systems faculty at Ohio University. In addition to his academic experience, Dr. Van Slyke spent ten years in the information technology industry in a number of technical, managerial, and marketing positions.

Dr. Van Slyke's current research interests are in electronic commerce, and information technology and education. Issues in electronic commerce of particular interest include factors relating to its adoption by individuals (especially the role of trust in adoption decisions), its adoption by small businesses, and differences in its adoption across cultures and across genders. Information technology and education topics researched are skills required of IT professionals, teams and teamwork, and technology mediation of distance learning.

Dr Van Slyke has published in a number of journals, including the *Communications of the Association of Computing Machinery, Information Resource Management Journal, Annals of Cases on Information Technology Applications*, *Industrial Management & Data Systems*, *Journal of Information Systems Education, Journal of Information Technology Theory and Application*, and *Information Technology, Learning and Performance Journal*. In addition, he has contributed chapters to several edited research compilations.

Dr. Van Slyke has taught a variety of graduate and undergraduate information technology courses, including Electronic Commerce, Database Administration, Systems Analysis and Design, and the Management of Information Systems. He has also lectured internationally on a variety of topics related to electronic business. In 2001, Dr. Van Slyke received the Galloway Award for Undergraduate Teaching.

Dr. Van Slyke received a Ph.D. in Information Systems from the University of South Florida. He also holds a Masters in Business Administration from Appalachian State University, and a Bachelors of Science in Business Administration from the University of Central Florida.

France Bélanger is the Director of the Center for Global E-Commerce and an associate professor of information systems in the Department of Accounting and Information Systems at Virginia Tech. Prior to her academic career, she held various technical, marketing, and managerial positions in large information systems and telecommunications corporations in Canada. She has also provided consulting services to corporations in Florida.

Dr. Bélanger's research interests focus on the use of telecommunication technologies in organizations, in particular for distributed work arrangements, electronic commerce, and distance learning. She has published in numerous Information Systems journals, including *Information Systems Research, Communications of the ACM, IEEE Transactions on Professional Communication, Information & Management, The Information Society,*

Information Resources Management Journal, Database, Office Systems Research Journal, e-Service Journal, and the *Journal of Information Systems Education.* Her first book, for managers, entitled *Evaluation and Implementation of Distance Learning: Technologies, Tools and Techniques* (Idea Group Publishing, 2000), was co-authored with Dr. Dianne H. Jordan. Dr. Bélanger's work has been funded by PriceWaterhouseCoopers, the Department of Education, and the Commonwealth of Virginia's Center for Innovative Technology.

Dr. Bèlanger has been teaching a variety of graduate and undergraduate technical and managerial IS courses, including Systems Analysis and Design, Database Management Systems, Managing Information Services, E-Commerce Security, Web Applications and E-Commerce, and many Telecommunications, Networks, and Data Communications courses. She also designed Web-based seminars for businesses, and taught continuing education courses on E-Commerce, the Internet, and Security both in Virginia and Florida. She received the Pamplin College Award for undergraduate teaching at Virginia Tech in 2001.

Dr. Bélanger received her Ph.D. in Information Systems from the University of South Florida. She has holds a Bachelor of Commerce degree from McGill University and a College Degree in Applied Sciences from Ahuntsic College.

CHAPTER 1

INTRODUCTION TO ELECTRONIC BUSINESS

LEARNING OBJECTIVES

After reading and completing this chapter, you should be able to:

■ Define electronic commerce and electronic business
■ Describe how electronic commerce and electronic business differ
■ Discuss the importance of electronic commerce
■ Describe the role of information and computer technologies in electronic business
■ Discuss why electronic business is growing rapidly
■ Explain why standards are important to electronic business
■ Provide examples of how some organizations are using electronic business

Opening Case: A Tale of Two Countries
(or How E-business Kept a Groom out of Hot Water)

Note: The following story is true. The names have been changed to protect the innocent (Sally) and the guilty (Jim).

Jim and Sally were engaged to be married in August. In order to help pay for the wedding and the subsequent honeymoon in Australia, Jim decided to take a short-term assignment in India during that same summer. While that meant that he would be out of the country for the last part of the wedding planning process, Sally agreed that the extra money would be worth it. (Of course, Jim was secretly glad to miss as much of the planning as possible. What he did not know was that Sally was also happy to have him absent for the last minute planning!)

So, Jim flew to Bangalore, India that July, happy in the knowledge that the trip was undertaken with the blessings of his bride-to-be. After two weeks in Bangalore, Jim realized to his immediate horror that Sally's birthday would occur in just a few days. Woops! Although Jim had already purchased some very nice jewelry for Sally from a local (Indian) craft emporium, there was no practical way to get it to her in time for her birthday. Jim was dumb enough to have almost forgotten his fiancée's birthday, but he was smart enough to know that he had better have a nice gift on her doorstep by her birthday.

Jim gave the crisis considerable thought. Then a possible solution occurred to him. What about buying something online? He remembered buying a book while on a long trip the previous summer. It was no problem for the bookseller to ship the book to any address Jim requested.

Seeing salvation in sight, Jim connected to the **Internet** and directed his Web browser to his favorite bookseller, "Buckets-o-Books." He thought for a moment, and then used the Web site's search function to look for books on Australia, the site of the upcoming honeymoon. Fortunately, Buckets has a good selection of travel books, and several potential gifts for Sally showed up in the search results. Jim read the online reviews from other Buckets customers. One of the books had almost unanimously favorable reviews so Jim clicked on the "add-to-cart" button.

Jim then clicked on the "view cart" button. The contents of his online shopping cart popped up on his monitor. He verified that the correct book was shown, and then went on to change the ship-to address to Sally's home address. Jim was also quite happy to see that Buckets would gift wrap the book, and would even add a gift card with a personal message from Jim. Jim pondered a few moments and came up with a nice sentiment for the card, typed the message in the appropriate box on the Web-based form, clicked "submit" and waited for an order confirmation screen to appear. After a few moments, the confirmation screen appeared, indicating that all had gone well with the purchase. Jim sighed with relief. Crisis averted.

A couple of days before Sally's birthday, Jim began wondering if the book had made it to Sally yet. He went back to the Buckets Web site and navigated to the customer service section, which allowed him to check the status of the shipment online. After a couple of minutes, Jim found the right area on the Web site and used the tracking number in an e-mail from Buckets that confirmed his order. Jim entered the number, clicked on "check status," and in a few minutes saw that the package was delivered the previous day. E-business to the rescue!

INTRODUCTION

The idea of conducting business transactions via electronic media, rather than face-to-face, has been an integral part of many businesses for several decades. Only recently, however, has the term "electronic commerce" entered the public consciousness. Although reliable statistics on the amount of commerce conducted electronically can be hard to come by, Forrester Research, a well-respected market research firm, estimates that by 2004, worldwide sales of goods and services conducted online will total U.S.$7.8 trillion.

While this is an impressive figure, it should be interpreted with a healthy dose of skepticism. It is important to understand that this is an *estimate*—at best, an educated guess. The actual total in 2004 will differ significantly from the estimate. Even the experts disagree. For example, Forrester estimates that electronic commerce between businesses in the United States will reach $1.5 trillion by 2003, while the Merrill Lynch estimate for the same period is $2.5 trillion. Fortunately, the precision of the estimate is not important to our point. The main point is that the amount of commerce conducted electronically is growing rapidly.

Chapter 1 provides an introduction to the concept of electronic business, including defining the term electronic commerce and the related term electronic business. This chapter also discusses why these ideas are so important to today's economy. In addition, we examine some potential explanations for the recent emergence of electronic business. This examination leads to a discussion of how electronic business is facilitated by standards. The chapter concludes with several examples of electronic business in a variety of industries.

ELECTRONIC COMMERCE AND ELECTRONIC BUSINESS DEFINED

There is a seemingly endless array of definitions for electronic commerce (e-commerce). However, most of the definitions seem to have two common elements. First, electronic commerce concerns some sort of economic activity. For example, sending an electronic mail message to a recording company inquiring about price or specifications of a product would be electronic commerce, while sending a message to your grandmother would not. The second common element is that the economic activity occurs via some electronic media, such as a computer network. So walking into the local music store to check the price of a compact disk is not electronic commerce, while checking the price on the World Wide Web is.

For the purposes of this book, we follow Wigand's (1997) widely accepted definition of **electronic commerce**—any form of economic activity conducted via electronic connections. Generally, the economic activity described occurs between *at least* two parties. The "at least" is important, it is common for an electronic commerce transaction to actually involve several parties. For example, purchasing an automobile online may involve the manufacturer, the dealer, a finance company, and an extended warranty provider, in addition to the customer. Taking this notion a step further, we tend to think of electronic commerce as crossing organizational boundaries. By this thinking, an employee checking a company's internal network to investigate vacation policies would not be electronic commerce.

A final note about the definition of electronic commerce is that it does *not* have to involve the Internet and **World Wide Web (Web).** While most e-commerce stories in the business and popular press involve Internet-based electronic commerce, it is a fact that much electronic commerce activity occurs outside of the Internet, instead occurring via privately owned data communications networks.

To recap, there are three main components to the definition of electronic commerce.

- Economic activity is involved.   2 parties.
- Interaction occurs electronically.
- The interaction typically crosses organizational boundaries.

There are an increasing number of electronic commerce experts who distinguish between electronic *commerce* and electronic *business* (e-business). In our view, the main difference between the two is that electronic commerce defines interactions between organizations and their customers, clients, or constituents. On the other hand, electronic business is a broader term that also encompasses an organization's internal operations. Our working definition of **electronic business** is the use of electronic communications networks to allow organizations to send and receive information. Note that this transfer of information can be entirely internal, unlike electronic commerce, which typically crosses organizational boundaries. Note that, like electronic commerce, electronic business does not have to utilize the Internet or Web.

Before we finish discussing definitions, two final notes on the definitions of electronic commerce and electronic business warrant mention. First, it is important to recognize that there are many who might disagree with certain aspects of our definitions. Since there is no universally accepted definition for either term, it is natural that some disagree with our specific definitions. Fortunately, the exact wordings of the definitions are not extremely important to the material presented in this book. Slight deviations in the definitions will not be a barrier to your understanding of the technologies behind electronic business. Second, starting with the next section, we use electronic business rather than electronic commerce because electronic business is the more encompassing term.

WHY IS ELECTRONIC BUSINESS IMPORTANT?

Many believe that a fundamental shift in the way business is conducted is taking place. Put simply, businesses are using information and computer technologies (ICT) to make their operations more efficient and more effective. On the surface, this is nothing new; businesses have been automating through the use of ICT for forty years. Recently, however, more and more organizations are not only using ICT to improve their internal operations, but are also changing the way they deal with customers and suppliers.

This is the real revolution. Without getting into a deep discussion of economics, business transactions almost always carry along excess baggage—operations that must occur for the transaction to take place, but that do not add any real value to either party. Economists sometimes call these inefficiencies "friction," or transaction costs. Put simply, ICT, when effectively applied, can drastically reduce transaction costs, which leads to better overall efficiency in the economy.

These lower transaction costs can result in a "win-win" situation for businesses and their customers. Businesses benefit from lower costs of operations, while customers may benefit from potentially lower prices and better service. We will discuss the benefits of electronic business for businesses and their customers in detail in Chapter 2. Another reason for the excitement surrounding electronic business is the Internet's capability to facilitate network effects. These effects are also discussed in Chapter 2.

So how much business is taking place online? In its April 2000 issue, *Business 2.0,* a leading electronic business magazine, reported a series of estimates and projections of the amount of commerce occurring over the Internet for a number of industries (Byron 2000). Table 1-1 shows some of the current estimates in U.S. dollars.

Notice how small a share of the overall business in these industries takes place over the Internet. Given all of the press coverage of online stock trading, you might think that most stock trading takes place over the Internet. As Table 1-1 shows, quite the opposite is true. A very small portion of stock trading (about 5 percent) occurs on the Internet. Another area that you might expect to be Internet-dominated is retail sales. However, the Internet accounts for just over one-half of one percent of the retail market. As you can see, despite the excitement surrounding e-business over the Internet, currently there is little of it.

However, the projections for 2003 tell a different story. Retail sales over the Internet are expected to grow to U.S.$62 billion, which is a 360 percent increase over 2000. Similar growth is also expected in other industries. While some of this growth simply represents growth in the industry, the increase in industry size only accounts for a small portion of the growth in online transactions. For example, the total market size of the health care industry is expected to grow from U.S.$1.4 trillion to U.S.$1.9 trillion (135 percent growth). In the

Table 1-1 Industry Markets and Internet Shares

Industry	Total Market	Internet Share	Internet Share in 2003
Construction	$1.7 trillion	$3.4 billion	$28.6 billion
Food services	$140 billion	$14 billion	$60 billion
Retail	$2.6 trillion	$16.8 billion	$62 billion
Utilities	$357 billion	$5.2 billion	$108 billion
Manufacturing	$4.2 trillion	$134 billion	$1.7 trillion
Finance	$1.9 trillion	$103 billion	$435 billion
Insurance	$500 billion	$450 million	$4.1 billion
Health care	$1.4 trillion	$6 billion	$178 billion

SOURCE: C. Byron, "Net Dry Rot," *Business 2.0* (April 2000): 195–210. © 2001 Time Inc
All rights reserved.

same period, Internet-based health care is projected to increase from U.S.$6 billion to U.S.$178 billion, an increase of almost 3000 percent.

As we said earlier, these projections must be viewed with some skepticism. However, even if the numbers lack some accuracy, the message is clear. Internet-based electronic business is only beginning. As organizations become more adept at electronic commerce and as consumers become more used to conducting commerce over the Internet, electronic business will continue to grow rapidly. Currently, we are only seeing the tip of the electronic business iceberg.

THE ROLE OF TECHNOLOGY IN ELECTRONIC BUSINESS

Why does the title to this book refer to "Electronic Business Technologies," rather than just "Electronic Business?" The answer is quite simple. None of the many benefits of electronic business are possible unless a wide variety of information technologies are working in careful concert with one another. See the story that opened this chapter for an example. An amazing number of technologies worked together to make Jim's use of electronic business possible. Let's review a *partial* list of the technologies involved. Table 1-2 lists the technologies along with a brief description of how they were used. Note that this list is not complete, either in terms of the technologies or their use.

Note how many different technologies were required for Jim's seemingly simple use of electronic business. Keep in mind that Table 1-2 is only a partial list. A complete list of all of the technologies involved would be several pages long. It is important to understand the technologies behind electronic business. This not only helps you grasp what is happening today, but may also help you see what direction electronic business will take in the future.

WHY NOW? UNDERSTANDING THE EMERGENCE OF ELECTRONIC BUSINESS

Why has electronic business exploded into the public consciousness so rapidly recently when, in fact, electronic business and the Internet have existed for many years? While there are a number of factors that may account for the emergence of electronic business, two seem particularly important: (1) the improvement in a number of related technologies and the convergence of these technologies, and (2) the concept of critical mass. This section discusses each of these factors, and how they relate to the rise of electronic business.

Convergence

The convergence, or coming together, of a number of technologies may, in part, account for the recent emergence of electronic business. Advances in the three broad areas of content, access devices, and transmission led to the convergence of these areas, which facilitated electronic business. Let us examine how these events occurred.

Content has become more digital. Everything from newspapers to music is now produced using digital technologies. For example, newspapers are produced using word processing and publishing software, music is recorded digitally, as are photographs and videos. Because this content is produced digitally, it is relatively easy and low cost to transmit the content over telecommunications networks such as the Internet, which facilitates electronic business. For example, if a manufacturer produces its product catalog digitally, the process of putting the catalog online as part of an electronic business Web site is made easier and less costly.

The past few years have also seen significant advances in network access devices, including personal computers. As the name implies, an access device is any piece of equipment that allows the user to gain access to a computer network. A wide variety of network access devices are used today, including personal computers; hand-held computers, such as the Palm Pilot; certain types of cellular telephones; some game consoles; and television set–top boxes, such as Web TV. Just a few years ago, network access devices were primarily limited to computers and terminals. Two aspects of the advances made in access devices are particularly important. First, the most widely used network access device, the personal computer, has been vastly improved, both in terms of capability and ease of use. Second, the greater variety of access devices expands the reach of networks into new areas.

Table 1-2   Some Electronic Business Technologies

Technology	Use
Personal computer	Runs Web browser software
Modem	Enables the personal computer to access the Internet through a phone connection
Routers	Helps direct the data across the Internet; other types of network hardware are also involved
Servers	Web, e-mail, and database servers were all used to handle different functions
Shopping cart software	Necessary to manage the purchasing process
Database management software	Stores and retrieves book data
Database to Web connectivity software	Allows data from the database to be accessed through a Web page
E-mail	Sends order confirmation messages
Shipment tracking software	Enabled Jim to see if the package had been delivered
Internet and Web protocols	Allow the Internet and Web to function

The personal computer of today is much more powerful in terms of computing speed and storage capacity than the computer of just a few years ago. As anyone who has "surfed the Web" on an early 1990s computer can tell you, this increase in capability makes using the Internet, or any other telecommunications network, a much more pleasant experience. In addition, the increased power of the modern personal computer allows for software that greatly improves ease of use.

Although it seems as though the point-and-click **graphical user interface (GUI)** has been in use forever, in fact it has only been popular since the late 1980s, with the rise in popularity of the Apple Mac and Microsoft Windows. (Note that the GUI was developed by Xerox in the 1960s, but was not popularized until much later.) The emergence of the GUI is important for two reasons. First, it makes computers in general much easier to use, which allows more people to make use of them. This increases the utility of making information available on networks more attractive, since most people access networks through personal computers (at least for now). We will explore this idea further when we discuss critical mass. The development of the GUI is also important because, when coupled with increased network and computer performance, the GUI allows for easier to use Web browsers, which we will discuss in a later chapter. For now, it is sufficient to understand that the development of a GUI-based Web browser not only made navigating the Web much easier, but also allowed for the mixture of text, graphics, and other media that characterizes today's Web.

The recent past has also seen the development of a wide variety of network access devices, as mentioned above. Why is the variety of access devices important? In short, the availability of many different access devices means that individuals and organizations have the ability to obtain access devices that fit their particular needs. Do you travel extensively? Then perhaps a hand-held or notebook computer fits your needs. Maybe a cellular telephone would work even better for you. If you want Internet and Web access but do not feel that you can justify the expense of a personal computer, you may find that accessing via a game console or set-top box is your best choice. If you do not want to tie up a television for Internet access, you may find that an Internet appliance such as Compaq's iPAQ works well for you. The availability of access devices that fit individuals' needs is expected to lead to more people having Internet access, which in turn expands the market for electronic business.

The third area in which technological advances have had a major impact on electronic business is network transmission. Although we cover network transmission technologies more completely in later chapters, a brief overview of some recent advances warrant discussion here. In order for electronic business to work, a vast amount of data must be moved across a network, such as the Internet. This leads to the need for fast, reliable network transmission. Not so long ago, most dial-up network access occurred using 2,400 baud modems. While these modems worked well for certain types of data communications, the demands of today's electronic business applications far exceed the capability of these older devices. The currently popular 56,000 baud modem is more than twenty times faster than the 2,400 baud device in use just a decade ago. The faster transmission speed translates into expanded capabilities for networked applications, such as electronic business applications. A product catalog complete with pictures that is impractical to deliver at slow transmission speeds becomes practical with faster access. While the use of very high-speed transmission technologies has been economical for large enterprises for some time, more recent developments, such as broadband cable and digital subscriber lines, bring similar transmission speeds into homes and small businesses.

While any of the developments discussed in this section might individually help facilitate increasing electronic business, the convergence of all of these developments led to an explosion in capabilities that correspondingly led to the recent explosion in electronic business. The emergence of online digital music serves as an example. The MPEG3 (MP3) standard for compressing digital music is a content technology that allows a song that would normally be several megabytes in size to be compressed into a single-megabyte file. (We provide more detail about MP3 in Chapter 8.) While this is an important development, without fast transmission speeds, transmitting even the compressed files would take too long for many potential users. However, with the emergence of high-speed access, a single megabyte song can be downloaded in a few moments. Once the song is downloaded, the advances in personal computers (which are network access devices) provide the processing power and storage capacity necessary to effectively play the MP3-encoded song. The result of the convergence of these technologies is a revolution in the recording industry. Several major recording labels now make a portion of their music catalogs available for download. These electronic business sites allow users to listen to samples of songs for free and then purchase and download select songs or albums for a fee. Figure 1-1 provides an example from the Web site of Vitaminic, a European company that aggregates and distributes electronically music from various publishers. The Web page in Figure 1-1 shows how you can listen to and download a song from Mississippi John Hurt. If you like the song, you can download it in MP3 format for a small fee. Downloading the song allows you to listen to it without being online.

The convergence of technologies is further illustrated in a new industry that has emerged from the MP3 revolution. There are now many companies that manufacture and market MP3 players. These players are actually highly portable, special purpose computers that are designed specifically to manage and play MP3 music. Some of these devices will soon mix content, access, and transmission technologies to allow users to access music libraries via the Web, and then download selected songs via wireless data transmission. As new technologies continue to develop, we will see an ever-increasing array of electronic business applications, most of which are currently beyond imagination.

Critical Mass

Another idea that may help explain the surging popularity of electronic business is the concept of critical mass. Put simply, for any communications technology (including the Internet and Web), the number of entities (people or organizations) using the technology tends to increase gradually until a certain number of users is reached. When this critical mass of users is reached, the utility of the technology becomes so great that there is an explosion in the number of users. The exact number that represents the critical mass of Internet users is a matter for academic discussion—it really does not matter to our discussion. However, the idea of critical mass is both interesting and important in that it helps us understand what is happening with electronic business.

To understand the concept of critical mass a little better, consider the telephone. If only two people or companies owned telephones, buying the third phone would only have value for those who needed to communicate with the two telephone owners. As more and more telephones were purchased, the utility of the next telephone sold would increase. At some point (critical mass), there would be enough phones in use to make owning one attractive to many people. The actual process of people choosing to use a new technology is much more complex

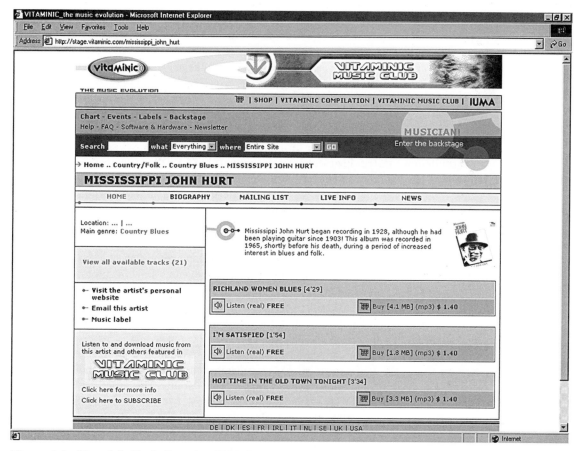

Figure 1-1   Vitaminic Music Download Web Page.

SOURCE: Mississippi John Hurt page, Vitaminic, http://stage.vitaminic.com/main/mississippi_john_hurt. Used with permission. © Vitaminic USA, Inc.

than this. There are many other factors that influence the process, and the critical mass point is very different for different types of communications technologies. However, in our view, the critical mass concept helps in understanding the seemingly rapid adoption of the Web.

Interestingly, when a communication technology reaches critical mass, there can also be a secondary impact on other, related technologies. A critical mass of one technology can "pull" the adoption of related technologies. For example, the number of personal computers in homes and offices certainly had an impact on the number of people using the Internet. We may soon see a similar phenomenon. When the number of wireless network access devices reaches a critical mass, we are likely to see an explosion in consumer-oriented applications that utilize wireless networking.

INTEROPERABILITY AND THE IMPORTANCE OF STANDARDS

When discussing the rise of electronic business, it is important to understand the concept of **interoperability,** which is the ability of systems running in different operating environments to communicate and work together. Interoperability is necessary for widespread electronic business—different types of computers need to be able to work with each other. Imagine if your PC running Microsoft Windows 2000 could not communicate with a network server operating under Linux. Since the Internet and Web facilitate interoperability, a user does not care what kind of server she is communicating with. The interoperability of the Internet and Web means that any client computer can communicate with any server, no matter what the operating environment.

There is a catch, however. All of the clients and servers must be following the same set of rules, or **protocols.** For example, the Internet uses a set of rules called the **Transmission Control Protocol/Internet Protocol (TCP/IP).** As long as all of the computers involved follow the TCP/IP rules, they can communicate with each other. There are many other sets of rules, which we discuss in detail throughout the book, that are important to electronic business. As long as everyone agrees to follow these rules, the computers can communicate and electronic business can occur.

While there are other ways to achieve interoperability, the Internet and Web operate on the idea of having standard sets of protocols that everyone must follow. This means that as long as you have a computer with software that can follow the protocols, you can access any server on the Internet that also follows the protocols. This interoperability is a major reason that an increasing portion of electronic business is occurring over the Internet and Web. The following story illustrates the importance of interoperability.

In the late 1990s, one of the authors worked for a company, GCA, that sold many different types of computer hardware and software, which it obtained from several different sources. Many GCA employees spent a considerable part of each day telephoning vendors to check product specifications, prices, and stock availability. This process often involved prolonged bouts of "telephone tag," beginning with the GCA employee calling a vendor and leaving a message. When the vendor's employee returned the call, the GCA employee was unavailable, which resulted in another message, and so on. What should have been a ten-minute process often stretched over several days.

In response to this situation, two vendors, HPC and WW, set up systems that allowed GCA and other customers to retrieve information electronically. Both vendors believed that making product information available online would significantly improve customer service, while at the same time lowering costs. HPC, a very large computer manufacturer, developed a proprietary solution that required special software to be installed on every computer that would be used to access the product information. The GCA employee who wanted to look up information about HPC products would have to run the special software, which would dial HPC's server through a dedicated modem. Fortunately, GCA did not use any Mac computers, since the software was not available for that environment. The interface for the HPC software did not follow any established standard, so the users had to learn a new piece of software. Basically, the system was relatively difficult to learn and to use. Because of this, most GCA employees gave up using the HPC software after a few attempts and went back to calling on the telephone.

The WW system was designed differently. There was no proprietary software required to use the system because it used established Internet and Web protocols. Any computer with an Internet connection and an up-to-date Web browser could access the WW system (including Macs). Since the entire system operated through a Web browser (which all of the GCA employees used frequently), there was very little to learn in order to use the system. Because no training and no special software were required, all of the GCA employees used the WW system extensively, which reduced telephone contacts significantly. WW saved money by having fewer customer service personnel, and GCA and other customers were very pleased because their questions were now answered almost immediately.

Both the HPC and WW systems provided the same functions, and were developed to solve the same problems. The main difference between the two systems is that the WW system relied on standards to allow interoperability, while HPC used a proprietary approach. From the customer's perspective, there was very little effort required to use the WW system. The HPC system simply required more effort than it was worth.

As the story illustrates, electronic business becomes much easier and more effective when standards are used to facilitate interoperability. As new technologies emerge, new standards must be developed. The future will see many new standards evolve through the cooperative efforts of many organizations. The establishment and widespread acceptance of these standards is a critical first step in a new technology becoming an integral part of the electronic business landscape.

ELECTRONIC BUSINESS EXAMPLES

In this section, we provide several examples of applications of electronic business. The examples are drawn from a number of different industries and represent several different types of goals for the use of electronic business. By reading the examples and visiting the associated Web sites, you should begin to get an idea of the broad reach of electronic business.

Priceline.com

Priceline.com is the second most recognized brand on the Web (behind Amazon.com). Its initial business was selling airline tickets on a "name your price" basis. An individual can log on to Priceline.com, enter an itinerary, and then state the price she is willing to pay for the ticket. Priceline's software then electronically contacts airlines that serve the requested route and provides them with the consumer's price. If an airline is willing to sell the ticket for the stated price, Priceline contacts the purchaser via e-mail, charges her credit card, and the airline issues the ticket.

One interesting aspect of Priceline.com is that it would be very difficult to establish this kind of business without Internet-based electronic business. All a consumer needs to use Priceline's service is Web access and a credit card, which means that there is a huge mass of potential users. Within two years, Priceline.com grew to approximately four million users, which represents an attractive market for potentially empty airline seats. Without the wide reach of the Web, Priceline's service would likely be too cumbersome and expensive to be practical.

Priceline's model is particularly well suited for "perishable" commodity items. Although there are certainly differences in various airlines, a ticket is to a large degree a commodity. More importantly, after a certain point in time, an unfilled airline seat becomes worthless. How much would you pay for a ticket to Honolulu—on a flight that departed yesterday?

Priceline.com is an excellent example of re-intermediation, which is simply the introduction of a new kind of "middleman." Initially, many experts believed that the rise in electronic business would lead to widespread disintermediation (the elimination of middlemen). While there has been considerable disintermediation due to electronic business, there are also a large number of new intermediaries who take advantage of the communications capabilities of the Internet and Web to provide valuable services to both buyers and sellers.

Priceline.com has added other product lines to its site. Now consumers can "name their prices" on mortgages, hotel rooms, automobiles, and even groceries. The success of Priceline.com has also spawned imitators. Expedia.com, an online travel agency, added a similar service for airline tickets called Price Matcher, which resulted in a patent-infringement lawsuit by Priceline.com. Many other companies have modeled their electronic business offerings after Priceline's buyer-driven model, and it seems that many more will follow.

United States Internal Revenue Service

The U.S. Internal Revenue Service (IRS) conducts electronic business in a number of ways. For example, businesses are able to file certain types of tax returns electronically. This is convenient for the business owners since some accounting software is capable of filing these returns automatically. In addition, the process increases the IRS' internal efficiency because labor-intensive and error-prone manual data entry is eliminated. Recently, the IRS began allowing individual taxpayers to file their taxes electronically, which holds similar benefits.

In addition to electronic filing, the IRS maintains an extensive customer (taxpayer) service–oriented Web site. The focus of this site is providing information to taxpayers, and the Web site offers a dizzying array of documents, including question and answer files, notices, and actual tax code. In addition, tax forms for 1992 through the current year are available for download, saving taxpayers the effort of tracking down forms from a library, accountant, or other source. The information and forms available on the Web site also saves the IRS money through the elimination of labor costs associated with answering questions and providing forms.

Note that the IRS' Web site offers documents in four different formats. The existence of different formats offers an interesting challenge for organizations. An organization must decide which of the many available formats to use when offering documents on its Web site. On the surface, you might think that the organization should offer all documents in a variety of formats since this makes documents more easily available to a variety of visitors. However, this can be costly in terms of maintenance. Each different format represents a huge number of additional files that must be created and maintained. Of course, this is less of a problem for static (unchanging) documents.

The use of electronic business by the IRS is an excellent example of the "win-win" situation that can result from the effective use of electronic business technologies. Taxpayers benefit from the improved convenience offered by the Web site and electronic filing. The government benefits from the significant improvements in efficiency. A major reason that electronic business is so popular is because it affords the opportunity for providing improved customer service while lowering costs.

NewView Technologies

Another example of an effective application of electronic business technologies is NewView Technologies (previously e-STEEL Corporation), an online marketplace that brings together buyers and sellers of steel-related products. Started in 1999, NewView Technologies' goal is to use electronic business to bring efficiencies to the steel marketplace.

NewView Technologies is an example of a business-to-business hub, which brings together multiple buyers and multiple sellers. Some hubs, such as NewView Technologies, are dedicated to a particular industry, while others serve a specific business process, such as human resources.

The main thrust of NewView Technologies is the e-STEEL Exchange. The Exchange allows buyers to create inquiries regarding products, while sellers offer products for sale. The product inquiry (buying) process proceeds as follows:

1. The buyer defines the product in which he is interested.

2. The buyer defines the commercial terms he is willing to accept, including product price, payment terms, delivery terms, and the desired time frame.

3. The buyer selects the target audience for the inquiry. The audience can consist of a single supplier, selected multiple suppliers, or all suppliers in the marketplace.

4. The buyer and seller negotiate. If an agreement is reached, electronic documents listing the terms of the sale are sent to both parties.

Suppliers who wish to make products available for sale follow a similar process. The NewView Technologies Web site also allows suppliers to search all product inquiries made by buyers, and buyers to search all supplier product offerings. When buyers and sellers reach an agreement and a transaction occurs, NewView Technologies charges a small percentage of the transaction (less than 1 percent) as a service fee. The seller pays this fee—the service is free to buyers.

The NewView Technologies marketplace is another example of a new intermediary brought about by the existence of electronic business technologies. Once again, the result is a win-win situation for buyers and sellers. Buyers are able to easily investigate a large number of product sources, and sellers are able to reach more potential customers.

ORGANIZATION OF THE BOOK

In general, this book takes a "top-down" approach by covering broader topics first, then going into more depth about particular issues later. Each chapter includes the following features.

- Chapter objectives
- Opening case study
- Summary
- Review questions
- Exercises, including hands-on activities for some chapters
- Discussion points

These features are all designed to help you gain a better understanding of the material covered in each chapter. However, you must also do your part. Take the time to actually read the chapter objectives before you jump into the chapter text. This alerts you to the important aspects of the chapter. Also take the time to read and think about the opening case study, which is designed to provide a context to anchor your understanding of the material, making it more meaningful. The review questions at the end of each chapter provide you with a way to check your knowledge of the information covered in the chapter. The exercises, on the other hand, are intended to help you synthesize different topics and to act as additional learning experiences for specific topics. Each chapter also has discussion points. These help you apply the material in the chapter by preparing an in-depth discussion of a topic. Using all of the learning features in each chapter helps maximize your learning experience.

SUMMARY

This chapter discusses several core concepts related to electronic commerce and electronic business. Both terms were defined and the differences between the two were explained. The importance of e-business is increasing daily. This chapter provided some explanations of why e-business is becoming so important.

The focus of this book is on technology. This chapter explained why understanding information technologies is so important to understanding e-business. Without the underlying technologies, e-business could not exist. In addition, by understanding the role of technologies in e-business, it becomes easier to anticipate how emerging technologies will change the e-business landscape.

Electronic business has existed for many years. So why is there so much interest in e-business today? This chapter offered two possible explanations—convergence and critical mass. A number of technologies in several areas have converged, making e-business vastly more practical and useful. For example, advances in data communications technologies and personal computers combine to make providing complex multimedia over the Internet possible. Another reason for the rise of e-business is that a critical mass of users and e-business sites has been reached.

A core concept that helps explain how e-business works is the concept of interoperability, which is simply the ability of different kinds of systems to work together. The Internet and Web are based on open standards. Anyone who follows these standards can access the Internet or publish Web sites. It does not matter if he is using Intel and Microsoft-based systems, Macs, or Linux-based workstations. As long as he follows the standards, the different systems can work together. Without this interoperability, the Internet and Web would not function, and neither would the e-businesses that utilize them.

KEY TERMS

electronic commerce (e-commerce)
electronic business (e-business)
graphical user interface (GUI)

Internet
interoperability
protocol

Transmission Control Protocol/
    Internet Protocol (TCP/IP)
World Wide Web (Web)

REVIEW QUESTIONS

1. (a) Define electronic commerce.

(b) Define electronic business.

(c) How do electronic commerce and electronic business differ?

2. (a) Explain the concept of transaction costs.

(b) How does electronic business impact transaction costs?

(c) Explain how electronic business can result in a "win-win" situation for businesses and their customers.

3. (a) In general, what portion of the overall economy occurs using electronic business?

(b) Discuss how this is expected to change in the next few years. Cite specific industries in your answer.

4. Why is it important to understand information and communication technologies when trying to understand electronic business?

5. Name five technologies used in electronic business and explain the role each plays in electronic business.

6. Provide two possible explanations for the recent rise in electronic business.

7. This chapter discussed three technology areas that, due to recent advances, have converged.

(a) Name and describe each of these areas.

(b) For each area, discuss some of the advances that are important to electronic business.

8. Name four types of network access devices.

9. Explain the concept of critical mass as it relates to electronic business.

10. (a) What is interoperability?

(b) Why is interoperability important to electronic business?

EXERCISES

1. Find three up-to-date projections for the size of electronic business in the next three to five years.

(a) Prepare a report of these projections. For each projection, describe (1) the projections (the numbers), (2) who made the projection, and (3) the market segment or industry represented in the projection (e.g., retail, energy, etc.).

(b) Discuss your assessment of the projections. How do they compare with each other? How accurate do you think they are? What factors should you consider when assessing the accuracy of electronic business projections?

2. Describe the process you followed to find the projections in Exercise 1. What resources (search engines, databases, etc.) did you use? What did you like/dislike about each? Describe any methods or Web site you used that were particularly useful or frustrating.

3. Describe an incident when you or someone you know used electronic business effectively. Include the following in your discussion.

(a) Description of the problem/situation

(b) How electronic business was used (what sites and tools you used)

(c) Your evaluation of the effectiveness of the use of electronic business in this situation

4. Use the Web to find the price of the book *Sick Puppy* by Carl Hiaasen at three online booksellers. (Your instructor may instruct you to search for some other book or product.)

(a) Describe the process you used in your search.

(b) Compare and contrast the three booksellers' sites in terms of (1) ease of use, (2) tools provided to assist you, and (3) other features of the sites that you found particularly useful or frustrating.

(c) Which bookseller's site did you prefer? Why?

DISCUSSION POINTS

1. Discuss how e-business impacts your daily life. How does e-business impact your actions as a student? As a consumer? As an employee (if you are working)?

2. Instant messaging allows you to easily see whether someone with whom you want to communicate is online and to exchange messages with her if she is online. Instant messaging is different from email in that instant messaging allows for immediate exchange of messages in a more conversational manner than e-mail. Discuss how the concept of critical mass applies to the use of instant messaging.

RELATED WEB SITES

Business 2.0: www.business2.com

Compaq: www.compaq.com

Expedia.com: www.expedia.com

NewView Technologies e-STEEL Exchange:
   exchange.e-steel.com

Priceline.com: www.priceline.com

U.S. Internal Revenue Service: www.irs.gov

Vitaminic: www.vitaminic.com/

REFERENCES

BYRON, C. 2000. Net dry rot. *Business 2.0* (April): 195–210.

WIGAND, R. T. 1997. Electronic commerce: Definition, theory, and context. *The Information Society: An International Journal* 13 (1): 1–16.

IMPACTS OF ELECTRONIC BUSINESS

LEARNING OBJECTIVES

After reading and completing this chapter, you should be able to:

- Discuss the impact of electronic business on the economy
- Discuss electronic business' impact on organizations
- Discuss electronic business' impact on individuals
- Name and describe four major categories of electronic business
- Define the term "business model"
- Describe the most popular electronic commerce business models

Opening Case:
The Convenience of Online Stock Trading

The dramatic rise in stock prices in many countries spurred the interest of individual investors worldwide. Mike Harrison was no exception. The soaring Dow Jones Industrial Index and NASDAQ caught Mike's attention. For many years, Mike used a traditional stockbroker to place trades, typically following a conservative buy-and-hold strategy. Mike began to wonder if it might be worthwhile to become a more active trader. Some of his friends were making big money buying and selling stocks on a short-term basis. A few of them even took a "day-trading" approach—they often bought and sold the same stock in a single day! Although Mike was a bit skeptical of day trading, he was willing to risk a little money on more aggressive trading. He had recently experienced some good fortune on a speculative stock. When attending an alumni function at his alma mater, he listened to a speech by a fellow alumnus who several years earlier had started a computer services firm, CXPS, Limited. The speaker discussed the artificial depression of CXPS stock due to some temporary market conditions. Mike thought that the speaker made a good case, so after some consideration, Mike called his broker and bought one hundred shares of the stock at $20 per share. In just a few short months, CXPS stock had climbed to almost $30. Mike reasoned that if he only speculated in companies that he knew something about, he could probably experience similar success.

Mike was a little confused about one thing, however. When he bought or sold stocks through his broker, there was a fairly high fee—typically $75. So, Mike asked Lisa, one of his day-trading friends, how she was able to make any money if she was paying a large commission on every trade. Since Mike's plan was to only buy a few shares at a time, he did not think his profits could ever make up for the large commissions. This was not a problem with his buy-and-hold strategy, but if he was going to buy and sell daily, the price increases would have to be substantial to offset the commission.

Lisa smiled and said, "Don't use your regular broker. Set up an account with one of the online brokers. My online broker only charges $10 per trade!" "Only $10?" Mike asked. Lisa, who spent a lot of time on the Web, explained that by having clients place their trades via a Web site instead of the telephone, the online brokers saved a lot of money, so they could afford to charge lower commissions. This made perfect sense to Mike, so he opened an account with Lisa's online broker. After doing a little research, Mike bought a few shares of some companies through the online account. The stocks went up, as expected, and he cashed out with a tidy profit.

In the meantime, the stock price of CXPS started on a fantastic rise. CXPS announced a complex strategy change that revolved around providing services to Internet companies. This was the height of the "dot-com" craze, so in just a few weeks CXPS stock had jumped to almost $70 a share. Mike knew that he should probably sell some of the CXPS stock to take advantage of the high price. He was pretty sure that the stock was not really worth $70. However, Mike had become spoiled by the convenience of his online broker. Every time he thought about having to pick up the phone, wait on hold, or even worse, play telephone tag with his regular broker, he found a reason to put off the call.

Soon, Mike became busy with other matters and never got around to selling the CXPS stock. He did, however, continue to trade online—it was quick, easy, and inexpensive. Then, one day he noticed the CXPS stock was falling—rapidly. But Mike was so busy at work that he just could not seem to find the time to call his broker. At about this time, the "dot-com" fever cooled, and so did CXPS's price. Today, Mike continues to hold one hundred shares of CXPS at $5 per share. He keeps the stock as an unpleasant reminder of the convenience of online trading, or more accurately, the inconvenience of conventional trading.

INTRODUCTION

As Mike's story illustrates, the advent of electronic business is having a profound impact on individuals, organizations, and the economy. As is true with many consumers, Mike and Lisa enjoy the convenience of interacting with organizations over the Web. They also enjoy the lower costs. The online brokers are able to offer these low prices because of the efficiencies gained by applying e-business technologies to improve their operations. Traditional brokers (many of whom now offer online trading) lost commission revenue to the online brokers. So we can see how e-business technologies impact many different levels of the economy.

Chapter 2 explores the impact of e-business with the goal of helping you understand its importance. It is also important to understand that there are several categories of electronic business. This chapter provides a taxonomy of four categories of electronic business. In addition, descriptions and examples of each category are given.

When attempting to understand the impact of electronic business on organizations, it is helpful to have knowledge of electronic commerce **business models.** Providing an all-inclusive listing of electronic commerce business models is a never-ending task—new business models emerge rapidly. However, this chapter's treatment of electronic commerce business models introduces some of the more important and interesting models, including examples of how several of these models are implemented.

IMPACTS ON THE ECONOMY

It is difficult to browse through any business-oriented periodical without reading about the "new economy." While there is still much debate over the exact nature of this new economy and whether the "old" economic rules apply, it is clear that the increasing application of electronic business has had and continues to have a significant impact on the global economy. The exact impact of electronic business on the economy will not be known for many years. However, there are several areas in which we have already witnessed significant effects. This section discusses these effects with the goal of providing a high-level understanding, rather than a detailed discussion of economic theory.

The "New" Economy

In his popular book, *New Rules for the New Economy,* Kevin Kelly (1998) asserts that there are three distinguishing characteristics of the new economy. Understanding these characteristics and their impact is the key to understanding how to prosper in the new economy.

First, the new economy is global. National borders and long distances mean less when dealing with digital products than when dealing with physical products. As a result, it is possible to move intangible, digital goods across the world and across borders rapidly and relatively easily. While it may take days to ship a physical book from the United States to India, the digital form of the same book can be transmitted electronically in moments.

The second distinguishing characteristic is that the new economy prefers the intangible to the tangible. Products such as software are really just ideas, although as a reviewer of this book pointed out, this is a little like saying that the Mona Lisa is just paint and canvas. Although there is considerable mental effort and creativity that goes into most software, there is not any physical form of the product. While software may be sold on compact discs as a matter of convenience, there is nothing to prevent that same program from being sent from the publisher's server to a customer's computer electronically. The same can be said for most information-based products.

Finally, the new economy is, in Kelly's words, "intensely interlinked." While economic entities have always been interlinked, in the emerging economy these linkages are intensified. This is due to the ease with which entities can communicate. As communication technologies continue to improve rapidly, it becomes easier and cheaper for organizations to coordinate their activities. For example, the Web allows electronic marketplaces, such as NewView Technologies (discussed in Chapter 1), to operate efficiently. These types of marketplaces represent linkages among many different organizations, and these linkages are a hallmark of the new economy.

The debate over just how new the new economy is and whether the "old" rules still apply will rage for many years. However, it is clear that the game has changed. The stock market is a good example. Electronic business technologies enabled online stockbrokers to revolutionize the industry. Several years ago, it was cost prohibitive to make small-quantity stock trades. Buying ten shares of XYZ Corporation at $10 a share may have carried a commission charge of $50. Today, that same $100 transaction might cost as little as $7.95. This opened the stock market to small investors, and many individuals began to trade stocks actively, which may be at least partially responsible for an unprecedented increase in the Dow Jones Industrial Average and NASDAQ. The remainder of this section explores several ways in which electronic business impacts the economy. Understanding its effects is important to understanding the role of technology in the economy.

Economic Efficiency

It is beyond the scope of this text to provide an extensive discussion of transaction-cost economics. However, as briefly mentioned in Chapter 1, one possible result of the effective application of e-business technologies is lower transaction costs. In a perfectly efficient economy (which does not exist in the "real" world), the cost of a transaction is zero. This means that there is no value being consumed by the mechanics of completing a transaction. Unfortunately, transactions always carry some excess economic baggage in the form of transaction costs. For example, when you purchase a candy bar at the local store, there are costs associated with paying a clerk to handle the transaction—the costs of counting and safeguarding the cash used to pay for the candy bar, among others. These transaction costs represent inefficiencies in the economy that are sometimes referred to as "friction."

E-business technologies have the potential to help reduce this economic friction. Consider, for example, ordering a pair of running shoes from a catalog merchant. You have two options for placing the order—postal mail or telephone. If you fill out an order form and mail it to the merchant, someone there must enter your order into the merchant's system. This is an example of a transaction cost—the merchant must pay an employee to enter your order. If you place your order by telephone, the merchant still incurs a transaction cost because an employee must take your order and enter it into the system. Contrast this process to purchasing from an online merchant. In this scenario, you access the merchant's Web site, find the shoes you want to order and specify the size, click on the "Buy" button, answer a few questions, and the order is transmitted directly to the merchant's order fulfillment system. The merchant does not have to pay an employee to interact with you. This is one reason why so many businesses are excited about the potential of e-business—e-business technologies have the potential to save businesses serious money by lowering transaction costs.

Of course, there are also costs associated with building and maintaining the online catalog and order system. These costs must be factored in when discussing the economic efficiency of e-business. For many small businesses, the development and maintenance costs may not be offset by the associated savings in personnel costs. For example, a large catalog organization may have hundreds of customer service representatives (CSRs) assigned to taking telephone orders. Eliminating half of them represents savings that may be significant enough to offset the development and maintenance of the online service.

However, a very small business may have only one person who takes phone orders. Unless the business is able to shift all customers to online ordering, they may still have to employ the single CSR. As a result, there may not be sufficient savings to offset the development and maintenance of an online sales presence.

When transaction costs are reduced, a portion of the inefficiencies in the economy disappears, resulting in a more efficient economy. In general, this is good for most participants in the economy.

Network Effects

For some products, particularly communications products, the value of the product is, at least to some degree, a function of the number of people or organizations using the product. To illustrate this point, consider electronic mail (e-mail). If only you and I have e-mail, it does not offer much value. When another person starts using e-mail, its value increases for you and for me, since we can now communicate with two other people, instead of just each other. The fact that three of us are now using e-mail makes it more attractive to other potential users. As more and more people join the e-mail network, it becomes increasingly valuable, which attracts even more users.

Network effects can lead to explosive growth. Consider the story of Hotmail, a pioneer in free Web-based e-mail. Hotmail first allowed customers to sign up for its service on July 4, 1996. By December, Hotmail had over one million customers. How did this happen so quickly? Because the value of an e-mail account increased rapidly as each new user signed up. Here's a simple example. If four people have e-mail, there are twelve distinct communication paths. (This assumes that we count each connection twice, once for each direction of communication.) If two more users sign up, there are now thirty communication paths. Adding only two more users more than doubles the number of communication paths. You can calculate the number of paths by using the formula $n(n-1)$, where n equals the number of members of the network. If only one thousand people have e-mail, there are almost one million (999,000) possible communication paths. If each path adds value to having e-mail, you can see how an e-mail account quickly becomes quite valuable as more people sign up. Be sure to remember network effects when reading the discussion of business-to-business e-business later in this chapter.

Globalization

Information technology, particularly network-related technologies, essentially makes the world a smaller place. Today, it is possible for a product design firm in New York to collaborate efficiently and effectively with a manufacturer is São Paulo. Recall the opening case for Chapter 1. It was possible for Jim to order a book from a U.S. bookseller while in India. Electronic business greatly reduces physical location barriers. In many cases, it simply does not matter where you are located. Some even go so far as to declare, "Geography is dead." While this is an interesting notion, it is not really true. When dealing with a tangible product, the physical distance between buyer and seller still impacts delivery costs. Other geographic issues, such as customs regulations, are also clearly impacted by distance. Even digital products are subject to issues involving national borders. For example, adult digital content that is legal in one country might not be in another. The important point to remember is that physical space is less important today due to the advent of electronic business, and in the future it is likely that the physical location of customers or trading partners will become even less important.

The following example illustrates how the Internet enables globalization. One research area of interest to the authors is differences in perceptions of electronic business among consumers in different countries. As part of this research, it became necessary to have a survey translated from English to Brazilian Portuguese. The authors were referred to a translation firm located in Brazil. Using Internet-based electronic mail, the survey was sent to the translators, who provided an estimate for the job via return e-mail. Ultimately, the translation was performed and the Portuguese version was sent back to the authors. The entire transaction occurred over the Internet. No international mail or telephone calls were required. Today, such stories are commonplace.

It is important to understand that it is not enough to simply develop a Web site in a particular language and expect users from the targeted country to flock to the site. Countries differ in more than just language. A major barrier to global e-business is understanding and dealing with local cultures and laws. For example, consumers in India make most of their purchases face-to-face with local merchants. Americans, on the other hand, are quite used to distant transactions, since catalog shopping has been popular in the United States for many years. Which consumers do you think are more comfortable with Web-based shopping? Privacy laws also differ greatly from country to country. The European Union has much stricter privacy protections than the United States. This difference has been a hurdle to e-business between the two.

As you can see, e-business has a number of important economic effects, which are summarized in Table 2-1. Individual organizations are also affected by the application of e-business technologies. We discuss these effects in the next section.

Table 2-1 Impacts on the Economy

Impact	Explanation
Global	Distance and national borders are less important when dealing with digital products.
Move to intangible products	Information-based and digital products (as opposed to physical products) are becoming increasingly important parts of the world economy.
Stronger interlinks	Interorganizational and interpersonal linkages become more important and more practical as communication and collaboration technologies improve.
Improved economic efficiency	E-business technologies, when properly applied, can reduce the economic friction by lowering transaction costs.
Network effects	The value of communication technologies depends in part on the number of people using the technologies. Network effects lead to explosive growth in e-business communication technologies.

IMPACTS ON ORGANIZATIONS

The emergence of e-business impacts organizations in a number of ways, some positive and some negative. In this section you will learn about many of these effects, including how e-business technologies create these effects and what they mean to the management of organizations. Note that the discussion is general in nature—the exact impact of e-business on any given organization depends on many factors, not the least of which is the quality of its e-business efforts.

Operational Efficiency

Perhaps the most often-touted benefit of e-business for organizations is the potential for tremendous improvements in operational efficiency. By using e-business to interact with trading partners, organizations can "trim the fat" from their operations without reducing effectiveness. While the emergence of Internet-based e-business has certainly heightened the interest in improving efficiency through information technology, in reality organizations have used IT for this purpose for many years in the form of electronic data interchange.

The terms **supply chain management** and value chain management are often used when discussing how organizations can improve efficiency through e-business. For our purposes, the two terms are interchangeable, so we will use supply chain management. The supply chain is basically all of the activities and organizations involved in producing a final product or service. According to the Supply-Chain Council, an industry group, supply chain management "includes managing supply and demand, sourcing raw materials and parts, manufacturing and assembly, warehousing and inventory tracking, order entry and order management, distribution across all channels, and delivery to the customer" (Frequently Asked Question page 2002). Figure 2-1 illustrates a simple supply chain. Note that actual supply chains are much more complex than the one illustrated, with many more organizations and linkages involved.

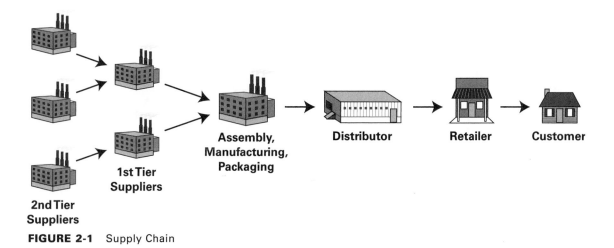

FIGURE 2-1 Supply Chain

Supply chains are often quite complex, involving many organizations that must effectively interact with each other. Broadly speaking, there are at least two primary ways in which the application of e-business technologies can improve the efficiency of a supply chain. First, e-business can be used to bypass some of the links in a supply chain. This is known as **disintermediation** and was introduced in Chapter 1. Figure 2-2 shows how the supply chain in Figure 2-1 could be shortened by eliminating the distributor and retailer. The manufacturer now sells directly to the consumer.

By eliminating links in the supply chain, organizations eliminate the communication and coordination costs associated with those links. In addition, profits may increase because the markup added by the downstream organizations can now be captured directly by the manufacturer. Some manufacturers pass along a portion of this savings to customers in the form of lower prices. For customers and manufacturers, this is a win-win situation—customers receive lower prices and manufacturers receive higher profits. Organizations that choose this strategy must be careful to avoid channel conflict, which is discussed later in this section. Of course, it may be difficult for certain organizations to eliminate some links. For example, some manufacturers may require the warehousing services of distributors. It is also possible for one intermediary to be replaced with another. A good example of this is delivery services. A manufacturer that "goes direct" to its end customers must replace the product delivery services commonly offered by retailers. (Of course, before the middlemen were eliminated, the manufacturer had to ship to the wholesaler, but this is generally a small number of large shipments. When shipping directly to the end customer, there are a large number of small shipments.)

The second way in which e-business can make supply chains more efficient is by lowering the cost of communication and coordination among the various members of the supply chain. A typical supply chain involves a large number of organizations, all of which must communicate orders, billing and payment information, shipment dates, and a seemingly endless array of other information. Such communication is expensive and time consuming. Further, if information is not communicated in a timely and accurate manner, unnecessary costs are incurred. By using information technology to communicate, organizations can

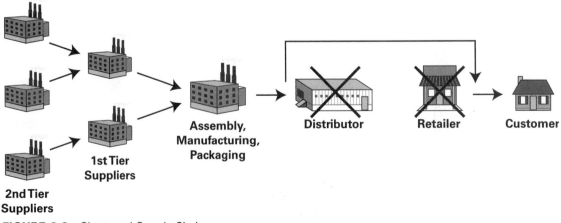

FIGURE 2-2 Shortened Supply Chain

enable faster, more accurate, and lower cost information exchanges with their trading partners. A partial list of information flows in a supply chain is shown in Figure 2-3.

Although electronic data interchange (EDI) has been used for many years to facilitate information exchange in supply chains, the Internet is particularly useful for exchanging supply chain information. Because the Internet and Web are based on nonproprietary standards, it is relatively inexpensive for trading partners to use the Web for communication exchange. This partially overcomes a limitation of traditional EDI, which is the expense of joining a private, proprietary network. Since the Internet is public, there is little cost involved with joining the network. Because the Internet is based on standards, any organization that has access to the Internet can potentially join a supply chain's communication network.

Recall the story of HPC from Chapter 1. WW uses the Internet and Web technologies to communicate with their customers. This is a simple, but very effective, example of supply chain management. The error-prone, time-consuming, and often frustrating paper- and telephone-based information exchanges of the past now occur almost instantly, with few errors and much less frustration. Figure 2-4 diagrams how WW uses the Internet to facilitate communication with its trading partners.

E-business technologies may also play a key role in enabling enterprise resource planning (ERP) systems. ERP systems help an organization tie the various aspects of its operations together by replacing separate, disconnected software applications with a single multi-mode application. The key component of an ERP system is a shared database that contains data about all aspects of an organization. For example, an organization could replace its separate accounting, manufacturing, and human resource systems with an ERP system. The ERP system makes it much easier for the different areas to share information.

While there are many advantages to ERP systems, they are very complex and difficult to implement. In particular, ERP systems can be very difficult to adapt to a particular organization's needs. This difficulty has led to many examples of implementation failure, and even more examples of budget overruns. Major ERP system vendors include SAP, PeopleSoft, Oracle, and J.D. Edwards.

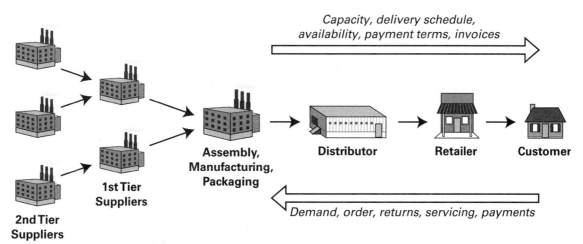

FIGURE 2-3 Information Flows in a Supply Chain

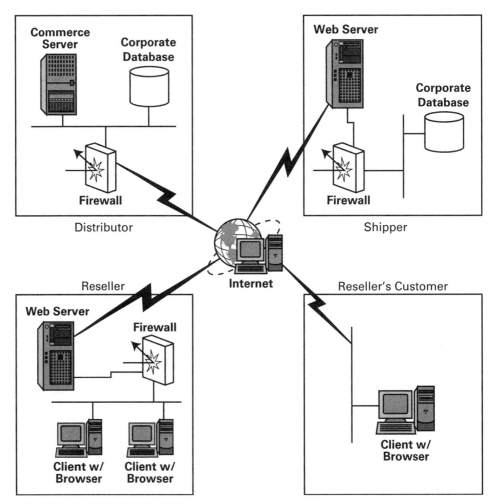

FIGURE 2-4 Web-Enabled E-business Application

Channel Conflict

Organizations using e-business technologies to shorten their supply chains must be aware of the potential for channel conflict. **Channel conflict** occurs when two or more channels compete for the same sale of the same product. E-business channel conflict most often occurs when a manufacturer begins to sell directly to end customers, while also selling to intermediaries who sell to some of those same customers.

When a manufacturer begins to sell directly to end customers, businesses that currently sell to those same customers understandably become concerned. In some cases, there is not much the retail businesses can do. But in other cases, the retailers are able to thwart the manufacturer's efforts. A major determining factor in who prevails in channel conflicts is the relative power of the manufacturer and the retailers. In the case of the airline industry, when airlines began launching their consumer-oriented e-business efforts, travel agents lacked the power to demand that the airlines withdraw their efforts. In an attempt to gain the upper hand, the American Society of Travel Agents called upon the U.S. government to block a plan by several major airlines to form their own travel consortium. Similar battles are raging in the music industry, where retailers are suing Sony over its highly aggressive moves to draw customers away from traditional music retailers.

As e-business continues to grow, manufacturers will continue to struggle over how to best balance the potential benefits of disintermediation with the very real threat of channel conflict. In the meantime, it will be interesting to watch as the battles continue to develop.

New Markets

For some organizations, e-business technologies may be the conduit to new markets. Because e-business eliminates many barriers related to physical location, an organization can use e-business to reach markets that were previously too distant to be practical. Do you know where Amazon.com's headquarters is located? What about Amazon's Web servers? Even if you do considerable business with Amazon, you probably do not know much about its physical location—basically you do not care because the physical location does not matter to you. As the opening anecdote of Chapter 1 illustrates, you can place an order with Amazon from any physical location with Internet connectivity. While physical proximity is important for shipping purposes, location is of no consequence when it comes to reaching the customer.

New Products

Some organizations are using e-business technologies to develop and market new products. The ease with which businesses can connect with customers allows existing businesses to add to their product portfolios, and also allows new businesses that have developed new products to emerge.

Many of these new products are heavily information-based. Priceline.com allows customers to "name their price" on airline tickets, among other products. On the surface it appears that Priceline.com is selling airline tickets. However, deeper consideration reveals that Priceline.com is actually selling information to airlines. Through their Web site, Priceline is able to determine the price point at which a specific customer is willing to purchase a seat on a particular flight. In effect, this information is sold to an airline, which is willing to pay Priceline a fee for handling the transaction.

New Competition

Properly applying e-business technologies can represent tremendous opportunities for businesses to improve efficiency, reach new markets, and develop new products. Many companies are deriving significant benefits from e-business. But e-business technologies can also have a negative impact. The same technologies that allow a business to enter new markets also represent a threat from competitors entering the business' market. This competition may come from newly founded businesses, from existing competitors, or even from existing businesses that are new to an industry.

An industry that is all too aware of the threat from e-business is the travel industry. Just a few years ago, when a consumer or business wanted to book a seat on a flight, they called or visited a traditional travel agent. Then online travel agencies began to spring up. Companies such as Travelocity and Expedia chipped away at traditional agencies' business. Soon the airlines themselves got into the act. Today, most, if not all, major airlines have Web sites that not only allow online reservations, but often offer premiums, such as discounts or additional frequent flyer miles, to travelers who are willing to bypass travel agents and book directly. Many hotel operators and automobile rental companies offer similar Web-based services. The impact of e-business on the travel industry is so strong that there has been a shift of power in the industry. Travel agents now wield considerably less power. One result is that airlines now pay lower commissions to travel agents. So, those travel agencies that have not taken advantage of e-business technologies have lost customers and now earn less money on each ticket they sell.

Electronic Business Investments

The carrot of the promise of positive effects from e-business, and the stick of the potential for new competition leads many organizations to aggressively undertake e-business projects. Contrary to the misconception that e-business is inexpensive, successful large-scale e-business projects require significant investments in people and technology.

E-business skills, such as Web site design, Java and ASP programming, and Web server administration, were not part of computer science and information systems curricula just a few short years ago. As a result, there is a general shortage of people with these kinds of skills, which means that adding e-business capabilities to an organization can be quite expensive. There are many approaches to solving the skills problems, including retraining existing employees and outsourcing e-business projects. However, at present, all of these approaches come at a high price. While time will tell how long the skills shortage persists, acquiring the skills necessary for e-business development and implementation currently remains a high-cost necessity.

Many organizations must also make significant investments in technology. Serious e-business projects require robust information technology infrastructures that are not only able to satisfy current needs but are also able to handle the potential for explosive growth. Underestimating capacity carries potentially disastrous consequences. One recent example involves the encyclopedia publisher Britannica. In an effort to offset falling revenues from the sale of hardback encyclopedias, Britannica announced plans to launch an online encyclopedia that would be supported by advertising—its use would be free, at least initially. Soon after the announcement, Britannica proudly announced a launch date for its online product. When the day came, most users who tried to access the site were unable to get a response. Instead of being able to research the report due tomorrow, little Billy (or Billy's parents) were only able to get an error message from a Web browser. Britannica seriously underestimated demand, and as a result seriously undersized their Web infrastructure. They were forced to shut the site down, bring in high-priced consultants, and try again. For a period of time, visitors to the site were greeted with a "come back later" message.

Britannica's experience illustrates two important aspects of e-business. First, e-business is expensive. Any large-scale e-business project requires considerable investment.

Companies who underestimate the expense of designing, implementing, and maintaining e-business systems will see those systems fail to live up to their potential. Britannica's story also illustrates the negative impact a widely publicized failure can have on a company's reputation. Britannica has long been a highly respected brand name. This name was most certainly tarnished by the initial failure of their Web site.

Britannica is not alone in underestimating traffic and technology capacity needs. Many Web merchants and other e-business companies have faced similar challenges. Some merchants who thought they had properly sized infrastructures to handle traffic to their Web sites were surprised when the number of visitors spiked during holiday shopping periods.

Keep in mind that Web-based e-business is still very new. Is it surprising that many mistakes are made in such a new area? Companies are feeling their way—experts have only recently begun to gather the data and experience necessary to make accurate estimates of technology needs. Until organizations gain a solid understanding of Web site traffic patterns and other e-business technology management factors, we will continue to read about failed efforts and relaunches of e-business sites. Eventually, however, organizations will understand e-business' impact on IT infrastructures.

Market Changes

In some cases, the emergence of e-business can actually change the structure of a market. The stock market is a prime example. Prior to the development of discount stockbrokerages, relatively few individuals engaged in active stock trading. A major reason for this is that commission structures for buying and selling stocks were so high that trading just a few shares of a stock was not economical. It was not uncommon for a broker to charge $100 for executing a trade. That commission immediately reduced any profit from the trade. So unless you had enough money to buy and sell large blocks of stock, the high commissions involved prevented you from active trading.

Say, for example, that you thought XYZ Inc., now trading at $5 per share, was going to increase in value to $7 per share. You're willing to invest in one hundred shares. A $100 commission on the purchase puts your total cost for the shares at $600. Your assessment is correct and the stock increases to $7 per share so you decide to sell. The proceeds from the sale are $700, minus another $100 commission for a net of $600; which is exactly what the stocks cost you. Your net profit from the trade is zero—not a very good investment.

Online discount brokers change the picture dramatically. If you are using E*Trade, a popular online stockbrokerage, each trade costs you about U.S.$15. Now the one hundred shares of XYZ cost U.S.$515 to buy. When you decide to sell at U.S.$7 per share, your net proceeds using E*Trade are U.S.$685. Now your net profit on the XYZ stock is U.S.$170, which is not a bad return on a U.S.$500 investment.

By taking advantage of e-business technologies, brokerages are able to offer significantly lower commission rates to customers who place their orders online. The brokerage incurs much lower transaction costs on a stock trade. They need far fewer stockbrokers to interact with customers, fewer phone lines, much less physical office space, and so on. Some of these savings are passed on to the customer in the form of lower commissions.

The lower commissions offered by online brokerages has, at least in part, led to the dramatic increase in the number of individuals actively trading stocks. Some economists believe that a result of more individuals investing in the stock market has been the unprecedented rise in the volume of the U.S. stock market. Other markets may soon see similar transformations. One market to watch is that of recorded music. As discussed in Chapter 1, the MP3 technology may enable a shift in control in the music industry.

The impact of the application of e-business on organizations is summarized in Table 2-2. E-business also impacts individuals. These effects are the topic of the next section.

IMPACTS ON INDIVIDUALS

Many of you have just started a new term, complete with new classes, new instructors, and new textbooks. Just a few years ago, students across the world purchased textbooks in basically the same way they had for decades. A new term meant a trip to the campus bookstore, standing in long lines, wandering endless aisles in search of the required books. For many students, this was a hated experience—few people fondly recall standing in line at their alma maters' bookstores. Today, however, the situation is changing because of e-business.

On many campuses, students are turning to the Web to purchase their textbooks, rather than waiting in long lines. Several online textbook merchants have recently emerged to challenge the traditional campus bookstores. In fact, some campus bookstore chains now have their own Web stores. For example, Folletts, a large campus bookstore chain, launched eFollets to compete with online-only bookstores, such as eCampus. Now while students are at home on break, they can jump on the Web and check several sites for the texts for the upcoming term. They simply point, click, and pay, and in a few days they receive their textbooks in the mail. The online shopping is not only convenient, it also allows for easy comparison among different stores, possibly leading to lower prices.

As you can see, e-business not only impacts organizations. Individuals' lives are also changed by e-business. As was the case with organizations, some of the impacts are positive, while others are, at least for some people, negative. In this section, you will learn about these impacts.

Table 2-2   Impact of E-business on Organizations

Impact	Explanation
Operational efficiency	E-business technologies allow businesses to eliminate and/or reduce costs.
Channel conflict	Using new channels (such as Web-based, direct-to-customer sales) may cause conflict with existing marketing channels.
New markets *new products*	E-business technologies allow organizations to explore new markets with little regard for geographic location.
New competition	Lowering geographic barriers may allow new competitors to enter the marketplace.
E-business investments	Organizations may feel that they have to invest heavily in e-business technologies in order to stay competitive.
Market changes	The application of e-business technologies may alter the structure of some markets, such as stockbrokering and music.

Greater Convenience

Most studies of why consumers use the Web for e-business cite convenience as the most important reason. In a 2001 study of online shopping by Gartner, Inc., almost half of those surveyed cited convenience as the only reason to shop online. Only 2 percent cited lower prices as the only reason to engage in online shopping (Pastore 2001). When you think about it, this makes sense. It is now possible to shop for a seemingly endless variety of products and services from the comfort and convenience of your home or office. Remember the story of Jim and Sally from Chapter 1? Jim was able to shop for a birthday present from an American bookstore even though he was in India—how convenient!

As discussed earlier, e-business technologies allow organizations to reach customers with little regard for the customers' physical location. This also works from the customers' perspective. Customers can purchase from merchants located virtually anywhere. (Keep in mind that legal barriers may prevent some products from being shipped to certain locations.) Students who buy their textbooks online are not particularly concerned with the location of the online bookstore, although the location may impact shipping costs.

Consumers can also shop online twenty-four hours a day, seven days a week—the Web is never closed. There is no need to wait for a store to open, or to worry about crowded aisles or parking lots, although very large numbers of shoppers can bog down the performance of an online store. You can shop at 3:00 A.M. while in your bathrobe and slippers. In many ways, online shopping is the ultimate in convenience.

All is not completely rosy, however. As it exists today, online shopping also suffers from some drawbacks. For example, with today's technologies, it is difficult to communicate the physical aspects of a product. You cannot touch and feel fabric, try on a pair of shoes, or slam car doors to assess the quality of a car. It is interesting to note that there are technologies under development that promise to simulate touch and feel.

Because of the distance that separates buyer and seller in e-business, there is a time delay between placing orders and receiving some products. If you order nutrition bars from an online health food store this morning, you are not going to be able to eat one for lunch. Digital products are an exception. It is possible to purchase software and download it at essentially the same time. A nice feature of acquiring digital products online is that not only is it possible to receive the product immediately, but shipping costs are eliminated.

Greater Efficiency

Individuals may also benefit from greater economic efficiency through e-business. As noted earlier, e-business technologies allow for improved economic efficiency through lower transaction costs. Another aspect of this benefit is lowering what economists call search costs. Whenever you buy a product or service, you conduct a search. Typically, there is some correspondence between the complexity of the search and the impact (cost, etc.) of the product or service. For example, you will spend more time searching for a new automobile than you would for a candy bar. For most consumer purchases, the main costs of the searches are associated with the time involved, although there are also some tangible costs, such as gasoline. Applying e-business technologies can help consumers reduce search costs.

Consider the process of finding and purchasing a new automobile. There are dozens of automobile makes and models on the market. Sifting through all of the choices is a time-consuming task. Differentiating among the models takes considerable research—buying and reading buyer's guides, visiting dealers, and talking with friends. Once you have identified the specific model you want, you still are faced with choosing a car dealer, which consumes even more time. As anyone who has gone through this process can tell you, searching for and purchasing a new automobile takes substantial time and effort.

Applying e-business technologies changes the picture. It is now possible to research, select, and even purchase automobiles online. There are a number of Web sites devoted to assisting consumers in their search for a new automobile. One of the best known is Edmunds. For many years, Edmunds published a well-respected magazine for automobile enthusiasts. Now Edmunds has a Web site with a wide variety of information on new and used automobiles. If you are interested in a new automobile, you can go to the Edmunds Web site and research prices and product specifications, read independent reviews and reliability ratings, and perform other automobile-related research. You can even obtain an appraisal of your current vehicle. Once you have decided on a model and how you want the car equipped, you can jump to a car-buying Web site such as Carsdirect.com or Autobytel.com. Although different services operate differently, they all basically send the specifications of your desired automobile to dealers in your area who then provide a price. You can then select the dealer and arrange for financing and the purchase and delivery of your new auto. All of this can be done without ever leaving home and in a fraction of the time it would take without e-business technologies.

It is easy to see how Web sites like Edmunds.com can lower search costs, but there is a less obvious impact of such e-business sites. Consumers can "level the playing field" with car dealers by using information found on the Web. In any economic exchange, such as the buying and selling of a car, parties can gain advantage when they possess information that is unknown to the other party. Economists call one party having more information than the other *information asymmetry.* Generally, whoever has more information comes out ahead. For many years, automobile dealers have enjoyed a significant information advantage over consumers. Information that can be obtained from Edmunds and other Web sites helps tip the information balance towards the consumer. When you research a new vehicle through Edmunds, you can find out the retail price for the vehicle, *and* you can learn what the dealer pays for it and what special financial programs are available to the dealer. You can use this information to negotiate a better price. In fact, some people believe that the wide availability of formerly confidential information is actually causing widespread changes in how automobiles are sold.

The Web makes product comparisons much more efficient for products ranging from printers to washing machines. Many product comparison Web sites have popped up in the last few years. In addition, some merchants build comparison features into their Web sites. For example, Netmarket.com, an online merchant allows customers to perform a side-by-side comparison of products. Having ready access to such information allows consumers to comparison shop much more efficiently. There is no need to spend time traveling from store to store in search of products to compare. Of course, consumers do need to be aware that there is the potential for merchants, in particular, to display certain items more or less favorably than others. Even product comparison sites that do not sell merchandise may have underlying motives that are unknown to consumers. Even in the digital age, "let the buyer beware" is good advice.

Increased Choice

Earlier in this chapter, we discussed how e-business technologies can allow businesses to reach customers with little regard for their physical location. The reverse is also true—customers can use e-business to purchase from businesses that may not be located nearby. In the e-business world, merchants all over the globe are a few keystrokes and mouse clicks away. This results in vastly increased range of choices for consumers. For example, many small towns only have one or two bookstores. Residents in these towns now have the ability to purchase from dozens of online bookstores conveniently. In earlier times, residents of rural areas have relied heavily on catalog mail ordering to buy products not carried by local merchants. To a degree, the giant retailer Sears made its mark by servicing small towns and rural areas through its massive catalog. People in areas without concentrations of competing retailers still rely heavily on catalog shopping. So how is e-business different? Key differences between catalog and online shopping include the nature of the catalog and how potential customers locate merchants.

While a printed catalog can include quite a bit of information, online merchants can take advantage of e-business technologies to not only include more product information, but to make an online catalog more interactive. Consider the Netmarket example discussed earlier. The customer decides which products to compare—Netmarket does not make this decision for the customer. This interactivity is impossible to implement in a print catalog.

Another key difference in catalog and online shopping is in the way merchants and consumers connect. In catalog shopping, one way the connection is made is by the merchant sending an unsolicited catalog to the consumer. This commonly occurs when the merchant rents a mailing list that includes the consumer's name and address. One of the problems with this method is that rarely does a particular catalog arrive just when the consumer is seeking a product included in that catalog. So enjoying the convenience and increased choice of catalog shopping often relies on saving piles of catalogs until you need those products, which is rather inconvenient. Contrast this method of connecting consumers and merchants with that of the online world. While there are many ways in which consumers and online merchants learn of one another, let us concentrate on two. If you want to purchase a book online and are familiar with an online bookseller, you can simply connect to the Internet, enter the merchant's address, and search its site for the book. Even if you are not familiar with any online bookstores, you can go to one of the many "portals," such as Yahoo! or Excite, and use their facilities to find bookstores. Or you can take a chance and guess at the Web address of a traditional bookstore, such as Borders or Barnes & Noble. Often you succeed and are able to find the traditional bookstore's Web site. Unless you have to go on an extended search, any of these methods are more convenient than saving a stack of printed catalogs on the off chance that you may want to order from one of them in the future.

An interesting application of e-business technologies is Web-based customer self-service systems. A customer self-service system is a component of a **customer relationship management** (CRM) system, which we discuss in more detail in Chapter 8. In the "old days," most organizations offered only traditional, phone-based customer service. You may have experienced the frustration of being on hold for long periods, waiting for a customer service representative to help you. However, some organizations recognized that emerging technologies offered the opportunity to provide a new type of customer service—customer self-service. For example, many credit card companies use interactive voice response (IVR) technologies to allow customers to perform routine tasks, such as checking balances, without interacting with a representative. Today, this form of customer service is routine. As the use of the Internet and Web expanded, organizations saw a new opportunity to offer expanded means of customer service. Many of these organizations developed extensive customer service Web sites that allowed customers to perform a variety of tasks. These newer methods of customer service offer attractive options for some customers. You now have the choice of using IVR-based, Web-based, or traditional representative-based customer service. Chapter 8 explores both customer self-service and CRM systems in more detail.

Potential for Lower Prices

Applying e-business technologies also has the potential to lower prices, particularly in certain product categories. Although most studies cite increased convenience as the primary reason for shopping online, many consumers are also attracted by the potential for lower prices. It is important to note that there is no conclusive evidence that online prices are consistently lower than prices from traditional merchants. However, there are some forces at work that can help bring about lower prices.

One factor that helps lower prices is increased competition online. Web merchants, especially new businesses, need to attract customers. In order to do this, they must pull customers from traditional off-line merchants. They must also compete with other Web merchants. There are many strategies for attracting customers. One of the most popular is to attract customers through lower prices. When several Web merchants are competing in the same market, customers benefit, perhaps through lower prices. Lower prices may also come about when Web merchants must compete with established traditional stores.

One reason many experts expect prices to be permanently lowered because of e-business is that, when properly applied, e-business technologies can lower the costs associated with business transactions. We discussed this previously. Although businesses cannot sell below cost forever, they can permanently lower prices when their costs are permanently lowered. For example, if a business reduces the cost of completing a sale from U.S.$10 to U.S.$2 by applying e-business technologies, any portion of that cost reduction can be passed along to customers in the form of lower prices. A good example of this are the "online only" discounts offered in the travel industry. Many airlines, hotels, and automobile rental companies provide incentives for customers to place their orders online rather than over the telephone. These businesses want to interact with customers over the Web because it is more cost effective. (There is an added incentive in eliminating travel agent commissions.)

One impact of the increased choice enabled by e-business is that Web-savvy consumers can now perform more extensive product and service searches with less expense and effort than was previously possible. Web-based searches are much more cost-effective than physically traveling from merchant to merchant in search of the best price/service combination.

Earlier we discussed how the Web can facilitate the purchase of an automobile. The emphasis of that discussion was on researching the many competing models. However, e-business can also facilitate comparing the offers of different dealers for the same automobile. For example, suppose that your research led you to the conclusion that a Ford Explorer XLT is the right vehicle for you. You can go online and use one of several car-buying services to request quotes from local dealers for your Explorer. Before e-business, you would have to travel to each dealer, describe in detail the model and options you want, and hope to receive a reasonable price quote. Then, the only sure way to determine whether that quote was competitive was to travel to another dealer and go through the same process all over again. At best, this was a time-consuming arrangement. Using e-business, you can accomplish basically the same thing with very little investment of your time or effort.

Not all impacts of e-business are positive, unfortunately. There are many unresolved issues related to e-business that may result in unfavorable impacts on individuals. We will focus on three of these: access inequities, the potential for fraud, and privacy considerations.

Access Inequities

As information technology becomes even more central to our everyday lives, those without access to these technologies increasingly suffer. In this chapter, we have learned the many benefits of e-business. However, how will people without easy access to the required technology benefit? Although this is an extremely complex issue, the short answer is that they won't.

Even in the most developed countries, there are large numbers of people who do not have access to computers. In developing countries, only the wealthiest have such access. A detailed discussion of the exact numbers is not required to understand the main point— many individuals are missing out on the benefits of e-business. On the surface, this may not seem like a large problem. After all, these people are simply conducting business the way they always have. They are not any worse off; they just are not any better off. This is a naive view of the issue. Because they cannot take advantage of e-business, people without access to the required technologies are in effect paying higher prices for the same goods than those people with access. The problem is compounded by the fact that those without access are also the people who can least afford to pay relatively higher prices. After all, most people who are well off financially would have access to e-business technologies.

Product purchasing aside, there are perhaps even more important consequences of unequal access. As e-business continues to expand, the associated skills and knowledge will become requirements for many jobs. We are not talking about knowing how to program in Java, or how to connect a Web front end to a mainframe database. Instead, we are talking about more basic tasks, such as using a Web browser, being able to navigate the Web, and understanding how to use electronic mail. For most reading this book, those skills are laughably simple—you may have been using the associated technologies for many years. Those without easy access to a computer and the Internet, however, may have had little opportunity to gain these skills. Keep in mind that even in developed countries, many schools lack adequate technology to allow students sufficient opportunity to interact with computers and the Internet. Students without easy access to computers and other IT will not be able to gain the required experience and, as a consequence, are less likely to become proficient in their use. In addition, individuals without the required technology or skills are not able to make use of the rich variety of information that is accessible over the Web. Research indicates that individuals with the skills and backgrounds necessary to use computers enjoy significant wage advantages in the employment market. The so-called wage gap is already widening. If a large number of today's students fail to gain these IT skills, further increases in the already growing wage gap may occur.

As time goes on, the consequences of unequal access are likely to become more severe. We are writing this chapter in the midst of the closest U.S. presidential election of modern times. As you may recall, there was considerable controversy regarding the nature of some ballots in one county in Florida. The claim was that these ballots were designed in such a way that some voters became confused and inadvertently voted for a different candidate than they intended. You might be wondering what this has to do with e-business. By 2004, some expect most U.S. states to allow online voting. In fact, online voting was tested in one U.S. state in the 2000 primary elections. What do you think the impact of widespread online voting will be? There would be three ways to vote—online, at a polling location, or via a mail-in absentee ballot. Voting online would be by far the most convenient of the three, just as shopping online is often more convenient. Is it fair that some citizens will be able to vote from the comfort of their homes without the hassle of requesting an absentee ballot, while those without Internet access are forced to wait in long lines? There would be a very real possibility that those without Internet access would be seriously underrepresented in the electorate, which could potentially result in underrepresentation in government. Later in this chapter, we will discuss e-business between governments and citizens. During this discussion you should keep the potential consequences of unequal access to information technology in mind.

Currently, there are many initiatives to allow access to information technologies in public facilities, such as libraries. However, it remains to be seen if these efforts will be enough. Some believe that if we do not address and correct access inequities soon, we will be heading down a slippery slope that will create serious consequences for many years to come.

Potential for Fraud

According to the National Consumers' League, in 2001 consumers in the United States lost over $6.1 million to Internet fraud. As is the case with any new marketing media, such as the Internet, legitimate organizations and individuals are not the only ones who recognize the potential opportunities. Many crooks and con artists also see the potential and migrate their fraudulent activities to the new media.

Judging from articles in the popular press, the biggest area of concern for most people is the potential for credit card fraud. There are several ways in which credit card fraud might be perpetrated against both businesses and consumers. Perhaps the biggest area of concern for most consumers is the potential of having their credit card number stolen while in transit over the Internet. However, it is much more likely that unwary consumers are defrauded by willingly providing their credit card number or other personal information to an unscrupulous merchant. It is extremely easy and inexpensive to build a very convincing e-business site and put it on the Web. Web sites from honest and dishonest merchants are hard to differentiate by simply viewing the site. A dishonest merchant can easily post a Web site, entice customers with fantastic bargains, collect payments, then disappear without ever delivering the promised goods.

Businesses are also vulnerable to credit card fraud on the Internet. Most consumer-oriented e-business occurs using credit card payments. These transactions fall into a category that credit card companies term "card not present" transactions. Since the cardholder and merchant are not physically in the same location at the time of the transaction, it is difficult for the merchant to authenticate that the person engaging in the transaction is, in fact, the cardholder. In a "card present" transaction, the merchant simply matches the signature on the receipt with that on the card, or perhaps requests an identification card. This kind of authentication, of course, cannot occur for e-business transactions. As a result, merchants are at risk from dishonest consumers who use stolen credit cards, which is a major concern since the merchant is typically not compensated for any fraudulent transactions.

Eighty-three percent of online merchants feel that online credit card fraud is a problem, according to a 1999 survey conducted by CyberSource Corporation, a vendor of software for online transactions, and Mindwave Research, an online research company. The same survey contends that although online purchases account for only 5 percent of all credit card transactions, these online transactions account for almost 50 percent of all credit card fraud. Experts believe that there will soon be a peak in online credit card fraud, after which it will decline. This is similar to what happened with telephone shopping.

Despite the common perception that Internet-related fraud is primarily illegally-obtained credit card numbers, according to the U.S. Federal Trade Commission, the number one source of Internet-related consumer fraud complaints are online auctions (Top Ten Dot Cons 2000). Potential for fraud exists on both sides of an online auction. Fraudulent sellers can fail to provide merchandise, or may send the purchaser merchandise that is not what was described in the auction. This is a particular problem with collectable items because the distant nature of the transaction prevents inspection prior to the sale. Dishonest buyers may fail to send payment as promised or may pay with bad checks or stolen credit cards. In addition, sellers are at some risk of the winning bidder refusing to pay for the auctioned goods. While the seller would not lose the goods (they would not ship prior to payment), they would have to incur the expense of time and money of a new auction.

In order to instill confidence in online auctions, most auction Web site providers now offer some sort of an escrow service. When an escrow service is used, the buyer sends the payment to the escrow service, which withholds the payment from the seller until the buyer verifies that the goods have arrived and match the description provided in the auction. Since the buyer trusts the escrow service to not pay until the buyer is satisfied, the risk of engaging in the transaction is eliminated. Laws against writing bad checks or using stolen credit cards afford some protection for the seller. At the very least, the seller can refuse to ship the goods until the check is cleared, so they have less risk.

Most online auction companies also provide a means for buyers and sellers to rate and comment on each other. Buyers are encouraged to check the ratings of sellers and the associated comments. If the seller has sold many goods using the auction site and has generally received high ratings and favorable comments, the buyer may be more confident of the seller. Sellers can also use the ratings of buyers to assess the sincerity of their bids.

There are also many other kinds of fraud that can be perpetrated on the Web. The U.S. Federal Trade Commission produced a list of the top ten online frauds, which are listed and described in order below (Top Ten Dot Cons 2000). The current list is available from the FTC Web site.

- *Internet auctions*—This was described previously.
- *Internet access services*—Consumers are mailed a check, which they are instructed to cash. Many do, believing that it is "free money." However, they later learn that by cashing the check they are obligated to a long-term contract for Internet access. The contracts commonly carry large cancellation and/or early termination penalties.

- *Credit card fraud*—Consumers are offered access to adult-content Web sites, but are required to provide a credit card number to verify that they are of adult age. Many consumers have later found that dishonest promoters have made large charges to their credit cards. Many defrauded consumers are reluctant to lodge complaints due to the circumstances under which they provided the credit card number.

- *International modem dialing*—This is another fraud related to adult-oriented material. Consumers can gain free access to the material by downloading software commonly called a viewer or dialer. Later, many of these consumers have seen extremely high long-distance charges appear on their telephone bills. This occurs because the downloaded software will disconnect the consumer's modem, then reconnect it through an international long-distance number.

- *Web "cramming"*—Consumers are offered a "no obligation," free Web site for a short trial period. However, some consumers later discover charges on their telephone bills. Others receive bills, even though they have never agreed to continue the service.

- *Multilevel marketing plans/pyramid schemes*—These frauds are analogous to those offered in the off-line world. Although some multilevel marketing plans are legal and legitimate, others are illegal pyramid schemes. In these pyramid schemes, the membership fees of later members are used to pay those who joined earlier.

- *Travel and vacation*—These frauds begin with offers of trips and vacations with many extra features at very low prices. Some consumers receive substandard accommodations, while others find that they must pay large undisclosed fees.

- *Business opportunities*—Of course, not all business opportunities offered over the Internet are fraudulent. However, some unscrupulous operators prey on consumers' desires to make "easy money." As with pyramid schemes, these frauds frequently rely on e-business technologies only for promotional purposes. However, other scams involve Web-based business opportunities.

- *Investments*—Some promoters entice consumers to make initial investments in a day-trading service with the promise of large returns on their investment. However, some consumers fail to understand that large returns are generally associated with high risk. While some may receive attractive returns, others lose their entire investment.

- *Health care products and services*—Some businesses make invalid claims of "miracle cures" for serious health problems. Few of these remedies provide the promised benefits. What makes this particular fraud worse is that consumers suffering from illness may not receive required medical care while taking the purported cure.

It is important to understand that this list includes only those forms of fraud about which the FTC receives the most complaints. This does not mean that all offerings in the listed categories are fraudulent. Certainly, there are many vacation offers, health care products, and investments that are perfectly legitimate. However, pursuing the list makes it clear that fraud can absolutely be perpetrated using e-business technologies. It is important for consumers to realize that simply because a company has a professional Web site does not mean that it or its offerings are legitimate.

Privacy

Another potentially negative aspect of the online world is the online invasion of individuals' privacy. While invasion of privacy is also a problem in the off-line world, the technologies that allow easy sharing of information can also be used to violate privacy. Privacy is a major concern with e-business. In fact, incompatible privacy regulations are seen as a potential barrier to global e-business. Barriers to e-business are discussed in Chapter 3, and privacy is considered more fully in Chapter 10.

Table 2-3 summarizes the impact of e-business on individuals. This completes our overview of the impact of e-business. The next section focuses on understanding the different types of e-business.

CATEGORIES OF ELECTRONIC BUSINESS

Organizations and individuals use electronic business in a seemingly endless variety of ways. Listing every manner in which e-business is currently being used is an impossible task. Before the description could be printed, new applications of e-business technologies would emerge, making the description out-of-date. Rather than trying to give an exhaustive list, we discuss several categories of e-business.

There are three types of entities that can engage in e-business: businesses, consumers, and governmental agencies. If we draw a circle for each of these entities, then draw arrows to indicate all possible connections between the entities, including two entities of the same type, we come up with six connections; business-to-business, business-to-consumer, consumer-to-consumer, government-to-business, government-to-consumer, and government-to-government. Because government-oriented e-business is an emerging area, we combine government-to-consumer and government-to-business into one category called government-to-constituent. Figure 2-5 illustrates these connections.

For each of the non-governmental categories of e-business (B2B, B2C, and C2C), the issue of business models is important. A business model is simply how a company generates revenue. There are three components to a business model. First, it should describe the basic architecture of the business, including the flow of products, services, and information, as well as descriptions of the various entities involved and their roles. Second, there should be a description of the potential benefits for the entities involved. Finally, sources of revenues should be described. Within each appropriate category of e-business, we provide examples of business models that apply to that category. Note that our intent is not to provide an exhaustive list of all possible business models for a category. Rather, our goal is to provide you with representative examples.

The discussion of business models in this section draws from a number of sources, chiefly Michael Rappa's Web site, "Business Models on the Web" (2002), Paul Timmers' article "Business Models for Electronic Markets" (1998), and Merrill Warkentin's e-commerce portal (2002).

E-BUSINESS IN PRACTICE

Tips for Successful Online Shopping

1. **Use common sense!** This is the most important tip for protecting yourself while online. Most, but not all, online fraud occurs when people do not stop to think about what they are being asked to do. As with off-line fraud, the main mistake most people make that allows con artists an edge is being greedy. If a "deal" seems too good to be true, it probably is, and you should steer clear.

2. **Be cautious about sharing your personal information.** Be aware of organizations that want to know your social security number (in the United States) or other identity number. Be certain that you know with whom you are dealing before sending any highly sensitive information via a Web site (or any other means). Identity theft is a growing problem in some countries. Refusing to share identifying information with unauthorized parties can reduce your risk. Even when you are dealing with an organization that legitimately requests personal information, only share that information if you are certain the Web site is secure.

3. **Only provide credit card information if the merchant's site is secure.** Even when dealing with legitimate operators, there is a slim chance of being victimized by someone intercepting your credit card number while it is in transit over the Internet. You can lower your risk by making sure that you only enter your credit card information when you are certain that the site is using proper security techniques. For example, you can tell that a site is using Secure Sockets Layer (SSL) by looking for a lock in the bottom right corner of an Internet Explorer window, or a key in the bottom left corner of a Netscape Navigator window. Also, the Web address should start with https:// instead of just http://. Security, including SSL, is discussed in detail in Chapter 10. Never send credit card numbers or other sensitive information through electronic mail.

4. **Only pay with a credit card or through an escrow service.** This tip is particularly important when you are dealing with organizations with which you are not familiar. Most legitimate online merchants have the ability to either accept credit cards or work with an escrow service. In some countries, using a credit card limits your liability in the case of a fraudulent transaction. For example, in the United States, consumers are only liable for the first U.S.$50 of unauthorized credit card charges. In short, avoid merchants that insist that you pay only with cash or check.

5. **Be very careful when doing business with merchants you don't know and trust.** Look for the Better Business Bureau seal or other third-party certification, but be careful of bogus certification. When you are in doubt, check the business' reputation with other consumers, the Better Business Bureau, or law enforcement agencies in the business' area. Also, be wary of businesses that do not provide a physical address and phone number.

6. **Make sure that you understand the offer.** Many occurrences of what consumers consider fraud come about because consumers do not fully understand the offers they accept. For example, you may agree to a free trial offer of a service without realizing that you are also agreeing to continue the service after the trial period expires unless you cancel the service in writing. Often, extending the service involves a significant fee. Also, be sure to understand shipping charges, delivery time, and return policies. Be particularly careful to clarify any "restocking" fees, which some merchants apply when you return a product. In addition, you should watch out for refurbished products, which are often offered on auction sites. Many times, astonishingly low prices are possible because the products offered are not new, but are used products that have been refurbished. Note that there is nothing wrong with purchasing refurbished products-in fact, you can often save significant money by buying them. It is important, however, to understand that you are not buying a brand new product.

Business-to-Business

In terms of number and value of transactions, e-business among businesses is the largest category by far. This form of e-business is called business-to-business and is abbreviated B2B. Deloitte Research and Forrester Research estimate that by 2003, business-to-business e-business marketplace volume will reach almost U.S.$1.4 trillion. By comparison, the same groups estimate that the business-to-consumer marketplace will reach only U.S.$200 billion. Note that both for-profit and not-for-profit businesses are included. Not only is business-to-business the largest category of e-business, it is also the oldest. The first form of e-business was electronic data interchange (EDI), which is simply companies exchanging data electronically rather than on paper. Businesses have been using EDI for decades—long before commercial use of the Internet was permitted and long before the Web existed.

In the past, only businesses that exchanged huge amounts of data could justify the expense necessary to implement EDI. EDI is quite complex and requires a considerable initial investment. The savings on each transaction or other data exchange were quite small, so unless two trading partners regularly exchanged large volumes of information, the costs could not be offset. In contrast, today even businesses that are only casual trading partners can utilize newer forms of e-business.

A major application of business-to-business e-business is supply chain management, which we discussed earlier in this chapter. However, there are many other ways in which businesses use e-business technologies to interact with each other. One of the most talked about applications is the business-to-business exchange, which is sometimes called a business-to-business hub. A business-to-business exchange is much like a stock or commodities exchange—the exchange connects multiple buyers and multiple sellers. Without some sort of an exchange, each buyer and seller must interact directly with each other seller or buyer, as shown in Figure 2-6. As a result, practical considerations prevent many buyers from seeking more than a few sellers. Likewise, sellers may find it prohibitively expensive to seek smaller potential buyers.

With a B2B exchange, however, buyers and sellers simply need to have the ability to interact with the exchange. The exchange matches buyers and sellers. It is not necessary for the parties to interact directly with each other. This situation is diagrammed in Figure 2-7. Notice how much simpler the interactions are from the perspective of the buyers and sellers.

The popularity of B2B exchanges is evidenced by their explosion in the last few years. Broadly speaking, there are two types of B2B exchanges—vertical exchanges and functional exchanges. Vertical exchanges focus on a particular industry. For example, Chemdex, an early B2B exchange, focused on the life sciences industry, while the e-STEEL Exchange offered by NewView Technologies operates in the steel industry, as the name implies. Functional exchanges, on the other hand, cut across industry lines and focus on a particular business function. Functional exchanges include i-MARK in the maintenance, repair, and operations function, and Employease for human resources.

Several approaches to B2B exchanges exist. Catalog aggregators combine the product offerings of many sellers into what is in essence a "super-catalog." Buyers are attracted by the simplicity and convenience of purchasing a wide variety of items from a single source. The catalog aggregator makes money through listing fees and/or transaction fees. The catalog approach works well when buyers and sellers engage in many transactions for low-priced products.

Table 2-3 Impact of E-business on Individuals

Impact	Explanation
Increased convenience	Consumers gain the ability to shop with less regard for time or location.
Increased efficiency	Consumers incur lower transaction costs, which results in greater economic efficiency.
Increased choice	Consumers can reach a greater variety of providers of products or services due to fewer limitations of location.
Potential for lower prices	Increased economic efficiency on the part of businesses may be passed along to consumers in the form of lower prices. Increased competition may also lower prices.
Access inequities	Individuals without the technology or knowledge to utilize e-business may suffer.
Potential for fraud	Fraudulent organizations and individuals are able to use e-business technologies to reach more potential victims.
Invasion of privacy	E-business technologies used for information sharing may lead to privacy invasions.

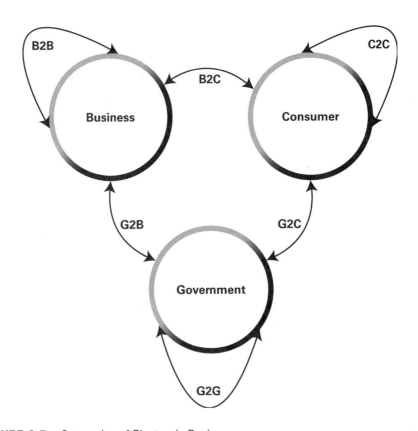

FIGURE 2-5   Categories of Electronic Business

Chemdex was an example of a catalog aggregator. Their Web site listed the suppliers that were members of the exchange. Buyers could purchase from any of these suppliers via the Chemdex Web site. In December 2000, Ventro, the company operating the Chemdex exchange, shut down the exchange along with the associated Web site. However, Chemdex remains an interesting pioneer of B2B e-business.

Some exchanges use an auction model. In an auction exchange, buyers typically bid on items posted for sale by sellers. Assuming that there are multiple bidders for an item, prices increase until the auction expires, at which time the highest bidder "wins" the auction and purchases the item at the bid price. Reverse auctions also exist. In a reverse auction, a buyer requests an item. Potential sellers then bid against one another to win the sale. Each successive seller bid drives the price of the item down until no more bids are offered or the auction ends. The auction model is best suited for non-standard products or perishable products.

One interesting example of a B2B exchange that uses an auction model is Altra Energy Market. Through its Web site, Altra Market Place, buyers and sellers of energy can trade bids and offers just as they would in a traditional commodities exchange. All bids and offers are made over the Web. Buyers and sellers are anonymous to each other at the time of bidding. Similar auctions exist in many other industries.

The market exchange model is also used by some B2B exchanges. The exchange model works best for standard, near-commodity products. With commodity products, there are few or no differences among different suppliers' products. For some product categories, all products that meet certain standards are considered to be equivalent. For example, grade A large eggs all meet the same standards, regardless of which farm produces the eggs. Businesses that follow the market exchange model generate revenues by charging a fee for each successful transaction that occurs using the exchange. Generally, this fee is paid by the seller.

The B2B exchange HoustonStreet is a good example of the exchange model. HoustonStreet provides a market for buying and selling electricity. Much like a traditional commodity exchange, the HoustonStreet Web site provides immediate, up-to-date trading prices. Power companies interested in selling their excess electricity are able to check current prices, then set their price and offer the electricity for sale. Power companies in need of electricity can likewise check current prices and, if those prices are satisfactory, purchase the electricity.

The final form of B2B exchange we discuss is the barter model. These types of exchanges work well when organizations have reciprocating assets. Reciprocating assets are different products with values that can offset one another. For example, perhaps you have a bicycle that you want to sell, and I have a pair of roller blades I am willing to part with. If we both feel that the items are of equal value, we may agree to trade one for the other. What makes the barter arrangement so attractive is that both of us are using a non-performing asset to acquire a performing asset. In the simple example, the non-performing asset is just an item that we're not using any more and the performing asset is an item that we anticipate using. The organization that runs the barter site generates revenue by charging a fee for each barter transaction facilitated by the site.

An interesting business model that sometimes fits into the B2B category is the affiliate model. Amazon.com is the pioneer of the online affiliate model. Amazon will pay a finder's fee to anyone with a Web site that directs business to Amazon. Web site owners can place a link to Amazon's Web store on their Web site. Whenever a visitor

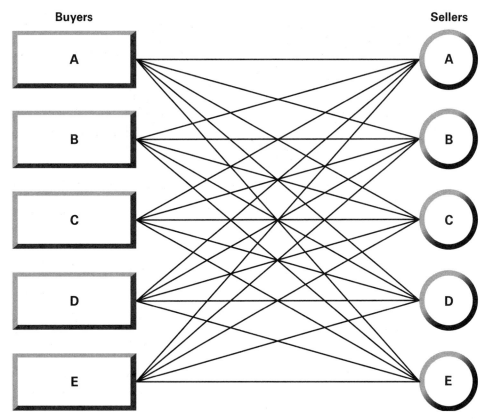

FIGURE 2-6 Direct Buyer/Seller Interaction

clicks through to Amazon and makes a purchase, Amazon pays a percentage of the income from the sale to the originating Web site owner. The strategy behind the affiliate model is different in that rather than trying to aggregate many buyers into a single portal, the affiliate model seeks to find Web users on whatever site they happen to be visiting. More than a few businesses have discovered that becoming an affiliate offers a new revenue stream. For example, The Motley Fool, a U.S.-based company that provides investment education, is an affiliate of Amazon. Visitors to the Motley Fool's Web site can "click through" to Amazon to purchase investment-oriented books. When this occurs and a purchase is made, The Motley Fool receives a commission from Amazon.

Many e-commerce companies have followed Amazon's lead and implemented affiliate programs of their own. Many companies using the affiliate model, including Amazon, allow both individuals and businesses to become affiliates. So, while we include the affiliate model in a discussion of B2B e-business, the discussion could also take place in the context of B2C e-business.

Generally, discussion of B2B e-business focuses on interactions among multiple businesses. However, an argument can be made for including interactions between businesses and their employees in this category. Of course, applying e-business technologies to these

Buyers   **Sellers**

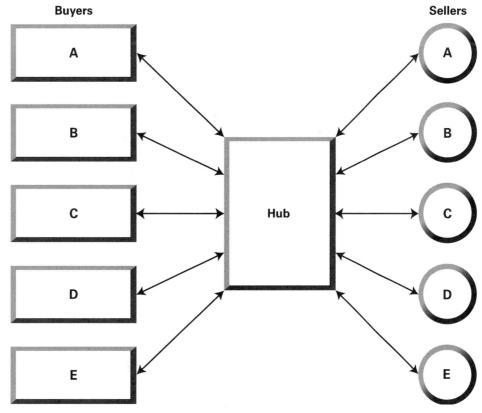

FIGURE 2-7   B2B Exchange/Hub

interactions offers the potential to cut costs while improving effectiveness. For instance, many organizations allow employees to manage their own benefits through a Web site. An example of this is an employee changing insurance coverage. Business-to-employee e-business systems hold the potential to significantly lower costs for organizations while increasing convenience for employees.

It is important to realize that the discussion in this section only scratches the surface of B2B e-business and of B2B exchanges. There have been entire books written on B2B e-business. Hopefully, the discussion has given you a taste of what B2B e-business is all about and of the wide variety of ways in which e-business technologies are applied to interactions among businesses. We now turn our attention to how e-business technologies are being applied to interactions between businesses and consumers.

Business-to-Consumer

Electronic business between businesses and consumers is a growing and highly publicized category of e-business. Business-to-consumer, or B2C, e-business was almost nonexistent just a few years ago. Today, however, an ever-growing army of consumers now turns to the Web when searching for products or services.

Many consumer-oriented e-businesses have been started since 1996. So far, the number of failures far exceeds the number of successes. While some in the press claim that this is a spectacular failure of e-business, we are more inclined to believe that this is simply a matter of learning how to use a new business medium. Whenever new ground is broken, there will be more failure than success, at least initially. Over time, however, we believe that businesses and consumers alike will learn what to expect from e-business. Expectations will become more realistic, and weaknesses in the technology will be overcome. As these changes occur, you will begin to see more and more success stories. Just as it was a mistake to expect too much from B2C e-business, so is it also a mistake to write it off as just a passing fancy.

There are many different forms of business-to-consumer e-business—in fact, there are too many to possibly cover in this chapter. Rather than even pretending to provide a comprehensive listing, we will discuss several of the more common forms of business-to-consumer e-business. In addition, we provide an example of each form.

Electronic stores (also known as eShops or eTailers) follow the electronic merchant business model. This form of e-business is essentially traditional catalog shopping translated for the Web. However, this does not imply that electronic stores (eStores) do not make effective use of e-business technologies. Rather, we compare them to traditional catalog shopping because both involve customers browsing through product offerings, making selections, and purchasing products. In contrast to traditional "brick and mortar" catalog merchants, Web-based stores are not subject to the limitations of printed catalogs. It is important to understand that some of the most successful Web merchants are also successful off-line. Many traditional catalog merchants have migrated onto the Web, as have traditional non-catalog merchants. For example, Lands' End, often touted as a highly successful catalog merchant, has a popular electronic store. Barnes & Noble, a "brick and mortar" bookstore, responded to the threat posed by Amazon.com by opening its own electronic store.

A lesser-known example of B2C e-business is Supergo Bike Shops. As the name implies, Supergo is a retailer of bicycles and bicycle-related products. One aspect of Supergo that makes it particularly interesting is that it conducts business through physical retail stores, a print catalog, and a Web-based electronic store. This is an example of a "clicks-and-bricks" merchant. Supergo has been effective at translating its knowledge of catalog-based selling to the Web portion of its business. Notice how the Supergo Web site, shown in Figure 2-8, also promotes its physical stores. Also note the "Hottest Deals" section. One advantage of an electronic store from the retailer's perspective is that, unlike a print catalog, the online store can be updated regularly. If a manufacturer of bicycle helmets offers Supergo particularly attractive pricing on a soon-to-be-outdated model, Supergo can quickly modify its Web site to promote the "hot deal." Supergo actually uses a sophisticated personalization system to select "hot deal" products for individual consumers.

Supergo is an example of a specialty retailer that has created an online presence. Another category of electronic stores is the "superstore." As is the case with traditional physical superstores, online superstores offer a wide range of products. Netmarket.com, mentioned earlier in this chapter, is a good example of an electronic superstore. Netmarket sells thousands of products, ranging from towels to refrigerators. Interestingly, Netmarket's origin is as an off-line membership-only catalog merchant. However, Netmarket has made the transition to the online world quite well. Recall the earlier discussion of Netmarket's product comparison feature, which is a good example of the effective use of e-business technologies.

Netmarket organizes its electronic shop into different departments, including electronics, computer and office, and home and garden, among others. In addition, Netmarket has two other unique areas in its Web store. The Factory Outlet section of Netmarket offers close-out and refurbished items at a deep discount. The offerings change often, depending upon what Netmarket wants to move out of inventory.

Even more unique was the Haggle Zone, which Netmarket spun off into a stand-alone Web site. The Haggle Zone allowed customers to negotiate the prices of products. Once a product was chosen, the customer chose a virtual haggler with which to negotiate. The negotiation would go back and forth until either a price was agreed upon, or the virtual haggler "decided" that the customer was not bargaining faithfully and terminated the transaction. Much care was taken to make the virtual hagglers realistic. They would make counter-offers, and would chastise customers for not "playing fair." Each haggler had a different personality. All of this was done to make the online bargaining experience more realistic and more enjoyable. Although Haggle Zone was an interesting idea, it was ultimately unsuccessful; the site is no longer available.

Online auctions are another type of B2C e-business. (Business-to-business online auctions also exist.) Businesses that follow the auction model generate revenue by charging sellers a fee for each item sold. Additional revenue is sometimes gained by providing other services, such as payment escrow or order fulfillment. Web-based auctions make particularly good use of e-business technologies. Using the Web allows auction-based businesses to reach a much wider audience than is possible otherwise. In addition, computers are able to manage the bidding process efficiently, eliminating the need for skilled auctioneers.

One interesting application of e-business technologies in the auction world is uBid's BidButler. The BidButler enables you to specify an opening bid and a maximum bid. If the opening bid is exceeded by another bidder, BidButler will automatically increase your bid. This continues each time your bid is beaten until your maximum bid price is reached. By using BidButler, you do not have to closely monitor your bid—the system will monitor the bid for you.

Perhaps the most widely known online auction business is eBay. However with uBid, all transactions occur between the customer and uBid. eBay, on the other hand, is simply a listing service. Sellers pay eBay to list items for sale and customers pay the seller, either directly or through an escrow service. We discuss eBay later in this chapter in the section on consumer-to-consumer e-business.

Another category of B2C e-business that has its roots in the off-line world is the electronic mall (eMall). Electronic malls are similar to traditional shopping malls in that rather than selling goods directly to consumers, the mall rents space to merchants. In the case of the eMall, this space is on a Web site. Many electronic malls specialize in a certain product category or industry. For example, Fashionmall.com specializes in clothing and other fashion-related products. Retailers pay Fashionmall.com to put links to their Web sites on the Fashionmall.com site. As is the case with a physical mall, premium space costs more. For example, retailers pay extra to be included on Fashionmall.com's home page.

All of the categories of B2C e-business mentioned so far are designed to facilitate transactions between businesses and their customers. There are two categories of sites that are not sales transaction-oriented. Instead these types of sites focus on promotion and customer service.

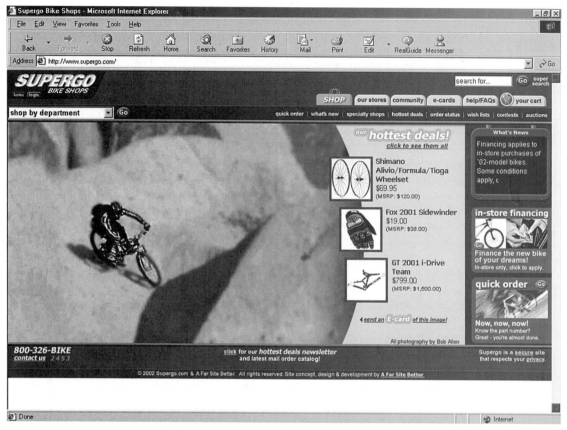

FIGURE 2-8 Supergo Bike Shops Web Store

SOURCE: Supergo.com home page, Supergo.com, http://www.supergo.com. © Supergo.com and A Far Site Better.

Many businesses have found that they can effectively and efficiently offer customer service over the Internet. Of course, many sales-oriented sites include customer service functions, but there are sites that were created for the sole purpose of providing customer service. These are especially popular in the computer industry. Providing software updates, answers to frequently asked question, and how-to pages online is not only less expensive for the business, in many cases it is also more convenient and effective for the consumer. Note that although we are discussing customer service sites in the context of B2C e-business, they are also widely used in B2B e-business.

One example of a customer service-oriented e-business site is that of Hewlett-Packard, a manufacturer of computer hardware and other electronic equipment. Hewlett-Packard allows customers to access support information for a variety of products through a Web site. It is interesting to note that Hewlett-Packard provides a link to their sales-oriented e-business site on their customer service site. Why would Hewlett-Packard do this? Many prospective customers visit customer service sites to learn about products they are considering purchasing. Once the prospective customer satisfies their questions, they may wish to make a purchase, and the link allows them quick access to the sales site. As is often the case in the off-line world, it is imperative to make the sale before the customer leaves the store. By providing the link to the sales-oriented site, Hewlett-Packard keeps the customer in its Web environment, increasing the likelihood of making the sale.

Some businesses make use of the community-building capabilities of the Web to allow customers to post and answer product-oriented questions. For example, suppose that you recently acquired a new computer and have problems with the modem. You could go to the community forum section of the manufacturer's Web site (assuming it has one), and look for postings of similar problems. If you do not find the help you need, you can post your own message requesting assistance. Typically, the manufacturer has technicians assigned to monitor and respond to postings. However, it is also common for one customer to answer another's question. From both the business' and the customer's perspective, such forums, when properly implemented and run, are quite powerful customer-assistance tools.

It is also possible for community building to be a source of revenue. When using the community model, an organization makes its money either by charging members a membership fee or selling advertising (or both). The Motley Fool, which we discussed earlier, is a good example of a business that makes use of the community model. A major attraction of The Motley Fool is its large community of active, knowledgeable investors. Membership in the community was free for many years. However, in 2002 The Motley Fool began charging an annual fee for access to its community forums. These fees are likely to represent a significant source of revenue. An interesting aspect of the community model is that its real value comes from the customers who make up the community's membership. While the company provides the technological framework for the community, the members add the valuable content.

Interestingly, The Motley Fool also makes use of other business models. For example, it also makes money from advertisements placed on its popular Web site. This is called (not surprisingly) the advertising model. Many of the most popular and widely recognized names on the Web make use of the advertising model. Note that although we are discussing the advertising model in a section on B2C e-business, it could also be included in the B2B section, since both the advertisers and the company selling the advertising are businesses. However, many of the best-known examples of companies that use the advertising model are consumer-oriented Web sites. Examples include Web portals such as Yahoo!, Excite, and Lycos. Search utilities, such as Google, also use an advertising-supported model. These businesses do not charge people to utilize the services offered by the business. Rather, revenue comes from companies that wish to place advertisements, such as banner ads, on the business' Web pages. This is similar to the model used by radio stations across the globe. Listeners do not pay for the privilege of listening to the radio station's broadcasts. However, organizations that want to reach those listeners pay the station to include the organizations' advertisements in the station's broadcasts. As you might imagine, the most visited Web sites command the highest advertising fees, just as the most listened-to radio stations do.

The subscription model can be applied to B2C e-business. With this model, revenue is generated through subscription fees. Often, companies that follow the subscription model provide a limited amount of content for free, but require a subscription for unrestricted access. Many of the organizations that use the subscription model are traditional brick-and-mortar businesses that also use the subscription model for their offline operations. Examples include *Consumer Reports* and the *Wall Street Journal*. Of course, there are also Web-only businesses that use the subscription model.

Sometimes an organization uses a Web presence to promote its offline business. An example of a company with a promotion-oriented Web site is Tommy Hilfiger, a clothing manufacturer. The "Tommy" Web site does not sell any products—it exists to help promote the company's products. The portion of the site shown is intended to familiarize customers with Tommy Hilfiger's fall product line. Fashion-conscious consumers can visit the company's Web site to get an early look at the upcoming trends. Also, notice that the Tommy Hilfiger Web site offers ClubTommy, which allows fans of the company's fashions to gain access to "inside" information, celebrity chat sessions, and fashion previews. Clubs such as these help create closer ties between businesses and their customers by making the customers feel like they are part of a special community.

Consumer-to-Consumer

Business-to-business and business-to-consumer electronic business are the most widely discussed categories of e-business. However, as Figure 2-5 illustrates, e-business also takes place among consumers, which is called consumer-to-consumer, or C2C, e-business. There are several forms of C2C e-business, but by far the two most popular are C2C auctions and classifieds.

The emergence of eBay provides evidence that there is a sizable market for C2C e-business. A quick visit to eBay's Web site shows that at any moment, tens of thousands of consumers are buying and selling through eBay. Books, china, used computers, furniture, collectables, and almost anything else you can think of is for sale on eBay or similar auction Web sites, such as Amazon.com's auction site. While these auctions certainly allow businesses to post items for sale, many consumers post their unwanted items rather than letting them collect dust in the garage. There are some consumers who have become so adept at selling items through eBay that their activities have actually become a business. Figure 2-9 shows the categories of products available on eBay. Note that each of these product categories includes many sub-categories.

Although eBay is not available in all countries, in part due to local laws governing auctions, as of this writing there are eBay sites for the United States, Australia, Canada, France, Germany, Japan, and the United Kingdom. The wide venue of eBay allows consumers to reach a much greater audience for their goods than they would by placing a classified ad in the local paper or holding a yard sale.

Listing an item for sale is relatively simple, even for a novice computer user. The fees charged by eBay are low, in most cases less than U.S.$2. In addition, eBay provides features and services that help facilitate conducting business with someone you do not know, and buying a product you cannot see. For example, eBay is affiliated with Billpoint, a company that enables individuals to accept credit card payments. Also, as mentioned earlier in this chapter, buyers and sellers are able to rate one another using the "Feedback Forum." This encourages both to faithfully carry out the transactions. Otherwise, poor ratings could seriously harm their online reputations. Finally, eBay partners with an escrow service, Escrow.com, that will hold a buyer's payment until the buyer verifies that the merchandise has been received in good order. The escrow service will likewise withhold refund payments until the seller verifies that the returned merchandise is received. A portion of eBay's description page for the Feedback Forum is shown in Figure 2-10.

Why is a feature such as the Feedback Forum necessary? The Feedback Forum is designed to help eBay customers assess how much they should trust sellers. It is important to understand that trust plays an important role in all business, but it is especially important in e-business because the buyer and seller interact through the use of technology rather than directly. In traditional business, the customer pays for the merchandise or service when it is received. This is not the case with e-business. The customer pays for the merchandise, then several days later receives it. Because the customer does not take possession of the merchandise at the time of payment, the customer must trust the merchant to faithfully carry out the transaction. In an eBay transaction, the merchant may really be an individual, rather than an organization. By looking at other buyers' feedback about the seller, the buyer can determine whether or not she should trust the seller to carry out the transaction. Without mechanisms such as the Feedback Forum and escrow services, far fewer consumers would be willing to take the risk of purchasing from other consumers online.

Recently, eBay merged with another company oriented towards facilitating C2C e-business—Half.com. Half.com allows consumers to sell their unwanted books, music, movies, and video games via the Web. Currently, there are over seven million items listed for sale on the Half.com e-business site. Instead of using an auction model like eBay, Half.com uses more of a classified advertisement approach. In exchange for paying a commission of 15 percent to Half.com, consumers can post items for sale at a fixed price—there is no bidding. In contrast to most classified advertising schemes, on Half.com if the item does not sell, the customer does not pay for the listing. This makes listing items for sale very attractive, since there is no risk to the seller, other than the time involved in posting the listings. In addition, paying a percentage commission rather than a flat rate makes it possible to sell low-priced items. Think about it this way. You want to sell your used CD of the Beatles' *White Album* and think that U.S.$7 is a fair price. You could place an ad in the classified section of the local newspaper. But if that ad cost you U.S.$5 to place, selling the CD would not be worth the effort. In fact, if the CD did not sell, you would be out U.S.$5. On Half.com, you can post the CD for U.S.$7, and when and if it sells, you only have to pay the 15 percent commission, which is a little over U.S.$1. If the CD does not sell, you pay nothing.

When a seller's item is sold, Half.com sends an e-mail notification to the seller, who replies to acknowledge that the item will be shipped. Then, Half.com verifies that the item has been received by the buyer and sends the seller a check. Checks are sent to sellers either once or twice a month, depending on the seller's sales volume.

How can companies such as Half.com and eBay make money when they charge such low fees to sellers? The answer is that they have learned how to effectively apply e-business technologies. The incremental cost of posting one additional item to either site is almost zero. The process of listing items, placing bids, or purchasing items is entirely automated. There is no need for human intervention (as long as the systems function properly). If any of these functions required employees to talk to customers on the phone, for example, there is no way that the listing fees and commissions could be so low. These and similar sites are good illustrations of how the proper application of e-business technologies can enable businesses that otherwise could not exist.

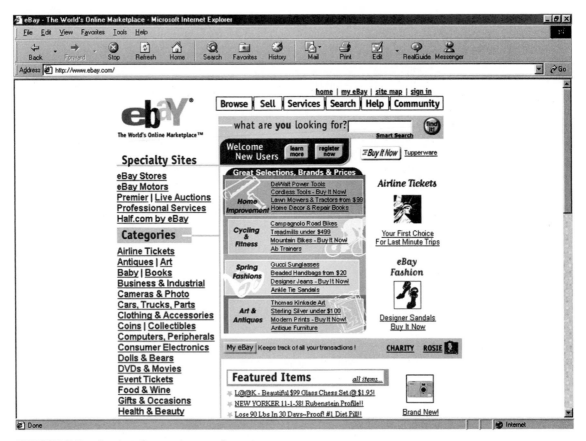

FIGURE 2-9 Product Categories on eBay

Source: eBay home page, eBay Inc., http://www.ebay.com/. These materials have been reproduced with the permission of eBay, Inc. COPYRIGHT © EBAY, INC. ALL RIGHTS RESERVED.

Government-to-Constituent

The final category of e-business that we will discuss is e-business between governments and their constituents, which we call G2C e-business, although others call it electronic government, or e-government. Many progressive governments are utilizing the Internet and Web to help facilitate communications with and service delivery to both private citizens and organizations. Note that rather than having separate categories for government-to-business and government-to-consumer, we combine the two into the category of government-to-constituent.

We have learned that e-business technologies can be applied by businesses to provide improved customer service. In a similar manner, governments can use e-business to improve their interactions with their constituents. In Chapter 1, we saw how the U.S. Internal Revenue Services makes dozens of tax forms and information bulletins available on the Web. Of course, national and regional governments in many countries use the Web to improve service delivery. For example, the Orange County, Florida government uses the Web to provide various types of information and services to its citizens.

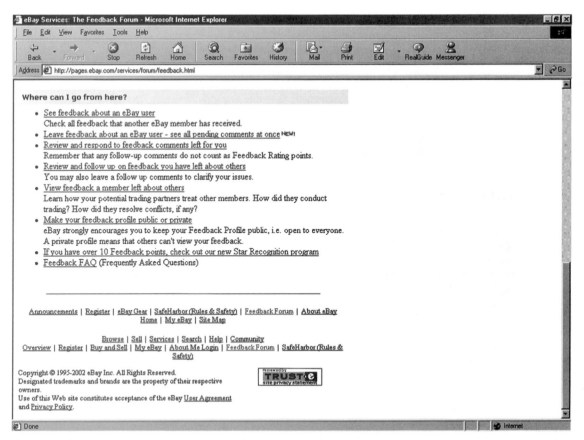

FIGURE 2-10   eBay Feedback Forum

Governments and their citizens must interact in many ways. Permits and licenses are required for many activities, such as constructing a building or driving an automobile. Regulations must be checked. Taxes and fines must be paid. When face-to-face or telephone interaction are the only forms of service available, long lines and waiting on hold are often the result. Sometimes you must travel to or call many different government offices just to track down required information. Electronic business technologies allow shoppers to avoid long lines at the mall. These same technologies can help citizens avoid long lines at city hall.

Governments around the world are investigating how to apply e-business technologies in order to more efficiently and effectively serve their constituents. For example, in April 2000, the Australian Commonwealth Government released its online government strategy. There is sufficient interest in G2C e-business that technology companies such as IBM, and prestigious consulting firms such as Booz-Allen & Hamilton have divisions devoted to electronic government.

At the moment, many governmental e-business efforts are simply online reproductions of the off-line structure. However, some governments are building electronic government portals that are similar to private Web portals, such as Excite and Yahoo!. These portals provide well-organized, single points of entry into the e-business structure of the government, just as Web portals attempt to provide a single, organized point of entry to the Web. We are in the early days of G2C e-business, but many believe that in a few years, using e-business technologies to interact with governments will be commonplace.

Keep in mind that the discussion offered here is not intended to provide a complete listing of all possible e-commerce business models. However, the business models described in this section are among the most widely used and allow you to gain a better understanding of e-commerce. Many e-commerce businesses that did not sufficiently consider their business models are now buried in the dot-com graveyard.

SUMMARY

Electronic commerce is impacting all levels of economies worldwide. As e-commerce technologies continue to mature and as individuals, organizations, and governments increase their understanding of how to best apply these technologies, the impact of e-commerce will only increase. This chapter provided an overview of these effects at three levels: economies, organizations, and individuals. One important point made in each of these discussions is that there are both positive and negative impacts of e-commerce. We must strive to understand how to take advantage of the positive aspects of e-commerce, while minimizing the harmful effects.

We also divided e-commerce into four categories: business-to-business, business-to-consumer, consumer-to-consumer, and government-to-constituent. In addition, different types of e-commerce applications were discussed within each category.

Finally, the chapter defined the term "business model," and discussed the importance of business models in e-commerce. In addition, we discussed a number of commonly used e-commerce business models and examples of each.

KEY TERMS

business model

channel conflict

customer relationship management

disintermediation

supply chain management

REVIEW QUESTIONS

1. (a) Identify and describe three ways e-commerce impacts economies.

(b) Identify and describe three ways e-commerce impacts organizations.

(c) Identify and describe three ways e-commerce impacts individuals.

2. (a) Briefly explain the concept of transaction costs.

3. (a) What are network effects?

(b) Explain how network effects can help explain the spread of communication technologies, such as electronic mail.

4. Explain how e-commerce technologies impact supply chains.

5. What threats do organizations face from e-commerce?

6. How can e-commerce technologies help consumers increase their economic efficiency?

7. Identify and briefly describe three areas of e-commerce-related fraud. Be sure to discuss how e-commerce technologies are used to perpetrate each fraud.

8. (a) What are the four categories of e-commerce described in this chapter?

(b) Give a specific example of each category.

9. (a) What is a business-to-business exchange?

(b) Name and briefly describe each type of business-to-business exchange discussed in this chapter.

10. Describe each category of business-to-consumer e-commerce discussed in this chapter.

11. Give two examples of consumer-to-consumer e-commerce.

12. (a) Define the term "business model."

(b) Why are business models important in e-commerce?

13. Name and describe each of the e-commerce business models described in this chapter.

EXERCISES

1. You are interested in buying a new automobile. Use Edmunds.com and other automobile-related Webs sites to do the following.

(a) Identify three models that satisfy your needs. List the following information for each model.

- The make and model of the vehicle
- The price if the vehicle is brand new
- The price of a one-year-old vehicle
- The fuel economy of the vehicle
- The monthly payment for each new and used model selected; use a 10 percent down payment and 10 percent interest for forty-eight months

(b) Describe how you used e-commerce technologies in researching your selections. What Web sites did you use? How did you find these sites? Describe the most and least useful aspects of each site.

2. You need a new set of golf clubs (or some other product assigned by your instructor). Use eBay to locate three sets of clubs that will meet your needs. Once you have found the three sets, read the Feedback Forum postings for each seller. (If you find a seller who does not have any postings, select a different set of clubs.)

(a) Describe your assessment of whether you would feel comfortable purchasing the clubs from each of the sellers. Why do you feel this way? What influence did the Feedback Forum postings have on your assessment?

(b) Which set of clubs would you buy? Why?

3. Find examples of three of the business models discussed in this chapter. Your instructor will tell you which three models to investigate. Do not use the examples mentioned in the chapter. For each example:

(a) Describe the business and the business model being used.

(b) How does the company generate revenue?

(c) Explain how e-commerce technologies help the company implement its business model.

(d) Do you think that the business model is viable? Explain your answer.

4. Locate and investigate four Web-based affiliate programs other than Amazon.com. Explain how each program operates, including what fees are paid.

5. Locate three Web sites for state or local governments. On each site, locate two activities that you (if you were a citizen of that area) can complete online, rather than in person or by mail. For each activity, describe the activity and the process used to complete it online. Rank the three sites in terms of (a) organization, (b) content, and (c) usefulness.

6. Find three government sites and critique how they are organized, what they offer, etc. Look up your local government's Web site. What can you do using your government's Web site? Are there any additional services you'd like to see? Explain.

DISCUSSION POINTS

1. With a classmate, debate whether the overall impact of e-business is positive or negative for (a) organizations and (b) individuals.

2. Discuss the potential impact that might result from individuals having unequal access to e-commerce technologies.

3. Prepare arguments for and against the following statement: "Governments should make full use of e-business

technologies to allow more convenient access to information and services. People without access to the Internet can still use traditional ways to access government. They aren't any worse off than before."

4. Following the controversy surrounding the 2000 United States Presidential election, there has been a push to use electronic voting. Discuss the advantages and disadvantages of using electronic ballots.

RELATED WEB SITES

Altra Energy Market: www.altranet.com

Altra Market Place: www.altranet.com/browse.php/market_place/

Barnes & Noble: www.bn.com/

Billpoint: www.billpoint.com

Consumer Reports: www.consumerreports.org

eBay: www.ebay.com

Edmunds: www.edmunds.com

Employease: www.employease.com

Encyclopedia Brittanica: www.britannica.com

eSTEEL Exchange: exchange.e-steel.com/

Excite: www.excite.com

Expedia: www.expedia.com

Fashionmall.com: www.fashionmall.com

Google: www.google.com

Half.com: www.half.com

Hewlett-Packard: www.hp.com

Hotmail: www.hotmail.com

HoustonStreet: www.houstonstreet.com

iEscrow: www.iescrow.com

iMARK: www.imark.com

J. D. Edwards: www.jdedwards.com

Lands' End: www.landsend.com

Lycos: www.lycos.com

The Motley Fool: www.fool.com/index.htm

National Consumers' League: www.nclnet.org/

Netmarket: www.netmarket.com

Oracle: www.oracle.com

PeopleSoft: www.peoplesoft.com

SAP: www.sap.com

Supergo Bike Shops: www.supergo.com/

Tommy Hilfiger: www.tommy.com

Travelocity: www.travelocity.com

Wall Street Journal: online.wsj.com/public/us

Yahoo!: www.yahoo.com

FURTHER READINGS

GILBERT, A. and B. BACHELDOR. "The Big Squeeze." *Information Week Online* (27 March 2000): http://www.information-week.com/shared/printArticle?article=infoweek/779/prchannel.htm&pub=iwk.

RANSDELL, E. "Network Effects." *Fast Company* 27 (1999): 208.

REFERENCES

Frequently Asked Questions page. 2002. Supply-Chain Council. http://www.supply-chain.org/Resources/faq.htm.

KELLY, KEVIN. 1998. *New rules for the new economy: 10 radical strategies for a connected world.* New York: Viking Press.

PASTORE, MICHAEL. 2001. Convenience key to successful holiday season. CyberAtlas.com (31 October 2001): http://cyberatlas.internet.com/markets/retailing/article/0,,6061_914131,00.html.

RAPPA, MICHAEL. 2002. Business models on the web. http://digitalenterprise.org/models/models.html.

TIMMERS, PAUL. 1998. Business models for electronic markets. *Electronic Markets* 8 (2): 39.

Top Ten Dot Cons page. Federal Trade Commission. 2000. http://www.ftc.gov/bcp/conline/edcams/dotcon/.

WARKENTIN, MERRILL. 2002. eBusiness models. http://www.mis-professor.com/ecomm/bizmodls.shtml.

CHAPTER 3

BARRIERS TO ELECTRONIC BUSINESS

LEARNING OBJECTIVES

After reading and completing this chapter, you should be able to:

- Understand and discuss perceptual barriers to e-business
- Understand and discuss societal barriers to e-business
- Understand and discuss legal and ethical barriers to e-business
- Understand and discuss organizational barriers to e-business
- Understand and discuss cultural barriers to e-business
- Understand and discuss a number of technical barriers to e-business

Opening Case: A Tale of E-business in Two Countries

Note: The following fictional account is based on the actual conditions that existed in the two countries, India and the United States, at the time of the writing. Two points should be made. First, conditions may have changed substantially by the time you read this. Initiatives are underway in India that are likely to lead to significant improvements in its telecommunications and technology infrastructures. Second, and more importantly, the following story is not intended to demean India or its citizens in any way. From personal experience, the story's author knows that in India there are vast numbers of very bright people with substantial technological skills. In fact, India is quickly becoming a center for information technology development. Much of the world's software development currently takes place in India and it is likely that India's share of the software development pie will only increase in the future.

The American Experience

Sally, a typical, middle-class, American consumer is looking for a gift for her brother's upcoming birthday. She really does not feel up to dealing with the mall crowds and the associated traffic and parking headaches, so she decides to do some Web shopping. Sally turns on her recently purchased PC, which is reasonably well equipped for Web surfing and cost about U.S.$1,000. The PC is a bit of a luxury, but she had no trouble paying for it on her U.S.$3,500 per month salary. Once the PC is up and running, she dials out to her Internet service provider (ISP). The connection is made at over 50 Kbps, which is not as fast as her connection at work (where she also has Internet access), but it is fast enough. Sally checked into getting higher-speed access through her cable TV provider, but decided that the extra speed wasn't worth the extra cost. Still, it is nice to have choices.

Sally does not know what to get for her brother, so she spends some time browsing some of her favorite shopping sites. She looks at clothes on J. Crew's Web site, electronics on BestBuy.com, books on Amazon.com, and compact discs on CDnow.com. It's almost like visiting the mall, but from the comfort of home. She finally decides that a CD player would be a great gift. Sally is a savvy shopper, so she decides to do a little comparison shopping and jumps over to Crutchfield's Web site (Crutchfield is an established mail-order supplier of electronics). Although Sally has never bought anything from Crutchfield before, she is not too worried about the possibility of fraud. She knows that if Crutchfield does not deliver the CD player, she can file a dispute with her credit card company and will not have to pay the charges.

Being a procrastinator, Sally has waited until almost the last minute to find her brother's gift, so she is glad that Crutchfield offers a variety of shipping options. Overnight shipping is too expensive, so Sally settles for second-day delivery via one of the well-known shipping services. Since she has used this service many times, she is confident that it will deliver the CD player on time.

The Indian Experience

Ram is similar to Sally in some ways. He is a typical, middle-class consumer. However, Ram is a typical, middle-class *Indian* consumer. Unfortunately, like Sally, Ram is also a procrastinator and needs to buy a gift in a hurry. Ram's choices are more limited than Sally's. Ram does not own his own computer. Even though his monthly income of Rs 20,000 (U.S.$465) puts him solidly in the middle class, it's nowhere near enough to afford a Rs 50,000 computer. Even if he had a PC, Internet access is difficult to afford. An Internet connection through VSNL, the Indian government's primary Internet service provider, costs around Rs 600 for twenty-five hours of connection time. Unlimited Internet access is relatively unknown in India. Phone service quality can be poor in Ram's area, so getting a good dial-up connection is not guaranteed. So, even if Ram could access the Internet from home, he's not sure if the connection would be good enough to make surfing the Web enjoyable.

Even though Ram does not have a home computer, he still has the option of visiting one of the many "Internet café's" that exist in his city. Their prices can be a bit expensive, at about Rs 100 per hour, and Ram has to travel into the city to get to one of the cafés. Ram decides to go to the café and rent time on one of their computers. After some searching, he finds a book that would make a perfect gift. Unfortunately, the site where he found the book is for a U.S., not an Indian, company. This presents a problem, since Ram wants low shipping costs and to pay in Rupees. He searches for an Indian company that offers the same book, and luckily is able to find one. However, Ram has never heard of this company, which is not surprising since it is in Mumbai, and he is in Bangalore.

This makes Ram nervous. He is used to dealing with merchants and vendors face-to-face. Ram recalls an unpleasant experience ordering something over the phone. When the product was still not delivered after two months, he threatened to sue the merchant. This was a hollow threat, however, and the merchant knew it. It would have been too expensive and time consuming to sue over a few hundred rupees. His credit card company was no help in resolving the dispute. It is too bad that there is not a better way to resolve disputes between customers and merchants. In the end Ram decides that it is just too much trouble to try to buy the book over the Web—he is better off going to his regular bookstore.

Differences in the Experiences

As can be seen from the narratives, the experience of Sally, the American consumer, is much different from that of Ram, the Indian consumer. For many American consumers, the online shopping experience is often enjoyable. The picture is quite different in India. While the Indian consumer may be just as technologically knowledgeable as the American consumer, several barriers hinder Web-based shopping in India.

INTRODUCTION

Although the use of electronic business technologies continues to expand rapidly, there are many barriers that may hinder the expansion of e-business. These barriers vary in nature. Some are technical, while others are organizational. Some exist at the societal level, while others pertain to the perceptions of individuals. Understanding these barriers, and how and why they may inhibit the use of e-business, is important to understanding how to apply e-business technologies.

This chapter examines these barriers in detail, and also discusses efforts underway to overcome these barriers. One point to take away from this chapter is the importance of nontechnical barriers. Many of you reading this book are planning careers in technical areas. As technologists, we tend to look for technology-oriented solutions to most problems. It is simply our orientation. However, we hope that by reading this chapter, you will gain an appreciation for the importance of non-technical issues related to e-business. Unless all of the barriers, technical and nontechnical, discussed in this chapter are overcome, e-business will never reach its full potential.

As you read this chapter, keep in mind that, although we use categories of barriers to organize our discussion, the barriers do not always fall neatly into one category or another. Fortunately, it is really not important whether a barrier is cultural or societal. The important fact is that the barriers exist and must be dealt with.

PERCEPTUAL BARRIERS

Individuals' perceptions represent one class of barrier to e-business, particularly in the case of business-to-consumer e-business. Make no mistake about it—the way individuals perceive e-business is a key determinant of whether or not they use e-business systems. If individuals or organizations think that e-business is too difficult, or that it does not fit with how they prefer to conduct business, or that they should not trust online merchants, they will not use e-business technologies. In this section, we discuss several perceptions that are related to individuals' decisions to use or not use e-business. Understanding these perceptions and how they are formed will help you understand how different aspects of e-business design may influence perceptions in a way that will lead more people to take advantage of e-business.

Before continuing with our discussion, it is important to understand clearly that it is the potential customers' perceptions that matter, not some independent expert's assessment. A good example is consumers' perceptions of complexity (which we discuss later in this section). There are a number of ways in which the actual complexity of a system can be measured. While this is certainly important, in this section we are concerned with perceptions, not objective reality. Perceptions influence behaviors, both directly and indirectly, through attitudes. Even if a system is, by objective standards, not complex, if I perceive it to be complex, I am less likely to use that system. Similar statements can be made about any of the perceptions discussed in this section.

Trust

One of the most important barriers to the use of e-business is the level of trust that individuals and organizations are willing to place in businesses selling goods and services online. Trust is important in all forms of e-business, whether business-to-business or business-to-consumer. In short, if people and organizations do not trust those using e-business to provide goods and services, they will not engage in e-business transactions. Think about it from your own perspective. If you did not trust a merchant, would you do business with that merchant?

What is trust? Trust is a very complex concept—one that applies to many different aspects of our lives. Trust impacts our interpersonal relationships, as well as our business relationships. There are both cognitive and emotional aspects of trust. In addition, there are many factors that may influence trust. For the purposes of this chapter, we will rely on the definition of trust proposed by Hosmer (1995), which is the expectation that the other party will behave in accordance with commitments, negotiate honestly, and not take advantage, even when the opportunity arises.

Trust is typically not an "all-or-none" proposition. In most cases, the degree to which you are willing to trust another falls somewhere between total trust or a complete lack of trust. It is often convenient to speak of trust or a lack of trust as if those were the only two options. However, it is important for you to remember that trust usually lies somewhere on a continuum between those two extremes.

Interestingly, trust is a dynamic concept. The level of trust you are willing to place in another changes over time as you become more familiar with the other party through experience or other knowledge. For example, the first time you make a purchase from a particular online merchant, you may not be willing to place much trust in it. However, if that purchase turns out well, your trust of the merchant is likely to increase. Of course, the reverse is also true. If the purchase turns out badly, your level of trust in the merchant will probably decrease.

Why is trust so important to e-business? There are a number of characteristics of e-business transactions that make trust important. First, e-business transactions occur at a distance. In a face-to-face transaction, the buyer and seller interact directly with each other. The buyer can inspect the goods for sale, touching and feeling the products in order to assess their quality. In addition, once the goods are paid for, the buyer takes possession of the goods immediately. In a distant transaction, such as those in e-business, the buyer cannot see the goods and, unless the product is digital, cannot take possession immediately. Because of this, the buyer must trust the seller to supply the goods as promised—to ship the correct products in a timely manner. In addition, the buyer must trust the merchant to faithfully describe the goods (to not inflate their quality, for example). Finally, the buyer must trust the merchant to take care of any problems. For example, if the products shipped are not the correct size, or if they are not what the buyer expected, the buyer has to trust the merchant to accept the return of the products.

Another factor that makes trust important in e-business is the fact that technology is involved. When business relationships are mediated by information technology, it is important to understand that the technology can impact the nature of the relationship. Without getting too theoretical, you can think of the technology as causing static in the relationship. One reason is that people and organizations have only been interacting through technology for a short period of time relative to how long they have been interacting face-to-face. This can cause some uneasiness. For example, people must have confidence that the online business has sufficient knowledge of e-business technologies to provide adequate security to protect private information, such as credit card numbers. Otherwise potential customers will not be willing to make purchases from that online business.

What are the attributes of trust? Studies of trust in commercial exchanges have shown that trust includes many components. However, we feel that there are four perceptions that are the most important in the context of e-business:

- Predictability
- Reliability
- Technical competence
- Fiduciary responsibility

What is important is not some independent expert's assessment of these characteristics. It is the perception of the potential e-business customer that is important. So even if a Web business is extremely technically competent, if potential customers do not feel that the business is technically competent, they will not trust the business. These components are defined and their importance to e-business is discussed below.

Predictability

Predictability pertains to the customer's assessment of his ability to "know" what the actions of the e-business organization will be. This is related to, but not the same as, consistency. A customer may have some expectation that a trading partner will act consistently. However, it is possible that the partner's actions may change, which lowers consistency. However, if the reason for the change is understood, and if the customer uses this understanding to adjust predictions, predictability will not suffer.

Perceptions of predictability impact trust—the more predictable you find a merchant, the more trust you are willing to place in that merchant. An example may help you understand why this is so. Let's assume that you deal with two Web CD merchants, Cool CDs and Terrific Tunes. When you place an order with Cool CDs, it always sends a confirmation e-mail message the next day and it always tells you when you can expect to receive your CDs. In addition, your CDs arrive within the time period promised. When a CD is out of stock, Cool CDs informs you of this in the confirmation e-mail, and you do not expect that CD to arrive any time soon. Because you generally know what Cool CDs is going to do—it is predictable—you are willing to trust it as an online merchant. Terrific Tunes, on the other hand, typically leaves you in the dark as to what it is going to do. Sometimes it sends e-mail confirmation, sometimes it does not. Even when it does, it does not inform you whether or not the CDs you ordered are in stock, so sometimes a shipment arrives, but some CDs are missing. You can never tell what is going to happen; Terrific Tunes, in your experience, is not predictable. As a result, you do not think that Terrific Tunes is worthy of your trust.

Reliability

Another perceptual component of trust in e-business is reliability, which we define as the correspondence between what a party says and what it does. When you think someone is reliable, you believe that she is acting in accordance with statements and agreements. As was the case with predictability, the more reliable you feel a merchant is, the more willing you are to trust them. Let's consider another example. If Cool CDs promises to ship all orders of in-stock products within two business days, and in your experience it lives up to this promise, you are likely to feel that Cool CDs is reliable and you are more likely to trust it.

Technical Competence

Perceptions of trust also depend on perceptions of technical competence. The importance of how potential customers perceive the technical competence of an online retailer was mentioned earlier. If potential customers do not feel that the Web merchant has enough technical knowledge to properly carry out transactions and protect sensitive information, they are not likely to trust the merchant. Even if the merchant wants to act appropriately, if you feel that it does not have the technical competence to carry out the desired actions, trust suffers. An experience of one of the authors illustrates how perceptions of technical competence impact trust and e-business use.

The author was going to participate in a fifteen kilometer road race. As a proponent of e-business, he was happy to learn that the race organizers had contracted with a race management company to provide online race registration. He clicked on the registration link on the race Web page and was transferred to the registration Web site. He entered the required information and clicked on the "secure payment" link. However, when the supposedly secure payment Web page opened, he noticed that the site was not actually secure. (You can tell this by looking at the lock or key icon on the Web browser and by looking for "https" in the address window.) Since he was not familiar with the management company, he assumed that it did not know how to properly implement transaction security. In other words, his perception of the technical competence of the management company was low. As a result, he did not trust the management company to actually protect his credit card number. Rather than use e-business to sign up for the race, he picked up the phone and registered.

Fiduciary Responsibility

The final component of trust we want to discuss is fiduciary responsibility. Although you may not be familiar with the term "fiduciary responsibility," it is actually a fairly simple concept. In terms of businesses and customers, fiduciary responsibility is the obligation of the business to act on behalf of the customer, even when the customer does not have the knowledge or experience to judge the business' actions. The higher you perceive the fiduciary responsibility of an organization to be, the more you will trust that organization. One business relationship in which fiduciary responsibility is often mentioned is that between attorneys and their clients. Due to fiduciary responsibility requirements, attorneys are required to act on their clients' behalf, even when the clients lack the knowledge to evaluate the attorneys' actions.

A good example of an e-business relationship in which fiduciary responsibility is important comes from online travel agencies. When you ask an online travel agent to provide you with the lowest fare for an airline ticket, you trust the agent to act on your behalf, even though you probably do not have sufficient knowledge of ticket prices to judge the agency's actions. In part, the level of trust that you place in the agency is determined by your perceptions of the agency's fiduciary responsibility. Table 3-1 summarizes the trust-related perceptions discussed in this section.

Impact of a Lack of Trust

What are the consequences of a lack of trust? There are two major consequences of trust in the context of e-business. Trust in a Web-based organization in part determines whether a consumer will use e-business to interact with the organization. It also impacts how heavily the consumer will monitor the relationship. Research indicates that the lower the level of

Table 3-1   Perceptual Components of Trust

Component	Definition
Predictability	Ability to "know" what the action of the other party will be
Reliability	Assessment of whether the other party will act in accordance with their promises and obligations
Technical competence	Assessment of whether the other party possesses the knowledge and skills necessary to carry out promised or expected actions
Fiduciary responsibility	Assessment of whether the other party will act on your behalf, even if you lack the knowledge to properly judge their actions

trust you place in an online merchant, the less you will interact with that merchant. The same is true in business-to-business e-business—less trust leads to less use overall. However, it may be that other reasons for using the online business outweigh the lack of trust. What happens in this case? Although there is no research that we know of to back up our opinion, we believe that when your level of trust is lower you will spend more time monitoring the online business. For example, a colleague of one of the authors made a purchase using an online auction. He had several reasons for using the auction even though he had no experience with the business. Despite the fact that he interacted with the business, he did not have a high level of trust. Because he did not trust the business, he called his credit card company at least once a day to check for unauthorized charges. This monitoring continued even after his order arrived. The auction company demonstrated that it was worthy of trust, and, as a result, our friend still makes periodic purchases from the auction company. Because he now has a higher level of trust in the business, he no longer spends much time monitoring his transactions with it.

How can online companies build trust? There are two key elements to understanding how companies can build their customers' trust. First, remember that there are at least four components of trust, which we discussed earlier in this section. By taking actions that improve customers' perceptions of these components, companies can build trust. Second, successful interactions with a business can increase the level of trust a customer is willing to place in the business. Of course, taking actions that help build trust will also help increase positive customer interaction.

Let's look at some ways online organizations can help improve customers' perceptions. Recall that perceptions of predictability help create trust. Clearly posting stock availability, processing times, and shipping times will help customers more accurately predict when to expect their orders to arrive, which will improve perceptions of predictability and trust. For example, Sierra Trading Post®, a Web and catalog merchandiser of outdoor-related products, provides accurate estimates for shipping times and costs on its Web site, as shown in Figure 3-1. We can vouch for the accuracy of the estimates through experience with Sierra. By being willing to quote shipping estimates, Sierra increases customers' perceptions of predictability and trust. Businesses using e-business should also include on their Web sites clear policy statements covering issues such as how they handle product returns.

Other Customer Perceptions

There are several other perceptions that are important when customers, both businesses and consumers, choose whether or not to use e-business to interact with an organization. By understanding these perceptions and how they influence use, online businesses can take steps to improve the perceptions and, in turn, e-business use. It is critical to realize that what is important is the potential users' perceptions of e-business, not that of some independent expert. Many perceptions thought to be related to technology use have been studied. However, we limit our discussion to six that have been widely supported by research and relate to potential users' perceptions of the characteristics of an innovation. So, they are collectively referred to as "perceived innovation characteristics." If you are interested in learning more about how new ideas and products move through society, you should

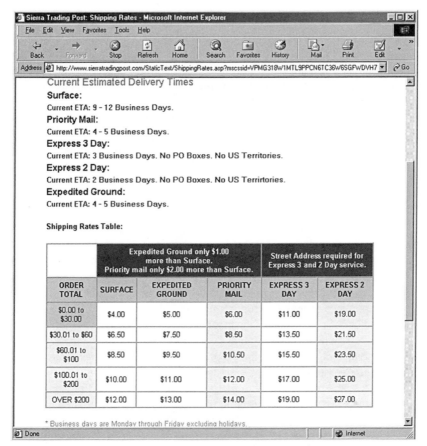

FIGURE 3-1   Sierra Trading Post Shipping Information Screen

SOURCE: Sierra Trading Post home page, http://www.sierratradingpost.com/. Used with permission.

read Everett Rogers' excellent book, *Diffusion of Innovations* (1995). The following discussion draws from this source and one other (Tornatzky and Klein 1987).

Perceptions of three innovation characteristics enjoy the most consistent support from research. Perceptions of **relative advantage, complexity,** and **compatibility** seem to consistently influence the use of an innovation. Other perceptions, including **visibility, result demonstrability,** and **trialability** are also thought to influence use, although there is less research evidence with respect to these characteristics.

Potential users' perceptions of the relative advantage of using e-business influence their eventual use of the technology. Relative advantage is defined as the degree to which an innovation is seen as being superior to its predecessor. There is substantial evidence to support the idea that perceptions of relative advantage influence consumers' ultimate use of an innovation, regardless of the nature of the innovation. For many consumers and businesses, one of the most important reasons to use e-business is convenience. The concept of relative advantage and convenience are closely related. Improved convenience is one factor that may increase perceptions of relative advantage. Others might include lower prices and greater choice. The more advantageous someone feels the use of e-business is, the more likely he is to use the technology.

Organizations interested in promoting the use of e-business can take steps to increase potential users' perceptions of the relative advantage. For example, promotional campaigns can emphasize the advantages of e-business, such as convenience and increased choice. It is also important that organizations keep the importance of perceived relative advantage in mind when designing e-business systems. Building in features that make the use of e-business more advantageous are likely to increase perceptions of relative advantage, which will, in turn, increase use. Features that are not easily reproduced in an offline environment may be particularly successful in increasing perceptions of relative advantage. A good example is product comparison. Many Web merchants offer customers the ability to dynamically build side-by-side comparisons of products. This is much more difficult to do offline, so it is likely to increase perceptions of the relative advantage of e-business over the offline alternatives.

Perceptions of the complexity of e-business also influence its use. Perceived complexity is simply the degree to which an innovation is seen by the potential user as being relatively difficult to use and understand. The harder it is to use or understand e-business in the users' view, the less likely they are to use e-business technologies. The concept of complexity is essentially the opposite of user friendliness. Manufacturers have long recognized the importance of making products user friendly. Factors ranging from the position of knobs and buttons to the size of the numbers on a clock influence complexity. For example, many more people use cassette tapes than ever used reel-to-reel tapes. Although cost and size are also factors, one reason for the popularity of cassette tapes is a result of their relative ease of use compared to reel-to-reel tapes. With a cassette, all you have to do is pop it in the player and press play. With reel-to-reel tapes, you must first complete a tedious threading process before you can listen to the tape. We see constant attempts to reduce the complexity of e-business technologies. For example, integrating electronic mail client software into Web browsers helps reduce perceptions of complexity. Companies using e-business must pay close attention to how complex their Web sites are. A commonly heard e-business-related complaint is that some businesses' Web sites are too hard to navigate. Perhaps you have experienced this frustration yourself. If so, you are less likely to use that Web site again - increased perceptions of complexity lead to decreased use.

As we mentioned earlier, it is perceptions that matter, not objective reality. This is particularly important to keep in mind when considering perceived complexity. Much time and effort is put into measuring the complexity of e-business systems. However, what ultimately matters is users' *perceptions* of how difficult the systems are to use. If all of the objective measures show that a system is not complex, but users still perceive the system to be complex, use suffers. Of course, objective measures of complexity are important and should be considered when designing an e-business system. If the objective measures show a system to be complex, it is very likely that users will also perceive the system to be complex. However, it is equally important to consider users' perceptions.

Perceived compatibility is defined as the degree to which an innovation is seen to be compatible with existing values, beliefs, experiences, and needs of users. Although the importance of compatibility is not discussed as often as relative advantage or complexity, our research indicates that compatibility is actually more closely related to e-business use. If any innovation, including e-business, is perceived to be incompatible with potential users, it is less likely to be used. Some system designers recognize the importance of compatibility. This is demonstrated by the use of **metaphors** in systems. One e-business example of the use of metaphors is the shopping cart. An example of an online shopping cart from Sierra Trading Post® is shown in Figure 3-2. Most business-to-consumer e-business sites, and many business-to-business sites, use a shopping cart metaphor to help users understand how to purchase items. When you are shopping online, you browse the product offerings, placing items you wish to buy in a virtual shopping cart. Once you have placed all of your desired products into the cart, you click on the "check out" button and complete your purchase. This is essentially the same process followed in many countries when you shop in physical stores. By using the shopping cart metaphor, e-business system designers increase the perceived compatibility of Web-based shopping, which increases its use.

The importance of many other perceptions have also been studied. We briefly discuss three of these. Perceptions of the result demonstrability of an innovation influence its use. Perceived result demonstrability refers to the degree to which potential users find the outcomes of using an innovation apparent. A related concept is perceived visibility, which refers to perceptions of how apparent the actual use of the innovation is. If I see you using an online retailer's Web site, it impacts visibility. If you tell me about ordering something online, it

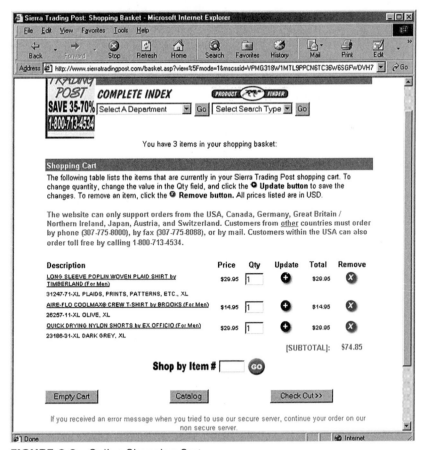

FIGURE 3-2 Online Shopping Cart

SOURCE: Sierra Trading Post, Inc., http://www.sierratradingpost.com/. Used with permission.

affects my perceptions of result demonstrability. Both of these perceptions have a positive relationship with use; increasing perceptions of result demonstrability or visibility increases use.

The final perception we discuss is perceived trialability, which refers to perceptions of the degree to which an innovation can be used on a trial basis before confirmation of the adoption must occur. A less formal way of putting it is that perceived trialability is whether potential users feel that they can "try it before they buy it." (Do not take the "buy it" part too literally.) When potential users feel that they must make significant investments in time, effort, or money in order to find out whether or not something is worthy of use, its use is less likely. This is the logic behind free trial offers, which have been used successfully by organizations such as America Online and other Internet service providers. Table 3-2 provides a summary of the perceptions discussed in this subsection.

In this section, we have seen how e-business users' perceptions can influence their use. Companies that wish to take advantage of e-business must pay attention to these perceptions and take steps that will lead potential users to view the use of e-business favorably. In the next section, we discuss societal barriers that are not related to perceptions, but rather are based on objective facts.

SOCIETAL BARRIERS

In the last section, we discussed some barriers to e-business that result from individuals' perceptions of e-business. In this section, we discuss barriers that exist at a higher level—the societal level. These are larger issues that cannot be addressed by individual organizations; overcoming these barriers requires the coordinated efforts of individuals, businesses, not-for-profit organizations, and governments.

Telecommunications Infrastructure

In the developed world, consumers and businesses often take their country's telecommunications infrastructure for granted. However, in many nations, reliable telephone

Table 3-2 Perceived Innovation Characteristics

Perception	Description
Relative advantage	Degree to which an innovation is seen as being superior to its predecessor
Complexity	Degree to which an innovation is seen by the potential adopter as being relatively difficult to use and understand
Compatibility	Degree to which an innovation is seen to be compatible with existing values, beliefs, experiences, and needs of adopters
Result demonstrability	Degree to which the outcomes of using an innovation are perceived to be tangible
Visibility	The perception of the actual visibility of the innovation itself, as opposed to the visibility of outputs
Trialability	Based on adopters' perceptions of the degree to which an innovation can be used on a trial basis

service is rare. Although dial-up telephone lines are only one method of accessing the Internet, the lack of quality telephone service is typically symptomatic of a weak telecommunications infrastructure. Simply put, since e-business relies on telecommunication networks, a poor telecommunications infrastructure presents a significant barrier to the application of e-business technologies. There is a direct relationship between a sound telecommunications infrastructure and sound e-business—in essence the telecommunications infrastructure facilitates e-business.

Even when the telecommunications infrastructure is sound, access to the infrastructure is beyond the reach of individuals in many areas. This is because access may be prohibitively expensive relative to the wages of many individuals. In most of the developed world, paying for a home telephone line consumes a relatively small percentage of household income. If you make U.S.$40,000 a year, paying U.S.$25 per month for telephone service is not much of a burden. However, if you only make U.S.$4,000 a year, the monthly fee may be beyond your reach.

Poor infrastructures are not limited to developing countries. Even in the developed world, many rural areas suffer from substandard infrastructures. While reliable telephone service is commonly available, e-business may still suffer due to the quality of existing equipment and the lack of high-speed connectivity options, such as digital subscriber line technology. For example, in the United States in 2000, the percentage of central city households with high-speed Internet access was almost twice that of rural households. Throughout the world, as people and organizations continue to adopt e-business, the demands placed on current infrastructures will increase dramatically. The use of e-business technologies will suffer unless telecommunications providers continue to improve infrastructures.

Access Inequities

Many reading this text spend large parts of their days in university environments in which Internet access seems to be everywhere. In addition, many of you also have a computer and Internet access at home. So, it may seem to you that pretty much everyone has access to the Internet. In fact, this is not the case. A large portion of the population does not have easy access to computers or the Internet. This is the case even in economically developed countries. For example, according to the U.S. federal government's Digital Divide project, over 86 percent of U.S. households with incomes in excess of U.S.$75,000 have access to the Internet. For households with incomes under U.S.$25,000, only 33 percent have Internet access (National Telecommunications and Information Administration 2000).

What are the consequences of this lack of access? It may be helpful to break the discussion into two broad areas—skills and benefits of e-business. Individuals who lack technological skills find themselves unable to qualify for many better-paying jobs. While other skills are certainly important, IT skills are at the core of knowledge work, and knowledge work is where much of the job growth will be in the future. The chain of consequences is clear. Those without access to IT will not gain the skills necessary to fully participate in the knowledge economy, which potentially holds severe economic consequences.

You may think that primary and secondary schools are equipped with computers. Aren't they teaching students computer skills? Our research shows that in many cases, even though schools do have computers, most students spend very little time gaining IT skills. There are several reasons for this. Teachers may lack the knowledge necessary to teach computer skills. More likely, it is very difficult to fit the teaching of computer-specific skills into the curriculum—there simply may not be enough hours in the school day. Regardless of the reason, the fact remains that many students are not learning IT skills, which may cost all of us in the long run.

A second consequence of lack of access to a computer and the Internet is that individuals are not able to fully benefit from the advantages of e-business. As we have discussed in other chapters, e-business holds significant benefits for consumers - for example, greater convenience, more choices, and lower prices. Obviously, those without access to the necessary technology cannot realize these benefits. Keep in mind that in most cases, those without access could actually benefit the most from e-business. Typically, these are low-income families. They have tight budgets that do not allow for computers and Internet access. It follows that those with the tightest budgets stand to gain from the greater choice and potentially lower prices available through e-business.

As IT professionals, it is incumbent upon us to help society overcome these access inequities. We can volunteer to help teachers learn how to integrate computers into their curricula. We can help wire schools for Internet access. We can help refurbish older equipment for use in schools. We can go into the schools and teach students how to use computers and the Internet. All of these activities certainly require an investment of time and effort. However, it is an investment that may well pay off beyond our wildest expectations.

Information Technology Skills Shortage

In order to take advantage of e-business technologies, organizations must have large numbers of skilled workers. A report from the U.S. Department of Commerce (1997) cites an Information Technology Association of America estimate that in 2000 there would be more than eight hundred thousand unfilled information technology jobs in the United States. A recent survey by the same organization reveals that more than three-quarters of the information technology executives surveyed believe that workforce barriers represent a hindrance to e-business. Twenty-six percent think that workforce barriers are a strong hindrance and 52 percent believe that workforce barriers are a moderate hindrance. Applying the basic economic law of supply and demand, we can see that the IT skills shortage drives up the cost of all IT projects. Since specialized e-business technology skills are in even shorter supply, e-business projects are especially susceptible. In many cases, organizations find that they must hire consulting firms in order to gain e-business expertise. Of course, this drives up costs even further.

The workforce shortage is a serious concern for all countries, but for developing countries it is even more serious. Unfortunately, developing countries may stand the most to gain from e-business. One reason that developing countries face more serious problems from the skills shortage is that many of these countries face a "brain drain" where many individuals with IT skills leave the country for higher salaries in other nations. Because of this, even when training and education programs are put into place, some people may leave the country after completing the programs, which prevents the developing country from taking advantage of the skills.

An interesting consequence of the skills shortage is the emergence of an IT "food chain." According to Arnold and Niederman (2001), skilled workers from less developed countries move to richer nations where salaries tend to be substantially higher. This, unfortunately, increases the digital divide between richer and developing nations.

How can the skills shortage be reduced? The best hope is well-planned education and training programs. In many countries, IT-related education programs are experiencing record enrollments. It is difficult for traditional educational institutions to keep pace with the demand. As a result, innovative education and training programs need to be developed in order to help meet the demand. For example, retraining programs may be able to help those with outdated or under-demanded skills gain valuable IT skills. In addition, it may be necessary to make better use of IT in the delivery of education. Industry has learned how to apply IT in order to improve efficiency. Now educational institutions are putting considerable effort into using IT to improve the efficiency of education delivery. The IT skills gap is large and expanding. A combination of approaches, hopefully all coordinated, will be required to erase this gap. Until this happens, the gap will remain a barrier to e-business growth.

Although, at a societal level, addressing the IT skills shortage requires actions beyond the reach of most individual organizations, there are steps that an organization can take that may help it overcome the negative impacts of the shortage. Organizations that develop and follow an overall human resource strategy are typically better equipped to deal with the IT skills shortage. A human resource strategy should include recruitment and selection, performance appraisal, reward programs, and employee development (Agarwal and Ferratt 2001). Organizations may find that changing the structure of jobs to be more flexible and more enriching may help retain skilled employees (Arnold and Niederman 2001). Employee retention is a major issue for organizations implementing e-business systems. Because of the skills shortage, retaining employees is critical; finding replacements is likely to be difficult and expensive. It is important that firms take a long-term view of their investments in human resources. One key aspect of retaining IT workers is making the work they do interesting and rewarding. For example, rotating workers among a number of jobs often helps keep workers from feeling that their jobs have become stale. Providing training to enable workers to gain new skills can also help retain employees (Agarwal and Ferratt 2001). However, this is a bit of a double-edged sword; the newly gained skills also make the workers more attractive to competing employers. For this reason, many organizations require some sort of commitment from employees before putting them through significant training. Often, these commitments involve a promise from the employee to stay with the organization for a specific length of time. If this promise is broken, the employee is responsible for reimbursing the organization for the cost of the training.

LEGAL AND ETHICAL BARRIERS

There are also legal and ethical issues that represent potential barriers to e-business. Since doing business across public networks, such as the Internet, is relatively new, there is a need for new legislation to establish the "rules of the road" for e-business. The need is particularly acute in consumer-oriented e-business. In addition, there are some complex ethical issues that must be addressed if e-business is to achieve its potential.

Digital Signatures

One area in which new legislation is required to facilitate e-business is digital signatures. In the offline world, handwritten signatures serve two main purposes. First, they can be used to authenticate the identity of the signer. For example, when you use a credit card to make a purchase at a store, the clerk may ask for another form of identification. By comparing the signatures on the credit card and the other identification, the clerk can be sure that you are, in fact, the owner of the credit card. The second purpose of signatures is nonrepudiation, which simply means keeping someone from claiming that he did not enter into some agreement. Let's assume that you sign an agreement to maintain a membership with a health club for one year. If you later try to deny that you entered into the agreement, the club's management simply has to point out your signature on the agreement. The presence of your signature prevents you from denying the agreement.

Digital signatures are intended to provide authentication and nonrepudiation in the online world. In 2000, the U.S. Congress passed the Digital Signatures Act, which legislates that digital signatures carry the same legal weight as written signatures. Although there are still some issues to be resolved, many see this act as being important to the development of multi-party e-business.

Consumer Protections

If business-to-consumer e-business is to achieve its potential, consumers must be sufficiently protected from dishonest operators and from honest errors committed by ethical businesses. This reality makes the area of consumer protection a potential barrier to e-business. In traditional face-to-face transactions, consumers have the opportunity to visually inspect merchandise to assess its quality and suitability. This is not possible today with e-business transactions (unless the products are digital). Therefore, consumer protections must be established to provide security for consumers making online purchases. You are much more likely to purchase a pair of shoes online if you know that there are protections in place to help you if you are not satisfied with your purchase.

There are several types of consumer protection, some legislated, some simply common practices that help facilitate business-to-consumer e-business. One example of a legislated form of consumer protection is the presence of small-claims courts in the United States. Most jurisdictions in the United States have less formal courts that are designed to decide on low–dollar value disputes. For example, if you feel that an automobile repair shop did not perform services for which you paid U.S.$200, you could file a claim against the shop in small-claims court. Typically, filing and arguing such a claim does not require the assistance of an attorney, which makes the process feasible for a U.S.$200 dispute. Enabling the economically feasible resolution of small-claim disputes helps eliminate some fears associated with e-business. Without small-claims courts, consumers may feel that they have little recourse when they feel that they were not treated fairly by an online business. Would you pay a lawyer U.S.$200 an hour to help you resolve a U.S.$200 claim. Probably not. However, if you have the ability to take action yourself in small-claims court, you may be more likely to pursue the matter.

Another form of legislated protection in some countries is limited consumer liability for unauthorized credit card transactions. In the United States, there is a $50 limit of liability for fraudulent credit card use. (Some other countries have similar provisions.) This means that when an unauthorized person uses your credit card, you are liable for a maximum of $50, subject to certain restrictions. Consumers in the United States have much less to worry about when using their credit cards online because of this protection. Even if their credit card information is intercepted during an online transaction, the maximum financial liability is relatively small. Some credit card issuers have gone a step further and have stated that consumers are not liable for *any* fraudulent use of their credit cards that results from information being intercepted during online transactions. Of course, these credit card companies are hoping to boost e-business and the use of their cards, since the vast majority of business-to-consumer e-business transactions involve the use of a credit card.

In some countries, credit card companies also help resolve disputes between cardholders and businesses. If a cardholder feels that merchandise or services purchased with a credit card does not meet the promised specifications, she can report the situation to the credit card company. The company will then help resolve the dispute. In simple matters, such as merchandise that was ordered and paid for but never received, the credit card company will refuse to pay the merchant and will credit the cardholder's account.

One of the authors recently made use of this service. Upon checking a monthly credit card bill, the author noticed a charge from an unknown company, which happened to be a dot-com. He went to the company's Web site and realized that it was a Danish company that stated on its Web site that it could not carry out transactions to the United States. Since the author resides in the United States, the credit card company was quickly satisfied that an error had been made and immediately issued a credit to the author's account. You can see how this dispute resolution service facilitates e-business. A consumer does not have to place as much trust in an online merchant when the credit card company is willing to help resolve disputes. Trust is still important, however.

Another example of a form of consumer protection based on common practice is the "no questions asked" return policy. Many online merchants follow the lead of catalog merchants and allow consumers to return merchandise regardless of the reason for the return. Such policies make consumers much more comfortable with ordering products they cannot try on or inspect. For example, not too long ago, one of the authors was shopping online for a pair of running shoes. He found a good deal on the Web site of Road Runner Sports, a catalog merchant that successfully made the transition to the Web. There was a problem, however. The shoes had all of the desired characteristics, but the author's size was not available. However, the next smaller size was in stock. Since this particular brand of shoes typically ran a little larger than normal, the author decided to take a chance and order the smaller size. Before doing so, however, he checked Road Runner's return policy and saw that it would refund the purchase price if the shoes were returned in new condition. This turned out to be important. When the shoes arrived, the author tried them on and quickly realized that he had make a mistake—the shoes were too small. Fortunately, all it cost was a small shipping charge. Road Runner Sports made good on its pledge to accept returns, even when there was no error on its part. The author received his refund. Even though Road Runner Sports did not make any money on this transaction, its liberal return policy will help retain the author's business.

Many countries do not have the same level of consumer protection as the United States. For example, India does not have a small-claims court. Other countries do not have credit card liability limits. The governments and merchants in these nations must address consumer protection laws and practices if e-business is to flourish.

Intellectual Property Rights

Intellectual property rights represent a barrier that has legal, ethical, and technical aspects. The battles over property rights in the digital music arena illustrate the importance of the issue. Both Napster and MP3.com faced possible bankruptcy as a result of losing lawsuits for violating intellectual property rights.

What are intellectual property rights? Just as individuals in most societies can own real property, land, homes, and the like, so can individuals and organizations own the rights to intellectual property, such as software, music, artwork, and writings. It is just as important to protect the ownership rights of intellectual property as it is to protect ownership rights of physical property. Laws to protect intellectual property have been in effect for many years. For example, this book is protected by copyright laws. You are not allowed to copy any portion of this book without obtaining proper permission from the copyright owner. When we were preparing the book, we had to obtain permission to use each illustration or screen shot used in the text.

There are three forms of intellectual property protection—copyrights, patents, and trademarks. Copyrights are used to protect rights in the fields of software development and the arts, such as literature, artwork, and music. Patents are generally used to protect inventions. For example, a new process or a new product design may be patented. Finally, trademarks and service marks are used to protect names and symbols that allow us to differentiate products from one another. For example, the familiar Microsoft Windows symbol is trademarked, as is the name "Coca-Cola."

How is the protection of intellectual property related to e-business? First, a significant portion of e-business activities involve intellectual property. All of the content of a Web site, for example, is the intellectual property of the Web site owner. While there are laws to protect the intellectual property rights of the Web site publisher, it is also the responsibility of the publisher to not violate the rights of others. Some e-business models revolve around digital goods that are, in essence, intellectual property. For example, many businesses following the subscription business model rely on intellectual property to form the core content of their offerings. These models may not be feasible if intellectual property rights are not protected. In addition, companies must ensure that they respect the intellectual property rights of others—they must not publish others' works without proper permission. Both Napster and MP3.com found themselves in legal battles because of intellectual property rights violations.

Intellectual property rights also represent a threat to the globalization of e-business. Or, the globalization of business represents a threat to intellectual property rights. At present, there are no globally uniform laws or enforcement activities regarding intellectual property rights. For example, software copyright laws are not as strict, nor are they as strictly enforced, in some countries as they are in others. This may lead to some companies being reluctant to make software available for download from the Web for fear of unfettered duplication and distribution of their intellectual property. The very nature of the Internet makes widespread distribution of digital goods a simple matter. Finding ways to stop the distribution of intellectual property via Web servers in foreign countries is a difficult issue. As companies explore markets in many countries, the territorial nature of intellectual property laws makes enforcing property rights in multiple countries expensive and complex. In short, there is much work to be done in making the processes of obtaining and enforcing intellectual property rights internationally smoother and less expensive.

Another interesting area related to intellectual property rights has been called "link liability," or more formally, contributory copyright infringement. Let's assume that you produce a Web site focused on blues music. Your site contains a link to a site that offers MP3 versions of classic blues songs for download. Unfortunately, you are not aware that the linked site does not have permission from copyright holders to publish the songs. You may be liable for contributing to the copyright infringement of the linked site, simply because your site helps direct traffic to the download site. What you view as simply an innocent link to an interesting Web site may be seen by copyright holders, and possibly the courts, as a violation of copyright laws. See the Universal Pictures versus Movie List E-business in Practice box for an account of a 1999 dispute over deep links. An article on Salon.com magazine provides a good overview of the deep linking issue. The Web address for the article is given in the Further Readings section at the end of this chapter.

Trademark infringement is sometimes an issue with domain names. (Domain names are the last parts of Web addresses, such as ebay.com or irs.gov. They are discussed fully in Chapter 4.) Several years ago, the practice of domain name poaching was commonplace. Domain name poaching involves registering a widely recognized name in the hopes that the company associated with the name would be willing to pay a sizable fee for the rights to the domain name. For example, an individual might have registered the domain lakers.com in the hope that the Los Angeles Lakers basketball team would agree to pay for the rights to use it. This was a lucrative strategy for some individuals who saw the opportunity early on, before many companies started registering their own domains. Trademark law did not fully address whether the use of a word in an Internet domain name constituted a trademark violation.

The problem was so widespread that The Internet Corporation for Assigned Names and Numbers (ICANN), the authority overseeing Internet domain names, instituted a domain name resolution process, known as the Uniform Domain Name Dispute Resolution Policy (UDRP). (The complete rules for UDRP are available at http://www.icann.org/udrp/udrp-rules-24oct99.htm.) This process allows an independent panel to settle domain name disputes, which has severely cut down on domain name poaching. However, there are still disputes over domain names, with each party believing that it has the right to the domain name in question. For example, Delta Airlines was not able to obtain the rights to the delta.com domain name from the Internet service provider deltaComm Development, the firm that legitimately held the rights to the domain name, until 2000.

The final intellectual property rights issue we discuss has the potential to be a serious barrier to the spread of e-business. Recently, the issue of patenting business processes has been in the news. Business processes (ways of conducting business) can be patented, which prevents other companies from using the same processes without the

E-BUSINESS IN PRACTICE

Universal Pictures versus Movie List

An interesting legal battle occurred between Universal Pictures and Movie List, a company that uses the Web to show trailers of upcoming motion pictures. Movie List's Web site contained "deep links" to previews of movies on the Universal Pictures Web site. What makes this case interesting is that Universal did not object to Movie List making certain trailers available. After all, Universal's own Web site actually contained the content. All Movie List did was link to the trailers on the Universal Web site. Universal objected to Movie List not creating links to Universal's home page, but rather creating links directly to the trailers. Such links are called **deep links** because they are links to pages or content buried deep within the linked-to Web site.

Universal's complaint was basically that the deep links from the Movie List site allowed Web users to bypass content on the Universal Web site that it wanted users to see before they could view the trailers. For example, Universal may have wanted users to have to see various banner ads for upcoming movies before being able to access the desired trailer.

After much correspondence among the publisher of Movie List, Universal, and Movie List's Internet service provider, Movie List agreed to link only to Universal's home page and not directly to any trailers. The final straw seemed to be the Internet service provider's threat to shut down Movie List's Web site, which the provider claimed it was legally bound to do. The correspondence between Universal's attorneys and Movie List is available at http://www.movie-list.com/universal.html. It makes for fascinating reading.

permission of the patent holder. The first widely reported cases of companies seeking to enforce their business process patents involve two e-business companies, Amazon.com and Priceline.com.

Amazon brought suit against Barnes & Noble, a rival bookseller, for infringing on Amazon's patent for its "1-Click" ordering process. As the name implies, the "1-Click" process allows repeat Amazon customers to place an order with a single mouse click. Barnes & Noble developed a similar system, which it called "Express Lane." Amazon claimed that "Express Lane" violated its patent on the "1-Click" process. Amazon was successful in obtaining an injunction against Barnes & Noble, forcing it to stop using "Express Lane."

In October 1999, name-your-price pioneer Priceline.com sued Microsoft over Expedia.com's hotel price-matching system. (Expedia.com is a subsidiary of Microsoft.) Priceline claimed that Expedia's system violated Priceline's patent of the name-your-price system. The suit was settled when Microsoft agreed to pay unspecified royalties to Priceline. Expedia continues to offer name-your-price services, but now pays royalties to Priceline for the right to do so.

The eventual impact of business process patents on e-business remains to be seen. It may turn out that these patents actually spur innovation in business processes. There are two reasons for this. First, businesses may be more willing to spend time and money developing innovative processes if they feel that the processes can be protected through patents. Without such protection, businesses may be reluctant to incur the development expense. Why make a big investment in developing new processes if it is a simple matter for all of your competitors to copy the processes? It may be better to let your competitors spend the money, and then copy their processes. If all organizations felt this way, no one would be innovating. A second reason is that businesses would have few choices in responding to competitors' innovating processes. Since the processes would likely be protected by patents, businesses would either have to ignore the impacts of the new processes (a choice that could well lead to negative consequences), or develop new, competing processes. For example, if Barnes & Noble cannot copy Amazon's "1-Click," it may have to develop new, innovative processes to compete with Amazon.

It is also possible that business process patents may end up hindering e-business. If patents are granted too freely, a useful innovation may only be used by a single company, the one holding the patent. An example comes from Amazon's patent of its Internet-based customer referral system, which is more commonly known as the associate program. The system is a process by which Web site publishers can refer customers to Amazon's Web site, and in return receive a commission on any resulting sales. Since this sort of system was widely used on the Internet, critics maintained that the process was not new or novel, which is a requirement for receiving a patent. If Amazon's patent had been enforced, many organizations selling on the Web would have been denied an important source of customer traffic. This, of course, would have harmed the development of online business. In short, the impact of widespread granting and enforcement of business process patents potentially creates burdens for many companies while benefiting only a handful of patent holders.

As you might imagine, patent laws differ from country to country. The laws in the United States are, in some respects, different from those in the European Union, Japan, and other countries. Until international consensus is reached, organizations wishing to patent business processes must contend with these differences. To understand more about the potential harm to e-business from business process patents, read the article "The Problem with Internet Patents." The reference for this article is found in the Further Readings section at the end of this chapter.

Controversial Issues of Electronic Business

Most of the interest in e-business focuses on applications that are clearly beneficial to their users. However, there are also applications of e-business technologies that may actually be harmful for at least some users. Our purpose is not to debate the relative merits of these applications; rather our intent is to illustrate some uses of the technologies that may be harmful. We discuss these issues under the umbrella of barriers because legislative efforts to limit these applications may also inadvertently limit other, less controversial uses of e-business technologies. In this section, we discuss several questionable applications of e-business and how they may represent barriers to e-business.

One application of e-business that many find undesirable pertains to material of an adult nature, which is sometimes known as pornography, delivered via the Web. One of the most important characteristics of the Internet and Web is that they make materials widely available. While this is usually a good thing, sometimes it makes material available to those for whom it may be inappropriate. Many parents are particularly concerned about their children either purposely or inadvertently viewing adult material on the Web. In fact, several companies offer software, called filters, that allows parents to block access to inappropriate Web sites. Similar software is used by public facilities, such as libraries and schools, that may feel the need to supervise what patrons view.

On the surface, it may not be obvious how controlling access to adult material is a barrier to e-business. There are at least three ways in which the wide availability of adult material on the Web is a barrier to e-business. First, some parents or school administrators may be reluctant to allow their charges to access the Web for fear that they may access adult material. This, in turn, may lead to fewer consumers utilizing e-business. A second problem is that filtering software sometimes blocks access to non-pornographic Web sites. For example, filtering software may be set to block sites that mention the word "breast" frequently. Unfortunately, this results in blocking sites that discuss breast cancer, breast enhancement, or other women's health issues.

A third reason is that legislation to control adult material on the Web may limit personal liberty. One example of such legislation is the Children's Internet Protection Act, which was passed by the U.S. Congress in 2000. One provision of the act is that schools and libraries will be required to employ filtering software in order to prevent children from viewing pornographic material. Failure to do so results in the loss of federal funding. Several groups, including the American Civil Liberties Union and the Electronic Privacy Information Center, are expected to challenge the act on a number of grounds.

A final issue related to adult material on the Web is that there is not widespread agreement on exactly what constitutes pornography. Laws and standards vary widely across countries and even within countries. The global nature of the Web makes this a thorny problem. For example, consider the case of a company in Amsterdam using the Web to publish adult-oriented material that is legal in the Netherlands. However, this material is accessed by someone in a country with laws against publishing the material. Are any laws broken? If so, by the publisher or by the user? How can governments police such activity when publishers are outside their jurisdictions? Perhaps there should be no policing. In any case, there is no widespread agreement on these issues. In addition, jurisdictional questions are not limited to adult material—there are similar questions related to other Web-based activities.

Another source of debate is how to deal with groups that post so-called hate messages on the Web or send such material via e-mail. The problems associated with hate groups are similar to those of adult material. Should groups or individuals be allowed to post hateful, potentially dangerous, literature on the Web? If not, who should stop them?

There are a growing number of groups using the Web to promote violence or hostility against other groups. The Simon Wiesenthal Center, a Los Angeles-based organization that tracks such groups, estimates that in 2000 there were three thousand hate groups on the Web, which is more than double the fourteen hundred reported in 1999. Many of these groups are based in the United States, where free-speech rights protect their activities. There is considerable debate on how to deal with these groups. For example, should it be allowable for hateful material to be posted or accessed using public university computing equipment? Some countries have passed laws against hate material on the Internet. For example, in Canada it is illegal to disseminate hate propaganda over the Internet. Germany bans all neo-Nazi material. On the surface, it seems that such activity should be banned. But in the United States, it would be a violation of civil rights laws. And the question of who decides what constitutes acceptable material is critical. There is a fine line, or possibly no line, between banning hateful material and censorship.

How do the online activities of hate groups represent a barrier to e-business? Basically, the potential barrier comes from steps that are or may be taken to restrict online hate group activities. Legislation designed to curtail hate groups' online activities may indirectly impact legitimate e-business activities. For example, an online auction may run afoul of some laws if it allows a copy of Adolf Hitler's *Mein Kampf* to be auctioned through its Web site. Monitoring against potential violations of laws in multiple jurisdictions could easily become time consuming and expensive, particularly if an organization does business in many different countries.

The final controversial application we discuss is online gambling. The laws governing gambling vary significantly from country to country. In fact, it is quite common for laws to differ among areas within a country. For example, in the United States, gambling laws differ from state to state; casino gambling is legal in some states, but not in others. Recently, however, Internet-based gambling has emerged. Online gambling allows betting through Web sites that simulate casino games, sports books, or other gaming activities. Differences in gaming laws are much easier to deal with in the world of physical gaming locations than in cyberspace. There is little to prevent a user who lives in an area where casino gambling is prohibited from logging on to an online casino. Even those who favor less restrictive gambling laws tend to agree that minors should be restricted from engaging in gambling activities. This is easy to carry out in a brick-and-mortar casino, but is much more difficult when dealing with a virtual casino.

It is also possible that Internet-based gambling increases the risk to those addicted to gambling. Two factors contribute to this. First, gambling online is a much more anonymous activity than going to a casino. Second, online gambling is much more accessible than offline gambling. Regardless of physical location, the addicted gambler can access a variety of online casinos through the Internet. While this may be a great convenience for those who gamble responsibly, it can be a tragic convenience for an addicted gambler.

Governments differ in their approaches to regulating Internet-based gaming. For example, Great Britain was one of the first governments to react officially to online gambling. In a 2000 report from the Gaming Board for Great Britain, it was recommended that online gambling be legalized and regulated. In contrast, Australia placed a moratorium on the licensing of Internet-based gambling houses (Rose 2001).

The primary threat to e-business from online gambling comes from the possibility that laws designed to regulate or prohibit Internet-based gambling may lead to further regulation of other online activities. Laws created with good intentions often have unintended effects in the long run. It is possible that gambling regulations may be used as precedent to over-regulate other, less controversial, activities.

Taxation

The issue of taxation also represents a potential barrier to e-business. Put simply, there is considerable dispute over how to tax business conducted electronically. For example in the United States, individual states derive a significant amount of revenue from taxing the sales of goods and services. The tax laws vary widely from state to state. For example, in some states, food and medicine are not subject to sales tax. In other states they are. The same is also true of taxes on services.

Even if laws were more uniform, the question of *which* governing body should receive any taxes due is a contentious issue. In face-to-face sales, the question of jurisdiction is simple—the state in which the sale occurs is entitled to collect taxes on the sale. The question is not so clear in electronically mediated sales. In e-business, it is common for the customer to be located in one state, the business' headquarters in another, the server in a third state, and the shipping warehouse in a fourth state. Which state gets to tax the sale? Technically speaking, most states require the end consumer to pay tax on any sales that occur out-of-state. However enforcing this requirement is problematic. As a result, most states rely on merchants to collect and pay sales taxes. But to which state is the tax due? For the moment, states in the United States have agreed to a temporary moratorium on the taxation of interstate Internet-based sales. This situation will not last forever, and eventually the issue must be resolved. Even the current moratorium poses problems. Traditional merchants are not happy with the moratorium because they feel it gives an unfair advantage to Internet merchants. Since the Internet merchants do not have to charge sales tax, they have a built-in price advantage of several percent. For big-budget purchases, this advantage can translate into a significant savings for the consumer. Since the portion of retail sales occurring over the Internet is still small, many are willing to let the tax question sit, for now. As the value of Internet-based retail sales increases, states will not be so willing to give up the tax revenue, and the question will have to be settled.

The taxation problem extends across national borders. Taxation laws and mechanisms differ greatly among countries. For example, the value-added taxes common in much of the world are virtually unknown to most Americans. While multinational corporations are well equipped to deal with cross-national taxation issues, smaller companies may not be. As e-business makes world markets accessible to smaller businesses, international taxation issues may become problematic for smaller, inexperienced businesses. Most of the points raised regarding the taxation of Internet-based commerce across state borders in the United States also apply to commerce that crosses national borders.

Privacy

As individuals and businesses continue to use e-business in increasing numbers, an equally increasing amount of information about these same individuals and businesses is collected and stored. If the parties involved are knowledgeable about the data being collected and how those data will be used, there is not a problem. The problem occurs when users either do not know what data are being collected, or do not know or consent to how the data should be used. The question of the degree to which the privacy rights of individuals should be protected is another barrier to e-business, particularly global e-business. On the surface, it seems obvious that privacy rights should be protected, but the common standard applied differs from country to country. For example, privacy laws in the European Union are much stricter than those in the United States, which implies that U.S. companies who want to do business in the European Union must follow the E.U. standard. However, the issue is not that simple.

In the United States, the common approach to privacy regulation has been self-enforcement. When the European Union put more stringent privacy regulations in place with a Directive on Data and Privacy in 1995, U.S. companies were reluctant to comply. This reluctance came from the knowledge that customer data represents a valuable resource that can be used not only for direct marketing, but also as a separate source of revenue. Businesses in the United States commonly sell customer data to other businesses.

Representatives from the United States and the European Union have hammered out a compromise called the **Safe Harbor Privacy Principles.** Seven principles comprise the framework for the Safe Harbor Privacy Principles. These principles outline requirements for how businesses must inform customers about privacy issues and provide options for them with regard to privacy. In addition, the principles dictate in broad terms how customer data should be secured and access granted, as well as how the guidelines should be enforced. Table 3-3, which is adapted from a draft of the principles, shows and describes each of the principles.

Disputes and occasional consumer uproars over privacy issues continue. For example, the Web advertising service DoubleClick came under fire for its user profiling activities. The Center for Democracy and Technology organized an electronic mail protest of DoubleClick's practice of tracking the online activities of consumers. Until privacy practices are made consistent, and all organizations doing business online learn to properly respect individuals' right to privacy, we can expect these disputes to continue. As long as they do, some people will be reluctant to provide personal information online, and e-business will suffer.

Cultural Content Quotas

The governments of some countries have long been concerned about the impact of foreign media content on their countries' cultural identities. The fear is that prolonged exposure to foreign cultures through the media may dilute the cultural identity of a nation. A number of

Table 3-3   Safe Harbor Privacy Principles

Principles	Description
Notice	Customers must be notified of how their information will be used, and to whom it may be transferred. In addition, contact information for the organization should be provided.
Choice	Customers should have the option to decline to participate (opt-out) in any data collection or use situation.
Onward transfer	Customer permission must be obtained before any personal information may be transferred.
Security	Reasonable precautions must be taken in order to protect personal information against loss, misuse, or alteration.
Data integrity	Information collected should be used only for the originally intended and disclosed purposes.
Access	Individuals must be able to access, correct, change, or delete their personal information.
Enforcement	Organizations must take appropriate action to ensure that personal information is protected. The misuse of personal information must carry negative consequences.

countries have had local cultural content quotas for TV and radio for many years. For example, Australian content rules have required commercial television to broadcast a variety of Australian-produced programs. Canada has similar requirements—English-language Canadian radio stations are required to broadcast 35 percent Canadian content. The requirement is even more stringent for French-language stations (Media Awareness Network 1999). Table 3-4 shows some of the content-related rules in Australia.

Why might content quotas represent a barrier to e-business? In a nutshell, governments could choose to block access to or shut down sites that do not comply with quotas. While most believe that this will not happen, the possibility exists. One reason that it is unlikely that the quotas will be strictly enforced is the difficulty of such enforcement. With television and radio, there are relatively few points of origin for the broadcasts. Contrast this with the Internet, which has millions of servers. It is virtually impossible for governments to monitor the content of all of these servers.

ORGANIZATIONAL BARRIERS

In order to take advantage of e-business technologies, there are a number of barriers that individual organizations must overcome, as opposed to the barriers over which organizations have little control. Organizations must work hard and be willing to invest money and time in learning how to apply e-business technologies to their operations. Harnessing the potential of e-business is difficult and hazardous. Taking the wrong step at the wrong time can put a business in bankruptcy. However, not embracing e-business may ultimately be even more hazardous. Businesses that bury their heads in the sand and do not take steps to overcome the barriers discussed in this section may soon find themselves swallowed up or simply destroyed by their more forward-thinking competitors.

Corporate Culture and Organization

To use a trite, but accurate, phrase, the only constant of e-business is change, and many businesses have tremendous difficulty dealing with change. Unfortunately, some

Table 3-4   Australian Television Content Regulations

Category	Required Australian Content
Programs (6:00 A.M. to midnight)	55%
Commercials	80%
Children's programming	260 hours per year; 50% Australian
Pre-school programming	130 hours per year; 100% Australian
First release documentaries	20 hours per year of Australian content

SOURCE: Screen Producers Association of Australia, "A Submission to the Productivity Commission Review of Broadcasting Legislation" (2000): http://www.spaa.org.au/submission/subm_06.html.

organizations are ill-equipped to deal with change. There are many potential causes for this. We will focus our discussion on three of them: resistance to change, organizational structure, and management expertise.

Taking advantage of e-business technologies requires change for most organizations. In many cases, this change is massive. Sometimes applying e-business technologies requires companies to completely rethink how their processes work and how they interact with their customers, suppliers, and employees. Throughout this book, we discuss how companies and industries are shaken up by e-business. Organizations that successfully embrace e-business must be able to deal with change quickly and effectively. For example, travel agents who recognized how e-business was changing their industry and adapted accordingly may actually benefit from the shift. Those who did not see the impact of e-business, or who lacked the ability to change, are far less likely to benefit.

If you have taken a management course, you have probably discussed resistance to change. Put bluntly, most people and most organizations do not like change. Change requires learning new ideas and processes, upsetting long-entrenched routines, and a myriad of other potentially troublesome events. Because of this, many individuals in organizations resist management's efforts to invoke change. Sometimes, certain individuals in an organization are quite justified in their resistance to the changes brought about by e-business—it may cost them their jobs. Recall that in earlier chapters, we discussed how e-business can make organizations more efficient. One source of this increased efficiency is workforce reduction. How would you react to changes that you thought would cost you your job? You might well mount heavy resistance to the change.

Organizations that hope to take advantage of the many benefits of e-business must overcome the natural resistance to change. All stakeholders—employees, suppliers, customers, and shareholders—must be convinced that the change is worthwhile from their particular perspectives. Making the case for massive change requires considerable managerial skill. The case for change must be made well in advance of the actual implementation. In fact, the organizations that can best adapt to e-business, or any other changes, are those that have organizational cultures and structures that foster flexibility.

Quite often, the organizations that are best equipped to deal with change are those that are actually designed with flexibility in mind. The structure of these organizations may be quite different from the traditional hierarchically oriented structure. Having a highly layered organizational structure can lead to inflexibility. A detailed discussion of organizational structure is beyond our scope. It is enough to understand that having many management layers can hinder an organization's ability to adapt quickly. Flexible organizations tend to make use of technological and organizational innovations to flatten their structures, which can lead to greater flexibility.

A lack of managerial expertise can be a barrier to effectively applying e-business technologies. For example, managers must have the skills necessary to overcome resistance to change. However, there are many other managerial skills that must be present in organizations that hope to successfully implement e-business. Perhaps the most important and most evasive ability that managers must possess is the ability to understand how e-business technologies might impact their organizations and their environments. Forecasting the impact of e-business represents the foundation upon which all other plans and actions rest. If managers miss the mark here, even the best conceived and implemented plans are destined to fail. The key to being able to understand the impact of e-business is a solid understanding of the organization and its environment, combined with an understanding of the role of information technology. In addition, a knack for being able to think "outside the box" (not rely on conventional thinking) is helpful.

Once an understanding of the impact of e-business is gained, it is necessary for managers to have the ability to develop an effective plan of action. It is not enough to see where the organization should be; a map for reaching that destination must also be developed. Striking a balance between speed and careful planning can be difficult. The rapid pace of change in the e-business world demands quick action. However, proceeding without a clear plan is just as dangerous as a slow reaction. In our work with organizations seeking to take advantage of e-business, we often see organizations that simply do not have clearly defined plans for integrating e-business into their operations. These organizations are characterized by frequent changes in direction. In many cases, these changes result in the organizations never accomplishing anything of substance with respect to e-business. It is imperative that managers have the capability to formulate effective plans, and the discipline to resist the urge to act without planning.

Finally, managers must have the knowledge necessary to carry out their plans. Implementing any massive organizational change is difficult. Not only are project management skills necessary, but the task is complicated by the need for changes in organizational structure. In addition, the heavy reliance on information technology makes the implementation even more complex.

During the implementation of the e-business plan, it is necessary for managers to have the ability to marshal the required resources and gain cooperation from various areas of the organization. It takes a skilled manager to gain the cooperation of people who may be negatively impacted by the change. Even employees who do not perceive a danger from e-business may be reluctant to cooperate. Sometimes this is a matter of not wanting to share information, sometimes it is simply a matter of not wanting to invest the time required. Regardless of the reason, because e-business cuts across functional areas of the organization, considerable managerial skills are necessary to gain access to the information and people required to implement the plan.

It is important to realize that e-business may require customers and suppliers to change some of their processes. In the case of customers, the reason may be obvious. Why should a company make goods and services available on the Web if customers do not use the system? In the case of business-to-business relationships, considerable input and buy-in from customers may be necessary for success. E-business systems may also need to connect to suppliers' e-business systems. The skills required to gain the cooperation of these external stakeholders may differ from those required to gain cooperation from those inside the organization.

Many organizations realize that they are lacking in some areas of required expertise. This is one reason that it is common for consultants to assist in e-business planning and implementation. Most of the large business and IT consulting firms have e-commerce or e-business divisions that employ experts in most aspects of e-business. While engaging these experts carries a high price, undertaking e-business projects without the necessary management expertise often proves to be even more expensive in the long run.

Lack of Viable Business Models

In the last chapter, we discussed the importance of business models. Regardless of whether an organization is using e-business technologies, a workable business model is a requirement for long-term success. Recall that a business model is simply a blueprint or plan for how a business makes money. While any successful business must have a workable business model, the relative lack of experience in e-business leads to a corresponding lack of viable business models. Because we are just beginning to gain experience with and an understanding of e-business, there are fewer good business models to learn from than there are in the offline world. Until organizations gain sufficient experience, a lack of workable business models will continue to hinder the development of e-business.

Beginning in mid-2000, the popular press began declaring the death of the dot-com companies. Many of the companies that had been touted as new economic miracles were beginning to fail after losing vast sums of money. For example, the online toy retailer eToys announced in January of 2001 that it was laying off most of its workforce and expected to run out of money by March. There are numerous similar examples. Why did these companies fail? There are many reasons, but one important explanation is that their business models simply did not work.

As this chapter is being written, many pundits believe that the clicks-and-mortar companies (those that have both an on- and offline presence) will be the ultimate winners in e-business. It is too soon to tell if these pronouncements are correct. However, it is useful to examine why this is a reasonable expectation. These companies do not have to come up with completely new business models. In many cases, they are simply extending existing business models, while at the same time using e-business technologies to improve their operations.

Lack of Planning

Organizations are under tremendous pressure to take advantage of the benefits offered by e-business. As a result, many managers rush to implement e-business strategies without taking the time to develop effective plans. While not advisable, the lack of careful planning is understandable. If competitors are not yet taking advantage of e-business technologies, managers may feel that there are opportunities to gain significant "first-mover" benefits if e-business projects can be implemented quickly. If competitors are utilizing e-business, managers are pressured into a timely response in order to minimize possible loss of market share. In any case, managers perceive that they must make haste in implementing e-business projects. The result is often a rushed planning effort, which often ultimately leads to failed e-business projects.

There have been many widely reported failures of initial e-business efforts. Even large, respected, and IT-savvy firms, such as IBM and Wal-Mart, have seen their initial forays into e-business fall flat. Interestingly, in some cases, these firms have pulled the plug on early e-business efforts, only to return with successful projects later.

Uncertainty about Organizational Structure

The final organizational barrier we discuss concerns the impact of e-business on the structure of organizations. Two issues are pertinent. First, there is some question as to where responsibility for e-business should reside in an organization. The second issue is how e-business will impact existing organizational structures.

Where in the organization should responsibility for e-business reside? Many IT professionals feel that the natural place for e-business is in the IT department. However, it is important to understand that e-business is, by its very nature, interdisciplinary. It involves marketing, accounting, purchasing, and other functional areas. So, the question of responsibility for e-business is not clear.

The extensive application of e-business technologies may lead to changes in existing organizational structures. The bulk of these changes occur because of the communication and coordination efficiencies enabled by e-business technologies. By using networks to connect various aspects of the organization, and by using network-enabled applications, organizations may be able to streamline their structures, while at the same time improving internal operations. For example, **intranets** have helped many organizations improve their internal operations.

The use of e-business technologies may allow organizations to take advantage of organizational structures that were not previously viable. For example, many organizations are making extensive use of **telecommuting,** which allows workers to spend all or some of their working time at home, rather than at an office. Taking advantage of telecommuting requires nontraditional supervisory structures since supervisors cannot simply walk through the office to check on employees. In addition, many organizations are employing the concept of the **virtual organization.** In a virtual organization, partners come together to work on specific projects. When the project is complete, the partnering organizations go their separate ways, possibly to join other virtual organizations. E-business technologies facilitate the operation of virtual organizations.

In addition, taking advantage of external e-business opportunities may require structural changes. These changes may be necessary in order to gain the flexibility necessary to respond to rapidly changing environments. For example, traditional multilevel management hierarchies may be too slow to respond to e-business opportunities or threats. Communicating up and down through the many levels consumes valuable time. And it is quite common for the quality of the information to degrade as it passes through multiple management levels.

Internet Abuse by Employees

Increased access to the Internet in the workplace poses an interesting problem for organizations. Many organizations recognize the potential benefits of giving employees access to the Internet. However, some employees use the access for non-work-related purposes. As a result, many organizations are quite concerned about employee abuse of the Internet. The importance of this topic is made evident by a special section on Internet abuse in the

January 2002 issue of *Communications of the ACM,* which is included in the Further Readings at the end of this chapter.

An obvious consequence of inappropriate use of the Internet by employees is lost productivity. When a worker is surfing the Web for pleasure, no work is being done and productivity is lost. Time spent sending or reading personal e-mail messages also results in lost productivity.

However, there are less obvious potential consequences. What are the consequences of an employee accessing offensive material while at work? Is an organization liable for sexual harassment penalties if a worker accesses pornographic material and then shows that material to a coworker? Is there any liability if a company does nothing to prevent employees from accessing copyrighted music using office computers?

The use of the Internet and Web for non-work-related tasks is widespread. In a 2000 survey by Vault.com, 82 percent of the employees surveyed admitted sending non-work-related e-mail messages from work; 88 percent reported surfing the Web for recreation during work. In some cases, the amount of time spent on this surfing is substantial. More than 35 percent of the workers said that they spent thirty minutes or more a day on recreational Web browsing (Vault 2000). Interestingly, this is a global problem. A survey of workers in Singapore found remarkably similar results to the Vault.com survey. In the Singapore survey, 76 percent of the workers reported sending personal e-mail messages during work and 80 percent reported engaging in recreational Web use while at work (Lim, Teo, Loo 2002).

Aligning Internet use with business priorities requires considerable effort on the part of an organization's management. An effective Internet policy management effort requires several components. The cornerstone of this effort is a clear, well-communicated Internet usage policy, which spells out exactly what the organization considers acceptable and unacceptable Internet use. It is critical that employees be made aware of the organization's policy; it is not enough to simply draft a suitable document. The organization's end-users must be trained in what constitutes Internet abuse and the consequences of such activities. Monitoring tools are another key component. These tools allow organizations to keep track of the Internet-related activities of workers. Monitoring tools should include a variety of options for reporting activity. Finally, the organization must develop and apply appropriate discipline measures (Simmers 2002). Without enforcement and discipline measures in place, some employees may be unwilling to modify their behavior to comply with the organization's Internet use policy.

CULTURAL BARRIERS

The e-business is global in scope. Because the core platform of the Internet is worldwide, many organizations hope to use e-business technologies to establish a global presence, or to improve their overseas operations. However, becoming global requires more that simply making a Web site available to potential customers around the globe. There are a number of issues that organizations with global ambitions must address.

Language

For many, the most obvious barrier to global e-business is language. It is clear that doing business in most countries, whether face-to-face or using e-business technologies, requires using the local language. Not surprisingly, research shows that customers are significantly more likely to use Web sites with content presented in their languages, even if they are fluent in other languages. Businesses running Web portals recognized this early on. A visit to Excite reveals that its portal is available in many languages. Further, the content for each country's site is tailored to that country. In other words, the content of Excite's Brazilian site differs from that of its Australian site.

On the surface, it may appear that making a Web site available in several different languages is not an insurmountable task. However, the difficulty in maintaining Web site content in multiple languages should not be trivialized. Consider that most e-business Web sites today are not simply static "brochure-ware" sites—the content of many sites is very dynamic. In fact, many e-business sites are database driven. A considerable amount of their content is actually derived from data in a database. For example, product names and descriptions may be stored in a back-end database. These data may then be put into a Web site in response to requests from users. Multilingual Web sites present potential problems for database-driven Web sites. Databases may need to be redesigned and additional data may need to be stored. For example, product names and descriptions may need to be stored in several languages, which complicates the database.

Electronic business software providers recognize the problems of localization and are offering products and services to help organizations that wish to do business in multiple countries. For example, in early 2001, IBM announced an updated version of its WebSphere e-business development software that is designed to help organizations overcome some of the barriers of global e-business. The software allows organizations to manage Web pages in multiple languages from a single site. In addition, users can easily switch between languages. The software also enables prices to be displayed in multiple currencies.

Compatibility

The success of a global e-business presence requires more than simply translating the content of a Web site. Barriers to success still exist if the e-business site is not compatible with local custom and conditions. A common practice in one country may make customers feel uncomfortable in another. One of our favorite examples comes from the common use of the shopping cart metaphor, which we discussed earlier in this chapter. Many sales-oriented Web sites use a virtual shopping cart to allow users to accumulate items for purchase. For users in many countries, this is a very natural process that fits with their past experiences. However, in other countries, shopping carts are almost nonexistent. Customers in these countries may find the virtual shopping cart unsettling and incompatible with past experiences.

Other customs that vary from country to country may present barriers to global e-business. A major hurdle is that consumers in many countries are not used to distant transactions. In the United States, for example, many consumers are quite comfortable with long-distance shopping, since catalog shopping is common. However, in most countries, almost all consumer purchases are made face-to-face with merchants.

Clearly, the idea of making purchases over the Internet is incompatible with this. The popularity of credit cards is another factor that may be important. In many countries, credit card purchases are rare, which presents a problem for e-business merchants, since the vast majority of consumer purchases online are made using credit cards. Companies that wish to do business in countries where credit cards are not popular face the task of devising alternate payment methods. The final local custom we discuss concerns product return policies. In some countries, merchants readily accept merchandise returns. In the United States, many businesses have a "no questions asked" return policy. We discussed the importance of such policies earlier in this chapter. In some other countries, merchants are not as willing to accept returns. Businesses that want to entice customers to shop online should take care to explicitly state return policies. Otherwise, consumers who are not used to being able to return merchandise may be reluctant to shop online. They may perceive the risk of online shopping to be high out of fear of being "stuck" with unwanted purchases.

Making Web sites compatible with users in multiple countries is a formidable task. Not only are there technological hurdles, but organizations must gain a deep understanding of the culture of each of the countries. For organizations that already have a presence in each country, the required knowledge may be available within the organization. However, those without a local presence may have to enlist the assistance of local partners in order to gain success. It is imperative that businesses understand the various countries in which they hope to do business. Otherwise, there is little chance for success.

Payment Infrastructure

Another difficulty faced by e-business companies in some countries is the lack of a modern payment infrastructure. For example, the vast majority of B2C e-business transactions take place with the use of credit cards. However, in many developing countries the use of credit cards is rare, even by the relatively affluent. In a number of countries, secure, stable electronic means of reliably making and receiving payments are not widely available. Since a reliable payment infrastructure is an important component of an overall e-business infrastructure, the lack of such a system hinders the growth of e-business. Some are calling for the increased development of alternatives to credit card payments, such as cash-on-delivery or a prepayment system. It remains to be seen which, if any, of these alternatives will prove viable. In the interim, the use of consumer-oriented e-business will not reach its potential, particularly in developing countries.

Multiple Currencies

The ability of e-business systems to deal with multiple currencies is also a barrier to global e-business, although it is more of a globalization issue than a cultural issue. As organizations seek to conduct transactions across national borders, the ability of systems to deal with multiple currencies becomes more important. A global e-business system must be able to price goods in the local currencies of customers. In addition, clearing payments in multiple currencies can be problematic. Organizations may choose to establish banking relationships in all countries in which they do business, or they may invest in a multicurrency payment system.

On the surface, handling multiple currencies does not seem like a major technological hurdle. However, the task is made more difficult by frequent exchange rate fluctuations. The systems must be able to keep track of these fluctuations. In addition, policies must be clear as to when currency conversions will occur. Will the rate in effect at the time of the order be used, or will the rate at the time of shipment be used?

OVERVIEW OF TECHNICAL BARRIERS

A number of technical barriers must be addressed in order for e-business to flourish. Some of these are discussed in detail elsewhere in this book. For example, security technologies are covered in Chapter 10. In this chapter, we want to focus on how these technology-related issues represent barriers to e-business development, rather than considering details of the technologies themselves.

Interoperability

Interoperability, as defined in Chapter 1, is simply the capability of different kinds of systems to interact. In Chapter 1, we discussed how interoperability is a cornerstone of e-business. Technologies related to e-business are developed continuously. Many researchers and developers are busy searching for ways to expand the capabilities enabled by the Web. While this development is crucial to the growth of e-business, there is a down side. Some emerging technologies have the potential to negatively impact interoperability. An example comes from Java, a programming language developed by Sun Microsystems. (Java is discussed in Chapter 5.) When Web developers began using Java to add interactivity to their sites, only users with the latest versions of certain Web browser software could utilize the new capabilities. Those using older versions (which may have only been a few months old) received error messages when accessing a Web site that used Java.

Have you ever had a similar experience? It is likely that you have, since many similar examples exist. One that the authors seem to run into frequently concerns Shockwave, which is software that allows the use of "rich media" content on Web sites. In order to properly view a site using the Shockwave technology, you must have Shockwave Player software installed on your computer. Since Shockwave is not currently a standard technology, interoperability suffers.

Sometimes a technology becomes so popular that it becomes a de facto standard. In such cases, there is little impact on interoperability in the long run. The Portable Document Format (PDF), developed by Adobe, is an example of this. The Portable Document Format allows images of printed pages to be displayed as printed. For example, a newspaper could convert its back issues to PDF files and make them available to subscribers over the Web. The Portable Document Format technology was developed as a proprietary technology by a private company. However, Adobe made the technology required to read files in PDF format available without charge. (Adobe charges for the software required to create PDF files.) In addition, the reader software was available for many operating environments. As a result, PDF files created in any operating environment can be read on any system running the reader software, regardless of the environment.

Over time, an interesting thing happened. Many individuals and companies wanted the capabilities enabled by PDF technology. As a result, there was considerable demand for the Adobe conversion software. Since the PDF file-reading software was available for free, organizations wishing to distribute page images simply published the PDF documents and instructed users to download the reader. Over time, the Portable Document Format became a de facto standard. Today, many new personal computers come with the PDF reader pre-installed, and most Web browsing software automatically launches the reader when encountering pdf files. The key to the PDF format becoming a standard was interoperability. As new technologies emerge, interested organizations need to be mindful of the importance of interoperability. Any technologies that fail to enable easy interoperability are likely to fail.

Security

Many businesses and individuals alike routinely send sensitive data across the Internet. These data must be protected—network-enabled e-business requires a high level of security in order to be successful. Unfortunately, the Internet was not originally designed to be a highly secure system. The good news is that a number of technologies have been developed to increase the security of the Internet and Web.

Since e-business security is discussed extensively in Chapter 10, we only provide a brief overview of the topic here. Our point in this chapter is only to help you understand how inadequate security technologies can hinder the development of e-business. There are many security threats in e-business. It is helpful to break the threats into two categories—threats to data and threats to systems. Since the Internet is a network of networks, data that are transmitted via the Internet typically pass through a number of networks in order to reach their destination. At any point during the transmission, the data are subject to being intercepted. Once the data are accessed by unauthorized individuals, they are subject to misuse or alteration. The implications of intercepting data such as credit card numbers are obvious. However, other types of business data are equally important. Imagine the potential damage to a company if its competitors could gain access to sensitive e-mail communications.

The nature of the Internet also opens the door to security threats related to systems. By design, the Internet is an open network. In theory, unless security measures are implemented, any computer on the Internet can access any server on the Internet. As a result, organizations must be careful to secure their systems against unauthorized access. Organizations that fail to take the proper precautions risk potential theft or destruction of valuable data. An additional threat to systems comes from viruses that proliferate across the Internet. Even if access to servers is restricted, those with access may unknowingly transmit destructive viruses.

Connectivity to Existing Systems

If e-business is to live up to its potential, it is necessary to connect newer, Web-based systems to existing systems. This is a straightforward process in some cases. However, typically connecting the Web-based systems to "back-end" legacy systems is complex, time-consuming, and expensive. There are a number of issues that make connecting Web-based and back-end systems difficult. Typically, the back-end systems are legacy systems that were developed many years ago. These legacy systems tend to be large, complex, and sometimes poorly documented. As a result, great care must be taken when linking them to the e-business Web-based front-end systems. In addition, the newer systems often exist in completely different operating environments. The older systems are typically mainframe-based. Unfortunately, most of these systems were not designed with interoperability in mind. As a result, complex, expensive software, called middleware, is required to translate between the old and new systems. The topic of connectivity to existing systems is discussed more thoroughly in Chapter 8.

Internet "Pipeline" Capacity

More and more individuals and organizations are making use of e-business every day. Most of this activity occurs over the Internet. As a result, there is an ever-increasing amount of traffic on the Internet. Unless the capacity of the Internet "pipeline" is continually increased, the increased activity may bring data traffic to a crawl. In the early days of the Internet, most traffic consisted of simple text. Today, however, advances in multimedia technologies result in an increasing portion of transmissions that consist of large image, sound, and video files. Web sites may contain dozens of high-resolution photos of products. Music is routinely sent across the Internet. Video clips are e-mailed to multiple recipients with a single click of the mouse. All of this transmission of large multimedia files threatens to clog the Internet pipeline. It is important to understand the differences in file sizes among text and various multimedia formats. A typical page of text contains about 2 KB of data. In contrast, a near-CD quality MP3 file of Cream's three-minute song *After Midnight* is about 2,000 KB. A short video clip may be 20,000 KB. You can see how additional network capacity is necessary in order to keep up with the increasing traffic.

The problems that can be caused when capacity does not keep up with demand are illustrated by the Napster phenomenon. As you may recall, Napster is software that allows Internet users to share MP3-format music files across the Internet. Basically, any Napster user could download music from any other Napster user on the network. Napster was an almost instant hit, particularly on college campuses. Before university network administrators knew what hit them, campus networks across the world saw tremendous increases in traffic, which resulted in serious slowdowns. Administrators soon discovered that a large portion of their networks' traffic consisted of MP3 files. As a result, many universities blocked Napster-based transmissions. Although some administrators did this because of legal issues, many were even more concerned with the cost of increasing network capacity.

Web Organization

The Web is chaotic—there is no overall organizing or categorizing strategy. This is one reason for the proliferation of search engines. The lack of organization is a very real problem for those interested in e-business. If customers cannot easily locate desired products or services, much of the convenience of e-business is lost. Think about it this way. When you move to a new city, it is often frustrating to shop for products or services. Once you make friends in the area, and once you have gotten to know the city better, shopping becomes much easier. A similar situation exists on the Web. There are significant differences, however. In the offline world, there are many long-proven organizing schemes to help customers locate businesses. Telephone directories, business directories, and media advertisements all exist for the purpose of helping customers locate businesses. There are some attempts at similar devices in the e-business world, but none are as universal or widely used as their offline counterparts. For example, most cities have only one or two business directories, such as the "Yellow Pages." There are dozens of similar directories on the Web. How can businesses know which to utilize, or even which ones exist? If you want to purchase a monitor for your computer from a local store, it is a relatively easy task to open the telephone directory and locate computer stores in your area. You may also peruse newspaper advertisements to look for bargains. Performing the same task if you want to buy the monitor online is a much less defined task. If you have some experience shopping online, you might have some favorite Web merchants or comparison sites. However, most people have far less experience with online shopping than they do with shopping offline.

SUMMARY

Electronic business technologies offer many potential benefits to organizations and individuals. However, there are a number of barriers to the growth and use of e-business. Unless these barriers are overcome, e-business will not live up to its potential. Chapter 3 helped you understand some of the barriers to e-business.

Perceptions are important. This chapter pointed out several perceptions that influence decisions to use or not use e-business to interact with trading partners. Trust is one of these. If individuals and organizations do not trust their trading partners' use of e-business technologies, they are not likely to use e-business. Four factors influence trust: predictability, reliability, technical competence, and fiduciary responsibility. Other perceptions also matter. How potential users see the relative advantage, compatibility, and complexity of using e-business impacts their decisions to use or not use the technologies. Organizations that wish to use e-business must pay close attention to how customers perceive factors discussed in this chapter. Otherwise, the use of e-business may suffer.

There are also barriers to e-business that individual organizations may not be able to impact. This chapter discussed a number of societal barriers that must be addressed at a higher level. For example, the telecommunications infrastructure in many developing countries, and in some rural areas of developed countries, hinders the use of e-business. Inequities in access to the technologies necessary to use e-business can also slow the growth of e-business. There is also a worldwide shortage of skilled information technology workers. Overcoming this shortage is critical to e-business achieving its potential.

This chapter also introduced you to the impact of several legal and ethical issues that may present barriers to e-business use. Examples of legal issues include the acceptance of digital signatures, consumer protections, and intellectual property rights. One of the more recent developments in this area concerns business method patents. There is the potential for both positive and negative effects on e-business from business method patents. The chapter also discussed other legal and ethical barriers to e-business, such as taxation, cultural content quotas, and privacy concerns.

Organizational barriers may also hinder e-business. The widespread use of e-business is new to many organizations. As a result, some organizations are struggling with how to ingrain e-business into their organizations. This chapter provided a discussion of some organizational issues that might negatively impact e-business, including corporate culture, the lack of viable business models, lack of planning, organizational structure, and Internet abuse by workers.

E-business is a global phenomenon. However, as organizations try to take their e-business efforts across national boundaries, they face a number of obstacles. One obvious problem is producing content in multiple languages.

Less obvious is the impact of compatibility on use. Customs vary from culture to culture. Web designers often violate cultural norms, which can negatively impact compatibility, and limit the use of e-business.

This chapter concluded with an overview of technical barriers to e-business. You were already aware of the importance of interoperability, but the chapter introduced you to other technical barriers, including security, connectivity to existing systems, and the Internet's capacity. The final technical barrier discussed was the general lack of organization to the Web. The lack of an overall organizing strategy makes finding information on the Web difficult, especially for inexperienced users. This difficulty presents a barrier to the use of e-business.

KEY TERMS

compatibility

complexity

deep link

intellectual property rights

intranet

metaphor

relative advantage

Safe Harbor Privacy Principles

telecommuting

virtual organization

REVIEW QUESTIONS

1. Define each of the following:

(a) Metaphor

(b) Telecommuting

(c) Intranet

(d) Portable Document Format

2. Why is trust important to e-business?

3. Name and describe four factors that comprise trust.

4. Name and describe three perceptions (other than trust) that impact decisions to use or not use e-business to interact with organizations.

5. An organization wants its customers to use e-business technologies to interact with the organization. Describe the necessary steps to positively impact the following perceptions (as they relate to e-business):

(a) Trust

(b) Relative advantage

(c) Complexity

(d) Compatibility

6. Reports indicate that there is a worldwide shortage of information technology workers. How does this shortage present a barrier to e-business?

7. Why are consumer protections important to e-business?

8. What are business process patents?

9. How might business process patents have a positive impact on the growth of e-business?

10. How might business process patents have a negative impact on the growth of e-business?

11. Describe three negative uses of the Web.

12. Name and briefly describe the Safe Harbor Privacy Principles.

13. What is a cultural content quota? How do these quotas represent a barrier to e-business?

14. How does corporate culture impact a company's use of e-business technologies?

15. Name and describe at least four cultural barriers to e-business.

16. Name and briefly discuss four technical barriers to e-business.

EXERCISES

1. Do all search engines return the same results? Try an experiment to find out. Use at least four search engines to search for the phrase "intellectual property rights." Compare the results. Which search engine gave you the best results? How much did the results differ? Discuss how any inconsistencies you found my have a negative impact on e-business.

2. Visit the Web site of an online merchant (Suggestions: Sierra Trading Post (http://www.sierratradingpost.com/), Amazon.com (http://www.amazon.com), Road Runner Sports (http://www.roadrunnersports.com), Dell (http://www.dell.com), or Buy.com (http://www.buy.com)). Identify features of the site that may impact potential customers' perceptions of each of the following: trust, relative advantage, complexity, and compatibility. Describe each feature and explain how it might impact the perception. Offer suggestions to the merchant for changing the site to improve these perceptions.

3. Find at least three IT training and/or educational programs in your area (other than the program in which you are enrolled). What skills are taught? What background is required for admission? What is the duration of the program? How much is the tuition? Do any of the programs put a special emphasis on e-business skills? Discuss the programs you identified in terms of reducing the IT workforce shortage.

4. Try to find each of the following for sale on the Web (your instructor may assign you other products); (1) a Trek brand mountain bike, (2) double-pane windows, and (3) solid oak bookshelves. What techniques did you use to locate the goods? What worked well? What did not work well? Discuss your experience in terms of technological barriers to e-business.

5. Read DoubleClick's privacy policy (available at http://www.doubleclick.net/us/corporate/privacy/default .asp?asp_object_1=&). How reasonable do you think its privacy policy is? Discuss how privacy concerns impact the growth of e-business.

DISCUSSION POINTS

For each issue below, prepare an argument in support of or in opposition to the statement.

1. Deep links should be considered violations of copyright. The owner of a Web site should be able to control how other pages link to its site.

2. Public access Internet facilities (such as libraries and school computer labs) should restrict access to adult-oriented Web sites.

3. Web sites that advocate hatred of any group should be banned.

4. Some Web sites require you to register to gain access to free content or services. It is ethical to give false personal information in order to gain access to the free content or services offered through these sites.

5. Universities should restrict e-business applications that consume large amounts of bandwidth, but do not directly add to students' education. For example, the universities that banned trading MP3 files using Napster were justified in their actions.

FURTHER READINGS

Perceptual Barriers

JARVENPAA, S.L., N. TRACTINSKY, L. SAARINEN, and M. VITALE. "Consumer Trust in an Internet Store: A Cross-Cultural Validation," *Journal of Computer-Mediated Communication* 5 (2) (available online at http://www.ascusc.org/jcmc/vol5 /issue2/jarvenpaa.html).

Technical Barriers

Internet Traffic Report, http://www.internettrafficreport.com/.

Macromedia. Macromedia Shockwave White Paper, http://sdc.shockwave.com/software/shockwaveplayer /whitepaper/.

Legal and Ethical Issues

GURLEY, W. "The Trouble With Internet Patents," Fortune.com (19 July 1999): http://www.fortune.com/indexw.jhtml ?channel=artcol.jhtml&doc_id=43712.

HANSEN, E. "DoubleClick Under E-mail Attack for Consumer Profiling Plans," CNET News.com (2 February 2000): http://news.cnet.com/news/0-1005-200-1539478.html.

Interactive Travel. "The Pain of the Delta Domain," Elliot.org (14 May 1998): http://www.elliott.org/interactive/1998/delta.htm.

MASON, D. Four Ethical Issues of the Information Age," *Management Information Systems Quarterly* 10 (1): 5–12.

ROSENBERG, S. "Don't Link or I'll Sue," Salon.com (12 August 1999): http://www.salon.com/tech/col/rose/1999/08/12/deep_links/index.html.

U.S. Department of Commerce. Web site on the Safe Harbor Principles, http://www.export.gov/safeharbor/.

Cultural Barriers

GUTZMAN, A. "Globalization of E-commerce: Are You Ready?" Internet.com (17 May 2000): http://ecommerce.internet.com/solutions/tech_advisor/article/0,1467,9561_365241,00.html.

Societal Barriers

ARNOLD, D. and NIEDERMAN, F. (Eds.) "Special Section: The Global IT Workforce." *Communications of the ACM* 44 (7): 31–54.

United States Department of Commerce. "America's New Deficit: The Shortage of Information Technology Workers," (1997) http://www.ta.doc.gov/reports/itsw/itsw.pdf.

Organizational Barriers

ANANDARAJAN, A. (Ed.) "Special Section: Internet Abuse in the Workplace." *Communications of the ACM* (January 2002): 45 (1): 53–87

REFERENCES

AGARWAL, R. and FERRATT, T. 2001. Crafting an HR strategy to meet the need for IT workers. *Communications of the ACM* 44 (7): 59–64.

ARNOLD, D. and NEIDERMAN, F. 2001. The global IT workforce. *Communications of the ACM* 44 (7): 31–33.

HOSMER, L. 1995. Trust: the connecting link between organizational theory and philosophical ethics," *Academy of Management Review* 20 (2): 379–403.

LIM, V., TEO, T., and LOO, G. 2002. How do I loaf here? Let me count the ways. *Communications of the ACM* 45 (1): 66-70.

Media Awareness Network. 1999. Media issues: Cultural sovereignty. http://www.reseau-medias.ca/eng/issues/stats/isssov.htm.

National Telecommunications and Information Association. 2002. A Nation Online: How Americans are Expanding Their Use of the Internet. http://www.ntia.doc.gov/ntiahome/dn/index.html.

ROGERS, E. M. 1995. *Diffusion of innovations.* New York: The Free Press.

ROSE, I. N. 2001. Understanding the law of Internet gambling. Gambling and the Law (27 April 2001): http://www.gamblingandthelaw.com/internet_gambling.html.

SIMMERS, C. 2002. Aligning Internet usage with business priorities. *Communications of the ACM* 45 (1): 71–74.

TORNATZKY, L., and KLEIN, K. 1982. Innovation characteristics and innovation adoption-implementation: A meta-analysis of findings. *IEEE Transactions on Engineering Management* EM-29 (February 1982): 28–45.

United States Department of Commerce. 1997. America's New Deficit: The Shortage of Information Technology Workers. http://www.ta.doc.gov/reports/itsw/itsw.pdf.

Vault. 2000. Results of Vault survey of internet use in the workplace. http://www.vault.com/surveys/internetuse2000/index2000.jsp.

CHAPTER 4

THE INTERNET AND WORLD WIDE WEB FOR E-BUSINESS

LEARNING OBJECTIVES

After reading and completing this chapter, you should be able to:

- Understand the basic functioning of client/server architecture
- Differentiate between the Internet and the World Wide Web
- Describe the Internet, its origin, and its current implementation
- Describe the core technologies that comprise the Internet
- Describe the core technologies that comprise the World Wide Web
- Understand the similarities and differences between the Internet and intranets
- Discuss issues and concerns of management with using the Internet for electronic business

Opening Case: eBay.com

In the early 1990s, Pierre Omidyar and his wife were discussing ways for her to trade, buy, or discuss with others her collection of over four hundred Pez candy dispensers. Mr. Omidyar went on to create an online centralized location for this. The Internet provided him with a means to connect this central location to users worldwide. Hence was born eBay.com in 1995. It has now become the largest online trading community for person-to-person trading. It is available internationally twenty-four hours a day, seven days a week, and there are five to ten million persons registered on the auction site in a given year. Figure 4-1 shows the main Web page for eBay.

In 1999, eBay had revenues of more than U.S.$225 million, representing a net income of close to U.S.$11 million. In 1998, the company went public, meaning that it started issuing stocks for sale on the stock market. eBay's business model is a dream for businesses, with almost no variable costs, no inventory, and no shipping costs. Since eBay does not take possession of items, and the company's income comes from fees that the auction site's users are paying (five to six percent of the items' value), profit margins are large. Sellers retain control of their assets until the items are actually bought by someone else, and then they take care of delivery themselves.

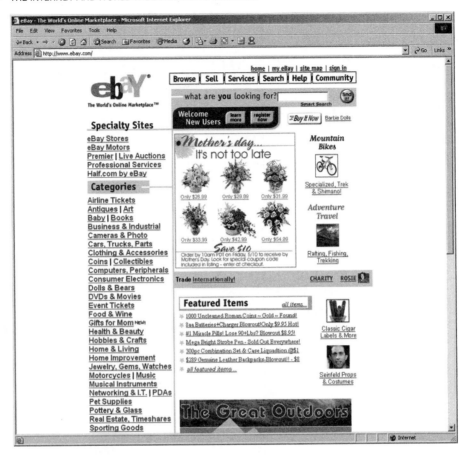

FIGURE 4-1 eBay Web Site

Today, eBay receives, on average, fifty million hits a day. The number of items available on the auction site has risen to more than four million. Other services have been added to the site, such as a library, a magazine, and discussion groups. Payments can be made electronically. One of the payment services is Billpoint—an agreement with Wells Fargo that allows customers to use credit cards to purchase items on eBay, even though the sellers are individuals without credit card processing capabilities. Billpoint provides buyers and sellers on eBay great payment convenience. eBay also provides some insurance on transactions to protect consumers from potentially fraudulent sellers. Another function is the ability to trade only locally in a particular region (for goods that may require inspection, for example), or globally.

In 2000, eBay acquired a competitor called Half.com. Half.com is also a person-to-person trading environment, but one that allows sellers to establish a fixed price at which their items sell. Conversely, eBay's model is a "freewheeling auction method" where prices are established by the "market." When it first acquired Half.com, eBay created a link from its Web site to Half.com's Web site. However, in late 2001 eBay wanted more integration of the fixed price model on its own Web site, which it plans on doing by taking control of back-end technology and customer service for both companies.

Not surprisingly, eBay had to improve substantially its technology infrastructure between 1995 and today. Each day, there might be twenty to thirty thousand brand new registered users. With the constant increases in its number of users, items, and functions, the company's servers sometimes became overwhelmed; this resulted in shutdowns in the summer of 1999. It is estimated that these shutdowns, which lasted close to a day each, cost the company millions of dollars and loss of goodwill by numerous customers. In response to these issues, eBay outsourced some of their **back-end technologies** (Web servers, database servers, and Internet routers) to AboveNet Communications, Inc. (acquired by Metromedia Fiber Network, Inc.) and Exodus Communications (currently in Chapter 11 bankruptcy) in 2000. These companies own high-speed Internet connections, providing eBay.com with high-speed links between its servers and the Internet, and therefore its users. These backbone networks use fiber optic links running at up to 622 Mbps. Yet, the company grows constantly. For example, it grew between 40 percent and 70 percent each quarter of 1998 and 1999. This requires substantial growth capabilities in its technology infrastructures. The company's approach to **capacity planning** has been to implement technology infrastructures to support five to ten times the anticipated demand. As eBay's infrastructure grew, the company placed various services on a number of different servers to avoid problems such as auction site crashes bringing down the rest of the communication facilities of the company. In September 2001, eBay announced that it would use International Business Machine's (IBM's) WebSphere e-commerce suite to replace its existing infrastructure.

The Internet made a company like eBay.com possible. Today's technology infrastructures are critical to its success. The Internet provides worldwide access to individuals twenty-four hours a day, seven days a week. Can you think of other technologies besides the Internet that could have allowed the auction site to be created and linked to consumers worldwide? What other factors can explain eBay's success? Remember that eBay was the first widely known online **person-to-person trading** site. The company gained reputation and visibility as the first mover in this area, and has since remained abreast of its competition.

INTRODUCTION

Business-to-consumer electronic business, as seen in Chapter 2, has become increasingly popular. The largest portion of this type of electronic business is conducted over the Internet. The Internet is also a significant communication backbone for non Web-based B2C, as well as business-to-business (B2B), transactions, which are increasingly conducted using Internet, **intranet,** and **extranet** platforms. Intranets use Internet technology for internal networks, such as corporate networks that are protected by a firewall. We will discuss intranets later in the chapter, and firewalls in Chapter 10 (Privacy and Security in E-business). Extranets use Internet technologies to create networks that connect trading partners. Since these networks are key to a number of electronic business environments, we will focus this chapter on presenting the basic technologies that serve as platforms for the Internet and the World Wide Web. We will begin by discussing the client/server architecture, which is the core of most networks. We will explore in-depth what the Internet really is. We will also compare and contrast the World Wide Web with the Internet. While many individuals consider these two entities to be the same, it is not the case. The World Wide Web is a **hypertext** based graphical interface to worldwide Internet resources. The World Wide Web is one application that uses the Internet as its communication network.

CLIENT/SERVER ARCHITECTURE

The client/server model of computing has become a central concept of computer networks, such as the Internet. In short, a **client/server architecture** is an architecture in which processing and storage tasks are divided between two classes of network members, clients and servers. The concept is actually quite simple. Clients are all processes that request services from servers, which are all processes that respond to requests from clients. Note that we use the term "processes" when referring to the roles of clients and servers. It is important to realize that most computers are capable of being used as clients or servers. A well-equipped computer can easily serve in either capacity. Some computers are specialized to be only clients or only servers, but most computers can be used as either.

One often confusing aspect of the client/server architecture is whether "server" refers to hardware or software. In common usage, it can refer to either. For example, if you say "My department needs to get a faster server," you are probably referring to buying a new computer (hardware). However, what makes this new computer a server is the software it is running. As we mentioned earlier, almost any well-equipped computer can be used as a server. So, what makes a computer a server, rather than a personal workstation, is the software it is running and the function it serves. There are specially designed computers that are intended to be used as servers and not personal computers. These computers typically have more expansion capabilities than personal computers and may actually look different. Do not be fooled, however; what makes these computers servers is the software they run.

You are likely to be very familiar with one system that uses a client/server architecture—the Web. When you surf the Web, you are probably using a Web browser, such as Netscape Navigator or Microsoft Explorer. When you do so, your computer system is acting as a client. When you enter a URL or click on a hyperlink, your software makes a request for a document from another computer, which is known as a Web server. The server, in turn, services your request and transmits the document to your computer. Then your Web browser displays the requested document. You can see how the work is divided between the client (your computer) and the server (the Web server).

In a client/server architecture, the client actually has two tasks. As we have already mentioned, the client makes requests to servers. The client is also responsible for the user interface, which is sometimes called the presentation. For example, the Web browser software (which is a client process) not only requests documents from servers, but must also display those documents and allow the user to make requests by typing a URL or clicking on a link. The servers must store all of the documents and be able to respond to requests from clients. Figure 4-2 illustrates a typical client/server architecture in which the clients connect to the server through a network.

Client/server computing is a type of **distributed computing.** Distributed computing architectures spread processing across a number of computers, as opposed to centralized computing, which uses a single computer to do all processing. Users access the main computer through terminals and a telecommunications network.

The basic client/server architecture is sometimes called a two-tier architecture. The basic idea has been extended into **three-tier** and **n-tier** architectures. A three-tier architecture, which is illustrated in Figure 4-3 divides processing into three layers; the presentation layer, the application layer (also known as the business logic layer), and the data layer. In the two-tier architecture, the business logic commonly resides on the client. Basically, the three-tier architecture extends the two-tier architecture by breaking out application data processes into

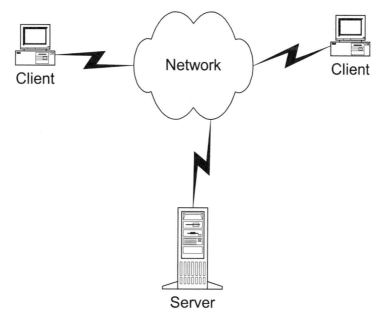

FIGURE 4-2   Client/Server Architecture

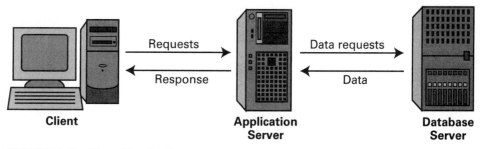

FIGURE 4-3   Three-Tier Architecture

separate layers. Further division of tasks can also occur, resulting in additional tiers. In general, we refer to an architecture with more than three tiers as an n-tier architecture.

In a three-tier environment, clients request services from the application server, which determines which data are required to satisfy the request, then requests the data from the database server. For example, an order entry operator might want to check the available stock of New Balance 580 running shoes. The operator enters the request by typing the appropriate stock number into a form on his computer, which is acting as a client. The operator's computer sends a request for the inventory information to the application server. The application server determines what data are required to satisfy the request, then asks the database server for those data. The database server locates the data, then sends them to the application server. The application server may need to perform processing tasks on the data. For example, there might be a rule that inventory levels are always reported with a 5 percent cushion. If so, the application server would deduct 5 percent from the actual inventory level, then send the adjusted figure to the client, which would then display the data in an appropriate format.

Middleware

Client/server and n-tier systems are often heterogeneous, which simply means that they use different types of systems and operating environments. For example, a system may use both Oracle9*i* and SQL Server as databases. Sometimes making different environments work together requires special software, called middleware. Middleware makes it possible for different software applications to communicate with one another; in other words, middleware enables interoperability. For example, some middleware links database systems to Web server software. Using middleware frees application programmers from writing the code necessary to enable the communications.

There are a number of different classes of middleware, including transaction processing (TP) monitors, object request brokers (ORB), remote procedure call (RPC) systems, and message-oriented middleware (MOM). Transaction processing monitors keep track of transactions as they progress through the system. In addition, TP monitors may perform load balancing tasks. Object request brokers allow applications to request and receive objects in an object-oriented environment without having to know anything about the servers on the network. Remote procedure call systems let programs on client computers run procedures on servers. The client program simply sends the appropriate arguments to the server, which executes the procedure using those arguments. One drawback to RPC is that it is synchronous, which means that the application sending the RPC must wait for a response before continuing. As you might have guessed, this can slow processing considerably. Message-oriented middleware enables clients to send messages to servers, then proceed with other processing while waiting for the server to respond. The MOM collects and stores the messages until the appropriate server is ready to accept them. MOM is particularly useful in workflow applications, which typically involve a number of processing steps. MOM is asynchronous, so the sending application can continue processing while waiting for a response. Middleware is discussed in more detail in Chapter 8.

Advantages and Disadvantages of Client/Server and n-Tier Architectures

Client/server architectures have been widely touted as being the salvation of many IT departments. As is often the case, the reality is somewhat less positive than the early promise. There are a number of clear advantages to client/server computing. However, there are also a number of disadvantages that are just as clear. In this section, we briefly discuss the main advantages and disadvantages of client/server and n-tier architectures.

There are a number of advantages that organizations may gain by using n-tier architectures. Of these, three seem to be the most important: (1) scalability, (2) interoperability, and (3) reliability. **Scalability** basically means the ability to increase or decrease computing capacity. For example, an organization would need to increase its computing capacity as it adds new employees. An organization's systems may also need to grow in response to new applications, such as Web-based selling. By their nature, well-designed n-tier systems are generally thought to be more scalable than centralized systems. In part, this is because of the modular nature of the client/server architecture. Up to a point, additional users can be added simply by adding inexpensive client computers. Of course, at some point, there would be too many clients for the database and/or application servers to handle. Then, additional servers would be added to the system.

Interoperability, is the ability of different types of systems to interact with each other. As we pointed out, interoperability is a key enabling factor for e-business. Multitier systems, in general, have a higher level of interoperability than do centralized systems. In part, this is due to the modular nature of client/server architectures. Because client/server architectures are modular, organizations demand the flexibility to utilize components from different vendors. For example, some clients may run Microsoft's Windows 2000, while others run Apple's Mac OS. On the same system, there may be a database server from Sun Microsystems running under Solaris and an application server from IBM that uses Linux. Because their customers demand the ability to build systems using a variety of components, many hardware and software vendors adhere to industry standards (such as TCP/IP), which allow interoperability with other products that follow the same standards. Middleware also plays a role in enabling interoperability in client/server architecture.

When properly designed, n-tier systems are highly reliable. Recall that in n-tier architectures, there are many different clients and servers. (Most systems have multiple database servers and application servers.) Because of this, it is not likely that a failure of any single component will cause the entire system to go down. If one of the servers in a n-tier system fails, functions of the system that do not require that particular server continue to perform normally—only part of the overall system ceases to function. Of course, any process that depend on that server are unavailable. In a centralized computing environment, when the central server fails, the entire system is unable to function.

There is an additional advantage of n-tier computing that is worth mentioning. Since the client computers are responsible for user interface and presentation tasks, the use of graphical user interfaces (GUI) is facilitated. Using a GUI requires significant computing power. In centralized systems, using GUIs would likely overtax the processing capacity of the central server. In an n-tier system, each client (commonly a PC) typically has sufficient power to deal with a GUI. Why is the use of GUIs important? In short, because they are generally easier to use than command-line based interfaces, which allows many more people to take advantage of information technology.

Unfortunately, there are also some serious drawbacks to n-tier computing. We discuss three of the more important drawbacks: (1) complexity, (2) hidden costs, and (3) less mature management tools.

As you know, n-tier architectures contain many different components that constantly pass data among each other. All of this communication requires close coordination, which leads to complexity. To understand why this is so, consider completing a class project by yourself and as part of a team. In many ways, completing the project by yourself is less complex. You do not have to schedule meetings, resolve disagreements, distribute tasks, or share information. Completing the project as part of a team (ideally) means that you must set up ways to communicate among team members and coordinate the members' efforts. But once all of the communication and coordination systems are in place, teams can handle large projects more effectively than individuals. This is very similar to computing using n-tier architectures. Communication and coordination systems must be carefully designed, which can be very complex and costly. In the long run, however, the high short-term costs are often offset by long-term savings.

Organizations implementing n-tier architectures may find that they incur some unexpected costs. Two of the most common hidden costs are training and staffing. Because implementing n-tier architectures requires specialized skills, organizations may have difficulty finding trained. When such individuals are available, they often command high salaries. An alternative available to organizations is to train their existing personnel, which is also costly. Determining which approach to take can be a difficult decision. Of course, an organization may choose to pursue both approaches. Regardless of the approach taken, hiring people with solid n-tier skills can be costly.

The final drawback to n-tier architectures is that they are less mature than centralized architectures. This means that standards may not be as well developed and that management tools may not be as robust. For example, network management tools for centralized systems have been in use for several decades. In this time, they have become quite powerful. By contrast, enterprise scale n-tier network management tools have been available for a much shorter period of time. As a result, they are not as robust as their centralized system cousins. As you might expect, the situation is changing—n-tier tools are improving rapidly. Hewlett-Packard's OpenView and Computer Associates' Unicenter are two popular network management systems. Table 4-1 summarizes the advantages and disadvantages of client/server computing.

THE INTERNET

The Internet is a worldwide network of networks. Devices called **routers** are used to interconnect the various networks around the world. Every host or computer that is a full participant on the Internet has a unique address called an **Internet protocol (IP)** address.

Origin of the Internet

In 1969, the United States Defense Advanced Research Projects Agency (DARPA) connected four host computers nationwide for their military research units, which included universities that were conducting research projects for them. Through various stages of evolution, ARPANET (see Table 4-2) was created. The network continued to grow until, eventually, it was split into a network for the military (MILNET) and a network for academics (Internet) in 1983. The Internet then grew by absorbing various

Table 4-1 Advantages and Disadvantages of Client/Server Computing

Advantages	Disadvantages
■ Scalability	■ Complexity
■ Interoperability	■ Hidden costs
■ Reliability	■ Less mature management tools

Table 4-2 Brief Overview of Internet History

1969	ARPANET is formed
1983	ARPANET is split into INTERNET and MILNET
1985	BITNET (CUNY's network including Canadian universities) is completed
1986	NSFNET is created by the National Science Foundation for leading U.S. universities and government agencies
1988	NSF installs high speed backbone and connects thirteen regional Internet networks
1990s	Commercial networks begin connecting to the Internet

networks worldwide until the early 1990s, when all of them formed a linked network of networks, resulting in today's Internet. Since then, the Internet has grown substantially, with over 150,000 interconnected networks today (see Figure 4-4), and more than seventy million host computers connected (see Figure 4-5).

Internet Tools and Applications

Most students today are familiar with the Web and have typically used it to conduct research; find general interest information, such as the latest football game scores; or even conduct some electronic commerce transactions by acquiring goods or services, such as

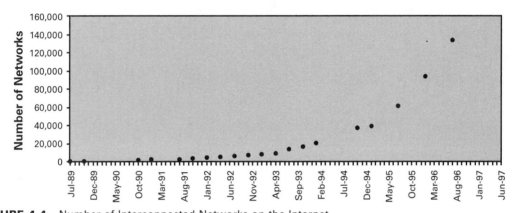

FIGURE 4-4 Number of Interconnected Networks on the Internet

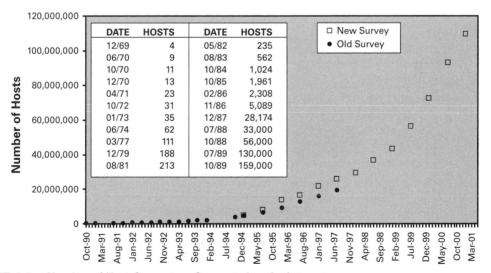

FIGURE 4-5 Number of Host Computers Connected to the Internet

computers. The Internet, however, supports a much broader set of applications than just the Web. Some of them, such as Gopher, Veronica, or Archie, used to be very popular, but have given way to new and easier methods of accessing the information (the Web). The most popular of these tools is the use of the Internet for electronic mail exchanges. Other tools briefly described in this section include **listservs, File Transfer Protocol (FTP),** real-time discussion tools, **newsgroups, remote logins,** peer-to-peer, and groupware.

Electronic Mail

E-mail is the most common application on the Internet. Electronic mail allows you to send messages anywhere around the world. Anyone that has an e-mail address can receive your messages (unless they work in a secure environment that does not let your mail into their system). The Internet is often used as the intermediary between two private networks that maintain their own mail servers. An owner of a mail server must assign an e-mail address to you. For example, if you pay an **Internet service provider** for connection services, the company should provide you with an e-mail address. Most companies, organizations, and institutions today have their own mail servers and can create as many e-mail addresses as their server can manage. Several organizations or companies also offer free e-mail accounts on the Web (e.g., Yahoo mail, Hotmail, etc.). Mail servers exchange messages using a variety of standards. The Internet mail standard is called **Simple Mail Transfer Protocol (SMTP).** There are other mail standards that exist and are used worldwide. Some of them are presented in Table 4-3.

There are a wide variety of electronic mail packages available commercially or for free. Most of these packages support **MIME.** Multi-purpose Internet Mail Extensions (MIME) is a set of specifications for sending attachments with e-mail messages. If two persons exchange e-mail messages, they can share attachments of all sorts, even if they use different mail packages, as long as both of their mail packages support MIME. MIME has extended the use of e-mail to share images, video, and audio clips, as well as text files and executable files. Unfortunately, it is the ability to transfer executable files that has led

Table 4-3 Common Electronic Mail Standards

Standard	Description
Post Office Protocol (POP)	A standard that allows users to prepare their mail ahead of time, reply to mail, and connect only for the time it takes to upload and download incoming and outgoing mail. This is a very important protocol for users who travel a lot and prefer to do most of their mail activities offline. However, it is being gradually replaced by another standard, Internet Mail Access Protocol.
Internet Mail Access Protocol (IMAP)	A standard that basically offers the same functionality as POP, but also allows users to leave their mail messages on the server after having read them instead of having all of them transferred to the client computer.
X.400	A standard for interconnectivity of mail packages. It allows mail to be sent from one mail application to another incompatible mail application (if vendors support X.400 in their products).
Common Messaging Calls (CMC)	A standard that is similar to X.400, but simpler. It supports a large number of vendors.

to the viruses that have been spreading throughout computer networks. We will discuss viruses and other threats to security in Chapter 10.

Listserv

An extension of e-mail capabilities is the use of listservs. Listservs are mailing lists that are used by individuals with similar interests to share information and create discussion groups. One of the authors is a member of several academic information systems listservs, a stock market discussion listserv, as well as a listserv on multi-hull boating. While formats to subscribe to listservs vary, you typically have to subscribe and unsubscribe to a list by:

1. Sending an e-mail to listserv@hostname (where hostname is the name of the server)

2. In the body of the text, including only the commands "subscribe list Your Name" (where list is the name of the list) or "unsubscribe list Your Name"

E-BUSINESS IN PRACTICE

How E-mail Works

Many of you probably send and receive e-mail messages every day. Did you ever wonder how a message gets from your computer to your friend's computer? Although setting up and maintaining an e-mail server is complicated, understanding how e-mail works conceptually is actually pretty simple. This figure illustrates how a message travels from your computer to your friend's computer. We have left out some of the details, but the example should give you a good idea of the basic process.

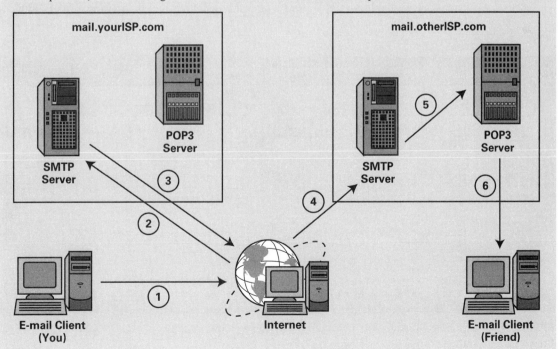

Note that these are the addresses used to subscribe or unsubscribe. To send messages to the list, you usually have to send to *list@hostname.* Proper instructions should be sent to you once you subscribe to a list. Sometimes, instead of *listserv* you may need to send your subscription or unsubscribe requests to *majordomo@hostname.*

File Transfer Protocol

File Transfer Protocol (FTP) is a key function on the Internet that allows users to move files back and forth between **nodes** on the network. For example, it is very useful for retrieving files from public sites around the world. When files are loaded on such public sites, FTP is said to use **anonymous FTP.** Even when you use your Web browser to access files and click on download links, FTP is the protocol that is used to actually transfer the files. The FTP protocol allows files to be transferred irrespective of the computer types or operating systems used, as long as the computers understand the FTP protocol. Different types of files, such as ASCII and binary files, can be transferred using FTP. Most applications and files today require the use of binary transfer. In recent years, several new FTP applications have been developed. These are much easier to use than the old command line approach to FTP that required users to know the commands and type them at a DOS-like prompt.

To start an FTP session, you must connect to the **remote server.** You must know either the name of the server or its IP address. You must then specify if the session is an anonymous FTP session (public site) or a secure site connection. For an anonymous session, most FTP programs will use *anonymous* as the logon id and your e-mail address as the password. For secure servers, you must have a user identification and a password on that server, and must have been allowed by the administrator to do FTP sessions. Figure 4-6 presents an example of an FTP session connecting to the United States' Internal Revenue Service using WS_FTP LE from Ipswitch, Inc. A large number of FTP applications are available on the Web as shareware (minimal fee) or freeware (free). Some of

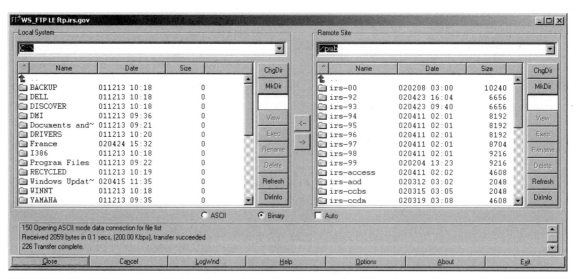

FIGURE 4-6 FTP Session with U.S. Internal Revenue Service (ftp.irs.gov)

SOURCE: Ipswitch, Inc., 1999. Used with permission.

the most popular include CuteFTP, FTP Voyager, WS_FTP, Netzip Download Demon, Hotline Connect Client, and Serv-U.

How do find out which files are available to you on the Internet? Most of the time you either hear from a friend or conduct a search using a Web search engine. Several years ago, the Archie system was developed to index most files that were available on public servers. You must know the name of the file or part of it, though, for searching through Archie. With today's rapidly growing number of public sites and files available, Archie has grown substantially. If you do not know the file you are looking for, your best bet is to use a Web search engine. For example, if you want to find out what software is available for chatting on the Web, using the keywords "Internet chat software" on a search engine will provide a number of sites from which software for Internet Relay Chat is available. Search engines will be discussed in the section on the Web in this chapter. Many FTP programs also have handy directory management functions (create directories; delete, rename, or copy files; etc.), which can be used just like file managers.

Internet Relay Chat

Internet Relay Chat (IRC) is a multi-user chat application that allows individuals to communicate synchronously using the Internet as the communication backbone. People can use virtual "channels" to meet and discuss topics of interest to them. It can be used by groups of people or just two individuals. It is a very useful communication tool for typing messages in real-time to anyone connected around the world. For example, it was used extensively during the Persian Gulf war (1991) to provide updates worldwide on what was happening. To use IRC, you must simply download or obtain a client IRC software, which then allows you to connect to the IRC network of servers. An example of a popular IRC program (although it performs more functions than simple chat applications) is ICQ ("I seek you") from ICQ, Inc. ICQ allows individuals to "logon," and alerts them when others they are seeking to communicate with are available online. This is done in the background while the user performs other functions on her desktop computer. Once individuals who want to communicate with each other are all available, and there could be many in a group, they can use the software's chat facility, message sending facility, file transfer capability, or e-mail facilities. In addition, ICQ can be used to launch other applications, such as Microsoft's NetMeeting **teleconferencing** application.

There are actually businesses that furnish online chat services. For example, HumanClick enables Web site operators to add chat facilities to their sites. Visitors can click on a chat link, which alerts the Web site operator that a visitor needs assistance. The visitor and the operator can then interact through a chat facility. Many Web merchants are using chat technologies to make Web shopping seem more personal.

Instant Messaging

Instant messaging software, such as AOL Instant Messenger, allows the Internet to be used much like an online pager. Using instant messaging software, you can send a quick message to a friend. The message will pop up on your friend's computer almost immediately after you send the message. Your friend can then reply to your message. In essence, you and your friend are using a private chat room to interact. Of course, for this to happen, you and your friend must both be online and running the instant messaging software. Most instant messaging systems allow conferencing, which allows several users to interact as a

E-BUSINESS IN PRACTICE

How Instant Messaging Works

Although using instant messaging does not require understanding how it works, instant messaging is a good example of a network-enabled application. So, we thought you might be interested in knowing how it works. The description that follows is generic rather than being related to any particular instant messaging system. However, most systems work in a similar fashion.

Before you can participate in instant messaging, you must have the appropriate instant messaging client software. If you do not already have the right client software, you must download and install the client. Once the software is installed, you can begin messaging. This figure illustrates how instant messaging works.

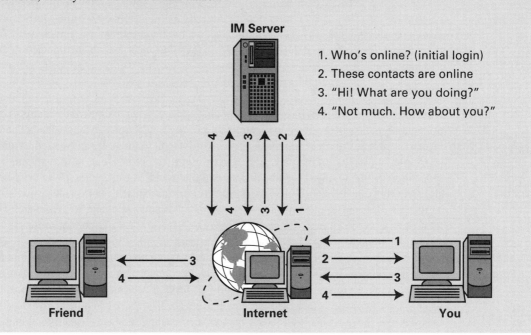

IM Server

1. Who's online? (initial login)
2. These contacts are online
3. "Hi! What are you doing?"
4. "Not much. How about you?"

Friend   **Internet**   **You**

group. For example, Yahoo! Messenger allows up to ten users to interact in a single conference. A recent development related to instant messaging is that many systems now allow voice-based messaging. Essentially, this is similar to making a telephone call, although the quality will not be as good. You can even combine the conference and voice capabilities to allow voice-based conference calling. Generally, conference calls require either sophisticated telephone systems or the use of a fee-based conference facility. For now, both conferencing and voice messaging are free from many providers, such as Yahoo! and MSN.

As the name implies, the advantage of instant messaging is that the messages appear almost immediately. E-mail messages, in contrast, are not received immediately—your friend must check for messages, which may happen automatically or manually.

Currently, there are several popular instant messaging systems. Among the most popular are those from AOL, Yahoo!, ICQ (I-seek-you), and MSN. Unfortunately, there are no standards for instant messenger systems, so the various systems may not interact. This means that someone using AOL Instant Messenger and someone using MSN's software cannot send messages to each other.

In the early days of instant messaging, most people used messaging for non-business use. However, today instant messaging use is becoming widespread in businesses. For example, programmers on a software development team can use instant messaging to "discuss" a bug in a section of code. Many teams within organizations are utilizing instant messaging systems as an inexpensive way to improve communications. It will be interesting to see how popular instant messaging use becomes within organizations.

Newsgroups

Newsgroup applications allow users to read and post messages to various **electronic boards** on the Internet. They are often referred to as **bulletin boards** or **discussion groups.** Users carry on discussions relevant to the particular newsgroup to which they are connected, and the system then organizes those discussions in an orderly fashion. Users must have a news reading program available to read the newsgroup discussions. The newsgroups are organized hierarchically, like Internet domains. For example, rec.music.rock is a recreational discussion group for individuals interested in music, and more particularly rock music. Some examples of high-level newsgroup domains are presented in Table 4-4.

Remote Login Through Telnet

This function allows users to connect to other computers on the Internet from their local system. It is very useful for connecting to a remote computer, such as your main server to check your electronic mail messages when you are half way around the world. It is also used extensively to access public sites, such as libraries or government databases. Today, many of these functions have been updated to take advantage of the Web and the Web browser.

Peer-to-Peer

In early 2000, an Internet-based application called Napster exploded into the public's consciousness. (Recall that in Chapter 3, we discussed the legal issues associated with Napster.) Once you download and install the Napster software, you can enter an artist's name or the name of a song and then receive a list of users who have the desired songs stored on their computers' hard drives. You can then download the song (or songs) from another user's computer.

Napster is one of a number of programs that utilize **peer-to-peer (P2P) networking.** Peer-to-peer networking has existed as a network architecture for many years. In these types of networks, all computers act as both clients and servers, which allows any computer to access the files stored on any other computer on the network. Programs such as Napster and Gnutella use the peer-to-peer concept to allow file sharing and other applications across the Internet. When you run the P2P application, you gain access to files stored on others' computers that are online and running the application at the same time, and they gain access to your files.

One of the more interesting P2P-related projects is Freenet. Freenet uses members' computers to create a global information storage and dissemination tool that anyone can use to view or distribute

Table 4-4 Examples of Newsgroup Categories

news	For discussions of news networks and software
rec	For discussions of recreational activities
sci	For discussions of scientific research and applications
soc	For discussions of social issues

almost any kind of information. One of Freenet's goals is to overcome the potential censorship of controversial material. To this end, Freenet allows anonymous posting of material and also does not have any centralized control or administration.

Organizations are reexamining P2P networking in order to avoid some of the costs associated with server-based file sharing. The future of P2P in the corporate environment is unclear. Time will tell whether P2P applications become an essential element of organizational information technology architectures or simply fade away.

Groupware

Groupware is not really new; in fact its roots go back to research work done in the 1980s. However, the advent of the Web has made groupware accessible to a much wider audience. It is important to recognize that not all groupware is Web based. Groupware can be run on most types of networks. As you might guess from its name, groupware is software that is designed to facilitate the work of groups. There are many different types of groupware, ranging from messaging systems and shared calendars to systems that allow custom development, such as Lotus Notes.

The dimensions of time and place are often used to classify groupware. Groups who meet in the same physical location are said to be colocated, or face-to-face; otherwise the group is called a distance group. When the members of the group come together at the same time, the group is said to be synchronous. When members are not all together at one time, the group is asynchronous. Of course, a single group can be classified differently on different occasions. The importance of the classification scheme is simply to understand different types of groupware applications. Figure 4-7 illustrates the classification scheme with example groupware applications.

Groupware over the Web, which tends to support distant rather than colocated groups, is becoming increasingly popular. The ability to access groupware functions though a Web browser is very advantageous, as is being able to access the groupware simply by accessing the Internet. Otherwise special software and telecommunication connections are required to use distance groupware. Organizations that wish to use Web-based groupware can choose to install and maintain their own groupware systems. Two of the more popular are Lotus Domino, which is based on Lotus Notes, and Microsoft Exchange. If an organization does not want to maintain its own groupware, it can use a groupware service provider. In fact some of these providers will let you use their groupware for free. Typically, these kinds of services are advertising supported, although others use the free service to promote more

	Same time (synchronous)	Different time (asynchronous)
Same place (colocated)	■ Group decision support systems ■ Voting ■ Presentation support	■ Shared computers
Different place (distance)	■ Videophones ■ Chat ■ Shared whiteboard	■ Discussions ■ E-mail ■ Workflow

FIGURE 4-7 Groupware Classification Scheme

advanced fee-based services. An example of a free groupware provider is Epls FastWorker, which provides rather complete functionality, including threaded discussions, task management, and document sharing. Epls uses the free Web-based service to promote the use of its groupware on private LANs, for which Epls charges a licensing fee. One of the most popular free services is Yahoo! Groups (http://groups.yahoo.com), which was born from a free groupware service called eGroups. Yahoo! Groups has many useful group support features, including file sharing, chat, shared calendars, and voting. Since Yahoo! Groups is a free service and many students are familiar with Yahoo!, many student groups use the service to help them organize and manage group projects. Organizations that use groupware must be careful to consider security and privacy issues. This is especially true when using Web-based groupware, and when using a groupware service provider.

THE WORLD WIDE WEB

The World Wide Web, also known as WWW or simply the Web, is the hypertext-based graphical interface to worldwide resources. It is one of the applications that uses the Internet as its communication network. It is also the application that, besides electronic mail, is growing at the fastest rate of all Internet services. Many would also say that it is the Web that created the growing demand for Internet services and is behind the Internet's spectacular growth. Figure 4-8 shows the phenomenal growth in the number of Web sites available on the Internet.

The Web originated from development at CERN, a European nuclear research laboratory. The first graphical Web browser that was available was Mosaic, created by the National Center for Supercomputing Applications (NCSA) at the University of Illinois in Urbana-Champaign. Today's popular Web browsers are mainly Netscape's Navigator and Microsoft's Internet Explorer, although several others exist. The browser is the window

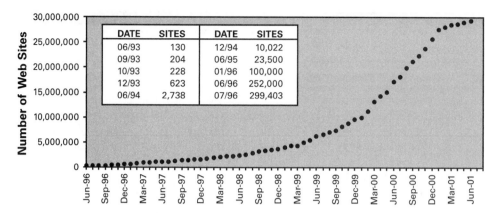

FIGURE 4-8 Number of Web Sites on the Internet

Source: Hobbes' Internet Timeline, http://www.zakon.org/Robert/internet/timeline/. Copyright © 1993–2001 by Robert H. Zakon.

into the resources of the Internet. It allows users to browse and find information located anywhere around the world.

Hypertext

The core technology behind the Web is the use of hypertext, which was actually conceptualized years before the advent of the Web. The word hypertext is derived from "a computer interface to text." It is a presentation format that allows users to view some information and to expand the information when needed by clicking on words that are identified as **hyperlinks** to other documents. Hypertext can be thought of as nonsequential writing that allows multiple types of data to be incorporated into files (e.g., text, images, graphics, videos, animated images, audio, and virtual reality environments). A document can be linked to specific sections of another document, which can then be linked back to the main document, or linked to any other document. Using hypertext, users can navigate through a text nonsequentially, or shift from one section of text to another section of text without a prearranged sequence. By simply clicking on the links, users navigate through this sea of documents rather easily (see Figure 4-9). Hypertext documents are created using a language called HyperText Markup Language (HTML). Chapter 5 presents an overview of HTML, while an online appendix (www.wiley.com/college/vanslyke) includes detailed HTML information, tutorials, and resources.

HTTP

HyperText Transport Protocol (HTTP) is the protocol that governs the interaction between browsers and Web servers. All pages (documents) on the Web have **Uniform Resource Locators** (URLs), which are used by the protocols to locate the resources. URLs have a format similar to this: http://www.cob.vt.edu/Pages/Main.html.

In this address, *www.cob.vt.edu* represents the server or machine name where the documents are stored. *Pages* represents the path or directory structure on the server for getting to the directory where the pages are stored. *Main.html* is the name of the file or page that is being accessed. Note that URLs could also be used to locate other protocols such as ftp://www.cob.vt.edu/FTP/file.html.

RECENT INTERNET APPLICATIONS

In recent years the Internet has seen an increase in the number of applications making use of its worldwide network. Two of these recent trends are worth mentioning: **desktop teleconferencing** and **voice over IP (VoIP).**

Desktop Teleconferencing

Desktop teleconferencing allows individuals at several remote locations to use a software package to connect to each other and communicate in real-time. Once connected, users can use a text-based **chat facility** (similar to the Internet Relay Chats discussed before); use audio communication if they have microphones, speakers, and appropriate drivers (often limited, however, to two users at a time); see each other if they have Web or digital cameras (also often limited to two users at a time); draw on a shared whiteboard; and even share Windows-based applications, such as Microsoft Word or Excel. Figure 4-10 shows an example of a desktop conferencing session using Microsoft's NetMeeting application.

With more and more bandwidth (speed capacity of communication channels) becoming available, the Internet is now capable of supporting desktop teleconferencing around the world. Three of the most popular desktop teleconferencing packages are

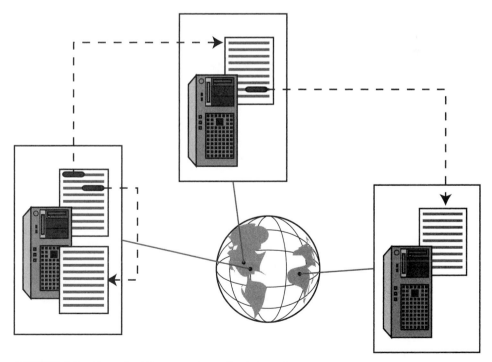

FIGURE 4-9 Hypertext Documents on the Internet

FIGURE 4-10 Example of a Desktop Teleconferencing Session using Microsoft NetMeeting

Microsoft's NetMeeting, CUseeMe (originally developed at Cornell University), and VDOPhone Internet. Some of the application packages are sold as shareware and some are free. While there are some limitations, such as the quality of audio or video, the advantages of real-time communication anywhere guarantee a bright future for desktop teleconferencing.

Voice over IP

Internet phones are one of the latest trends in Internet applications. Voice over IP (VoIP), also known as **Internet telephony,** allows individuals to have "phone" conversations over the Internet and intranets using the **TCP/IP protocol.** It started in the mid-1990s with personal computer to personal computer phone calls. These connections required that two individuals conversing with microphones and speakers use the same software package. The connections were extremely choppy, and when you were conversing with someone, you would hear your own voice as you spoke.

Then came Internet phones, which used technology similar to that used for chat rooms. This is called **streaming audio.** Today, there are Internet phones that require others to use the same technology, and there are also connections possible between personal computers and regular telephones. Using servers and regular phone connections, some companies allow users to use their computer to dial someone's regular home or business phone. For example, dialpad.com used to offer free long-distance calls anywhere in the United States if the user was willing to use the company's system and see their running ads while talking to someone. There are over one hundred Internet telephone applications, with products such as Microsoft's NetMeeting, Intel Internet Phone, Netscape's CoolTalk, IDT's Net2Phone, Hotcaller, or Callrewards. Some of these require computer-to-computer connections, while others require only one user, "the caller," to have a computer. Some are free and some must be purchased.

The technology is fairly straightforward. Computers equipped with microphones or regular telephones connected to VoIP ports are connected to the company's Internet access. As employees talk, their voices are **digitized** and then split down into packets **(packetized)** that are carried over the network using the Internet Protocol, just like computer data would. For example, a Japanese trading house company called Kanematsu Corporation uses VoIP for long distance faxes and calls in Japan. It reports savings of 60 percent on their monthly phone bills.

While "free" long-distance calling is the main appeal of this technology, there remain several problems associated with VoIP.

- The quality of the sound depends on the speed of users' Internet connections and the current Web traffic at the time of the call. Hence, the quality is not only lower than regular phone calls, but also inconsistent. None of the providers can yet guarantee quality of service for VoIP. The speed or bandwidth issue is the greatest barrier to the growth of VoIP at this moment.

- VoIP connections may not work from behind a firewall (a security feature preventing outsiders from accessing a network, which we will discuss in Chapter 10), limiting access for many individuals.

- There are still some incompatibility issues that need to be resolved for complete interoperability between different VoIP systems.

- Regulation may limit the growth of VoIP. Long-distance and local phone companies have been arguing with the Federal Communications Commission (FCC) that Internet Service Providers are competing with them, and should therefore be regulated. At the writing of this book, VoIP is still unregulated and the effects of potential regulation are unknown. However, many long-distance and local phone companies now charge "access fees" to make up for lost revenues.

Even with the current limitations of the VoIP technology, the IDC Corporation predicts that VoIP will grow to over 135 billion paid minutes by 2004. Some of the reasons for its continued growth recently, even with low quality, include low cost and compatibility with existing equipment. As Voice over IP grows, a closely related product that will also gain popularity is Fax over IP (FoIP).

Decision Point

Now that we have covered the basic Internet applications, one of the first questions managers of e-businesses will have to answer is whether or not their company should use the Internet. The following questions can help guide managers in the related decisions that must be made.

- Should we give Internet and Web access to our employees?
- Which tools should be made available (e-mail, Listservs, Web, IRCs, FTP, Newsgroups)?
- Should we use teleconferencing for our communications?
- Should we use Voice over IP for our communications?
- Should we use the Internet for our e-business infrastructure?

STRUCTURE OF THE INTERNET AND THE WEB

In this section we explore the basic structure and core technologies of the Internet and the Web. One of the main reasons that the Internet has grown so rapidly in recent years is the basic architecture on which it is built—the client/server computing model—which was discussed at the beginning of the chapter. But the standard protocol on which the Internet is based is also critical to its success.

Network Protocol: TCP/IP

One of the main elements of the Internet is the **network protocol** used by clients and servers to communicate on the vast Internet network. The network protocol sets the rules for communication between the computers (known as nodes) on the network.

There are several network protocols in use throughout the world. Among these are IBM's **Systems Network Architecture (SNA)** and **Advanced Peer-to-Peer Networking (APPN),** Xerox's **Internetwork Packet Exchange/Sequenced Packet Exchange (IPX/SPX),** and **User Datagram Protocol (UDP),** to name only a few. However, by far the most popular of these protocols for communication on the Internet is the Transmission Control Protocol/Internet Protocol (TCP/IP).

At one point in the history of the Internet, the military decided to standardize it on the TCP/IP network architecture. It is now the most popular network protocol used. TCP/IP is a network protocol that is comprised of two main components: TCP and IP. TCP is responsible for the overall network transport function (known as transport layer functions), while IP is responsible for addressing and routing (known as network layer functions). The following paragraphs provide a very high-level description of what TCP and IP do. An in-depth networking course is required to understand the details of each function, including the numerous other functions performed by TCP and IP that are not described here.

The sending computer's TCP protocol takes the information that is being sent to another computer on the network (this might be an intermediary computer) and breaks it down into smaller chunks of data called packets. TCP will number the pieces and include TCP control information. The receiving computer's TCP will open the TCP control information and reassemble the data in the right order.

The Internet Protocol is responsible for **addressing** and **routing** functions within TCP/IP. The routing function determines the best route for the information to get to the intended receiving computer. This is similar to you picking up a map of your state to determine the best way to get to another city (because there's a good concert playing there!). You have to take into account potential accidents, shortcuts, and traffic

E-BUSINESS IN PRACTICE

Advanced Topic in IP Addressing

The IP numbers are really 32-bit long addresses. In other words, an address would look something like this:
10000000101011001010101100100101
This being hard to remember, the 32-bit address is split into 4 bytes, like this:

10000000 10101100 10101011 00100101
Each byte is then converted into its decimal equivalent and separated by a period:
128.173.171.37

information you've just received. The addressing function determines the addresses to be used to ensure that the information reaches its destination. It is similar to determining the address of all the members of your family before you send your Christmas cards. In Internet talk, every computer needs to have an IP (Internet Protocol) address to be connected to the Internet and participate in the communication exchanges. IP addresses are currently composed of four numbers separated by periods, such as 128.173.171.37.

Connecting to the Internet

If someone asks you, "Are you on the Internet?" what would be your answer? What do you need to do to connect to the Internet? These are very important questions for anyone wishing to participate in electronic business via the Internet. Connecting to the Internet basically means that you have a connection established to one of the servers on the network of networks—servers that are connected together worldwide on a permanent basis. Whether it is the middle of the night or the middle of the day, servers that are part of the Internet remain connected to other servers that are part of the Internet. So your answer to whether you are connected to the Internet or not depends on your type of connection. If you have a permanent connection (have a permanently assigned IP address), then you're on the Internet. What if you don't have a permanent IP address? An IP address can be "loaned" to you for the duration of your connection (for example, if you're dialing up from home to your school).

Hardware for Internet Connections

There are several ways to connect to the Internet. One that many students are familiar with is to use a home computer to "dial into" the university's system, at which time you are "on" the Internet. Another way is to have a direct, permanent connection, such as those in the computer laboratories at your university or in your professors' offices. In this case, the computers are connected to a **local area network (LAN),** which is in turn connected to other networks using high speed links. Either way you connect to the Internet, there are some basic hardware, software, and configuration requirements that must be met.

A local area network (LAN) provides direct connections between personal computers, and sometimes hosts, in a limited geographic area (usually less than five kilometers). The two most popular LAN architectures currently on the market are the **Token Ring** and the **Ethernet** (see Figure 4-11). To be connected to the LAN, each station must have a LAN card installed in the

Ethernet Hub

Token Ring Hub

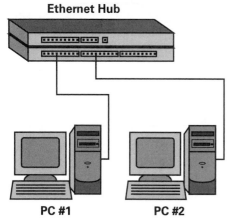
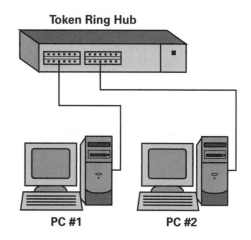

PC #1   PC #2

PC #1   PC #2

FIGURE 4-11   Ethernet and Token Ring LANs

computer. This card is called a **network interface card (or NIC),** and can be bought in any computer store, including online computer stores. A cable then connects this card to the LAN's hub. The **hub** is a box containing a high-speed medium that allows all the computers connected to it to communicate together. Hosts can also be connected to the hub to provide more storage and functions to the stations on the LAN. If the server system (host) has an established permanent connection to the Internet, then every station on the LAN is "permanently" connected to the Internet as well, if the proper software is installed (See Figure 4-12).

LANs allow connections within small geographic areas, usually a department, building or campus. But how can you connect to the Internet if you are at home and do not have access to a LAN there? There are two options. First you can be connected on a high-speed network that is itself connected to the Internet. Typically you must lease a connection with a telecommunications company or an Internet service provider. They provide the network and their servers are typically linked to the Internet. Some of the popular ways to connect like this include ISDN (integrated services digital network), DSL (digital subscriber lines), or cable modems. These networks will be described in more depth in Chapter 6 (Telecommunication Technologies for E-business).

Companies also want direct connections between their servers and other servers connected to the Internet. They usually acquire these direct connections from telecommunications corporations or Internet service providers as you would for your home. However, there are additional networks they would consider, such as Frame Relay, Asynchronous Transfer Mode (ATM), and leased T-carrier lines. Again these networks will be described in more depth in Chapter 6.

For most students and most of the general population wishing to connect to the Internet, a **dial-up connection** is the most financially feasible alternative. Dial-up connections require the user to have a computer (and appropriate software) with a modem and communication software. Configuration of the communication software will be discussed in the following section. Using a regular phone line, the user dials into a server that is connected to the Internet (see Figure 4-13). This server can be an organization's (university, corporation, or agency) server, or an Internet service provider's (ISP) server. The costs are usually none or very small for connecting to your company or university, and very reasonable for connecting to an ISP. For example, a 56 Kbps (kilobits per second) line to connect

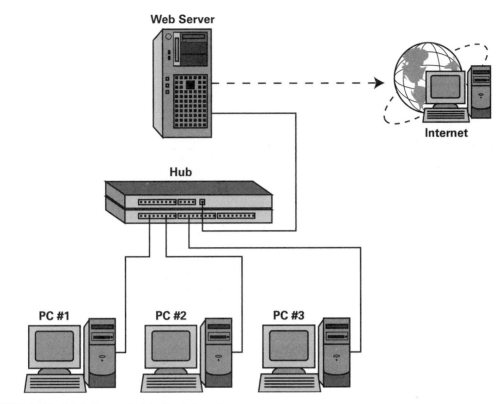

FIGURE 4-12   LAN Connected to the Internet

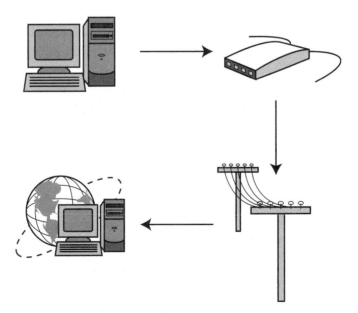

FIGURE 4-13   Connecting to the Internet from a Home Computer

to an ISP in the United States can be leased for U.S.$15.95 to $29.95 per month. (56 Kbps could be thought of as sending two full pages of written text every second.) For these fees, some ISPs allow simple connections to the Internet with e-mail facilities and some storage space to load your own Web pages. Other ISPs offer customized interfaces and access to their own databases of information. Some of the most well-known commercial online providers include America Online (AOL), CompuServe, Delphi, Microsoft Network (MSN), and Prodigy. Most phone companies also offer Internet connection services, as do a large number of small- and medium-sized ISPs worldwide.

Recent advances in telecommunication technologies have provided new options for Internet connections. One that is very popular is the use of cable modems, which require a connection with a cable company. These connections run at much higher speeds than regular phone line connections. They make use of the same cables that are used for cable television. Some installations support two-way communication, allowing the cable connection to be used for uploading data from your computer to the host you connect to, and for downloading data. Other cable connections are one-way only, allowing you to download from the server at high speed but requiring you to use a regular phone line for uploading. In either case, the major advantage of cable modems over regular phone lines is speed at a reasonable cost (currently about twice as much as dial-up connections). The main disadvantage is that cable modem connections are susceptible to speed variations based on the number of users on the **local loop.** So as long as your neighbors do not use cable modems for Internet connections, you get incredible speed. When many join, however, the speed of the individual connections deteriorates rapidly.

The second popular option is digital subscriber line services (DSL). These services make use of regular phone lines with new equipment that allows the connection to be completely digital. Speeds are **asymmetrical.** Downloading speeds are fast; from 1.2 to 6.0 Mbps. Uploading speeds are slower (640 Kbps). This is often sufficient for Internet usage, though, since most of the traffic is from the server to your computer (when downloading a Web page, text, programs, and images are downloaded). When you request a Web page, this request, which is in the form of a few lines of text, is the only traffic from your home to the Web server (upload). DSL will be described in more depth in Chapter 6.

Decision Point

Once an e-business has decided that the Internet is appropriate as an infrastructure to support its business, it must decide how it will be connected to the Internet. The following questions can provide guidance when making those decisions. First, management must ask, "How will we connect to the Internet?"

1. If the answer is a direct "always connected" connection:
    a. Will we use a LAN internally?
    b. Will we use cable modems?
    c. Will we use DSL?
    d. Will we use another communication network (see Chapter 6)?
    e. Will we use a telecommunications provider or an Internet service provider?

Note that a Web server must be permanently connected for customers to use it, and therefore, a permanent direct connection is required if a company is going to use the Internet to sell products or offer services.

2. If the answer is a dial up connection:

    a. Will we connect to an Internet service provider?

    b. Will we connect using an existing server (company, organization, school)?

Software and Configurations for Internet Connections

At the beginning of this section we described TCP/IP and highlighted the fact that to be part of the Internet you must have an IP address. No matter how you are connected to the Internet, your workstation must have communication software that is configured for connecting to the Internet. For permanent connections, such as those for individuals connected to a LAN, there are four main features that must be configured: the IP address, the **DNS servers,** the **gateway,** and the net mask. These are described below. There are several ways to find out your configuration information. For Windows users, the IP, DNS, gateway address, and net mask can be configured directly into the TCP/IP settings. To do this, you must go to the control panel and access properties of the network connections. Figure 4-14 shows a typical TCP/IP properties screen. Another way to find this information is to run from a DOS prompt (Start, Run under Windows) the winipcfg.exe file.

IP address

As we have seen in the section describing TCP/IP, one of the main features you need to be part of the Internet is an Internet Protocol (IP) address. Where do you get this address? What does it mean?

Each IP address is composed of two parts, a computer name and its domain name. Several of the most common high-level domains are presented in Table 4-5. Of course, not all domains are equally popular. The famous dot-com (.com) is obviously the most popular, with 36,672,100 hosts registered as a dot-com by April 2001 (The 25 most popular top-level domains 2001). This represents approximately 79 percent of the host computers. The second most popular high-level domain is .net, with 13 percent of the hosts, or 32,952,900 hosts. The third in popularity is .edu, with 7,771,300 hosts.

The Internet Corporation for Assigned Names and Numbers (ICANN) was formed in 1998 as a nonprofit, private sector corporation by a coalition of business, technical, academic, and user communities with interests in the Internet. It coordinates the assignment of Internet domain names, Internet protocol address numbers, and protocol parameters and port numbers so that there are unique numbers and names assigned globally. The organization also ensures that the **root server system** of the Internet operates properly.

ICANN is the organization that assigns high-level domain names and blocks of addresses to organizations, which can request an A, B, or C network class (see Table 4-6). Once organizations get one or many blocks of addresses, they are then responsible for assigning IP addresses within their blocks. There are actually five classes of addresses. Class D and E addresses are reserved for special purposes and organizations cannot request them. For example, Class D addresses are used for **multicasting.** Multicasting allows multiple

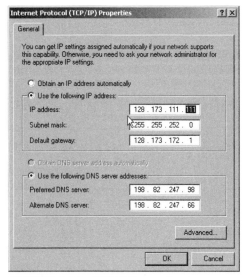

FIGURE 4-14 TCP/IP Properties
Configuration Screen for Windows

computers with the same multicast address to receive the same message sent to that one address. Even though the message is sent only once to the address, all members of the set receive the information.

As can be seen from Table 4-6 an organization that uses a class A network has approximately sixteen million addresses it can use and assign to its members. A class B network allows sixty-five thousand addresses. For example, a university that uses a class B network, such as 128.173, would have approximately sixty-five thousand IP addresses it can assign to students, faculty, staff, and other members of its community. As with everything else on the Internet, the number of domains used has seen exponential growth in recent years (see Figure 4-15).

IPv6 What happens if an organization needs thirty-two thousand addresses? It needs a Class B network categorization to have enough addresses. Looking at Table 4-6, one can imagine that we are going to run out of IP addresses soon if organizations always request classes containing far more addresses than they need. With more and more devices being introduced on the market that require their own IP addresses, the current addressing scheme (called IPv4) will run out of addresses. It currently supports four billion addresses, with 74 percent in North America, 17 percent in Europe, and 9 percent in Asia/Pacific. As a result, IPv4 is slowly being replaced by the **IPv6 (version 6)** addressing scheme proposed by the **Internet Engineering Task Force.** IPv6 expands the IP address size from the current 32 bits to 128 bits. In this case there will be 16 bytes for each address. This should relieve the pressure on addresses for some time. However, the implementation of IPv6 will likely require the operators of millions of Web servers worldwide to change or upgrade their operating systems.

Domain Name System (DNS)

Do you know your best friend's IP address? Do you know your own? You probably don't know your or anyone else's IP address. But you probably know many people's Web

Table 4-5 Some Common High-Level Domains

Original (pre-2001)		Newer (post-2001)	
.com	Commercial organizations	.aero	Aeronautical organizations
.edu	Educational institutions	.biz	Business organizations
.gov	Governmental institutions	.coop	Cooperatives
.mil	Military organizations	.info	Informational organizations
.net	Network organizations	.museum	Museums
.org	Other organizations (nonprofit, etc.)	.pro	Professional organizations

Note: There are also a huge number of domains that refer to country codes, such as .ca for Canada, .uk for United Kingdom, or .au for Australia.

Table 4-6 Classes of IP Addresses

Class	Example	Number of Networks Possible per Class	Number of Addresses per Network
A	50.x.x.x	128	16,000,000
B	128.173.x.x	16,000	65,000
C	192.12.56.x	2,000,000	256

addresses. What about your favorite shopping site or your favorite sports news site? It is very likely, again, that you would remember these sites' addresses. Why? Because they are given names that are easy to remember, and that make some sense to you and other users. For example, your university's main Web site probably ends with .edu. The last part of the address makes it easy to indicate that it is an educational institution.

For example the computer named *france.cob.vt.edu* is the same computer that has the address 128.173.175.107. In reality,

- "france" is a computer that has a unique IP address
- "cob" is the group that manages this computer (College of Business)
- "vt" is the university that owns these groups of addresses (Virginia Tech)
- "edu" is the national group (or domain) for educational institutions.

Other common domains were presented in Table 4-5.

Don't be fooled though. The names of the various sites and servers are useless if they cannot be transferred into actual IP addresses, since these are the addresses the computers use to recognize each other on the network of networks. Note also that the name of the computers may not be directly related to the numbers of the IP address. In the previous example, 175 does not directly mean cob (College of Business). Another indication of this is company Web sites, such as www.yahoo.com or www.microsoft.com, that are composed of two or three names but still have 32-bit addresses.

So how do these addresses get translated from names to numbers? That's the role of the Domain Name System (DNS). Your university probably has one or two servers (a backup server is always recommended) dedicated to handling domain name requests.

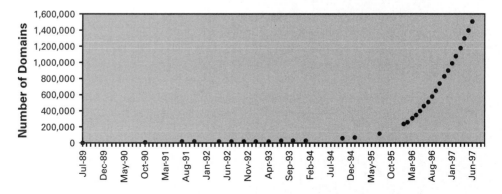

FIGURE 4-15 Number of Domains Registered on the Internet

SOURCE: Hobbes' Internet Timeline, http://www.zakon.org/Robert/internet/timeline. Copyright © 1993–2001 by Robert H. Zakon.

When a computer needs to send a message to another computer for which it doesn't know the IP address, it requests that address from the DNS server. This is the process known as **address resolution.** The DNS server knows the address if it is within its own pool of addresses or if someone else has already asked for the same address. If the DNS server does not know the address that is requested, it requests it from a root DNS server (higher up in the hierarchy of domains). For example, the DNS server for france.cob.vt.edu would request an unknown address from the edu DNS server. The process goes on until the address is found and sent to the computer that is waiting to send the message.

If you know the IP address of a server, however, you can request to connect directly to that server. For example, if you know the address of your server and the DNS server is down (and you don't have a backup DNS server), then you will still be able to connect. The downside, though, is that if someone decides to change all of their information to another server (transfer all of the pages of their Web site to another server system), the IP address is not valid anymore, but the application (name) address could remain the same (assuming it is "deleted" from the original server). The domain name information can be updated to point to the new IP address, and in this case knowing the old numbers would not be useful.

Gateway

The gateway is the computer that isolates your own local area network from the rest of your networking environment. It is your connection to the outside world. The term gateway is an older term that has been replaced by router in Internet terminology (and represents improved technology, too). As we've seen, the Internet is made up of multiple networks connected together. The routers are the systems that actually interconnect all of the networks. By providing the address of your "gateway" in your TCP/IP configuration, you are telling your computer's software where the "door" to the other networks is.

Subnet Mask

Subnets are smaller networks that, when connected, make up an organization's network. For example, several organizations have different local area networks (LANs) for each department within their organization. To facilitate the communication between computers within their subnets and between subnets, the subnet mask is added to the TCP/IP configuration. The role of the subnet mask is to identify which computers are part of a computer's subnet, and which are not.

The typical subnet mask takes the form of 255.255.255.0. When translated into its 32-bit address, this is equal to 11111111111111111111111100000000, or twenty-four "1" bits followed by eight "0" bits. The subnet mask indicates that all computers that have the same first three bytes (first twenty-four bits) in their address are part of the same subnet. When a computer wants to send a message to another computer, the TCP/IP protocol compares the address of the requesting computer with the address of the destination computer. Looking at the subnet mask, TCP/IP can then determine if the message should go outside the subnet (and send it to a gateway) or not.

The following are subsets of computers installed in one organization.

- Station 1   128.173.175.49
- Station 2   128.173.175.89
- Station 3   128.174.188.32
- Station 4   128.174.179.32

If station 1 wants to send a message to station 2, the destination address is compared to its own. Given a subnet mask of 255.255.255.0, the station will conclude that station 2 is within its subnet since the first three bytes of its address (128.173.175) are the same as the first three bytes of the destination computer's address (128.173.175).

Now imagine that the subnet mask is 255.255.252.0 (or 1111111111111111 0000000000000000). Remember that each number is representing a byte of eight bits. Every byte numbered 255 is actually 11111111. In this case any addresses with the same first two bytes would be part of the same subnet (like stations 1 and 2, or 3 and 4).

Dynamic Addressing

Most students will not have computers constantly connected to the Internet. They do not have their own IP addresses, but usually request that an IP address be assigned dynamically to them for the duration of their session (this is requested in the TCP/IP properties information as seen in Figure 4-14). There are two major ways to assign addresses dynamically: **Bootstrap Protocol (bootp)** and **Dynamic Host Control Protocol (DHCP).** The explanations of the inner workings of the protocols are beyond our scope, but it should be known that dynamic addressing requests are usually done for clients connecting from a dial-up connection. In addition to DHCP or bootp, which dynamically assign addresses, one of two communication protocols must be used to actually establish the remote connection. Those communication protocols are **CSLIP** and **PPP,** which you must identify in your modem configuration (for example in Dial Up Networking under Windows).

Compressed Serial Line Internet Protocol (CSLIP) is a very simple protocol that allows two computers to connect using TCP/IP over a point-to-point telephone line connection. A **point-to-point connection** means that a connection goes directly from one point to the other, and there are no intermediary nodes or lines that can be connected in between. When students dial in from their home to their university's computer, they establish a point-to-point connection for the duration of their transmission. The fact that the protocol is compressed simply means that **data compression algorithms** are used to reduce the amount of data being transmitted, improving your line's performance. CSLIP is very limited in terms of error control and addressing, however, and is slowly being replaced by PPP.

Point-to-Point Protocol (PPP) is a newer protocol for point-to-point connections. Its main improvements over CSLIP are the addition of error control information and the fact that it supports network protocols other than TCP/IP.

Sockets

You might have noticed that some addresses on the Web are followed by a colon and a number. For example, in the format of 128.173.175.49:80, the last number represents the port of a particular application to be accessed on the computer. When such a port number is added to the IP address, we call this combination a **socket.** The purpose of such addresses is to connect directly to specific application software on the server, such as a Web server application.

INTERNET VERSUS INTRANET

The basic Internet technologies and related applications described in this chapter can also be used internally by an organization. When used this way, they are said to form an *intranet.* Intranet applications are typically protected by firewalls from outside access, and are being used extensively in today's businesses and organizations for a variety of applications. Examples of popular intranet applications include:

- *Dissemination of corporate documents*—Organizations maintain a large number of corporate documents, such as annual reports, employee benefit guides, emergency procedures manuals, and so on. Rather than print a large number of copies, these documents can be made available to all employees online.

- *Searchable directories*—Many organizations are large enough that it would be difficult for a single employee to know all others. When organizations are global (worldwide) the problem is even greater. Searchable directories are like the old phone books corporations used to publish. By making these directories available online, organizations can keep them more up-to-date, and include additional information, such as electronic mail addresses and Web page links.

- *Unit or individual pages*—Individuals might have the opportunity to create their own Web pages as a mechanism to share their knowledge. Work units, such as departments or divisions, can also create pages, providing information to all individuals within the corporation needing access to information about their divisions.

- *Software distribution*—The intranet can be used to provide software to the organization's employees. When various software applications need to be upgraded, the organization can acquire the proper number of licenses and make the software available for download on the intranet. This reduces the number of CD-ROMs or disks that must be transferred between individuals, avoiding the risk of losing, damaging, or destroying them.

- *Collaborative applications*—A large number of collaborative tools can be loaded on the intranet, such as electronic mail, chat facilities, conferencing software, or groupware such as Lotus Notes. Individuals within the organization can then use these to perform tasks with their colleagues.

THE INTERNET AND BUSINESS-TO-BUSINESS CONNECTIONS

When organizations use the Internet to conduct business with other companies outside of their organizational boundaries, they are often said to use an *extranet*. Extranets use Internet and Web technologies to provide services and information to users outside the organization, but with restricted access (as opposed to the Internet). They are considered an extension of intranets, used to provide access to outside stakeholders of the organization.

Obviously, organizations that use the Internet as a backbone to conduct their daily business need better connections than dial-up. There are two main types of connections used by companies to connect to an information service provider: dedicated circuits or packet switched circuits. Examples of dedicated circuits include T-carrier lines and digital subscriber lines (DSL). Examples of popular packet or circuit switched services include ISDN, Frame Relay, and Asynchronous Transfer Mode (ATM). These connections will be described in more depth in Chapter 6.

MANAGERIAL ISSUES FOR INTERNET-BASED ELECTRONIC BUSINESS

There are several issues that managers must take into consideration before launching their company into Internet and Web-based electronic business ventures. One of the reasons most often cited for reluctance to do business on the Internet is security. Other reasons include managerial control and legal, organizational, and cultural barriers. Most of the barriers to electronic commerce were discussed in Chapter 2.

What makes the Internet different than previous technologies? Why do we suddenly feel our security and privacy are threatened by this network? In reality, giving your credit card number to a store over your cordless phone may be less secure than sending it over the Internet. So why don't we worry about it? Because we hardly hear about phone hackers. Accessing such information one phone at a time is not worth the effort, and the challenge of "breaking the codes" does not exist. In the case of the Internet, however, there has been a proliferation of hackers whose focus is on breaking codes and accessing private and confidential information. By gaining access into even just one main commercial server, a hacker can access financial and personal information for several thousand individuals at the same time. Some of these stories are then publicized widely (there are probably many more incidents that are not publicized), so everyone is informed about the security threats of the Internet. We will discuss security and methods of improving it in more depth in Chapter 10.

Another area of concern for organizations when deciding whether or not to allow Web access to employees is the lack of control the organization has on what employees do with this access. One issue that arises is the illegal copying of software available on the Internet. If employees download such software, the firm might be held responsible for the illegal copies. Another issue is whether employees will shirk their duties to spend office hours surfing the Web. Another major issue is employees downloading free software from the Web. Even if intentions are good, such as getting a utility to improve a computer's performance, employees might end up downloading viruses. Once a virus is on a computer within the organization, it can spread easily to other computers.

Who Governs the Internet?

Managers like to know who they are dealing with when they conduct business transactions. It is reasonable, therefore, that they would want to know who governs the Internet if they are going to use it as a backbone for their electronic business initiatives.

There is no one governing body that has "control" over the Internet. Because it is made up of multiple networks linked together, multiple parties own and manage parts of the Internet. So, for example, your university manages its own part of the Internet. It is up to the university to establish rules of usage and control the content that is included on its servers.

Several groups of individuals also perform more general management tasks. Volunteer organizations include the Internet Engineering Task Force (IETF), the responsibilities of which include discussions of operational and technical problems and standards for the Internet, and the **Internet Society (ISOC),** which attempts to establish standards for the Internet. Another organization that has broad responsibilities is ICANN, the central organization that assigns IP addresses to organizations upon request, as previously discussed.

E-BUSINESS IN PRACTICE

Frequently Asked Questions about Internet2

What is Internet2?

Internet2 is a not-for-profit consortium, led by over 170 U.S. universities, developing and deploying advanced network applications and technology, accelerating the creation of tomorrow's Internet. With participation by over sixty leading companies, Internet2 recreates the partnership of academia, industry, and government that helped foster today's Internet in its infancy.

Is Internet2 a separate network? Will Internet2 replace the current commercial Internet?

Internet2 is not a separate physical network and will not replace the Internet. Internet2 brings together institutions and resources from academia, industry, and government to develop new technologies and capabilities that can then be deployed in the global Internet. Close collaboration with Internet2 corporate members will ensure that new applications and technologies are rapidly deployed throughout the Internet. Just as e-mail and the World Wide Web are legacies of earlier investments in academic and federal research networks, the legacy of Internet2 will be to expand the possibilities of the broader Internet.

How will Internet2 benefit current Internet users?

Internet2 and its members are developing and testing new technologies, such as IPv6, multicasting, and quality of service (QoS) that will enable revolutionary Internet applications. However, these applications require performance not possible on today's Internet. More than faster Web or e-mail, these new technologies will enable completely new applications, such as digital libraries, virtual laboratories, distance-independent learning, and tele-immersion. A primary goal of Internet2 is to ensure the transfer of new network technology and applications to the broader education and networking communities.

What kind of technology will be needed to use the advanced Internet applications and technologies?

We expect the capabilities needed to use new technologies and applications being tested and developed by Internet2 and its members to be built into upcoming generations of commercial products. Internet2 corporate partners are working closely with the Internet2 community to expand the capabilities of their products and services, as well as the global Internet. For example, just as most personal computers sold today include the ability to use the Internet, tomorrow's commercial products will include the ability to use advanced networking capabilities.

Does Internet2 have publicly traded stock?

Internet2 is a not-for-profit research and development consortium and does not have publicly traded stock.

What is the relationship between the Next Generation Internet (NGI), Internet2, and other advanced networking initiatives?

The university-led Internet2 and the federally led NGI are parallel and complementary initiatives based in the United States. Internet2 and NGI are already working together in many areas. For example, through participation in an NSF NGI program, more than 150 Internet2 universities have received competitively awarded grants to support connections to advanced backbone networks, such as Abilene and the very high performance Backbone Network Service (vBNS).

Internet2 is also forming partnerships with similar advanced networking initiatives around the world. Working together will help ensure a cohesive and interoperable advanced networking infrastructure for research and education, and the continued interoperability of the global Internet.

Why are universities taking the lead in Internet2?

University research and education missions increasingly require the collaboration of personnel and hardware located at campuses throughout the country in ways not possible over today's Internet. Moreover, universities are a principal source of both the demand for advanced networking technologies and the talent needed to implement them.

Researchers, instructors, and students at Internet2 universities are able to explore capabilities beyond today's Internet as they teach and learn and conduct science in disciplines ranging from the fine arts to physics.

How much is being invested in Internet2 and where is the money coming from?

Internet2 members have committed to actively collaborate in the development of advanced networking technologies and applications. For Internet2 universities, this means providing high-performance networking on their campuses—investing to upgrade their campus networks and connecting to a national Internet2 backbone network.

For Internet2 corporate partners, this means actively collaborating with Internet2 universities and

E-BUSINESS IN PRACTICE

in Internet2 initiatives. Internet2 universities have committed over U.S.$80 million per year in new investments on their own campuses and corporate members have committed more than $30 million over the life of the project. In addition, Internet2 member institutions may receive funding in the form of competitively awarded grants from the NSF and other federal agencies participating in the federal Next Generation Internet initiative.

What about educational institutions that are not Internet2 members?

Participation in Internet2 is open to any university that commits to providing on-campus facilities that will allow advanced applications development. The investment this requires may be more than many institutions can manage right now. However, Internet2 also supports collaboration by Internet2 universities with non-member institutions. Fifteen years ago, connecting to the Internet could be as expensive as participating in

Internet2 today. As the technology dropped in price, the entire academic community benefited from the efforts of the initial research participants. Deployment of Internet2 technology will follow a similar pattern.

What are some of Internet2's long-term goals?

A key goal of this effort is to accelerate the diffusion of advanced Internet technology, in particular into the commercial sector. In this way, Internet2 will help to sustain United States leadership in internetworking technology.

Internet2 will benefit non-university members of the educational community as well, especially K-12 and public libraries. Internet2 and its members aim to share their expertise with as wide a range of computer users as possible. This approach characterized the first Internet and it can work again today.

SOURCE: Information reproduced from Internet2's Frequently Asked Questions Web site (http://www.internet2.org) with permission.

Internet2

As you can remember from the beginning of this chapter, the Internet was developed by researchers, military and academic, to rapidly exchange research information. As you also know, the Internet has now grown into a worldwide network available to everyone, and is being invaded by all types of commercial organizations. Researchers have for some time now been thinking that it is time to upgrade the Internet into a completely new network. Thus is born **Internet2.** Internet2 is a trademark of the University Corporation for Advanced Internet Development (UCAID).

Internet2 is a consortium of over 170 universities that, in conjunction with business and government partners, are working on the development of a higher speed network. Given that more and more fiber optic links are available today, this higher speed network is highly feasible. Indeed, Internet2 is currently available, and a number of universities have begun implementation. There are three goals stated for Internet2 (UCAID 2000):

- "Create a leading edge network capability for the national research community"
- "Enable revolutionary Internet applications"
- "Ensure the rapid transfer of new network services and applications to the broader Internet community."

Internet2 development and implementation will undoubtedly have a major impact on the current Internet. However, given its focus on the research community, the precise implications for electronic business are not yet known.

CLOSING CASE: DIALPAD.COM

The first wave of Internet telephony started in the early 1990s. Originally, Internet telephony meant that a person could "talk" to another person using personal computer to personal computer connections. Individuals had to use the same software package (e.g., teleconferencing applications discussed in this chapter). Of course, voice connections tended to be quite choppy, and the synchronous transmission modes used meant that users could talk and hear themselves speak at the same time. In the second wave of Internet telephony, voice connections from personal computers to telephones were made possible. One company that supported and used this model is Dialpad Communications, Inc.

Dialpad is a privately owned company started in 1996 as Serome Technology, Inc. in San Jose, CA. At its inception, the company offered Voice over IP (VOIP) consulting services to local area companies. The company, now based in Santa Clara, CA, has become one of the United States' leading Voice over IP companies. In 1999, the company began offering one of the first Internet phone services to consumers who use their personal computers to call anyone on their residential, cellular, or business phones in the United States. This allowed users surfing the Web to make calls at the same time, using their computer and Internet access connection. All the user needed was an Internet account and a computer with a sound card, which had to be full duplex. The user also needed a microphone and a speaker, or a combination microphone and earphone headset, which increased the quality of communication. The original setup also allowed users to make computer-to-computer calls (see figure 4-16).

With these free long-distance calls, Dialpad became known to millions of users. While the quality of the sound was not always very good, and sometimes the service was not always available during peak hours, free calling remained a significant marketing tool to gain new users and retain existing ones. So how did the company make money? Originally Dialpad was an advertising-supported company. The company's business model was based on advertising and sponsorship revenues, along with licensing fees for some of the company's software designs and features that other companies would use (Dialpad designs and patents a variety of VoIP technologies), and backend revenue sharing with e-commerce and opt-in e-mail partners (it showed banners to users while they were conversing). Each phone call cost the company a fraction of a cent, easily covered by advertisements.

Today, building on its expertise and the experience the company developed with its early business models, Dialpad has turned into a full-blown Voice over IP company. It offers calls throughout the United States and internationally. It has over fourteen million registered customers. However, it has done away with unlimited free calls. Consumers can pay a monthly fee for a number of minutes (at this writing it was U.S.$9.99 per month for four hundred minutes anywhere in the United States). There is still a free call option called "trial calls" which are limited to five minutes at a time, available for free calling in the Unites States or Canada. Businesses can use Dialpad's software or services for establishing Voice over IP networks for their company. For example, in October 2001 Dialpad announced its Enterprise Access solution, which allows companies to use their existing telecommunications equipment to connect to an IP network for low cost voice communications. Using a T-1 (or higher) connection (direct high-speed line), the company connects to an IP backbone provider. Using Dialpad's patented products, the voice packets are prioritized and sent from the company's PBX (private branch exchange) directly to the IP network, delivering voice and fax service.

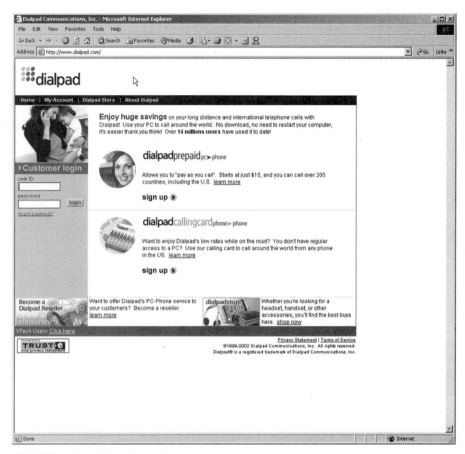

FIGURE 4-16   Web Site of Dialpad Communications

SOURCE: Dialpad Communications home page, http://www.dialpad.com/. Used with permission.

Discussion: When should a company consider Voice over IP for their business calls? What do you think of Dialpad's approach to building its reputation by offering free phone calls? Would this have been possible without a network such as the Internet? Use what you have learned about Voice over IP to predict the future of the Fax over IP (FoIP) application. Recall that some of the issues with using VoIP include the quality of voice communications available when the Internet is used, since the quality is very much dependent on the speed of the Internet connection available. The services may also be much more difficult to implement if the calling computer is behind a corporate firewall. And finally, a company cannot afford reduced voice quality during peak hours of the day.

SUMMARY

In this chapter, we presented a broad overview of the Internet and the World Wide Web, beginning with the client/server computing architecture, which enables

businesses to utilize the Internet and World Wide Web to their advantage. Client processes request services (such as data) from servers. Clients also are responsible for the user interface. Server processes respond to requests from clients. The basic client/server architecture has been expanded into three-tier and n-tier architectures. In the three-tier architecture, servers are divided into application servers and data servers. N-tier architectures contain additional layers of servers. Advantages of n-tier architectures include scalability, interoperability, and reliability. Drawbacks include complexity, hidden costs, and less mature management tools.

The Internet is a network of networks. To be a participant on the Internet, workstations and servers must have an Internet Protocol (IP) address. They must also have a connection to an Internet service provider, either directly through a LAN or a high-speed communication network, such as ISDN, Frame Relay, ATM or DSL, or through a dial-up connection. Dial-up connections can connect individuals to an organization's server (company, university, or government), or directly to an Internet service provider.

The World Wide Web (Web) is a hypertext-based graphical interface to Internet resources. Hypertext can be thought of as non-sequential writing that allows multiple types of data to be incorporated into files (e.g., text, images, graphics, videos, animated images, audio, and virtual reality environments).

Intranets are networks that utilize Web and Internet-based technologies and are used within organizations. One of the main features of intranets is the use of a firewall to prevent access to the organizations' servers from outside the organizations (and sometimes to prevent access to the Internet from inside the organizations). For companies wishing to offer Web-based access to selected outsiders, an extranet can be used.

Managers have many concerns when considering the Internet as a core technology for their electronic business strategies. These concerns include security, employee access to the Web, illegal copying of software, and viruses. Because companies use the Internet more and more for electronic business, several researchers and their partners have developed Internet2, a faster network with restricted access.

KEY TERMS

addressing
address resolution
Advanced Peer-to-Peer
    Networking (APPN)
anonymous FTP
asymmetrical
back-end technologies
Bootstrap Protocol
    (bootp)
bulletin boards
capacity planning
chat facility
clients
client/server architecture
CSLIP
data compression algo-
    rithms
desktop teleconferenc-
    ing
dial-up connection
digitized
discussion groups
distributed computing
DNS servers
Dynamic Host Control
    Protocol (DHCP)

electronic boards
Ethernet
extranet
File Transfer Protocol
    (FTP)
gateway
groupware
hub
hyperlinks
hypertext
HyperText Transport
    Protocol (HTTP)
Internet2
Internet Engineering
    Task Force
Internet phones
Internet protocol (IP)
Internet Relay Chat
    (IRC)
Internet service provider
Internet Society (ISOC)
Internet telephony
Internetwork Packet
    Exchange/Sequenced
    Packet Exchange
    (IPX/SPX)

intranet
IPv6 (version 6)
listervs
local area network
    (LAN)
local loop
middleware
multicasting
Multi-Purpose Internet
    Mail Extensions
    (MIME)
network interface card
    (NIC)
network protocol
newsgroups
n-tier architecture
nodes
packetized
peer-to-peer (P2P)
    networking
person-to-person trading
point-to-point connec-
    tion
PPP
remote logins
remote server

root server system
routers
routing
scalability
servers
Simple Mail Transfer
    Protocol (SMTP)
socket
streaming audio
subnets
Systems Network
    Architecture (SNA)
TCP/IP protocol
teleconferencing
three-tier
Token Ring
Uniform Resource
    Locators (URL)
User Datagram Protocol
    (UDP)
voice over IP (VoIP)
Wide Are Information
    Service (WAIS)

REVIEW QUESTIONS

1. Define the following terms:

(a) Client/server architecture

(b) Client

(c) Three-tier architecture

(d) Internet chat

(e) Groupware

(f) Peer-to-peer

2. Describe the functions of the client and the server in client/server architecture.

3. Name and describe the three tiers of the three-tier architecture.

4. Discuss the advantages and disadvantages of multi-tier architectures.

5. Discuss how multi-tier architectures facilitate the use of graphical user interfaces.

6. What is the function of middleware in a multi-tier architecture?

7. What is the Internet?

8. What is the Internet electronic mail standard?

9. What is MIME? What is it used for?

10. What is a listserv?

11. What is the protocol commonly used to transfer files on the Internet?

12. What is an Internet Relay Chat?

13. Describe a situation in which you would use each of the following:

(a) Electronic mail

(b) Chat

(c) Instant messaging

14. How do you subscribe to a listserv?

15. Describe how e-mail works.

16. Describe how instant messaging works.

17. Use the time/place groupware classification grid to classify each of the following:

(a) Voting

(b) Electronic mail

(c) Chat

18. Name and briefly describe four types of middleware.

19. Describe a situation in which middleware would be required.

20. What language is used to format hypertext documents?

21. Describe the concept of hypertext.

22. What is a URL? What it its purpose?

23. Write the basic format of a URL and describe what each part of the URL is.

24. Describe two recent Internet applications gaining popularity.

25. Describe the main components of the client/server architecture.

26. What is middleware?

27. What is a network protocol?

28. Explain the main functions of the TCP/IP protocol.

29. Describe the various ways to connect to the Internet.

30. What are the main elements that must be configured in TCP/IP settings?

31. What classes of network addresses are available to organizations, and how many addresses do they each contain?

32. Explain when dynamic addressing is used in Internet connections. Which protocols are used for this?

33. What is a point-to-point connection?

34. What is an extranet?

35. What is an intranet?

36. What are the major issues managers must consider before using the Internet for electronic business?

37. Describe how the Internet is managed. Who is in charge?

38. What is Internet2?

EXERCISES

1. Partner with one of your classmates. Both of you should download a popular instant messaging system. Use the system to discuss a class project or other issue. Discuss your experience. How effective was the interaction? What advantages and disadvantages does instant messaging have versus using e-mail? Face-to-face? Telephone?

2. Explain the differences between a two-tier, three-tier, and n-tier client/server architecture and give an example in the context of a university where each of them might be found.

3. A company is establishing a new client/server environment. One of the decisions it has to make is what type of middleware to use. Briefly explain the different types of middleware it could select, and give at least one main advantage and one main disadvantage for each.

4. Explain how the 32-bit addresses of the current Internet Protocol addressing scheme function.

5. What are the four classes of IP addresses available with IPv4? Explain the limitations of this addressing scheme and discuss what is being done to address this issue.

6. How are IP names related to IP addresses? Describe the process used to convert IP names into IP addresses.

7. What is a socket? What is a gateway? What is a DNS server?

8. List four major domain names.

9. Describe three possible ways to become a participant in and connect to the Internet.

10. For each of the methods of participation on the Internet outlined in Problem 6, describe the necessary configuration.

11. Think of an Internet business opportunity. Identify the major strengths and the major weaknesses of using the Internet for this business. Identify the technology strategy you would use for connecting your business to the Internet.

12. Discuss the probable reasons that the IP number specification scheme is running out of addresses.

13. Describe to someone not familiar with the topics discussed in this chapter why several addresses are needed in your TCP/IP configuration to be able to connect to the Internet. Describe each address and what role is performed.

HANDS-ON PROJECTS

1. Use the customer service chat facility of a Web merchant. Describe your experience. What did you like/dislike about using chat for customer service?

2. Set up a Yahoo! Groups (http://groups.yahoo.com/) (or other groupware system assigned by your instructor) for a team project. Use the groupware to help you communicate and coordinate your project. What did you like about the experience? What did you dislike?

3. Assuming you have completed hands-on exercise 2, write a report on your experiences with the groupware. What did you like about it? What did you not like about it? What features did you find the most useful?

4. Sign up for an e-mail list using the digest format. You can locate lists of interest to you at http://www.webcom .com/impulse/list.html#Search, http://search.yahoo.com /bin/search?p=mailing+lists, and http://www.liszt.com/.

5. Find your TCP/IP information. Bring this information to class and get in groups of four or five students (can also be discussed with the whole class). Compare your TCP/IP information with that of the other students.

(a) What addresses are different between the students?

(b) What addresses are the same?

(c) For the two questions above, explain why the addresses are different/similar.

6. Compare the costs of establishing a dial-up connection to the Internet in your area with the costs of connecting by cable modem, ISDN, and DSL.

7. Research Voice over IP (VoIP) products. Select and download two that are either freeware (available for free) or that offer a test version. Use the two products several times and identify their main advantages and weaknesses. Prepare a recommendation report for whether VoIP should be used for a small e-business selling clothing online.

8. Search on the Internet for the five best priced Internet service providers. Identify which one you would select and discuss why.

9. Research the most up-to-date status of the Internet2 project. Discuss its potential implications for electronic commerce.

10. Determine the e-mail standards supported by your current or preferred electronic mail application package.

DISCUSSION POINTS

1. Read the article "Copyright Law and the World Wide Web" on the book's Web site (http://www.wiley.com/college/vanslyke). Answer the following questions:

(a) What are you allowed to copy from someone else's Web page?

(b) What are you not allowed to copy?

(c) What do you do if you want to "borrow" an image?

(d) Which images are copyrighted?

(e) Can you "borrow" HTML code from another site?

RELATED WEB SITES

Dialpad Communications, Inc.: www.dialpad.com

Epls FastWorker: www.epls.com/epls_fw/eplsFwOV.html

Freenet: freenet.sourceforge.net/index.php?page=whatis

HumanClick: www.humanclick.com/products/index.htm

ICQ, Inc.: www.icq.com

FURTHER READINGS

eBay, www.ebay.com

FITZGERALD, J. and Dennis, A. *Business Data Communications and Networking.* New York: John Wiley & Sons, 1999.

GOODIN, Dan. "New Internet Protocol Still Has Many Hurdles to Clear," *The Wall Street Journal,* 14 May 2001, B5.

ICANN. "ICANN Announces Selections for New Top-Level Domains," http://www.icann.org/annoucements/icann-pr16 nov00.htm.

Internet Society, http://info.isoc.org/guest/zakon/Internet /History /hit.html

KROL, Ed. *The Whole Internet: User's Guide & Catalog.* Sebastopol, CA: O'Reilly & Associates, 1994.

PANKO, R. R. *Business Data Communications.* Upper Saddle River, NJ: Prentice-Hall, 1997.

REFERENCES

The 25 most popular top-level domains. *InternetWeek,* 16 April 2001, 13.

UCAID. 2000. About Internet2. http://www.internet2.edu.

CHAPTER 5

ELECTRONIC BUSINESS APPLICATIONS DEVELOPMENT

LEARNING OBJECTIVES

After reading and completing this chapter, you should be able to:

- Describe the differences between programming, scripting, and coding languages
- Read and understand an HTML-formatted document
- Recognize and differentiate between several HTML writing tools
- Understand the differences between HTML and DHTML, between HTML and XML, and between HTML and ASP
- Read and understand a JavaScript-formatted document
- List the basic components and functioning of the Java programming language
- Identify other development languages for e-business
- Determine which programming or coding language is appropriate for developing a given Web-based electronic business application

Opening Case: Amazon.com

Technological advancements in telecommunications, such as the Internet, have revolutionized the way companies conduct business. Amazon.com is one company that not only became possible because of the Internet, but that also makes extensive use of the technologies available today to gain competitive advantage over other e-retailers. Today, Amazon.com (Figure 5-1) is recognized as the leader in the **virtual store** industry.

Amazon.com started operations in July 1995 as an Internet-only virtual retail bookstore. The vision of its founder, Jeff Bezos, was that the Internet would offer fast, easy, and enjoyable shopping for consumers. As of the writing of this book, more than twenty-nine million people from more than 160 countries have shopped at one of Amazon's Web sites. The company operates sites in five countries: France, Germany, Japan, the United Kingdom, and the United States. The headquarters of Amazon.com are in Seattle, Washington.

While investors originally thought this was a "losing idea," Jeff Bezos went forward with the launch of Amazon.com. During Amazon's infant stage, the main offerings were books and music. The company also used **push technologies** to send subscribers the reviews of newly published titles, to send suggestions of titles that might be of interest to

139

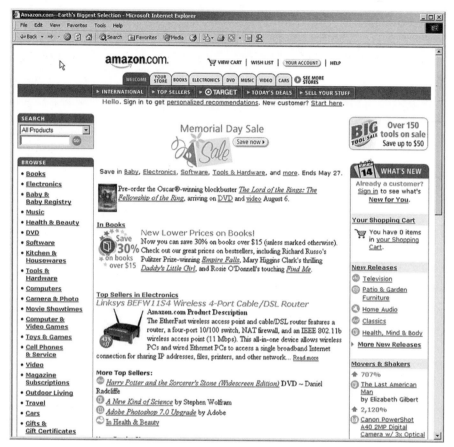

FIGURE 5-1   Amazon.com

SOURCE: Amazon.com home page, http://www.amazon.com. Courtesy of Amazon.com, Inc.

them based on historic data from their previous orders, or to allow them to submit their own review of a recently published book. Amazon also provided information and entertainment services through its Internet Movie Database. Today, the product set has been expanded to include videos, DVDs, music, toys, games, electronics, and more. The company made U.S.$2.7 billion in sales in 2000, resulting in a net loss of U.S.$417 million. Many investors have happily put their money in Amazon.com stocks, which have sold at a phenomenal rate. The stock price hit an all-time high of more than U.S.$113 per share on December 9, 1999, but then dropped with the NASDAQ in April 2000, and then further with the decline of the stock market in 2001. In 2000, Amazon was rated as the number two Web retailer in the United States (Pastore 2000). Amazon—the most popular site on the Web—has yet to turn a profit.

Amazon.com has taken many steps to ensure its growth and continued success. One has been to develop an information technology infrastructure to conduct all aspects of its e-business. Amazon.com uses enterprise computing—the company purchases all of the hardware and software necessary to operate its online stores, and hires its own staff of developers to create the e-business site. The infrastructure for Amazon.com must support immensely high traffic (millions of hits per month), requires a large database to store catalogs of products that may change constantly, and requires customization of forms, pricing tables, and other elements of its sales cycle.

Amazon has been an innovator and a leader in the field of Web commerce. Using its own staff and infrastructures, Amazon can build features and functions that allow it to be unique and competitive in the marketplace. In this dynamic business environment, it has attempted to capitalize on its first-mover advantage by patenting the systems and methods it has developed. Some of these patents have been granted even though competitors have argued that the systems were already in the public domain. The company has more than ten such patents based on the products and services it developed to operate its business. For example, two of the patents relate to the security aspects of transmission of credit card information. Two of the most heavily discussed patents that Amazon has received include one-click shopping and the associates program. One-click shopping allows customers to acquire goods quickly and conveniently by clicking on an icon to perform their acquisitions. The company sued Barnes & Noble after it received the patent to stop its competitor from using this technology.

Another combination of technology and marketing that Amazon patented is its associate program, or customer referral system. The customer referral system allows Amazon to widen its marketing reach by working in cooperation with associated Web site owners, usually content sites. Products mentioned on the associated Web sites have links that send consumers directly to Amazon's Web pages for those products, so the user will purchase the product from Amazon. If a user buys a product from Amazon, the referring associate site owner receives compensation. For example, Adobe's Web site directs consumers to buy Adobe books from Amazon.com. Today, Amazon operates the largest affiliate program, with more than 430,000 sites, according to an article in the *Roanoke Times,* 24 April 2000, entitled, "Content Sites Find Ways to Mind Their Stores." The entire system, including associate registration, customer purchases, referral tracking, payment, and reporting, is completely automated. The idea is to connect content sites to e-retailers. It's a way to drive traffic to cyber shops. Marketing partners receive commissions on traffic driven to the Amazon site. The patent is officially called the Associates Program. Amazon claims that the patent is based on automation of registration and other functions, which is accomplished through innovative technology. Other companies argue that it is common sense and that they use similar programs but may not have patented them, stating that Amazon's patent requests fail the basic tests of novelty and non-obviousness.

Amazon.com has a host of other applications developed or being developed to make purchasing more convenient for its customers. For example, it has developed online shopping applications accessible from Internet-ready wireless telephones or Palm Pilots. Mobile customers can monitor the status of their purchases, access more in-depth comparison information, and check shipping availability for products. This is a huge market with expectations of 204 million Internet-enabled smart phone users by 2005. Wireless phone Internet shopping ability is a result of Amazon.com's *Anywhere Initiative,* which seeks to find new ways for customers to find, discover, and buy anything online, anytime, anywhere.

Amazon.com pioneered electronic retail shopping and marketing with sheer will, determination, and business savvy. This company simply would not exist without the insight of its management team to take first advantage of the most current, powerful, ever-improving telecommunications technology. Its growth relies on both being first and using the e-business applications it develops in a competitive way.

How hard do you believe it is to develop such systems (those that were patented)? How does a company come up with ideas for new systems to develop? Note the company's focus on developing applications to make shopping online easy, convenient, and fun. Amazon provides its future associates with easy-to-implement features and necessary software (plug-ins). How difficult is it to build systems that are easy for others to use? Do you think that Amazon was right in requesting patents for its developed applications?

INTRODUCTION

There are a wide variety of development environments that are available for Web-based electronic business applications. In this chapter we discuss and present examples of the following languages: **HyperText Markup Language (HTML)** and **Dynamic HTML (DHTML), Active Server Pages (ASP), Extensible Markup Language (XML), JavaScript, Java,** and **Perl/CGI.** It is important to differentiate between a markup language and a programming language. A markup language adds information to text to format it or describe how it is to be used. Conversely, a programming language is used to write programs or applets that perform functions over and above formatting and displaying text. Programming languages can be used simply to create actions on Web pages, or they can be used to add complete functionality to Web and non-Web environments. The biggest challenge for managers responsible for electronic business is deciding which development environment, including hardware and software platforms, they should invest in. The decision is even more challenging when you consider that substantial investments must be made in hiring and/or training programmers in the particular language(s) selected.

In the previous chapter we discussed the technologies behind Web-based electronic business. Now that we understand better the Internet and the Web, as well as the client/server architecture that serves as their foundation, we will present the various tools that can be used for developing such Web-based electronic business applications. It should be noted that this chapter presents an overview of the various development environments for the Web. Each warrants its own textbook. The purpose of this chapter is not to make a developer of the reader, but to provide you with enough background information on these different technologies to be able to distinguish between the various programming environments, and select those most appropriate for each organization that wants to have a Web presence. Further information on some of these programming languages is provided in the online appendix accompanying the book.

TERMINOLOGY

Programming, Scripting, or Markup Language?

It is important to distinguish between the types of tools that are available for developing electronic business Web-based applications. Some tools actually allow the users to write functionality for their Web pages, or even to link their Web pages to new applications. Others really only format the text you have.

Where are the differences? First and foremost, the complexity of the tools and the time it takes for someone to learn them. More complexity usually means more functionality. If an individual wants to add a complex function, let's say a mortgage calculator, to his Web site, then a **programming language** is required. On the other hand, if someone simply wants to show his data in a tabular format, simple **markup languages** (such as HTML) can be used. Here are some definitions that may help shed some light on these differences:

- *Markup language*—This tool adds information to the text to format and structure it, and describes how it is to be used. Markup languages were developed to allow text to be displayed in more than a single font and type size. Today they allow text and the codes to be stored in a single document so that the **interpreter** can read and format the text according to the codes. Examples of coding languages include HyperText Markup Language (HTML), **Virtual Reality Modeling Language (VRML),** Dynamic HTML (DHTML), **Standard Generalized Markup Language (SGML),** and Extensible Markup Language (XML).

- *Programming language*—This tool is used to write **programs** or **applets** that perform functions over and above formatting and displaying text. Programming languages can be used simply to create actions on Web pages, or they can be used to add complete functionality to Web and non-Web environments. Programs written with programming languages are typically compiled or interpreted. A **compiler** takes the program written in text and turns it into machine code. The interpreter interprets this machine code. For example, when the user tries to link to a page that contains a call for a program, the browser acts as an interpreter, reading the machine code and interpreting it to "run" the program (these are called runtime systems). Examples of programming languages include Java and Perl/CGI (as well as all other traditional programming languages, such as C++, COBOL, Fortran, Pascal, and the like). Programming languages are often classified by generation (first, second, third, and fourth) and/or by type (structured or object). In **structured programming,** the programs are broken up in chunks of code, sometimes named **routines,** which are called from other routines or subroutines. **Object programming** involves defining **objects,** which can contain both data and behaviors. Several books discuss these programming concepts in depth.

- *Scripting language*—**Scripting languages** have grown out of traditional programming languages. They add functionality and interactivity to electronic business Web pages without the need for separate compilers. They are interpreted directly by the browser. They do not, however, have the sophistication of traditional programming languages for creating complex applications, and they do not provide a method to check for user errors the way compilers can. Examples of scripting languages include Active Server Pages (ASP), JavaScript, and **VBScript.** Scripting languages are typically interpretive—they are interpreted at run-time, or they are compiled and executed as they are run by the browser. As we shall see later, ASP is a **server-side scripting** language (some actions are taken on the server instead of by the browser on the client), while the other two are client-side scripting languages.

Program, Document, Script, or Applet?

Another set of terminology that may confuse many is that used for the files that are being run on our computers. It is a question of terminology, and each of the development environments listed above uses different names for these files. To add to the confusion, some vendors even give particular names to files written using their programs. In general, however, you will see the following definitions:

- *Program*—The word program is typically used with programming languages. The program is the file that the programmer actually writes and debugs (for many hours, as anyone who has done programming knows). Once it is compiled, it is usually called an executable file.

- *Document*—The word document is usually used to refer to HTML files or other marked-up files. It has no particular meaning except that for HTML it refers to a document that starts with the <HTML> **tag** and ends with the </HTML> tag (we will discuss tags in a later section).

- *Script*—Files that contain **scripts** are often called script files. However, in Web-based environments, scripts are often integrated into HTML documents.

- *Applet*—Applets are Java programs. They are in executable form (they have been compiled) and are loaded on a Web server, but they are executed by the browser, when the browser requests them. In addition, applets have been designed with some limitations on writing capabilities so that when you download an applet it won't "decide" to format your hard drive, which, of course, a full Java program could do (we'll discuss security issues in Chapter 10). A new term is now used to refer to Java programs that are written to run on the server side, and these are called **servlets.**

Other Terminology

Programming is a science in itself, and we cannot in one chapter cover the basics of programming, languages, and techniques. There are many more complex sets of tools, such as runtime systems, objects, pseudocode, bytecode, virtual machines, or ActiveX controls. While it is beyond the scope of this chapter to cover all of these topics, there are numerous excellent programming reference guides and tutorials available for those interested in this area.

MARKUP LANGUAGE: HTML

HyperText Markup Language (HTML) is the main language that has been used for developing the Web pages we see today. HTML is created through the use of codes called *tags*. Several tools can be used to create HTML files. Modifications to HTML have been made over the years, and this is why there are several versions of HTML. Nevertheless the basic structure of HTML has remained the same. (Changes between versions typically involve more tags included or supported).

HTML is used to format hypertext documents. As we saw in the previous chapter, hypertext documents allow documents to reference each other as needed in a hyperlink structure. HTML documents are coded using the following rules:

- Tags are included in angle brackets (smaller than (<) and greater than (>) signs). For example the tag for formatting text as a paragraph would be <P>.

- Most HTML tags envelop the text with a beginning tag and an ending tag. Ending tags include a slash (</tag>) to indicate it is an end tag. For example, if we want to italicize a certain word, we would code it this way: This text is to be <i>italicized.</i> On the browser, this would read as: This text is to be *italicized.*

- The good news for those who will code HTML documents is that it is totally case insensitive, with the exception of file names. It is possible, for example, to write a heading level 2 tag as <H2> and then end it with </h2>. However, all file names that are referred to in the document must be written in exactly the same case mix as the original file name. For example, if I want to create a hyperlink to another file named ChapTer1.htm, I would use the following tag: <A HREF="ChapTer1.htm"> text </a>. Note: This case sensitivity for file names is why you must type exactly the name of the page, including lower and upper case characters, when you try to access a Web page using your browser.

All HTML documents follow the same basic structure. A basic HTML document is composed of two parts: a head and a body (or a frameset—discussed in Appendix A, available online at http://www.wiley.com/college/vanslyke). Detailed HTML coding instructions, tutorials, and useful links are provided in Appendix A. Following is a coding example for a very basic HTML document.

```
<HTML>
<HEAD>
<TITLE> Title of Document </TITLE> </HEAD>
<BODY>
<H2> First HTML Example </H2>
<P> This is a paragraph of text on the page </P>
<A href= "file2.html"> Linked Page </A>
</BODY>
</HTML>
```

Figure 5-2 shows how this coding would actually appear when processed by a Web browser.

All HTML documents must start and end with the <HTML> and </HTML> tags, respectively. These indicate to the browser that the files are indeed HTML files (the browser assumes this when it sees the file extension .htm or .html). The </HTML> should be the last tag of the file.

The head part of the document is where information about the document is stored. For example, if you use a Web editor to create an HTML file, a META tag (<META>) will be created indicating the tool used. You can also use META tags to describe the document or provide a list of keywords for search engines. Of course, these must be nested within (placed between) the <HEAD> and </HEAD> tags. Another tag that is used in the head of the document is the <STYLE> tag, which will be described in more depth in the

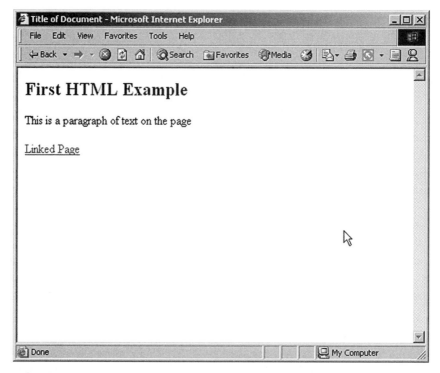

FIGURE 5-2 Basic HTML Document as Presented in a Browser

DHTML and JavaScript sections of this chapter. The STYLE tag allows you to define exactly what your document should look like.

Another information element typically included between the <HEAD> and </HEAD> tags is the title of the page. This tag is very important because browsers use it when users surf the Web and access your page. When they add your page as a bookmark or favorite page, for example, the text between the <TITLE> and </TITLE> tags is used to describe the page. Therefore, you should include something useful in the title. For example, if you have a series of pages that contain chapters of an online book, having a <TITLE>Chapter 3</TITLE> tag is not very useful. There might be thousands of "Chapter 3" bookmarks out there. You should include instead the name of the book, the site information, and then the chapter number.

Note that all the information included in the head of the HTML document *does not appear* on the Web page. The title will appear in the upper left corner of your browser window, next to your browser identification. Anything you want to see on the page must be included between the <BODY> and </BODY> tags. There, you can have different levels of headings defined (<H1> to <H6>), paragraphs (<P>), lists (<OL>, <UL>, <DL>), tables (<TABLE>), forms (<FORM ...>), images (<IMG ...>), hyperlinks (<A href ...>), and more. It should also be noted that frames may replace the body of a document. Frames are a way to divide the browser window into multiple sections that can be accessed independently. We see this a lot with navigation indexes on Web pages. Frames are also very easy to code using the <FRAMESET> <FRAME> </FRAME> </FRAMESET> tags. All of these tags, plus numerous others, are provided in Appendix A (available online at http://www.wiley.com/college/vanslyke), which is dedicated to HTML coding.

Alternative Tools for Writing HTML Documents

The previous example and Figure 5-2 presented a very basic HTML document. How do you know all of the HTML tags that can be used? How does one code the attractive and complicated pages on the Web? Actually, many people have written HTML documents without any knowledge of HTML tags. How did they do that? They used one of the numerous **HTML assistants** or editors, available on the Web, pre-packaged with other application software, or as separate applications from computer and software retailers.

Before you run off and decide you do not need to know HTML to write Web pages, you should understand more precisely what the HTML assistants do for you. An HTML document is a text file that is saved in **ASCII** format. The browser opens up the file because it knows from the extension (.htm or .html) and the <HTML> tag at the beginning of the file that it is an HTML file. It then uses all of the HTML tags to format and display the content as requested. Everything on a Web page that is not text or a tag is actually stored in a separate file. For example, all images, image backgrounds, and programs are stored separately and are "called" within the HTM L file (linked through special coding). The HTML document is what puts it all together.

There are three main ways to code the HTML files: writing directly to an ASCII file using a text editor such as Microsoft's Notepad or WordPad, using an HTML assistant or converter, or using an HTML editor. There are also numerous Web management tools. These environments provide not only Web design tools, but also utilities for managing pages, links, access, security, and more.

Coding the Hard Way

Hard-core HTML users started their Web environments by coding HTML directly into ASCII files. Many of them still prefer to code this way because their coding is much cleaner than some of the other methods. Of course, to code files this way you must know HTML tags, or at least know where to go when you need to know certain HTML tags.

Given that an HTML file is an ASCII file, the best way to start coding "the hard way" is to use a plain text editor (such as Microsoft's WordPad or UNIX's vi). Then, all coding and text are written into the file. Once the file is complete, it must be saved as a text file (ASCII) with an extension of .htm or .html. Saving it with another extension doesn't make it a non-HTML file, but your browser is programmed to start when an .htm or .html file is accessed.

That's all there is to it. Using the basic coding presented in Appendix A (available online at http://www.wiley.com/college/vanslyke), you can write your own Web pages this way. To test your pages before you actually store them on a public Web server, just open up your preferred browser and open the file with the .htm/.html extension. When it is ready, you can upload it to your Web server in the appropriate directory, which should have been defined by the administrator as a public read-only environment. Note that if you work in a UNIX environment, you must also make the file "public" read-only for it to be accessible on the Web. Most Web administrators create standard directories, such as ftp and www, for their users and make them public read-only by default. Administrators also often define certain file names that can be recognized as the first page that is read in a Web server directory. The most popular are index.html, main.html, or home.html. They allow you to write your Web address directly to the directory without specifying the file name (for example, one author's Web site is currently defined as www.cob.vt.edu/belanger/, and the main file is called index.html, but it is not necessary to specify it to access it). Ask your administrator for the file name that is being recognized as the starting page on your Web server.

Coding with HTML Assistants and Converters

Today, many individuals do not wish, or have no time, to learn HTML tags. Several options are available for those individuals. First, they can use their regular applications, which have HTML assistants embedded in them. For example, one can write a Microsoft Word or Excel document and use the HTML assistant (File, Save as HTML) to convert the document into HTML. The HTML assistant basically takes the formatting you have given to your original file and adds all HTML tags it deems necessary to make the formatting look exactly (or as close as possible) as you had intended. When you use such an assistant, a <META...> tag is added to the HTML file that describes which tool was used to produce the document. Other **converters** that take existing documents and convert them into HTML exist on the Web (available for download). These converters exist for all environments today, including Macintosh, UNIX, and PC, and work with documents written in everything from LaTeX to PageMaker to PowerPoint.

Converters and assistants suffer from a few limitations. First, when you want to make changes to the document, assuming you don't like what it looks like once converted to HTML or because new functions/text need to be added, you must often change the original document and reconvert it. Another limitation is that converters tend to add a large number of codes that you wouldn't use if you were coding by hand. For example, when you use a template to create a document, it adds particular font sizes, types, and spacing to your basic document. You can then change the fonts and sizes by selecting text and clicking on the proper font, size, etc. When the converter changes your document, it adds codes for all spaces you didn't select to be changed to the new font, creating tags for all blank spaces in the original template font. Imagine now all of the blanks, double-bolded words (selected twice to be bolded because of other text around them), and so on, that are frequently created when you write in the original application. Codes are added for all of these. Try saving a document as HTML using an assistant, then review the coding in a text editor. Compare all of the codes that were added to the codes you would have actually used if you did it the hard way. This superfluous coding will not likely affect how the HTML document appears when viewed with a Web browser, but it can create problems if the document is going to be used in conjunction with another program or converted to another type of document. And sometimes it can just be confusing.

Coding with HTML Editors

Assistants and converters are typically used by individuals who will only sporadically create Web pages and do not want to spend the time to learn HTML, and do not care whether the code is clean and efficient or not. There is another group of individuals who code a lot of HTML documents and who do not wish to retype some of the tags all the time. For those individuals, an HTML editor is the best option. **HTML editors** are applications used specifically for writing HTML documents. They make it easy to insert images, add links to other pages, and format the text the way one wants it to appear in a browser. HTML editors vary substantially in their complexity and capabilities. Some are basic personal computer–level applications (such as Microsoft's FrontPage), while others are complete Web page management systems that keep track of pages, linked files, and hyperlinks. They allow **Web masters** to manage the Web environment. For example, when the address of one page is changed, the system allows the Web master to view all pages that have that link in them and update all of them at once.

Validating Code

There are so many HTML tags, so many assistants and converters, that it is easy to create code that is complex, is unreadable, and may not perform as desired. No matter which of the above methods you have used to develop your code, it is usually a good idea to test your code and "clean it" of extraneous tags. You can first test documents by opening them with a Web browser, as described before, but sometimes you want to actually go a little further into the testing. Fortunately, some generous minds on the Internet have created **validators** to check HTML code and have provided them for free.

The most recent HTML version is 4.0, which was published in December 1997. One of the main changes between HTML 3.2 and 4.0 is the use of **Document Type Definitions (DTDs)** in HTML 4.0. Document Type Definitions provide an "external definition of the document structure" (Martin 1999, 23). In other words, a DTD contains information about the data, or content of the Web pages. It defines every aspect of how a new set of tags can be used. This can include which elements are available for use on the Web page, in what sequence they must appear, how often they may be used, how they can be nested, or the attributes they may contain. In other words, the document contains the rules that define the elements of the Web page, and the structure of the language that is used. We will discuss DTDs in more detail when explaining Extensible Markup Language (XML).

OTHER MARKUP LANGUAGES

HTML is the main markup language in use today for creating Web pages. Most Web pages also make use of scripting and programming languages, which will be discussed in a later section of this chapter. There are other markup languages that exist, but that are not as commonly known, either because they are relatively new or because their use is limited.

Standard Generalized Markup Language (SGML)

Standard Generalized Markup Language (SGML) is a very sophisticated markup language from which HTML was actually derived. HTML is therefore considered a subset of SGML. SGML is both large (containing a huge number of tags) and complex. Few SGML documents exist on the Web, but they are out there. Interleaf offers a Web browser plug-in for viewing SGML documents.

Dynamic HTML

One of the limitations of HTML-generated pages is that movement or action of individual elements is not possible. In other words, the pages are static. Movement is often added by inserting **animated gifs,** or images that move. But the rest of the pages remain static. But dynamic HTML (and the rest of the languages we present in this chapter) allows Web pages to contain elements that move or change based on the user's actions. DHTML is a combination of basic HTML and features from scripting languages.

Style Sheets

The basic component of DHTML that adds dynamism to Web pages is the use of style sheets. **Style sheets** define the display properties of the Web pages (as separate from the structure that you define in basic HTML tags). For example, style sheets would describe the various lists used in a document. Following is an abbreviated version of a simplified style sheet.

```
<STYLE>
H1
   {margin:0in;
   margin-bottom:.0001pt;
   page-break-after:avoid;
   mso-outline-level:1;
   font-size:12.0pt;
   font-family: "Times New Roman"}
DIV.Section1
   {page:Section1}
OL
   {margin-bottom:0in}
UL
   {margin-bottom:0in}
</STYLE>
```

The <STYLE> and </STYLE> tags encapsulate the style sheet definitions. This set of tags is included in between the <HEAD> and </HEAD> HTML tags described earlier.

In the example above, a style sheet defines some specific HTML tags (H1, DIV, OL, and UL). For each tag, the **display attributes,** or how the text is to be displayed, are presented in curly brackets ({}) after the tag. For example, a level 1 heading (H1), which is already defined with a specific format in basic HTML, is modified here to include a left margin of zero inches (i.e., left justified) and 0.0001 point margin after the heading (creating some space between the heading and the text of the next element); it does not allow page breaks directly after the heading; it is used as a level 1 heading when an outline is automatically generated; and it is set in Times New Roman 12 point font.

This shows only one style sheet, and only shows parts of it. When multiple style sheets are used within the same document, building on each other, we have **cascading style sheets (CSS).** Style sheets are templates that define a hierarchy of styles that can be applied to each HTML tag. There are three levels at which style sheets can be applied to documents. The first is the **inline style,** where the style attribute is placed within the tag itself in the body of the document. For example, <P style= "font-size:7.0pt;font-family:Times New

Roman"> is an inline style that establishes that this paragraph is in 7-point Times New Roman font. If you save a Microsoft Word document as HTML using the "save as Web page" tool, the coding you will see will be slightly different than that shown here.

The second level of styles that can be defined is **embedded style sheets,** which you can see in the <STYLE> </STYLE> tags as presented in the earlier example. Finally, the third level is **linked style sheets.** Linked style sheets use a separate file containing the style sheet linked into the document you are writing using a LINK tag in the head section. For example, you would see the following tags: <LINK href="mystyle.css" rel=STYLESHEET>. In this case, *mystyle.css* contains all of the style definitions you want to use in your document, but you can override them with embedded or inline style sheets. They can be overridden because the browser first looks for inline styles, then embedded style sheets, and then linked style sheets for each element it "sees" in the file.

JavaScript within DHTML

The second major "element" that makes DHTML possible is the use of JavaScript. JavaScript will be described in more depth later in this chapter. Basically, JavaScript commands (scripts) are used to dynamically position items on HTML pages, provide dynamic content, or to create **events.** Events are actions taken by a user (mouse movement or keyboard use) that are recognized by the JavaScript software. Once an event is recognized, it can be used to trigger different responses. Some typical events are presented in Table 5-1.

The way these "events" are used is shown in the following example.

```
<DIV ONMOUSEOVER="showtext ('Smile')"
  ONMOUSEOUT="hidetext ('Smile')">
<IMG SRC="Smile.gif">
<DIV ID="Smile" CLASS =<"texthide">
<P> This is a beautiful day! <BR> Give a smile to those
<BR> who need it most:
the sad and angry!
</DIV>
```

The result of this coding is shown in Figure 5-3. The first screen shows the resulting Web page before the mouse is moved over the image, and the second screen shows the same Web page when the mouse is moved over the image. Detailed explanations of these events and the codes are presented later in the section on JavaScript. In this file, moving the mouse over the image triggers the *showtext* event, while moving the mouse elsewhere (out) triggers the *hidetext* event.

How does this all fit together? We learned about style sheets earlier. Events and JavaScript are used to trigger new style sheets to be "called" when certain events occur (as detected by the browser). The pages can therefore be made "dynamic." For example, a user moving the mouse

Table 5-1   Some JavaScript Events

JavaScript Event	Description of How Event Is Triggered
ONCHANGE	Entering data in a field on a form
ONCLICK	Clicking a mouse button
ONMOUSEMOVE	Moving the mouse
ONMOUSEOUT	Moving the mouse off an item on the page
ONMOUSEOVER	Moving the mouse over an item on the page

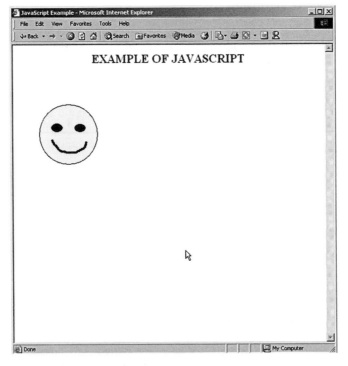

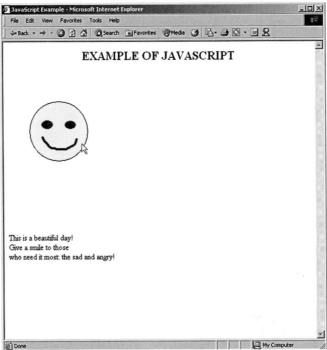

FIGURE 5-3 Example of Using JavaScript Events

over a word may see an image or text definition of this word (without going to another page). The following are the basic steps for creating such DHTML pages (Cintron 1999):

1. Write a style sheet.

2. Give a NAME (tag) to the HTML element that will result from the action (which is called the target).

3. Give an event attribute that calls a JavaScript function to the HTML element where the action will be triggered **(activating element).**

4. Write the JavaScript function that will modify the **target element.**

This is a simplified version of what needs to be done to create dynamic HTML pages. A model defining the interaction of all these elements (style sheets, HTML, and JavaScript) was written by Netscape (which also created JavaScript to add dynamism to its browser, Navigator). This model is called the **Document Object Model (DOM).** It is a "structure that gives object properties to a document loaded in the browser" (Cintron 1999, 140). Using DOM, an element can be moved, added, or deleted from a document dynamically. Microsoft also has its own Document Object Model. DOM has also been recommended for Web page design by the World Wide Web Consortium (W3C).

Virtual Reality Modeling Language (VRML)

When Web masters want to include three-dimensional (3D) images on their Web pages, they can consider the use of virtual reality for their pages. This can be done with the use of Virtual Reality Modeling Language (VRML). VRML is a file format for sharing 3D environments on the Web. Like most markup languages, it is **platform independent,** meaning it can run on different types of computing environments (such as UNIX, Windows, Mac, etc.). The files created with VRML are called **worlds.** These worlds can include hyperlinks to other worlds or Web pages, and they can be animated and allow user interaction. The VRML tags are used to represent the geometry and the behaviors of objects in the worlds. Some objects are simple, such as cubes, while others are complex, such as humanoids (as you see in video games). VRML is not limited to creating game-like Web pages, though. For example, scientific visualization or analysis of financial data are two excellent applications of 3D environments. There is a consortium, **Web3D Consortium,** which oversees the changes to these standards. Recently, a new language, called **X3D (Extensible 3D),** has been proposed to replace VRML (as XML, which is discussed next, is proposed as a potential replacement of HTML).

Writing VRML

Like HTML, VRML can be written using a plain text editor. However, you must have a VRML browser to be able to "test" your pages. Several such software applications, as well as VRML editors, are available as freeware, trial versions, or shareware on the Web. For example, popular VRML editors include Virtue3D, ParaGraph's Virtual Home Space Builder, Caligari's Pioneer, ModelWorks Software's VRML Express, blaxxun interactive's blaxxun3D, ParallelGraphics' VrmlPad, and IDS's V-Realm Builder, to name a few. In writing VRML worlds, you can also make the VRML coding interact with Java and JavaScript (both defined later in this chapter) to provide even more additional functions.

Viewing VRML

The VRML browsers are **plug-ins** that complement your Web browser. Examples of popular and free VRML browsers include: Cosmo Player (Cosmo Software, now owned by Computer Associates) for Windows, Macintosh, and Irix platforms; WorldView (Intervista Software) and blaxxun Contact (blaxxun interactive) for Windows platforms; VRML4Linux (Gerall Kahla) for the Linux platform; and Cortona and Islands (a multi-user VRML browser) (ParallelGraphics). These browsers typically support VRML 1.0, which was originally adopted in 1995, and VRML 2.0, which was adopted in 1996 and contains "moving worlds." VRML 97 was released in 1997, but is very similar in content to VRML 2.0.

Extensible Markup Language (XML)

Extensible Markup Language (XML) is said to be the next great Web language. Like HTML, it provides a way to structure documents, but it also gives meanings to the elements that are in the document. Just like HTML, XML is a subset of SGML. Some of the functionality found in SGML that was not provided in the original HTML (namely Document Type Definitions) is included in XML.

In XML, you must define your own tags, which is an important difference between XML and HTML. In XML, you can define more precise elements. For example, you could define *person* as a tag. Every time you refer to a type of person in your document, a specific format that you have defined would be used (once you use the tags properly), and you would specify the attributes of the particular person you are including in this specific area of the document. For example, you could define the following person: <PERSON gender = "m" type = "dependent"> Peter Smith </PERSON>. The great advantage of extensibility (the flexibility of creating your own tags) could also turn into a disadvantage if every individual creates her own tags, without any consistency. Sometimes the best documents are those in which only a few tags are defined, and those are used in a consistent manner.

Coding in XML

Writing XML documents is very similar to writing HTML documents. The tags even look similar. Like HTML, an XML file is a text-based file, but it is saved with an .xml extension. The file starts with an XML declaration: <?xml version= "1.0"?>. If the file is created using an existing DTD, it can be incorporated into the file by the following command: <!DOCTYPE person SYSTEM "person.dtd">.

The structure and syntax of XML is very clearly defined, and the rules are easy to follow. Below are some of the most important syntax requirements for XML:

1. XML tags are enclosed in angle brackets (lesser than (<) and greater than (>) signs), just as in HTML. XML tags also include attributes or parameters. For example, if *employee* is defined as a tag, the particulars for each employee can be defined using attributes, as follows:

   ```
   <EMPLOYEE type="salaried" gender="m"
   condition="fulltime">Mike Jones</EMPLOYEE>
   ```

2. All tags must have an end tag. Just as in HTML, end tags in XML are preceded by a slash (/). However, unlike HTML, all empty tags must also be ended, or

closed. Empty tags are those that do not surround any content. For example, the image tag <IMG src="file.gif"> does not require an end tag in HTML, but would have to be closed in XML. Empty tags are therefore written slightly differently in XML, with the addition of a space and a slash at the end of the tag, such as <IMG src="file.gif" />. The other types of tags that surround content, called container tags, typically require an end tag in HTML, and definitely do in XML.

3. The values of XML attributes must be surrounded by quotation marks ("value"). While in HTML experienced coders always recommend the use of quotation marks around values (color="red", for example), there are many instances when not putting the quotation marks has no negative effect on the Web page. In other words, quotation marks are considered optional for certain attributes. In XML, however, all attributes' values must have quotation marks.

4. While HTML tags are totally case insensitive, allowing you to use capital letters, lower case, or even mixed case within the same document, XML is case sensitive. Since you define your own tags, you can decide to assign two different formats to <PERSON> and to <person>.

5. Comments can be included, as in HTML, with the <!— comments —> tag (where *comments* are the actual comments in the file).

6. Tags must be nested properly. While HTML allows you to overlap tags (although it is considered sloppy coding), such as <FONT size=+2> <U> Text </FONT> </U> (the end of the underline tag, </U>, should precede the end of the font tag, </FONT>), XML does not.

By following the above rules, you can define XML documents fairly easily. The most important part of coding XML is to (1) plan ahead by examining the documents you want to code and the elements that comprise those documents, and (2) create your own tags while making sure they are used consistently within the organization. It is extremely important that all persons using XML in an organization use the same coding scheme. This will require communication between everyone involved, while keeping excellent documentation. In programming, some of the most challenging work is maintaining coding/programming that has been created by someone else and for which no clear documentation exists. XML coding is no exception.

The goal in XML is to create structured documents. Three main steps should be followed:

1. *Planning and analysis*—Look at all documents, how they are interrelated, and what is common between them. Decide on the styles you want (not necessarily the format; for example, should this be a table or a list?). This is a very important step, and enough time should be allotted to complete it thoroughly.

2. *Writing the Document Type Definition (DTD)*—Although this is not a necessity, these rules or guides that you create will allow you to compare your created documents to the expected outcomes. If this is done thoroughly and properly, the next step is much easier.

3. *Marking up the XML document*—Starting with DTDs, the documents are then tagged. This resembles using HTML to tag a document, with the exception or main difference that there is not a specific set of tags you can use. It is important to start with existing DTDs in the organization before going on to create your own set of tags.

You can insert tags as you create a document (content), or you can create the document and then go back to insert tags. The browsers need to be able to recognize the XML tags, interpret them, and display the information. At the writing of this book, there is some support available in the most recent versions of Netscape Navigator and Windows Internet Explorer. XML can also be read by style sheet languages, such as CSS (Cascading Style Sheet) and **XSL (Extensible Style Sheet).** XSL is an XML-based language that details how XML documents will be formatted. The use of XSL allows the content (the actual page content) to be separated from the representation of the content (the style sheet). For example, a tag called <BOX> can be defined in XSL to display a box format (which would be clearly defined in the XSL style sheet). The XML document would contain the <BOX> tag everywhere the coder wishes to display the information within a box (e.g., <BOX> This text is boxed </BOX> would appear as $\boxed{\text{This text is boxed}}$). Using XSL, a Web page can be rearranged for printing without the need to download a different version of a document. This is used, for example, by Web-based magazines that offer a "printable" version of their articles.

XML uses, just as DHTML and JavaScript do, the Document Object Model (DOM) that we discussed earlier. Again, it is important to note that XML is used not just for displaying information on a Web page (like HTML), but rather serves as a structure for documents, and provides documentation for what this structure is. Finally, it should be noted that XML, like all other tools that are currently in use for Web development of electronic business, has a number of tools, editors, online documentation, and test sites available on the Web. What does a complete XML document look like? It depends very much on an organization's style sheets, DTD, and other tags of importance. Following is a very simple but complete XML document for a bookstore.

```
<?xml version = "1.0"?>
<BOOK>
<TITLE> Evaluation and Implementation of Distance
Learning </TITLE>
<AUTHOR> France Belanger </AUTHOR> and <AUTHOR> Dianne
H. Jordan </AUTHOR>
<CHAPNO> Chapter One </CHAPNO>
<CHAPTITLE> Introduction </CHAPTITLE>
<CHAPTER>
<P> Since the dawn of human history … </P>
<P> The 20th century has seen … </P>
</CHAPTER>
</BOOK>
```

There is, of course, more to XML than what we covered here, but by now you should understand the basic concepts of XML and why it is so flexible compared to HTML.

Why XML for E-business?

Many believe XML is the next Web language. Why is XML so popular? What can it do that HTML can't do, besides flexibility of tags? To understand the importance that XML can have for today's Web environments, it is important to note that many applications used by corporations for their operational systems cannot display information in HTML even though these applications need to exchange information over the Internet. The Internet protocols discussed in the previous chapter are used for the transmission of messages over the Internet. However, there is also a need for a standard for the data formats to be understood by the various systems that will use them. That's where XML can help. For example, if you are sending an HTML document containing course information, there is no way to "dissect" the information automatically with HTML (since only formatting tags are used). However, using XML, a set of tags such as <SYLLABUS>, <TEXTBOOK>, <CREDIT_HOURS>, and so on can be used so that the actual content of the document can be processed automatically by systems. This is particularly important for database-driven e-business systems where each XML tag can correspond to a field in the underlying database. This is something that the pre-defined sets of HTML tags cannot do.

XML Standards and Applications

As previously discussed, one of the major advantages of XML is that it is very flexible. With flexibility, however, comes the need to standardize so that companies who want to use XML for transferring information to each other can understand each other's data. For example, if Company A uses <CLIENT_NAME> </CLIENT_NAME> as a set of XML tags, but Company B uses <CUSTOMER_NAME> </CUSTOMER_NAME>, the two companies' systems will not be able to process each other's data. Given this situation, industries need to develop some common languages to conduct electronic exchanges of data using XML. As a result, several industries are developing **"vertical XML vocabularies"** that include XML tags for use within their industry. An example of this is **Electronic Business XML (ebXML),** sponsored by the United Nations Centre for Trade Facilitation and Electronic Business (UN/CEFACT) and the Organization for the Advancement of Structures Information Standards (OASIS). The intent is for ebXML to become the global e-commerce standard for computer-to-computer information exchange.

E-BUSINESS IN PRACTICE

Will XML replace HTML?

After reading the preceding sections of this chapter, there should be no doubt that XML and HTML, while similar, are very different in what they can do for an e-business' Web environment. It is argued that the "next generation of HTML will be reformulated in XML under the name of XHTML (extensible hypertext markup language)" (Amor 2000, 336). This new language will combine a core set of HTML tags with the flexibility of XML tags. It seems likely that this will occur. The reason? Because XML has numerous advantages over HTML. Below are some of the key advantages (Amor 2000, 337):

1. *"Browser presentation*—XML can provide more and better facilities for browser presentation and performance through the use of style sheets."

2. *"Information accessibility*—Information is more accessible and reusable due to the flexibility of XML."

3. *"Richer content*—Through the use of new markup elements, it is possible to create a richer content that is easier to use."

4. *"SGML compatibility*—As XML files are compatible to the SGML standard, they can be also used outside the Web in an SGML environment."

5. *"Tailored document types*—Document providers and authors are able to create their own document types using XML and are not restricted to the set of markup elements in HTML. It is possible to invent new markup elements."

The design of the standard started in 2001, as an online, easy-to-translate equivalent of EDI (Electronic Data Interchange). However, at the end of 2001 there still remains much to be accomplished before ebXML can be used significantly for commercial transactions.

Wireless Markup Language

There is also a new markup language called **Wireless Markup Language (WML)** used to create Web pages for micro-browsers. Micro-browsers are toned down versions of browsers that can be used on wireless devices, such as smart phones or personal digital assistants (PDAs).

SCRIPTING LANGUAGE: ACTIVE SERVER PAGES

Active Server Pages (ASP) is a scripting language created by Microsoft for server-side scripting. It is free and already built into the Microsoft Windows 2000 and XP operating systems. Plug-ins can be added to older versions (Windows NT or 95/98). With ASP, it is possible to create dynamic and interactive Web server applications, one of the most popular being collecting and analyzing input data from online HTML forms. ASP automates form handling, which used to be performed with more complex CGI scripts. The Perl/CGI language will be described later in this chapter. While Microsoft developed ASP, other companies, such as ChilliSoft, offer their own ASP tools.

The ASP code is mixed in with the actual HTML tags, but unlike the HTML tag, it is never actually seen by the browser. Typically, users can "run" ASP code with their standard browsers (even though they may not know they are running this code). The Web server application, Internet Information Services, on Windows 2000 or XP runs in conjunction with a small dynamic link library called ASP.DLL on the server. When a user requests a file from this server that contains an ".asp" extension, the ASP.DLL library handles the interpretation of the page, generating an HTML page that is then handled by Internet Information Services (like every other HTML file on the server).

There are many reasons that make ASP a very interesting scripting language to learn. First, it is relatively easy to learn, and it can handle many advanced functions. ASP can be used to create Web applications that interact with databases or other applications. For example, it is possible to use ASP code to populate a Web page with information from a database. The information can be updated as often as the database itself is updated. The downside is performance. Not being a full-fledged programming language, ASP does not provide well-engineered applications, even if it is optimized. However, as we will discuss in the Perl/CGI section, CGI scripts have a lot of overhead. Every time a CGI script is requested, the server must initiate the CGI compiler to translate and compile the program. Conversely, there is no compiling necessary for ASP (it is a scripting language).

Writing ASP Code

ASP is usually written by using a combination of HTML tags and some scripting. Many developers use VBScript as the scripting language, although JavaScript, Perl, and Python are other popular options. These languages will be briefly discussed in a later section of this chapter. Following is an example of a simple ASP file using VBScript.

```
<%@ LANGUAGE = "VBScript" %>
<HTML>
<HEAD> <TITLE> Form Processing </TITLE> </HEAD>
<BODY>
<%
First = Request.Form("First")
Last = Request.Form("Last")
Previous = Request.Form("Previous")
%>
<% Response.Write First %>
<% Response.Write Last %>
<% If Previous = "yes" then %>
Previous Visitor
<% Else %>
New Visitor
<% End If %>
</BODY>
</HTML>
```

Let's assume the file in the previous example is called *process.asp* and is stored on the server where the related HTML pages are stored. In the HTML file that uses this script, a form would be created for registering visitors using the <FORM> tag as follows: <FORM method = "Post" action = "process.asp">. The rest of the form would include input values for first name, last name, and whether the visitor had been to the site before or not. In the HTML file, those input variables would be defined as "First," "Last," and "Previous." Note that these are the variables we are requesting in the ASP file. The *Response.Write* expression sends information to the browser. The <% and %> envelop our scripting information. The first line of the file identifies which scripting language is used. Once the data are entered by the user and the script is activated, the program will print the first name (First), last name (Last), and either Previous Visitor or New Visitor, depending on the answer provided.

SCRIPTING LANGUAGE: JAVASCRIPT

One of the problems with HTML files is that they are text files, which means that they cannot perform "actions" in response to user requests. This is where scripting languages like JavaScript can add some dynamism to the HTML pages. The original JavaScript program was released under the name LiveScript by Netscape (for Navigator 2.0). We discussed JavaScript a little bit in the section on DHTML, since DHTML uses it for acting on style sheets, so we will build on that discussion in this section.

JavaScript can be entirely written within the HTML page, and is interpreted by the browser to execute tasks in response to user actions (event driven). An example of a simple action that users can perform is to move the mouse over sections of a Web page. A JavaScript routine can be written so that different text or menus appear as the user moves the mouse around the Web page. The following example shows how a JavaScript routine can be incorporated into a regular Web page.

```
<HTML>
<HEAD> <TITLE> JavaScript Example </TITLE> </HEAD>
```

```
<SCRIPT language="javascript">
function showtext(text) {
 … code to show text ….
}
function hidetext(text) {
 …. code to hide text …
}
</SCRIPT>
<BODY>
<H2 align=center> EXAMPLE OF JAVASCRIPT </H2>
<DIV ONMOUSEOVER="showtext ('Smile')"
 ONMOUSEOUT="hidetext ('Smile')">
<IMG src="Smile.gif">
 <DIV id="Smile" CLASS =<"texthide">
 <P> This is a beautiful day! <BR> Give a smile to those
<BR> who need it most:
 the sad and angry! </P>
 </DIV>
</BODY>
</HTML>
```

The JavaScript routine is included within the <SCRIPT> and </SCRIPT> tags. The code for showing and hiding the text is not presented here. Within the body of the HTML file, the script is called upon. When the mouse is moved over the Smile image (gif), then the text is displayed (ONMOUSEOVER). And when the mouse is moved away from the image, the text disappears (ONMOUSEOUT="hidetext ('Smile')"). This example is similar to one presented earlier, and the result can be seen in Figure 5-3.

Components of JavaScript

As with most programming languages, there are some basic components that are included within JavaScript documents. Some of these components include a variety of data types (boolean, number, string, array, or object), operators (arithmetic, comparison, logical, or assignment), statements, and a structure for all JavaScript programs.

In JavaScript, there are only three main types of statements used: if-else, for, and while-do. The first type of statement allows the browser to evaluate some condition to decide which portion of code to execute next. For example, some simple code using an if-else statement follows:

```
If day = "Sunday"
   {count += 2}
else
   {count += 1};
```

This simply makes the JavaScript add two to the *count* variable if the day is Sunday, or add one to the *count* variable for any other day of the week. The for and the while-do statements are **loop statements.** Loop statements perform certain actions until a given condition is met. An example of the for statement follows:

```
For (count = 0; count < 10; count += 1);
```

In this statement the initial value of the variable *count* is set to zero. The second part of the statement indicates to continue performing the action until the condition of *count* being smaller than ten remains true. The last part of the statement is the action, in this case adding one to the value of *count*.

Finally, the while-do statements are similar to for statements in that they create a loop. The format is as follows:

```
While (count < 10) {count += 1};
or
Do {count += 1} while (count < 10);
```

In the first statement *count* is increased by one until it reaches nine (smaller than ten). When the *count* equals ten no action is taken. In the second statement *count* is also increased by one until it reaches ten. The main difference between the two statements is that the condition is checked first in the first statement.

Structure of JavaScript Documents

There are some specific rules for creating the structure of a document in JavaScript (as for any other programming language). In this case the main rules are (Cintron 1999):

1. The JavaScript is included within the <SCRIPT> </SCRIPT> tags in the HTML file.
2. Functions and blocks of statements in JavaScript are enclosed in curly brackets { }.
3. Evaluation/comparison expressions in JavaScript are enclosed in parentheses ( ).
4. Array elements in JavaScript are indicated by square brackets [ ].
5. Comments are either enclosed between slashes (/) if on a single line, or /* and */ if running onto multiple lines (not <!— and — > as in HTML).
6. JavaScript statements should end with a semicolon (;) although most browsers are quite forgiving on this.

The following example shows a very simple HTML page with JavaScript that can be used to make sure a student enters his social security number on a form called *studentinfo*. Note that the script itself (*checkSSN*) is called from within the body of the document, but is written before the body.

```
<HTML>
<HEAD> <TITLE> Checking Student SSN Example </TITLE>
</HEAD>
<SCRIPT language="JavaScript">
<!— function checkSSN ( )
{if (document.studentinfo.studentSSN.value = =" ")
   {alert ("You need to enter your SSN");}
   }
—>
</SCRIPT>
<BODY>
<P> Please enter your Social Security Number and click "submit" </P>
```

```
<FORM name=studentinfo>
<INPUT type=text name=studentSSN>
<INPUT type=button name=submit value=submit
onClick=checkSSN( );>
</FORM>
</BODY>
</HTML>
```

Using JavaScript for E-business

JavaScript is fairly easy to code and can be used to add dynamic content to an e-business' Web site. It can also be used to reduce network transmission of erroneous data. For example, one of the ways that JavaScript can be used by e-businesses is for verifying user input on forms, as done in the previous example. In the example, if the value submitted for the *studentSSN* field is empty (" "), then a warning message appears (*You need to enter your SSN*). Since the script is run from within the browser, the data can be verified for completeness before they are sent for processing. For the user, this saves reloading the page or retyping the information to correct the wrong input. For the e-business, it reduces the transmission load on the network since only complete data are sent for processing. Of course, large e-businesses will tend to use more sophisticated programs developed in robust programming languages to handle their customers' data. JavaScript was never intended to be such a general purpose programming language. Nevertheless, it is easy to code, can be used for fast prototyping of dynamic content on Web pages, and provides quick execution (since the source is loaded with the Web page). It also has good interfaces to other programming languages, such as Java. It is therefore an excellent language for small e-businesses.

PROGRAMMING LANGUAGE: JAVA

Java was originally developed by Sun Microsystems. It is an object-oriented language that has two main and highly publicized advantages: (1) It is designed to run on any platform, including hardware and software. (2) It offers **reusability.** While we discuss Java in this chapter within the context of developing Web pages for electronic business, Java is a full-fledged programming language that can be used to develop applications that may have nothing to do with the Web. Remember from our previous discussion that Java programs are called *applets* (for small applications). However, the term *servlets* is also used to refer to Java programs running on the server side of client/server environments.

If a company says that it is a "Java shop," you may want to ask what "flavor" of Java it is using. The various companies that offer Java compilers and development tools have made some slight variations in how the Java code is written. So if you write a program with one development tool, you may not be able to compile it with another one. Note that this applies to only a few products, and most are 100 percent Java compatible. In addition, once you've learned the basics of Java, you can easily navigate between the different products. Table 5-2 lists some of the Java compilers currently available on the market.

Table 5-2 Some Current Java
Integrated Development
Environments (IDEs)

Product	Company
Java WorkShop	Sun Microsystems
JBuilder	Borland (Inprise)
JFactory	Rouge Wave
VisualAge for Java	IBM
Visual Café	Symantec
Visual J++	Microsoft

Web Pages with Java

We cannot teach you how to program Java applets in this chapter. A complete course in Java is required to fully understand the process. However, you should be able to recognize when Web pages call Java applets. You should also understand the various files stored on the different platforms and how they work together in making some of those glitzy pages you see on today's Web sites.

When writing a Java applet, one uses a text editor or a Java development tool. If you remember the earlier discussion on HTML, you will notice that the basic idea is the same. A plain text editor allows you to write any program, it is the codes or tags you use in the file and how you store and name the file that makes the difference. In the case of HTML, we stored and named the files as .htm or .html, and we used the <HTML> </HTML> tags. The browser interpreted those tags to present your Web page. In Java, we will store the file that contains the Java program with a *.java* extension. This indicates to the compiler that the file contains a Java applet. In contrast to HTML, though, we now need to compile the file, as it cannot be read as is. To do this we will use a **Java compiler (javac),** based on the development environment selected (see Table 5-2 for some IDEs).

Once the program is compiled (this can be easily done using drop down menus with most of the earlier mentioned programs, which all have debugging tools available), the compiler creates a separate file with a *.class* extension. This is the binary file that will be called into the HTML document and can be executed (see Figure 5-4).

The Java files are called **active documents.** An active document is one that actually performs functions (in contrast to our static HTML files). When a browser requests an active document from a server, the server returns a program that the browser can then run locally. The **Java binary file** (*.class) is this file, which is stored on the server. When the user's browser requests the HTML document from the server, which contains the call for the .class file, the server sends the HTML page back to the browser, together with the executable file. This file is then translated and run (executed) by the browser locally. In other words, the Java file is executed on the client. Note that this is why you need a browser that supports Java to access certain sites. Figure 5-5 summarizes how Java is incorporated into Web pages. Note that some Java programs are run on the server (called *servlets*) instead of being transferred to the client.

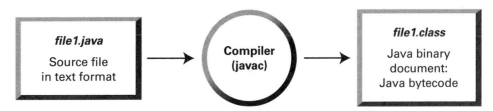

FIGURE 5-4 File Formats in Java

Incorporating Applets into HTML Documents

There are currently two ways to call an applet within an HTML document:

1. Use the APPLET tag, which is used with HTML version 3, or

2. Use the OBJECT tag, which is used with HTML version 4.

The applet tag uses the basic form of:

```
<APPLET codebase="http://web.page.org/directory"
code="test.class" width="150" height="120"> </APPLET>.
```

The APPLET tag is incorporated into the HTML file in which you want the applet to appear. The codebase is the path, including either the URL up to the file name or just the directory structure if the executable file is located on the same server. The code is the actual program file with the .class extension. Attributes can be added to the applet, including size attributes (height/width), alignment (align), and description of the applet (alt). As with most HTML tags, there are many more attributes that can be added to the APPLET tag, but they are beyond our discussion.

The object tag is similar, but is considered more general. Its form is as follows:

```
<OBJECT codebase="http://web.page.org/directory"
classid="test.class" width="150" height="120"> </OBJECT>
```

One can easily note that the codebase, height, and width attributes are the same as in the APPLET tag. The code is replaced with the classid, which is also the actual executable file in this case. Similar additional attributes used by the APPLET tag can be used with OBJECT. However, the OBJECT tag also includes a codetype attribute that the programmer can use to tell the browser what kind of object is included in the classid attribute. In addition, the OBJECT tag can include some DHTML tags such as STYLE, ID, and CLASS, as well as JavaScript type tags such as ONMOUSEOVER, ONMOUSEMOVE, ONCLICK, etc.

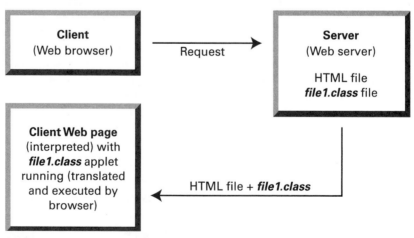

FIGURE 5-5   Web Environment with Java

Writing Java Applets and Servlets

As previously discussed, writing Java applets requires a course in Java programming. However, there are some basic rules for writing the programs, which are fairly easy to follow and provide a better understanding of what the fuss over Java is about. Before you get started you must understand that Java has basically three components:

- Programming language—the coding used to create the programs.
- **Runtime environment**—the environment that is used to run Java programs, such as development tools, compilers, etc.
- **Class library**—Java has a large library of objects that are already written, which you can use to create your own applets. This definitely makes writing applets easier. All you need to do is learn what is available within the libraries. Some of the key libraries available are listed in Table 5-3.

Learning what is available in the Java libraries is the key to mastering the Java programming language. How do you use the libraries presented in Table 5-3? They contain **classes** that have already been written, so you simply need to import them into your program. For example, instead of programming by hand all of the codes needed to create a drop down menu, you can borrow it from the class for drop down menus. The same can be said of buttons, windows, etc. When you want to write such an applet, the first thing you do in your file is to import all of the classes you will need (to borrow from). For example, the beginning of an applet may look like this:

```
import java.applet.*;
import.java.awt.*;
public class test extends Applet {.......};
```

In this case, you are importing all classes (hence the *) from the applet and awt libraries. You will then create a new class (test) that will build upon the Applet class (which exists within the java.applet library). What does extending mean? Because the Applet class is already written, it contains numerous functions. One key to Java is the concept of **inheritance**—when you create a subclass to an existing class, it inherits all of the properties and methods included in that existing class. This allows code to be reused for all classes that need the same functions. You should also note that in this example, the new class you are defining

Table 5-3   Java Libraries

Library	Description
Java.applet	Includes classes that provide graphical support for applets
Java.awt	Abstract Windowing Toolkit; includes classes that provide GUI elements
Java.io	Includes classes for input and output support
Java.lang	Includes the basic classes for the core language; they do not need to be imported
Java.net	Includes classes for networking
Java.util	Includes a variety of miscellaneous classes

is test. The file you are creating therefore needs to be called test.java (remember it is not compiled yet!). The rest of the java file contains variables and methods. Once compiled, the file will be called *test.class*. The following example presents a simple Java program.

```
package sampleapplet;
import java.awt.*;
import java.awt.event.*;
import java.applet.*;
public class Visit extends Applet implements
ActionListener
{
 //Declare a counter
   int count = 0;
 //Declare and create a textfield and a button
   TextField info = new TextField("There have been no
visitors registered");
 Button register = new Button("Please register");
 //Initialize the applet
 public void init()
 {
 //add the button and (non-editable) textfield to the
applet
   add(register);
   info.setEditable(false);
   add(info);
 //have the button listen for the action event
   register.addActionListener(this);
   }
 public void actionPerformed(ActionEvent e)
 {
 //user clicked button
 if (e.getSource() == register)
 {
         count++;
        info.setText("There have been "+count+" visi-
tor(s) registered");
 }
 }
}
```

Let's see what the program does. We already know about importing libraries and defining and extending the public class. The next three lines define three new variables for the visit class. The *count* variable is an integer, the *info* variable is a text field, and the *register* variable is a button. The next two **methods** define what shows up on the page, and then what happens to it. The init( ) is usually called every time an applet is loaded, and it initializes the variables and setups on the display. In this case a new button is displayed on the screen with the words "Please register" written on it. It is then set to read-only (cannot be edited, so the users won't change the text), and set to react to the event. Notice we did not have to write the code to draw the button because it is part of the java.awt library. The next line adds the info variable, which is set to state that no visitors have registered yet.

The second method provides the action. The method called *action* is invoked when the event *e* is triggered (by pressing the *register* button). If the Button called "Please register" is clicked, then the *count* variable is increased by one (*count++*), and the info variable is changed to say: "There have been 1 visitor(s) registered." Notice that the variable *count* is used within this sentence by including it with + signs on each side. Figure 5-6 shows this code once it has been compiled and called within an HTML file.

The action takes place on the user's browser. So the code in the example does not serve the role of a counter of hits on a Web site (which requires much more complicated programming or the acquisition of an existing tool). If the user closes her browser and reopens to access the same Web page again, the counter is set back to zero (the application starts running again). However, as long as the browser is opened, the Java applet is resident and ready to change the count of registered visitors every time she clicks the button.

Other Java Capabilities

Java is a much more complex and complete language than what we have portrayed in this chapter. For example, it is possible to add animation in Java programs by repainting the displays using paint, update, repaint, artman, or other commands. Java and HTML can

FIGURE 5-6   The *Visit.class* Applet

also interact directly by using, among other elements, parameters. If you want to learn Java, you can download free or trial versions of some of the compilers. Then, get yourself a good book and start experimenting.

Differences Between Java and JavaScript

It should be fairly obvious to you, after reading the preceding sections, that Java and JavaScript are quite different, although they use the same object-oriented approach. Some of the key differences are highlighted in Table 5-4.

JavaScript is easy to code and is typically used by less experienced developers who want to add interactivity to their Web sites. For client side applications (programs run by the browser), JavaScript can replace client-side Java. Conversely, Java is for experienced programmers. It is a powerful programming language that is being used by many electronic business Web sites for advanced functions and dynamism. The two languages interoperate well, but they are technically, functionally, and behaviorally different.

OTHER POPULAR LANGUAGES FOR E-BUSINESS DEVELOPMENT

In this section, we identify and very briefly describe some popular languages used to create e-business applications. Each language has its strengths and weaknesses, and the choice of language is very often the result of a company's current environment and the preferences of the company's developers.

Programming Language: Perl/CGI

Perl/CGI existed before JavaScript, VBScript, and Active Server Pages, to name a few. Perl stands for Practical Extraction and Report Language. It is a text processing language that runs on servers. The Perl language is used to write CGI scripts (Common Gateway Interface). It is an established protocol for transmitting data between Web server applications and Web browsers. Since it has been around for a long time, you will frequently see Perl routines being called by HTML documents. Most form processing on the Web has been done using CGI scripts since the FORM tag was implemented. You can identify these programs by their .pl

Table 5-4 Some Differences Between Java and JavaScript

	JavaScript	Java
Name of programs	JavaScript (or scripts) on server: server-side	Applets on server: servlets
Language	Scripting language	Programming languages
Storage format	Source text	Bytecode
Integration	Scripts embedded within HTML	Applets are stored separately from HTML files
Shared control	Can control Java applets	Cannot control JavaScript
Interaction between programs	Can interact with HTML and Document Object Model	Works by itself, can be "called" by others
Interpretation	Interpreted by client but not compiled	Compiled on server (to bytecode) and interpreted client

extension. For example, a typical form starts with the following FORM tag: <FORM method="post" action="cgi-bin/register.pl">. When the user hits the "submit" button, the browser accesses the Perl/CGI script named in the action attribute. In this case the cgi-bin is the directory where the scripts are kept on the server, and the Perl program is called *register.pl*.

Perl is an **interpreted language,** which means the programs are compiled when they are run. Like other languages, the best way to learn Perl is to get a good book or access one of the numerous online resources available on Perl, and then write and compile programs. Fortunately, not only are there excellent resources available online, but Perl compilers are also installed on a large number of servers. You might want to check your work or school server to see if any such compiler is installed. The other option is for you to download a Perl compiler from one of the several Web sites that offer them, such as Perl.com.

Differences Between CGI/Perl and Java

Java is taking over a lot of functions on servers (servlets) that were typically performed by CGI scripts. Some of the reasons why Java is slowly replacing the CGI scripts include the greater efficiency of Java for handling requests (on the server) and the general advantages of Java as a language. CGI scripts require the server to initiate the CGI compiler and translate and compile the program every time a request is made for that script. Conversely, servlets (java) remain active and can be used whenever, without recompiling, translating, or initiating. In addition, Perl programs, although very efficient, are harder to read than Java programs. Given that Java offers **portability (platform independence),** and that it can be used for standalone programs (not just Web applications), one can see that it has much to offer in replacing CGI scripts.

Scripting Language: VBScript

VBScript is another common scripting language for Web browsers that is interpreted by the browser. However, VBScript was developed by Microsoft and is only supported by Microsoft's Internet Explorer. It is a subset of the Visual Basic language that can be embedded into HTML files, just as JavaScript can. VBScript can be used to add interactivity or dynamism to Web pages. It is tightly integrated with Internet Explorer and Microsoft's operating systems, which is both an advantage (can do highly sophisticated applications) and a disadvantage (does not run on other operating systems and/or browsers).

Programming Language: Python

Python is an object-oriented programming language (like Java). It uses very clear syntax that is simple to understand for developers with experience using Java, Perl, or other similar languages. It is portable (like Java) so it can run on a large number of platforms (operating system environments), and can interact with C or C++ applications. Finally, the source code for Python is freely available.

INTEGRATED E-BUSINESS DEVELOPMENT ENVIRONMENTS

In order to develop business-to-business or business-to-consumer Web sites and applications, companies hire programmers who use some of the languages described in this chapter or use development environments that integrate several existing e-business tools. For example, auctioning software exists. If a company wants to start a marketplace on widgets, it could decide to ask its programmers to develop an auction system, or alternatively buy one that already exists. Some companies prefer to use existing tools to increase their productivity. Others prefer to develop their own to retain their competitive advantage and intellectual property.

To facilitate development of e-business environments, a large number of small and large corporations have started to offer electronic business integrated solutions. This may involve combining existing products with the skills of contracted developers to customize applications to clients' needs. Companies can also outsource all of their electronic business development, the hosting of their Web site, and maintenance of their applications. Products to support Web development are often called Web application servers. There are hundreds of such products available on the market today. Table 5-5 summarizes some of the most popular ones. A more complete list can be found at the Application Server Zone.

Decision Point

We discussed a large number of development environments in this chapter. How is a company to choose which environment to use for its e-business development? The following decision points may help you picture the series of decisions that must be made by the manager in charge of this decision.

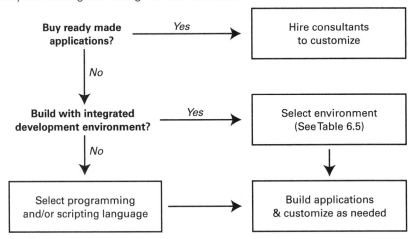

MANAGERIAL ISSUES

Selection of Development Environment

After reading this chapter, it should be obvious that languages abound for developing electronic business Web environments. This leads to a difficult question for managers: in which one or ones should they invest? The perfect environment for one company might not be at all suitable for another. For example, very small companies can get away with using a Web development tool as simple as FrontPage to create their initial Web presence. Clearly, large and established corporations will want to use more sophisticated development environments that will not only provide them with glitzy, high-quality Web sites, but also with tools to track activity on their Web sites and provide added value to their customers. Small firms typically make use of FrontPage, ColdFusion, JavaScript and DHTML. Why? Because they are easy to learn and use, and the initial investment is small. DHTML and JavaScript (or VBScript) can be used to connect small databases to Web sites, or to add dynamism to the sites on the client side. Conversely, large corporations will have to support larger databases and will also want to create dynamism on the server side to handle large quantities of user inputs. Languages such as Perl and Java, or development environments such as WebSphere or WebObjects, would be appropriate for such projects. For medium-sized firms, any language might be appropriate, including Active Server Pages.

Managers cannot base their decision only on the fact that a certain language is the "hot" language right now and that everyone talks about it. The decision to use one or more languages has several implications that managers should consider. Some of these considerations include:

- *Integration of languages*—A company might have a number of different development environments. The development tools must be able to mix and match properly. For example, several of the integrated development environments presented in Table 5-5 make use of Java. It would make sense for the firm's other software development projects to use Java (although it may not be the case). Most of the time, it is actually useful to have several tools in use, as long as they integrate well together.

- *Training*—Changing a development environment or adding a new development environment to the company's existing list requires training existing programmers and/or hiring new programmers. Since most companies want to keep their programmers, they often prefer to offer training to bring them up-to-date. Training considerations include the cost of courses and the loss of productivity for those individuals in training. Hiring external programmers might reduce the training needed, but training will still be required for the business-specific environment.

- *Hardware/software*—If a new development environment is considered, managers must also evaluate whether new hardware and/or software is required to support this new development environment. They should also have someone investigate the compatibility of existing tools, hardware, and software with the new environment.

- *Life span*—One of the most difficult tasks for those deciding on which new development environment to implement is the evaluation of the life span of these development tools. How long will this language be around? For example, XML is said by many to be the next big thing on the Web. How much should managers invest in XML? Is there another competing language that may take over in a few years? All of these are very difficult questions, and there is more speculation than information available in the public domain.

Table 5-5 Some Application Server Products

Product	Company	Details	Web Page
Avenida Web Server	Avenida	Server-side Java technology; standard edition comes with four servlets; difficult integration	www.avenida.co.uk
BEA WebLogic Enterprise Platform	BEA Systems	Has two types of products: WebLogic Server and WebLogic Server Developer Center; can connect to Java environments	www.weblogic.com
ColdFusion	Macromedia (bought product from Allaire)	Works with Java; has pre-built building blocks; good for database connections; very popular	www.macromedia.com
Borland Enterprise Server	Borland	Developed by Inprise; builds on open standards (Java, C++, etc.); builds on Sun Java	www.inprise.com
eXcelon	Object Design	Good for database connections; uses XML; difficult integration with existing business software	www.exceloncorp.com
FrontPage	Microsoft	A Web development tool for small businesses or individuals	www.microsoft.com
WebSphere Commerce	IBM Corporation	Offers suite with many editions; also offers payment processing and integration services products; builds on Java; for small- to large-scale projects	www.ibm.com
SilverStream eXtend	SilverStream	Has several products: Director, Composer, Application Server, Workbench; to build and deploy complex web applications	www.silverstream.com
Sybase EAServer	Sybase	Builds on Internet standards (Java, C++, etc.); good for integration of multiple platforms	www.sybase.com
WebObjects	Apple	Application server environment for large-scale projects; provides integration	www.apple.com

Development Life Cycle

For creating an electronic business Web site, developers should follow the same process as for any other information system application. This means that the development process should follow a traditional **systems development life cycle** (SDLC) (see Figure 5-7), or a prototyping approach.

Under the traditional SDLC, requirements should be thoroughly analyzed first. This includes both the business side requirements (what do we want to gain from this site?), as well as the design requirements (what tools do we currently use? how much compatibility is required with existing systems? what are the most up-to-date tools available?). Once planning and analysis have been completed, the initial design should be created. Once the design has been approved and tested, the Web site should actually be developed (unless you use a prototyping approach). Before it is put into operation with real users accessing it, though, the Web site should be thoroughly tested. There are so many companies offering services and products on the Web today, that if one company's Web site has major glitches, users may not come back. Finally, once in operation, the Web site must be maintained.

Maintenance of a Web site requires a lot of effort. Such maintenance can include all of the following:

- Making sure someone responds to requests/comments sent to the contact information provided on the site

- Maintaining any links from the site to other sites (links constantly change, get dropped, or refer to obsolete pages)

- Making sure the site uses recent versions of software but supports older versions (new features are neat, but when changing to a more recent software package, it is important to support users trying to access the site with older software)

- Updating the site when business information changes

- Restructuring the site when new pages are needed; when doing this, it is important to keep the old site active and add a referring link, so that customers who have not updated their links to the new pages are not "lost"

The life cycle presented above is a very abbreviated version of the life cycle you may have learned about in other information systems courses. There is an additional challenge faced by today's electronic business Web developers. Most business leaders want to be up and running in electronic business right away. They do not want to hear that it's going to take two years to develop a site. It might be too late by then, with too many other companies having taken advantage of the market. This puts a lot of pressure on the developers. In this case, using outside programmers or integrated solutions might be the best alternative.

Web Site Design and Usability

A key element of Web site design is the actual content of the Web site. Too many graphics or colors that are too aggressive are just two examples of issues in design that may prevent many customers from doing business on a particular site. Unfortunately, many Web programmers forget that content is the key. A good Web site provides added value through content, not just flashy design elements. One of the best ways to ensure that content is valuable is to go through several **storyboards** before actually designing the site. Storyboards are paper-based layouts that show what the various pages of a Web site are, what their content is, and how they are related. Going through several versions of these storyboards, verifying content with the appropriate users and managers, is one way to avoid cluttered Web sites or Web sites that offer little value.

One key factor to which Web site designers must pay attention is **usability.** Usability is a combination of factors, such as navigation, shopping carts, etc., that, in combination, affect the experience users have with a system. Usability of a Web site will impact its subsequent use by customers. For example, Forrester Research reports that 50 percent of potential sales are lost when visitors to a

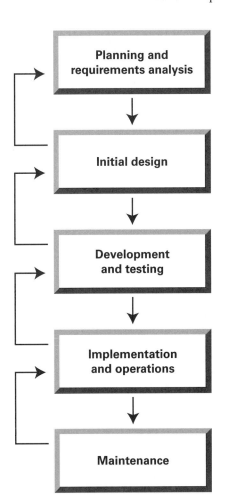

FIGURE 5-7 Traditional Systems Development Life Cycle

Web site cannot find what they are looking for (Manning 2000). Some key usability concepts include ease of navigation, value of material presented, and quick downloads (limited number of images). We will discuss usability of Web sites in more depth in Chapter 9, and we will provide examples of how usability can be enhanced for an e-business' Web site.

Browser Support

In selecting a Web development environment, e-businesses must take into account the varied levels of support provided by browsers for the various environments. For example, recall that not long ago it was common to see sites that required the use of a Java-enabled browser. Browsers that were not "up to date" were rerouted to an older or different Web site (or simply did not load!). Today, most browsers support Java. As new features are added and new versions are developed for the various Web development environments, however, companies must ensure that "older" versions of their sites are available for users who have not upgraded their browsers. Similarly, some tools, such as JavaScript, result in differing implementations depending on the user's browser. As a result, some Web pages are not displayed properly with certain browsers. This is why some sites actually include the statement, "Site best viewed with [browser name]." The solution is for e-businesses to either use features that are supported by all browsers (so that customers don't get frustrated when they can't load a page), or provide multiple versions of their Web pages for use with the different browsers.

SUMMARY

This chapter provided an overview of several of the most popular development environments for electronic business on the Internet. We began by differentiating between markup, scripting, and programming languages. Typically, programming languages are more complex and require a longer learning curve, but are much more flexible and complete. Most of the real programming languages used for Web environments can also be used for non-Web applications.

We briefly overviewed three coding languages. HyperText Markup Language (HTML) is the core tool for Web pages. We described its basic rules for document formatting, including the head and the body of the document. We also presented some basic tags that are used, although to really learn HTML, you should use Appendix A (available online at http://www.wiley.com/ college/vanslyke). We discussed related languages to HTML, including SGML, DHTML, VRML, XML, and WML. SGML, Standard Generalized Markup Language, is the root from which HTML was derived, but is much more complete and complex. It is not used extensively on the Web. Dynamic HTML (DHTML) makes use of HTML, together with JavaScript and style sheets to add dynamism to HTML pages. Virtual Reality Modeling Language (VRML) allows developers to create virtual reality worlds that can include 3D environments on the Internet. Extensible Markup Language (XML) is the most recent contender as the development tool for the

Web. It allows tags to be customized to the organization. It is therefore more complete than HTML, and yet fairly easy to learn. To make good use of XML, you should define Document Type Definitions (DTDs) that contain all style requirements to include with your coding. Finally, WML is used for designing pages to be accessed by wireless devices.

We then discussed two scripting tools: JavaScript and Active Server Pages. JavaScript was developed by Netscape. The scripts are incorporated within the HTML file. They allow functions to take place in response to user actions. Active Server Pages is a server-side scripting tool developed by Microsoft. It combines the use of HTML and one of four scripting languages. It is used more and more in the market for handling form data from Web pages.

We also discussed the Java programming language. Java is an object-oriented programming language developed by Sun Microsystems. It is a complete language that can be used for non-Web applications as well. We then presented a number of other popular Web development tools, such as Perl/CGI, VBScript, and Python. Finally, we presented some electronic business integrated development solutions.

The chapter concludes with a discussion of managerial issues, including how to decide which Web development environments to use, the use of a development life cycle, Web site design and usability, and issues of browser support.

KEY TERMS

activating element
active documents
Active Server Pages (ASP)
animated gifs
applets
ASCII
cascading style sheets (CSS)
classes
class library
compiler
container tags
converter
display attributes
Document Object Model (DOM)
Document Type Definitions (DTDs)
Dynamic HTML (DHTML)
Electronic Business XML (ebXML)
embedded style sheets
empty tags
event
Extensible Markup Language
    (XML)
Extensible Style Sheet (XSL)
HTML assistant
HTML editor

HyperText Markup Language
    (HTML)
inheritance
inline style
interpreted language
interpreter
Java
Java binary file
Java compiler (javac)
JavaScript
linked style sheets
loop statements
markup language
methods
object programming
objects
Perl/CGI
platform independent
plug-ins
portability (platform independence)
program
programming language
push technology
reusability
routines

runtime environment
scripting languages
scripts
server-side scripting
servlets
Standard Generalized Markup
    Language (SGML)
storyboards
structured programming
style sheets
systems development life cycle
tag
target element
usability
validators
VBScript
vertical XML vocabularies
Virtual Reality Modeling
    Language (VRML)
virtual store
Web master
Web3D Consortium
Wireless Markup Language (WML)
worlds
X3D (Extensible 3D)

REVIEW QUESTIONS

1. Define the terms programming language, scripting language, and markup language.

2. Identify languages that produce applets.

3. Identify languages that produce scripts.

4. Explain the basic structure of HTML documents.

5. Explain how a Web browser recognizes HTML documents.

6. Identify the three rules for writing HTML tags.

7. Identify some of the tags that can be found in the head section of an HTML file.

8. Identify and discuss the pros and cons of the different methods that can be used to write HTML documents.

9. Describe the purposes of the Standard Generalized Markup Language (SGML) and its relationship to HTML.

10. Describe the components of Dynamic HTML (DHTML).

11. Explain what the Cascading Style Sheets standard is.

12. Identify the three levels of hierarchy in cascading style sheets.

13. Describe what a JavaScript event is.

14. Describe what the Document Object Model (DOM) is.

15. Describe the functions of the Virtual Reality Modeling Language (VRML) and its potential business uses.

16. What is X3D?

17. Explain the role of Document Type Definitions (DTDs) in Extensible Markup Language (XML).

18. Identify and describe the main steps required to write an XML document.

19. How do you recognize an XML document before it is opened? After it is opened?

20. List the syntax requirements for XML tags.

21. Explain the purpose of the WML language.

22. Briefly describe what Active Server Pages is intended for.

23. What are the components of ASP?

24. Which scripting languages can be used in ASP?

25. Identify and briefly describe the components of JavaScript.

26. What are the three types of statements used in JavaScript?

27. List the rules for structuring JavaScript documents.

28. Identify the various formats a Java document goes through before it is used by the Web browser.

29. Describe what an active document is.

30. Identify the two ways to incorporate an applet into an HTML document.

31. Describe what a servlet is.

32. Identify the components of the Java programming environment.

33. What is the purpose of Java libraries?

34. Explain the concept of inheritance.

35. Identify two of the most popular advantages of Java.

36. Describe the purposes of Perl/CGI and how they compare to Java and Active Server Pages.

37. Identify and describe some of the key issues faced by managers with electronic business development responsibilities.

EXERCISES

1. Outline the similarities and differences between HTML, DHTML, and XML.

2. Which of the languages discussed in the chapter are interpretive languages and which are compiled languages?

3. Create an HTML document with the topic of "the best student organizations to belong to." The Web page should have a heading that reads: Best Student Organizations to Belong To. It should then have three short paragraphs each describing one of the three best student organizations to belong to, and why you think they are the best.

4. A small business is trying to link its Web page to a regional economic development Web site located on the server www.ccc.org (This is a fictional site created for this exercise). The code for the link is: <A HREF= http://www .ccc.org/Main.html>. The link fails to work. What could be some causes of the failure?

5. XYZ Corporation has had a Web page online for a long time. Its pages provide good content about the company and its products, but they are fairly static. As XYZ wants to enter the electronic business world, it wants to include more dynamism in its Web pages. Management would like to have banners, collect customer information online, and provide moving pictures for products, so that customers can see different views. What language should it consider for creating these news pages? Make sure you describe the pros and cons of your solution.

6. I have defined a style sheet that contains definitions for heading levels 1, 2, 3, 4, and 5 (H1, H2, H3, H4, H5). They all use 14 pt. fonts. I have then linked it into my DHTML document. Within the DHTML document, I have used the <STYLE> </STYLE> set of tags to define heading levels 3 and 4 as using 12 pt. fonts. In the text I also used the following lines: <H3 style= "font-size:11.0pt"> and <H2 style= "font-size:11.0pt"> for every H3 and H2 heading. What will my fonts be for headings level 4 (H4), 3 (H3), 2 (H2), and 1 (H1) in my text?

7. The Extra video store keeps information, among other things, about videos, CDs, customers, and employees. It wants to create a dynamic Web site where customers could enter reviews about the videos they have rented, where employees could provide suggestions for videos to rent, and where video and CD products could be displayed on revolving shelves. Create a list of tags that could be used in XML for Extra's Web site.

8. A company has coded the following information:

<A href= "file2.html"> <b> This is a link to file 2 </a> </b>.

What will HTML display on the Web browser? What would XML display on the Web browser? Why?

9. Compare and contrast ASP and Perl/CGI for forms handling.

10. Write the JavaScript statements that would be used to do the following.

(a) Set the price at 5.00.

(b) Verify if the age is greater than 18. If it is, add 5.00 to the price.

(c) If it is not, add 0.50 to the price, but do not let the price reach 8.00.

11. You are writing a Java program. You will create a window that will include buttons, functions, and access to an external database. You want this program to be called TheBest. Write all of the lines of the beginning of your program until you define TheBest.

12. Outline the similarities and differences between Java and JavaScript.

13. ABC Corporation is a small company with limited financial means. It has about five hundred regular customers. They buy from the company once a month on average. The company has decided to collect customer information on its Web site by having customers fill out Quality of Service forms. The forms can be submitted online by pressing a submit button. ABC is wondering which language to use for handling the processing of the forms. Which do you recommend, and why?

14. A couple is starting a small company while keeping their "day" jobs until this small online company really takes off. They both have used computers a lot, but they are not really programmers. They can learn, though. Should they use pre-packaged software? Should they hire someone to develop their Web site? Should they invest in a course and develop their Web site themselves? What other pitfalls should they be wary of before embarking on this adventure?

HANDS-ON PROJECTS

1. Think of a small business venture that you are aware of, or that you would be thinking of starting, which would benefit from an online presence. Identify the main business goals and outline the advantages and disadvantages for this company to go online. You will then prepare a layout of what its Web pages should look like (on paper). This is the design portion. Then you will implement the Web site. Using HTML (after you have gone through Appendix A, which is available online at http://www .wiley.com/college/vanslyke) or an HTML editor, create its Web site. The Web site should contain at least the following:

- Important business information
- Contact information, including an e-mail link
- Links to other relevant sites
- At least two pages and some navigation between the pages
- At least one image per page, but nothing too big

2. Find on the Web the sites of the companies and organizations mentioned in this chapter. Identify what the most up-to-date versions of their software applications or languages are. Identify what major changes these latest versions include.

3. Select a Web page from your university's Web site. Print the source code (either as a screen shot when viewing the source code with your browser; or by using the "file, Save as" function and opening the source file in a text or HTML editor, and then printing). Then walk through the source code and identify what the various portions of the source code are, and what they do. Make sure you also identify whether scripting languages are used or whether outside programs are called from within the HTML code.

4. Compare all of the development environments presented in the chapter with respect to costs of hardware required, software, and personnel. Personnel costs should include programming costs, as well as managing/maintaining the environment.

5. Set up a contest with your colleagues. Select a Web page from your university's Web site that contains at least five pages of code. Save the source code in a separate file, and save all images used as well. Go through the code and eliminate every tag that is not absolutely necessary for the page to still look exactly the same. The student with the most minimal code that has kept the page content and format intact wins.

DISCUSSION POINT

"XML is the most powerful Web language available today, and it is here to stay." Debate this statement, highlighting the pros and the cons of XML and its competing languages.

RELATED WEB SITES

Amazon.com–U.S.: www.amazon.com

Amazon.com–France: www.amazon.fr

Amazon.com–Germany: www.amazon.de

Amazon.com–Japan: www.amazon.co.jp

Amazon.com–United Kingdom: www.amazon.co.uk

Application Server Zone: www.appserver-zone.com

Forrester Research: www.forrester.com

Internet Movie Database: www.imdb.com

Perl.com: www.perl.com

FURTHER READINGS

Active Server Pages Guide page, Microsoft Developers Network library. Microsoft Corporation. http://msdn .microsoft.com /library/default.asp?URL=/library/psdk/iisref/aspguide.htm.

Amazon.com, http://www.amazon.com.

Bullard, Len. "Authoring VRML 1.0." VRML Site Magazine (December 1996): http://www.vrmlsite.com/dec96 /spot1.html.

Burnard, Lou. "What Is SGML and How Does It Help?" *Computers and the Humanities* 29 (1995): 41–50; http://www.hcu.ox.ac.uk/TEI/Papers/EDW25/.

Cover, Robin. "SGML: General Introductions and Overviews." in The XML Cover Pages, http://www.oasis-open.org /cover/general.html, 28 June 1999.

Extensible Markup Language (XML) Activity Statement page. World Wide Web Consortium. http://www .w3.org/XML /Activity.

Extensible Stylesheet Language (XSL) Version 1.0: W3C Recommendation page. World Wide Web Consortium. 15 October 2001: http://www .w3.org/TR/xsl/.

Gibbs, Mark. "Making your Web Pages Active." Network World 16 (12 April 1999): 36.

Goodman, Danny. *Dynamic HTML: The Definitive Reference.* Cambridge, MA: O'Reilly & Associates, 1998.

HTML Tutorial page. World Wide Web Consortium. http://www .w3schools.com/html/default.asp.

Levitt, Jason. "Microsoft's Active Server Pages: A Primer." Information Week 756 (11 October 1999): 82.

Bell, G., A. Parisi, M. Pesce. "The Virtual Reality Modeling Language: Version 1.0 Specification." VRML List Moderator, 1995: http://www.vrml.org/VRML1.0 /vrml10c.html.

XML Tutorial page. World Wide Web Consortium. http://www .w3schools.com/xml/default.asp.

REFERENCES

AMOR, Daniel. 2000. *The e-business (r)evolution.* Upper Saddle River, NJ: Hewlett-Packard Professional Books.

CINTRON, Dave. 1999. *Fast track Web programming: A programmer's guide to mastering Web technologies.* New York: John Wiley & Sons.

MANNING, Harley. 2000. *Why most Web sites fail.* Cambridge, MA: Forrester Research.

MARTIN, Teresa A. 1999. *Project cool guide to XML for Web designers.* New York: John Wiley & Sons.

PASTORE, Michael. 2000. Top e-tailers of February 2000. Internet.com, 13 March 2000: http://cyberatlas.internet .com/markets/retailing/article/0,1323,6061_320111,00 .html.

CHAPTER 6

TELECOMMUNICATION TECHNOLOGIES FOR E-BUSINESS

LEARNING OBJECTIVES

After reading and completing this chapter, you should be able to:

- Understand the basic components and functioning of Electronic Data Interchange (EDI)
- Describe the basic characteristics of wide area networks
- Explain the differences between leased circuit and switched networks
- Describe the basic features of T-carrier lines
- Explain the concept of virtual private networks (VPN)
- Describe the basic features of digital subscriber line (DSL) networks
- Describe the basic features of integrated services digital network (ISDN)
- Describe the basic features of the frame relay network
- Describe the basic features of asynchronous transfer mode (ATM) network
- Explain the concept of value added networks
- Identify the main wireless networks for m-commerce
- Understand the managerial concerns of network selection, network security, and network management

Opening Case: Federal Express Corporation

E-businesses, small and large, make extensive use of courier services to deliver their products directly to each other or to consumers who shop online at their Web sites. Two of the most well known worldwide delivery services are United Parcel Services (UPS) and Federal Express (FedEx). This case describes some of the telecommunication infrastructures used at FedEx.

Federal Express was founded in Little Rock, Arkansas, in 1971. It is a publicly traded company that concentrates on creating end-to-end delivery services and business solutions. Through the use of a superior physical telecommunications network, FedEx delivers more than five million packages or letters every day. It also uses a powerful virtual network to handle more than one hundred million electronic transactions daily.

Federal Express Corporation is a U.S.$20 billion business made up of several units: FedEx Express, FedEx Ground, FedEx Custom Critical, FedEx Trade Networks, and

FedEx Freight (see Table 6-1). It has become such a successful company that the name of the company is often used in the English language as a verb that means to send something via courier (e.g., "I will fedex this to you tonight").

Information Technology at FedEx

FedEx has an information technology budget of more than U.S.$1.5 billion per year. Technology is one of the three core assets of the company (along with their transportation infrastructure and human resources). Every FedEx employee, from package couriers to data analysts, has some interaction with technology. As such, the company is often regarded as one of today's leading edge information technology companies (Wetherbe 1996). The success of FedEx is based on rapid delivery services, combined with competitive pricing and value-added technology. The company claims to be able to deliver packages in more than 210 countries within twenty-four to forty-eight hours. In order to achieve this success, the company had to rely heavily on technology, such as bar code scanning and real time tracking. The company also uses a number of software applications and devices to optimize its delivery services.

FedEx revolutionized the overnight package delivery business when it introduced the ability to track packages, and to complete transactions over the Internet using the company's proprietary InterNetShip application. One technology that the company introduced to keep track of vital routing and tracking information is the SuperTracker, also called the micro-wand. The SuperTracker is a handheld device used by Federal Express couriers that scans information from a bar-code label affixed to each package. Digitally Assisted Dispatch System (DADS) terminals are installed in each FedEx van or truck to upload data information for every package delivered or picked up. Data is exchanged by connecting

Table 6-1 Federal Express Corporation

Name	Headquarters	Purpose
FedEx Express Corporation	Memphis, Tennessee	World's largest express transportation company; connects markets in more than two hundred countries with global transportation network
FedEx Ground	Pittsburgh, Pennsylvania	Specializes in small-package shipping; second largest provider of ground small package delivery services in the United States; includes a new service called FedEx Home Delivery
FedEx Custom Critical	Akron, Ohio	Specializes in non-stop door-to-door delivery of special, time-specific critical shipments within the United States, Canada, and Europe
FedEx Trade Networks Inc.	Memphis, Tennessee	Offers full service brokerage trade consulting and information technology, which fully integrates regulatory compliance for imports and exports, document preparation, and archiving; provides e-clearance for electronic, quick customs clearance
FedEx Freight	San Jose, California	Provider of next and second day delivery in the continental United States

the SuperTracker to the DADS terminal. The package information is then communicated directly from the truck to the centrally located tracking system via FedEx owned satellites. DADS terminals and the FedEx satellites are the core of FedEx's private wireless data network. The combined use of the SuperTracker, DADS terminals, and satellite connections allows FedEx to know where all packages are at all times. FedEx customers also benefit from this information since the company has created a Web site for customers to track their own packages online, a feature that reassures many customers about the effectiveness of the delivery service. In addition, customers, large and small, also have the ability to produce their own shipping labels online. Once completed, FedEx receives an electronic notification to pick up the package.

In addition to using the Internet to allow customers to track their packages, FedEx takes advantage of Internet technologies in their complex company-wide intranet system available to all FedEx personnel worldwide. It provides access to important documentation and package tracking information. The company also offers software decision support tools and communication tools on the intranet. The intranet is connected to an outside network, allowing electronic communications between employees and customers.

M-commerce

The previous paragraphs only give a high-level overview of some of the technologies used at FedEx. The company prides itself in being on the leading edge of information technology use in the transportation, information, and logistics business. As a result, it is not surprising that FedEx is one of the leading companies in using **mobile commerce,** or **m-commerce,** a topic that we will discuss in more depth in this chapter. In March 2001, FedEx announced its partnership with w-Technologies to extend its wireless networks beyond the vans and trucks to the couriers themselves. In other words, the wireless network used by the company to track packages is extended to the handheld devices used by the couriers. They enable the couriers to provide tracking information, e-mail tracking results, or even get directions to FedEx depots. For example, couriers are able to scan packages at the door so that tracking data is entered into the system sooner, and so they can access the company's information network to answer customers' questions immediately.

The new wireless connectivity augments the existing capabilities of the DADS wireless network previously discussed. This network, however, is optimized for vehicle communications. The company therefore contemplates newer public wireless networks, such as **2.5G** and **3G networks,** to implement its future wireless applications. The company is also considering **Bluetooth** technology for some of its new wireless applications, such as improving the communication between SuperTrackers and DADS terminals, or between terminals and label printing equipment in the FedEx trucks and vans. Today, newer terminals installed in the trucks can send data to the central tracking system in several ways, including a telecommunication company's wireless network, a satellite network (in areas where coverage is spotty), or via a Spectrum24 wireless LAN when the trucks are at depots.

FedEx also provides wearable computers that can be used by employees loading packages at central facilities to scan packages as they move from facility to facility. Another wireless effort is FedEx's agreement with AvantGo, announced in April 2001, to augment its Web site with wireless applications to allow customers to use their wireless devices, such as smart phones, to track their FedEx packages while away from their home or office computers. These are just some of the examples of new infrastructures that FedEx implements and constantly upgrades to take full advantage of wireless networks.

Summary

FedEx is a leading-edge company in the use of information technology to support its business. As a matter of fact, the company could not exist today without its technological infrastructure. The company always strives to use more advanced technologies to improve its delivery and service to customers, and wireless networking has become one of its main network infrastructures. New applications will continue to be evaluated by the company to retain its leading edge, such as voice recognition. How can this improve their already existing advanced wireless network? What other leading edge telecommunication networks could be advantageous for this company? What is the next step for this company to maintain a competitive advantage over other courier services?

INTRODUCTION

Electronic business is not limited to Web-based shopping. In fact, the business-to-consumer market is not the largest of the e-commerce segments in terms of transaction values and revenues. As seen in Chapter 2, business-to-business electronic commerce is the largest segment. Some of these transactions between companies are conducted via the Internet, but a large portion are conducted using other telecommunication networks. This chapter describes the most common of these telecommunication networks, which can be used to interconnect organizations or to connect individuals to organizations for conducting electronic commerce transactions.

Most of the telecommunication networks described in this chapter fall into the wide area network (WAN) category. A wide area network (WAN) is a network of computers that spans a large geographic area. It is important to realize that these networks form the core of the telecommunication structures available to today's organizations, not just for electronic commerce but also for all electronically supported business functions that need information exchanges. Irrespective of whether a company decides to venture into electronic business applications or not, it will most likely need some sort of telecommunication backbone to conduct its business in today's global economy. A telecommunication backbone is the core structure that is used to transmit digital and voice data from one location to another. Several of these networks will be discussed in this chapter, including wireless networks for electronic commerce (otherwise known as m-commerce for mobile commerce). The chapter concludes with three very important managerial issues: network selection, network management, and network security.

NON–WEB-BASED E-BUSINESS

Chapter 4 presented the Internet as a network that can be used for e-business, and particularly for Web-based e-business. On the other hand, a large number of e-business transactions are conducted over non–Internet-based networks, particularly for the business-to-business segment. The first of these non–Internet-based infrastructures that truly connected organizations for conducting business transactions electronically was Electronic Data Interchange (EDI).

Electronic Data Interchange (EDI)

Electronic Data Interchange (EDI) involves direct computer-to-computer exchange of information between companies using a standard format. The standard format allows companies to perform very specific business functions with one another, such as billing, purchasing, payments, and more. EDI is the precursor of what is now termed business-to-business electronic commerce. The first EDI systems were implemented decades ago in an effort to lower transaction costs between business partners. Early adopters of EDI believed it would give them significant competitive advantages. For some, those advantages were indeed realized.

Figure 6-1 shows a typical (but simplified) EDI arrangement in which all electronic documents are transferred via telecommunication networks. There could be four different networks used in this exchange: one between the buyer and supplier, one between the supplier and its bank, one between the buyer and its bank, and one between the two banks. Conversely, all partners might be connected to the same network. All of the documents are electronic, and there is no need to reenter information into the computerized systems at any point in the communications. The electronic exchanges illustrated in Figure 6-1 represent a simplified set of transactions that would occur between two companies and their

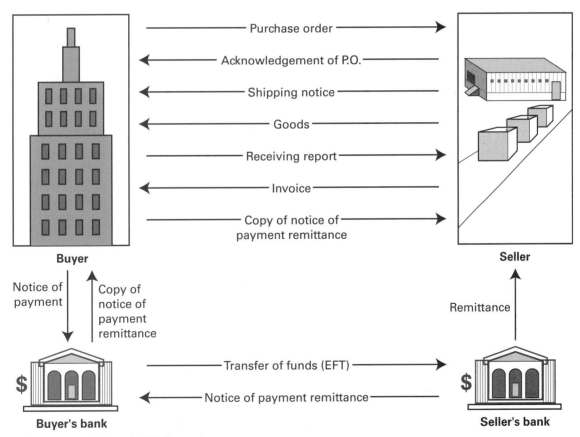

FIGURE 6-1 A Simple EDI Example

banks for one single sale. Typically, however, multiple sales occur between two companies. In addition, other transactions, such as returns and back orders, need to occur during the sales process. Furthermore, banks may exchange several notices with their clients. As you can see, numerous transactions occur when companies do business together, and EDI allows them to save time and costs by performing these exchanges electronically.

Components of EDI

There are several components required for EDI transactions to occur between two trading partners. These include the EDI software needed to translate the documents from the companies' own formats to standardized formats, a telecommunication network, and legal agreements.

Software Each company has internal systems that produce purchase orders, invoices, and other traditional business documents. These documents follow the format of the proprietary or acquired applications that the company uses. This format, of course, might be completely different than the format used by other trading partners. To perform an EDI transaction, therefore, a number of processes must occur. For example, in Figure 6-1, the data are first extracted from one of the computer systems (e.g., a purchase order on the buyer's system). The data are then translated into a transmittable EDI standard format using an EDI translation software. This is called the *outbound transformation.* The message is then transmitted. On the receiving computer (e.g., the seller's system), the message is translated from the standard EDI format into the computer format of the seller's application by another EDI translation program. This is called the *inbound transformation.* Finally, the data are downloaded into the seller's application. This set of processes must occur for every document exchanged. Several value added networks (discussed in a later section) provide software programs to perform these translations for companies that subscribe to their networks. Otherwise, companies must own EDI translation software that works with their computing environment.

Standards We have mentioned several times that EDI uses a standard format. Why is this needed, and what is that format? Because companies do not use the same application software to process their internal data, documents sent in a proprietary format would be useless on other companies' systems, since the documents would not be understood by these companies' applications. Therefore, for the documents to be exchanged seamlessly between companies, a standard format needed to be designed. In North America, the ANSI ASC X12 standard is used to conduct most EDI transactions. This standard (set of specifications for format and exchange of documents) was originally developed by large corporations, and is now under the control of the American National Standards Institute (ANSI) and the Accredited Standards Committee (ASC). For example, ANSI ASC X12 would specify that a bill of sale must contain specific fields with specific characteristics. Following the same rules on both sides of the transaction allows two systems to communicate with each other. To do this, software is implemented to translate each system's document characteristics into the EDI standard. Meanwhile, in Europe, another standard, called EDIFACT, was developed by the United Nations. There are other EDI standards in existence, including WINS and TDCC, but they are less popular and less widely used than X12 and EDIFACT. Differences exist between worldwide standards, which require companies to have even more translation software. This can be prohibitively expensive. Efforts are being made to develop a standard that would merge ANSI ASC X12 and EDIFACT into one international standard.

Telecommunication Network Many large companies often choose to develop their own private networks to conduct EDI transactions with their main partners. These wide area networks can be implemented using dedicated lines or switched networks. We will cover those in the next section of the chapter. This approach tends to be costly and complex, but there are substantial savings in transaction costs to be achieved. For many small and medium enterprises, however, it is often simpler and more cost effective to use value added networks (VANs) to conduct their EDI transactions, particularly if they have to connect to multiple trading partners. Value added networks are wide area networks provided by common carriers or information systems providers that provide not only the underlying wide area network, but also additional services, such as **store-and-forward messaging, protocol conversion, speed translating,** data handling, and **packet assembly and disassembly.** Additional examples of services offered by VANs to companies willing or able to pay for them include audit trails, backups, and extra security. By providing these services, VANs allow companies with different (incompatible) systems to communicate.

An example of a popular EDI service is mailboxes maintained by a VAN. Companies can leave their transactions stored on the VAN's server until they are ready to retrieve them. This way, companies can process batches of transactions at one time for greater efficiency. For example, an e-business can retrieve accumulated orders every hour, instead of one by one, for processing. Similarly, a person who manages a small online retail store and also holds a day job can leave transactions on the VAN's server and process them during her lunch hour or after work. (It would be very difficult to run a business this way, but many owners of small dot-coms have done this.) With the advent of the Internet as a communication platform for business, connection costs to access VANs have been reduced substantially, allowing a growing number of smaller firms to participate in EDI. We will discuss VANs in more depth later in this chapter.

Legal Agreements Last, but not least, companies engaging in EDI transactions must sign a number of legal agreements determining their responsibilities, level of information sharing, and a host of other contracting arrangements that bind their trading relationship.

Benefits and Weaknesses of EDI

Today, many companies in a variety of industries conduct EDI transactions to reap some of the potential benefits EDI offers. By allowing transactions to be standardized and to be conducted electronically (without the need to recopy or reenter information), EDI offers a number of strategic, operational, and opportunity benefits, which are summarized in Table 6-2. Most benefits reported by companies center on corporate efficiency, but there are also competitive advantage benefits that can be achieved through lower costs, tighter links to customers, or increased product differentiation. Some estimates suggest that 70 percent of all computer input has previously been an output of another computer. Reducing reentry of such data reduces potential sources of errors. Some companies also estimate that an electronic transaction costs them one-tenth the cost of handling and processing a paper-based transaction (The ABC of EDI 2000). Other benefits include reduced lead time between order placement and product receipt, reduced lead time in payment receipt, and increased inventory supply and claim processing information for customers.

EDI is not a perfect system for everyone. As previously discussed, the costs of implementation can be very high. To implement an EDI system, hardware and software must be purchased, installed, and maintained, and connection fees to a telecommunication system or a VAN

Table 6-2 Some Benefits of EDI

Strategic Benefits

- Faster billing cycle
- Ability to adopt new business processes, such as just-in-time manufacturing techniques
- Ability to win new business or retain existing customers due to business efficiency
- Ability to respond quickly to highly competitive new market entrants

Operational Benefits

- Reduced costs (paper and processing costs)
- Improved cash flow (with electronic invoice and payment)
- Error reduction
- Acknowledged receipt

Opportunity Benefits

- Enhanced image
- Competitive edge
- Improved corporate trading relationships

Source: The ABC of EDI page, Welsh Development Agency, 2000: http://www.edi.wales.org/feature4.htm.

must be paid. EDI partnerships were often started by large companies that had captive sets of suppliers. For example, a large food chain decided to implement EDI in collaboration with a large bank, and required its suppliers to use EDI to transact with it. Those wishing to keep or gain this large customer needed to conduct their transactions via EDI, even though the costs might have been prohibitive for them. For the large players with numerous transactions conducted online, these costs are quickly repaid, but for those with low volumes of transactions, it may take a long time to recover these implementation costs.

The inflexible structure of EDI can also make it difficult to deal with international transactions. For example, exchanging documents with different currencies or different types of postal codes requires that a large number of blank spaces be allotted into the standard to allow for these differences (e.g., a Canadian company that would allocate six spaces for postal codes (with a format of A1A 1A1) actually has to allocate ten spaces if it wants to do business in the United States (where zip codes have the format of 11111-1111)). Finally, an important difficulty associated with EDI that managers often realize only after they have started to implement it is the integration of EDI software with their (often outdated) internal systems, a difficulty often greater than the connections and translations required for communications with their partners.

Traditional EDI versus Business-to-Business Systems

Over the years, EDI evolved from a one-to-one system between two trading partners to a multiple partner environment. Every partner joins a trading network to reap some of the numerous rewards of EDI. In this multi-partner environment, EDI allows easy transmission of documents across systems that are incompatible in hardware and software. However, this communication requires that documents be in a very strict standard format. This is both an advantage and a disadvantage of EDI systems. Standardizing the format allows for fast processing and support for the multiple environments. It also allows the documents that are exchanged to always be unambiguous. However, today companies want to exchange more and more electronic documents for an ever-growing number of business processes, and many companies want to make use of the less expensive Internet for these transactions. To replace the inflexible EDI formats and conduct less structured (but by no means unstructured) transactions, many companies have started to implement new business-to-business systems. XML is increasingly used to conduct these B2B document exchanges among multiple partners.

As discussed in Chapter 5, XML offers some standard formats for documents, but it is very flexible. One of the big problems with B2B exchanges using XML is the necessary agreement regarding names and coding terms. For example, if one company decides to code its standardized documents in XML using the term *client* (<CLIENT> Mr. Jones </CLIENT>) but its trading partner uses the term *customer* (<CUSTOMER> Mr. Jones </CUSTOMER>), their respective systems won't be able to understand each other (e.g., the first company's system wouldn't find any client information in the second company's document). Resolving those semantic issues is a major task when several trading partners are trying to conduct transactions together. This is why industries develop their own XML standards, such as ebXML (E-business XML), to standardize the terms to be used by B2B trading partners. Hence, we are going back to standardized formats, but avoiding (it is hoped) the level of structure that made EDI more restrictive. Again, however, it is the large players in the market that tend to force their semantics on the smaller players.

Decision Point

An e-business wishing to conduct electronic transactions with its business partners must decide whether to use traditional EDI systems or newer business-to-business systems. The following decision chart can help them in this decision process.

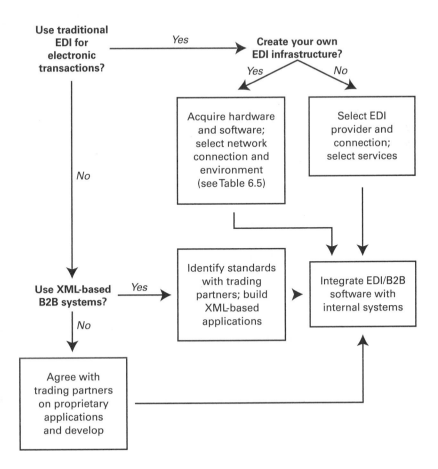

WIDE AREA NETWORKS

Wide area networks (WANs) provide connections over a large geographic area, such as a city, state, province, county, country, or even several countries worldwide. Building a wide area network is a major task, and most companies rely instead on renting, subscribing, or leasing WAN services from a telecommunications company (common carrier) or a specialized information systems provider. There are numerous WANs available commercially in the world. Some WANs follow the same standards worldwide, but most have some differences in how they are implemented, depending on the region of the world where they exist. All networks, however, fall into two broad categories: **dedicated circuit networks** and **switched networks.**

Dedicated Circuit versus Switched Networks

One of the first decisions to make when a company is choosing a network for e-business implementation is the type of connection it wants. If it wants to establish a network between specific locations where there will be a constant flow of transactions, either within the company or with a trading partner, it can consider dedicated circuit lines, which provide permanent connections between two locations. An organization can lease such lines from a telephone company (telco), or build its own dedicated circuit (e.g., install a line between two buildings, assuming the company owns the land in between or gets permission). The other option is to use a switched network, which allows companies to pay for **access points** to the network and/or for the traffic they generate on the network. These networks are maintained by telcos or other providers, and are shared by many users (subscribers). Alternatively, a company can build its own network, requiring it to install **switching equipment** and software, and acquire connections for the communication between this equipment.

Dedicated Circuits

When a telecommunications carrier establishes an end-to-end connection between two customers (such as your company and a service provider), they are said to establish a **circuit.** It is important to realize that establishing a connection between a business, say in Atlanta, and its business partner, say in London, England, requires the use of multiple transmission media, switches, routers, and other devices. Nevertheless, if a circuit is leased from a carrier, the subscriber pays for the end-to-end connection irrespective of what devices are being used in between. This is the main difference between leasing or buying a network connection from a provider, and establishing your own. Few companies, only the very large ones, actually establish their own complete networks since they have to acquire lines, install switching equipment and numerous other devices and software, and, most importantly, spend a lot on personnel who implement and maintain the operation of the network. Most firms usually have a combination of some internal networks and some use of a carrier's or service provider's network. When a company leases a dedicated line, it pays for the line whether it is fully used all the time or not.

Digital and Analog Dedicated Circuits

Circuits are the actual line connections used to build networks. Circuits can be **analog** (or **voice-grade**) or digital. Table 6-3 shows the progression of speed for various circuits.

Table 6-3 Basic Circuits and Speeds

	Line	Speeds
Analog	Voice-grade	2.4 to 56 Kbps
Digital	64 Kbps circuit	64 Kbps
	T-carrier	
	T-1	1.544 Mbps
	T-3	44.700 Mbps
	T-4	274.176 Mbps
	E-carrier	
	E-1	2.048 Mbps
	E-3	34.400 Mbps
	Higher E-carrier available	
	Fractional T-1	128 Kbps
		256 Kbps
		384 Kbps
		768 Kbps
	SONET	
	OC1	51.840 Mbps
	OC3	156.000 Mbps
	Higher SONET networks available to 9.952 Gbps	

Typically, analog circuits are not used for large scale e-business since they are the slowest and the most prone to errors. However, Web-based e-businesses must realize that many consumers accessing their Web sites have only analog lines at home. These lines can run at a maximum speed of 56,000 bits per seconds, or 56 Kbps. Because analog lines are so slow, e-businesses must try to make their Web sites' response times better, for example by limiting the number of large size images, or by offering text-only pages.

There are several levels of digital circuits available, from simple 64 Kbps lines to multi-gigabit per second (Gbps) lines (trillions of bits per second). The most commonly used circuits for medium- to large-scale e-business are **T-carriers** (also called digital service lines) in North America and **E-carriers** in Europe. A T-1 circuit, for example, runs at 1.544 Mbps (millions of bits per second). The highest speed digital lines that exist today are the **SONET (synchronous optical network)** circuits. SONET is the wide area network name, and the speeds are rated as **optical carrier (OC)** in North America, going from 51.84 Mbps to 9.952 Gbps. There is an international version of SONET called **Synchronous Digital Hierarchy (SDH).**

Of course, the speeds achievable by the various types of circuits depend on the medium used. For example, SONET lines can only be implemented on fiber optic cables. Voice-grade lines, conversely, use copper wires. Higher speed lines typically require a better medium (fiber optic cabling is the fastest medium). Another concept that influences speeds achievable is **multiplexing.** Multiplexing is the capability of including several communication channels on one medium—having ten computers send data simultaneously over one wire, for example. T-carrier lines use multiplexing. For example, the T-1 circuit multiplexes twenty-four channels (of 64 Kbps) on one line. The E-carrier multiplexes thirty channels per line. The fact that these lines are multiplexed allows carriers to sell only parts of the line in what are called fractional T-carrier services. Companies that cannot afford a full T-1, for example, could lease 384 Kbps lines. When several circuits are leased or established, a company is said to have a network.

Virtual Private Network

A **virtual private network** (VPN) is a connection over a public network that a company uses for its internal purposes. The network uses encryption to secure information as it passes from one gateway to another. Instead of simply leasing lines between two sites and managing the network of lines itself, a company may decide that all it wants to do is use a network without having to maintain it. This is the role of the virtual private network. The telecommunication carrier from which the VPN is leased handles all maintenance on the network, freeing the company to focus on its e-business. A recent trend in VPNs is to use the Internet as the underlying network for communication between user sites. The network appears to be private to the users even though the Internet serves as the **backbone.** The main advantage of using such a VPN is lower costs. The disadvantages, however, are worth considering. Not only is the use of the Internet for company traffic a security risk, but also the overall traffic on the Internet is unpredictable. Other popular infrastructures for VPNs include **ATM** and **frame relay** networks, which will be described in the next section. The cost of a VPN is a function of the number of users that need access to the network, which can range from forty to forty thousand; the features selected; and the support offered by the VPN provider.

Digital Subscriber Line (DSL)

Telecommunication companies continuously try to develop higher speed networks. The growth of the Internet, the Web, and now Web-based e-business furthers this need for high speed networks. While companies can afford to acquire permanent connections at high speeds (such as T-1) for their business, users connecting from their home (or small businesses that use home offices) need something faster than the 56 Kbps leased lines available but at a reasonable cost. In response to this market requirement, telecommunication companies have designed a new modem technology to use existing twisted-pair cables that are wired to most people's homes for high-speed digital links. Thus was created **asymmetric digital subscriber lines (ADSL),** also simply called **digital subscriber lines (DSL).**

There are actually a number of different types of DSL networks, including **HDSL (high rate DSL), VDSL (very high speed DSL), RADSL (rate adaptive DSL),** ADSL, and others. However when individuals talk about DSL, they usually mean ADSL, which is an asymmetrical network. This means the speeds are different for **upstream communication** than for **downstream communication.** Upstream communication is from the user's home to the service provider. Downstream communication is from the provider to the user's home. The maximum speeds achievable with DSL are 6 Mbps downstream and 640 Kbps upstream. The actual rates depend on the distance between the home and the service provider, how much of the network uses copper wires, the type of wires, the type of equipment used, and other error potentials. Why is downstream communication faster, and why is that important? DSL is targeted to Internet users. As a user browses the Web, pages that contain text, images, and programs (such as Java applets) are downloaded. This requires higher speeds because more data need to be transferred (more bits). When the user requests a page, however, the data that is sent from the user's computer to the provider is only a GET request, which contains several lines of text. This requires much less speed, as only a few kilobytes of information are transmitted.

Why can you achieve higher downstream speeds? One of the important components of a transmission network is the transmitting equipment. Service providers have high-end equipment that can generate stronger signals than the equipment the user would have at home. This is part of the reason they can generate higher speeds for downstream signals. To acquire a DSL service, the user must install a DSL modem and pay the line fee. The main advantages of DSL are the permanent connection that is established to the Internet (similar to dedicated leased lines) and the higher speed of transfers. The disadvantages of DSL include competing standards (with the different types of DSL available) and the lack of availability outside most urban areas. The biggest competitor to DSL for the consumer market is **cable modems,** which make use of cable television connections. For small e-businesses, T-carrier or ISDN (discussed next) tend to be more popular options.

Switched Networks

When a company creates a network using dedicated circuits, it has to determine exactly which two points will be connected. With the changing world of e-business, it may be difficult to have a fixed number of locations that need to access each other. For example, a small e-business owner may design his business so that it is completely run on the Web, allowing him to travel anywhere and still run the business. For companies needing such flexibility, subscribing to a switched network may be the best connectivity solution. A switched network allows the company to send data back and forth between multiple locations without the need to establish direct connections between those locations. Instead, the company needs to provide or acquire connections between their offices and "the network."

Switched networks are found in two categories: **packet-switched** and **circuit-switched** networks. The most common circuit-switched network commercially available to companies for e-business or other telecommunication applications is **ISDN (integrated services digital network),** while the most common commercially available packet-switched networks include frame relay and ATM (asynchronous transfer mode). An older network called X.25 is still available, but it reaches a maximum speed of 64 Kbps. Another newer service called SMDS (switched multimegabit data service) is fast, but generally too expensive and not yet widely accepted. These last two networks are therefore not discussed in this chapter.

Integrated Services Digital Network (ISDN)

Integrated services digital network (ISDN), as its name implies, is an all-digital network. It uses twisted-pair copper cables wired to the homes of consumers and to businesses. The basic premise of ISDN, when it was first launched many years back, was that it would be "the" network to homes, which would carry voice, data, and video signals together. It was very slow to be accepted, however, because upgrades to equipment and lines were necessary. As a result, new competing technologies were being developed. While still marketed and used today, these other alternatives provide major competition to ISDN in the American marketplace, and further hinder its growth. In Europe, deployment of ISDN was a lot more successful.

ISDN works by providing multiple channels in one medium (the cable) using multiplexing techniques. The basic rate ISDN (called **ISDN-BRI)** offers two channels at 64 Kbps (called B channels) and one 16 Kbps channel (called the D channel) for control information. Consumers who use ISDN in their homes would typically acquire this type of ISDN. For commercial use, ISDN also offers a primary rate interface **(ISDN-PRI),** which provides twenty-four to thirty channels at 64 Kbps each (resulting in speeds of up to 1.544 Mbps or 2.048 Mbps). These ISDN networks (basic rate and primary) are called **narrowband ISDN,** or simply ISDN. A newer generation of ISDN was created using broadband technology and is called **BISDN or broadband ISDN.** Broadband technology allows multiple channels of communications on the one medium at varying speeds (instead of fixed speeds like 64 Kbps). This, again, is done using multiplexing techniques.

Frame Relay

Frame relay is a second-generation packet-switched technology, replacing the older X.25 networks. Frame relay offers speeds from 56 Kbps to 44.736 Mbps. It is a very good alternative to T-1 service between multiple sites since its costs are much lower. This is due to the fact that every location only needs to be connected to the frame relay network, not to all of a company's other locations, to be able to transmit to any location. For example, a company can replace ten lines connecting their five sites with frame relay access for each site (see Figure 6-2). Each line connecting to the frame relay network is typically a local connection (instead of expensive long distance line connections). The company still has to pay for the five lines to the access point (called **point of presence,** or **POP),** but these five local lines probably cost much less than the ten long distance lines needed previously to connect all sites to one another.

The frame relay network takes the incoming **packets** (unit of data in which messages are split up for transmission over the network) and converts them into its own structure for transmission over the network. At the other end of the frame relay network (the receiving access point), the packets are reconverted into the data structure of the company's system. One of the characteristics of frame relay is that the network does not perform error control during the transmission. Error control is only performed at both ends of the network, allowing frame relay networks to achieve high transmission speeds. Companies can negotiate with carriers on the level of frame relay service they wish to acquire. They agree on a **committed information rate (CIR),** which is the guaranteed speed provided on the circuit. Typical speed packages for CIR are 56 Kbps, 128 Kbps, 256 Kbps, 1.544 Mbps, 2.058 Mbps, and 45 Mbps. A **maximum allowable rate (MAR)** can also be negotiated, which is the maximum speed that the network will try to provide if it has the available capacity. This leads to an important feature of frame relay—support for **data bursts.** Data bursts are peaks of network traffic that occur at certain points in time, which are above the regular rate of traffic agreed to and/or generated by the user. Finally, it should be noted that large companies can build their own frame relay networks by installing frame relay switches and software and providing connections between them. This requires the company to also operate and maintain the network.

Asynchronous Transfer Mode (ATM)

Asynchronous transfer mode (ATM) is also a packet-switched network, so its functioning is similar to frame relay. One of the main advantages of ATM is that there are various speeds available, and a company can negotiate the particular speeds that it needs for its business operations. The main differences between ATM and frame relay, besides the technical functioning of the network, is that ATM offers much greater speeds than frame relay, but at greater costs. In fact, the lowest speeds of ATM networks start at the higher end of the frame relay networks, making the two networks very complementary. ATM transmission speeds vary between 25 Mbps and 2.46 Gbps. Smaller e-businesses will tend to use frame relay, while larger e-businesses might need the speeds of ATM. Another important feature of ATM is its excellent support of data bursts (peaks of network traffic), like frame relay.

When negotiating ATM speeds, there are four grades of services that the company can consider:

- **Constant bit rate**—The provider guarantees a transmission rate and makes sure that users do not exceed that rate.

- **Variable bit rate**—The provider and the company agree on a normal usage rate and a faster burst rate for unexpected high volume transfers.

- **Available bit rate**—The provider guarantees a minimum capacity and will support bursts when it has available capacity to do so.

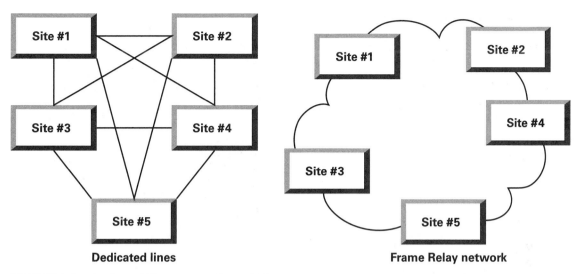

FIGURE 6-2   Dedicated Lines versus Frame Relay

- **Unspecified bit rate**—The provider does not guarantee a specific rate and will transmit all it can within its available capacity.

Companies can also negotiate a quality of service contract and assign priorities to messages. While the speeds stated above are the minimum and maximum speeds that ATM can provide, the most common speeds in use commercially today for ATM are 156 Mbps and 622 Mbps. The flexibility or **scalability** of ATM, however, allows companies to change (increase or decrease) their speed requirements as needed (depending on the agreement with the service provider). While some consider ATM to still be quite costly, we should see increased use of this network in coming years as its cost falls and its cost structure becomes even more flexible. A (large) company that wishes to operate its own ATM network can build it with the proper hardware and software. It would be quite expensive to do so, but it is becoming a popular alternative to dedicated circuits for creating virtual private networks.

The Internet

This chapter focuses on telecommunication systems for e-business. It must be noted that the Internet is also a wide area network composed of numerous WANs and LANs that are interconnected worldwide. We described in Chapter 4 how the Internet suffers from a few major weaknesses when it is considered for business-to-business electronic commerce. The main weakness we discussed is security (to be covered in Chapter 10). Another issue for companies is the reliability of the network. Companies want to be able to control their networks if their businesses depend on it. In using the Internet it is very hard to hold one party accountable for the whole network. For example, banks would not consider using the Internet as a backbone to transfer funds between their ATMs (automated teller machines) and their offices. Yet many companies do consider the Internet as an alternative connectivity option to the WANs discussed in this chapter.

Decision Point

We have discussed a number of different wide area networks. An e-business that decides to use a wide area network to connect its offices, or to connect to its business partners (for B2B applications), must choose between the different types of connections available. The chart below can help managers in this decision process.

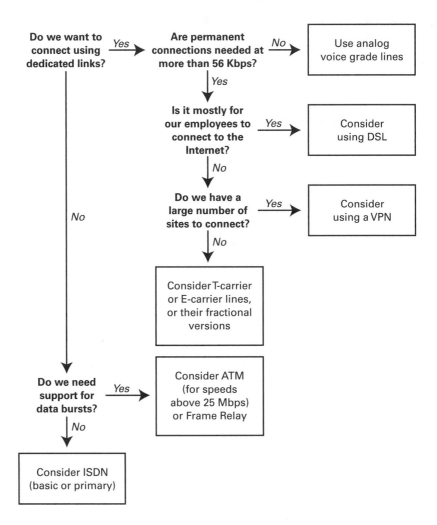

VALUE ADDED NETWORKS

Value added networks (VANs) are a particular type of wide area network that provide services in addition to the underlying telecommunication system (which is typically a packet switched network). Recall that VANs are the primary networks used for Electronic Data Interchange (EDI). Some of the features and functions a company can request in selecting a VAN include Internet connections, translation and conversion software, communication services, and consulting services. A more extensive list of features and functions is presented in Table 6-4.

Table 6-4 Some Typical VAN Features

VAN Feature	Description
Consulting services	Provides consulting services to the VAN subscribers for technical support, implementation, or evaluation of information systems services
EDI to e-mail	Provides software on the VAN to send EDI documents to electronic mail formats; e-mail responses are then converted back to the EDI format required by the subscriber's system
EDI to FAX	Provides software on the VAN to send EDI documents to fax machines; fax responses are then converted back to the EDI format required by the subscriber's system
FTP connection	Allows the use of the FTP protocol (see Chapter 6) on the VAN
Help desk services	Provides a help desk the VAN subscriber can call for technical and user support
Implementation services	Provides help in implementing the EDI system for the VAN subscriber
Internet browsing	Allows members connected to the VAN to surf the Internet
Syntax compliance checking	Performs checks on the syntax of EDI documents sent on the VAN
Translation software	Provides software on the VAN that performs translation between the company's system data and the EDI format selected
VAN interconnects	Provides a service to connect to other VANs

Source: CAMP Inc., http://ectools.camp.org/ecedi/vandir_main.html. [Author: This address is no longer valid.]

An example of how a VAN can be used is presented in Figure 6-3. In this case, a company connects to the VAN to transact with different business partners, and this is done seamlessly, even if each of the partners has a different computing environment.

VAN providers charge fees for the services they provide. While some services can be bundled together for pricing purposes, using VANs tends to be more expensive overall than simply acquiring or leasing a communication link (WAN) for which no services are provided besides the agreed upon transmission rates (and quality of service). However, when a company considers that it does not have to pay for specialized network personnel, maintenance of the network, and individual connections to each one of its business partners, a VAN can represent substantial savings. The VAN provider also handles technical issues. An additional benefit is that many VAN providers are interconnected today, allowing a company on one VAN to transact with a company on a different VAN. Some of the most important benefits of using a VAN instead of direct connections or private networks between trading partners are outlined in Table 6-5.

VAN Providers

There are a large number of VAN providers worldwide. Several providers offer services locally in their respective countries. Others offer international data exchange services and have a presence in most industrial countries worldwide. Some of the most well known international VAN providers include EDS and GE Global eXchange Services. Each country, however, has its own set of leaders. In the United Kingdom, for example, TRADANET is one of the most widely used VANs (The ABC of EDI 2000). In the United States, leaders can also be found in the telecommunication companies, such as Bell Global Solutions, AT&T, or MCI Telecommunication Corporation. However, there are numerous providers, large and small, and some have market specializations (such as

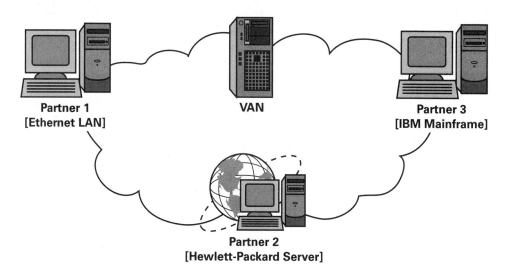

FIGURE 6-3 VAN Connection to Several Trading Partners

the insurance business). A search for "value added networks" in a Web search engine will result in an extensive listing of several such providers.

How much would a VAN connection cost? Prices vary substantially and might be out of date by the time you read this book. However, just for illustrative purposes, one company, CTI Communications, charged the following fees in the United States at the beginning of 2001: U.S.$25.00 per month for an analog interface (a dialup connection to the VAN), plus U.S.$5.00 per Megabyte of data sent/received. In addition, the initial one-time software setup fee for a Microsoft Windows-type interface was U.S.$995.00. These costs are very reasonable, but it must be remembered that these are for dialup connections at 28,000 or 56,000 bits per second. Digital lines, such as ISDN, can also be used, but for a different fee.

Other considerations in selecting a VAN include whether the VAN provides services for doing business with the government, what EDI standard is supported, what VANs the company's trading partners use, and of course, cost and connection alternatives. VANs can charge by the amount of connection time used, or by the amount of data sent, or both, or by any other payment scheme they may negotiate with individual companies.

WIRELESS NETWORKS AND M-COMMERCE

One of the areas of e-commerce that is rapidly growing is m-commerce, or mobile commerce. The idea of m-commerce is fairly simple—offer users the potential to conduct business transactions wherever they are using a wireless network. When people talk about m-commerce, however, they include a variety of nontransaction functions. Basically, any services that can be accessed using wireless handheld devices fit into this category. This includes handheld devices used to browse the Web, as well as handheld devices used by mobile workers in need of wireless connections to their offices. The growth of m-commerce can be attributed to a number of factors, such as the development of newer and smaller technologies, more mobile populations worldwide with connection

Table 6-5 Some Benefits of VANs

- One connection to many partners
- Most computer hardware supported
- Most operating system software supported
- Most protocols supported
- Interconnection between VANs
- Expertise on recent EDI technologies and standards
- Multiple data formats supported
- Technical support provided
- Value added component (additional services provided)

needs, deregulation of many telecommunication markets, and the fact that implementing wireless media is often cheaper than implementing wired networks in countries where such networks need upgrading.

The expectations for m-commerce are very high, but slow to materialize in certain markets, particularly in the United States. There are millions of users in Japan and some Scandinavian countries, such as Finland (home of the Nokia corporation) who already use their cellular phones to buy goods and services and access Web information services. Figure 6-4 shows estimated revenues for the global m-commerce market in the early twenty-first century. It is clear that Europe and Asia are leading the way in the m-commerce market, and will continue to do so for a number of years.

What seems to prevent some markets from grasping the m-commerce trend as rapidly as others? First is the lack of agreed-upon standards. For example, in the United States, numerous standards for wireless services, and changes to them, have been developed over the last few years. As companies are evaluating the best routes into wireless services, they try to determine which standard will be viable and recognized. A wrong move into the wrong standard can mean wasted investments in money and time, and future useless technologies. The businesses have the unenviable choice of moving too soon into a losing standard, or too late into a lasting standard. This has slowed the growth of m-commerce in this market. Conversely, in Europe there was an early agreement on the technical standards for wireless services. This resulted in less risk of making a wrong

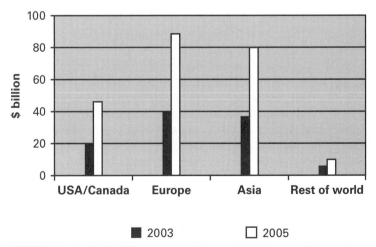

FIGURE 6-4 Global M-commerce Transaction Revenue Forecasts

Source: David P. Hamilton, "Going Places: Mobile Commerce Takes the Internet into a Whole New, Uncharted World," *The Wall Street Journal,* 11 December 2000, R3. Original data from McKinsey & Company.

technological choice. They invested in technologies and services that followed the agreed upon standard because they believed it would not change for many years. Innovative designs and new technologies were therefore brought to market, and m-commerce has grown substantially in the European markets.

Another issue with m-commerce networks worldwide is the limited bandwidth available from wireless media as compared to achievable speeds on line-based networks (previously described in this chapter). Most wireless networks today use cellular technologies, which often run at only 14.4 Kbps and can have spotty coverage in nonurban areas. Another major issue with the growth of m-commerce is the interface for users on handheld devices. While a cellular phone can be made small with advanced battery technology and lightweight materials, a Web browsing interface requires a minimum screen size to be effective. Similarly, keyboard functions on a cellular phone are often awkward, especially for men with bigger hands. As the screens cannot be made as wide as computer monitor screens, only portions of Web pages or long e-mail messages can be seen on the phone. The two main types of devices used for m-commerce on wireless networks are the PDA (personal digital assistant) and the **smart phone.** PDAs typically include small address databases, scratch pads, and other functions that used to be provided on electronic agendas. In addition, they allow users to send e-mail or access the Web through wireless connections. Smart phones are cellular phones with display screens that allow users to do things similar to those they would do on a PDA.

Wireless Networks

There are several alternative wireless networks in existence today. These include satellite networks, microwave and **infrared** communications, **paging systems, spread spectrum radio,** other radio frequencies, and **local multipoint distribution services (LMDS).** Most of the m-commerce frenzy, however, is centered on cellular technologies and **wireless LANs** and personal area networks. Cellular networks are established by erecting cellular towers (antennas) that can transmit or receive a signal over a certain geographic area, called a cell. Antennas are placed so that cells are overlapping (see Figure 6-5). This allows users to travel in their cars without being disconnected as they move from one cell to the other. When the user dials a number on her cellular phone, the closest tower will pick up the signal and retransmit it to the company's switching office. When the user is being called, the towers will broadcast a signal to the user's cell phone and, if it is turned on, the phone will accept the call. There can be several networks available, so the phones are programmed to accept signals from specific providers.

The first cellular technologies available used analog signals. The **AMPS (Advanced Mobile Phone Service)** standard, launched in the early 1980s, was the most widely used in the United States. The service used two bands, A and B, so that two companies could be present in every market. Each band used half of its bandwidth to send and half of its bandwidth to receive signals. Analog services provided less clarity on the line than newer digital technologies, and provided less security. Cellular phone companies also disliked the technology because it required a lot of precious bandwidth for each phone connection. At its peak, in 1990, AMPS had close to twenty million subscribers in the United States (Evolution of mobile communications 2002).

As the use of cellular phones grew in popularity, and with the need for more secure connections, companies began developing digital cellular services. Today, cellular phone

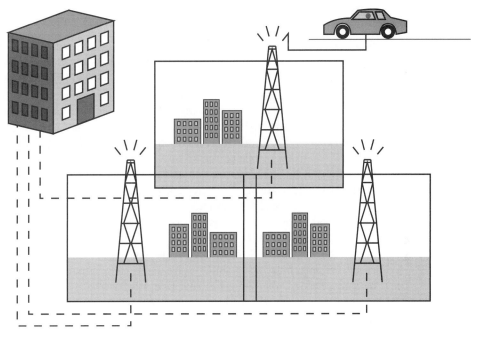

FIGURE 6-5   A Cellular Network

companies can place a large number of users on their digital networks. Most of these digital networks allow digital voice communications, the transfer of data, and simple text messaging. The digital networks are usually referred to as **personal communication services (PCS).** One problem is that there are many different alternative standards for PCS. Some of the most common include:

- **CDMA (code division multiple access)**
- **TDMA (time division multiple access)**
- **GSM (global system for mobile communication)**
- **D-AMPS (digital AMPS)**
- **PDC (personal digital communication)**

Europe standardized on the GSM technology. In the United States, both CDMA and TDMA are used (as well as other technology standards). Japan uses the PDC standard. The basic differences between the technologies include how conversations are sliced up and turned into digital signals, and how conversations are multiplexed on the network. These differences result in different performance levels, although they tend to be invisible to users today. Which is best? Experts do not agree. Some say that Europe has a better cellular service. Others say that this is simply due to the fact that they use only one standard. Today, networks can converse with one another, irrespective of which standard is being used. Nevertheless, wireless telephone equipment companies still struggle with which standard to support.

Wireless Application Protocol

In the summer of 1997, Ericsson, Nokia, Motorola, and Unwired Planet, founded the WAP Forum to create the **Wireless Application Protocol (WAP).** It defines sets of protocols to allow operators, manufacturers, and application providers to handle the differences between each wireless service provider. The WAP Forum has grown since its founding to include more than one hundred members from many different countries and many different areas of wireless communications, such as terminal and infrastructure manufacturers, operators, carriers, service providers, software houses, content providers, and companies developing services and applications for mobile devices. These companies have joined together to develop WAP in the hopes that there would be one unique global standard for wireless Web applications. Unfortunately, it is rare in information and telecommunication systems for only one standard to exist worldwide, and wireless Internet connections are no exception. A competitor to WAP called **i-mode** is being used in the Japanese and European markets.

A WAP transmission follows some of the same protocols that are used for a line-based transmission. However, the media and servers used by WAP differ from land-based systems. First the mobile device sends its original request through the wireless network. Second, the request is sent to a **WAP proxy server.** The WAP proxy server accesses the requested Web server and scans the server for WML (Wireless Markup Language) pages. WML is similar to HTML with the exception of being formatted for small handheld devices. If the Web page supports WML, the page is sent to the WAP proxy server. If the Web page does not support WML, the HTML code is sent to an HTML filter, which changes the format of the page to WML so that the page can be viewed on the screen of the mobile device. Once filtered, the page is sent to the WAP proxy server, which then sends the page back through the wireless network to the handheld device (see Figure 6-6).

Companies wishing to participate in m-commerce have to develop scaled down versions of their Web sites, which can be loaded on the wireless devices using WML. WAP has not been a great success. In Europe, less than 10 percent of mobile subscribers use WAP (Peering round the corner 2001). Some of the reasons include its low transmission speed for display of cut-down Web pages, the availability of multiple non-compatible WAP versions, and the lack of good WAP-enabled sites.

I-mode

I-mode, which provides wireless Internet service, is WAP's biggest competition for m-commerce. The standard provides for presentation of cut-down Web pages on small color screens in mobile phones. I-mode was launched by NTT DoCoMo, Inc. in Japan in February 1999. NTT DoCoMo has captured 60 percent of the Japanese mobile-telephone market, and more than two-thirds of its subscribers have also signed on for i-mode. As of late 2001, i-mode had more than twenty-seven million active subscribers paying an average of U.S.$20 per month, composed of monthly charges for the service at ¥300 ($2.50), plus ¥2.4 (2 cents) per kilobyte downloaded. In addition, a number of DoCoMo-approved i-mode sites have subscription fees of about 300 yen monthly. DoCoMo takes 9 percent commission on those fees and passes the rest of the money to the publishers of those Web sites.

I-mode can be used to access Internet services, such as browsing Web sites or sending electronic messages. Many wonder why i-mode is so successful compared to WAP.

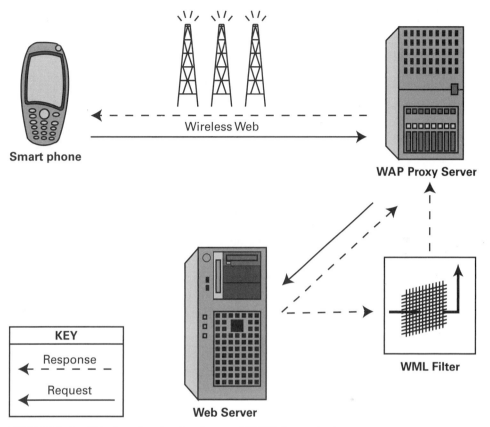

FIGURE 6-6   Wireless Application Protocol (WAP) Transmission

Experts suggest that the differences between the successes of WAP and i-mode are more due to social and environmental factors than to technological factors. An example of an environmental factor is the lack of easy access to wire-based Internet connections in Japan, as compared to the United States, where fast wire connections are easily available. Similarly, personal computer penetration is much lower in Japan than in the United States, and charges for dial-up Internet access are much higher. Another huge difference is that wireless coverage in Japan and Europe is very extensive, while there are still many "gaps" in wireless coverage in the United States. Finally, but not least, there is the business model used by NTT DoCoMo, which returns money to the Web site providers that develop i-mode enabled sites. Wireless providers do not have such arrangements in the United States and Europe, which leads to very few WAP-enabled Web sites.

Personal Area Networks

One type of network that is gaining increasing popularity is the **personal area network.** A personal area network (PAN) is a wireless network connecting a computer to its peripheral devices or other computers. For example, a PAN can be created between a personal digital assistant (PDA) and a desktop computer so that the two devices are synchronized (information is updated in both devices at once). A PAN could also link a PDA to a mobile phone to exchange phone numbers, and could simultaneously link to a wireless headset to create a hands-free audio environment. Office peripherals can also be interconnected wirelessly, allowing a laptop, digital camera, or PDA to connect to a fax machine, printer, or scanner. For example, you could place a digital camera in front of a printer and print your new pictures. A number of technologies can be used to create these PANs, and the most popular ones include Bluetooth, the **IrDA (infrared), and WiFi (wireless Ethernet LAN).** Bluetooth, WiFi, and another wireless technology called **HomeRF** all use an unregulated radio frequency for data transmission (the 2.45 GHz bandwidth), so there are many interference concerns with these competing technologies.

Bluetooth

Bluetooth is a standard for wireless communications between computers, cell phones, printers, scanners, and other devices. Bluetooth's name comes from the Viking king Harald Blatland. He was the first Christian king of Denmark, and in the tenth century, he unified warring Viking tribes. The name Blatland, which translates to Bluetooth in the English language, was given to him because of his discolored teeth, which resulted from his taste for blueberries and blackberries. The Bluetooth Special Interest Group chose the term to emphasize its effort to unify different groups to develop a worldwide standard for wireless communications.

Bluetooth technology operates on the globally available 2.45 GHz unlicensed radio band. It avoids interference from other signals by having its signal hop on different frequencies. Bluetooth devices can be ten meters (thirty feet) to one hundred meters (three hundred feet) apart, depending on the power level of the devices. Bluetooth technology provides a data transmission channel and up to three voice channels. The data channel supports asymmetric and symmetric data transfers. Asymmetric data transfers are supported at a maximum rate of 723.2 Kbps in one direction while permitting an operating rate of 57.6 Kbps in the opposite direction. The symmetric operation rate is 432.6 Kbps.

The basic Bluetooth network structure is called a **piconet** (see Figure 6-7). A piconet is formed by a master device and one or more slave devices. Each piconet uses different **hopping frequencies.** The maximum number of active slaves in a piconet is seven. However, that limit only refers to active slaves, and up to 256 additional slaves can be synchronized to the master in a nonactive way. These inactive devices are also called **parked devices.** Each parked device remains synchronized with the master and can rapidly become active and begin communication within the piconet. Two or more piconets can exist in the same wireless coverage area since they use different frequency channels. When two piconets overlap in their coverage area, it is called a **scatternet.**

IrDA (Infrared)

IrDA stands for Infrared Data Association, an organization devoted to wireless infrared data transmissions. Unlike Bluetooth, IrDA is based on infrared technology, which is limited to short line-of-sight transmissions. The IrDA recommends that for reliable data transmissions, two infrared devices be placed within one meter of each other and with less than a thirty-degree angle between them. Infrared cannot travel through walls or obstructions, and it is harder to connect multiple devices. However, the IrDA argues that the limited range of infrared is an advantage because it offers greater security and simplicity than the radio technology of

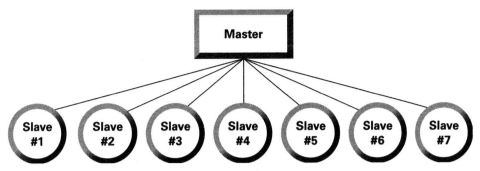

FIGURE 6-7   Structure of a Piconet under Bluetooth Technology

Bluetooth. With infrared technology, there is little doubt as to where the data are sent. With Bluetooth, however, it is possible to send data to an unintended destination within the range. The IrDA also touts its advantages in speed, cost, and installed customer base. Infrared devices typically transfer data at 4 Mbps, with potential for 16 Mbps. Another advantage to infrared technology is cost: infrared transceivers add only U.S.$1 to $2 to the cost of a device. Since it is so cheap to implement, infrared devices are widespread in notebook computers, printers, handheld devices, and more. However, many early infrared devices could not communicate due to proprietary protocols and competing standards.

Wireless LAN 802.11b

Another widespread wireless technology is the IEEE standard for **wireless Ethernet, 802.11b.** Commonly known as WiFi, the 802.11b standard uses the same 2.45 GHz bandwidth space as Bluetooth. Since it uses radio technology, it can penetrate through walls and obstructions without dropping the signal. The WiFi standard supports data transfer between devices at up to 11 Mbps. It has a greater range than Bluetooth, but consumes more power and has a much steeper price tag. Also, the WiFi devices are physically larger in nature and are harder to fit into smaller handheld devices. Bluetooth is geared towards devices such as cell phones and PDAs, for which lower cost, lower power consumption, and smaller size are critical factors. WiFi, on the other hand, is geared towards notebook and desktop computers, for which power usage and size are less of an issue.

2.5G and 3G Networks

The cellular networks we described earlier are referred to as 1G and 2G networks. First generation (1G) mobile networks are analog mobile phone services (such as AMPS). The second generation of mobile networks includes the digital mobile phone systems currently available (CDMA, TDMA, GSM, etc.). New 3G mobile networks will offer broadband transmission with speeds of up to 2 Mbps, allowing high-speed wireless access to the Internet, e-commerce transactions, entertainment, and information services from anywhere. In an effort to ease the cellular market from the current 1G and 2G networks to the more advanced 3G networks, an interim network capability, deemed 2.5G, is being implemented. Whereas 1G and 2G networks were circuit switched networks, the new 2.5G and 3G networks are packet switched networks.

Circuit switched networks work by creating a dedicated connection through the network. This path is then used for all communications between the two devices. Packet switched networks allow much greater use of the entire network by breaking up messages into packets that can take any network route to get to the destination, thus avoiding congested parts of the network. Table 6-6 presents some comparisons between the current 2G, 2.5G, and 3G networks.

3G systems evolved from incompatible 2G systems, such as CDMA, GSM, and TDMA. They combine the features of these networks in a standard called IMT-2000, which ensures the compatibility and interoperability of different systems in 3G. The 3G networks also support W-CDMA, a standard proposed by Ericsson. W-CDMA is short for Wideband CDMA. It allows transmission of text, digitized voice, video, and multimedia at data rates of up to 2 Mbps in a fixed or stationary wireless environment, 384 Kbps in a slow mobile environment (walking), and 144 Kbps in a fast mobile environment (driving).

3G networks' higher bandwidth will allow new wireless services, such as video conferencing and multimedia streaming. 3G can also be used for creating a **virtual home environment** in which a roaming user will have access to the same services she has at home or in the office. This will be achieved through a combination of transparent terrestrial and satellite connections. The potential applications are limitless, from personal video and voice communication on a global scale to worldwide television access. Corporate mobile users are expected to be the majority of early subscribers. On October 19, 2001, Hutchison 3G announced that it was collaborating with 3G LAB to develop multimedia applications for the wireless environment, such as full voice coverage, video and audio streaming, live news broadcasts, music on-demand, multimedia messaging, and interactive games. Currently, Ericsson is the world's leading 3G supplier. The company predicts that the revenues will increase from U.S.$30 million today to approximately U.S.$21 billion by 2004 in m-commerce alone. NTT DoCoMo launched its 3G service, called FOMA (Freedom of Multimedia Access), in late 2001. The FOMA network offers i-mode access at much faster speeds than existing phones. Users have access to a number of new applications, from video telephony to the simultaneous use of data and voice services.

Table 6-6 Comparisons of 2G, 2.5G, and 3G Networks

	2G	2.5G	3G
Speed	10 Kbps	64–144 Kbps	144 Kbps to 2 Mbps
Example: time to download a three minute MP3 song	31–41 minutes	6–9 minutes	11–90 seconds
Features	Phone calls	Phone calls/fax	Phone calls/fax
	Voice mail	Voice mail	Global roaming
	Simple text messaging	Large e-mail messaging	Large e-mail messaging
		Web browsing	Web browsing
		Navigation/maps	High-speed Web navigation/maps
			Videoconferencing
			TV streaming
			Electronic agenda meeting reminder

MANAGERIAL ISSUES

Network or Provider Selection

We have seen in this chapter that there are many alternative telecommunication networks that support e-business applications available to companies. How is a manager able to decide which network best suits the company's needs? There are several factors that must be considered in making this decision. Table 6-7 summarizes some key factors.

Network Applications

The telecommunication networks described in this chapter can be used for all of a company's telecommunication needs or for e-business applications. In selecting a network, the information technology executive must consider the particular applications for which the network is intended, both current and future. Companies need to consider all of their telecommunication requirements before deciding on a network. Why is the selection of the network so dependent on the applications to be used? Because different applications have different key requirements that must be met. For example, if a bank wishes to establish online banking services for its customers, security will be more

Table 6-7 Network Selection Criteria

Criterion	Examples of Factors to Consider
Applications	■ How many locations need connection to the network? ■ How many users will be connected to the network? ■ What will the network be used for? ■ What applications need to be supported?
Speed	■ How much traffic will there be on the network? ■ Is the traffic going to be regular or will there be peaks (bursts)? ■ Is there a need for different upstream and downstream speeds? ■ What is the maximum speed requirement?
Cost	■ How much is the company willing to spend? ■ Will we need specialized personnel? ■ What is the maintenance cost for the network? ■ Is there a fixed fee or a fee based on traffic? ■ How much does the equipment cost for connecting to the network? ■ Should we lease network connections or build our own network? ■ Did we include all costs in the analysis (network, equipment, personnel, training, maintenance, etc.)?
Reliability	■ How critical is the network to our business? ■ Who is responsible for fixing network problems?
Flexibility and expandability	■ How easy is it to increase the bandwidth when needed? ■ Can new access points be acquired within the same contract? ■ Can we change our network connections when our requirements change?

important than speed. A company that wishes to use videoconferencing for e-learning (distance training of its employees) will require a high speed network because of the bandwidth requirements of videoconferencing applications. The applications selected will also depend upon the estimated number of users (important to determine potential traffic); the number of locations, offices, or individuals that will be connected (to establish the number of access points or leased lines); and whether traffic will be constant or have peaks (bursts of data). This information will also help determine the best network for each application. It is key to understand that applications have to be considered within a portfolio. Some networks might have slack, or unused bandwidth, that could be efficiently used for other applications.

We can categorize the telecommunication application requirements into three segments: use the network as a backbone for internal transactions and communications, use the network as a communication backbone with external entities to the organization, or use the telecommunication network as a backbone for conducting electronic transactions with external entities. Each category highlights different core requirements.

Backbone for Internal Communication and Transactions When choosing a WAN, companies must consider the type of application for which they are going to use the network. While the frenzy of electronic commerce has brought many to think of the network as the gateway to the outside world, the largest portion of companies' communications is still typically internal. Employees within the company need to communicate; applications need to be accessed from all of the company's locations; documents need to be transferred among offices. Two examples of applications requiring an internal communication backbone are a worldwide communication network and an intranet.

Companies that have worldwide offices, or even a large number of offices within a country or region, need a backbone for their communications. In running the day-to-day business of the company, individuals need to exchange information, share expertise and knowledge, exchange documents, have discussions, collaborate on projects, and perform other communication-based work processes. In selecting a WAN for this environment, companies are usually very careful about security, since corporate information, such as customer information or trade secrets, are a major source of competitive advantage in most industries.

We discussed in Chapter 4 how companies use Internet technologies within their organizations to create intranets. Examples of how companies use intranets include dissemination of information to their employees, facilitating administrative processes with online forms, and facilitating knowledge sharing by including expert information systems. It is important to understand that using Internet technologies does not mean that the company actually uses the Internet. Rather, the company could use any of the telecommunication systems described in this chapter with the TCP/IP protocol and browser-like applications to support its intranet.

Backbone for External Communications E-business involves all electronically supported processes required to conduct business. In today's marketplace, companies have to communicate with the outside world for nonbusiness transactions, be it with their own employees, other companies, or the government. Two examples of external communication applications that require telecommunication systems are **telecommuting** and teleconferencing.

Telecommuting or telework is the concept of employees working away from their traditional offices and using telecommunication technologies to maintain a link to that office.

Telecommuters can work from home or a variety of other locations. The whole area of telecommuting is a field of study in itself with numerous sociological, organizational, and individual impacts. For the purposes of our discussion, though, the important aspect of telecommuting is the communication link to the office. What kind of networks should a company allow? For sporadic telecommuters, some companies simply offer dialup links at 56 Kbps. In these situations, the company, hopefully, pays for the employee's second phone line. Companies that offer telecommuting on a large scale and on a regular basis can offer direct connections between employees' homes and offices. Two of the most popular alternatives today for such network connections are ADSL and ISDN, where these networks are available. Companies generally pay service providers for the connections rather than providing the network connections themselves.

Teleconferencing encompasses three types of conferencing tools: data conferencing, voice conferencing, and video conferencing. Voice conferencing resembles the conference calls that have been used for ages in business. Today's voice conferencing applications can also use IP networks (voiceover IP), as discussed in Chapter 4. Data conferencing applications use a variety of tools to allow online collaboration between remote people. The famous "chat" software is an example of a data conferencing application (refer to Chapter 4). Other examples include shared whiteboards and shared applications. Video conferencing applications use video signals, allowing individuals to see each other. As discussed in Chapter 4, teleconferencing technology can be used internally (for training sessions, for example) or externally (to conduct meetings at a customer site with remote experts, for example). Some companies use large-scale conferencing rooms for teleconferencing. Others use desktop teleconferencing, which employs inexpensive or free application software installed on workstations and connections via the Internet. The first option is very expensive, while the second option is relatively inexpensive. The important factor, though, is that the network required to support large-scale conferencing is very different than that required for desktop conferencing. As already stated, most desktop conferencing uses the Internet as a backbone. Given that high bandwidth is required to exchange video signals, the company should have a high-speed link to its information service provider. In large-scale conferencing, dedicated links between the two offices can be leased, or a company can build its own network. In either case, bandwidth is the major factor to take into consideration.

Backbone for External Transactions The core of the e-commerce concept is that transactions are conducted using electronic media. All of the telecommunication systems described in this chapter can be used for conducting external transactions. Some are more appropriate for business-to-consumer e-commerce, while others offer more advantages for business-to-business e-commerce environments. Refer to the beginning of the chapter for a discussion of EDI and B2B electronic commerce. Examples of external transactions outside of the B2B market segment include online banking and online shopping.

There are two types of online banking. The most popular type today is using a browser that supports a high level of encryption to access one's account via the Internet. Another type of online banking is available from some banks for individuals who prefer not to use the Internet to conduct their banking transactions. The bank only needs to provide a modem pool that allows users to connect over regular phone lines. Banks usually provide a toll free access number, and all banking is done using software applications that the banks provide.

For companies in the retail and service industries that conduct online transactions directly with consumers, the Internet provides an ideal medium for access to the companies' sites. There are many examples of these, such as Amazon.com, eBay, and many more. The companies must provide security on their servers. They must also have servers with enough processing power and memory to handle the multiple requests that are being made at peak times. Finally, the companies must also have high bandwidth networks connecting them to their information service providers. As being online is their business, most of them will contract with more than one information service provider so that network failures will not stop their operations. What type of network should they use to connect to their information provider? Most companies use plain old digital dedicated lines, such as T-1s and T-3s. The dedicated lines do not suffer from network congestion when other companies' traffic increases, and they use fairly reliable technologies.

There are a large number of other external transaction applications. For each application, important questions need to be investigated before selecting a WAN: What kind of bandwidth do we need to run this application? How many users do we expect for this application? How reliable does the network need to be for this application? How much will this application grow? How much security is needed for this application?

Speed

One of the important criteria to consider before selecting the type of telecommunication systems to use for e-business is the speed of the network. Each type of network usually has a maximum achievable speed. It should be noted that maximum speeds are often theoretical since factors such as transmission errors or lower quality equipment can reduce the effective speed of the networks. Nevertheless, speed is a key criterion for selection of telecommunication systems. But what do these speeds really mean? Figure 6-8 shows the time it would take to transfer a 1 megabyte (MB) file using various networks. This file could include large text sections and two or three pictures. The file would occupy two thirds of a two-sided 1.44 MB diskette.

As can be seen from Figure 6-8, the speed of the network will have a significant impact on the response time and should therefore be considered when evaluating the different networks for one's electronic business applications. Why not always go for the highest speed network? Because higher speed networks cost more. So one of the compromises a manager must make in choosing a network is to balance the cost and the speed. The idea is to find the network that offers the most speed possible for the least cost possible. This relationship, however, is not linear, so there are some speeds that can be achieved without substantially greater costs.

Cost

In evaluating costs, the company must be careful to consider more than the connection fee and transfer rate fees (such as CIR for frame relay or CBR for ATM). Evaluation of costs should include installation costs, equipment costs, personnel costs for operation and maintenance, and any training costs required for the network operators. A careful evaluation must be made of the fixed rate costs and the peak rate costs (for networks supporting burst transmissions). Companies should evaluate whether they want to create their own network (only leasing the lines but owning and maintaining the equipment), leasing a complete network (such as a VAN), or even outsourcing all of their telecommunication systems needs.

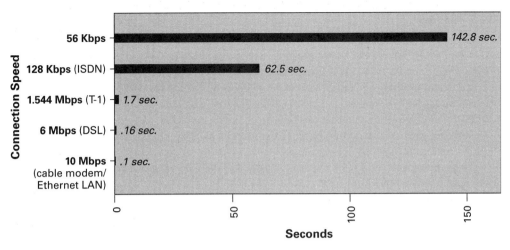

FIGURE 6-8   Transfer Times for 1 MB file

Reliability

When a company enters the world of electronic business, it becomes even more dependent on its telecommunication network than it was in the past. Who is responsible when the network goes down? How long will it take to repair network elements and bring the network back up? How long can the company's business survive without the network? When a manager starts answering these questions, she quickly realizes how crucial the network is for the company's business. While a backup plan is a necessity in this environment, considering these questions prior to selecting a network is even more important. For example, the Internet is unreliable for network traffic. If a bank requires its transactions to occur instantaneously, for example, to take advantage of international discrepancies in exchange rates, it cannot afford to use the Internet (this is in addition to the security issues). A leased circuit network requires additional backup leased lines so that when one circuit is down, another line can be used. A packet switched network, such as frame relay or ATM, can survive when one link or one node is down since another route will be found on the network. These are considerations that the IT manager must take into account in a network decision.

Expandability and Flexibility

Telecommunication networks represent major investments for companies contemplating implementation of electronic business. The cost of the equipment for establishing networks is usually fairly high, and is in addition to servers, stations, software, and other costs to establish the electronic business applications. Before choosing a network, a company should consider its long-term growth plan. Some networks allow easy expandability. For example, if a company uses the Internet to run its business-to-consumer electronic shopping mall, it can add servers, stations, and locations quite easily. On the other hand, two companies that establish a B2B link between themselves using a T-1 line must add two lines if an important third business partner needs to be added to the exchange (if they want a direct link), one to each of the existing partners.

WAN Summary

The above criteria can help an IT manager decide which network to implement for his company. Similarly, the criteria can be used in evaluating service providers should the company decide to outsource or lease most of its telecommunication capabilities. An additional criterion is security of data. This is discussed briefly later in this chapter, and an in-depth discussion is provided in Chapter 10. Table 6-8 presents a summary of the telecommunication solutions presented in this chapter. While these are the most common networks commercially available today, other networks exist and might be appropriate for specific companies. Speeds continue to rise, costs continue to fall, but the basic considerations in selecting a telecommunications network should not change in the foreseeable future.

When should any of the above networks be used? We discussed previously in this section criteria that can be used to evaluate which network is best for various situations. A typical example is a small business using a T-carrier or E-carrier line to connect its e-business site to an Internet service provider. Large companies also use T-carriers for connecting various offices together or for B2B links to business partners. Dialup voice grade lines are usually not a good choice for e-businesses. They are, however, the most common method of connection for consumers. Similarly, DSL connections are a good choice for consumers to browse the Web, but large companies can also use them to provide telecommuting connections for their employees. ISDN connections of the basic type (BRI) can be used for employee remote access as well, or for connections between company offices. Primary rates (PRI) can be used by small businesses for connections to Internet service providers, or by large companies for interoffice connections. Frame relay and ATM networks provide low cost connections when multiple sites need to be connected together. A small business with lower data rate transfer needs would prefer frame relay, while large businesses with requirements for

Table 6-8   Summary of Telecommunication Networks

Network	Speeds	Comments
Dedicated circuit networks		
Voice grade: dialup or lease	2.4–64 Kbps	
T-carrier	1.544–44.7 Mbps	High speed networks require fiber optic cabling
Fractional T-carrier	128–768 Kbps	
SONET	51.84 Mbps to 9.952 Gbps	Not widely available for commercial use
Digital subscriber lines (ADSL)	56 Kbps to 6 Mbps	Asymmetrical, typically for Internet use
Switched circuit networks		
Integrated services digital networks (ISDN)	128 Kbps to 2.048 Mbps	Different standards worldwide
Frame relay	56 Kbps to 44.736 Mbps	Very good for bursty data
Asynchronous transfer mode	25 Mbps to 246 Gbps	Very good for bursty data
Others		
Value added networks (VAN)	Varies	Pay for additional services
Wireless cellular networks	9.6–19.2 Kbps	Will be faster when 3G is fully implemented
Virtual private networks (VPN)	Varies	Can use any of the above networks for internal purposes

higher speeds would prefer ATM (with speeds starting approximately where frame relay speeds end).

Network Management

Network management is one of the biggest challenges for information systems professionals dealing with corporate networks. As companies increasingly embrace e-business, they become even more dependent on their networks, increasing the stakes for everyone involved in maintaining the networks in operation. The many functions of network management include fault management (finding and diagnosing errors), configuration management (knowing the status of all devices in the network), performance management (ensuring that agreed-upon service levels are maintained in the network), security management (providing all aspects of security for the network), and accounting management (providing statistics on network usage). A complete discussion of network management is beyond the scope of this text. The e-business manager should be aware, however, of the importance of the network management function if the company is to setup its own network.

Fortunately, there are hardware and software tools available to help manage networks. Hardware tools can help evaluate line traffic and determine where hardware problems are occurring. Software tools include all kinds of network management software. Most manufacturers of equipment and operating systems have some network management software tools available or built into their products. Integrating large diverse networks, however, requires integrated network management tools. Two main standards exist for network management software: SNMP and CMIP. **Simple Network Management Protocol (SNMP)** is the Internet network management protocol and is widely used. **Common Management Interface Protocol (CMIP)** is an international standard for network management that is incompatible with SNMP. In recent years, it appears that SNMP is taking over the integrated network management tool market.

Network Security

We cannot discuss telecommunication systems without talking about the issue of security. We will cover security in-depth in Chapter 10. All transactions that are conducted in business, whether internally or externally, need to include some level of security. You might say that it is not very important to you whether someone hacks into your e-mail account to see what you've been telling your friends. It would matter to you, however, if they used your account to send unwanted or offensive messages to other people. When we start talking about transactions involving personal information or money, the issue of security becomes even more important. Tools that can be used to enhance security include firewalls, encryption, and authentication methods. However, the network is still the key entry point for hackers and other ill-intentioned parties. For example, the Internet provides a greater security risk than using a provider's ATM network. It is therefore important that a company deciding which wide area network to use as its main telecommunication system consider the security levels that can be offered for each network.

Closing Case: Britannica.com

Encyclopedia Britannica, Inc. is an old brick and mortar company established in 1768 in Edinburgh, Scotland and currently headquartered in Chicago, Illinois. It defines itself as a "leading provider of learning and knowledge products," and many believe Britannica to be "the" encyclopedia company. Indeed, the company's main business has been printing encyclopedias to which worldwide scholars contribute. Since 1936, a new version of the encyclopedia has been printed every year with new facts and figures. Through various acquisitions, the company continued to grow over the years, with encyclopedias and other materials published for Japan, Korea, China, Taiwan, Italy, France, Spain, Latin America, Turkey, Hungary, Poland, and many other countries. Yet, in the early 1990s, with the advent of the Internet, the company realized that its printed sources of information were receiving competition from Web-based resources, even though the company produced an online version of its encyclopedia for educational databases as early as 1981, and on CD-ROM in 1989. In 1994, the company started its venture into the world of e-business with its first Web-based encyclopedia. Britannica.com was created. It allows users to call up encyclopedia entries online, and offers various other services.

In 1999, Kent Devereaux, the senior vice-president of Britannica.com, decided that the company needed to make another bold move to continue to take advantage of the digital world by moving into m-commerce. His idea was to take advantage of the new trend of users surfing the Web with Palm Pilots or cellular phones. Within one year, by December 2000, the company started offering access to their Web site through wireless Palm devices and some Web-enabled mobile phones. The company was able to launch its wireless-enabled Web site through various partnerships, most importantly with Palm, Inc., and rapid programming. One of the advantages that the company had was that its Web site was already using XML, making translation of these pages to WML pages much quicker. Britannica decided to allow free access to its wireless-enabled Web site for Palm and mobile phone users. The company then became an official content provider for OmniSky Corporation, a wireless-modem manufacturer. Today, Britannica.com has established a large number of such partnerships in its quest to become a leader in m-commerce. Britannica.com hopes that providing such wirelessly accessible content is going to become such a premium service that consumers will be willing to pay for it. Do you think this will happen? How else could Britannica.com take advantage of the m-commerce potential? What should be their next venture into e-business?

SUMMARY

This chapter describes telecommunication networks that can be used to implement electronic business applications. Many electronic commerce applications and transactions are conducted over non–Web-based systems. One example of a mostly non–Web-based e-business environment is Electronic Data Interchange (EDI). EDI was the precursor of today's B2B electronic commerce market segment. EDI involves the transfer of electronic documents between trading partners in a standard format. The two most common EDI standards are X12 and EDIFACT. The fact that a standard format is used provides strategic, operational, and opportunity benefits. EDI and B2B e-commerce make use of wide area networks (WANs) for their network connection alternatives.

Wide area networks provide connections over a large geographic area, which can be a city, state, province, county, or country. WANs are divided into dedicated circuit and switched networks. Dedicated circuit networks offer permanent connections between locations. The chapter presents analog and digital circuits, digital subscriber lines (ADSL/DSL), and SONET as dedicated circuit networks. Switched networks offer companies the possibility to pay for access points to the network, and for the traffic used. Integrated services digital network (ISDN), frame relay, and asynchronous transfer mode (ATM) are switched networks presented in the chapter. We also discussed value added networks (VANs) and virtual private networks (VPNs). A virtual private network (VPN) is a public network leased by a company for its internal communication needs. Value added networks are wide area networks that add various services to the telecommunication connections. VANs are used extensively for EDI applications.

Analog lines are mostly used for dialup connections. Digital lines can be leased at varying speeds. High-speed digital lines commonly used in the United States include T-carrier and fractional T-1, ranging in speeds from 64 Kbps to 274.176 Mbps. In Europe, similar lines are called E-carrier and have similar maximum speeds but start at 2.048 Mbps. Digital subscriber line (DSL) is an asymmetrical network typically used to connect homes to the Internet. An asymmetrical network is one in which the upstream speed (going from the home to the provider) is not the same as the downstream speed (going to the home). DSL speeds range from 56 Kbps to 6 Mbps.

Integrated services digital network (ISDN) is an all-digital network offered in two rates. The basic ISDN (BRI) runs at 128 Kbps (two 64 Kbps channels) and the primary ISDN (PRI) runs at 1.544 Mbps (twenty-four channels at 64 Kbps). A newer version is broadband ISDN, or BISDN.

Frame relay is a packet-switching technology that offers speeds from 56 Kbps to 44.736 Mbps. Companies pay only for access points and traffic transported on the network. Two rates companies can negotiate with the provider are the committed information rate (CIR) and maximum allowable rate (MAR). Asynchronous transfer mode (ATM) is another packet switched network, with speeds ranging from 25 Mbps to 2.46 Gbps. It has four rates that can be negotiated: constant bit rate (CBR), variable bit rate (VBR), available bit rate (AVR), and unspecified bit rate (UBR).

M-commerce is the use of wireless networks to conduct e-business transactions. Many people define it more broadly, for example, to include Web surfing on a cellular phone. M-commerce is more popular in Japan and Europe than in the United States. The networks for m-commerce have evolved from first generation systems, which were analog, to second generation systems that provide digital phone networks, and the future third generation systems that will provide broadband higher speed cellular networks. Numerous standards exist for the digital mobile phone networks. CDMA and TDMA are standards used in the United States. GSM is a standard used in Japan and Europe. Wireless Application Protocol (WAP) is a standard for connecting wireless devices to the Internet. Its competitor is i-mode, a popular wireless standard developed by NTT DoCoMo. Personal area networks (PAN) connect computers to each other and peripherals wirelessly. Technologies for PAN include Bluetooth, WiFi (wireless Ethernet), HomeRF, and infrared (IrDA). Future wireless technologies include 3G networks.

Selecting a wide area network involves comparing telecommunication networks with respect to support for the applications a company wants to run, speed, cost, reliability, flexibility, and expandability. Managerial issues for telecommunication systems, in addition to network selection, include network management and network security.

KEY TERMS

2.5G network	(asymmetric) digital	Bluetooth	code division multiple
3G network	subscriber lines	broadband ISDN	access (CDMA)
access points	(ADSL or DSL)	(BISDN)	committed information
Advanced Mobile Phone	asynchronous transfer	cable modems	rate (CIR)
Service (AMPS)	mode (ATM)	circuit	Common Management
analog (voice-grade)	available bit rate	circuit-switched	Interface Protocol
ANSI ASC X12 standard	backbone		(CMIP)

constant bit rate
data bursts
dedicated circuit networks
digital AMPS (D-AMPS)
downstream
    communication
E-carriers
EDIFACT
Electronic Data
    Interchange (EDI)
frame relay
global system for mobile
    communication
    (GSM)
high rate DSL (HDSL)
HomeRF
hopping frequencies
i-mode
infrared
Infrared (IrDA)
integrated services digi-
    tal network (ISDN)
ISDN-BRI

ISDN-PRI
local multipoint
    distribution services
    (LMDS)
maximum allowable
    rate (MAR)
mobile commerce
    (m-commerce)
multiplexing
narrowband ISDN
network management
optical carrier (OC)
packet assembly and
    disassembly
packets
packet-switched network
paging systems
parked devices
personal area network
personal communication
    services (PCS)
personal digital commu-
    nication (PDC)

piconet
point of presence (POP)
protocol conversion
rate adaptive DSL
    (RADSL)
scalability
scatternet
Simple Network
    Management
    Protocol (SNMP)
speed translating
spread spectrum radio
store-and-forward
    messaging
switched networks
switching equipment
Synchronous Digital
    Hierarchy (SDH)
synchronous optical
    network (SONET)
T-carriers
TDCC
telecommuting

time division multiple
    access (TDMA)
unspecified bit rate
upstream communication
value added networks
    (VANs)
variable bit rate
very high speed DSL
    (VDSL)
virtual home
    environment
virtual private network
WAP proxy server
wide area network
    (WAN)
WINS
Wireless Application
    Protocol (WAP)
wireless Ethernet LAN
    (WiFi)
wireless Ethernet,
    802.11b
wireless LANs

REVIEW QUESTIONS

1. What is a WAN?

2. What is EDI? How does it work?

3. How are EDI and B2B e-commerce systems related?

4. What are the components of EDI?

5. Identify the main benefits of EDI.

6. What are the two main EDI standards?

7. What are value added networks?

8. Explain the main differences between dedicated circuit and switched networks.

9. What is a circuit?

10. What is an analog signal?

11. What are the main digital leased circuits available today?

12. What is fractional T-1?

13. What is the difference between T-carrier and E-carrier lines? Where are they used?

14. What is a virtual private network?

15. Describe the digital subscriber line network.

16. Explain what an asymmetrical network is.

17. What are some of the advantages of switched networks?

18. What is integrated services digital network?

19. What are the two types of ISDN networks and what differentiates them?

20. Describe the frame relay network.

21. What is the committed information rate (CIR)?

22. Describe the ATM network.

23. List the grades of services offered with ATM.

24. Describe two value-added network services.

25. What is m-commerce?

26. Describe the most common wireless networks for m-commerce.

27. What is WAP?

28. What is i-mode?

29. What is a personal area network (PAN)?

30. What is Bluetooth?

31. Describe the purposes of the 802.11b standard.

32. Describe how infrared communication can be used to create a PAN.

33. List five network evaluation criteria and explain them.

34. What is network management?

35. Identify the two main network management protocol standards in use today.

36. Explain why network security is an important issue.

EXERCISES

1. A company uses electronic mail to send notification of shipments of material to its customers. Is this EDI or e-commerce? If e-commerce, what type of e-commerce? If EDI, what makes it EDI? If not EDI, what would make it EDI?

2. A company uses X12 EDI to trade with a business partner. Another company wants to start doing business with them but uses an EDIFACT EDI with its partners. Can the companies use EDI together? What would they need?

3. Why would anyone connecting from home to the Internet want to use ISDN when regular phone lines work fine and are fast enough?

4. If you have an ISDN line installed, do you just pick up the telephone and dial the number of the party to whom you want to send data? Explain.

5. For each of the following situations, give several potential reasons why the company could have selected the type of network it did:

(a) Company A sends data between its New York and Washington, D.C. offices. It uses a dedicated circuit network.

(b) Company A sends data between its New York and Washington, D.C. offices. It uses a switched network.

(c) Company A sends data to Company B. It uses a dedicated circuit network.

(d) Company A sends data to Company B. It uses a switched network.

(e) Company A sends data to Company B. It uses a VAN.

6. If you wanted to acquire digital dedicated lines and you needed a speed of approximately 500 Kbps at your peak rate, which network connection would you select?

7. A company offers its employees the possibility of connecting to the office from home. Should the telecommunications manager be more concerned about network management or network security?

8. You work for a medium-sized company that has offices in New York, Atlanta, and Washington, D.C. In each office LANs are installed. You must decide on a network to interconnect them. The first decision is whether you want to outsource the network completely or manage it yourself. How will you make that decision? What are the important criteria?

9. Continuing on exercise 8, you decided to acquire a network from a telecommunications company or service provider. Which networks are not good alternatives? Which networks are good alternatives? Why? Which network will you choose? Why? How would your answer change if you knew that you will need to expand substantially by adding new offices in three years?

10. Why would a company install a virtual private network?

11. What type of company or user needs an ADSL line? Why?

12. For each of the following situations, pick a network and one alternative network. Explain your choice.

(a) Internet connection from home

(b) Telecommuting to an office with constant need to be connected

(c) Business-to-business transactions with a company's partner

(d) Offering Web-based shopping to customers

(e) Communication backbone between office in Paris, France and London, England

(f) Desktop teleconferencing for employee training in more than three hundred cities

13. Explain why the downstream speed is different than the upstream speed in ADSL. What is the advantage of this? What is the disadvantage? What makes it possible to do that?

14. Why is the ISDN PRI network the same speed as the T-1 connection?

15. What rates do you need to negotiate when you use a frame relay network?

16. What is the main advantage of using frame relay instead of leased lines?

17. What are the various rates used in ATM? Do you need to agree on all of them?

18. You want to select a VAN for doing EDI with another business partner that will use the same VAN provider. What minimum features should you have?

19. Is WAP a cellular standard? Why might content providers (Web sites) prefer to support i-mode instead of WAP?

20. Explain the main differences between the various cellular standards in use today. Which is the best? Why?

21. Which generations of mobile phone systems are used in today's marketplace?

22. Explain for each of the network selection criteria why they are important in selecting the network.

23. Explain why network management and network security are two very important issues for the telecommunications manager in charge of networks.

24. You must select a wireless network to connect all of the computing devices in your two-story home. What are your options? Which one will you choose? Why?

HANDS-ON PROJECTS

1. Research on the Internet information about two other EDI standards besides X12 and EDIFACT. Describe who uses them and where they are used, what their differences are with X12 and EDIFACT, and why we don't hear as much about them.

2. Research on the Internet or by calling telecommunication companies and Internet service providers the costs of the various networks presented in the chapter for your area. Assume you are representing a small business that needs a link to the Internet.

3. Research the most popular VANs in your area. What kinds of services do they offer? What are the prices for these services?

4. Research the SONET network. What is its current status? Is it widely available? Who uses it? What is the current standard?

5. Investigate the exact costs and all the hardware needed for you to install an ISDN line in your home to a service provider. Do the same for a DSL line.

6. Research newer and faster networks that could replace some of the technologies described in this chapter.

7. Find information about the 3G wireless networks mentioned in the chapter and find the current costs to implement them.

DISCUSSION POINTS

1. "In the future all networks will be interconnected anyway, so we should use the Internet for all electronic business transactions." Discuss this statement with your classmates.

2. Split your class into several groups of three or four people. In each group, rate each of the network selection criteria in order of importance. Compare your findings with the rest of the class and discuss your reasoning for the rankings you provided.

FURTHER READINGS

BÉLANGER, France, and Dianna H. Jordan. *Evaluation and Implementation of Distance Learning: Technologies, Tools and Techniques.* Hershey, PA: Idea Group Publishing, 2000.

CARR, H. H., and C. A. Snyder. *The Management of Telecommunications: Business Solutions to Business Problems.* Chicago: Irwin, 1997.

CTI Communications' IP Value Added Network page. CTI Communications. 2001: http://www.cticomm.com/van.htm.

FITZGERALD, J., and A. Dennis. *Business Data Communications and Networking.* New York: John Wiley & Sons, 1999.

GREENSTEIN, M., and T. M. Feinman. *Electronic Commerce: Security, Risk Management, and Control.* Boston: Irwin McGraw-Hill, 2000.

HAMBLEN, M. "U.S. Wireless Industry Eyeing Japan's I-Mode Success." *Computerworld* March 22, 2001, http://www.computerworld.com.

HOUSEL, T. J., and E.W. Skopec. *Global Telecommunications Revolution: The Business Perspective.* Boston: Irwin McGraw-Hill, 2000.

PANKO, R. R. *Business Data Communications.* Upper Saddle River, NJ: Prentice-Hall, 1997.

REFERENCES

Evolution of mobile communications page. 2002. International Engineering Consortium. http://www.iec.org/online/tutorials/umts/topic01.html.

Peering round the corner. 2001. *The Economist* 360 (8235): 6.

The ABC of EDI page. 2000. Welsh Development Agency. http://www.edi.wales.org/feature4.htm.

WETHERBE, James C. 1996. *The World on Time*. Santa Monica, CA: Knowledge Exchange.

CHAPTER 7

CLIENT/SERVER TECHNOLOGIES FOR E-BUSINESS

LEARNING OBJECTIVES

After reading and completing this chapter, you should be able to:

- Explain various types of server functions
- Identify the strengths and weaknesses of various server and network operating systems
- Know the different server hardware available in today's marketplace
- Identify server hardware and peripherals
- Know how to size a Web server
- Know the different client technologies available in today's marketplace
- Understand the choices of being hosted or hosting for e-business server implementation
- Understand the factors to consider in selecting client and server technologies

Opening Case: Skiviez.com

Have you ever thought of starting your own electronic business? With the falling prices of information technologies, the increased availability of easy-to-use Web development software, and the booming economy of the late 1990s and early 2000s, several university students just like you have tried, and many with success, to establish their own Web-based businesses. One such student was Robert Clark, a graduating senior at Virginia Polytechnic Institute and State University, who started his own business, called Skiviez.com, during his last semester of school. Robert was already involved in Web development, taking up small contracts to help pay for his studies. He also had a vision that selling underwear online was a promising market.

The first step in Robert's business endeavor was to develop a business plan for his company. In his plan, he covered the basic structure of the company, the marketing efforts, the industry analysis, the financial analysis, a technology analysis, and other background information. The plan called for the business to be an "Internet retailer of premium quality men's and women's underwear." The Web site had to be designed to allow customers to search by brand or style, and each item would have to allow a 360-degree view of the product so that customers could fully view every item before buying. Additional desired features included optional gift wrapping, and a selection of other gifts, such as underwear in a beer mug, wineglass, or coffee mug. In order to support this kind of Web structure, the technology infrastructure would require a top-quality information system with inventory management, fast transaction processing, customer management, shipping, and flexibility to add features as the business grew.

Robert identified seven key success factors for his business, including the Web design and the speed of the site. Having built Web sites for other companies, Robert felt comfortable that his Web design would place him in an advantageous position with respect to his competitors. However, the speed of the Web site was a key concern. The first decision he had to make was whether to host the Web site on his own server or contract with an external organization to host his Web site. In order to be able to answer this question, Robert had to evaluate various technology infrastructures. In doing so, several questions came to mind. Which **operating system** should he use? How many servers should he have or use? What type of servers? What kind of Internet connection would be best? What processor speed should the servers have? How much storage? How much **main memory?** What kind of **peripherals** should he consider? What brands are the best? Which database should he use for inventory? Robert spent quite some time answering these questions and evaluating various alternatives. What would you have recommended?

SERVER TECHNOLOGIES

Introduction

Chapter 4 introduced the basic concepts of **client/server computing** and discussed how they could be applied to e-business. In this chapter, we explore further the hardware and software technologies for servers, peripherals, and clients that one should consider for an e-business implementation.

There are different types of servers that a company must consider when it wants to implement e-business applications. The most obvious one for B2C e-commerce is the **Web server,** where the company's Web site is hosted. However, it is important to realize that a Web server by itself will not be useful if there are no other servers used for running the business functions. For example, receiving orders via a Web site form is only the first step in making the transaction. The order must be stored somewhere **(database server),** processed by a business application **(application server)**, and printed if a paper invoice is sent to the customer **(print server)**. These are just some of the examples of the types of servers a company may need to run its e-business. Each server function is usually implemented by one or more software programs.

For a small business, all of these servers could be found on one machine. In this case, we would have a **two-tier client/server** environment; one tier is the server computer that contains all of the server functions, and the other tier is the **client** accessing these server functions. For larger businesses, these different types of servers could actually be hosted on different machines, in this case creating an **n-tier client/server** architecture. Figure 7-1 shows an example of some differences between using one or multiple servers for e-business applications. The figure assumes that there is a Web site for consumers to access, a database that keeps track of orders, and a separate application that is used to process the orders and print invoices. Most e-businesses use a database to store such information as product specifications, orders, or customer records. Separating the database from the Web server has the added advantage of adding security since the database can be kept inside

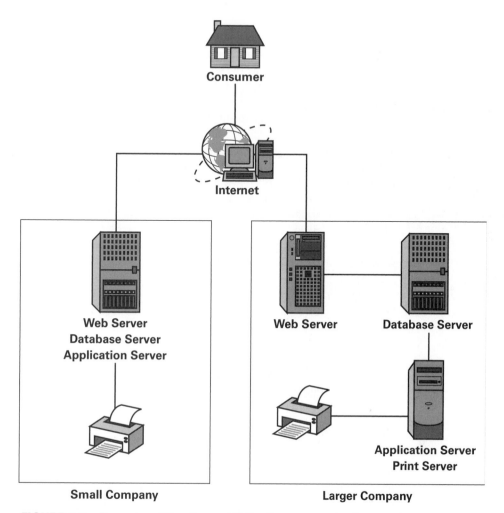

FIGURE 7-1 Examples of Two-tier and N-tier E-commerce Implementations

the corporate walls, protected by a **firewall**, while everyone can access the Web server. Firewalls and other security features will be discussed in Chapter 10.

Types of Servers

In Figure 7-1 there are four types of server functions that must be performed for conducting the B2C e-business transactions. These represent some of the many types of servers that can be used for e-business. Having servers specialized for specific applications allows managers to optimize each server for each operation. For example, a database server will require more disk space than a communication server. The database server will also typically require a high-end computer with high levels of processing power available. In this section, we present the various types of servers that are most commonly used. Note again that based on the client/server architecture, several server functions can actually be performed on one or many physical machines.

File Server

One of the first services used extensively when LANs became popular was the **file server** function. The basic role of the file server is to become the central location where information is stored and accessed by multiple clients. The file server could be thought of as an extended hard drive for each client. The disk drives of these servers can be mapped using software functions that make the file structure appear like that of any other drive on the user's system. This makes it very user friendly. Some organizations prefer that users employ a **file transfer protocol (FTP) program** for moving files between the clients and the server. The mapped drive or the FTP program allow users to store, copy, delete, or retrieve data files, or even to execute programs directly. When a program is executed from the server, the program is brought into the **RAM storage space** of the client and run from there. In a true client/server computing environment, it can also be run directly from the server.

There are many advantages to the use of file servers, which are also called application servers. One advantage is that the server provides a central storage location from which administrators can backup user files. If the backup is performed regularly, all user files are safe from potential destruction. Since users rarely backup their own computers, this environment provides a greater protection of data for the company. Another advantage of storing files on a server is that it allows users to access the servers from many locations. Files stored on a PC's hard drive are typically only accessible from that PC (if they are not shared). Conversely, files designed to be shared on a server can be accessed from home, the office, or other places. In addition, two individuals with proper access to the server's file systems can share their work. However, there are also concerns about security, since anyone obtaining a valid password can view, use, or delete most files. The file server functions are integrated in most modern operating systems.

Print Server

Also integrated into most modern operating systems, print server services allow multiple users access to high-end printers. Very often, it is prohibitively expensive to give each person her own high-end laser printer. The solution, and one of the main reasons for the growth of **LANs** in the 1980s, is to share the resource, in this case the printer. The setup of a print server is quasi-transparent to the user. The user gets to print to a **virtual port** instead of a real port. The implementation is slightly more complex. The print server must accept all the requests from the users and put them in a print queue, which will hold the files until the printer is free.

Web Server

The role of the Web server is to host Web pages. As with every other server, it must have an operating system and applications specifically tailored to its role. One of the key features to look for in a Web server is the speed of processing. If the business is going online and numerous customers are going to try to access the company's Web site at the same time (people all seem to shop at the same time, of course), it is crucial that the speed of the system be able to handle the volume of transactions. The e-business site must therefore be able to handle regular traffic and peak demands. The last section of this chapter will describe the main factors used in sizing a Web server. The Web server, like every other server, is only as fast as its slowest component. In an e-business environment, the Web site **response time** can make the difference between a user returning to the site for more acquisitions and a user never returning to the site. The two most popular Web servers today are the Apache Web server, and the iPlanet Web server. Both will be described with their respective operating systems later in this chapter.

Database Server

A crucial part of an e-business' technology infrastructure is its database. This is where customer information is stored, including contacts, orders, billing, and payment information. The core of a business is often the information that is being received and sent to customers, information that is stored in the database. The database server holds the database or databases for the organization. In selecting server hardware for a database server, storage capacity will undoubtedly be one of the key factors. In selecting database server software, there are some key requirements that must also be met. Support for **data integrity,** multiple access, and **scalability** are some of those key requirements. Data integrity ensures that the data in the database are consistent, accurate, and valid. This is especially important when multiple users access the database at the same time. For example, if multiple customers are trying to place orders on a Web site simultaneously, the database should be able to handle the requests by storing the orders, updating the inventory, and updating the customer information without any information being lost.

Two of the most popular database environments for e-business are Oracle's Oracle9*i* Database and Microsoft's SQL Server. The SQL Server is built to run on the Windows operating system, while Oracle9*i* can run on a number of different platforms. Because it is designed for just one family of operating systems, SQL Server is said to be faster. However, Oracle provides better support for some functions. It also has a large install base, meaning that Oracle skills are more widely available. Being used widely in business, Oracle becomes a natural choice for many companies when they start considering setting up an e-business component to their operations. Oracle, however, will typically cost more than SQL Server, which is also the best of all databases in terms of ease of use. As a result, SQL Server seems to be a good database for small and mid-sized organizations (Dyck 1999). The two main weaknesses of SQL Server, however, include the lack of programmability for those who write their own business applications to connect to the database, and the fact that SQL Server offers less multimedia support.

Some very small companies have also used Microsoft Access for their database environment. Unfortunately, Access does not have the integrity support required for running truly multi-user environments with large volumes of transactions. Several other database server environments exist on the market and can be used for e-business systems when one takes into consideration their benefits and limitations. For larger systems, other database environments include IBM's SQL/DS, DB-400, or DB2; and Progress' Progress RDBMS. For desktop systems, Corel's Corel Paradox and Lotus' Approach may be appropriate. A survey of database server environments for Web data conducted by Zona Research, Inc. for the last two quarters of 1999 revealed that SQL Server was the most used database server application for Web data (Zona Research 2000). The same survey showed that SQL Server was followed by Oracle, PC-level databases (Approach, Access, etc. grouped together), flat files (not stored in databases), DB2, Sybase, IMS, Informix, DB/400, and Ingres.

Communication Server

When a company has a large volume of outside data communications, a **communication server** could be very useful. The role of the communication server is to handle all communication specific tasks for the internal network. The server will most likely require much less storage than a database server, but it must be able to handle the company's traffic. Examples of communication functions handled by a communication server include remote access, such as allowing you to connect to the university from home; handling communication protocols; and performing identification verification. **Gateway services** perform connections from inside the organization to the outside world. To do this, gateway services will translate the company's **network protocols** to those of the outside system. Firewalls (discussed in Chapter 10) could be considered specialized communication server services. Some communication servers handle very particular types of communications, a few of which are discussed in the following paragraphs.

Mail Server   As you might have guessed, a mail server is responsible for handling electronic mail-related tasks on a network. The mail server accepts incoming messages and then distributes them to the appropriate users' mailboxes. In addition, the mail server accepts messages from internal users, then sends internal messages to the appropriate mailboxes and sends external messages out to the Internet. Electronic mail is discussed in detail in Chapter 4.

FTP Server   An FTP server allows an organization to provide users with the ability to download and/or upload files to or from remote locations. In many cases, organizations use FTP servers to let users access the latest versions of software. For example, Hewlett-Packard has a number of FTP servers that allow its customers to download the latest versions of drivers for printers, CD drives, and other hardware. Microsoft uses FTP servers to distribute updates for most of its software products. Some organizations use FTP servers to allow employees to share files. While electronic mail attachments can also be used for this purpose, FTP servers tend to be more robust, handle errors more effectively, and often allow for larger file transfers. (Many mail systems limit the size of attachments.) Examples of FTP servers include Ipswitch's WS_FTP Server and Shadow Op Software's Dragon Server. In addition, some Web servers, such as Apache, Microsoft IIS, and iPlanet Web Server, include FTP server software.

Chat Server   Some organizations using e-business are using chat technologies to let customers interact with customer service representatives in real-time. (We provide an example of this in the next section.) Many organizations feel that this method of providing customer service gives customers the immediate help they desire at a lower cost than using the telephone. Other organizations are using chat technologies to allow employees to interact in low-end teleconferences. In many cases, organizations that utilize chat technologies choose to install and run their own chat servers rather than rely on third-party services. Chat servers allow users to set up private "rooms" that have restricted access. More advanced chat servers feature voice and video support. Popular chat servers include IRCplus 2000 and Pendulab's Chat Blazer Enterprise.

Fax Server   Although it may seem that electronic mail is eclipsing facsimile document transfers, the fact is that most organizations still make heavy use of fax machines. Fax servers allow users to skip the paper aspects of faxes while still utilizing the basic technology. For example, a training company can use a fax server to send the latest course calendar to clients without ever actually printing the calendar on paper. The fax server will use a list of fax numbers to send the calendar to clients, who will receive the calendar on their fax machines (or fax servers) just as with any other fax document. Fax servers can also receive fax documents and route them to individual users' computers. Users can then view the documents on their computer monitors or print the documents if hard copies are required. Esker Software's FaxGate and VSI-Fax Network Server, and Captaris' RightFax Enterprise are widely used examples of fax server software.

List Server List servers allow electronic mail messages to be sent to a large number of users automatically. For example, the authors belong to a list called ISWORLD, which serves the academic information systems community. If we are seeking input on a research project, one of us can post a message to this list and that message is then distributed to everyone on the list. This all happens without human intervention. This is an example of a two-way list, through which users can interact with others on the list. Generally any user can post a message. Some lists are one-way only, which means that the list owner can distribute messages to everyone on the list, but list members cannot interact with each other. This type of list is quite common. Uses include newsletters and announcements. List server software may also archive messages according to discussion threads (topics). This frees users from having to store messages on their own computers. Many list servers also allow users to choose a digest format for receiving messages. When using a digest format, a user receives a periodic (e.g., daily or weekly) message that contains a compilation of all of the messages during that period. Many users find this option to be less intrusive and more efficient than individual messages. This is not surprising since an active list may generate dozens of messages a day. L-Soft's LISTSERV and Great Circle Associates' Majordomo are among the most widely used list server software.

Groupware Server

Groupware servers facilitate communication and information sharing among members of a work group. Groupware software may include features such as shared calendars, document repositories, discussion lists, and conferencing. While it is possible to use third-party groupware servers, many larger organizations find it more effective to have their own groupware servers. This allows for more flexibility and control over the environment. We discuss groupware later in this chapter. Lotus Domino, Novell Groupwise, and Microsoft Exchange are popular groupware servers.

Multimedia Server

As more users gain high-speed access to the Internet, the use of multimedia will increase. Because of the increasing importance of multimedia, some organizations are installing special servers to deal with multimedia files. Some of these servers are specialized for a particular format. For example, some radio stations use RealNetwork's RealSystem servers to allow listeners beyond the reach of the stations' signals to listen to the stations' programs. Other applications of multimedia servers include archiving presentations and video-based product demonstrations. Of course, it is possible to employ multimedia on a Web site without using a special multimedia server. Site performance may be improved, however, through the use of a multimedia server. **Streaming multimedia** (such as RealAudio) may also necessitate the use of a special-purpose server. Widely used multimedia server examples include RealSystem, Apple's Quicktime, and Microsoft's Windows Media Server.

Proxy Server

A proxy server is an intermediary between a user and the Internet. In its common form, a proxy server intercepts requests for Internet resources, such as a Web page, from a user workstation. The proxy server then checks its cached resources to see if it includes the requested page. If it does, then the proxy server sends the cached copy of the page to the user. If not, the proxy server requests the page from the appropriate Web server, then forwards the contents of the page to the requesting user. The user never receives data directly from the Internet—all data go through the proxy server. The main reasons for using a proxy server are protection and performance. When proxy servers are part of a firewall, they keep inappropriate data (such as destructive programs) or unauthorized users out, and keep private information (such as organizational secrets) in. Firewalls are discussed at length in Chapter 10. Many proxy servers maintain a cache of frequently requested resources. Requests for these resources are satisfied more quickly when cached than when coming directly from the Internet. Some proxy servers also maintain logs of traffic and scan incoming resources for viruses. Deerfield.com's WinGate Pro, Netscape Proxy Server, and Microsoft Proxy Server are examples of proxy server software.

As you can see, there are many types of specialized servers that improve the effectiveness of e-business systems. As the range of e-business applications continues to expand and as organizations become increasingly dependent on e-business, the variety of servers will expand even further.

Decision Point

Now that we have discussed various types of server functions required to run an e-business, it is time to stop and reflect on which of those services an e-business may wish to have. The following questions can help the e-business manager in this decision-making process.

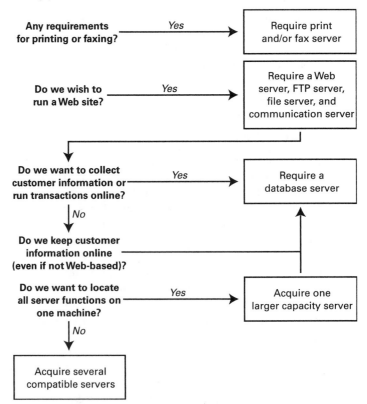

Server and Network Operating Systems

Different types of operating systems can be used on server hardware, such as **UNIX, Linux, Windows, Macintosh,** and **OS/2.** What is important for e-business applications is that the server operating system selected is network capable—it is able to function within a network. Most operating systems today (in their recent versions) have this capability. In the next section of this chapter we present various server hardware. Most people focus on the hardware when they are evaluating possible choices for servers. However, selecting the server operating system is just as important as choosing the right hardware. It is, after all, the operating system that manages the hardware. In addition, the operating system must be able to run the applications needed for the e-business, including running the Web site if it's a Web server, the database if it's a database server, or the applications for application servers.

A **network operating systems (NOS)** is a fairly complex program that can be used to manage internal resources (like a server operating system), as well as the resources on a local area network. Some of the functions of network operating systems include managing one or several servers, managing one or more printers on the network, managing the interconnection between the stations on the local area network, managing users both locally and remotely, managing system security, supporting applications, and managing client/server functions. Basically, the network operating system coordinates and manages the resources and the sharing of those resources on the network.

Operating Systems for Web Servers

The most popular operating systems for small and mid-range servers include UNIX, Linux, Windows, and OS/2. Some of these operating systems, such as UNIX and Linux, can also operate on very large systems. We will explore these further in this section. You should note, however, that numerous other operating systems exist, in particular for larger systems, such as IBM's OS/390 and DEC's VMS. Also be aware that this section provides a very high level overview of these systems, which continually evolve.

Windows 2000/ME/XP Microsoft Corporation is the creator of the Windows family of operating systems. The most recent versions of these operating systems (as of late 2001) are Windows 2000, ME, and XP. Windows ME (Millennium Edition) is a typical Windows workstation-level operating system originally intended to replace Windows 98. However, it never really caught on, and Windows XP was soon created to replace it. Windows XP comes in a professional and home edition. The professional edition is setup for networking environments, while the home edition is "clean" (few icons) and simple to use.

Windows 2000 was released in early 2000 and offered major improvements over the previous version (Windows NT) in terms of **reliability,** scalability, ease of use, and support for more hardware devices—more than eleven thousand of them, according to Microsoft. Windows 2000 is marketed as a network operating system (NOS), providing file sharing and peripheral sharing for networks of microcomputers. The operating system supports multiple users, applications, and servers, a large number of peripheral devices, and many network administration tools. The functions supported by Windows 2000 depend on the version acquired.

- *Professional*—supports small- to medium-sized companies
- *Server*—more powerful system; designed to support database intensive applications

- *Advanced Server*—most powerful version; designed to support online transaction processing, data warehousing, Web-site hosting, large-scale Internet service hosting, and large-scale scientific and engineering simulations

The advantage of selecting Windows 2000 as the operating system for a Web server is that it is ready to run Web sites with its built-in **Internet Information Server** 5.0 (IIS). The IIS must be installed (it won't install by default), but is included on the Windows 2000 disk. IIS contains an **FTP server** (file transfer), an **HTTP server** (Web server), and an **SMTP server** (an Internet mail server).

UNIX   UNIX is a very robust server operating system, which can support networking and complex applications. One of its components is the **Network File Service (NFS),** which provides built-in functions to support file server services. It can be used on desktop computers, as well as on very large scale servers and mainframe computers. The basic UNIX operating system offers only a text-based interface, not very user-friendly for the general user population, but very efficient for hard-core network users and programmers. Graphical interfaces are also available today. UNIX has existed since 1970 at Bell Labs, which makes it one of the oldest, and therefore most stable, operating systems. It is a streamlined operating system, meaning that the operating system code is relatively small (compared to Windows, for example). This makes the code efficient and explains partly why UNIX systems operate quickly. It can support network functions easily, and has a wide variety of applications written to work on it. Like Windows 2000, it can support many applications, users, servers, and printers on the network. It also deals easily with interconnections of multiple networks, supporting both local and remote users efficiently.

Linux   Linux is a derivative of the UNIX operating system concept, although the core (UNIX kernel) has been rewritten completely. Linux is an **open source** operating system. This means that the source code of Linux is available for free on the Internet. This sets this operating system apart from all others. However, different companies have started to market different versions of Linux. Of course, some have advantages over others. Some will run small-scale e-business operations, while others are capable of running very large-scale operations. At the time this book was written, the two most popular versions were Red Hat and Caldera's OpenLinux 2.2.

Why would anyone buy Linux if it is free on the Web? The two main reasons include technical support and additional software features and applications. When a company decides to implement Linux company-wide as its underlying structure for all applications, or even for only its e-business applications, it becomes dependent on making sure the software works all the time. Since Linux is free, the technical support provided is limited to discussion groups and individuals willing to offer answers to questions on dedicated Web sites. This group of users, however, is very dedicated, and tries to provide fixes and answers for bugs quickly. Nevertheless, companies want more insurance of technical support and are willing to pay the price for this. Buying Linux also allows companies to acquire all supporting applications and utilities needed to make the system efficient. And Linux is still relatively inexpensive compared to other operating systems.

One of the important differences between Linux and Windows with respect to running Web servers is that Linux is not a Web server by itself, just an operating system. Just like Windows has the IIS for running a Web server, Linux requires the use of a Web server application. The Apache Web server is often used in conjunction with Linux. Like UNIX,

Linux has fast execution because it has relatively small and efficient code. It also offers network support functions. The two negatives for Linux will tend to disappear over time. First, there is the technical support issue discussed above. As companies implement more and more Linux-based systems, opportunities will exist for companies to start specializing in providing Linux support. The second negative is that, being relatively new, there are fewer applications being developed or supported on the Linux operating system. This issue is also slowly disappearing as Linux becomes more widely used.

OS/2   While Windows 2000 and UNIX are discussed extensively in the trade press, IBM's OS/2 was the first truly **multitasking** operating system (keeping two or more programs running at the same time). Launched in 1987 with a command line interface, OS/2 has evolved into OS/2 Warp, which includes a universal network client that allows an OS/2 machine to connect not only to IBM's system network architecture (SNA), but also to virtually any network systems, including Windows 2000 and NetWare. OS/2 is a network-capable operating system, supporting network connections in the client/server environment, in particular with its Warp Connect and Warp Server tools. Warp Connect allows clients to access network resources, while Warp Server allows stations to act as servers on a network. In addition to all of the operating system functions typically supported, such as support for local and remote users, OS/2 Warp includes **speech recognition** software and mobile office services (allowing a mobile user to keep files synchronized between offices).

NetWare   Novell's NetWare is not a server operating system per se, but rather a network operating system (NOS). In fact, NetWare was *the* NOS on the market for a very long time. Most corporations considered NetWare to be the best on the market. It was very comprehensive and was able to function on any size network, from very small to very large. Back in 1995, Novell's NetWare had close to 70 percent of the NOS market (DiDio 1995). However, in recent years Microsoft Windows NT and then 2000 have continued to chip away at NetWare's market share. Some say it is because NT was marketed more strongly than NetWare, while others say that it is because Microsoft has been more responsive to user requirements by constantly adding functionality to its operating system. One of the recent "improvements" in NetWare is the support of the TCP/IP protocol, the main protocol behind the Internet.

Solaris and iPlanet   **Solaris** is an operating system from Sun Microsystems, and it was primarily designed to run on Sun's workstations (SPARC), although a large number of other hardware platforms are supported, including Intel-based platforms. Solaris is a UNIX-based operating system, like Linux. Sun claims that the operating system was developed with the Internet in mind, using TCP/IP as its core network protocol for more than fifteen years. The newest version also includes support for **IPv6** Internet addresses, and a mobile IP standard for mobile computing. It can support small systems or very large systems. It even supports clustering of servers (discussed in the server configurations section presented later in this chapter). It originally used the Apache Web server application for hosting Web sites. Eventually, Sun created its own Web server application, called iPlanet, in collaboration with Netscape, to run on its operating system and others. iPlanet is a complete Web server application with security features and numerous tools to host dynamic Web pages. It can run on other UNIX platforms, such as Red Hat, AIX, or HP, as well as on some of the Windows operating systems.

Apache   As previously discussed, some operating systems, such as Windows 2000, have built-in Web server functions. For other operating systems, vendors prefer to keep their operating systems streamlined (and hopefully more efficient) by not adding such functions. Instead, they support Web server applications that run on their operating systems. One of these Web server application programs, which is by far the most popular on the market, is the Apache Web server. The Apache project is an open source program that can be used for Internet Web server platforms with software such as Oracle Corporation's AIS or IBM's WebSphere. It can also be used with other technologies to perform complex Web server functions, beyond those of hosting Web pages. Apache servers are used on Linux, as mentioned previously, and also on UNIX systems, and even on older Sun Solaris systems. Apache can also run on Windows server systems.

Summary of Server and Network Operating Systems

Selecting a network operating system is a challenging task. Many criteria should be taken into consideration in the evaluation of the different options. For example, it is important to investigate the types of hardware and application programs supported, the performance requirements, the stability of the operating system, the support provided, and TCP/IP compatibility for Internet-based e-business systems. Table 7-1 shows some of the relevant criteria and comparisons of the operating systems discussed in this chapter. We must note that other operating systems exist, for example, for portable devices (such as Windows CE) or for very large systems (such as IBM's OS/390). It is also important to realize that companies often have to use more than one operating system internally, either because of migrations, mergers, new application requirements, or just because of change in IT management. The good news is that many applications are portable between several operating systems. The fact that your e-business application was developed in Java under Windows does not prevent it from running under UNIX. You will probably have to recompile the programs, and maybe make adjustments to some of the systems for performance reasons, but at least you don't have to start everything from scratch.

Which of the above systems are the most popular? It depends on what type of application we are discussing. For Web servers, the Linux and Apache combination is a very popular option. One leading organization that determines Web server software in use in the world is Netcraft. The company's January 2001 survey of Web sites received responses from 27,585,719 sites. The results show that Apache dominated the Web server market between June 2000 and January 2001. The problem with these types of surveys, however, is that it is very difficult to measure which servers are actually *actively* using which operating system (see E-business in Practice: Who's Web Boss? Linux or M'soft?). Another problem in comparing operating systems and Web server applications is that Web servers are utilized differently, with some using mostly "static" sites made up of ordinary HTML code, and others using dynamic pages with **server side scripting,** such as **Active Server Pages (ASP)** or **Common Gateway Interface (CGI)** pages.

Server Hardware

Today's Web servers typically use one of three types of processors: Intel Pentium, Alpha-based, or Sun Microsystems processors. The most common of these processors for servers is still the Intel processor. Computers are often classified as **microcomputers,** minicomputers, **mainframes,** and **supercomputers.** The microcomputer is typically a single-user computer. The minicomputer is a multiple-user computer that runs multiple applications simultaneously. The mainframe is a much larger computer offering the capability to run multiple applications and support information processing for multiple users, but in even greater numbers. Finally, the supercomputer tends to be used to compute large numbers of mathematical compilations as quickly as possible. What is important to realize is that a server can be any of those computers. On the other hand, the operating systems previously discussed may not work on all machines. For example, Linux cannot run in its original version on a PDA, but there are versions of most operating systems that are designed for running on very small (e.g., Windows CE) or very large machines (e.g., IBM OS/390). For the purposes of our discussion in this section, however, we will focus on small business computers.

There are a large number of manufacturers of server technologies worldwide. Some of the popular brands include Compaq, Dell, Hewlett-Packard, IBM, Gateway, Micron, and more. Most manufacturers produce quality equipment, which makes it hard to decide which one is best for a given environment. Cost is one of the first factors that people consider in making their selection. However, when selecting a server for an e-business environment, customer service and support, warranty, and reliability of the equipment should be prime considerations.

Dual Processor Servers

Servers can have dual processors. A **dual processor** server can improve the overall speed of a site or server application. Unfortunately, a dual processor server does not mean that the overall speed doubles from that of a single processor server. Since the processors make use of slower components, such as hard disk drives, memory, and other peripherals, the overall speed is restricted by these interactions. In addition, multiple processors always require some coordination and communication. As each processor is added, there is less total value added to the combination. Nevertheless a dual processor does offer several advantages.

The actual megahertz, or speed, of the processor indicates the speed of the central processing unit. A typical user might not notice a difference between a 500 and a 550 MHz computer. On the other hand, everyone would notice the difference between a 160 MHz

Table 7-1 Server and Network Operating System Comparison

	Cost	Range of Hardware Supported	Range of Applications Supported	Performance	Stability
Windows 2000 (NT)	Moderate to high	Modest	Large to very large	Good	Modest
UNIX	Moderate to high	Very large	Large	High	High
Linux	Free download	Very large	Limited to modest	Good to high	Very high
OS/2	Moderate to high	Modest	Modest to large	Good	High
Solaris	Free download	Modest to large	Modest to large	High	High
NetWare	Moderate to high	Modest	N/A	Highest	High

SOURCE: Adapted from Curt M. White, *Data Communications and Computer Networks: A Business User's Approach* (Cambridge, MA: Course Technology, 2001).

E-BUSINESS IN PRACTICE

Who's Web Boss? Linux or M'soft?

Despite popular wisdom and the usually jubilant claims of open source folk, Linux and Apache do not dominate the Internet. In fact, they hold only a tenuous 1.67 percent market share lead over Windows-based Web sites.

An entirely new survey methodology employed by Netcraft, considered the world leader in doping out what sites use which software, sheds new light on the net. The new numbers hold major implications for the exploding thin Web server market, where Windows and Linux are in a death match for dominance. The Netcraft numbers hint, but don't explicitly prove, that Windows may lead in the corporate and commercial Web sectors, as Microsoft claims.

In theory, there are 17 million Web sites out there. Netcraft's conventional count indicated that 6.1 million of them run on Linux servers and only 3.6 million run on some species of Windows. Netcraft concluded that Linux had a 14.4 percent lead over Microsoft.

Ah ha, but now Netcraft has reinterpreted its data in light of new technology it's come up with and decided that its old conclusion is wrong and that Linux has less than a 2 percent lead.

Netcraft says now that only 7.7 million of the total universe of 17 million sites are "active" Web sites. Netcraft has a new "active site methodology" that discriminates between active sites and those that exist in name only. Active sites are "produced by real people crafting HTML," Netcraft says. "Name only" sites are legitimately registered but previously couldn't be distinguished and were counted as if they were real sites. They typically consist of a single Web page with a message like "under construction" or "this name available for sale."

Cybersquatters looking to make a quick buck by selling their domain names own some of the nearly ten million template sites. Individuals and companies who have grabbed names for a multiplicity of reasons own the rest, and it seems that the companies that host the vast majority of template sites use Linux and Apache, a situation that previously inflated the Linux-Apache market share claims.

According to Netcraft's new methodology, Linux really has only 29.99 percent of the market, or 2.3 million sites. Windows is a hair behind at 28.32 percent with 2.2 million sites. Solaris still comes in a distant third with 16.33 percent of the market, or 1.2 million sites. All other operating systems combined—from Mac to mainframes—hold 23.59 percent, or 1.9 million sites. Netcraft says it couldn't figure out what operating systems were used on 1.76 percent of the Web, or 132,862 sites.

Commenting on the radically different view of the Web it's now offering, Netcraft says, "NT and Windows 2000 are much more fully represented in this analysis, but the success of Linux with the hosting companies is also very clear." Netcraft says Solaris "is being pushed further up-market by the combination of Linux and NT, and does well in specific high-volume transaction environments such as Internet brokerage."

Netcraft's numbers also strongly hint that personal Web sites represent a huge piece of the Linux market share, with a few individual Web-hosting companies running Linux responsible for hundreds of thousands, if not millions, of those sites. That would leave Windows well in the lead as the operating system of choice at serious corporate and e-business sites.

Netcraft's new analysis significantly changes the size of the huge lead that the free Apache Web server supposedly holds. Web-hosting concerns using Apache are home to 6.2 million template sites. With template sites stripped out, Apache's share of the "active" Internet drops from 62.53 percent to 59.56 percent. That's still more than respectable, of course, but again lots of those active sites are personal, not business-related. And it's not uncommon for 100,000 Apache-on-Linux sites to be hosted on a single server.

In contrast, after about 1.5 million template sites hosted on Internet Information Server are dropped from the calculations, the Microsoft-IIS market share increases from 20.36 percent to 26.84 percent. The AOL/Netscape piece of the pie, with almost 1 million template sites stripped out, drops from 6.74 percent to a trivial 2.61 percent.

SOURCE: Stuart Zipper, 4 August 2000: http://www.linuxgram .com/article.pl?sid=00/08/04/0935383&section=128. Reproduced with permission of the LinuxGram. © 2000 LinuxGram.

and a 550 MHz computer. The choice of speed is counterbalanced by the cost factor. The faster the processor, the more likely an e-business' customers will have better response times. However, there are other elements in the network that can limit the speed of the customers' access even if the company has the fastest processor on the market. Remember from our discussion in Chapters 4 and 6 that the customers' connections to the Internet might be slow, and that an e-business must account for that in its Web design.

RAM for Servers

Another component of the server hardware that is important to consider in selecting a server is the amount of **RAM (random access memory**) available. The RAM of a computer is what allows it to run multiple applications at the same time. Today's operating systems make more and more use of RAM, forcing us to increase the amount we buy when we acquire a computer. The same is true for server machines. Many experts would suggest that the absolute minimum RAM for a server, even for a very small business, should be 128 MB. This could be sufficient for a print server or some application servers, but it would be insufficient for a Web server environment. As applications increase in complexity, size, number, and ease of use, more RAM is needed. For an e-business Web server, for example, many would recommend a minimum of 256 MB. Serious servers with database and e-mail tools can have up to 4 GB (gigabytes) of RAM. Fortunately, the cost of RAM has been steadily decreasing, making it inexpensive and easy to upgrade most servers.

Server Auxiliary Storage

Servers must also have storage space. Obviously, a database or a file server will require much more storage space than an application server. Fortunately, storage in the form of hard drives has also been steadily decreasing in price. At the same time, applications and operating systems make more and more use of storage. For example, when you browse the Web, a portion of your disk drive is being used to store the files (pages) you look at temporarily. If you have not configured your system to automatically delete them regularly, and you never delete them manually, your hard drive is cluttered with such files, using a lot of space.

RAID (Redundant Arrays of Independent Disks) Technology

Hard drives, or auxiliary storage, are mechanical devices (there are some moving parts in a hard drive, which means that there are some access delays due to the moving parts). E-businesses might want to improve their overall response time by using multiple hard drives. **RAID (Redundant Arrays of Independent Disks)** is one technology used for accessing multiple hard drives. A RAID controller reads and writes to several hard drives (four hard drives is a typical RAID configuration, as shown in Figure 7-2), which allows it to store parts of files on each of the drives. These several smaller parts of the file can then be accessed simultaneously (instead of one large file being accessed by one drive).

An alternative use of RAID technology is to enhance a site's security by providing backup facilities. In this scenario, two of the drives are used to store parts of the files, while the other two are used as backup. Backups performed in this way use a process called **mirroring,** in which the same data is stored on several "mirrored" drives. When

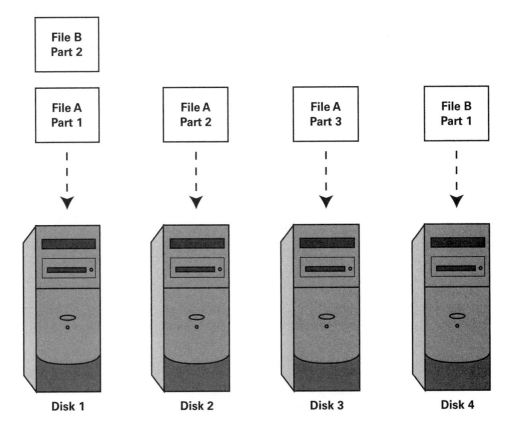

FIGURE 7-2   RAID Technology Using Four Disks

considering RAID technology, the total amount of storage space required is the first decision point. The company must then decide on how many disks to use, taking into account the number of disks that will be mirrored.

Other Server Peripherals

Students should be familiar with most of the technologies presented in this section, so consequently, the discussion is very high level. The section is only intended to provide an overview of the peripherals that managers must consider when they acquire a server environment for their e-business.

Monitor

Selecting a monitor and video card for servers should be one of the easiest tasks. Only the Web master, server operator, or owner of the company (who often takes on all of these roles!) uses the monitor. Therefore, the monitor does not have to be top of the line in terms of size, color, or features, unless the operator of the server also uses it for regular tasks (which is not recommended). Costs should drive this decision. Note that for client hardware, monitors should be carefully selected, as they are the users' interfaces with the systems. If users have poor interfaces, they will probably dislike the system and may discontinue its use.

Network Equipment

If the server is part of a three-tier or n-tier environment, it must be linked to the other servers. A **local area network (LAN)** is probably the best solution for connecting the servers internally (unless they are located at various sites, in which case one of the networks described in Chapter 6 could be used). The most popular LANs today are still the **Ethernet** and the **Token Ring.** In each case, a **hub** is used to connect the servers together, as well as any workstations or PCs that need access to the servers. Hubs are fairly inexpensive, even for a 10/100 Mbps Ethernet LAN. Each server or client that needs to be interconnected also needs to have a LAN card (a network interface card or NIC), either Token Ring or Ethernet, depending on the selected hub. LAN cards fit into available slots inside the server's case. An alternative to a hub is the use of a **switch.** The switch is similar to the hub, but does not function the same way internally (with respect to how the stations and servers communicate with one another).

Backup Systems

One of the key features needed for any e-business to run its operations, whether it uses several large-scale servers, one small server, or even just a few desktop workstations, is a backup system. How crucial is backup? Given the complexity of our technology installations and our dependence on computers today, backup is indeed a key element. Traditionally, home users tend not to backup their data...until something happens to their files. Ask for a show of hands in your class. How many students have performed a backup of their files in the last week? Month? Six months? Year? Ever? You'll be surprised by the results. For companies, however, backup is often the key to survival, particularly if their business operations involve any online components.

Backup capabilities require a combination of hardware and software tools. Most operating systems described before have built-in backup utility software. Other backup software is available from a wide variety of vendors. Most backup utilities compress files. **Data compression** reduces the total number of bits used to represent a set of data items using a compression algorithm. For example, several standard backup utilities offer a four to three compression ratio. Therefore, data normally using 100 kilobytes of space would be stored using only 75 kilobytes ($[100 \div 4] \times 3$).

The next decision is which medium is going to be used to store the backed up files and applications. For small businesses or home users, backup options include **ZIP disks** and **CD-ROMs.** ZIP drives can be external or integrated (internal). Disks can currently contain 100 or 250 MB of data, enough space to store a high volume of large files, including database files. The optical disk is a device similar to the CD-ROM, but programmable. CD-ROMs (compact disk read-only memory) can also store a large number of files. The capacity of the original CD-ROM (120 mm disc) is approximately 600 MB of data. The data are saved on an **optical disk** using a CD burner. Once files have been stored on the CD, however, they are not erasable but can be read multiple times. This means that, contrary to the ZIP disks, the CD cannot be reused. However, CDs are fairly inexpensive, so weekly backups would not represent a major cost over a year.

Cartridge and tape backup systems are also available for reasonable prices today. These systems use **magnetic tapes.** A plastic ribbon covered with a metal oxide coating is used to store the data. The older tapes were open reel, which had to be mounted on a tape drive to be read or written on. Today's magnetic tape devices use tape permanently enclosed in plastic cassettes or cartridges, which are read by cartridge read/write devices. Both small and very large companies can use cartridge systems. For small companies, it is often a better choice than other media. For larger companies, it is often one of very few options they have to backup their huge amount of data.

Finally, a popular method of backup is to duplicate all files on disk drives. The cost of disk drives has been dramatically reduced over the years, making storage of the same data twice a reasonable backup strategy for many businesses today. Of course, in this case, the files must be stored on two different disks to make sure that if one crashes the other is still available. When the updating of the files is done on the two disks simultaneously, the process uses mirrored disks. Everything is written, updated, or deleted from the two disks at the same time. This provides an exact copy of everything on a disk. These disks can be on two different devices or on one, using the RAID technology previously discussed.

The costs of these various backup options vary substantially. The cheaper alternatives include the ZIP drives and the **CD burners,** followed by tapes and cartridges, and finally mirrored disks. In addition to cost, the choice of which backup alternative is better for a company depends on the amount of storage needed, the expertise available, and the types of systems it has. New technologies are also regularly tested, such as **magneto-optical drives,** which use lasers and reflected light to sense data values, or **USB (Universal Serial Bus)** storage devices, which connect into a USB port and are becoming popular alternatives to ZIP disks, particularly for laptop users.

Uninterrupted Power Supply

Just like backup systems, a very important feature that a company should consider when acquiring a server for the purposes of e-business (or any business purpose) is the **uninterrupted power supply (UPS).** Electricity is needed for all computers to work, and without it companies cannot operate their computers, servers, or networks. E-businesses cannot afford, therefore, to be dependent only on the power company's supply of electricity. The UPS provides electricity when the main power supply is shut down. The amount of time that the systems can keep running on this alternative source of current depends on the amount of money spent for the UPS system. Some very small systems can provide power for one or two servers. Very large UPS systems support mainframes or server farms (a large number of servers).

Printers and Scanners

It is unlikely that you will see servers in networks that do not have at least one printer attached. While many users may have their own personal printers connected to their workstations, **network printers** tend to be high-end printers supporting large volumes of printing at reduced costs. The printers are often better quality than the locally attached printers. Printers come in all varieties. You can choose between laser, ink jet, or dot matrix; you can select color or black and white. Printers can also be used as copiers, or can function only as printers. It is beyond the scope of this book to discuss all printers. The important point we wish to make is that selecting a printer is also important in the overall implementation of servers for an e-business, at least until we reach the days of the so-called paperless society.

A **scanner** is a device used to input images and text from a paper format to an electronic format. While many businesses may not see the need for a scanner, a small dot-com or a small business that wishes to use its own pictures and photographs to create its Web page needs to be able to create digital versions of these images. That's what the scanner is for. For example, a small online clothing retailer who wants to create an online catalog of its products could use a scanner to present pictures taken at its latest clothing line demonstration. A sports travel organization might wish to scan pictures of its latest trips to show potential customers. The scanner can be used for any of these, as well as scanning text. A **digital camera** may also be used in lieu of a scanner. Digital cameras will be discussed under the client technologies section. How does a scanner work? The scanner moves over the image and converts it dot by dot, line by line into a stream of binary numbers, each representing a single point on the image. This point is known as a **pixel.** The pixels can then be reproduced on the computer screen or saved in files.

Decision Point

Assuming that the e-business has decided on its basic server and operating systems, it must now decide on which peripherals are needed. Basic decisions, such as which printers and scanners to use, are not presented below. However, the following questions might help guide the decision-making process for other peripherals.

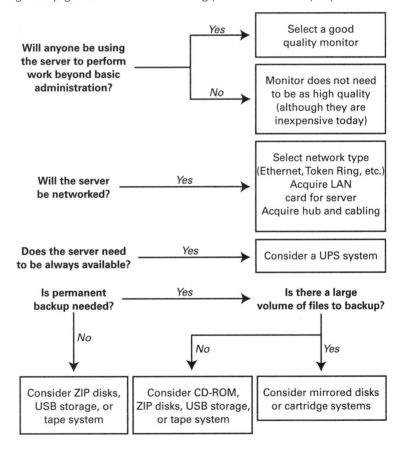

Server Configurations

We have discussed most of the server hardware and software you will encounter in implementing e-business operations. The servers, however, can be implemented in different configurations. For example, some servers are designed for one specific function. These are called **thin servers.** Another way to configure servers is to include them in **server farms,** in which multiple servers are collocated and connected.

Thin Server

A new term has recently been introduced in the client/server architecture terminology: the thin server. The idea of thin servers is to have pre-configured network "appliances" dedicated to a single network function. In general, servers are seen as the major central computer that performs a number of functions, including storing files, dealing with communications, or performing mail and Web services. The thin server approach dedicates a less expensive and less complex machine to a very specific function. For example, a thin server can be used as a Web server. Another thin server would be dedicated to e-mail services. A third one can be dedicated to handling local area network administration functions. Network administrators really like the idea of the thin servers because they are less expensive and easier to setup, maintain, and control. Of course, for companies that need multiple functions managed by a server, but without a high volume of transactions to justify separate servers, this is not a solution. Large companies, on the other hand, should clearly consider the thin server as a good alternative client/server solution. An example of such an appliance-type server is Dell Computers' PowerApp.web server. It is designed for one and only one purpose: to host Web sites. All features of the operating system that are not needed to host a Web site have been removed. This results in a reasonable price, and provides for quick setup and easier maintenance.

Server Farms and Server Collocation

The idea of server farms or **server clustering** is to tie servers together to distribute software loads and better manage server failures. Clustering really became popular with Digital Equipment Corporation's VAX minicomputer systems, which could be strung together. Most clustering today is done on UNIX-based systems with proprietary applications allowing servers to be connected in powerful and **fault-tolerant systems.** More recently, NOS have been upgraded to support server clustering in Intel-based personal computer hardware. However, server clustering remains a very complex implementation. It involves combining network hardware, using **middleware** and operating system clustering software, and building custom applications to have a seamlessly functioning cluster of servers. Some of the required functions include **load balancing** (between the various servers), **server failover** (transferring load to another server in case of a failure), and data mirroring (duplicating all data on two separate disks). Most PC-based networks offer one or two of the above functions, but rarely the three functions together. Within the next few years, however, server farms or server clustering for PC-based networks should be a common server configuration. One of the issues, however, with collocating the servers is the potential security problem it creates. Having all data and processing in one location can result in business losses, or even in the closure of a business if a disaster of any kind strikes this location. This is especially an issue for smaller organizations.

Sizing a Web Server

Before determining which server a business should acquire for its e-business environment, the size of the server must be determined. This step is called Web server **capacity planning.** How do you do this? It is a very difficult task to estimate the future traffic on a Web site. At best, what you will have is a good approximation of the expected traffic, or an educated guess. Some servers are easier to size, for example a database server, if you know exactly how many clients access the servers, for which applications, and how often the applications are typically used. For sizing Web servers, though, companies have generally few or no experienced people, technology changes very fast, the tools available are not very mature or well-tested, and there are few or no industry benchmarks against which to compare (Wong 1997).

There are basically three factors to consider in sizing a Web server: the level of user demand or traffic, the capabilities of the networking environment, and the nature of the Web page content that is to be available on the server. Therefore, before sizing a Web server, the company needs to ask important questions: Is this Web server going to be an intranet or an Internet server? What is the potential demand for access to this site? What is the speed of the connections the company has to the Internet or intranet? How many pages will be loaded? Will the Web server be generating data for access? (Trickett, Nakagawa, Mani, Gfroerer 2001).

Once the estimate has been completed for the regular expected traffic, other estimates should be calculated for peak periods (Mother's Day, Christmas, etc.) and for periods of time that will occur immediately after a given marketing campaign (coupons, rebates, etc.). In this case, it is very important to consider whether a server must be upgraded before the new marketing campaign starts. If the server is not ready to handle the load, it could prove disastrous, and even more disastrous if you try to upgrade during these new peaks of traffic.

User Demand or Volume

The user demand is generally measured in the number of hits per second. One of the most popular Web servers worldwide is home.netscape.com, with approximately 120 million hits per day (Wong 1997). If that load is spread over twenty-four hours, or 86,400 seconds, then the site averages approximately fourteen hundred hits per second. This average is called the sustained load. However, there could be demand peaks of more than double that. Let's say that peaks on the Netscape site run about three thousand hits per second. There will be periods of time when the server is relatively inactive. Since Netscape does receive a large number of hits, the company tries to keep image size low. Why? Because for each hit, images and text must be downloaded. In Netscape's case, it keeps the average page size to five kilobytes. Therefore, fifteen hundred hits at 5 kilobytes result in an approximately 8 Mbps (eight megabits per second) aggregate data rate (when all hits and the amount of data transferred are aggregated together). Using the sustained load allows one to size a server for that load, but peaks in demand must also be met. If peaks occur at times when customers would be buying a company's products online, poor response time may stop them from making purchases. Note also that transferring Web pages is only one function of the server. Other duties can include authentication, transferring protocol information, and establishing and managing the connections (which are called **sockets** in Web server terminology).

It should also be noted that **intranets** typically get fewer hits, on average, per day than Internet sites. Therefore, knowing whether the site is to be used for an intranet or for the Internet is important. In addition, sizing for an intranet is much easier since the total potential population of users is known.

Type of Content

Before determining the bandwidth requirements for the network to which the server is connected, we need to figure out what content is to be stored on the Web pages. The type of content will determine the storage requirements for the server. Obviously, images represent larger content than blocks of text. These two types of content, text and images, are found in most "static" HTML pages. Another type of content that must be considered is executable files or services. Recall from Chapter 5 that scripts are either sent to the client to be interpreted and/or run by the browser (such as Java applets), or executed on the server (such as CGI scripts). If a Web site makes extensive use of CGI scripts (e.g., numerous forms to be handled), then the server must be sized to handle these additional requests. Finally, applications such as search engines also require more powerful Web servers to accommodate the extra processing on top of handling client hits to the server.

Network Bandwidth

Once the number of hits has been determined, network consumption or bandwidth requirements need to be established. This process will require you to make certain assumptions. For example, the average HTTP get operation (to retrieve a Web page) retrieves about 13 KB (kilobytes) of data. Of course, some retrievals are much smaller (e.g., text only), while others are larger (e.g., images). Using the example of an e-business with one thousand clients and ten hits per day, this results in an aggregate rate of 1.3 KB per second, again a very low number.

For a small e-business, the number of hits tends to be much smaller. For companies with very busy sites, hits can be in the range of one hundred to one thousand hits per day (Wong 1997). Knowing how many clients are expected to connect to a Web site may help determine the expected aggregate data rate. If, for example, it is expected that one thousand clients will connect to the server per day, and that these clients will perform ten hits each, this results in a sustained number of hits of 0.1 per second, a very manageable load for servers. Another factor to consider is that while the server's processor may well be capable of handling the load, the bandwidth of the network on which the processor is connected will affect the overall response time and should be planned together with the size of the server. We discussed in Chapters 4 and 6 various limitations on network connections and various bandwidths available. Using an ISDN line at 128 Kbps would not be a problem in our previous example (1.3 kilobytes is roughly equal to 10.5 kilobits, and our system supports transfers of 128 kilobits per second). This example uses low estimates for the number of potential clients and the size of the transfers. It may be that the average hit is more like 25 kilobytes because of numerous images and executable files, changing all of our calculations. While this section shows how to estimate bandwidth requirements, several simulation tools can also be used in obtaining these numbers.

Summary of Sizing a Web Server

Following are the basic steps used in sizing a Web server. The steps should be useful to you, but it really is a matter of experience to become an expert at sizing Web servers. In addition, each vendor's server may have its particularities to take into account. Fortunately, vendors have realized the difficulty of the task for their potential customers and have prepared documentation and tools to facilitate their work. One example is IBM's document "Understanding IBM pSeries Performance and Sizing" available on their Web site (Trickett et al. 2001).

These are the first few steps to sizing a Web server:

1. Determine the expected number of hits per second. Use the number of expected potential clients and their average number of hits per day.

2. Determine the peak number of hits per second.

3. Determine the type of content to be stored on the server.

4. Determine the bandwidth requirements by looking at the average size of hits.

How important is it to have a site with a good response time? A 1999 report published by Zona Research (Pastore 1999) suggested that slow download times on e-commerce sites may cost merchants more than U.S.$4 billion each year. The study reports that more than one-third of users give up when download times are too slow. Sizing a Web server properly, then, becomes a very important task for an e-business.

CLIENT TECHNOLOGIES

The client is the part of any network or system with which the user typically interacts. It is therefore a very key technology. There are a number of client technologies available for the e-business. They can be classified as workstations or special terminals, such as **automatic teller machines (ATMs), kiosks,** and **point-of-sale devices,** or special input devices, such as cameras and **bar code readers.** Other client technologies include television **set-top boxes** and the whole set of mobile devices that can be used for **m-commerce.**

Workstations

Workstations, personal computers, or microcomputers are terms used to refer to the client device with which users interact. What factors should a manager consider in selecting workstations for employees? The key factors include cost, of course, as well as performance, features offered, compatibility with existing equipment, and the reputation of the vendor with respect to quality and support. Cost will depend on the brand and the features offered. Popular brands include Compaq, Dell, Gateway, IBM, Hewlett-Packard, and many more. Performance is often a result of processor speed and the amount of random access memory (RAM) available. The processor speed, measured today in megahertz or gigahertz, indicates the speed at which the processor can handle its tasks. Workstations, just like servers, can have multiple processors. Why is memory important to performance? More memory means that there are larger **buffer** spaces to hold additional data. This enables the system to continue processing while disks are being accessed because some of the needed data are held in memory. Having more data in memory may also reduce the number of disk accesses. More memory also means that there is more room to load some programs, at least partly, in memory to make them directly accessible, or it allows several programs to be loaded into memory. Several other internal features of a computer can also affect its performance. For example, performance can be increased with a faster clock speed, wider instruction and data paths, and faster disk access. It is beyond the scope of this book to explain all of these internal details.

Network Computer

Another type of client workstation that has gained popularity in recent years is the **network computer.** In the network computer, there is a lack of directly attached secondary storage capacity. The network computer must therefore rely on the server to supply its operating system and applications. There are several benefits to network computers. First, they tend to be somewhat cheaper than traditional PC workstations. They are also much easier to maintain. Updates can be loaded on the server and all network computers attached to that server are automatically updated with the most recent operating system or application. Another benefit for companies is that security is enhanced as employees cannot copy data onto diskettes, since no diskette drives are provided. Of course, they can still print the data on the network printer.

Portable Workstations

Laptops offer the same features as traditional workstations in smaller and lighter versions. Of course, lighter laptops will have fewer drives built-in, but most often additional drives can be connected outside of the computer. Some manufacturers of laptops include Compaq, Dell, Gateway, IBM, NEC, Toshiba, and others. In selecting a laptop, all of the criteria described for the traditional desktop workstation apply, but in addition, the company must consider the durability of the laptop and its weight. Laptops tend to be exposed to more adverse conditions, such as being left in a car under intense summer heat or freezing winter temperatures, or being dropped.

Workstation Peripherals

Some of the peripherals to consider include the mouse, the monitor and related graphics card, CD-ROM, ZIP drive for backups, speakers and sound cards, size of the hard drive, keyboard, Web camera, and the NIC card for a workstation that is part of a network. Monitors are important peripherals for client workstations because they are the windows to the applications for users. Displays are made up of thousands of individual pixels, or picture elements, arranged to make up a rectangular screen. Each pixel is a tiny square on the display. Common displays today have 768 rows of 1024 pixels (768 x 1024). Older screens had 480 x 640 or 600 x 800 pixels. Today, good quality displays support a large number of colors, and 1600 x 1200 pixels. Monitors also vary in the size of the display. Good quality monitors are important to reduce user fatigue (from looking too long at a screen) and to increase the quality of images in applications for which images are important. Graphics programs require large amounts of memory in the computer to display high-resolution images. Today, part of the memory requirement has been transferred to the graphics card installed within the computer, and to which the monitor is connected.

While the discussion above referred to a company acquiring monitors for its employees, consumers' monitor quality is very important for Web-based e-businesses. Consumers may or may not have high quality monitors in their homes. Therefore, just as a Web site design should take into account the possibility that consumers have low speed connections to the Internet (see Chapter 4 and previous discussion in this chapter), it should also take into account the possibility that they have lower quality monitors. In designing the Web site, the company should be careful not to include images that require high-end monitors to be displayed correctly.

Some of the other peripherals for client workstations were discussed in the server technology section, such as hard drives, random access memory (RAM), CD-ROM, Zip drives, and NIC cards. Others are fairly straightforward and do not require an extensive discussion, such as mice, speakers and sound cards, and keyboards. Another device that is gaining popularity among Web users as its price has gone down substantially in recent years is the Web camera. Web cameras allow a site to send a video image of people, events, or things in real-time. One of the most common applications of Web cameras is videoconferencing, which allows people to hold meetings online and see each other.

Workstation Operating Systems

Workstations require operating systems to make them run (and applications to make them useful). Typically, companies have the choice of the operating system they want to use. Most of the operating systems were presented in the server technologies section. We will not repeat this discussion here. Note that client versions of the server software are available, with fewer administrative tools and simplified code. For example, the Windows XP operating system is network capable, but is not designed to be used as server software since a number of functions (available in Windows 2000) are missing. While the operating system is critical for making computers work, the application software is the most important piece of the client workstation *from the users' point of view.* Users will use applications to perform their business functions. As long as their applications work well, users rarely care about what system is running behind the application to manage the computer's resources.

Transaction Terminals

Transaction terminals are computers designed for special purposes. You interact with many of them regularly. For example, in a typical week you probably go to several stores that use point-of-sale terminals, or you might go to the bank's ATM to withdraw some money, or you might even use the ATM functions at the point-of-sale terminal.

Automated Teller Machines (ATMs)

Automated teller machines (ATMs) are special purpose terminals that provide twenty-four–hour banking services to consumers. The terminals are linked directly to their respective banking institution, usually via a dedicated line connection. The terminals include a printing device (printing your transaction receipts), a keypad (for data entry), a magnetic card reader (for identification), a display screen, an envelope-receiving drawer, and a cash-dispensing drawer. Most businesses will not have to consider or acquire ATMs unless they are a bank or other financial institution (trusts, insurance, brokerage, etc.).

Point-of-Sale (POS) Terminals

Point-of-sale (POS) terminals are computers specially designed to operate at the place where sales are recorded. POS often include sales management and inventory control systems. Most POS terminals are connected to a bar code reader, which simply reads bar codes printed on products or their packaging. This eliminates the need to retype information, and therefore the possibility of human error, in addition to speeding up the process. As merchandise is scanned using the bar code reader, all information on the product stored in the computer's database (or central server) is available. This includes the price, specifications, and any discounts currently available. As the product is scanned and paid for by the consumer, the inventory levels are also reduced automatically in the database. This allows the business manager to know exactly what was sold, and what needs to be reordered. Using POS terminals has therefore made retail businesses much more efficient in controlling their inventory, and increasing their overall profitability.

POS terminals are built using the same computer technology with which you are familiar, but with added hardware and custom-written software. Some terminals are custom built,

Example of a Kiosk

SOURCE: Photo courtesy of High Technology Solutions, Inc.

while others can be bought in standard packages. Peripherals that a manager has to consider when selecting a POS terminal system include the type of display monitor to use, the display pole (where consumers see prices), bar code readers, printers, cash drawers, credit card readers, check readers, and more, depending on the complexity of the system.

Kiosks

Kiosks are one of the latest trends in e-commerce, although they have been used for other applications for several years. For example, information booths at some airports and shopping malls use the kiosk technology. Kiosks are special purpose terminals connected directly to an application. Consumers use the terminal to interact with an online system, which can be Web-based or not. The kiosks are nicely designed to attract the consumer. They are also very user friendly, often allowing consumers to interact with the system using a touch screen.

Companies use kiosks to provide their customers with access to their online catalogs or products. There are two ways that companies implement kiosks. Some companies add them to their retail stores, allowing customers to browse their online catalog for all of the products they cannot keep in store. Others use kiosks for access to their online catalogs in locations that are available twenty-four hours a day, seven days a week. For example, a luggage-making company might install a kiosk in an airport. Or a kiosk to sell tickets for shows could be setup outside a shopping mall. Some U.S. companies that use Web-based in-store kiosks include Staples, Barnes & Noble, Best Buy, and Kmart.

Television Set–Top Boxes

One special type of client technology is the set-top box. The set-top box is a connection box that is used to provide Internet access using a television and the services of an Internet service provider (ISP). Set-top boxes are usually slightly larger than cable boxes, and are typically placed on top of the television. The functions provided are similar to those of **WebTV** (a television that can also be used to browse the Internet for a monthly fee). The user can use his television for watching programs, but can then also connect to his ISP to browse the Web or manage an e-mail account. For the installation to work, the user needs a television, a phone line that connects to the set-top box, and an ISP. Regular phone lines work, although the modems are not always high speed. For example, several set-top boxes incorporate modems that operate at 33.6 Kbps. The computer software is built into the set-top boxes, with often only simple Web browsers and e-mail readers. Additional applications can sometimes be added to set-top boxes, but very rarely. Applications, however, would not be very useful as there are no hard drives, diskette drives, or any type of permanent storage. However, the great advantage of set-top boxes is that they can bring Internet capabilities to everyone, even those without computers, at a reasonable cost.

Client Configurations

In the client/server architecture, the processing logic and storage is shared between clients and servers. Another way to categorize the architecture beyond the two-, three-, or n-tier designation is by describing clients as fat or thin. This refers to the amount of application logic managed by the client system. There is no good answer to the question, *"Which approach is preferred?"* It all depends on each company's environment, users, applications, and computing philosophy.

Thin Client

In the **thin client** approach, the servers handle most of the application logic. Mainframe and large server vendors, such as IBM and Sun Microsystems, believe in this approach. Clients are toned down, requiring less expensive systems. These clients are most often network computers, with no auxiliary storage or diskette drives. Servers are more expensive, to handle the bigger load. The thin client approach offers several advantages. First is security, since sensitive data cannot be downloaded onto diskettes at user workstations. As discussed in the previous description of network computers, this environment offers easier maintenance and management, requiring changes to the operating system and applications only on the server. In addition, it is easier to manage software licenses when only thin clients are used. Some disadvantages of the thin client approach, however, include less local control for users, higher costs for larger servers, and the loss of some of the advantages of client/server computing, such as sharing the load between clients and servers.

Fat Client

In this case, the client handles most of the application logic. This is the approach promoted by personal computer software vendors, such as Microsoft Corporation. Regular PCs with high-speed processors, large amounts of disk space, and memory are used to load a large number of applications handled locally. One advantage of this approach is more local control. If some applications are used only by a small number of people within an organization, it may make more sense to have those applications locally stored on those few individuals' computers. Having **fat clients** can also reduce the users' dependency on the network for getting their work done. In the era of user empowerment, the fat client approach is more appropriate. However, the fat client approach also has disadvantages. Several copies of the same software are needed. Users will often be using different versions of the same software. This makes management and maintenance of the environment very cumbersome. Users are often not very good at performing backups of their own machines. If they have crucial data of use to the organization, the data may be lost if their computers crash.

Mobile Client Technologies

We discussed in the previous chapter the new trend of mobile commerce, or using mobile devices to conduct electronic transactions. Early mobile technologies included analog cellular phones, pagers, and some special purpose wireless terminals. Today, there are many advanced devices (besides portable computers) for conducting transactions electronically in the wireless world. These include the newer **digital phones, personal digital assistants,** and different types of **smart phones.** Recall from Chapter 6 that there are different wireless networks around the world, and that even within the cellular networks, different standards exist. The mobile client devices in this section are described in general terms, but you should be aware that very often specific devices support specific standards.

Personal Digital Assistants

Personal digital assistants (PDAs) started as electronic agendas. Consequently, they typically include simple address books, scratch pads, and other functions that used to be provided on electronic agendas. In addition, they now allow users to send e-mail or access the Web through wireless connections. An example of a very popular personal digital assistant device currently is the Palm Pilot.

Digital Cellular Phones

While users can't surf the Web with a simple digital cellular phone, these phones have improved greatly. In recent years, their capabilities have expanded beyond placing and receiving phone calls, while their physical size has been reduced considerably. For example, **text messaging** on digital cellular phones allows users to receive and read written messages. The only problem is that the messaging is often only one-way. The user cannot generate or reply to a message, just receive and view it. Digital phones also provide most services available on land-based phones, such as caller ID and call waiting.

Smart Phones

Smart phones are the next step in cellular technology, and the real entry into m-commerce. They combine a cellular telephone, a PDA, and access to the Internet. All of these elements are combined into one device that fits in the user's palm. Smart phones provide users with the ability to talk, send and receive e-mail messages, and access the Web. It should be noted that while a smart phone has Internet capabilities, it does not use the latest versions of Netscape Navigator or Internet Explorer to navigate the Internet. Because of the limitations of the phones' processors, memory, battery life, display screens, and keyboards, they were developed to offer less complex, smaller, and custom-designed information services to the user. A smart phone's browser is called a microbrowser.

Smart phones use the **Wireless Application Protocol (WAP)** that we discussed in the previous chapter. The Wireless Application Protocol allows users to access and search the Internet, and to send messages using wireless devices. WAP works on any platform and reformats the content of the page to fit the screen. The other wireless protocol, **i-mode,** works in a similar fashion. One major advantage with smart phones is that the content that is being browsed can be location-specific. For example, a user can download weather information and maps, and at the same time obtain up-to-date traffic information based on where she is. Another advantage of smart phones is that WAP has an advanced security protocol, the **Wireless Transport Layer Security (WTLS).** It provides mobile users with data integrity, privacy, **authentication,** and **denial-of-service** protection. A user can therefore enter her credit card number to make purchases from her smart phone with less worry about credit card number theft. Smart phones are common in Europe and Asia but have had a slow start in the United States.

How is the smart phone market today? Really going well, with many technology giants launching their own technologies and applications to seize part of this exploding market. For example, Microsoft Corporation has launched smart phone software called Stinger, which should let Microsoft Outlook users manage their e-mail remotely. Phone vendors should follow in this giant footstep and offer products that support Stinger. Mitsubishi already sells smart phones equipped with Microsoft Mobile Explorer, a micro-browser for GSM phones in Europe. They should be available in the United States by the time you read this book. Another example is Cisco, a company known for making and selling routers, which has recently rolled out a line of Web-enabled telephones.

There are a wide variety of technologies and services accessible and available with smart phones. Following are just two examples.

AvantGo.com AvantGo offers an information portal for smart phones that specializes in "bridge[ing] the gap between the Internet, wireless, and mobile technologies." It tries to offer for smart phone users what Yahoo! offers for Web surfers. The user simply estab-lishes a connection using his smart phone and selects the information of interest, which is then downloaded directly to the phone. The user does not need a desktop PC, and the information can be more relevant or customized for the user.

SportsFeed.com SportsFeed is a company specializing in real-time sports information. It began by providing sports statistics and team standings via the Internet to people's desk-tops using a Java applet. Now, with the advent of smart phones, the company is providing the same information to cell phone customers. SportsFeed.com uses a push method; it sends updates to the user's phone using text-messaging technology. The company, how-ever, does not use the WAP protocol.

The future of smart phones is bright, with newer technologies constantly being intro-duced. For example, smart phones manufactured by Nokia now support **Java** technology to complement WAP. The use of Java allows users to download applications from the Web to their smart phones. The **third generation (3G)** of wireless technologies, discussed in the previous chapter, will also provide more bandwidth so that users will have high-speed access to the Internet from their smart phones. In 3G, mobile phones will unite voice com-munications, Internet access, music, television, video, a video camera, videoconferencing, a personal computer, and much more. All of this will be included in a handheld device that will fit in a user's pocket.

Newer client technologies are constantly being developed to facilitate the use of electronic information in business. Some of the promising technologies include voice and speech recognition. For example, a new technology built and hosted by NetByTel of Florida is being used by the Office Depot chain for facilitating customer order taking. Using a voice recognition system that understands and interprets natural language phrases, customers can call a free phone number and "talk" to a system to place their orders (Johnson 2001).

MANAGERIAL ISSUES

Hosting or Being Hosted

One of the main decisions a manager must make when contemplating the implementa-tion of a Web site for electronic commerce is whether the Web site should be hosted within the company or outsourced to another company. Being hosted by a company that specializes in Web-site hosting has several advantages. First and foremost, these companies will monitor the systems twenty-four hours a day, seven days a week. They will therefore ensure that your Web site is online and functioning so that consumers can browse it and make purchases almost all of the time. If an e-business hosts its own Web site internally, someone must be in charge of this twenty-four/seven monitoring. For very large companies, there is usually someone already in charge of monitoring systems at night and during weekends. If you're starting your own e-business, however, it means that you must monitor the system yourself or assign the task to one of your limited number of employees. Another advantage is that hosting companies will typically have several high-speed data lines, such as T-3s or even OC3s. These provide quick access for consumers to all of the Web sites they are hosting. In addition, having several high-speed lines provides a backup network in case one of the lines breaks down. Another advantage of being hosted is that the hosting company should have several individuals with networking and other skills who maintain the technology infrastructures. As a customer, when you lease space for your Web site, you will have access to this technical assistance. Finally, another main advantage of being hosted is the relatively low cost, especially up-front costs, necessary to start the business. Since you do not have to buy a server and high-speed connections, your costs are limited to the development of the Web site (which you must pay whether you are being hosted or hosting your own site), the initial setup costs, and the monthly costs for being hosted, including the Internet connection.

There are also disadvantages, though, to being hosted. First, you have no control over the server environment, and are totally dependent on the provider. This is why it becomes very important to shop around for a provider when you want to be hosted, and ask other customers about the reputation and customer service history of the provider you are considering. The provider may limit the number of sites it allows on its server; it may limit the size of your Web site or the number of transactions it will "accept" before charging you more; and it will force you to use the software environment that fits its infrastructure. And, possibly the most important disadvantage for some companies, security can be an issue with being hosted. When the database is stored outside of an organization's offices, there is an increased risk of security breaches. Finally, but also very important, is the lack of control you have over the bandwidth available for your customers to make transactions on your Web site. Since multiple Web sites are typically hosted on a provider's server, your response time becomes dependent on the traffic that occurs on these other Web sites as well.

Hosting your own Web site has several advantages. First, you get to decide exactly what the server environment will be and have total control over it. Another advantage of hosting your e-commerce Web site is that the site itself can be tied directly to the other information systems of the company (order processing, etc.). Of course, one of the main advantages of hosting your own Web site is the added security you can provide by keeping all of your data in-house. However, there are also some major disadvantages related to hosting your Web site. First and foremost is cost. For a large company, this issue may not be a huge one, but for most Internet startups and small e-businesses, the costs of the hardware, software, and personnel needed for hosting a Web site can be prohibitive. Another disadvantage of hosting your own site is, of course, that you are responsible for the maintenance. This is linked to the higher costs we just mentioned, because you need someone to take care of the computer equipment, network connections, and software. Finally, one disadvantage to always consider with technology is the risk of the system becoming obsolete in a short time frame. You would then have to upgrade the system, which creates additional costs and headaches. Table 7-2 provides a summary of the advantages and

Table 7-2 Summary of Advantages and Disadvantages of Hosting and Being Hosted

Being Hosted (Outsource)		Hosting	
Advantages	**Disadvantages**	**Advantages**	**Disadvantages**
■ Twenty-four/seven monitoring of Web site ■ Several high-speed lines ■ Technical assistance ■ Low monthly costs	■ No control over environment ■ Security ■ No bandwidth control	■ Total control of environment ■ Integration with other information systems ■ Security	■ Costs ■ Maintenance ■ Technology obsolescence risk

disadvantages of each approach. Which one a company chooses depends upon the particular requirements and situation of that company.

Most of the previous discussion about hosting or being hosted covers the typical issues that a small- to medium-sized e-business might encounter. What about a larger firm? The same principles apply, but the resulting decisions might be different. Cost is always an issue, but usually less of a concern than for small firms. On the other hand, being hosted could be quite expensive and result in not-so-low monthly costs. Similarly, security might be a bigger issue because larger firms are more often targeted by malicious parties. Maintenance is usually less of an issue in larger firms, not because it is simpler, but because there might be a larger pool of skilled employees to tap into.

CLIENT/SERVER TECHNOLOGY SELECTION

We have discussed throughout the chapter various considerations for selecting client and server hardware and software. We summarize all of these considerations in this section. Cost, of course, is often a prime factor. Other very important factors in selecting the client/server technologies to use for one's e-business include the reliability of the equipment or software, the compatibility of the equipment or software with the existing environments, the availability of skills to support the selected equipment and software, the amount of growth expected for the next five years, the documentation and support provided by the vendor, the complexity of the implementation, and, of course, the performance of the desired equipment and software environment. Obviously, there are trade-offs to be made. It would be great if a company could afford for their new e-business site a server farm with ninety-six processors and terabytes of RAID disks. There would be no delays or response time problems for the company's consumers. However, this type of site would cost millions of dollars. The bottom line is that it is important to find the right balance between the requirements, wish list items, and the company's budget.

Finally, remember that acquiring operating systems and application software is not all there is to it. Utilities and programming tools are very important too. For example, a company should look into what kind of backup systems are available, what anti-virus software it needs to install, and what kind of **crash protection software** it should acquire. Crash protection software performs crash stalling, which fixes a problem or closes all applications properly when an application signals that it is about to crash to the operating system. Other utilities a manager should consider include remote access software to manage the system from a remote location, and uninstall software to properly remove unwanted applications.

REVISITING THE OPENING CASE: SKIVIEZ.COM

This chapter provided you with a lot of information on client/server technologies. Recall from the opening case that when Robert Clark was starting his business, he had to make numerous decisions on his technology infrastructures and whether to be hosted or host his company's Web site. What do you think Robert did?

First, Robert evaluated whether being hosted or hosting was best. He knew he had the technical expertise to develop and maintain the Web environment. However, he did not really want to worry about having to monitor the Web site twenty-four hours a day, seven days a week. He also believed response time should not be a major issue if he could find an appropriate provider to host his site. On the other hand, Robert wanted to design the site to be truly integrated with the other information systems he would develop. He also believed security was very important. After his first evaluation, he decided that hosting his own Web site was the best approach, and he started investigating various server configurations and operating systems. In the end, though, costs became the bottom line issue. He determined that being hosted would cost U.S.$200 for initial setup, $200 to $400 per month for being hosted (for a large Web site), and $20 to $100 per month for Internet connections. In comparison, he believed the server would cost between U.S.$5,000 and $10,000. He would then have to add U.S.$500 $1,500 per month for DSL or ISDN lines. And finally, he would have to support the system himself or hire a technology person with a salary between U.S.$40,000 and $50,000 per year. Robert contracted with a third party to host the Web site he developed for Skiviez.com (see Figure 7-3).

E-BUSINESS IN PRACTICE

E-business in Practice: Still Want to Start Your Own E-business?

If you still want to start your own business and you want to evaluate your technology infrastructures, you might find additional information at these Web sites:

Examples of providers for being hosted:

- Interland: http://www.interland.com
- ValueWeb: http://valueweb.com

Examples of technology providers for hosting:

Server hardware:

- Dell: http://www.dell.com
- Gateway: http://www.gateway.com

- Hewlett-Packard: http://www.hp.com
- IBM Corporation: http://www.ibm.com
- Micron: http://www.micronpc.com

Server software:

- Microsoft Windows: http://www.microsoft.com
- Linux: http://www.linux.org (one of many pages)
- IBM OS/2: http://www.ibm.com
- Solaris and iPlanet: http://www.sun.com
- Apache: http://httpd.apache.org/

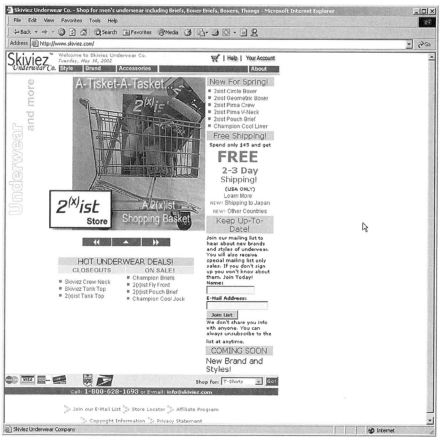

FIGURE 7-3 Skiviez.com

SOURCE: http://www.skiviez.com. Used with permission.

SUMMARY

This chapter presented the core client server technologies that can be used by a company, large or small, for e-business. There are many types of servers needed to run an e-business. Some of them include the file server, the print server, the Web server, the database server, and the communication server. All of them can be implemented on one or several machines. The most common operating systems used on smaller scale servers include Windows 2000 and XP, UNIX, Linux, IBM OS/2, and Sun Solaris. Other popular operating systems include IBM's OS/390, OS/400, and DEC's VMS. The operating system is responsible for managing and sharing the server's resources. Two Web server programs were also discussed, iPlanet and Apache.

When selecting server hardware, one must pay attention to the processor's speed, the random access memory (RAM) available, and the quantity of auxiliary storage available (hard disk). One alternative for high availability storage is RAID (Redundant Arrays of Independent Disks) technology, which involves multiple disks being accessed at the same time. Servers can also have dual processors, which involves two processors working together within one server. Other peripherals of importance when selecting a server environment for an e-business include the monitor, the network equipment (the LAN card and hub type), backup systems, uninterrupted power supply (UPS), and printers and scanners. Backup systems include the software application and the choice of media on which to store the backed up data. Choices include ZIP disks, optical disks (CD-ROMs), tape and cartridge systems (which use magnetic tape), or mirrored disks (which store the data on two or more auxiliary storage devices at the same time).

Servers can be configured as thin servers, where the server is stripped down to perform only one function, such as a Web server. Servers can also be configured in server farms or server clustering, where multiple servers are strung together. Considerations for sizing a Web server were discussed.

Client technologies include workstations, which can be configured as thin or fat clients. Special transaction terminals are designed for specific purposes. Examples include automated teller machines (ATMs), point-of-sale devices, and kiosks. Other client technologies include digital cameras, bar code readers, television set–top boxes, and mobile devices for m-commerce.

Important managerial issues with respect to client/server technologies include decisions of whether to be hosted or whether to host your own Web site. Each approach has several advantages and disadvantages, but often cost is the driving factor. Another managerial concern is how to select the right client/server technologies.

KEY TERMS

Active Server Pages (ASP)
application server
authentication
automated teller machines (ATMs)
bar code readers
buffer
capacity planning
cartridge
CD burners
CD-ROMs
client
client/server computing
Common Gateway Interface (CGI)
communication server
crash protection software
data compression
data integrity
database server
denial-of-service
digital camera
digital phones
dual processor
Ethernet
fat client
fault-tolerant systems
file server

file transfer protocol (FTP)
firewall
FTP server
Gateway services
HTTP server
hub
i-mode
Internet Information server
intranets
IPv6
Java
kiosks
LANs
Linux
load balancing
local area network (LAN)
m-commerce
MacIntosh (Mac)
magnetic tapes
magneto-optical drives
mainframes
main memory
microcomputers
middleware
minicomputers
mirroring
multitasking
n-tier client/server

network computer
Network File Service (NFS)
network operating systems (NOS)
network printers
network protocols
open source
operating system
optical disk
OS/2
peripherals
personal digital assistants
pixel
point-of-sale devices
print server
RAM storage space
random access memory (RAM)
redundant arrays of independent disks (RAID)
reliability
response time
scalability
scanner
server clustering
server failover
server farms
server side scripting

set-top boxes
smart phones
SMTP server
sockets
Solaris
speech recognition
streaming multimedia
supercomputers
switch
text messaging
thin client
thin servers
third generation (3G)
Token Ring
transaction terminals
two-tier client server
uninterrupted power supply
Universal Serial Bus (USB)
UNIX
virtual port
Web server
WebTV
Windows
Wireless Application Protocol (WAP)
Wireless Transport Layer Security (WTLS)
ZIP disks

REVIEW QUESTIONS

1. Explain the role of a file server, a print server, a Web server, a database server, and a communication server. Name and briefly describe five types of servers that are commonly part of e-business systems.

2. Identify the two most popular database servers currently available.

3. Explain the role of a server operating system.

4. Explain the role of a network operating system.

5. List the different versions of the Windows 2000 operating system and describe when each should be used.

6. What is the Windows 2000 operating system's Web server called?

7. Describe the main features of the UNIX operating system.

8. Describe the main features of the Linux operating system.

9. Describe the main features of the IBM OS/2 operating system.

10. Describe the main features of the Novell NetWare NOS.

11. What is Apache?

12. What is iPlanet?

13. Which processor is the most commonly found in small servers?

14. What is a dual processor server?

15. What unit of measurement is used to measure processor speeds?

16. Identify the main components of a server.

17. What is RAID technology?

18. Identify criteria to use in evaluating a server acquisition.

19. List important peripherals to consider in the selection of a server.

20. Identify the two most popular LANs available today.

21. Identify the different media used for backing up data.

22. Explain the role of an uninterrupted power supply.

23. Explain what a thin server is.

24. Explain what a server farm is. What is server clustering?

25. Identify the various software pieces that are needed on a client.

26. Identify the criteria used in evaluating the alternative workstations available.

27. Identify a large number of peripherals that can be considered when selecting a workstation.

28. What is a pixel?

29. What is a transaction terminal?

30. What is the purpose of an automated teller machine?

31. What is the purpose of a point-of-sale terminal?

32. What is the purpose of a kiosk?

33. What is a thin client?

34. What is a fat client?

35. What is a television set-top box? What is it used for?

36. Identify two types of mobile devices that can be used for m-commerce.

37. Describe the components of a smart phone.

38. What is the Wireless Application Protocol?

39. Explain the main differences between hosting a Web site and having a provider host it.

40. Identify the key factors used in sizing a Web server.

EXERCISES

1. Identify different types of server services that are needed for running an e-business. How different is the answer if the business is not an online business?

2. A medium-sized company wishes to install a file server, a Web server, a database server, and a print server. It has two machines to install these services on. It uses the Web server for hosting its company's Web page. It expects to have a large number of clients by the end of the year. It uses the database server to host the data collected from the Web, and to host all of its business systems. It has three thousand employees and sixty-eight business applications. Which server application should go on which machine? Justify your choices.

3. Prepare a comparison table of the advantages/disadvantages and features of the most recent versions of Oracle and SQL Server. When is each the most appropriate choice for a company?

4. Explain the main differences and the main similarities between the UNIX and the Linux operating systems. How does Sun Solaris compare to them?

5. Explain why some operating systems need an additional application, such as iPlanet or Apache, to host Web sites.

6. An accounting company has two servers connected through a local area network (LAN) to one hundred workstations. The company runs financial transactions for their clients, and therefore performs complete backups of their systems every night. Files backed up usually represent between 230 and 270 megabytes of data each night. Backup of previous nights are kept in storage for up to one year. What backup system and media do you recommend? Justify your answer. Make sure you calculate the total storage requirements.

7. One person's computer has 128 MB of RAM and another person's computer has 256 MB of RAM for the same peripherals and processor speed. Do you believe that one of these two person's computer will have more overall performance? Why? Why not? What is the role of RAM in overall computer performance?

8. Provide an additional example (not used in the chapter) of a business for which a point-of-sale terminal would be useful. Do the same for a kiosk.

9. Explain the difference between text messaging on a digital phone and text messaging on a smart phone. What technologies make these differences possible?

10. EFG Corporation wants to start venturing into the e-business arena. It currently sells specialized tea products to various retailers in the state of North Carolina. It has eleven employees: the president and owner, two administrative employees dealing with orders and billing, two

sales representatives, a secretary, and five employees dealing with shipping and packaging. The president, Bob, knows computers very well and has personally gotten involved in acquiring their current LAN. He thinks going on the Web might significantly increase their reach worldwide. He is considering whether to host the Web site or be hosted by another company. Highlight the pros and cons of each solution for him, taking into consideration and using the context of his business.

11. If a backup utility has a four to three ratio and you must store 156 MB of data. How much storage space is actually needed for the backup?

12. If a company has one thousand hits per hour on its Web site between the hours of 09:00 and 20:00 (9 A.M. and 8 P.M.), and 300 hits per hour the rest of the time, what is its sustained load? If the company's average hit is 18 kilobytes, what is its sustained aggregate data rate? The 18 kilobytes is based on its average page. The company builds another site with substantially more images and some CGI scripting. What will be the overall impact of implementing this new site?

13. Using the fictitious situation that follows, make a recommendation on an actual server for this company. You must select the brand, features, and peripherals that make the most sense. The company is fairly small, with ten employees and seven computers networked using an Ethernet LAN. It currently runs its business applications on individual PCs, but would like the database centralized on a server. It also wishes to start hosting its own Web site, through which it intends to increase its market share of the paper products it sells. It expects to have 1000 hits per day on the Web server for downloads of its catalog information, mostly text with some images. Its employees will generate fifty hits per hour to the database, downloading files each time of approximately 100 kilobytes each. Given its limited financial capacity, make sure to find the best—yet most price competitive—solution possible.

HANDS-ON PROJECTS

1. Identify a small business in your area and research the types of servers it uses for running its business. Make a recommendation on at least one additional type of server that might be of use to it. Evaluate the cost of this recommendation for it, and discuss the benefits it would get from adding this server application that would outweigh the costs.

2. Find out the most recent news regarding the Linux operating system. Is it still free? What is the most recent version available? What are the greatest concerns currently with respect to this operating system?

3. Find a company that uses Linux as its operating system and investigate why it chose this system over commercial ones.

4. Prepare a new comparison chart of the various operating systems discussed in this chapter using the most recent data you can find on the Web and in magazines. Is there a new operating system available? What versions are the most recent for each operating system? What did they add over previous versions?

DISCUSSION POINTS

1. "A medium-sized company should never need a mainframe as its server. A minicomputer, or even really just a microcomputer is enough." Is this sentence true? Why? Why not?

2. Discuss the ideas of thin clients, fat clients, and thin servers and who benefits the most from each approach. What should be the key considerations in making those choices?

RELATED WEB SITES

AvantGo.com: www.AvantGo.com

Skiviez.com: www.skiviez.com

FURTHER READINGS

Apache project, http://www.apache.org.

Brewin, Bob. "Microsoft Touts Smart Phones, Wireless Plans." *Computerworld,* 26 March 2001: http://www.computerworld.com/mobiletopics/mobile/story/0,10801,58956,00.html.

Burd, Stephen D. *Systems Architecture, Hardware and Software in Business Information Systems.* Cambridge, MA: Course Technology, 1998.

Dragan, Rich. "The Scalable Solaris 8 (Product Announcement)." *PC Magazine,* 4 April 2000: 64.

Englander, Irv. *The Architecture of Computer Hardware and Systems Software, An Information Technology Approach.* New York: John Wiley & Sons, 2000.

Fitzgerald, J., and Dennis, A. *Business Data Communications and Networking.* New York: John Wiley & Sons, 1999.

Garcia, Andrew R. "Benchmark Tests: Web Platforms (News Briefs)." *PC Magazine,* 23 May 2000: 154.

Mearian, Luca. "Staples Joins Kiosk Retailers."*Computerworld,* 5 February 2001: http://www.computerworld.com/managementtopics /ebusiness/story/0,10801,57381,00.html.

Panko, R. R. *Business Data Communications.* Upper Saddle River, New Jersey: Prentice-Hall, 1997.

Seltzer, L. "Serve It." *PC Magazine,* 8 June 1999: 163.

White, Curt M. *Data Communications and Computer Networks: A Business User's Approach.* Cambridge, MA: Course Technology, 2001.

REFERENCES

DiDio, Laura. "NetWare, NT Server to divide lion's share." *Computerworld,* 2 January 1995: http://www.computerworld.com/news/1995/story/0,11280,12994,00.html.

Dyck, T. "Microsoft SQL Server 7.0." *PC Magazine,* 1 August 1999: 221.

Johnson, A. H. "Helping Web sites take phone calls." *Computerworld,* 5 February 2001: http://www.computerworld.com /managementtopics/xsp/story/0,10801,57282,00.html.

Pastore, Michael. "Slow sites costing e-commerce dollars." *CyberAtlas,* 30 June 1999: http://cyberatlas.internet.com/markets/retailing/article/0,,6061_153991,00.html.

Trickett, Nigel, Tatsuhiko Nakagawa, Ravi Mani, and Diana Gfroerer. 2001. Understanding IBM pSeries performance and sizing: http://www.redbooks.ibm.com/redbooks/SG244810.html.

Zona Research, Inc. 2000. Where is Web data stored? (20 January 2000). Note: Zona Research no longer exists, so this article is no longer accessible.

Wong, Brian L. "Sizing up your Web server." *SunWorld,* October 1997: http://sunsite.uakom.sk/sunworldonline/swol-10-1997/swol-10-sizeserver.html.

CHAPTER 8

INTEGRATING BACK-OFFICE OPERATIONS

LEARNING OBJECTIVES

After reading and completing this chapter, you should be able to:

- Define the term "legacy system"
- Discuss issues related to legacy systems, including challenges associated with them and the reasons organizations retain legacy systems
- Discuss the importance of databases to e-business systems
- Discuss the importance of transactions to e-business systems
- Name and explain the ACID properties of transactions
- Discuss the main purpose of middleware
- Name and describe the main categories of middleware
- Discuss the importance of integrating legacy systems with e-business systems
- Describe the role of middleware in legacy system integration
- Describe the main characteristics of a data warehouse
- Describe the main components of a data warehousing environment
- Explain the "E/T/L" process of data warehousing
- Discuss the main goals of customer relationship management systems
- Use the CRM framework to categorize CRM technologies and applications
- Describe the purposes of primary keys and foreign keys
- Write simple Structured Query Language statements to insert, update, delete, and retrieve data

---

Opening Case: Red Robin International

The management of Red Robin International, a U.S.-based chain of 170 restaurants, faced a problem. Customer preferences vary widely according to geography. What sells well in Seattle in December may not do as well in Miami. Like many restaurant chains, Red Robin engages in menu "engineering," which means that they alter each location's menu to consider customer preferences (which, of course, change frequently), special deals from food and beverage suppliers, and inventory. For example, a chicken dish may be put on special for a location if that area's poultry supplier offers a special rebate if a certain volume is ordered. Red Robin's management knew what data they needed in order to engineer the menu for each region. Unfortunately, the necessary data did not exist in any single system; the data were spread out across a number of aging systems. As a result, when a regional manager wanted a special report, the request had to be made to a reporting specialist, who would then use Red Robin's antiquated reporting system to generate the requested report. The process was time consuming. It typically took twenty-four to thirty-six hours for a regional manager to receive a report. Often, this was too late to do any good.

At the core of Red Robin's problem was the fact that its operational systems were holdovers from the days before integrated systems were the norm. The product ordering system was completely separate from the restaurant sales accounting system. To make matters worse, the systems did not even use the same terms and numbers to refer to the same item. For example, cola might be item number 101 in one system and 202 in another. As you can imagine, this made it even more difficult to combine data across systems.

Red Robin's management knew that there had to be a better way; they needed to find an easier way to make data from operational systems available for decision-making. Making better decisions translates directly into bottom-line savings. For a restaurant chain the size of Red Robin, saving as little as 1 percent on food costs translates into hundreds of thousands of dollars.

Red Robin embarked on a serious effort to upgrade its decision support technologies. The key component of this effort is a data warehouse with hundreds of gigabytes of data that are available to managers through a Web-based interface. Now instead of having to wait a day or more to get information, managers can retrieve and analyze data quickly and effectively. To make the process even easier, a number of data cubes (multi-dimensional views of data) were created to track information in a variety of areas, such as sales by region and by time, product orders, and personnel costs. The new systems have resulted in millions of dollars in increased revenues and decreased costs. In a single incident, management discovered an error that led to a canceled order for U.S.$250,000 worth of unneeded items.

INTRODUCTION

When most people think of e-commerce and e-business, they think of the Internet and Web pages. Some people think of well-known dot-com companies, such as Amazon.com, while others envision the Web sites of more traditional organizations, such as Wal-Mart or Sears. However, regardless of the nature of the organization, a key factor in the organization's success is how well it is able to integrate its **back-office** operations with its e-business systems. What are back-office operations? Think of a hotel. When you think about a hotel, you probably think of the front desk, rooms, restaurants, and bars. Most people would not give much thought to the things that go on behind the scenes. However, unless such processes as bill preparation, employee payroll, and food and beverage ordering, are carried out efficiently and effectively, the hotel is not likely to be a success. These less visible, but critically important, functions are examples of back-office operations. In the Red Robin case, food ordering and personnel systems are examples of back-office operations.

Organizations that want to take advantage of e-business technologies must consider how to build systems that not only present a favorable interface to the customer, but also effectively integrate all of the operations that take place behind the scenes. Unless an organization is a start-up, it likely has existing operational systems that must be taken into account when designing e-business efforts. These existing systems are often called **legacy systems.** In many cases, legacy systems carry out their tasks quite well, despite the fact that they are based on older technologies. Organizations must decide whether to scrap legacy systems or try to use various methods of tying them into newly developed e-business systems. The first section of this chapter discusses legacy systems, including their benefits and drawbacks.

Middleware represents a major class of technologies directed toward integrating systems based on different platforms into a cohesive whole. Middleware systems act as translators between different types of systems, which allows these systems to interact. Many organizations use middleware to help extend the life of existing systems by connecting them to newer, network-enabled systems. This chapter describes several different types of middleware and discusses how they can be used effectively in e-business systems.

One of the most important tasks of many back-office operations is to carry out **transactions.** Almost any organization must deal with transactions. Examples of transactions include orders, bill payment, and billing for services provided. This chapter provides an overview of transaction processing, including a discussion of the importance of transactions to e-business and the characteristics of a "good" transaction.

The chapter proceeds by revisiting legacy systems in the context of integrating legacy systems with modern e-business systems. There are a variety of methods used to achieve this integration, and the most popular are presented.

The chapter continues by examining two applications that are directed at making use of the information generated and gathered by back-office systems. **Data warehousing** is used by many enterprises that wish to make data from a variety of systems available to decision makers. **Customer relationship management** (CRM) systems help organizations organize and utilize information about customers in order to improve customer satisfaction while maximizing profits.

Databases underlie most e-business systems. Regardless of the nature of the organization, data is a key organizational resource. Often a major goal of e-business systems is the better management and utilization of data resources. For those of you who are not familiar with relational database technology, this chapter provides an overview of database technology and discusses various methods for connecting e-business systems with databases.

LEGACY SYSTEMS

Legacy systems are simply information systems that are based on older technologies. Although this definition is not very complicated, it captures the spirit of what most people mean when they refer to legacy systems. In general, legacy systems are mainframe-based and utilize third-generation programming languages (such as COBOL) in combination with relational databases. Of course, there are many exceptions to this generality.

The Problem with Legacy Systems

Regardless of the exact operating platform and technologies involved, most legacy systems share many characteristics. First, they are based on older technologies. A prime example of this is that the majority of legacy systems are written in COBOL. For many years, COBOL was the dominant programming language for business applications. (In fact, most operating business applications are currently still in COBOL.)

Legacy systems also tend to be large and complex. It is common for a COBOL-based legacy application to consist of hundreds of thousands of lines of code. Often the logic of these programs is quite complex. Unfortunately, many large legacy applications are poorly documented and poorly structured. (Of course, poor program documentation and structure are not limited to legacy systems.) When you combine this with complexity and size, many legacy applications are very difficult to maintain. When changes need to be made to the logic of the program, it can be very difficult to track down the code that needs to be changed. Often, multiple changes must be made to affect a single functional change. The E-business in Practice box helps illustrate this point.

Most legacy systems were designed and developed many years ago. Some of them date back to the late 1960s. So in many cases, the designers and developers of the systems are no longer with the organizations. Of course, the relatively high turnover rate for IT workers sometimes makes this a problem even for recently developed systems. This means that some parts of the legacy systems are not well understood. When you consider this in combination with the size, complexity, and poor structure and documentation, you wind up with a system that is very difficult to maintain.

The fact that many legacy systems are "mission critical" makes them even more problematic. A mission-critical system is one that the organization cannot do without. This is not surprising. In the early days of data processing, organizations devoted

E-BUSINESS IN PRACTICE

A Simple Job Turns Complex

Many years ago, one of the authors had a client who owned a business that leased plants to companies in order to improve the appearance of their stores or offices. Once a company signed up, it was billed on a monthly basis for the service. The author's client wanted a program that could automate the generation of monthly bills and the tracking of payments. The author was able to find a relatively inexpensive system that met most of the client's requirements. However, when the system printed the bills, a line item for "discount" was printed on each bill. The client pointed out that this was not acceptable. Because each of his customers was charged a negotiated monthly fee, there would never be a discount applied. He was concerned that when clients saw the discount line on their monthly bills, they would wonder why they were not receiving some sort of discount. The candidate system could be modified, and the author told the client that it would be easy to alter the code to eliminate the discount line. After a little bit of searching in the program, the author found the line of code that printed the discount line. The code was quick altered to remove the word "discount," and the system was delivered to the client. When the client ran the first set of bills, some of them included the discount line. Of course, this led to a complaint to the author, who reexamined the code (more carefully this time). There were no less than a dozen separate places in the program where the discount line was indicated, depending on a number of logical conditions. In a well-structured program, there would only be one. After many hours of code editing and testing, the author was finally able to deliver a properly working system. Had the program been well-structured or well-documented, the job could have been completed in much less time.

resources to automating the most important organizational activities (that could be automated). Examples include the billing system for a utility company, an order entry system for a wholesaler, and a settlement system for a stockbroker. Basically, if a mission-critical system is out of operation for any length of time, the organization is in serious trouble. Since many legacy systems are mission-critical, making changes to them becomes very problematic. Any errors introduced during the modification can lead to serious problems for the organization.

The sheer number of legacy systems is a problem for many organizations. It is not unusual for a large organization to have hundreds of legacy applications. For example, according to an article in *Software Magazine*, Mellon Financial Corporation has over two hundred legacy systems with an average of five hundred programs per application (Frye 2000–2001). This translates to more than sixty million lines of programming code (most of it in COBOL). The volume of legacy code in many organizations means that a large percentage of the information technology budget is devoted to maintaining and updating legacy systems. It is a significant challenge to reduce this expenditure so that resources can be directed at developing new technologies and migrating to e-business systems.

Let us summarize the challenges of legacy systems.

- Legacy systems are large, often consisting of many thousands of lines of code.

- Legacy systems are complex.

- Legacy systems are often poorly structured and poorly documented.

- Legacy systems were designed and developed long ago by people who are no longer employed by the organizations that own the legacy systems.

- Legacy systems are often mission-critical.

- Many organizations have large numbers of legacy systems. In total, these systems may contain millions of lines of code.

You may recall the year 2000 (Y2K) problem that was prominently discussed in the popular press in the late 1990s. The Y2K problem was a great illustration of the problems associated with legacy system. A seemingly simple problem (change year fields from two digits to four digits) became a major project for IT departments around the world. Although the estimates vary, it is safe to say that a fortune was spent on overcoming the Y2K problem. According to the Final Report of U.S. Senate's Y2K Committee, solving the Y2K problem cost U.S. organizations an estimated U.S.$100 billion (Senate 2000). The U.S. federal government spent $8.5 billion on the problem. (Appendix II of the Report has a fascinating list of examples of Y2K glitches throughout the world.) Although the basic problem seems simple, the problems associated with legacy systems made the Y2K problem a global event.

Why Keep Legacy Systems?

You might be thinking that with all of the problems associated with legacy systems, why not simply replace them? To understand the answer, you should first understand why so many legacy systems are still around. Put simply, they work and they work well. Most legacy systems have been operating reliably for many years. Recall that many are also mission-critical. Organizations are not likely to scrap reliable systems for something new.

What if the new system does not function correctly? A major electricity provider found out the answer to this question. In the late 1990s, this company completed a long-term project to replace its legacy customer service system with one based on newer technologies. After much testing, the new system was declared to be sound. The company shut down the legacy system and switched operation to the new system. Shortly, the new system crashed. What worked correctly in testing did not work when the system went "live." After several days, the company was able to switch back over to the legacy system while the problems with the new system were corrected. Until the legacy system was back in operation, customer service was shut down. New accounts could not be set up, bills could not be prepared, and customers' questions could not be answered. As you can imagine, the situation was a nightmare for the company. This is not the only case of an organization running into problems when replacing legacy systems. So, you can understand why organizations might be hesitant to replace reliable legacy systems.

Legacy systems also tend to be high performance. These systems were designed from the start to be able to efficiently handle high transaction volumes. The architectures on which most legacy systems are based are optimized for transaction processing, which can result in high performance. Organizations are often reluctant to discard such efficient systems.

Finally, most organizations have infrastructures in place to keep legacy systems operational. For example, IT staff are skilled in the languages and platforms associated with legacy systems. If an organization migrates to newer technologies, considerable resources must be directed toward retraining existing staff or hiring people skilled in the new technologies.

So, as you can see, there are a number of reasons organizations may want to keep their legacy systems rather than scrapping them completely. Table 8-1 recaps the advantages of legacy systems. Because of their advantages, it is important to have a basic understanding of how legacy systems can be integrated into an e-business environment.

Integrating Legacy Systems into the E-business Environment

Almost any organization wishing to utilize e-business technologies must struggle with the question of how to best integrate legacy systems into an e-business environment. This question is critical when building a comprehensive e-business environment; being able to utilize well-functioning legacy systems may save significant money and time. In fact, much of the real work of e-business systems occurs through these legacy systems. So, integrating legacy systems into e-business environments is often a necessity. The alternative to integrating legacy and e-business systems is to rebuild the functionality contained in the legacy systems, which can be an expensive proposition.

Table 8-1 Common Advantages of Legacy Systems

- Legacy systems are reliable.
- Legacy systems are well-tested.
- Legacy systems exhibit high performance.
- Legacy systems can handle large volumes of transactions.
- Most organizations have infrastructures that maintain and support legacy systems.

In order to understand the integration issue, it is helpful to first understand some other areas, which we address in the following sections. First, we provide a discussion of transactions, which are at the core of many e-business applications. Then, we discuss a class of technologies known as middleware, which are directed at enabling different types of systems to work together. Then, we revisit the legacy systems integration question by providing a discussion of various methods of achieving this integration. Also, if you are not familiar with relational database technology, we suggest that you read the last section of this chapter.

TRANSACTIONS

Transactions are at the core of many e-business systems. If we asked you to name a few examples of transactions, you would probably have no trouble coming up with five or six off the top of your head. Buying a textbook, making a utility payment, and registering for a class are all examples of transactions. However, when discussing business systems, transactions have some very specific characteristics. In this section, we define the concept of a transaction and discuss the characteristics of a "well-behaved" transaction. These characteristics are known as the **ACID properties.** Also, we discuss the importance of transactions to e-business systems.

While there are many different definitions for the term "transaction," they all revolve around the idea of a set of operations that occur together. Basically, a transaction is a logical unit of work that typically involves a set of operations. Transactions have an "all or nothing" goal. We either want all of the operations involved in a transaction to occur, or we want none of them to occur. So, we take great pains to ensure that this "all or nothing" idea is enforced. The system must guarantee that if any one of the operations fails, then any changes made by other operations are "undone." Since the operations we speak of involve reading or writing data to a database, the database management system typically handles this chore. Let us look at an example in order to illustrate the importance of the "all or none" idea.

Suppose that your organization sells paint to hardware stores. A customer places an order for one hundred gallons of red paint. There are several database operations that must occur for this transaction to successfully take place. The system must:

1. Check the inventory table to make sure that there are one hundred gallons available
2. Check the price of one hundred gallons of red paint
3. Check the customers' credit availability to make sure there is sufficient credit for the transaction
4. Update the customers' credit availability to reflect the purchase
5. Update the sales table of the database to reflect the sale
6. Update the accounts receivable table to reflect the charges for the sale
7. Update the inventory table to reduce the number of gallons of red paint available
8. Update the shipping table to reflect that one hundred gallons of red paint should be sent to the customer

Of course, there are also other operations involved, but you should have the idea that even a relatively straightforward transaction involves many database operations. Now suppose that all of the operations occur except the last one (8). What are the implications? One implication is that you have an unhappy customer. Wouldn't you be unhappy if you were billed for one hundred gallons of paint that were never shipped to you? What happens if step 6 never happens? Now you have a happy customer that received the paint but was never charged for it. Of course, this is not good from your perspective; too many transactions like this and your company will be out of business. Another possible outcome of a partial transaction is inconsistent data in the database. For example, if the inventory level of red paint is never updated, the database would reflect one hundred gallons of red paint more than is actually in stock.

As you can see, there are serious consequences to a partially completed transaction. This leads us to one of the characteristics of a well-behaved transaction; **atomicity.** According to the atomicity principle, a transaction should be guaranteed to be atomic. So from a logical perspective, if a transaction cannot occur in its entirety, it should not occur at all. Transactions should also exhibit **consistency.** This means that a transaction that begins with the database in a consistent (valid) state should, after being completed, leave the database in a consistent state. If any part of the transaction fails, the database should be returned to its prior, consistent state. The concept of **isolation** means that any changes to the database that occur as the result of a transaction should be hidden from all other users (or transactions) until the transaction is complete. Finally, transactions should be **durable,** which means that any changes made to the database as a result of a completed transaction should persist even if later hardware or software failures occur. If a system failure occurs in the middle of a transaction, any changes made to the database as a result of that transaction are rolled back (undone). A transaction manager (which is sometimes called a transaction monitor) is used to ensure that transactions meet these principles. Table 8-2 provides a summary of the ACID properties.

Why are we discussing the concept of a transaction in a chapter devoted to integrating back-office and e-business systems? The short answer is that most activities that occur through e-business systems involve transactions. Even if the activity does not directly involve a transaction, the activity is likely to use data that is derived from many transactions. So, the correct processing of transactions is a critical part of a successful e-business system.

Now that you have an idea of what transactions are and why they are important, we turn our attention to a widely used, critical link between legacy transaction processing systems and more modern e-business systems. Middleware is often used to provide this link. In the next section, we provide an introduction to this important topic.

Table 8-2 The ACID Properties of Transactions

Property	Description
Atomicity	If a transaction does not occur in its entirety, it should not occur at all.
Consistency	If a transaction starts with the database in a consistent state, the database should be in a consistent state at the end of the transaction. If the transaction fails, the database should be returned to the starting state.
Isolation	Changes to the database from a transaction should be hidden from all other transactions until the transaction is complete.
Durability	Changes made to the database resulting from a completed transaction should persist, even if later hardware or software failures occur.

MIDDLEWARE

The various components of today's e-business systems often reside on different types of computers that may be running different operating systems. Making these **heterogeneous systems** work together can be a daunting task. Broadly speaking, there are two basic ways to achieve interoperability. One approach is for all of the various types of systems to follow a common set of standards. As discussed earlier in this book, the Internet and Web utilize this approach. All servers and clients on the Internet utilize TCP/IP and other standards to achieve interoperability. In this section, we discuss a second approach—the use of special software called middleware that is used to allow different types of systems to interact.

Middleware is software that is used to connect otherwise separate systems. More formally, the Software Engineering Institute (SEI) defines middleware as "connectivity software that allows multiple processes running on one or more machines to interact across a network" (Software Engineering Institute 2000).

Informally, middleware is often referred to as "glue" because it allows separate applications to stick together. Another term often used to refer to middleware is "plumbing," since middleware connects at each end to an application and allows data to flow through it from one application to another. A basic function of middleware is to translate data from one system for another. For example, middleware might allow users to utilize a Web-based application to pull data from a legacy database. The middleware would convert the data from the database into a form the Web application could understand and vice versa. Since so much data resides in legacy databases, middleware is often a critical component in an e-business system.

Following is a discussion of the three major categories of basic middleware: communication, data management, and platform middleware (Ulrich 2001).

Communication Middleware

As the name implies, communication middleware enables communication between heterogeneous, typically distributed applications. An early example of communication middleware is the use of remote procedure calls (RPC). Using an RPC, one application can request data from another program on the network without having to worry about developing a specific procedure for the remote computer. In essence, one computer sends a request for the remote procedure to the other computer. The programmer for the calling software does not need to understand the internals of the program on the responding computer. The programmer only needs to be concerned with following the RPC protocol, knowing what procedure to request, and knowing what arguments to send to the remote procedure. One example of an RPC protocol is the Distributed Computing Environment (DCE), the standards for which are published by the Open Software Foundation, which has been incorporated into The Open Group. Early RPCs were synchronous. This means that the calling software waits for a response, and does not continue processing until a response is received. Today, however, asynchronous RPCs exist that allow the calling application to continue processing while waiting for a response. As you might imagine, an asynchronous RPC is generally preferred.

Message-oriented middleware (MOM) is another type of communications middleware. With MOM, applications send messages that are stored until the server is ready to act upon them. The applications are free to continue with other processing while awaiting responses, which classifies MOM as an asynchronous method. This makes MOM particularly well-suited for applications that involve extended processes. An insurance claims application is a good example. The application might send messages to other systems using MOM to find out the limits of the policy, the estimated cost of the repairs, and so on. While the claims application waits for responses it can continue with other processing.

Two basic kinds of MOM exist. Message queuing MOM allows applications to send messages to a virtual waiting room (typically in the form of a file), where the messages sit until the receiving application is ready to receive them. The sending application only needs to know how to communicate with the MOM. It does not need to know how to communicate directly with the receiving application. Message queuing MOM is particularly useful when communication among applications is not reliable, for example in mobile computing. Message passing MOM pushes information to applications, rather than waiting for applications to request it. Pushing the information out is more efficient in certain situations. For example, a manufacturer's sales system may push new pricing information out to its customers' purchasing systems. One approach popular for message passing is the publish-subscribe model. In this setup, applications register their interest in a particular subject. Applications also may be registered to publish messages to a subject. When the publishing applications send new information, the MOM will pass that information to all applications that have registered an interest in that topic.

Data Management Middleware

The second category of middleware is data management middleware. Middleware in this category allows an application to access data that is not defined inside that application. For example, it may be necessary for data management middleware to translate information from the data format of a Web-based sales application to the data format of a legacy inventory control application. One example of data management middleware is SQL-oriented database access middleware. This kind of middleware is capable of translating a generic SQL request into the data access language utilized by the database management system that manages the data in question. This eliminates the need to program specific requests in the native language of each database management system from which an application must draw data. The major database vendors, such as Oracle, offer SQL-oriented middleware. Many data management middleware systems employ Java Database Connectivity (JDBC) and/or Open Database Connectivity (ODBC) standards as the core of their systems.

Platform Middleware

The final category of middleware we discuss is platform middleware. Examples of platform middleware include transaction-oriented middleware and object request brokers. A transaction processing (TP) monitor provides environments for the transaction-oriented applications that must access relational databases. TP monitors are particularly important when transactions must access and/or write data across a number of databases, which is quite common. One job of a TP monitor is to ensure that the ACID properties of transactions that we discussed earlier are applied. Another example of platform middleware is object request brokers, which allow applications to request services and send objects in an object-oriented environment. This allows heterogeneous networks to be used to distribute and share the objects that make up an application. Two competing architectures for ORBs are the Open Management Group's Common Object Request Broker Architecture (CORBA) and Microsoft's Distributed Common Object Model. Using ORBs, a client can request an object from a server without knowing where the server is on the network. In addition, it is not necessary for the client to understand the details of the server's interface. Although asynchronous ORBs exist, most used today operate synchronously.

While dividing middleware into neat categories is helpful for gaining a basic understanding, it is important to note that, in actuality, the categories are blurred. For example, some ORBs now have messaging and transaction processing. This blurring of lines does not really matter too much.

So far in this chapter, we have discussed the importance of legacy systems, transactions, and middleware. The legacy systems are at the heart of many back-office operations, and database technology is the core of many legacy systems. Transactions are a key element of many e-business systems. Middleware is one approach to tying various systems together into a cohesive whole. In the next section, we attempt to tie these topics together by discussing ways of integrating legacy systems into an e-business environment.

LEGACY SYSTEM INTEGRATION

There are literally billions of transactions carried out by legacy systems every year. As noted earlier, there are many reasons to continue using these systems rather than developing new applications to carry out the tasks performed by the legacy systems. As a result, many organizations are faced with the challenge of integrating existing legacy systems into network-enabled e-business environments. In this section, we provide an overview of some approaches to carrying out this integration.

Many network-enabled e-business systems must utilize data stored in the databases of legacy systems. Because of this, data integration is perhaps the most important aspect of legacy systems integration. Some approaches to data integration allow applications to access data directly from the legacy databases. These approaches are said to be noninvasive. Invasive approaches, on the other hand, involve transformations of the legacy data. This transformed data is then accessed by the e-business systems (Ulrich 2000). Note that much of the following discussion is adapted from a 2000 article by William Ulrich. We encourage those of you interested in legacy system integration to read this article, which is listed in the References section of this chapter.

Middleware is a key component of legacy system integration, including data integration. For example, a noninvasive approach to data integration is for an e-business application to connect to messaging middleware, which accesses data through an SQL call to the legacy relational database. The legacy database responds to the message with the appropriate data, which is sent through the middleware to the e-business application, which then presents the data to the user through a Web-browser.

Many transaction-oriented legacy applications utilize nonrelational data structures. (Relational databases separate data into a number of different tables rather than in one large table. They are explained in detail in the last section of this chapter.) In such cases, it may become necessary for an additional layer of middleware to selectively translate the required non-relational data into a relational database format. The relationally structured data is then accessed as described in the previous paragraph.

Sometimes it is worthwhile to completely reanalyze and redesign legacy databases. This invasive form of legacy data integration is quite complex, which translates into quite expensive. The structure of the data must be reanalyzed. Existing redundancies in the data (data that is stored multiple times in the database) must be reconciled. Typically, the data structures are made to conform to relational database rules. Because of the complexity involved in these tasks, most organizations choose to avoid this approach.

Remote procedure call middleware can be used to allow a Web-based e-business application to invoke legacy systems. This is common when transaction processing operations are carried out by legacy systems. One interesting use of this form of integration is to combine data from a number of legacy applications into a single, Web-based form. For example, a brokerage customer using a Web-based form to place a stock trade might see the results of the trade along with an update of account balances on a single browser-based form. This could take place even if the trade transaction was carried out on one legacy application and the account balances resided on another legacy system. This is a form of noninvasive legacy integration. Ulrich (2000) notes that these forms of integration are most useful when the legacy applications are relied upon to carry out specific, well-defined transactions that can be identified and invoked by the e-business application. Put differently, these approaches work well when the legacy applications do a good job of supporting the transaction needs of an organization, but the organization wants to allow Web-based access to the legacy applications.

Interestingly, the approaches to integration described so far have much in common with a previous round of legacy updating. When client/server computing became popular, there was a similar trend to make mainframe-based legacy applications available through client/server-based systems. A technique known as screen-scraping was a popular, relatively simple approach to enabling legacy application access through client-based graphical interfaces. Although this approach suffered from a number of drawbacks, it was quite popular because it was relatively simple and inexpensive. Many of today's efforts to integrate legacy systems into e-business environments are similar. Screen scraper software allows mainframe-based applications to utilize features such as radio buttons, check boxes, and pull-down lists. Conceptually, they work by intercepting screens from mainframe applications as they are transferred to a personal computer, then transforming the data from the mainframe, along with the design of the corresponding graphical form, into a more modern looking and acting graphically based screen. To the user, the transformed form looks like other graphically based forms. To the mainframe, the personal computer acts just like a standard terminal. This approach allowed organizations to quickly take advantage of the ease of use of graphical interfaces without having to redesign mainframe applications.

The techniques described so far are improvements on the screen-scraping approach, but they still do not represent true integration. This is because as noninvasive approaches, they do not enable modification of the compartmentalized, rigid structures of legacy systems. The legacy applications still operate like legacy operations. This can mean unnecessary redundancy and a lack of integration with other applications as well as other drawbacks.

Why are these approaches so popular if they do not represent true integration? Simply put, they are popular because they are relatively quick and easy solutions to the immediate problem of allowing Web-based access to legacy systems. A more comprehensive approach is to migrate existing legacy systems onto modern e-business architectures. This can be accomplished by building reusable components that are based on the business logic that exists in the legacy systems. These components can then be implemented in the e-business environment. Erlikh and Goldbaum (2001) note that the real value of legacy applications is in the business knowledge they contain rather than in their specific technical structure.

This business knowledge is typically in the form of business rules that are implemented through the legacy systems. The components' approach to legacy migration allows organizations to selectively extract these rules in a phased approach to migration. Because the business rules are based on the proven logic of the legacy systems, they have a high level of integrity. The components' approach, in a way, allows the best of both worlds. The high integrity of the legacy systems can be maintained, but true e-business integration of applications can occur. Also, when cross-platform languages (such as Java) are used to implement the new components, organizations gain the advantage of not being tied to a particular operating platform. Although the component approach is considerably more complex, time consuming, and expensive than some other approaches, many feel that in the long run, organizations will find that the benefits justify the efforts. If you are interested in learning more about component-based e-business architectures, we encourage you to read the *Communications of the ACM* article by Peter Fingar, which is listed in the Further Readings section at the end of this chapter.

Choosing the correct approach to legacy system integration is, of course, very complex and requires considerable expertise and experience. While it is well beyond the scope of this section to provide complete guidance for this problem, we can provide a simplified view, which is shown in the following Decision Point.

Decision Point

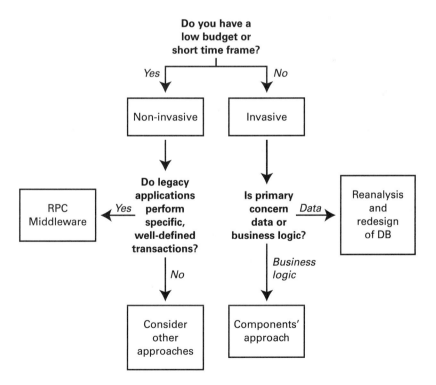

One important aspect of legacy system integration is making data from these systems available to decision makers. Data warehousing is a concept that emerged in the early

1990s that is directed at making data from transaction-oriented, operational systems available in a structure that is well-suited for decision support. In the next section we provide an overview of data warehousing.

DATA WAREHOUSING

So far in this chapter, our primary focus has been on operational systems, which are the systems that handle the day-to-day activities of an organization. However, it is important to understand that the value of the data generated by these systems extends beyond day-to-day operations. Unfortunately, the structure of the data in operational systems is not optimized for supporting decision making. As a result, there has been considerable work done in developing methods and technologies to structure data and make it available for decision support. In this section, we discuss the concept of data warehousing, which is directed at providing data for decision support.

Data Warehousing Defined

Data warehousing is "the process whereby organizations extract value from their informational assets through the use of special data stores called data warehouses" (Barquin 1997, 5). While this definition is accurate, it is more useful if you know what a data warehouse is. Ralph Kimball (1996, 310) (a widely recognized data warehousing expert) defines a **data warehouse** as "a copy of transaction data structured for query and analysis." A more detailed, and perhaps more useful, definition comes from another "big name" in data warehousing, Bill Inmon (2000). He defines a data warehouse in terms of the following characteristics.

- A data warehouse is a collection of databases that are designed for decision support.
- The databases are subject-oriented. This means that a data warehouse is organized around particular subjects, such as customers, employees, or products.
- The data in a data warehouse is integrated from a variety of sources that may be internal or external to the organization.
- The data in a data warehouse is often transformed from its original format in the source databases. For example, summary data rather than detailed data may be stored.
- The data in a data warehouse is time-variant, which means that there is a time dimension to each item of data. For example, rather than storing the current inventory level for a product, a data warehouse might store the inventory level at the end of each day. So, each inventory level would be associated with a particular date.
- The data in a data warehouse is nonvolatile. In theory, once an item of data is put into a data warehouse, it is never removed. Typically, this does not hold in practice, however. Many organizations find it more practical to "age" data in a data warehouse; only data from certain time periods is kept. For example, management may decide that the data warehouse should contain data from the last five years. If so, then data periodically is removed or archived to inexpensive media.

Now that you understand the characteristics of a data warehouse, it is appropriate to discuss the need for data warehousing. The data in operational systems tends to be transaction-oriented, meaning that the data are organized around the transactions the system is designed to support. In addition, the data are detailed. For example, the operational systems of a CD merchant would maintain the data associated with current orders placed by every customer. While this is fine for maintaining day-to-day operations, it may not be the best way to format the data for supporting long-term decision making. It may be more useful to aggregate the order data according to customer location, products, and/or time. For example, if management wants to get a sense of how sales are going over time, it is not necessary to look at each individual sale. It is more useful to look at the total sales for each product category for each week. A data warehouse can also combine data from different sources. Perhaps the CD merchant has physical stores as well as a Web-based store. It is possible that the physical and virtual stores have different operational systems. If so, the data can be integrated in the data warehouse. This would allow comparisons to be made, for example.

Components of a Data Warehouse

A data warehouse environment is made up of more than databases. There are a number of pieces that must work together in order for the data warehousing effort to be successful. These components are described here (Edelstein 1997).

Data Migration Tools

Data migration refers to taking data from source systems and loading them into the data warehouse. The tools that help in the migration process are critical because this migration is perhaps the most costly and time-consuming process in data warehousing. Data migration tools can be divided into three categories; data copying and replication, data transformation, and data cleansing. As the name implies, data copying and replication tools are used to make copies of the data in source systems so that they can be converted into forms more suitable for the data warehouse. Data transformation tools are used to perform this conversion. For example, data may be aggregated, and derived values (such as extended prices) may be calculated by transformation tools. Data cleansing tools are used to ensure that the data in the data warehouse are accurate. Inaccurate data in a data warehouse is more than a nuisance; it is a dangerous situation. The whole purpose of a data warehouse is to support decision making. Using inaccurate data, then, can lead to wrong decisions, which can lead to all sorts of unpleasant consequences (Paller 1997).

Metadata Repositories

Metadata is defined as data about data. In the context of data warehousing, metadata is data that describes the data in the data warehouse. The metadata is stored in databases called repositories. There are two broad categories of data warehousing metadata repositories— administrative and end-user. Administrative metadata describes data about source databases, data warehouse objects, and how the data from the source databases are transformed before they are moved to the data warehouse. End-user metadata helps those using the data warehouse form their queries and perform their analyses. For example, an end-user might refer to the repository to determine what a particular item of data is called.

Warehouse Data Stores

Warehouse data stores are the structures used to actually store the data in the data warehouse. Most warehouse data stores take the form of relational databases. However, organizations are increasingly using multidimensional databases. Relational databases conceptualize data in terms of two dimensions. Rows represent records and columns represent fields. Multidimensional databases go beyond this two-dimensional view. They are often conceptualized in terms of cubes, although there can be more than three dimensions. For example, a multidimensional cube might include the three dimensions of product, time, and location. This simplifies processing of queries such as "How many copies of *War and Peace* did we sell in the Northeast region?"

Tools for Data Retrieval, Formatting, and Analysis

This is perhaps the most varied category of components. A wide variety of decision makers utilize the data in a data warehouse. Query tools allow users to retrieve data from the data warehouse. Report generators are an example of formatting tools. Analysis tools include spreadsheet software (such as Excel), statistical analysis software (such as SPSS and SAS), and multidimensional analysis software. Two emerging developments in the analysis tool category are **data mining** and data visualization tools. Data mining tools help users discover patterns in the data. With most analysis tools, users know what questions they want to ask before using the tool. With data mining, users do not necessarily need to know what questions to ask; the software uncovers patterns for the user. Data visualization tools allow users to "see" patterns in the data. These tools allow users to build quite complex, three-dimensional representations of the data.

Management Tools

Data warehouse management tools allow those responsible for the operation of the data warehouse to perform their tasks more effectively. These tasks include controlling access to the data in the data warehouse, performance monitoring, and usage monitoring.

Now that you have an understanding of the various components of a data warehousing environment, let us examine how it all fits together. Figure 8-1 illustrates the data warehousing environment graphically.

Before actually designing and building the data warehouse, the systems storing the source data must be identified. Recall that these systems may include operational systems internal to the organization, as well as external data sources, such as industry and governmental data. The next step is to design and create the data warehouse. At the heart of this step is the data model. Specific data modeling methods have been developed for designing data warehouses. These include the star and snowflake models. Of course, the design of the data warehouse is critical to success. After the data warehouse is built and populated with terabytes of data, making changes to the structure is difficult and expensive.

Once the data stores for the data warehouse have been created, the **extract/transform/load (ETL) process** takes place. First, the data must be extracted from the source systems. As noted earlier there are tools that assist in this task. Organizations may also create their own programs for performing the extraction. When the data have been extracted, they must be transformed to fit the data warehouse's data model. Two different types of transformation will help you understand what happens in this process. As we noted earlier, data from source systems often must be **cleansed** before they are placed in the data warehouse. Why is this necessary? There are a number of problems that can occur when integrating data from multiple sources. One problem is that the same item of data may go by different names in different systems. For example, one operational system may use the term "price" to refer to the same data another system calls "cost." The opposite

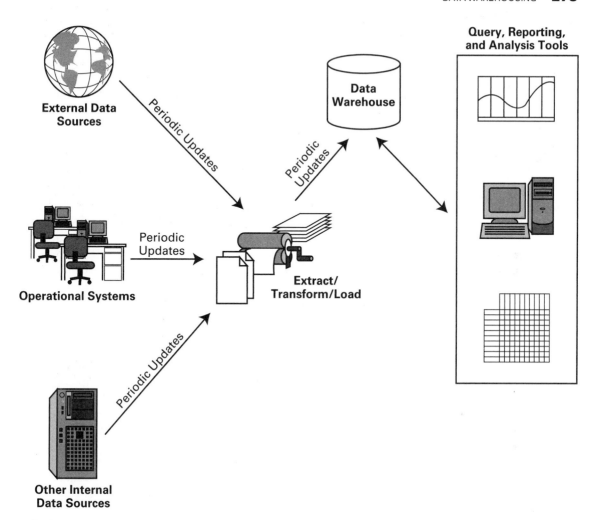

FIGURE 8-1   Data Warehousing Environment

problem can also occur. Two different source systems may use the same name for different items of data. For example, a purchasing system may use "price" to refer to the cost of acquiring a product, while in a sales system "price" refers to the price the organization charges for a product. A similar problem can occur even within a single operational system. An example of this is when different names are used to refer to a single customer. For example, an organization may provide products to the shipper FedEx. Various values may be used in one or more operational systems to refer to this customer, including "FedEx," "Fed Ex," and "Federal Express." These problems must be reconciled before the data are loaded into the data warehouse.

You should be aware that cleansing data is a huge task. Although conceptually it sounds relatively simple, in reality it is a difficult job. In fact, some data warehousing projects fail because of the inability to cleanse "dirty" data. One reason dirty data can be so difficult to detect is that it can take so many forms. Sometimes incorrect values come about as a result of users entering false values for required data fields when using operational systems. For example, a user may be required to enter a postal code on some data entry screen. If the correct code is not known, the user may enter something like "11111" or "12345." The operational system accepts the value and enters it into the database. This sort of dirty data is difficult to recognize. Of course, if the problem is not recognized, it cannot be corrected. There are many other common causes for dirty data. For a good overview of the problem, see the article "Data Cleansing: A Dichotomy of Data Warehousing?" which is referenced in the Further Readings section.

The second type of transformation we discuss is aggregation. Recall that data in a data warehouse is often aggregated in various ways. For example, we may want to aggregate individual sales into daily totals for each product. Of course, data may be aggregated in multiple ways. Product sales data may be aggregated by day, by customer, by region, and by salesperson. There is an interesting tradeoff that occurs during aggregation. There are two benefits to storing aggregated data, rather than detailed data. First, aggregating the data makes retrieval much faster. If data are not aggregated, it is possible for a retrieval operation to require complex joins that involve millions of records, which can be an extremely slow process. A second, less important, benefit is that storage requirements *may* be reduced through aggregation. Rather than storing the details of each sale during a particular day, aggregation allows for storing only the totals. It is important to understand, however, that it is also possible that aggregations can actually require more storage space than the detailed data. This occurs when the data are aggregated in many different ways. The downside to storing aggregated data is that the original detail of the data is lost. This is a problem if a user wants to investigate the data in ways not anticipated in the aggregations.

When the data have been transformed, they can be loaded into the data warehouse data stores. Of course, it is not sufficient to simply carry out the ETL process once. The process must be repeated periodically to reflect changes in the data from ongoing operations. Two interesting problems arise from the need to update the data warehouse. First, the proper update period must be determined. A balance must be found between the need for current data and the processing costs of performing updates. Fortunately, most data warehousing applications do not require current data, since data warehouses are oriented toward historical data. The second challenge is to determine which data in the source data systems have changed. The process of identifying and capturing the changed data is called changed data capture.

When the data warehouse is finally populated with data, a variety of query, reporting, and analysis tools may be utilized to allow decision makers to benefit from the data in the warehouse. As noted earlier, there are many different decision support tools. It is important to note that the data warehouse and query, reporting, and analysis tools are not sufficient for making quality decisions. Human expertise is required to interpret the analysis.

There is considerably more to data warehousing than we have described in this section. If you are curious and wish to learn more about the topic, we encourage you to refer to the Web sites and books listed in the Further Readings section at the end of the chapter.

Data warehousing is directed at helping organizations benefit from the vast quantities of data they gather. An important use of data warehouses is as components in a customer relationship management system. We discuss customer relationship management systems in the next section.

CUSTOMER RELATIONSHIP MANAGEMENT SYSTEMS

Customer relationship management (CRM) is an organized set of activities and technologies directed at understanding the needs of current and potential customers. The overall goal is managing the organization's associations with customers in a manner that maximizes customer retention and satisfaction, while also maximizing the organization's profitability. That is the academic definition of CRM, but we should provide a better idea of what CRM is all about. The basic idea behind CRM systems is to allow all "customer-facing" members and systems (those who interact with customers) of an organization to have a consistent view of each customer. An example may help illustrate.

Kim Harris is a customer of Quickie Computers, a major computer manufacturer that sells directly to home and business computer users. Kim is thinking about a new computer and she wants to talk to a Quickie sales representative about what is available. She calls Quickie's toll-free telephone number. A recorded voice responds with a menu of choices for Kim. She presses "2" to talk to a sales rep. Soon a sales rep named Mike is introducing himself to Kim. What Kim does not know is that in the minute or so she was waiting for someone to answer, Quickie's CRM system has identified Kim by her telephone number. Since Kim has contacted Quickie in the past, the CRM system retrieves her information and displays it on Mike's computer even before he answers the call. So, Mike is aware that two years ago, Kim purchased a Quickie 667 MHz system with a CD-RW drive, along with a four-page-per-minute color printer. Mike also sees that she contacted customer service several times in the two years she has owned the computer and that in each case her issues were resolved during the first phone call. He also knows that Kim has been thinking about a new computer for a couple of months; she called Quickie earlier with some questions about one of their special offers. The CRM system also reminds Mike that this month Quickie is offering a special rebate to customers who purchase a new Quickie 1.4 GHz Multimedia system (which includes a CD-RW and upgraded sound system) along with a twelve-page-per-minute color printer.

As you can tell from our little example, Mike is well equipped to take Kim's call. He knows what kind of computer she currently has (assuming she still has her Quickie 667 MHz). He knows that she has a slow printer. He knows that she will probably want to include a CD-RW drive in her new computer. Mike also knows that Kim has made use of Quickie's customer service several times and is likely to be happy with the service provided, since none of her issues required multiple calls. All of this information is provided by the CRM system. The system also includes analytical software that indicates that customers who have already inquired about a Quickie system are often influenced to make a purchase decision when offered a time-sensitive offer, such as the rebate. The CRM system was also able to analyze Quickie's current specials and identify the one best suited to Kim's situation.

CRM systems have three main goals, as illustrated in the example (Meta Group 2001). First, CRM systems help organizations manage multiple channels of interaction with customers in ways that the customers prefer. Like many organizations, Quickie has a number of communication channels it uses to interact with customers. Quickie has an extensive Web site where customers can examine product offers and specifications, place orders, and perform "self-service" customer service. Of course, Quickie also interacts with customers over the phone for inquiries, sales, and customer service. Other channels of communication include e-mail, automated phone systems, and "fax-back" services. The CRM system kept track of the fact that Kim typically uses the phone to talk to live representatives in her interactions with Quickie; so rather than directing her to an automated system, the system put her call through to Mike. You can imagine Kim's possible frustration if she had been made to suffer through seemingly endless phone menus and messages before talking to an actual person. (Many of you have suffered similar frustration.)

The second goal of CRM systems is to provide an integrated picture of the customer across the various customer-facing parts of the organization. In the example, by the time Mike took Kim's call, he knew her account and customer service history. If there were any unresolved customer service issues, Mike would be aware of them. Mike also knew that another sales rep had recently talked with Kim, and that the focus of the discussion was that she was beginning to think about a new computer. This goal is particularly helpful in customer service. Customers who call for service are generally already agitated (since they are usually dealing with a problem). They can quickly become even more agitated if they have to make multiple calls and repeat the entire story each time. The reverse is also true. One of the authors would not dream of changing Internet service providers because his was so effective in resolving a multi-call problem when he moved to a new home. Even though the problem took several calls to resolve, on each call the customer service rep knew what had occurred during the previous call. (As it turned out, the problem was with a bad connection in a piece of phone company equipment outside the author's house. Of course, this took a new modem and several hours on the phone to figure out.)

The third major goal of CRM systems is to enable the analysis of customer-related information. This information is gathered through interactions with customers, although external data (such as census data) may also be involved. This goal is also illustrated in the interaction between Kim and Mike. Remember when the system prompted Mike to inform Kim of the rebate? That particular special offer was selected through an analysis of the success of similar specials when offered to different types of customers. For example, the analytical functions of the CRM may have determined that potential customers who have previously inquired about a system are motivated to action by a time-sensitive special (such as the rebate offer). Table 8-3 summarizes the major goals of CRM systems.

The goals of CRM systems make them attractive to organizations. However, changing over to a CRM approach is not a simple matter. According to studies by Gartner Group and Meta Group (Ericson 2001), estimates of failure rates for CRM projects range from 55 to 70 percent. So, there is significant risk associated with making the transition to CRM. In order to be successful in this transition, organizations must look beyond purely technical issues. The ability to achieve buy-in from various areas of the organization and to change management skills are nontechnical keys to successful transitions. Of course, there are complicated technological issues that also must be addressed. The ability to deal with both nontechnical and technical issues are requirements for successfully implementing almost any e-business system, including those discussed in this chapter.

Table 8-3   Goals of CRM

- Manage multiple channels of interaction with customers
- Provide a unified view of the customer across the enterprise
- Analyze information collected to improve campaigns, services, and products

---

A Framework for Understanding CRM Systems

In order to better understand CRM, we use a variation of a popular framework developed by the META Group, an IT research and consulting firm (META Group 2001). The framework consists of two dimensions: customer life cycle and functional components. In this section we discuss each of these dimensions as they relate to the framework. Then we use the framework to help us organize a discussion of the various components that may be included in a CRM system.

Customer Life Cycle

The customer life cycle is composed of a series of phases that customers pass through when interacting with an organization. There are a number of variations on the phases, but they are all similar. We are using the EFTS version, which is often used in discussions of CRM. Other similar ideas include the customer service life cycle popularized by Ives and Learmonth (1984).

The customer life cycle consists of four phases: engage, transact, fulfill, and service. The combined phases are referred to as a cycle, because completion of one round of the cycle often leads to another round. This is illustrated by Kim's experience in our example. Kim was at the end of one cycle (for her current computer) and was beginning a new cycle (for the replacement computer). Note that in the following discussion we refer to products, but similar statements could be made about services.

Engage The engage phase of the life cycle deals with making the customer aware of the product. During the engage phase, the organization tries to generate customer leads, and subsequently convert those leads into new customers. A number of CRM-related functions are used when engaging potential customers. These include sales automation tools, marketing campaign management tools, and Web-based catalogs. An increasingly popular application related to engagement is e-mail marketing. You have probably received more than a few marketing-oriented e-mail messages. Many Web sites that require you to register before allowing you to access some content do so in order to target marketing messages, which are often delivered via e-mail. Today, many of these sites use opt-in marketing (also known as permission marketing) which offers the customer the option of signing up to receive special "e-mail only" offers.

Transact Activities associated with the actual purchase process occur in the transact phase. The goal of this phase is to efficiently and effectively complete the purchase process. It is critical that the transact phase go smoothly, otherwise customers may abandon their purchases. E-business technologies are closely linked with activities in the transact phase, even for non-Web purchases. One common example is payment technologies. Even when a customer orders a product over the telephone, e-business technologies are often used to connect to a credit card processing center in order to gain payment approval. In many cases, sales representatives use network-enabled systems to check inventory or perform other tasks. Another increasingly popular application associated with the transact phase identifies add-on products for customers. For example, when purchasing a printer, the system might recommend a cable to the customer. Often these add-on sales can account for more profit than the original purchase. Another interesting application is configuration software. Sometimes figuring out the right product to purchase may be difficult for many customers. For example, identifying the correct memory to purchase when upgrading your computer may be difficult.

There are literally dozens of different types of memory used in personal computers (and that is not even considering other electronic devices, such as digital cameras, MP3 players, and personal digital assistants). Picking the wrong type is at best inconvenient and at worst damaging. A good example of configuration software is Crucial's Memory Selector, which helps customers select the proper memory for a vast array of computers and other memory-dependent electronic devices. This Web-based system steps the customer through a series of choices leading to a listing of memory that is compatible with the customer's device, ensuring that the customer chooses appropriate memory.

Fulfill In the fulfill phase, activities are directed towards delivering the purchased product to the customer. E-business technologies are particularly important when a product is in digital form, such as digital music or software. In these cases, product delivery can take place using networks, such as the Internet. A popular example of a fulfillment-oriented application is package tracking. Many online merchants make very good use of package tracking systems from companies such as United Parcel Service and FedEx. Once a customer has completed the transact phase by placing an order, many organizations allow the customer to track the status of the order through a Web site. For example, Dell Computer Corporation's Web site lets customers check the status of an order from the time the order is placed. Once the computer (or other product) leaves Dell's warehouse, Dell's Web site connects to the shipper's tracking software to inform the customer of the progress of the order. Supply chain management (SCM) systems may also be used during the fulfillment phase. Although SCM systems are often not considered to be part of CRM systems, efficiencies are gained when CRM systems are able to interface with SCM systems.

Service The service phase of the customer life cycle is made up of activities directed toward supporting customers during their ownership of a product. These activities are what many people call customer service. Two widely discussed applications associated with the service phase are call center automation and customer self-service. Call centers handle incoming customer communication and include functions such as help lines and information inquiry and response. The term "call center" is actually a bit of a misnomer because it implies that customer contact is made via telephone calls. In actuality, many so-called call centers handle customers who use a variety of media to contact a company, including voice, fax, and e-mail. A major reason that call center automation is such a hot topic is that many organizations now realize that customer service calls are often opportunities to generate additional revenue. You may have experienced this, perhaps when dealing with a credit card company. Many credit card companies use customer service inquiries to offer additional products, such as insurance or other member services. In fact, some companies partner with other organizations to sell external products and services through incoming customer calls. For example, Capital One (one of the "big three" U.S. credit card companies) partners with companies such as Earthlink (a large ISP) to market external products. Customer self-service applications allow customers to help themselves rather than rely on customer service representatives. Web sites are a popular method for customer self-service. However, the sophistication and effectiveness of customer service Web sites vary widely. Some are limited to very simple "frequently asked question" (FAQ) pages, while others offer large databases with highly sophisticated search facilities. Information technology companies were pioneers in customer self-service. Manufacturers such as Sun Microsystems have allowed users network-based access to software patches, device drivers, and configuration instructions for many years (even before the widespread use of the Web). It is important to understand that other technologies, such as interactive voice response (IVR) and fax-back services, are also important components to an effective customer self-service strategy. Table 8-4 recaps the customer life cycle phases and provides some examples of CRM-related applications for each phase.

Functional Components

The second dimension of the CRM framework consists of a categorization of components of CRM systems. Components of a CRM system can be broken down into three categories: operational components, collaborative components, and analytical components. These are explained below.

Operational Components   The operational components of a CRM system help an organization improve day-to-day interactions with customers. Operational components include applications such as sales management, account management, and order management systems. In addition, many legacy systems may be operational components of a CRM system.

Collaborative Components   Collaborative components of a CRM system are directed toward improving the way in which organizations interact and collaborate with their customers. A number of interesting technologies can be included in this category. For example, many organizations have added interactive chat facilities to their customer service Web sites. In addition, many organizations use both automated response and traditional e-mail as efficient customer collaboration tools. The IVR systems mentioned earlier also fall into this category. A collaborative technology that is growing in popularity is the use of voice over IP (VoIP) technologies that allow a customer to talk to a "live" customer service representative while online. Two aspects of this technology are particularly attractive to companies. First, it allows customers to have voice interaction as an option, even

Table 8-4   Customer Life Cycle Phases

Phase	Description	Technologies/applications
Engage	Creating customer awareness of the product or service, goal of the engage stage is to generate leads and then convert those leads into customers	■ Sales automation ■ Campaign management ■ Web-based catalogs ■ Marketing
Transact	All activities associated with the purchase process	■ Product configuration ■ Product pricing ■ Order management ■ Payment
Fulfill	Delivery of the product or service to the customer	■ Package tracking ■ Supply-chain integration
Service	Supporting the customer during the ownership of a product or service	■ Call center automation ■ Issue tracking ■ Self-service ■ "Sell-up"

if their telephone line is tied up accessing the Internet. Second, VoIP calls are very cost effective; they are much less expensive than providing a toll-free number to customers.

Analytical Components   The final category is analytical components, which consists of technologies and processes that organizations can use to analyze customer data. A critical analytical component in most CRM systems is the data warehouse, which we discussed earlier. Data mining technologies and methods are often used to discover patterns in the data stored in a data warehouse. One analysis that many organizations find useful is customer segmentation (sometimes called customer clustering), which allows organizations to group customers that share certain characteristics. For example, Student Advantage, a company that provides college student-oriented marketing services, uses segmentation to place its student members into very small segments. This allows Student Advantage to provide extremely targeted marketing opportunities to a wide variety of clients. Data mining can also help in customer profiling. Customer profiling lets companies build a picture of a customer through data about customer interactions. These profiles allow companies to better anticipate customer needs and better predict customer behavior. For example, in the Quickie Computers story, customer profiling helped Quickie's CRM system profile Kim. Then behaviors of customers similar to Kim were analyzed in order to select the offer that was most likely to elicit a purchase.

Combining Functions and Technologies

Combining the customer life cycle with the CRM components' categorization results in a two-dimensional grid that we can use to classify various CRM functions and technologies, as illustrated in Table 8-5. Note that some technologies span a number of cells in the framework. This is because certain technologies are used in more than one phase in the customer life cycle. For example, a data warehouse can be used to analyze data resulting from or support decisions associated with any of the customer life cycle phases.

Table 8-5   CRM Framework

	Operational	Collaborative	Analytical
Engage	■ Sales force automation ■ Marketing automation ■ Lead processing	■ IVR ■ E-mail	■ Data warehouse ■ Data mining ■ Customer profiling ■ Campaign management
Transact	■ Order tracking ■ Legacy systems ■ Call center automation ■ Configuration management	■ Web storefront ■ E-mail	■ Data warehouse
Fulfill	■ Order tracking ■ Legacy systems		■ Data warehouse
Service	■ Customer self-service ■ Field service management ■ Call center automation	■ IVR ■ Web storefront ■ E-mail	■ Data warehouse ■ Data mining

Of course, Table 8-5 only offers a sampling of CRM-related technologies. There are dozens of technologies that may be included as part of a CRM system. Our intent is to give you a feel for the variety of technologies involved in CRM and to show you how the framework can be used to classify these technologies. Also, note that most of the technologies shown in the table are applications, which, of course, are enabled by a myriad of other technologies, such as programming languages, servers, and networks. The following sections provide brief descriptions of each of the technologies shown in Table 8-5. Note that we exclude legacy systems, data warehouses, e-mail, and Web storefronts from this discussion, since they are covered elsewhere.

Sales Force Automation

Sales force automation technologies include application software that provides a number of functions directed at making sales representatives more efficient and effective. Example applications include contact management, account management, and proposal generators. Many applications in this category make use of wireless communication technologies.

Marketing Automation

Marketing automation systems help organizations identify and reach top customers, prospects, and market segments. These systems automate mundane tasks, such as responding to requests for product literature. They also help organizations coordinate marketing efforts across the enterprise. In addition, they gather data on marketing efforts, such as response rates. These data can be analyzed in order to improve future marketing efforts.

Lead Processing

Lead processing systems are used to qualify, assign, and track sales leads in order to maximize the probability that the leads will turn into sales. For example, a lead processing system can analyze leads and assign them to the proper sales representatives based on location, product line, or other criteria. In addition, the system may link to external information sources to gather additional information (such as financial information) about the prospects.

Order Tracking

Order tracking systems use database technology to allow customers to determine the status of any order. For example, Dell Computer Corporation's order tracking system lets customers track orders through five steps in Dell's internal processing system: order processing, pre-production, production, delivery preparation, and shipment. In addition, Dell's Web site lets customers link to the appropriate shipper's Web site to track the progress of a shipment even after it has left Dell's control. Many organizations have similar systems, some of which are used internally by sales or customer service representatives to answer customer inquiries over the telephone.

Call Center Automation

Call centers are often the main contact point between an organization and its customers. Call centers handle a wide variety of functions, ranging from dealing with complaints to providing technical assistance. A critical component of call center automation is access to complete customer information, which may require integrating information from a number of databases and legacy systems.

Configuration Management

Configuration management systems are used to properly configure or choose complex products. For example, configuring a computer system correctly can be complex; choosing one option may require another option. Configuration management systems guide customers (or sales or customer service representatives) through the configuration process in order to ensure that the product meets expectations. Often these systems use sophisticated databases coupled with expert system technology.

Customer Self-Service

As discussed earlier, customer self-service systems allow customers to track down the solutions to problems without interacting with a customer service representative. Today, many customer self-service systems utilize a Web-based interface. A key part of a Web-based self-service system is the search technology used to help customers locate the appropriate information. One trend in this area is to use natural language processing to enable customers to perform complex searches without learning a specific search engine syntax.

Field Service Management

These systems help organizations with tasks such as scheduling, dispatching, and communicating with field service personnel. For example, when an elevator manufacturing company receives a service request, the field service management system identifies service technicians who are qualified to service the particular model involved. Then the system checks the schedules of those technicians and schedules the service call according to availability and location. Wireless communication technologies play a key role in many field service management systems.

Interactive Voice Response

Interactive voice response (IVR) technologies allow customers to use a telephone to navigate through various types of systems, such as product request systems or customer service systems. For example, many companies use IVR to let customers access account information. An interesting use of IVR is for conducting automated telephone surveys. Typically these surveys use pre-recorded questions to which subjects respond either by pressing telephone buttons or by speaking their answers.

Data Mining

Data mining tools are used to analyze data gathered through other components of a CRM system. Data mining helps identify patterns and relationships in the data. Data mining can help companies better understand the vast volume of data collected by CRM systems. For example, data mining can identify products that are often purchased together, which can help build product bundles that are more likely to be successful.

Customer Profiling

Customer profiling systems help organizations group their customers according to demographic characteristics or behaviors. This allows an organization to paint a picture of customers or prospects that can be used to better target marketing offers. An interesting development in the area of customer profiling is the emergence of Customer Profile Exchange (CPexchange), which is an XML-based standard for exchanging customer profile information.

Campaign Management

Campaign management systems help organizations plan, carry out, and analyze the results of marketing campaigns. An important feature of a good campaign management system is the ability to manage campaigns that utilize multiple channels, such as print, television, and e-mail.

DATABASE OVERVIEW

A collection of some sort of data sits at the core of almost any e-business system. It does not matter if you are talking about a Web portal such as Yahoo!; an online merchant, such as Amazon.com; or a business-to-business exchange, such as Altra Energy Technologies' ePower Marketplace. Almost any e-business system makes heavy use of data. Although the specific technology varies, in general terms, these collections of data are called **databases.** Formally, a database is a collection of **data** that is used by the systems of an organization (Date 2000). Informally, you can think of a database as a bucket of data from which an organization's systems retrieve data, or into which the systems place data.

Although the terms data and information are commonly used interchangeably, the two terms actually have different meanings. Data are raw facts, such as a prices, descriptions, or colors. (By the way, the word "data" is actually the plural form of the word "datum." However, "data" is commonly used for both the singular and plural forms. In most cases, we follow the common usage.) By itself, an item of data has no meaning. For example, is the number fifty, which is an item of data, good or bad? You cannot answer this question without knowing more. If it is an hourly pay rate, most people would think it is pretty good. If it is a score on a test for which there were one hundred points total and the average score was an eighty-seven, most people would think it is bad. In order to answer the question, we had to combine our single item of data with other data. Data that has been processed in some way is called **information.** In most cases the distinction between the two terms is unimportant. However, both authors teach database courses, so it makes us feel better to at least mention the difference.

Databases are managed by systems called **database management systems,** which we abbreviate as **DBMS.** A DBMS is responsible for creating, maintaining, and providing access to databases. Basically, the job of the DBMS is to shield users and application programs from all of the hardware and operating system details involved in storing and retrieving data.

There are several theoretical models that are used as the basis for database systems. However, in terms of e-business systems, the **relational database** approach is currently the most important. In the future, other approaches, such as object-oriented databases, may overtake relational databases in terms of importance, but for now relational databases rule. In the next section, we provide an overview of the structure of relational databases.

Overview of Relational Databases

Most of the databases used in e-business follow a model called the relational database model. Many popular database management systems follow the rules of this model. Examples include Microsoft Access, Microsoft SQL Server, Oracle, Sybase, and IBM's DB2. The overall goal of relational database systems is to provide flexibility in the use of data while minimizing the potential for inconsistencies in the data. Prior to the advent of relational databases, most application programs were responsible for maintaining their own data. This led to an abundance of redundant data. This, in turn, led to many problems with inconsistent data. The potential for data inconsistency occurs whenever an item of data is stored more than once. For example, if your address is stored twice in the information systems of your university, it is possible that you are listed as having one address in one file and another address in the other. You may have experienced this. Perhaps the library sends notices to your old address, but your grade reports go to your new address. This cannot happen if your address is only stored once. (Of course, it is possible that your address is incorrect even if it is stored only once. However, the data will at least be consistent.)

Relational databases follow a set of rules called **normal forms** that, when met, ensure that data inconsistencies cannot occur. A complete discussion of these normal forms could easily fill an entire chapter. So, we will simply say that these normal form rules must be followed, or inconsistencies may result. See the Further Readings section for references to more information on normal forms and the theory behind relational databases.

In order to understand how relational databases work, it is helpful to look at a manual database system. Suppose you had information about customers and orders stored on a piece of paper. The paper might look like the one shown in Figure 8-2. Note that we can identify a customer by its ID and an order by its order number. For this to work, we must have a rule that says we cannot repeat a customer ID or an order number.

Look closely at the data on the paper. Notice how customer number 101 is listed for four orders. Do you see that a different address is listed for order number 6? For order numbers 1, 8, and 10, customer 101 is located on Main Street, while for order number 6, customer 101's address is shown as South Street. Unfortunately, there is nothing in this method of storing data that prevents this kind of inconsistency from occurring.

Consider a different way of organizing your information. This time you use two sheets of paper, one with order information and one with customer information, as illustrated in Figure 8-3. You still need to be able to match customer information to orders (for example to get the customer's address). So, you need some kind of cross reference information on the order sheet to allow you to match an order to a customer. Since you know that there can only be one customer for each order, and that the customer ID number uniquely identifies a particular customer, you decide to add a customer ID for each order on the order sheet. This provides the cross reference that will let you link customer data with order data.

Order Number	Date	Total	Customer Number	Name	Street	City	State	Zip
1	October 1, 2001	$ 125.50	101	ABC Equipment	101 Main Street	Belle Isle	FL	32813
2	October 4, 2001	$ 200.72	102	Southern Services	75 Second Avenue	Orlando	FL	32809
3	November 15, 2001	$ 105.85	103	XYZ Distributors	995 Bobcat Way	Athens	OH	45701
4	November 26, 2001	$ 235.17	107	Knight Food Services	3234 Golden Street	Manhattan	KS	66505
5	December 17, 2001	$ 154.23	108	Quickie Computers	707 Commerce Avenue	Blacksburg	VA	24066
6	December 28, 2001	$ 245.00	101	ABC Equipment	500 South Street	Belle Isle	FL	32813
7	January 8, 2002	$ 175.35	107	Knight Food Services	3234 Golden Street	Manhattan	KS	66505
8	January 30, 2002	$ 168.30	101	ABC Equipment	101 Main Street	Belle Isle	FL	32813
9	February 13, 2002	$ 112.20	103	XYZ Distributors	995 Bobcat Way	Athens	OH	45701
10	February 22, 2002	$ 254.65	101	ABC Equipment	101 Main Street	Belle Isle	FL	32813

FIGURE 8-2 Single "Sheet" Database

Now if you need to put a customer's name and address on some report that also includes order information, you can simply look at the customer ID on the order sheet and use it to find the correct customer information. There is no way that you can have an inconsistency in the customer information (such as having two different addresses for a customer) because you are only storing each item of customer information one time. (If the organization wants to keep track of both current and past addresses for customers, a separate table is used to store address histories.)

Before we look at how relational databases work, we need to define some terms. First, a particular type of data, such as customer name, order number, or price is called a **field.** (Note that this same concept also goes by the name **column.**) A collection of related fields is called a **record.** Each row in Figure 8-3 shows a record. A collection of related records is known as a **table.** A database is made up of a collection of related tables.

A relational database works in much the same way as the two-sheet organization of customer and order data. Each table (which equates to each sheet of paper in Figure 8-3) consists of a group of related records, which are each made up of a group of related fields. Recall that each customer is identified by a unique value, as is each order. In database terminology, this unique identifier is known as the table's **primary key.** A relational database works by eliminating redundant data, except for overlapping values (fields) that can be used as cross references to link data from different tables together. These repeated fields are called **foreign keys.** A foreign key in one table is a primary key in a related table. When you are using a relational database and you need to combine data from different tables, the database management system looks at the foreign key values from one of the tables and finds matches in the primary key values of the other table.

Order Number	Date	Total	Customer Number
1	October 1, 2001	$ 125.50	101
2	October 4, 2001	$ 200.72	102
3	November 15, 2001	$ 105.85	103
4	November 26, 2001	$ 235.17	107
5	December 17, 2001	$ 154.23	108
6	December 28, 2001	$ 245.00	101
7	January 8, 2002	$ 175.35	107
8	January 30, 2002	$ 168.30	101
9	February 13, 2002	$ 112.20	103
10	February 22, 2002	$ 254.65	101

Customer Number	Name	Street	City	State	Zip
101	ABC Equipment	101 Main Street	Belle Isle	FL	32813
102	Southern Services	75 Second Avenue	Orlando	FL	32809
103	XYZ Distributors	995 Bobcat Way	Athens	OH	45701
107	Knight Food Services	3234 Golden Street	Manhattan	KS	66505
108	Quickie Computers	707 Commerce Avenue	Blacksburg	VA	24066

FIGURE 8-3 Two "Sheet" Database

Relational database designs are shown in a **logical schema.** There are several different ways to show a schema. One notation, which is commonly used in more formal database work, is shown in Figure 8-4. Each table is shown as a collection of fields, which are shown in rectangles. Primary key values are indicated with a solid underline. Typically, a foreign key is shown as a dashed underline, although some people use italic type because it is easier to do. The arrows point from a foreign key field to the primary key to which it refers.

Microsoft Access, a popular Windows-based database management system, shows a logical schema differently, although the same information is shown regardless of which method you use. In the Access schema, tables are shown as rectangles with the field names arranged vertically, rather than horizontally, as shown in Figure 8-5. Primary keys are shown in boldface type. Access does not use any special typeface to indicate foreign keys. However, you can tell when a field acts as a foreign key by looking at the lines that link tables together. As was the case with the logical schema in Figure 8-4, a line between two tables indicates that these tables are related to each other. In Access, the line connects a primary key to a foreign key field. In general, you can tell which is the primary key by

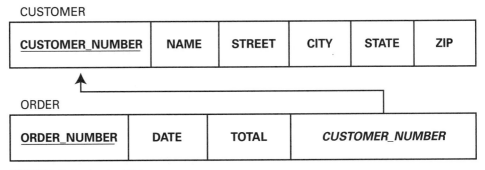

FIGURE 8-4 Logical Schema

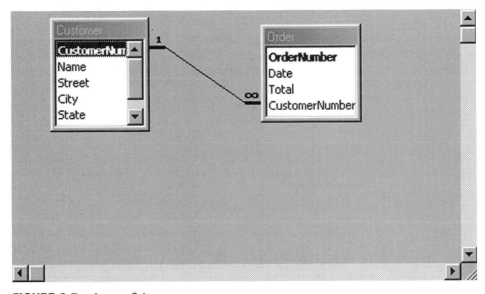

FIGURE 8-5 Access Schema

looking at the symbol at the end of the line. If the symbol is the numeral "1," that field is the primary key. If the infinity symbol is shown, that field is the foreign key. (The infinity symbol looks like a sideways eight (8).) There are some exceptions to this rule, but in general it works.

Now let us take a look at a simple database. This database consists of four tables—one representing customers, one representing orders, one representing products, and one that is used to link orders to products. This last table is called the ORDERLINE table because it represents the line items on an order. It is an example of what is sometimes called a linking table because its only reason for existence is to link other tables together. The schema for this database is shown in Figure 8-6. Note that in a "real" database there would probably be many other fields. However, we can make our point by using the small number of fields shown.

You might wonder why we need a special table just to link orders and products. Why not just use PRODUCT_ID as a foreign key in the ORDER table? This is a very reasonable question. This linking table is necessary because of one of the rules associated with the normal forms we mentioned earlier. This rule says that there can only be one value for each field in a given record. Since an order can contain many different products, using the primary key of the product table as a foreign key in the order table violates this rule. We cannot use the primary key of the order table as a foreign key in the product table because a product can be included on more than one order. The solution is to use the linking table ORDERLINE.

Now let us put some data into our tables. Figure 8-7 shows two of the tables from our database (CUSTOMER and ORDER) with some sample data. Notice how each foreign key (CUSTOMER_NUMBER) value in ORDER matches a primary key value in the

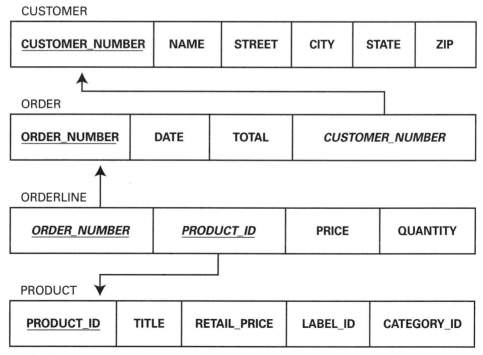

FIGURE 8-6 Order Database

Order Number	Date	Total	Customer Number
1	October 1, 2001	$ 125.50	101
2	October 4, 2001	$ 200.72	102
3	November 15, 2001	$ 105.85	103
4	November 26, 2001	$ 235.17	107
5	December 17, 2001	$ 154.23	108
6	December 28, 2001	$ 245.00	101
7	January 8, 2002	$ 175.35	107
8	January 30, 2002	$ 168.30	101
9	February 13, 2002	$ 112.20	103
10	February 22, 2002	$ 254.65	101

Customer Number	Name	Street	City	State	Zip
101	ABC Equipment	101 Main Street	Belle Isle	FL	32813
102	Southern Services	75 Second Avenue	Orlando	FL	32809
103	XYZ Distributors	995 Bobcat Way	Athens	OH	45701
107	Knight Food Services	3234 Golden Street	Manhattan	KS	66505
108	Quickie Computers	707 Commerce Avenue	Blacksburg	VA	24066

FIGURE 8-7 Referential Integrity

CUSTOMER table. One advantage of using a database is that the DBMS can enforce rules to ensure the integrity of the data. For example, we can tell the database to not allow negative values for quantities. One important type of integrity is called **referential integrity.** It says that every foreign key value has to match a primary key value in a related table. When you think about it, this is a very good rule. Otherwise you might be able to enter a customer number in an order that does not match any of the customer records. This would mean that later you would be unable to link this order to any customer, which, of course, is a bad thing.

You should now have a basic understanding of how relational databases are structured and the method used to link data from different tables. Now it is time to examine the method used by most relational DBMS for retrieving data from these databases. This is the topic of the next section.

Structured Query Language

The standard language for retrieving data from relational database management systems is the **Structured Query Language,** which is generally referred to as **SQL.** Of course, IT people like to turn acronyms into words whenever possible, so many people pronounce SQL as "see-qual." All popular relational DBMS that we know of use some form of SQL as a data manipulation language. In database terms, a data manipulation language is also used for data retrieval. Some DBMS offer alternatives to SQL for data retrieval. For example, Microsoft

Access allows you to use a method called Query By Example (QBE) for data retrieval. Access also supports SQL.

In this section, we provide a very basic introduction to SQL. Our purpose is not to turn you into a programmer. Rather, we want to give you a flavor for the language by showing you a few examples. SQL is actually very important to e-business systems because it is commonly embedded in programs written in other languages.

SQL code that accomplishes some task is usually referred to as an SQL statement, rather than a program. This is because SQL code is often embedded into the code of programs written in other languages. For purposes of following our discussion, you can break down SQL statements into two categories. One category includes statements that are used to change the data stored in a table. The other category includes statements that retrieve data, but do not change the actual data.

Three statements are used for changing the data in a table. An INSERT statement puts new records into a table. A DELETE statement is used to remove a record. When you want to change the values of one or more fields in one or more records, you use an UPDATE statement. We discuss each of these in turn.

The basic syntax of the INSERT statement is shown in the following code. When showing statement syntax in this chapter we use uppercase letters to indicate command words that must be entered as shown. Lowercase letters are used to show where you would enter parameters that vary. For example, the words INSERT, INTO, and VALUES are always entered exactly as shown. However, you would replace "table-name" with the name of one of the tables in your database. Finally, we use italics to indicate that something is optional. In the following code, the list of fields is optional.

```
INSERT INTO table-name
(field-1, field-2, …, field-n)
VALUES
(value-1, value-2, …, value-n);
```

As you can see, the basic syntax of the INSERT statement is fairly simple. There are only a few parameters that vary from one INSERT statement to another. Let us look at a specific example. Suppose you want to add a new product to your database. You could use the INSERT statement shown in the following code to accomplish this task.

```
INSERT INTO PRODUCT
(PRODUCT_ID, DESCRIPTION, PRICE)
VALUES
('555','CD PLAYER', 79.95);
```

Two other SQL statements are used to manipulate the data stored in the tables of a database. The UPDATE command is used to change values of one or more records in a table. The DELETE command is used to remove one or more records in a table. The basic syntax for these two commands is provided in the following code.

```
UPDATE    table-name
SET       column-name = expression
WHERE     condition
;
DELETE    FROM table-name
WHERE     condition
;
```

Although it is not required, both of these statements are usually issued with a conditional statement, which sets out logical conditions that must be met before a record is updated or deleted. In fact, you must be very careful when using these statements, otherwise it is possible that you could accidentally remove all records from a table or change all values of a column in a table to a single value. Sometimes these actions are appropriate, but typically you want the DELETE or UPDATE statements to act on a subset of the records in a table. In these cases, you must specify some conditional statement to limit the records affected.

In SQL, a WHERE clause is used to express conditions. For example, suppose you have decided not to offer the CD player entered into the database in the earlier code. You can remove this record from the database by using the DELETE statement shown in the following code. This statement only affects a single record—the one with a PRODUCT_ID value that matches 555. No other records are impacted. This is accomplished through the WHERE clause, WHERE PRODUCT_ID = '555'.

```
DELETE FROM      PRODUCT
WHERE            PRODUCT_ID = '555'
;
```

A condition in an UPDATE statement works in a similar manner. By specifying a condition, you limit the records that are impacted by the UPDATE statement. Suppose that you want to discount the product with the ID value 444 by 10 percent. The UPDATE statement in the following code accomplishes this task.

```
UPDATE     PRODUCT
SET        RETAIL_PRICE = RETAIL_PRICE * .9
WHERE      PRODUCT_ID = '444'
;
```

SQL also provides a method for retrieving data from one or more tables in a database. The SELECT statement is used for this purpose. A portion of the basic syntax for the SELECT statement is shown in the following code. Note that a complete discussion of the SELECT statement is beyond the scope of this chapter. See one of the SQL texts referenced in the Further Readings section for more detailed information.

```
SELECT    expression-1, expression-2, …, expression-n
FROM      table-1, table-2, …, table-n
WHERE     condition
ORDER BY result-col-1, result-col-2, …, result-col-3
;
```

All queries produce what is known as a record set, which is simply a set of one or more rows and one or more columns of data. We limit the columns included in the query results through the first line in the query. We use the WHERE condition to limit the rows included in the results.

Let us look at each line of the SELECT statement in detail. The first line starts with the word "SELECT" followed by a list of one or more expressions. Generally, these expressions are the names of columns from the tables referenced in the FROM clause in the query. However, it is possible to include constants (such as a number or string of characters) or an expression involving columns and/or numeric constants. The FROM clause is used to tell SQL what tables you want to include in your query. One important requirement of a properly constructed SQL SELECT statement is that all columns used in the query must be in one of the tables listed in the FROM clause. Otherwise, the query will produce an error message. All SELECT queries must include at least the first two lines. Everything else is optional. This includes the WHERE clause, which is used to include conditions for limiting the rows included in the query results. Note that these WHERE conditions can become quite complex and can include a set of conditions that must be met. We will look at an example of this later. The final line in the SELECT statement syntax shown in the previous code is used to control the order of the rows in the query results. The ORDER BY clause is optional. If multiple columns are listed in the ORDER BY clause, multiple levels of sorting occur. For example, if you included both the STATE and POSTAL_CODE columns in the ORDER BY clause of a query, results are sorted first by state. Then, within the results for each state, the results are listed according to postal code.

Let us consider some examples of SQL queries. Suppose you want to produce a list that includes the last name, state, and postal codes for all customers. You want the list to be in order of state, then postal code. The following query produces that list. Note that we like to put each column in a column list on a separate line. This is helpful when there are problems with a query; it is not a requirement. In fact, SQL will let you break lines almost any way you wish. Of course, it is not a good idea to try to break a line in the middle of a word. We also like to include the table name of a column along with its column name. For example, CUSTOMER.LAST_NAME means the LAST_NAME column from the CUSTOMER table. Once again, this is not a requirement, but some feel that it is a good habit to get into.

```
SELECT    CUSTOMER.LAST_NAME,
          CUSTOMER.STATE,
          CUSTOMER.POSTAL_CODE
FROM      CUSTOMER
ORDER BY  CUSTOMER.STATE,
          CUSTOMER.POSTAL_CODE
;
```

Notice that we did not limit the records to be included in our results. You can tell this because we did not include a WHERE condition. However, we did not include all columns in the CUSTOMER table in our query. We limited the columns by only specifying some columns in the column list of the SELECT statement.

How could you limit the results of the query to just those customers who are in the states of Ohio or Virginia? To answer this question, you must first know that we used abbreviations for the state values in the CUSTOMER table. The abbreviations for Ohio and Virginia are "OH" and "VA," respectively. There are actually several ways to write this query. One way is to use the word "OR" to express multiple conditions in a WHERE clause, as shown here.

```
SELECT    CUSTOMER.LAST_NAME,
          CUSTOMER.STATE,
          CUSTOMER.POSTAL_CODE
FROM      CUSTOMER
WHERE     CUSTOMER.STATE  =  'OH'
   OR     CUSTOMER.STATE  =  'VA'
ORDER BY  CUSTOMER.STATE,
          CUSTOMER.POSTAL_CODE
;
```

When you use the word "OR" in a WHERE clause, records that meet *either* of the conditions separated by OR are included in the results. If you want to include only records that meet *both* of a pair of conditions, you would use the word "AND" rather than OR. It is possible to use more than one OR and/or AND condition in a single WHERE condition. When mixing ANDs and ORs, you should use parentheses to group the conditions so that they are evaluated as you intended. Of course, expressing multiple conditions in a WHERE clause is not required. For example, if you want to look up information about a single part, you could use a simple WHERE condition that only includes a single condition.

It is common for a query to use data from multiple tables. In such cases, a join condition must be expressed in the WHERE clause of the query. Recall from earlier in this section that relational databases use overlapping values to match records from different tables. This is accomplished by matching a foreign key value from a record in one table to a primary key value in a related table. One way to express a join condition is to use a WHERE clause, as illustrated in the following code. This query shows the number and date of each order, along with the last name of the customer who placed the order. To retrieve the order data, we must include the ORDERS table, while the customer last name data comes from the CUSTOMER table.

```
SELECT    ORDERS.ORDER_NUMBER,
          ORDERS.ORDER_DATE,
          CUSTOMER.LAST_NAME
FROM      ORDERS, CUSTOMER
WHERE     CUSTOMER.CUSTOMER_ID = ORDERS.CUSTOMER_ID
ORDER BY ORDERS.ORDER_DATE
;
```

The join condition is expressed in the WHERE clause. Conceptually, when multiple table queries are performed, SQL creates a temporary table that includes all possible combinations of records from the tables involved. In our example, every record from the ORDERS table is combined with every record from the CUSTOMER table. Of course, not all of the records in this temporary table are correct. Only those records where the CUSTOMER_ID value from the ORDERS table matches the CUSTOMER_ID value from the CUSTOMER table are accurate. The WHERE condition tells SQL that the only records from the temporary table that should be included are those that meet this condition.

It is possible to combine join conditions with other conditions. For example, the query in the previous code is the same as that in the following code, except that the latter query only returns records in which the customer ID value is 111111. In other words, the results only include orders that were placed by this customer. Notice that we used the customer ID value from the CUSTOMER table, rather than from the ORDERS table. This was a somewhat arbitrary decision. We would get the same results if we used ORDERS.CUSTOMER_ID instead. (The execution speed of the query may vary according to exactly how the query is constructed. However, this detail is beyond the scope of this section.)

```
SELECT    ORDERS.ORDER_NUMBER,
          ORDERS.ORDER_DATE,
          CUSTOMER.LAST_NAME
FROM      ORDERS, CUSTOMER
WHERE     CUSTOMER.CUSTOMER_ID = ORDERS.CUSTOMER_ID
```

```
AND     CUSTOMER.CUSTOMER_ID = '111111'
ORDER BY ORDERS.ORDER_DATE
;
```

As you might imagine, there is quite a bit more to SQL than what we have discussed here. However, you should now have a basic understanding of the core of the language. We encourage you to investigate SQL further by reading one of the books listed in the Further Readings section and by practicing writing queries. The Web site for this book includes sample databases in Microsoft Access and standard SQL scripts that can be used to create the database. You can use this database for your practice.

E-BUSINESS IN PRACTICE

USING ASP WITH SQL

Active Server Pages (ASP) is a server-side scripting language from Microsoft that can be used to build dynamic Web pages. (Recall that ASP is discussed more fully in Chapter 7.) For example, many online merchants use ASP scripts to enable online catalogs. The ASP script takes input from the user (typically using a form), then builds a page with content that matches the input. For example, Buy.com (http://www.us.buy.com/default.asp) uses ASP to allow shoppers to search its catalog. Many ASP scripts use SQL to retrieve data from a database. The ASP code below illustrates the use of SQL. This script is used to validate a user's login and password by checking the user's entry against a database table. The section of the code in boldface type uses an SQL statement to perform the database query. Although the formatting of the SQL statement in the script (such as the quotation marks) differs, otherwise the SQL statements embedded in ASP scripts follow standard SQL syntax. To learn more about ASP and SQL, refer to one of the ASP books in the Further Readings section.

```
<% '* Receives user login and pass-
word and validates against
  '* the FacStaff table
Dim conTemp, stUserID, stPassword,
s, rsFacStaff

'* Translate form inputs into SQL
stUserID = Request.Form("txtUserID")
stPassword                         =
Request.Form("pwdPassword")


'* Construct SQL statement
s = "SELECT * FROM FacStaff " _
  & "WHERE UserID = '" & stUserID &
"' " _
  & "AND Password = '" & stPassword
& "';"


'* Open connection
set conTemp =
Server.CreateObject("ADODB.Connecti
on")
conTemp.Open "dsnTest", "sa", ""


'* Execute SQL to retrieve user's
record
set rsFacStaff =
Server.CreateObject("ADODB.Recordse
t")
set rsFacStaff = conTemp.Execute(s)
%>
```

SUMMARY

This chapter discussed a number of topics associated with integrating "behind the scenes," back-office operations with e-business systems. While many people think of Web sites when thinking about e-business systems, in reality much of the work of e-business systems is performed by back-office systems. Many of these fall into the category of legacy systems; they have been in place for many years and are based on older technologies. While legacy systems present a number of challenges to organizations, in general, they are robust, high-performance systems. As a result, many organizations are reluctant to part with existing legacy systems.

Transactions are key elements of many e-business systems. A transaction is a set of operations that must all occur for the transaction to be complete. If some operations in a transaction are completed, but others are not, the completed operations must be undone. A transaction should follow the ACID properties of atomicity, consistency, isolation, and durability.

Middleware is software that allows two otherwise incompatible systems to interoperate. Since many e-business environments consist of systems operating on a variety of platforms, middleware is often a key enabler of e-business. This is particularly true when e-business environments include legacy systems. The use of middleware is only one method of integrating legacy systems into e-business environments. This chapter provided an overview of this and other approaches.

The chapter also discussed data warehousing and customer relationship management systems. Data warehousing takes data from operational systems and transforms it into forms more suitable for supporting decision making. Customer relationship management systems help organizations better understand and interact with their customers. Both data warehouses and customer relationship management systems play a key role in the e-business environments of an increasing number of organizations.

Relational database technology is at the core of many legacy systems. The same can be said for most e-business systems; databases, particularly relational databases, are key components of many e-business systems. The core structure of a relational database is the table, which is made up of rows and columns. Relational databases prevent unnecessary redundancy while maintaining flexibility by following a number of rules known as normal forms. A key aspect of relational database theory concerns the use of foreign keys, which are matched to primary key values in related tables. Enforcing referential integrity ensures that the value of each foreign key in a database has a matching primary key value.

Structured Query Language (SQL) is the standard language used to create, maintain, and retrieve data from relational databases. All major relational database management systems use some version of SQL. This chapter provided an overview of some key SQL statements. The INSERT statement is used to put data into a database table. Data are removed using the DELETE statement, while data values are changed using the UPDATE statement. The SELECT statement is used to retrieve data from the tables of a database. A WHERE clause can be used with the UPDATE, DELETE, and SELECT statements to limit the associated actions to a subset of rows.

KEY TERMS

ACID properties	data cleansing	field	normal forms
atomicity	database management	foreign key	primary key
back-office	system (DBMS)	heterogeneous system	record
column	data migration	information	referential integrity
consistency	data mining	isolation	relational database
customer relationship	data warehouse	legacy system	Structured Query
management	data warehousing	logical schema	Language (SQL)
data	durability	metadata	table
database	E/T/L process	middleware	transaction

REVIEW QUESTIONS

1. What are back-office operations? Give three examples of back-office operations.

2. Describe five problems associated with legacy systems.

3. Discuss why an organization might choose to retain its legacy systems.

4. Contrast data and information.

5. Name and describe the ACID properties of transactions.

6. Explain why a transaction must be "all or none."

7. What is the purpose of middleware?

8. Name and describe the three major categories of middleware.

9. Provide an example of middleware from each of the three major categories. Briefly describe each example.

10. Explain why middleware is important when integrating legacy systems into e-business systems.

11. Contrast invasive and noninvasive methods of legacy system integration.

12. Describe the key characteristics of a data warehouse.

13. Explain the need for data warehousing.

14. Describe each of the following:

(a) Data migration tools

(b) Metadata repositories

(c) Warehouse data stores

15. Describe the E/T/L process.

16. Describe two types of data transformation that occur when operational data is transformed for data warehousing.

17. What are the benefits of storing aggregated data in a data warehouse? What is the drawback?

18. What is the main purpose of customer relationship management?

19. Name and describe the three main goals of CRM systems.

20. What are the four phases of the customer life cycle? Provide an example of a CRM technology or application that applies to each phase.

21. Name and describe the three categories of CRM system components.

22. Describe how unnecessary data redundancy can lead to data inconsistencies.

23. What is the purpose of a primary key in a table?

24. What is the purpose of foreign keys? Describe how they work.

25. In SQL, what statement is used to:

(a) Put data into a table

(b) Change the values of data in a table

(c) Remove data from a table

(d) Retrieve data from a table

EXERCISES

1. Visit the ScreenSurfer demonstration Web site (http ://support.screensurfer.com/). Interact with at least two of the mainframe systems included in the demonstration. Based on your interactions, comment on how the interfaces for these systems compare to other systems you frequently use (such as your university's Web site). Discuss the advantages and disadvantages of the "screen-scraping" approach to updating legacy systems. Use examples based on your interactions with the ScreenSurfer demonstrations.

2. Identify and briefly describe a legacy system that is used by your university. Why do you think that this system is a legacy system? How could the system be improved

(from the user's perspective) by the use of e-business technologies?

3. Describe an example of a transaction that you were a party to (for example, registering for a class or making a purchase). Break the transaction down into separate operations (for example, checking to see if there are seats in the class). Pick two of these operations and discuss the impact of having these operations fail while the rest of the operations occur successfully.

4. Describe a situation in which you performed customer self-service. What CRM-related technologies and applications played a part in your experience?

5. Locate a customer self-service Web site. Describe the site. What can customers do through the site? What benefits do customers gain by using the site? What benefits does the site provide for the organization?

HANDS-ON PROJECTS

Download (or create) the Wish-List database from the textbook's Web site. (http://www.wiley.com/college/vanslyke). The logical schema for the database and the ProductID table are shown below. Write and execute the SQL statements to do each of the following.

1. Insert the following rows into the PRODUCTS table. (A separate statement is required for each row.)

2. Delete the product with the ProductID value "122" from the PRODUCTS table.

3. Change the price of the product with the ProductID value "222" to 15.75.

4. Display the title, price, and availability of all products.

5. Display the last name and state of each customer. Put the list in order of last name.

6. Display the ProductID, title, and availability of each product that is "in stock."

7. Display the last name and state of each customer from the state of Georgia. (Georgia is abbreviated as "GA" in the database.)

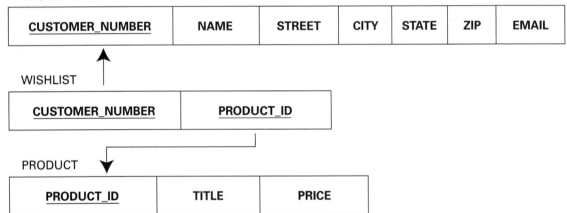

CUSTOMER

CUSTOMER_NUMBER	NAME	STREET	CITY	STATE	ZIP	EMAIL

WISHLIST

CUSTOMER_NUMBER	PRODUCT_ID

PRODUCT

PRODUCT_ID	TITLE	PRICE

ProductID	Title	Price	Availability
221	Just Like You	17.95	in stock
222	Hourglass	16.50	in stock
223	Man of Constant Sorrow	15.95	one week

DISCUSSION POINTS

1. Discuss ways in which your university could use a data warehouse? What challenges would have to be overcome to develop the data warehouse?

2. Discuss the pros and cons of replacing legacy systems. What alternatives are there for organizations that want to retain their legacy systems, but still want to take advantage of e-business?

3. One reason organizations use CRM systems is to gain revenue from call centers. (For example, when you call to check your credit card balance, the customer service representative might offer you additional products, such as insurance.) As a consumer, how do you react when a customer service representative tries to sell you something? Do you think that these kinds of activities will help or hurt organizations in the long run? Justify your answer.

FURTHER READINGS

Data Warehousing

BARQUIN, R., and H. EDELSTEIN. *Building, Using and Managing the Data Warehouse.* Upper Saddle River, NJ: Prentice Hall, 1997.

MOSS, L. "Data Cleansing: A Dichotomy of Data Warehousing?" *DM Review* 8 (February 1998): 46. Also available at http://www.dmreview.com/editorial/dmreview/print_action .cfm?EdID=828

Legacy Systems Integration

FINGAR, P. "Component-Based Frameworks for E-commerce." *Communications of the ACM* 43 (10): 61–65.

Object Management Group. CORBA Basics page, http://www .omg.org/gettingstarted/corbafaq.htm.

Active Server Pages

BUSER, D., C. ULLMAN, J. DUCKETT, J. KAUFFMAN, J. LLIBRE, and B. FRANCIS. *Beginning Active Server Pages 3.0.* Chicago: Wrox Press, 1999.

Databases

FORTA, B. *Sams Teach Yourself SQL in 10 Minutes.* 2d ed. Indianapolis, IN: Sams Publishing, 2001.

HOFFER, J., M. PRESCOTT, and F. MCFADDEN. *Modern Database Management.* 6th ed. Upper Saddle River, NJ: Prentice Hall, 2002.

WATSON, R. *Data Management: Databases and Organizations.* 3d ed. New York: John Wiley & Sons, 2002.

REFERENCES

BARQUIN, R. 1997. A data warehousing manifesto. In *Planning and designing the data warehouse,* ed. R. BARQUIN and H. EDELSTEIN. Upper Saddle River, NJ: Prentice Hall.

DATE, C.J. 2000. An introduction to database systems. Reading, MA: Addison-Wesley.

EDELSTEIN, H. 1997. An introduction to data warehousing. In *Planning and designing the data warehouse,* ed. R. BARQUIN and H. EDELSTEIN. Upper Saddle River, NJ: Prentice Hall.

ERICSON, JIM. 2001. The failure of CRM: Looking for someone to blame. *Line56* 2 August 2001: http://line56.com/articles /default.asp?ArticleID=2808.

ERLIKH, L., and L. GOLDBAUM. 2001. EAI's missing link: Legacy integration. *EAI Journal* 3 (April): 12–15.

FRYE, C. 2000-2001. Move or improve? *Software Magazine,* 20 (December-January), 38–43

INMON, BILL. 2000. What is a data warehouse? http://www.billin-mon.com/library/whiteprs/earlywp/ttdw.pdf

IVES, B. and G. LEARMONTH 1984. The information systems as a competitive weapon, *Communications of the ACM,* 27, 1193–1201.

KIMBALL, RALPH. 1996. *The data warehouse toolkit: Practical techniques for building dimensional data warehouses.* New York: John Wiley & Sons.

META Group. 2001. Integration: Critical issues for implementation of CRM solutions. Paper commissioned by Oracle Corporation, 15 February 2001. Available at http://www.ora-cle.com/applications/crm/metacrmwp.pdf.

PALLER, A. 1997. A roadmap to data warehousing. In *Planning and designing the data warehouse,* ed. R. BARQUIN and H. EDELSTEIN. Upper Saddle River, NJ: Prentice Hall.

Software Engineering Institute (2000). Middleware, http://www.sei.cmu.edu/str/descriptions/middleware_body.html.

ULRICH, W. 2001. E-Business integration: A framework for success. *Software Magazine* 21 (August/September): S4–S15.

CHAPTER 9

PROVIDING CONTENT FOR ELECTRONIC BUSINESS

LEARNING OBJECTIVES

After reading and completing this chapter, you should be able to:

- Discuss the business importance of content
- Discuss the importance of considering variations in users' technology when making content decisions
- Describe and discuss technologies and issues related to text-based content
- Understand technologies and issues related to content based on graphic images
- Understand technologies and issues related to network-enabled digital audio
- Understand technologies and issues related to network-enabled digital video
- Describe multicasting and contrast it with unicasting
- Discuss business uses for digital media
- Define usability
- Discuss the importance of considering usability when designing and developing e-business systems
- Describe the Technology Acceptance Model and how it applies to usability
- Describe how users interact with computer systems
- Discuss principles for attaining highly usable e-business systems

Opening Case: Listen Before You Buy

Recently, a friend told you about a new CD by one of your favorite groups, the duo of Dave Carter and Tracy Grammer. You go online to Amazon.com and use Amazon's search facility to look for the new CD. Whether you realize it or not, content has just come into play. When you searched for "Tracy Grammer," Amazon's e-business system generated a query that searched through Amazon's extensive database. The information contained in this database is an example of content, content that is quite useful to you at the moment. The database also contains content that is quite valuable to Amazon—the content attracts visitors to Amazon's Web site and makes shopping for products easy. Figure 9-1 shows the results of your search.

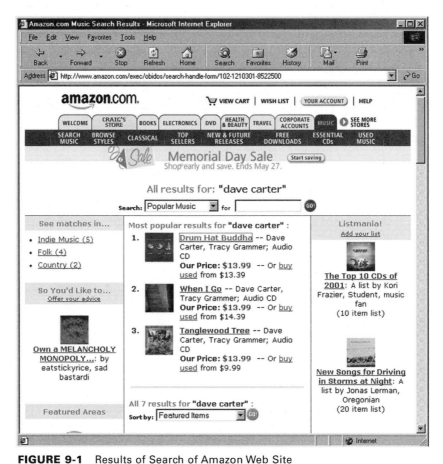

FIGURE 9-1 Results of Search of Amazon Web Site

SOURCE: Amazon.com search results page, courtesy of Amazon.com, Inc.

You recognize the first title as the one you are seeking, but you are not quite ready to buy the CD. You have been disappointed by new releases from favorite artists in the past. Before you are willing to buy the CD, you would like to be able to listen to some of the songs. So, you click on the "Drum Hat Buddha" link. Figure 9-2 shows the resulting Web page. Notice that this page shows you more information about the CD. The left-hand side of the Web page displays links to both editorial reviews of the CD and reviews by fellow Amazon customers. These reviews are also examples of content that is accessed through a database query. If you click on "customer reviews," Amazon's system will retrieve the requested reviews from the appropriate database and display them on a Web page. You can also listen to samples of some of the songs on the CD by clicking on "listen to samples."

You decide to skip the reviews for now and go straight to the song samples. This Web page is shown in Figure 9-3. As you have probably guessed, the song samples are also content. This time, however, the content is in a different form. The content is not text-based, but is in the form of sound files, which we usually refer to as audio files. In this case, the song clips use a format called RealAudio, which is an example of streaming audio. In essence, the term "streaming" means that the file will download while it is being

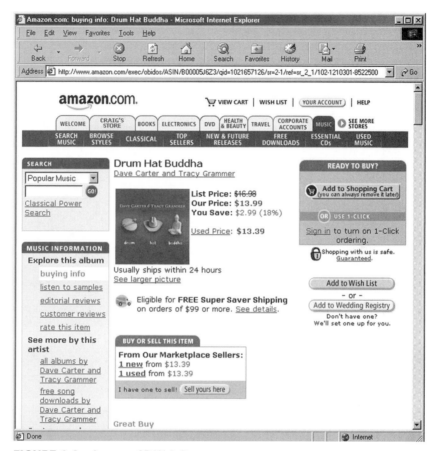

FIGURE 9-2 Amazon CD Web Page

Source: Amazon.com product page, courtesy of Amazon.com, Inc.

played. When using a streaming format, you normally cannot store the downloaded file for later use. If you want to hear the song clip again, the data will be downloaded again. We will discuss this and other audio formats later in the chapter.

The text-based content from Amazon does not require any special software. Your Web browser can display it. However, when you listen to RealAudio song clips, another application, RealPlayer is required. This application is not part of your Web browser, although your browser can probably open RealPlayer and send the song clip to it. If you do not have RealPlayer installed on your computer, however, you are out of luck. Before you can listen to the song clips, you have to download and install the RealPlayer software. Fortunately, the software is free for personal use.

You spend a few minutes listening to the song clips and like what you hear. You are still a little hesitant to lay out your money, so you decide to read the editorial reviews of the CD. The reviews are favorable, but just to be sure, you take a look at a few of the customer reviews. All of the customer reviews are enthusiastic, so you decide to go ahead and buy the CD.

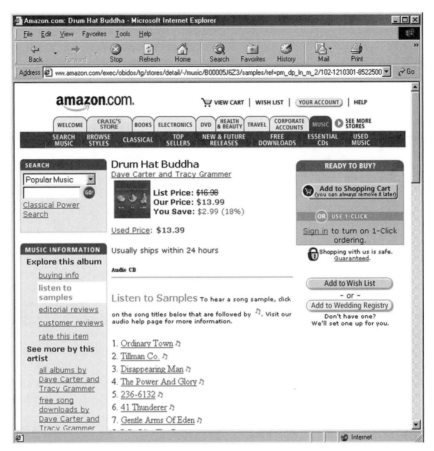

FIGURE 9-3 Amazon Song Clip Web Page

SOURCE: Amazon.com song sample page, courtesy of Amazon.com, Inc.

INTRODUCTION

Content is king—this phrase sums up the importance of content to e-business. Content is important regardless of the focus of an e-business system; it is the life-blood of an e-business system. Take just a moment to think about how you use e-business systems personally. Maybe you want to check on tickets for an upcoming concert. The Web site you use has many different types of content. There is text-based content on ticket prices, ticket availability, concert time and location, and so on. There might be graphical content also. For example, Ticketmaster's Web site lets you view an image of the layout of many concert halls, which can help you pick the best seats. Maybe the site also has song clips of the opening act, or even short videos of one of the act's earlier tours. All of this is content, and we will talk about the technologies that enable such applications in this chapter.

When you stop to think about it, the Web is really just a way to organize content, and the Internet is just a way to move content from place to place. Whether you are shopping for iron ore, checking stock prices, listening to a far-away radio station online, or viewing a training video on your PC, you are basically accessing content.

You can see how important content is by taking a closer look at the opening case. The first thing to notice is that content is what attracted you to the Amazon site. To find out about the new CD, you could have made a trip to your local music store. But you could not be sure that it would have the CD, or that store policy would allow you to listen to it. Also, the chances of running into someone in the store who had listened to the CD were slim. By going to Amazon's Web site, you knew that you could listen to tracks from the CD and that there was at least a decent chance that there would be some customer reviews available. You knew that Amazon's Web site would have *content* that was of value to you. Although Amazon makes money by selling products, the content of the site is what attracts potential customers. If Amazon's content is better than its competitors, customers are more likely to visit Amazon. Of course, many other factors, such as price, product availability, and customer service, impact customers' decisions about where to shop. However, if the content of a merchant's site is poor, the chances are that few potential customers will even bother to visit the site, much less actually make a purchase.

In this chapter, we provide an introduction to a wide variety of content-related technologies, ranging from text to video. We discuss content file formats, tools for creating the content, and tools for accessing the content. We also discuss usability issues associated with content. The first section of the chapter sets the stage by discussing the business importance of content. The second section covers the various types of content, and provides details on format options and tools for generating and accessing each type of content. The last section emphasizes the importance of considering usability when making choices about content.

BUSINESS IMPORTANCE OF CONTENT

The chapter's opening case illustrates the importance of content to Amazon's business. This is only one example of a business model that depends at least partially on the content of an organization's Web site. Recall the discussion of business models in Chapter 2. Amazon is an example of an electronic merchant, which we also called an e-tailer. Web site content is important to the success of companies using the electronic merchant business model. (Although we use the context of Web sites throughout this chapter, most of the points made would also apply to non-Web e-business systems.) For many electronic merchants, the bulk of their content is in the form of text. While text-based content may seem boring when compared with audio and video, skillfully dealing with text-based content is a key to success for electronic merchants. Visit any electronic merchant's Web site and you will see the importance of text-based content. All those boring, but important details, such as pricing, availability, and shipping times, are critical to helping the customer make an informed buying decision. The core of an electronic merchant's content is the product database, which typically includes such information as product descriptions, prices, availability, and other details. Most large electronic merchants tie the product database to the Web site. You will learn some ways to do this elsewhere in this book. Sometimes smaller merchants simply list product offerings with descriptions and prices.

The content of many electronic merchants goes far beyond simple product information, though. The Amazon example illustrates how a savvy merchant can use content in various forms to add value to its Web site. The customer reviews are a good example of how content can be used to attract potential customers in innovative ways. First, it is difficult for offline merchants to duplicate this feature. What are the chances that you will run into several people who have opinions on a CD you are considering in a local store? Second, the reviews build a sense of community among visitors to the Web site. As we discussed in earlier chapters, a sense of community can lead to regular visitors.

Many electronic merchants also build databases that contain information about customer preferences. For example, Amazon keeps track of items that registered users have purchased or placed on their wish lists. Sophisticated software can use this data to generate recommendations, such as those shown in Figure 9-4. One of the authors likes to use this feature of Amazon to find new music and books that might be of interest. You can probably imagine how this can help Amazon increase sales. Of course, Amazon is not alone in providing this kind of content. Many other electronic merchants have similar facilities.

To sum up, electronic merchants use content in two main ways. First, the content is used to provide information about product or service offerings. For many merchants,the a product database provides the core of this content. Second, content is used to attract potential customers and to influence customers' buying decisions. The reviews and song clips offered by Amazon are examples of this use of content.

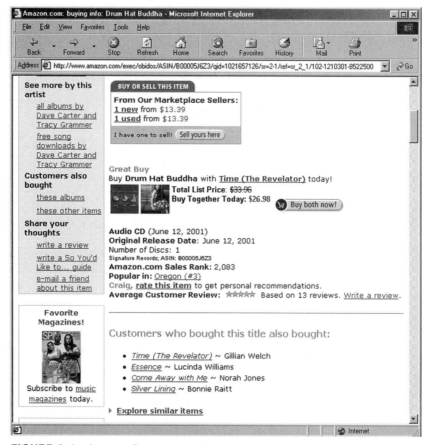

FIGURE 9-4 Amazon Recommendations

SOURCE: Amazon.com product page with recommendations, courtesy of Amazon.com, Inc.

Some business models revolve totally around content. The prime example of such a model is the subscription model. A well-known example of a business that follows the subscription model is the *Wall Street Journal*'s online component, WSJ.com. Like many companies using the subscription model, WSJ.com offers some content for free, but requires a subscription to access most of the content. Subscribers to WSJ.com can access all of the content found in the *Wall Street Journal,* in addition to content that is found only online. Another business and investing-oriented subscription site is RealMoney.com, which is the subscription affiliate of TheStreet.com. TheStreet offers a variety of free content aimed at those interested in investing. The RealMoney site, which requires a subscription, contains content that is perceived by many to be more valuable. For example, RealMoney provides commentary on markets and individual stocks throughout the day. In addition, the portfolios and stock picks of a number of experts are only available to subscribers of RealMoney.

An interesting aspect of these examples is how they both use free content to attract visitors, with the hope of turning nonpaying visitors into paying subscribers. Knowing what to give away and what to sell can be difficult. On the one hand, the free content must be of sufficient quality and value to convince visitors that the subscription-only content is worth paying for. This is particularly important if the company does not already enjoy a good reputation. On the other hand, the companies do not want to give away content that people would be willing to pay for. Many companies that follow the subscription model offer short-term trial subscriptions at little or no cost in the hopes that trial subscribers will find the content sufficiently valuable.

One particularly interesting example of a subscription model comes from a popular American radio talk-show host, Rush Limbaugh. As is the case with many radio and television shows, Limbaugh uses his Web site to promote his radio program. For example, fans who are traveling can find out what stations carry the show. Those who are unable to find the show locally can listen via streaming audio. What makes Limbaugh's site interesting is not the free, promotional content. What is interesting is that his program is sufficiently popular to entice many listeners to subscribe to RUSH 24/7, which is only available to paid subscribers. One feature of the subscription site is the archive of shows. Visitors to the free site can only listen to broadcasts of the show during certain times. Subscribers can access streaming audio of shows from the previous two weeks at any time. A more bizarre, and somewhat humorous example of subscription-only content is the Dittocam, which is live streaming video of Limbaugh's show. Although it is still too soon to tell whether sufficient listeners will subscribe, RUSH 24/7 is an interesting example of mixing free and subscription-only content.

Content is equally important to organizations that follow the advertising model. Companies that use advertising-based business models make money by selling advertising. Advertisers are attracted by the number of visitors (who are sometimes referred to as "eyeballs") a site can claim. What do you think attracts visitors? Of course, it's the content of a Web site. If a Web site's content is of poor quality, or if the design of the site makes content difficult to find or access, the site is unlikely to draw many visitors, which translates into lower advertising revenues.

Web directories and search engines are examples of Web sites that depend on content to draw advertising dollars. The directories Excite and Yahoo! are among the most successful generators of advertising revenue. It is no surprise that they are also among the leaders in Web site traffic. For example, in May 2001, Yahoo! was the third most valuable "property" on the Web in terms of unique visitors. In that month, the content of Yahoo! Web pages attracted more than fifty million unique visitors. The success of Yahoo! illustrates that it is not only the content of a Web site that matters; the organization of the content is equally critical. One of the things that makes Yahoo! so popular is that the content available through the site is very well organized. This organization helps make the site useful to visitors, which of course, helps increase traffic to the site. Yahoo! and Excite also offer content beyond their Web directories. For example, visitors can customize the appearance of the main Web page by including content such as stock prices, horoscopes, and weather information. Allowing visitors to customize the content of a page helps "lock in" the visitors to that particular site, which also helps attract advertising revenue.

Most people probably associate Web-based advertising with **banner ads.** According to some sources, however, **streaming ads** are more cost-effective than the traditional banner ads. These ads are called "streaming" because they utilize **streaming media,** which consists of audio and/or video that is transmitted continuously. With streaming media, the content starts to play almost immediately—the entire file does not have to be downloaded before the playback can begin. (We discuss streaming media in more detail later in this chapter.) Streaming ads utilize streaming media (usually both audio and video) to display ads that are similar to television ads. These ads seem to be much more effective at persuading viewers to click through to the advertised site. In one study, streaming ads achieved a click-through rate of 9.5 percent, versus only 0.5 percent for banner ads (ConsumerMarketingBiz 2001). As broadband connections become more widespread, some experts predict that streaming media, including streaming ads, will become even more important.

We could continue to discuss example after example of businesses that depend heavily on content for success. However, we hope that the few examples we have shared make the point that content is not simply a technology issue. The business aspects of content are equally important. The technologies are only one piece of the puzzle. Astute people must learn how to effectively translate the capabilities of the technology into functions that benefit the organization.

Considering Users' Technology

Many readers of this book probably access the Internet primarily through high-speed on-campus connections. While the performance of such connections is nice, sometimes the speed gives us a tainted view of the Web landscape—we may think that everyone enjoys this kind of performance. In fact, the opposite is true. Most users still access the Internet through slower dial-up connections. According to a 2001 report by The Strategis Group (Pastore 2001), broadband access will not surpass dial-up access in the home market until 2005.

Why is this important to a discussion of e-business content? The primary message is that most Web users will *not* have high-speed access, particularly users of business-to-consumer e-business Web sites. This means that Web sites that use multimedia intensive content may perform poorly over dial-up connections. Perhaps you have had the unfortunate experience of having to wait for a Flash introduction to load over a slow connection. (Flash is a proprietary method of including multimedia content on a Web site.) If so, you can sympathize with many home computer users.

It is important to offer alternatives for users with slow connections. In the early days of the Web, it was common to see text-only alternatives for many graphics-intensive Web sites. This was considered a must when a 14.4 KB connection was considered fast. Too many of today's Web site designers assume that everyone has a broadband connection, and consequently design very flashy, impressive sites that are essentially unusable over dial-up connections. To make matters worse, they do not offer alternatives for those without high-speed connections. The designers' ignorance results in potential users who decide that it is not worth the wait to access the slow Web sites. Remember, none of the advantages of e-business are realized if users choose not to use e-business.

Managing Content

One of the more difficult tasks faced by organizations wishing to utilize e-business is managing content. We have argued that content is critical to e-business. Just as successful organizations must properly manage money, people, and other resources, so must they manage content. Content is a major asset for organizations, and as such it must be managed effectively. Organizations have always been concerned with managing content. Filing systems for paper documents are an example of organizations' concern with content management. There are a number of goals that must be achieved for proper content management.

- *Security*—An organization must ensure that its valuable content is secured. This means that it should be protected against intentional or accidental misuse and destruction.

- *Accuracy*—Ensuring the accuracy of content is also a component of effective content management. This involves not only ensuring that content is accurate when it is first generated, but also updating content when appropriate. For data-oriented content, such as store locations and product prices, the need for accuracy is obvious. However, accuracy is just as important for other types of content, such as images. For example, suppose that a color choice for an automobile has been discontinued. The organization should make sure that no images of the automobile in the discontinued color are displayed on the organization's Web site.

- *Utilization*—Another aspect of content management is making sure that the content is available to those who need it. A major challenge is cataloging the content in a manner that makes it easy to locate. This can be especially challenging for images and videos, which are particularly difficult for many search technologies to deal with. A related issue is making the organization's Web designers aware of content that has already been developed in order to prevent duplication of effort. For example, a digital image of a product may have been created for product marketing literature. Web designers responsible for creating online catalogs should be provided with this image so they do not create a duplicate.

- *Updating*—An effective content management system should also provide tools that make it easy for users to update content. This can be challenging, since content is often repeated on various pages on an organization's Web site or intranet. Changing all occurrences individually is difficult and subject to inaccuracies.

- *Retirement*—Content can age over time, and at some point become obsolete. When this happens, a content management system should provide a way to properly retire this content. In some cases, it is erased completely; in others, it is archived.

A wide range of content management tools exists. Some of these tools are integrated within Web development systems, such as Microsoft FrontPage, while others are dedicated content management systems. Prices range from a few dollars to tens of thousands of dollars. Broadly speaking, there are two approaches organizations take when developing content management systems. Some organizations combine a number of "best-of-breed" systems, while others prefer to use a single, integrated system. In either case, implementing content management systems is a time-consuming, expensive, but necessary part of e-business.

In this section, we built the business case for the importance of content, discussed the importance of considering the technology of your users, and discussed the importance of content management. In the next section, we discuss the technologies associated with a number of different types of content, including text, static images, video, and audio.

CONTENT TECHNOLOGIES

There is a wide variety of content-related technologies. In this section, we describe major content technologies, including content protocols and generation and editing tools. The discussion is broken down according to the type of content, starting with text and progressing through page images, static graphics, video, and audio.

Text-Based Content

Despite the excitement surrounding newer forms of content, for many e-business users, text is still the content king. Think about your latest Web surfing session. The chances are good that most of the content you were seeking was text based (even though you may not have realized it at the time). Consider the opening case. On the surface, it appears that the focus of the search was on audio content (the song clips). However, most of the content involved was text based. The discography (list of recordings) was text. The track listings were text. The editorial and user reviews were text. Of course, there were other types of content on the Web pages, such as images and audio. The point is that the text-based content drove much of the browsing activity.

The importance of text-based content is maintained across different e-business applications. For example, in a business-to-business hub, most of the information is text based. Prices, product descriptions, and delivery terms are all text. When you renew your automobile license online using a government Web site, the form you use is text based. The pervasive nature of text in e-business applications is what keeps it in the shadows for many users. We are simply so used to seeing text on Web sites that we do not really notice it. We see text so often that it simply does not have the "cool factor" of other content types.

What technologies are used when dealing with text? The key to most interactive e-business sites is an up-to-date, well-designed database. While it is certainly common for e-business databases to contain nontext content, the bulk of information in most databases is text. Later you will learn how to connect databases to Web sites. For now, it is enough for you to understand that most interactive e-business Web sites are driven by underlying databases, and that most of the content of these databases is text.

Text-based content can come from many different sources. For many organizations utilizing e-business applications, a substantial portion of text-based content comes from existing databases (legacy databases). For example, a company selling products over the

Web may tie their Web site applications into existing inventory control databases in order to provide up-to-date availability data.

It is also quite common to draw content from sources outside the organization. For example, stock quote data is content that comes from the various markets. **Portal** sites primarily contain content from outside sources in the form of links to other sites. In fact, the purpose of most portal sites is to act as an organized gateway to outside content. (Keep in mind that corporate portals serve a similar purpose, but for content internal to an organization.) Recall that in the last section we discussed that content can be an important tool for drawing visitors to a Web site. Unfortunately, keeping content fresh can be very time consuming, which means very expensive. In response to this, a number of companies offer fresh content for a fee. (Some provide content for free, in exchange for the ability to post advertisements.) In fact, an entire content provider industry has evolved. One interesting example of a content provider that makes content available for free is Moreover Technologies. It will let anyone with a noncommercial Web site add to the site a limited set of Moreover's news content without charge. (See the Hands-On Exercises section of this chapter for an exercise involving this service.) Moreover has an impressive client list that includes such well-known organizations as AT&T, the UK Post Office, and *The Economist.* In essence, these and other companies outsource to Moreover the job of keeping certain types of content current. Moreover gleans information from more than three thousand online sources, selects and categorizes appropriate content, then makes this content available to clients. The company claims to generate more than one thousand news stories per hour.

The globalization of commerce leads to a text-related difficulty for many organizations; how to effectively translate content into multiple languages. In Chapter 3, we discussed barriers associated with globalization. One obvious hurdle is that of language. Organizations with e-business users across the globe must have an effective means of making important content available in multiple languages. Of course, one challenge is translating the content into the desired languages. A less obvious difficulty stems from the different character sets used by various languages. Often, special typefaces must be downloaded in order to display language-specific characters. A number of Web portal sites seem to deal with these content problems effectively. For example, Yahoo! offers Local Yahoo!s for more than twenty countries.

Fortunately, automated translation technology has advanced rapidly. There is a variety of software available that claims to translate popular languages. For example, Systran claims to translate between English and nine other languages, ranging from French to Chinese. Systran's Web site allows individuals to translate certain formats of text files, as well as Web pages. The example below shows the sentence-by-sentence results of using this service to translate a draft of the previous paragraph from English into Spanish.

```
The globalization of commerce leads to a text-related
difficulty for many organizations;
    El globalization del comercio conduce a una dificultad
    text-related para muchas organizaciones;
how to effectively translate content into multiple lan-
guages.
    cómo traducir con eficacia el contenido a idiomas
    múltiples.
In Chapter 3, we discussed barriers associated with
globalization.
    En el capítulo 3 discutimos las barreras asociadas al
    globalization.
```

```
One obvious hurdle is that of language.
   Un cañizo obvio es el de la lengua.
Organizations with e-business users across the globe
must have an effective means of making important content
available in multiple languages.
   Las organizaciones con los usuarios del e-negocio a
   través del globo deben tener medios eficaces de hacer
   el contenido importante disponible en idiomas múltiples.
Of course, one challenge is in translating the content
into the desired languages.
   Por supuesto, un desafío está en traducir el contenido
   en las idiomas deseadas.
A less obvious difficulty stems from the different char-
acter sets used by various languages.
   Una dificultad menos obvia proviene los juegos de car
   acteres diferentes usados por varias idiomas.
Often, special typefaces must be downloaded in order to
display language-specific characters.
   Las tipografías a menudo especiales se deben descargar
   para exhibir caracteres específicos a una lengua.
```

One interesting development in the area of translation comes from the Web search engine Google. In 2000, Google began offering translations of some non-English Web pages. As of Summer 2002, Google provided automatic translation services to English from French, German, Italian, Portuguese, and Spanish. More languages are likely to become available. Although this service is interesting and exciting, it does have difficulties. Frequently, navigation buttons are images rather than simple text. The fact that the buttons are images rather than text makes them untranslatable by the translation software. The automatic translation software examines the text on the Web page. It has no way of recognizing that the images (the buttons) are used to represent text. There are some features in later versions of HTML that may help ease this situation. For example, the software might translate the text in the ALT tags of images. Google actually does this. If you visit the Google search page, then search for UCM, you should see the original Universidad Complutense de Madrid home page in the search results. Then click on "translate this page." When Google displays the translated page, hold your cursor over one of the buttons and you should see the translated ALT tag text. (Since Web pages change frequently, these instructions may not work. In this case, you may either search for a different Web page translation, or consult this book's Web site at http://www.wiley.com/college/vanslyke for updated instructions.)

Even when translating text, the software is sometimes unable to make an accurate translation. This is illustrated by Google's translation of "Servicios Centrales," which Google translated into "Services Power Stations," rather than the more correct Central Services. Considering context as part of the automatic translation process is a considerable challenge. Experienced human translators are able to draw on their understanding of context to alter their translations from situation to situation. For example, the English phase "cool stuff" does not literally mean things that are somewhat cold. Automatic translation (sometimes called machine translation) may not be able to consider the context in order to correctly translate "cool stuff."

Despite the problems, we believe that Google's efforts are an indication of what is to come. Soon, automatic translations of Web pages may be the norm rather than a curiosity.

Formats for Text-Based Content

There are many formats that can be used to display text-based content. Typically, in e-business applications, text-based content is displayed in the HTML format, which we discussed in Chapter 5. All Web browser software is capable of displaying HTML content; no additional software is required. There are other widely used formats for text-based content that require software beyond a Web browser. For example, many Web sites provide text-based content in Microsoft Word format (which is commonly called .doc format). Viewing these documents requires the presence of a Word format external viewer. The Web browsing software must also be configured to launch the external viewer software when it encounters a Word format file.

Organizations that wish to make text-based content available online face other hurdles. One of these is the issue of finding effective ways to make formatted text documents and documents that mix text and images available to a wide array of users. Another difficulty comes from the fact that many documents were not originally intended for distribution using electronic media. There is a widely used common solution to both of these problems—using special document formats.

Much of the content of the Web consists of HTML documents. In many instances the use of HTML is not a problem. However, organizations that want to publish specially formatted documents often find the HTML format limiting in at least two ways. First, HTML editors do not normally offer the same degree of control over the appearance of a document that modern word processing and page layout software offers. This can be a problem for documents that require special formatting. For example, documents that are intended to be printed often do not fare well when formatted in HTML. You may have experienced this when printing an HTML document. Second, many documents are initially created and formatted in document formats other than HTML. Many documents, for example, are originally created using word processing software. While many of today's word processors allow users to save documents in HTML, it is much more common for users to save documents in the format native to the word processing software.

Fortunately, there is a single method that can help overcome these problems—the use of document viewing software. These "helper applications" allow Web browsers to launch the viewing software when special document formats are encountered. We talked about one of the most popular document viewers in a previous chapter. You may recall that we discussed the Adobe Acrobat Reader, which allows users to view documents saved in Adobe's Portable Document Format (PDF). According to Adobe's description of its format, documents that are converted to PDF maintain all of their original formatting, including fonts, colors, layout, and images, regardless of the software used to create the document. In Chapter 3 we discussed how PDF has become a de facto standard for making documents available electronically. Adobe makes the viewing software available for free through its Web site, which is a major reason PDF has become a standard. Of course, the technology also works quite well.

Almost anyone who wants to distribute documents electronically can use PDF. As you might recall, the software necessary to generate PDF files is not free. If you want to use PDF to publish your files, you must purchase Adobe's Acrobat. Interestingly, you would not use Acrobat to create the original document. Rather you create documents using other software, such as a word processor, then use Acrobat to convert those documents into PDF files. The Acrobat software can be used in conjunction with most popular word processing and document layout software. In addition, Acrobat is available for all major operating systems, such as Windows NT, Mac OS/10, and Linux, so most computer users can utilize the Acrobat Reader software. In fact, Acrobat Reader is even available for the Palm OS, so you can view PDF documents on your Palm Pilot handheld computer.

An interesting development related to text-based content is the growing popularity of electronic books. Adobe recently developed the eBook Reader, which allows users to read books on their desktop or notebook computers. One of the more interesting applications for this technology involves publishing textbooks electronically.

Some organizations that use certain word processing software distribute formatted electronic documents using the native format of the software. For example, many organizations use Microsoft Word as their word processing standard. Some of these organizations simply distribute documents in Word format. One problem with this approach is that individuals who do not have that particular word processing software may not be able to view the documents. Some word processing software publishers make viewers available for free in order to overcome this problem. For example, if you do not have Microsoft Word and need to view Word documents, you can download and install a Word viewer to give you this capability. It is important to note, however, that the viewing software only allows users to view the documents; they cannot edit using the viewer.

One problem with using proprietary word processing formats comes about when you need to share editable documents with others who do not use the same word processing software. For example, you may be working on a project with someone who uses Corel's WordPerfect, while you use Microsoft Word. Fortunately, there is a simple solution to this dilemma. Most professional-level word processors can read and write **Rich Text Format (RTF)** files. By saving your documents in RTF rather than Word format, your partner can easily open and edit the documents. Of course, your partner would also save the documents in RTF, not WordPerfect format.

Interestingly, there is one attribute—the ability to edit documents—that can be a major advantage or disadvantage for either PDF or word processing files. Files that are distributed in PDF format cannot be edited, although the technology does allow for "fillable" forms. If the content of the document is such that it should only be altered by the creator, then the absence of editing capabilities is an advantage. For example, many organizations make brochures available to the public using PDF technology. Clearly, only the organization or its agent should be able to alter the brochure. By using PDF, the document cannot be altered without access to the original file from which the PDF file was produced.

Of course, in many cases electronically distributed documents are intended to be changed. In this case, the PDF format would not be useful. Many organizations make boilerplate documents available to employees, who tailor the documents to their particular needs. In these cases, it is preferable to make the documents available in a word processing format so the documents may be edited. But distributing documents that should not be changed in a word processing format presents great risks.

Of course, not all text-based information is in the form of documents. Sometimes text-based data files are distributed electronically. For example, a university may distribute enrollment data via its Web site. There are two common methods used to distribute data of this sort. First, the data may be made available in the native format of a spreadsheet program or database management system. This method is most appropriate when an organization knows that those who require the data have access to the appropriate software. For example, an organization may place financial data on its intranet using Microsoft Excel if Excel is the standard spreadsheet program for the organization. The second method is to publish the data using a non-proprietary format. One of the most widely used data formats is the **comma-delimited file format.** In this format, each item of data is separated by a comma, and each record is typically on a separate line. Most spreadsheets and database management systems can import comma-delimited files, so the format is useful when the use of a particular program cannot be assumed.

Decision Point

This Decision Point can help you decide on the appropriate format for text-based content. Note that this Decision Point does not consider how to manage the content. It is only concerned with deciding on the appropriate format.

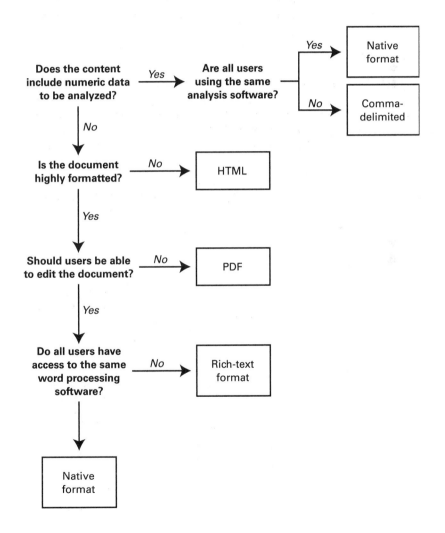

Of course, e-business content is not confined to text-based documents—much of the content on the Web consists of graphics, audio, and video. In the next section, we discuss graphics formats, including static and animated images.

IMAGE TECHNOLOGIES

You have, of course, heard the old saying, "A picture is worth a thousand words." Many times in e-business, the old adage rings true. Of course, as technology professionals, we want to use a more precise term than "pictures." In the technology world, we refer to pictures as **images.** Defined simply, an image is a visual representation of something. There are two main types of computer-based images: **raster** or **bitmap images** and **vector images.** Raster images, which are commonly called bitmap images, are composed of grids of spaces, called pixels or bits. Conceptually, each pixel is assigned a color in order to make up the image. The entire mapping of pixels is called a bitmap. In actuality, not every pixel is assigned a color. On any given row of the bitmap, only color changes must be noted. So, two images that are the same size in terms of dimension will vary in terms of the number of bytes used to define the image.

Vector images are defined through mathematical statements or commands that define lines and shapes. For example, a vector image may contain a circle that is defined by assigning a center and a diameter, along with other characteristics, such as color and width. The same circle displayed in a bitmap format would require assigning a color for each point on the circle. In general, when used properly, an image in the vector format results in a much smaller file size than one in the bitmap format. However, displaying images in vector formats typically requires software beyond Web browsers. As a result, most images on the Web are in bitmap formats and we discuss bitmap technologies in more depth. However, it would be a mistake to ignore the importance of vector images to e-business. Many organizations routinely distribute vector image files electronically. So, we also provide a brief discussion of some vector image technologies.

Raster Image Technologies

Raster images, also known as bitmap images, are much more common in Web-based e-business than vector images. In this subsection, our goal is to provide you with a basic understanding of the most important raster image formats, including how to choose the best format for a particular circumstance. We also introduce you to some commonly used tools for generating and editing raster images.

Currently, two raster image formats dominate the Web: the Graphics Interchange Format (GIF) and the Joint Photographic Expert Group (JPG or JPEG) format. A third format, Portable Network Graphics (PNG) is gaining in popularity and importance. By the way, if you want to sound like a Web insider, be sure to pronounce GIF as "jiff," JPG as "JAY-peg," and PNG as "ping." Although there are more than thirty raster graphics formats, our discussion focuses on the three formats mentioned above. In addition, we briefly discuss a few other popular formats. Keep in mind that entire books have been written about graphics formats. Our intent here is not to make you an expert on all current formats. Rather we want to help you become familiar with the formats that are the most important in an e-business context.

GIF

When you access a Web page that contains graphics, the chances are good that those graphics are either in GIF or JPG formats. The GIF format was developed in the mid-1980s by Compuserve, an early online service provider. In those days, modems were painfully slow. A fast modem ran at 1,200 baud. While this speed was fine for exchanging text, transferring graphics was extremely time consuming. In the same time period, there were many different operating environments for personal computers, which resulted in many compatibility problems when sharing files.

To address these problems, the GIF format was developed. There were two main goals underlying the GIF format. First, the format had to be platform independent. Second, the images had to be compressed. As you might have guessed, the compression results in significantly smaller file sizes, which translates into faster transmission. We will focus on the compression aspect.

When you save an image in GIF format, special software called an encoder creates a GIF data stream that contains all the information necessary to reproduce the image. When the image is viewed, decoder software reads the data stream and displays the image. The encoding/decoding scheme used by the GIF format is known as LZW. (The scheme is named for its inventors, Abraham Lempel, Jacob Ziv, and Terry Welch.) The degree of compression depends on the characteristics of the image. The LZW algorithm works on the basis of horizontal repetition. This means that a solid line of a single color offers the highest degree of compression. As the degree of horizontal repetition lessens, the degree of compression drops.

The LZW compression method results in **lossless compression,** which means that the original image can be reproduced exactly. There are some limitations to the reproduction, however. The original GIF format can only handle 256 colors out of a pallet of 16 million. (A newer version of the format can display more colors, but some popular software still limits GIF images to 256 colors.) While 256 colors may sound like a large number, when displaying certain kinds of images, such as photographs, 256 colors is not nearly enough. In practical terms, the limitation means that if an original image uses more than 256 colors, it will not reproduce correctly when decoded, which results in an image of poor quality. To illustrate, Figure 9-5 shows a photograph that has been converted to the GIF format, along with the original photograph. Notice how fuzzy the GIF image looks when compared to the original. Interestingly, if both files are set to the same resolution, the GIF file is larger—it is approximately twice as large as the original image.

A second drawback of GIFs is that the LZW compression algorithm is patented. As a result the code used for creating or reading a GIF file can only be used under license from Unisys. See the Further Readings section at the end of the chapter for more information on the LZW patent. We will discuss this situation further when we cover the PNG format.

JPG

The second most common graphics format on the Web is JGP. Unlike GIF, JPG can handle a large number of colors. The format stores image data as 24-bit color, which means that 24 bits of data are used to describe each pixel. This translates into more than 16 million available colors. In fact, as the name implies, it was designed specifically for compressing photographic images. The format is well suited to its task. Compression ratios can be as high as 20:1 without appreciable loss of quality. This compression comes at a price, however. Recall that GIF uses a lossless compression algorithm. The JPG format uses a **lossy compression** algorithm, which means that the quality of the image degrades when its file is compressed. Fortunately, the way the compression works takes advantage of limits in human visual perception, so typically the loss in quality is imperceptible. However, when the size of the image is increased, the loss in quality becomes noticeable. Figure 9-6 illustrates this by showing a portion of a JPEG version of the image in Figure 9-5 that has been magnified to twice its original size. You can see how much worse it looks than the original image.

A nice feature of the JPG format is that you can specify the degree of compression, which translates into the degree of quality loss. So, if you need a particularly high-quality image, you can specify a lower compression ratio. If file size is more of a concern than image quality, you can use a higher level of compression. You may have seen this in action when viewing "thumbnail" images in online catalogs. These images are relatively small, which hides quality loss. As a result, very high compression ratios can be used without noticeable loss in quality.

It may sound like JPG should be your image format of choice. However, this is not always the case. While JPG works well for photographs or photo-like images, it is not the equal of GIF when dealing with line art. This is why Web graphics such as bullets, lines, and icons are GIF images rather than JPG images. Figure 9-7 shows an original image saved in an uncompressed format called TIFF, then saved as a GIF image, and then a JPG image. Notice how the GIF image is of better quality, even though its file is smaller. The JPG image appears fuzzy, while the GIF image is true to the original. At the end of this section, we discuss some rules of thumb for choosing the most appropriate image format.

FIGURE 9-5 Quality Loss in GIF

FIGURE 9-6 Quality Loss in JPG

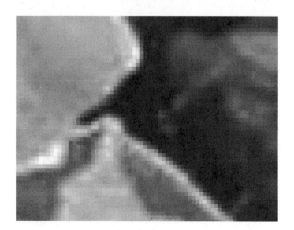

TIFF

GIF

E-Biz

JPG

FIGURE 9-7   Comparison of GIF and JPG

PNG

The final raster image format we discuss in detail is the Portable Network Graphics (PNG) format. The PNG format was developed to address problems with the GIF format. As is often the case, technology issues were not the only driving force behind the development of PNG. The primary driver was a business issue. Unisys, the company that holds the patent on the LZW compression method used in GIF, announced in 1995 that it was going to enforce its patent on LZW. As a result, commercial developers who utilize GIF encoding and decoding must pay a royalty to Unisys. This development drove a group of experts to develop the PNG format, which is royalty-free. Note that the Unisys patent is scheduled to expire in 2003.

The World Wide Web Consortium formally issued the PNG format specification in late 1996. Major Web browsers, such as Internet Explorer and Netscape Navigator, and graphics software packages, such as Adobe Photoshop and Corel PHOTO-PAINT, support the format. Some experts believe that, in time, PNG will be the dominant format on the Web, although this remains to be seen.

In addition to being royalty free, PNG also has other advantages over GIF. The compression method used is said to be superior to LZW while still being lossless. Also, when used properly, PNG compression results in smaller files than does LZW. A common rule of thumb is that a PNG image will be 10 percent to 30 percent smaller than the same image in GIF format. This is not universally true, however. Certain images, such as those with few colors, may compress more with GIF than with PNG. In addition, PNG supports up to 48-bit color. An interesting feature of PNG is progressive display, which means that during transmission, a low-resolution image appears quickly followed by a gradually improving image. PNG also allows you to control the amount of transparency in an image. With GIF, a single color can be set to be transparent, which improves the appearance of some images. However, GIF does not let you make a color semi-transparent, while PNG does. Finally, PNG images can contain searchable metadata about the image. For example, you can add text comments to a PNG image and these comments would be stored within the PNG file.

There are some drawbacks to PNG. Although most popular browsers offer some level of support for PNG files, this support is often incomplete. For example, some browsers have trouble correctly displaying PNG transparency. We expect that this situation will improve over time. See the Hands On Exercises section for a Web site that will let you check to see if your Web browser correctly displays PNG images. Another drawback to PNG as an alternative to GIF is that PNG does not support animation. A related format, Multiple-image Network Graphics (MNG), was developed to enable PNG-based animation. At present, there are a number of applications that can generate and edit MNG images. We expect that support for MNG will continue to grow.

As you can tell from our discussion so far, there are advantages and disadvantages to each of the formats. In Table 9-1 we provide an overview of the important

Table 9-1 Summary of Raster Image Format Characteristics

	GIF	JPG	PNG
Colors	256	Millions	Millions
Color depth	8-bit	24-bit	48-bit
Compression	Lossless	Lossy	Lossless
Typical efficiency	Good 10% to 30%	Excellent Often more than 90%	Very Good 30% to 50%
Browser support	Excellent; complete support on all major browsers	Excellent; complete support on all major browsers	Good; incomplete support on most browsers
Transparency	Full only	None	Full or partial
Animation	Yes	No	No (support under MNG format)
License required	Yes	No	No

characteristics of each format. But what do the characteristics mean in terms of advantages and disadvantages. Table 9-2 shows the major advantages and disadvantages for each format. How can you choose among GIF, JPG, and PNG? There are some widely used rules of thumb for making this choice. Table 9-3 summarizes these. In short, when dealing with photo-like images, use JPG if slight quality loss is acceptable, and use PNG if not. When dealing with images with relatively few colors, sharp edges, or embedded text, use PNG or GIF. Never use JPG for pure black and white

Table 9-2 Raster Image Format Advantages and Disadvantages

Format	Advantages	Disadvantages
GIF	■ Lossless compression ■ Supports transparency ■ Supports animation ■ Good compression, especially for images with large amounts of solid color. ■ Widespread browser support	■ Requires license fee ■ Only lossless for images with fewer than 256 colors ■ For some images, compresses less than PNG ■ No support for partial transparency
JPG	■ Excellent compression ratios ■ 24-bit color support ■ Millions of colors ■ Widespread browser support	■ Lossy compression ■ Sharp edges may appear blurred ■ No support for transparency ■ No animation
PNG	■ Lossless compression ■ 48-bit color support ■ Millions of colors ■ Supports full and partial transparency ■ Good compression ■ Progressive display	■ No animation support ■ Limited browser support

Table 9-3 Choosing a Raster Image Format

Format	Best use	Avoid
GIF	■ Images with large areas of limited colors ■ Line art ■ Logos ■ Cartoons ■ Buttons, icons and borders ■ Animations	■ Photographs ■ Images with more than 256 colors ■ When licensing is an issue
JPG	■ Photographs ■ Photo-realistic images ■ When slight losses in quality are acceptable in exchange for compression	■ Images with sharp edges ■ Line art ■ Images with embedded text
PNG	■ Images with large areas of limited colors ■ Line art ■ Logos ■ Cartoons ■ Buttons, icons and borders ■ Photographs and photo-realistic images when no loss in quality is acceptable	■ When compatibility with older browsers is an issue ■ Photographs and photo-realistic images when slight quality loss is acceptable

images. As PNG support becomes more widespread, we recommend using PNG rather than GIF to avoid any licensing problems.

As we mentioned earlier, there are many other formats for raster-based images. Since the three we have already discussed account for the vast majority of the images on the Web, we only briefly describe three other popular raster-based formats below.

Tagged Image File Format (TIFF)

This format is widely used for many imaging applications that involve making reproductions of paper-based images. For example, you may encounter TIFF when you use a scanner. In the context of e-business, TIFF is often used for medical imaging, electronic faxes, and other document imaging applications.

PCX

The PCX format was developed by ZSoft for its PC Paintbrush software, which was an early PC-based illustration program. Like TIFF, PCX is widely supported by electronic fax software and scanners. Applications of PCX are similar to those of TIFF.

Windows Bitmap Format (BMP)

The BMP format is the native Microsoft Windows bitmap image format. If you have used Microsoft Paint, you have used the BMP format. The BMP format is best used for small images, such as icons.

As we stated earlier, most of the graphics on the Web are raster-based. However, it is very important to realize that e-business goes beyond Web pages. So, it is important to have some understanding of non-raster image formats, which is the topic of the next subsection.

Decision Point

This Decision Point can help you decide on which of the "big three" raster image formats is most appropriate for a particular image. Note that there are times when the use of other formats is more appropriate. For example, when preparing the screen shots you see in this book, we used the TIFF format. This decision was made because TIFF is an uncompressed format, which offered the highest quality possible. File size was not a consideration, so compression was not necessary. However, for most network-enabled applications (such as Web sites), file size is a major issue, so compressed formats are often used.

The Decision Point makes two assumptions: (1) that you have already decided to use a raster, rather than vector, image format; and (2) that browser support for the PNG format continues to improve (which we expect).

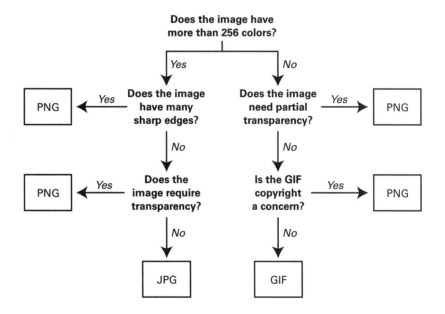

Vector Image Technologies

Many organizations use e-business applications that make use of vector-based images. For example, engineering firms routinely use e-business technologies to manage and share computer-generated engineering drawings. The same can be said for manufacturing and construction firms.

Vector images are sometimes called object images because you manipulate vector images by manipulating objects such as lines, circles, and polygons. Instead of representing an image as a set of rasters (individual points), vector images "think" in terms of geometric objects. For example, a line is not a series of pixels, it is a line that is ten units long and starts at the coordinates 0,0,0. There are at least three major advantages vector images have over raster images. First, vector images are more flexible. They can be resized without degradation in quality. The only size limitations come from the output devices. One file can be used to generate postage-stamp or wall-sized output (assuming your output device can handle these sizes). Second, a better output device will create a better-looking vector image, which is only partially true for raster images. Both of these advantages come from the fact that vector images use mathematical descriptions of objects, rather than bitmaps, to define an image. Finally, vector images are often smaller than the same images at the same level of quality stored as raster images.

There are also drawbacks to vector formats. Vector formats are not suitable for certain types of images, such as photographs. Images that contain colors that vary on a pixel-by-pixel basis are not suitable for vector formats. Earlier we said that the quality of a vector-based image depends on the quality of the output device. More specifically, this qualification is true for raster-based output devices, which includes most monitors and printers. Because of this, when vector images are displayed on low-resolution devices, quality suffers. Finally, reconstructing a vector image may take time, because each image object has to be drawn individually.

As was the case with raster images, there are many different vector image formats. However, unlike raster formats, determining which are the most important to e-business is difficult. One reason for this is that the vector formats tend to be proprietary. In addition, many formats are specific to one software package or to a particular family of software. For example, the DWG format, which is arguably the most common vector image format, is a proprietary format developed by Autodesk, publisher of AutoCAD, which is the most popular computer-aided drafting program. Using such formats might be a problem for consumer-oriented e-commerce. You would probably not want to post DWG images on a Web site unless you were sure that potential viewers had access to AutoCAD. In some cases, viewing software is available for little or no cost, as we discussed earlier in relation to PDF files. However, even if a viewer is available, it must be downloaded and installed. Casual users may be unlikely to bother with this.

How, then, are vector images used in e-business? In most cases, vector images are used in business-to-business applications, when each party involved has access to the proper graphics software. An example will help illustrate. Large construction projects involve literally dozens of different organizations working together, including architects, engineers, contractors, and others. All of these organizations must share considerable amounts of information. Much of this information is in the form of engineering and construction drawings. Perhaps you have seen blueprint versions of these types of drawings. Today most of these drawings are computer-based. The most popular tool for generating these types of drawings is AutoCAD, as we mentioned earlier. Assuming that the graphics standard for the project is AutoCAD DWG format, each of the organizations involved would have access to the AutoCAD software. A restricted access Web site could be set up to enable downloading and uploading drawings, allowing the organizations to quickly access the most up-to-date version of any drawing. For example, the electrical engineering firm could make revisions to a lighting plan. Upon notification of the revision, the lighting contractor could go to the Web site to retrieve the revised drawings. A key point in this illustration is that the project participants agreed to use a particular vector format, which is the only way this type of interactivity would be possible.

Of course, there are many different vector image formats used in e-business. We briefly discuss some of them below. Keep in mind that new formats emerge often, usually to address some weakness in the available formats. As a result, it is important to understand that there is no single format that is best. The key to deciding on formats is to understand the benefits and drawbacks of the formats under consideration and how these apply to your particular situation. The format that is best in one situation might lead to disaster in another. The formats discussed below are in alphabetical order, not in any rank order.

Drawing Interchange File (DXF)

The drawing interchange file format was developed and is maintained by Autodesk, the developers of the AutoCAD computer-aided drafting (CAD) software. The purpose of DXF is to allow users to exchange vector-based images. Most DXF files use ASCII DXF, but binary DXF is also available. Almost all personal computer-based CAD systems can read and write DXF files. As a result, DXF is widely used when users of different CAD systems need to share files. DXF viewers allow those without CAD software to view DXF-based images. See the Further Readings section for a reference to more information on the DXF format.

PostScript/Encapsulated PostScript (EPS)

PostScript, developed by Adobe, is really a programming language rather than a file format. Its main purpose is page description. PostScript has a reputation for being able to produce very high-quality images. Because of this, PostScript has emerged as an industry standard. Devices must integrate the ability to interpret the PostScript language in order to be able to display or print PostScript files. Most high-end output devices offer the ability to handle PostScript files. An attractive feature of the language is that images are scalable, so images can be printed at virtually any size without loss of image quality. PostScript files are actually stored in an ASCII format, so you can read and edit the code with a text editor. Following is an example of part of a PostScript file.

```
%!PS-Adobe-3.0 EPSF-3.0
%%BoundingBox:0 0 288 288
userdict begin
  /ok_EllipseDict 50 dict def
end
ok_EllipseDict begin
  /ok_Ellipse
  {
       ok_xOffset ok_yOffset moveto
       ok_x1 0 ok_xR ok_y1 ok_xR ok_yR rcurveto
       0 ok_y1 ok_x1 neg ok_yR ok_xR neg ok_yR
rcurveto
       ok_x1 neg 0 ok_xR neg ok_y1 neg ok_xR neg ok_yR
neg rcurveto
       0 ok_y1 neg ok_x1 ok_yR neg ok_xR ok_yR neg
rcurveto
       closepath
  } def
  /ok_Ellipses
```

Encapsulated PostScript (EPS) is used to include a description of a single page within a PostScript file. For example, an EPS file might describe a graph that is included in a PostScript document. Sometimes EPS files contain a preview image in a bitmap format. This allows devices that are not able to display PostScript images to preview an EPS image. Note that the preview is only a rough approximation of the EPS image. The EPS format has been widely adopted; most illustration software can produce EPS files. While generally included in discussions of vector formats, both PostScript and by extension EPS files can contain bitmap images. For example, the PostScript file for a company newsletter might contain a bitmap format photograph.

Macintosh Picture Format (PICT)

The PICT format is a lossless image format developed by Apple Computer. Files in the PICT format can contain both vector and bitmap images. Virtually all graphics software for the Macintosh can read PICT files.

Scalar Vector Graphics (SVG)

The SVG format is one of the more recently developed formats. It is also one of the most interesting in terms of emerging e-business applications. The SVG format was developed as an application of the Extensible Markup Language (XML). Two factors make this an exciting development. First, any browser that can understand XML should be able to display an SVG-format image. Recall that most vector formats are proprietary and can only be viewed with special software. Second, since SVG images are vector-based, they are scalable, which means that they can be displayed at different sizes, without losing image quality. Another advantage of SVG is that text can be embedded in the code for the image and this text can be recognized by search engines. This facilitates both searching and translation into other languages.

Windows Metafile (WMF)

The WMF format is used primarily in Microsoft Windows environments to exchange images. While WMF is generally considered a vector format, it can also be used to display bitmap images. The term metafile in this instance refers to a set of commands that can be used to display an image. Files in the WMF format cannot be displayed directly by most Web browsers. However, there are WMF viewer plug-ins available for Explorer and Netscape.

Now that we have discussed major image formats, we turn our attention to tools used to manage these images. In the next section, we provide an overview of some of major imaging software tools.

Software for Creating, Editing, and Managing Images

There are many different software tools that can be used to create, edit, and manage images for e-business. Of course, fully describing these tools would require many volumes. Providing a highly detailed look at even a single tool could easily fill an entire book. As a result, we do not intend to provide much detail in this section. Rather, our goal is to simply introduce you to a few of the more popular tools with the hope that this will give you a feel for the range of tools and the functions they provide. To this end, we discuss one example in each of three categories of image software: illustration, painting/photo editing, and diagramming. In addition, we cover an example of image management software. Of course, there are other categories of image-related software, but understanding these should help you gain an appreciation for the area. It is important to note that while we put each of these programs into a distinct category, in actuality there is considerable overlap. For example, we discuss Jasc Software's Paint Shop Pro as a painting program for creating and editing bitmap images. While Paint Shop Pro certainly fits into this category, it also offers vector image functions as well as image management. The categorization of a particular piece of software is not really important. What matters is that you understand the range of functions that are associated with creating, editing, and managing digital images.

Illustration Software

Illustration software is used to produce professional-quality drawings. The distinguishing characteristic of illustration software is the ability to create and edit vector-based images. In other words, illustration software lets you create images using objects such as lines, curves, circles, and polygons. As we discussed earlier, a major advantage of vector-based images is that they maintain their quality when scaled up and down. The only restriction on resolution is a result of the output device. Because of this, vector-based illustration software is often the choice of professional illustrators. The most popular illustration software packages are Adobe Illustrator, CorelDRAW, and Macromedia FreeHand. We will briefly describe CorelDRAW.

CorelDRAW is the core of Corel's CorelDRAW 10 Graphics Suite, which also includes a paint program, animation software, and a number of utilities. As the name indicates, CorelDRAW has gone through a number of versions. The current version (as this is being written), CorelDRAW 10, is considered to be one of the best illustration software packages. The program offers a number of useful features, including the ability to place objects on different layers, advanced font management, and the ability to write PDF documents. In addition, when dealing with multi-page documents, each page can be viewed at a different size and orientation. CorelDRAW also has the ability to apply various levels of shading and transparency. Paint Software

Paint software, which is also called image-editing software, primarily deals with raster-based images rather than vector images. In addition to allowing you to create raster images from scratch using paint-like tools, most paint software also includes facilities for editing digital photographs. Popular paint programs include Adobe Photoshop, Paint Shop Pro, and Micrografx Picture Publisher (Micrografx was acquired by Corel Corporation in 2001). We will focus our discussion on Paint Shop Pro.

Like CorelDRAW, Paint Shop Pro has been popular for many years. One reason for the popularity is that it offers considerable functionality for a relatively low price. Currently, Paint Shop Pro sells for around U.S.$100, which is about 20 percent of the price of Adobe Photoshop. Paint Shop Pro is known for being user friendly while still being powerful. For example, you can create custom line patterns and shapes. In addition, the software includes a number of special lighting and other artistic effects. For example, the software helps you retouch digital photographs. As is the case for most major paint programs, Paint Shop Pro offers a number of features related to photo editing. For more information on Paint Shop Pro visit the Jasc Software Web site, listed in the Related Web Sites section at the end of this chapter.

Diagramming Software

Diagramming software could be considered a subcategory of illustration software. However, diagramming software is typically used to create diagrams (as you may have guessed), graphs, charts, and other types of business-oriented graphics. Examples of the kinds of images created include network diagrams, flowcharts, and organizational charts. One of the most popular diagramming programs is Visio, which was originally developed by Visio Corporation, but is now sold by Microsoft. Visio is one of the personal favorites of the authors. We have been using the software to create diagrams for many years. In fact, many of the diagrams used in this book were originally drawn using Visio. Visio offers a "drag-and-drop" interface that allows users to place pre-drawn objects on the screen. In addition, the software has a connection feature that makes sure that lines connect to other objects precisely. These features, along with others, allow those of us with little artistic talent to create professional-quality diagrams. As an example, Figure 9-8 shows a Visio screen that illustrates a figure from Chapter 2 of this book. Notice the symbols on the left-hand side of the screen. All you have to do to use one of these in your drawing is to click on the symbol and drag it into place. Visio also enables users to create their own custom

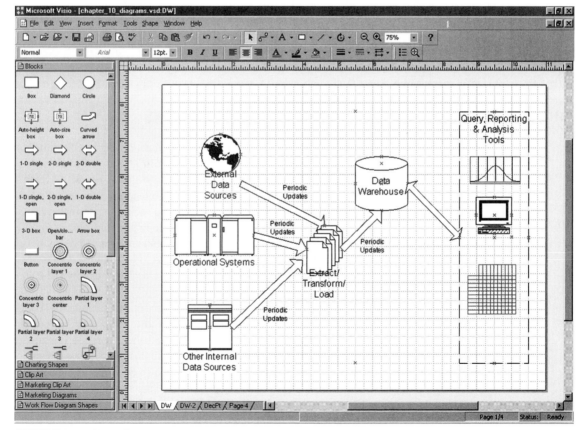

FIGURE 9-8 Visio Example

symbols and symbol libraries. There are several specialized Visio versions and add-ins available. For example, Visio Enterprise Network Tools is an add-in to Visio Professional that helps networking professionals create diagrams of their network infrastructure. You can learn more about Visio from the Microsoft Visio Web site, which is listed in the Related Web Sites section at the end of this chapter.

Image Management Software

We have learned that there are many e-business uses for images. In addition to using images for Web sites, we know that organizations routinely share different types of images across private networks. As an organization increases its use of images, the volume can quickly become overwhelming. Image management software is designed to help organizations deal with this problem. Although specific functions vary with the particular software package, most professional-level image management systems include facilities for cataloging, storing, and viewing images in a variety of formats. In addition, many systems support conversion of images between popular image formats. PhotoSoft's PhotoExplorer is an example of image management software. The software allows users to organize thumbnail versions of images into albums, which can then be browsed or searched. In addition, images can be viewed from a number of different angles. PhotoExplorer can also convert from or to many different image formats, including all of the formats we have discussed in this chapter.

So far, you have learned about text-based and image-based content technologies. Both of these have been utilized in network-enabled applications for many years, although the technologies continue to improve, even as you are reading this. Now we will examine newer content-oriented technologies. In the next section, we discuss digital audio, which is an increasingly important component of many e-business systems.

DIGITAL AUDIO TECHNOLOGIES FOR E-BUSINESS

Audio delivered over networks is becoming increasingly popular. Although still primarily focused on entertainment applications, **network-enabled audio** is poised to become an important business tool. Network-enabled audio is digital audio that is delivered over a communications network rather than other media, such as cassette tapes or compact discs. In this section, we provide an overview of some of the audio technologies that have e-business applications. Digital audio is an extremely complex topic. So, our goal is to give you a sense of the technologies and their applications to e-business, not make you an expert in digital audio. For those of you interested in learning more about digital audio, we provide some pointers to additional material in the Further Readings section at the end of this chapter.

Broadly speaking, there are two approaches to making network-enabled audio available to users. One approach is to enable users to transfer audio files from a server to their computers, then play the audio from their hard drives. We call this approach download audio. The other approach, known as streaming media (audio, in this case), plays the audio as it is being transferred to the user's computer, without actually downloading the audio file itself to the user's hard drive. Each of these approaches has its own set of technologies, and its own set of advantages and disadvantages.

Before delving into the various formats, however, it is helpful to understand a little about audio sampling and compression. Three main factors affect the quality of a digital audio sample: the sampling rate, the sampling resolution, and the number of channels. A series of samples is used to create a digital version of an audio event, such as a band playing a song or someone speaking. The sampling rate is simply the number of samples that is recorded in a given period of time. Sampling rates are usually expressed in samples per second. The higher the sampling rate, the higher the quality. A compact disc recording is typically sampled at a rate of 44,100 per second. A sampling rate of 8,000 per second results in telephone-quality sound. The second factor is the sampling resolution, which is expressed in the number of bits per sample. This is commonly called the bit depth. A higher bit per sample rate results in better quality sound. Finally, the number of channels refers to whether the audio is in mono (one channel) or stereo (two channel). All of these factors can be expressed in a single parameter by multiplying them, which results in a factor expressed kilobits per second, such as 128 Kbps. In the popular MP3 format, CD-quality audio can be achieved at about 128 Kbps, which results in a compression ratio of about 1:10.

Compression/decompression schemes (**codecs**) compress the audio (and video) files, then decompress them during playback. In most cases, the files are decompressed in real-time at playback, which requires considerable processing power. Fortunately, almost all current personal computers have sufficient processing power. There are many different codecs, each with its own set of strengths and weaknesses. Rather than framing our discussion in terms of codecs, we discuss various audio file formats. Keep in mind that if a format allows for compression, there is a codec involved.

Download Audio Technologies

Earlier in the book, we discussed Napster in the context of peer-to-peer technologies. As you may recall, the main use of Napster is to allow users to share digitally encoded music. This is an example of an application of download audio technology. In most cases, the audio files swapped on Napster were in the MPEG-1 Audio Layer 3 format, which is better known as MP3. Napster allows you to locate and download an MP3 file of a song from another user's computer. Once the file is downloaded to your computer, you can play the song as many times as you like without ever again connecting to the other user's computer. This is the main advantage of download audio technologies—once the file is transferred to a user's computer, the user can play the file multiple times without having to download the file again. Since multimedia files tend to be large, the resulting reduction in network traffic can be important. Unfortunately, download audio technologies suffer from a significant drawback; the entire file must be downloaded before playback can begin. This can make it unsuitable for some applications, which we will discuss later.

Although the MP3 format may be the download audio format with which you are most familiar, there are a number of download audio formats that may be used in e-business applications. In this section, we discuss, in alphabetical order of the format's acronym, the most popular formats.

Audio Interchange File Format (AIFF)

The AIFF is primarily used on Apple Mac computers. In fact, it is the default audio format for Macs. However, there is support for the format on other operating platforms. The format can compress files, but this compression not only degrades the quality of the sound, it may also cause problems with compatibility on non-Mac computers.

Sun/NeXT Audio (AU)

The AU format is widely used on computers running Unix and Unix-like operating systems. According to some, the AU format was the first audio format used on the Web. AU is a compressed format, but does suffer from relatively low sound quality.

Musical Instrument Digital Interface (MIDI)

MIDI is really not an audio file format. It is actually a file of instructions that can be read by a sound card in order to reproduce notes to be played. This results in very small files. The MIDI format is very commonly used in electronic musical equipment, such as synthesizers.

MPEG-1 Audio Layer 3 (MP3)

Today, the MP3 format is perhaps the audio file format most closely linked with e-business and the Web. The MP3 format uses compression technologies to significantly shrink the size of audio files, while maintaining sound quality. MP3 can achieve a compression ratio of 1:24, resulting in much smaller audio files. Audio quality suffers noticeably at compression ratios higher than 1:12, however. The ability to compress an audio file without significant degradation of sound quality is a major reason the MP3 format is so widely used for e-business applications. When transmitting audio across a network, the size of the audio file is very important. In effect, smaller files equate to faster transfer or download times. The MP3 format uses a lossy compression method, which results in the loss of some data during compression. So how can MP3 files maintain high-quality sound? Sound quality is maintained because MP3's compression scheme eliminates data that represents sounds that are beyond the range of human hearing. This results in near CD-quality sound. You can test the quality yourself by comparing a song in MP3 format to the same song on the original compact disc. Chances are you will not be able to tell the difference. One interesting feature of MP3 is that, while it is normally thought of as a download format, the files can also be streamed. Although MP3 is an international standard, and is extremely popular, it is not the native audio format for any of the popular computer operating systems. As a result, in the past it has been necessary to obtain special software to play MP3 files. Fortunately, this software is widely available and, in many cases, free. For example, stripped-down versions of MUSICMATCH and Nullsoft's Winamp are available for free. Even though the free versions of these applications lack some of the features of their for-fee counterparts, the programs tend to be quite capable. Installing special software in order to listen to MP3 files is becoming a thing of the past. For instance, newer versions of Microsoft's Windows Media Player are capable of playing a variety of formats, including MP3.

QuickTime (QT)

Although, the QuickTime format is generally thought of as a digital video format, it is possible to create a "movie" without a video channel, which in effect, results in an audio file. The QuickTime format is most closely associated with Macs, although the format is also supported on other platforms, including Windows. QuickTime allows compression and, like MP3, also allows for both streaming and downloading of audio files.

Wave (WAV)

The WAV format is the native audio format of the Windows family of operating systems. If your Windows-based computer plays sounds through its speakers when it starts up, when you receive an e-mail or when you shut down, for instance, those sounds probably come from WAV format files. It is possible to have either compressed or uncompressed WAV files. Sound quality is good for both, but even when compressed, WAV files tend to be large in comparison to files in other formats, such as MP3.

Windows Media Audio (WMA)

A more recent development in the world of digital audio is the WMA format, which many see as Microsoft's answer to MP3 and streaming audio. The format is very promising. Even when highly compressed, sound quality is quite good, even when compared with the original CD version. WMA seems to offer a better compression-to-quality ratio than MP3. In other words, when comparing files that sound the same to the human ear, WMA files tend to be smaller than comparable MP3 files. The format allows for streaming and downloading. One drawback to the WMA format is that it is proprietary, and therefore, is subject to licensing fees. However, Microsoft has waived licensing fees when WMA is incorporated into software that operates on a Windows platform. Although it is too early to tell, the WMA format appears likely to become a serious player in the digital audio market.

As you can see, there is a wide range of digital audio formats. After we discuss streaming audio formats, we will discuss how to choose among the various options. At that time, one very important consideration will be file size. Table 9-4 provides file sizes for a short (approximately 1 minute) music clip in the WAV, MP3, and WMA formats. Notice that the MP3 files and WMA files are approximately the same size. This may seem a little confusing at first glance. You may recall that one of the benefits of WMA is its compression scheme, which typically results in smaller files than MP3 *at the same level of quality.* Generally speaking, few people would be able to tell the difference between a 128 Kbps MP3 file and a 64 Kbps WMA file. So, when comparing files of the same audio quality, the WMA files are smaller.

Streaming Audio Formats

Recall that streaming audio files are played as they are received. You do not need to wait for the entire file to download before you can listen to the file. There are several advantages to this approach. First, it is not necessary to download an entire file in order to listen to part of a song or other piece of audio. This is very beneficial in terms of network traffic. Suppose that you use streaming audio to listen to an unfamiliar song. After a few seconds, you decide that the song is not for you and you stop the playback. Once you stop the playback, the network stops transmitting the corresponding audio file, which reduces network traffic. Another advantage of streaming audio is that the client computer only has to devote a small amount of storage to the file. The only storage needed is for a playback buffer, which is used to guard against "skips" in the playback caused by minor variations in transmission speed. Finally, the client application can adjust playback parameters to account for the connection quality and playback capabilities of the client computer.

We have already discussed three formats that are used for streaming audio. Recall that MP3, QuickTime, and WMA formats can all be streamed or downloaded. Rather than rehash

Table 9-4 Digital Audio Format File Size Comparison

	WAV	MP3	WMA
32 Kbps	1,626 KB	37 KB	40 KB
64 Kbps	1,626 KB	75 KB	77 KB
128 Kbps	1,626 KB	148 KB	152 KB
160 Kbps	1,626 KB	185 KB	189 KB

Note: WAV is uncompressed

these formats we limit our discussion here to formats not previously covered. In addition, we provide an overview of some of the more popular streaming media server technologies.

RealAudio (RA/RM)

RealAudio, the streaming audio format from RealNetworks, was the Web's first popular streaming media format. The first version of RealPlayer (now named RealOne), the client software for RealAudio content, was released in 1995. It remains popular, with more than two hundred million unique users as of late 2001. Content ranging from live sports broadcasts to music and movie clips is available in RealAudio format. Figure 9-9 illustrates this range by showing the RealGuide Web site. Production tools for producing RealAudio files allow compression, which significantly reduces file sizes. RealAudio files can be mono or stereo and can be optimized for different connection speeds. In theory, this enables those with dial-up lines to effectively listen to RealAudio streams. Our experience is that the listening experience ranges from poor to acceptable when using a dial-up connection. Sound quality is much better when using a broadband connection to listen to streams optimized for faster connections. The format allows for encoding ranging from 8 Kbps (suitable only for speech) to more than 96 Kbps (which is fine for high-quality stereo audio). At the high

FIGURE 9-9 Real.com Real Guide Screen

SOURCE: Real guide page, RealNetworks, http://realguide.real.com/. Used with permission.

end (96 Kbps), sound quality is roughly equivalent to MP3. Newer versions of this format allow both audio and video, so the more correct name of the format is RealMedia. In the early days of Internet-based streaming media, RealAudio technology was the clear choice. More recently, however, the advent of streaming MP3 and WMA has made the choice less clear. It will be interesting to track developments in this area.

Shockwave Audio (SWA)

One of the newest developments in the streaming audio market is Shockwave Audio, from Macromedia. Like MP3, the SWA format is capable of producing highly compressed audio files, while maintaining sound quality. One factor that makes the SWA format interesting is that many users already have the Shockwave client software installed on their computers. Perhaps you have visited a Web site that uses Shockwave Flash technology to add three-dimensional multimedia to the site. (See http://play.nike.com/play/play.html for an example.) The newest versions of the Shockwave player include support for Macromedia's Flash technology. The quality of SWA format audio is surprisingly good, even over a dial-up connection. One drawback to Shockwave is that it lacks the ability to do "live" real-time encoding. This makes other technologies, such as RealAudio, more suitable for live Web-based broadcasting. On the plus side, Shockwave does not require special server software, which is required with RealAudio

Other Formats

A number of the formats already discussed also can be used in streams. For example, MP3 format audio can be streamed rather than downloaded. One example of streaming MP3 use is WUMB, a Boston-based radio station. One of the authors (who resides in Florida) frequently listens to WUMB MP3-based broadcasts using the Winamp client software. The QuickTime format is often used for streaming audio, as is the WMA format.

Which streaming format is the best? As with most questions of this kind, the answer depends on the application and on the user audience. Answering this particular question is made more difficult by the rapid advancement of streaming audio technology. For several years, RealAudio enjoyed the lead. Recently, however, both Microsoft's WMA format and Macromedia's Shockwave have made significant advances. Frankly, this is a difficult question to answer. Even if we could offer a definitive answer, that answer would almost certainly be out of date by the time you read this. As a result, let us simply make two points. First, it is probably a good idea for organizations to not become too attached to any particular streaming format. Being able to effectively integrate newer, more advanced formats may be crucial. Second, the rapid technological advancement in this area is evidence that many people believe that streaming media is a very important e-business application. Companies such as Microsoft, RealNetworks, and Macromedia are pouring large amounts of money into becoming the leader in streaming media. They would not do this unless they believed streaming media to be a key technology for the future.

DIGITAL VIDEO TECHNOLOGIES

In many ways, digital video technologies for e-business applications are similar to the digital audio technologies we have already discussed. As with audio, video can either be downloaded or streamed. Also, some of the audio formats we discussed are either capable of carrying video, or have associated video technologies. Our focus in this section is on network-enabled digital video. There are many different uses for digital video, ranging from distribution of digital video discs (DVD) to movie clips over the Internet. We use the term "network-enabled" to indicate that the means of distribution is a telecommunications network, such as the Internet. We feel that at present, network-enabled digital video is more applicable to e-business, so we concentrate on these technologies. Keep in mind that digital video is an extremely complex topic—many books have been written on the subject. As a result, you should not expect to be an expert in digital video after reading this section. However, you will have a basic idea of what network-enabled digital video is about. We begin the section with an overview of the process of producing network-enabled digital video. This is followed by descriptions and brief discussions of the major formats used for network-enabled digital video.

Producing Network-Enabled Video

Whether you are an amateur putting a video of your cousin's fifth birthday party on the Web or a professional producer distributing a digital video of a major speech, you would use the same basic process to produce and distribute the digital video. Of course, the particular technologies and tools may vary, but the basic process is the same.

There are five steps to producing and distributing a digital video. Figure 9-10 illustrates the process.

1. *Record the video.* The original footage can be filmed using either a digital or analog video camera. Possible formats, in order of increasing quality, include VHS, Hi8, and MiniDV. Resolution for video is commonly expressed in horizontal resolution. Standard VHS resolution is 250 lines, Hi8 is 400 lines, and DV is 500 lines. While almost any camera can be used, the higher the quality of the original video, the better the overall results are likely to be. Other factors, such as lighting quality and the steadiness of the camera, also impact quality.

2. *Capture the original video on a computer.* Your computer will need a video capture card in order to accept the video from the original media. As with the camera, better quality hardware generally leads to better results (assuming that the user is competent). Your computer will need to have a large amount of disc space. Uncompressed, the file size of a good quality video clip can easily exceed 1 GB per minute. A number of factors dictate the quality of the captured video and the size of the resulting file. There is a tradeoff between file size and quality—higher quality means much larger files. We discuss quality considerations later in this section.

3. *Edit the video.* Editing the video is not always necessary, but in most cases, the quality of the final product can be greatly increased by careful editing. Popular consumer-level video editing software includes Adobe's Premiere, Ulead's MediaStudio, and Discreet's cinestream (previously Digital Origin's EditDV).

4. *Encode/compress the edited video.* Encoding (compressing) digital video is a critical step in the process due to the very large file sizes associated with digital video. When distributing video over a network, large file sizes equate to long download times. When encoding the video you must decide which format to use.

5. *Distribute the video.* Even though we are primarily concerned with network-enabled digital video, there are other means of distributing your final product.

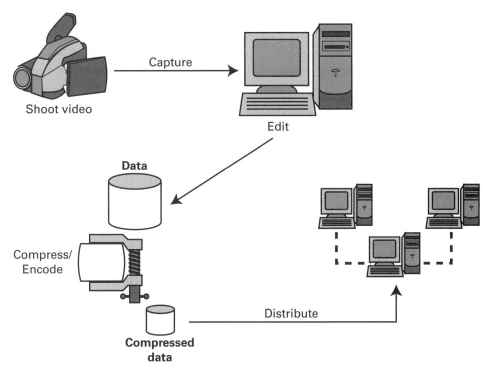

FIGURE 9-10 Digital Video Production and Distribution Process

SOURCE: Real guide page, RealNetworks, http://realguide.real.com/.

Many organizations record the video onto CD-ROMs for distribution. Using DVD is another popular choice. Assuming that you are going to distribute the video over a network, you must decide whether you are going to use a download or streaming replay method. Generally, streaming is a better choice for all but very short (one or two minute) videos. Streaming also has the advantage of better protection of your intellectual property. Since the viewer never downloads the entire file in a streaming arrangement, it is much less likely that an unscrupulous user will capture and redistribute your video.

Some Digital Video Considerations

A number of factors can influence the quality of digital video. First, the quality of the original video critically impacts the quality of the final product. While it is possible to enhance quality to a limited extent through video editing, a higher quality original usually leads to a higher quality final product. Second, the capabilities of your video capture card impact the final quality. Once again, higher quality cards generally lead to better final products. All other things being equal, a U.S.$5,000 capture card will offer better results than a U.S.$500 card. Finally, the parameters you choose for the encoding process impact the quality of the final video. These parameters not only impact quality, but also affect file sizes

Three main parameters set during the encoding process contribute to the quality of the final product. **Frame rate** refers to the number of frames per second your video will display. The standard frame rate for movies is about twenty-four frames per second. Television broadcasts (in the United States) display about thirty frames per second. Usually, anything less than fifteen frames per second results in jerky motion. The **frame size** refers to the amount of screen space (in pixels) that the video encompasses. This parameter is sometimes called the window size. These sizes should always have an aspect ratio of 4:3. Typically, 640 × 480 is considered full size. The final parameter is **color depth,** which is also called color quality. Color depth is usually expressed in bits, such as 8 bit or 16 bit. A color depth of 8 bits translates into 256 colors, while 16 bits gives you more than 64,000 colors. You can estimate the file size per second of a digital video by using the following formula:

$$\text{File size} = (\text{frames per second} \times \text{frame size} \times \text{color depth}) \div 8$$

So, a single second of uncompressed video with thirty frames per second, a 640 × 480 frame size, and 16-bit color results in a file size of about 18 MB. This translates into a little over a gigabyte per minute. A standard CD would hold less than one minute of video using these parameters. Cutting the frame rate to fifteen frames per second, the frame size to 320 × 240, and the color depth to 8-bit reduces the file size to a little more than 1 MB per second. These parameters result in video quality that is acceptable for many e-business applications. Now a CD can hold about ten minutes of video. Of course, a video captured using the second set of parameters is of lower quality than one using the first set. As you can see, there is a tradeoff between quality and file size.

Even with the second set of parameters, file sizes are quite large. For network-enabled applications, these large files must be highly compressed. This need is addressed through the encoding step in the process. Let us take a look at a few of the more popular formats that offer compression for digital video.

Digital Video Formats and Architectures

There are three main architectures for delivering streaming digital video over networks: Apple's QuickTime, RealNetworks' G2, and Microsoft's Windows Media. In this subsection, we discuss these three architectures. In addition, we provide an overview of two widely used digital video file formats: Audio Video Interleave and Moving Picture Experts Group.

A key component to any digital media architecture is the compression technology. The actual compression for digital video is handled by compression/decompression algorithms, which are called codecs. You may recall that we briefly discussed codecs in the section on digital audio. These codecs are very important. However, for nonexperts, it is usually more useful to talk in terms of formats than codecs. Since our goal is to give you an overview of digital video, we frame our discussion in terms of digital video formats and architectures rather than codecs. Also, we focus on the formats that are most likely to be used for network-enabled applications. One of the formats, MPEG-4, is an open standard, although there are proprietary implementations of the standard. A second format, AVI, is proprietary. The other formats—QuickTime, RealMedia, and Windows Media—comprise the "big three" and are all proprietary. Although we speak of these as formats, they are really multimedia architectures that are associated with the format. In our discussion of the "big three" we will talk about the format as well as the associated player software.

Audio Video Interleave (AVI)

The AVI format is a special application of Microsoft's Resource Interchange File Format (RIFF) specification. The format is widely used on Windows-based personal computers. AVI technology is widely supported, which means that there are many tools for creating, editing, and playing AVI files. In addition, the format supports a wide range of video qualities. This lets you make tradeoffs between file size and video quality. The Active Streaming Format (ASF) is replacing AVI as a Microsoft standard.

Moving Picture Expert Group (MPEG)

There are actually three MPEG standards that relate to digital video. MPEG-1 was developed in 1988 to allow VHS-quality video to be stored on and played from CD-ROM media. MPEG-2 followed in 1996 and is the standard for digital television and DVD. Of the most interest in relation to network-enabled digital video is **MPEG-4,** which became an international standard in 1999. The MPEG-4 standard is based on MPEG-1, MPEG-2, and QuickTime (which we discuss later in this section). The format supports video quality ranging from lower quality than a standard video conference all the way up to quality exceeding high-definition television. The jury is still out on MPEG-4. There seems to be some disagreement among experts as to the video quality that can be achieved. At the very least, MPEG-4 appears to be a digital media format to keep an eye on.

QuickTime

QuickTime is produced by Apple Computer, and is the native multimedia technology for Macintosh computers. To quote Apple's QuickTime literature, QuickTime is "a file format, an environment for media authoring, and a suite of applications." QuickTime is a mature technology—it was released in 1991. As a result, it is well supported on both Windows and Macintosh operating environments. Player software is also available for other operating systems, including Linux, Solaris, and Free BSD. Apple claims that there more than 150 million copies of the QuickTime player in use. The player supports all popular encoding formats for images, sound, and video. In fact it supports more than two hundred multimedia formats, including all of the ones we discuss in this chapter. (You can view a list on Apple's QuickTime Web site, which is listed in the "Related Web Sites section at the end of this chapter.) One nice feature of QuickTime is that a single QuickTime file can be streamed or downloaded. So, it is not necessary to create separate files for streaming and downloading.

RealNetworks G2

The G2 architecture from RealNetworks is arguably the world's most popular streaming media architecture. G2 is primarily intended for streaming media across a network, such as the Internet or a corporate intranet. The RealMedia player, RealOne, is the client application for the G2 architecture. RealNetworks also offers a number of software packages for creating, editing, and broadcasting streaming media. The G2 architecture uses the Real Time Streaming Protocol (RTSP) to control streams over IP networks, such as the Internet. The protocol allows "VCR-like" controls for pausing and positioning. Of course, these controls are only available when streams are archived. They are not available when viewing live streams. Figure 9-11 shows the RealOne (previously RealPlayer) client software. The positioning controls are circled in the upper left-hand corner.

FIGURE 9-11 RealOne Screen

SOURCE: RealOne is a trademark or a registered trademark of RealNetworks, Inc. Used with permission.

Windows Media

The final digital video architecture we discuss is Windows Media Technologies. Like the RealNetworks G2 environment, Windows Media supports RTSP. Since the Windows Media Player is included with every copy of every flavor of Windows, the Windows Media Technologies architecture has become very popular, even though it is the newest of the formats we have discussed. Not surprisingly, Microsoft has released a set of digital multimedia software tools to match RealNetworks' offerings, including authoring, serving, and playing software. The Windows Media Player can replay files in a variety of formats, including ASF, AVI, and MPEG. One interesting feature of the Windows Media Technologies is the Digital Rights Manager. This can be used to encrypt the multimedia content. In order to view the content, the user must acquire a digital license. This prevents the redistribution of the content. The technology allows for other applications, such as pay-per-view.

As you may have noticed, there are many similarities between digital audio and digital video. This should not be surprising, since most videos contain audio as well as "moving pictures." As a result of these similarities, many of the software tools associated with digital audio and digital video are the same. Of course, there are many tools that are particular to one or the other. Most of these specific tools are oriented towards content production. However, even these tools have some similarities. Regardless of the type of media, software tools are required to capture, edit, and distribute the content. In the next section, rather than discuss audio and video software tools separately, we concentrate on software that can be used for both audio and video.

STREAMING MEDIA SOFTWARE

In this section, we discuss the various types of software that are required to enable streaming media applications. Recall from our earlier discussion that there are five basic steps involved in streaming media production and distribution.

1. Record the original audio/video.
2. Capture the original on a computer.
3. Edit the computerized original.
4. Encode (compress) the edited original.
5. Distribute the encoded audio/video.

We use steps 2 through 5 as a framework to discuss digital media software. Two points are important for you to keep in mind. First, we are only scratching the surface of the available software for each step in the process. There are many more options than we discuss here. Our goal is simply to make you aware of the functions of each class of software and to make you aware of one or two leading products in each category. Second, although we frame our discussion in the context of streaming media, the software for steps 2 and 3 is also used for downloaded digital media.

Media Capture Software

Typically, digital video is originally recorded on a device that is separate from a personal computer. For example, a video camera may be used to record a video to tape, or a digital video camera may be used to record a video to digital storage media, such as a memory card. If the original is recorded in digital form, capturing may be a simple matter of connecting the camera or storage media to a computer and transferring the file holding the video from the recording device to the computer.

If the original is nondigital, the process is more complex. The content must be both digitized (converted into digital form) and transferred to the computer. In the case of video, a video capture card must be installed in the computer for this to occur. Once the capture card is installed, the next step in the process is to connect the video source to the computer and start the transfer. Basically, the capture process creates a bitmap image for each frame of the source. By adjusting the size and quality of these digitized frames, you can impact the size of the digitized file. For example, choosing a smaller frame size or lower color depth reduces the file size. Software such as VideoFramer from FlickerFree can be used to capture video from nondigital sources. A similar process is used to capture audio from an external device to a computer. Today, most personal computers come equipped with sound cards that are capable of performing audio capture from most source devices, such as CD and tape players. In addition, most operating systems, including Windows and Mac OS, include software to capture audio. For example, Windows 2000 includes Sound Recorder as part of the operating system.

Unfortunately, for clips longer than approximately thirty seconds, third-party software is required. One example is Cool Edit from Syntrillium Software Corporation. Cool Edit lets you record audio from any audio source that can be connected to your sound card. As the name implies, Cool Edit also includes audio editing features. Other software for audio capture includes GoldWave from GoldWave and SoundEdit from Macromedia.

Digital Media Editing Software

Most software that helps you capture digital audio and video also includes features for editing the file once it is captured. All three of the audio capture products mentioned in the last paragraph also include editing features. Cool Edit includes many features for editing digital audio files. For example, Cool Edit allows you to cut, copy, and paste sections of audio just as you would use a word processor to manipulate text. In addition, special effects, such as reverb and echo, are frequently included. You can also perform functions such as increasing or decreasing the bass.

DDClip from SoftLab-Nsk is capable of editing both digital audio and video. DDClip allows nonlinear editing, special effects inclusion, and many other features. Apple Computer's FinalCut is another example of a video editing tool. FinalCut includes advanced features, such as compositing, which allows you to combine multiple layers of elements like video, text, and audio. Adobe Premiere, Macromedia Director and Ulead MediaStudio are other examples of digital video editors.

Digital Media Encoding Software

Once the digital media has been captured and edited, it must be encoded into the format or formats of choice. Many of the same products that are used for editing digital media can also take care of encoding. One of the more popular tools for encoding is Cleaner from Discreet. Cleaner is capable of creating files in many different formats, including AVI, Windows Media, RealMedia, and QuickTime. One nice feature of Cleaner is the ability to batch process as many as two thousand files. This allows you to set up many files for encoding overnight. This is important because encoding is a complex, time-consuming process. Encoding large files can tie up your computer for considerable lengths of time, even with a fast processor. Another example of encoding software is Producer from RealNetworks. Producer has the capability to encode for either live or on-demand streaming media applications. In addition, the software lets you encode a single file that the RealMedia architecture will play back at up to eight different connection speeds. Producer also supports two-pass encoding. This process makes an initial pass through the file, analyzing the file in order to determine the best way to compress it. The actual encoding takes place on a second pass using the analysis performed in the first pass. Microsoft and Apple are among the other companies that offer encoding software.

Once your multimedia content is edited and encoded, it may be necessary to integrate different types of multimedia content into a single stream. While many of the editing packages allow this, a more recent development offers a standards-based solution. In the next subsection, we describe this technology, which is known as the Synchronized Multimedia Integration Language (SMIL).

Synchronized Multimedia Integration Language (SMIL)

The Synchronized Multimedia Integration Language is an easy-to-learn, HTML-like language that is designed to support the integration of various types of multimedia resources into a single "experience." The World Wide Web Consortium (W3C) developed the SMIL (pronounced "smile") standard. (See Further Readings for a reference to the W3C SMIL Web site.) The primary intent of SMIL is to allow content creators to synchronize various types of multimedia content into a single stream. For example, you might want to mix a video of a presenter with an audio track and presentation slides. All of this content must be synchronized in order for the presentation to make sense. Prior to the creation of SMIL, multimedia-editing software, such as Macromedia Director or Adobe Premiere, would be used to place the various elements together into a single "movie." (In this section, we use the term movie for convenience. In reality, an SMIL file need not contain any digital video at all.) A key feature of SMIL is that each element can exist in a separate file, possibly in separate locations. This is similar to the approach followed by HTML; various parts of a Web page can exist in different files on different servers. One advantage of this approach is that you can easily update one element of an SMIL movie without having to redo the entire movie. For example, if you need to update the presentation slides for a movie, you simply change the slides. There is no need to edit the SMIL file itself. Another advantage of SMIL is that you can easily integrate live streaming material with other, archived material. Finally, SMIL makes it easy to create several versions of the same movie. This is a handy feature if, for example, you need to feed a presentation to an audience in several languages. You can simply translate the audio elements and slides. Any video or images would remain the same for each version. Since the actual SMIL file is simply a text file, editing the original to point to new audio or slide files is a relatively simple task, similar to changing the location of an image in an HTML file. There are currently a number of software tools for authoring SMIL files. including GR*i*NS from Oratrix Development, and Confluent Technologies' Fluition. As the use of SMIL increases more tools will become available.

Digital Media Server Software

There are two ways to deliver streaming digital media over a network. Progressive download, which is sometime called "fast-start," delivers the content from a standard Web server, such as Internet Information Server or Apache. Since this method does not allow the user to control playback (such as pausing) it should only be used for relatively short clips. Generally speaking, organizations that are truly interested in network-enabled streaming media should invest in software that enables the second method: true streaming.

Streaming media server software utilizes special protocols that were developed specifically to deal with the demands of streaming media. QuickTime and RealSystem servers (called RealServer) use the Real Time Streaming Protocol (RTSP). The Windows Media server uses a Microsoft-proprietary protocol called Microsoft Media Server (MMS). While these are the three major streaming media servers, there are a number of others, including Nullsoft's ShOUTcast and Darwin Streaming Server, which is essentially an open software implementation of the QuickTime server.

A detailed discussion of the features of each server is beyond our scope, and frankly by the time you read this, the information would be out of date. However, there are several considerations that can help you decide on a particular server. First, cost is always a consideration. One thing to watch out for with streaming servers is that some, such as the RealServer, have tiered pricing structures—the more streams the server can serve, the higher the cost. The free version can serve up to twenty-five streams, the sixty-stream version costs U.S.$2,000, the one hundred-stream version costs U.S.$6,000, and the five hundred-stream version costs U.S.$10,000. In contrast, both QuickTime and Windows Media Server are free. Another factor to consider is the server's ability to handle growth. As you find more uses for streaming media, the size of your audience and the complexity of your content are likely to increase. You should be sure that your server choice can deal with the growth. An interesting feature available on some servers, such as RealServer, is the ability to monitor network conditions and alter the characteristics of the stream accordingly, in order to deliver maximum quality. RealServer calls this feature SureStream. It allows RealServer to adjust the stream for different users, depending on the quality of the user's network connection. Microsoft has a similar technology known as Intelligent Streaming. Microsoft uses the analogy of the layers of an onion to explain Intelligent Streaming. As the network path between the server and a client slows down, the server "peels" a layer of video data, which makes the stream smaller. When the connection improves, the layer is replaced. Support for pay-per-view applications is also a desirable feature in some applications. Both RealServer and Window Media Server offer this feature. Finally, in some streaming media applications, it is necessary to control access to the content, which requires an authentication process.

Your server choice also should be capable of **multicasting.** Typically, most network traffic is unicast. This means that each user that requests something is sent a different copy of the data. For example, if you and I are both listening to the same archived radio show, we both receive a different copy of the stream. As you can imagine, this can be inefficient, particularly when many users request the same stream. Broadcasting, on the other hand, sends a copy of the data to all users on a network, regardless of whether or not they request it.

Broadcasting also wastes resources, because each client must process the data, even if the data were not requested. Multicasting is in a sense a combination of these two approaches. In a multicast, a single data stream is sent, but a client must "join" the multicast in order to receive the data. Figure 9-12 is a conceptual view of multicasting.

Multicast streaming media does have at least one drawback. As is the case when viewing or listening to a live stream, the user has less control over the playback of the content. For example, the user cannot skip forward or backward, which is typically possible when accessing an archived stream.

The interest in multicasting led to the development of the Multicast Backbone (MBone). MBone is a virtual network consisting of parts of the Internet where multicasting is enabled. In other words, it consists of servers that are known to be capable of handling multicasts. These servers are known as multicast islands. When data is sent from one multicast island to another, it is encapsulated as a unicast and is sent to the next island. When this happens, the multicast is said to pass through a unicast tunnel. The non-multicast part of the Internet (the unicast tunnels) sees the multicast as a simple data packet. At the next island, the multicast router un-encapsulates the packet and sends the multicast on. Figure 9-13 illustrates the structure of the MBone.

Digital Media Client Software

The final piece of the digital media puzzle is the client software, which is typically called the player. Popular multimedia players include QuickTime, RealOne, and Windows Media Player, all of which we have discussed previously. There are other players also, such as Winamp. Most players can handle a variety of digital media formats. In addition, various controls are offered, including fast-forward, rewind, pause, and volume control. Most players also offer **skins,** which allow users to customize the appearance of their players.

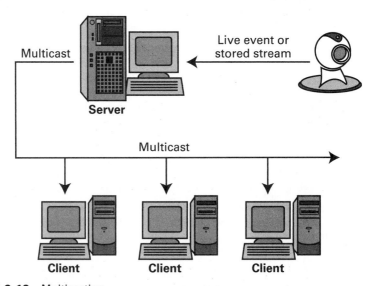

FIGURE 9-12 Multicasting

SOURCE: QuickTime API Documentation site, Apple Computer, http://developer.apple.com /techpubs/quicktime/qtdevdocs/REF/Streaming.4.htm.

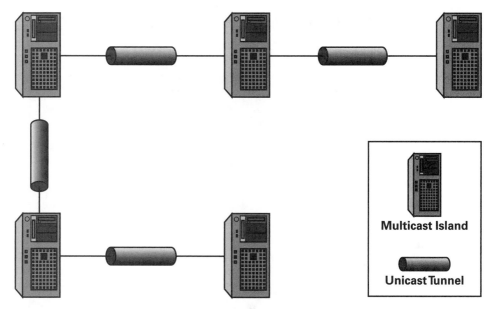

FIGURE 9-13   MBone Structure

SOURCE: "Multicast Streaming—An Introduction," Microsoft Corporation, 13 July 2001,
http://www.microsoft.com/ntserver/techresources/streaming/multiwp.asp.

One key feature of streaming media players is the ability to buffer playback. Buffering
stores a certain amount of streaming data before beginning playback in order to guard against
temporary interruptions in the data stream. Most players allow you to adjust the size of the
buffer by indicating the number of seconds to be held in the buffer. In some players, the user
can specify the buffer size in terms of bytes. It is also possible in some players to set the buffer
size to the available memory. Increasing the buffer can help compensate for poor network
connections. Figure 9-14 illustrates the buffer setting in Windows Media Player.

From Server to Desktop:
The Mechanics of Delivering Streaming Media

Now that you have an idea of the major architectures and software tools involved in network-enabled digital video, it may be helpful to briefly discuss the mechanics of how
these architectures actually deliver the video to the user's desktop. We will use
RealNetworks' architecture for our example. Keep in mind that even though we put this
discussion in the section on digital video, the same process applies for any streaming multimedia. Figure 9-15 shows a schematic of the delivery of streaming media. The text
below describes the steps in the process, as illustrated in the figure.

- Step A: The Web server delivers the initial Web page to the user's Web browser.
- Step B: The user clicks on the audio link, which causes the browser to send a
  request to the Web server.
- Step C: The Web server sends a **metafile** to the user's Web browser. In the
  context of streaming media, a metafile is a file with a URL (Web address) that

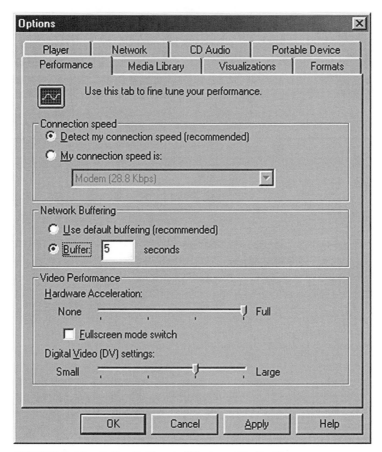

FIGURE 9-14 Buffer Setting in Windows Media Player

points to a streaming media source file. In the RealNetworks architecture, this is a .ram file. For Windows Media files, the file extension is usually .asx or .wmx; and for QuickTime, it is .mov.

- Step D: The Web browser automatically launches the media player software. Information from the metafile is sent to the player.

- Step E: The player requests the media file from the streaming media server. Note that for true streaming, this server is separate from the Web server. In this context server refers to software; it is possible for both the Web server and streaming media server software to reside on the same computer. However, for most practical applications, the two servers would be loaded on separate computers.

- Step F: The streaming media server sends the actual media file to the player, which begins replaying the video or audio.

In this section, we discussed the technologies that enable various flavors of network-enabled digital media. In the next section, we describe a number of ways in which organizations apply these technologies.

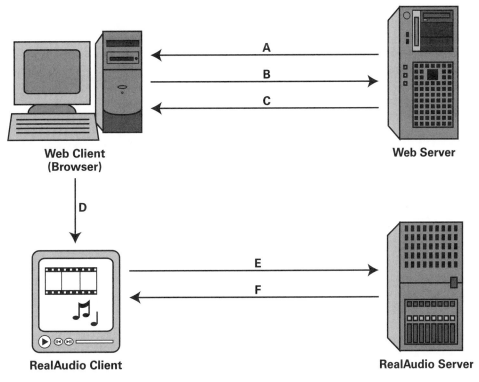

**Web Client
(Browser)**

Web Server

RealAudio Client

RealAudio Server

FIGURE 9-15 Streaming Media Delivery

BUSINESS USES FOR NETWORK-ENABLED DIGITAL MEDIA

Now that you have a basic understanding of digital media technologies, it is time to turn our attention to some organizational applications of these technologies. The e-business applications for digital media are many and varied. As the technologies continue to improve, even more applications will arise. In this section, we provide a brief look at a variety of these applications. Note that our list of applications is by no means exhaustive—many other examples exist.

Network-Enabled Training

One of the most promising applications for digital media is network-enabled training. Providing training to employees is a major cost source for many organizations. Training is expensive for many reasons. Employees must be given time off from their regular duties. Training professionals are generally well-paid. Often, employees must travel to training centers, which results in travel and lodging costs. Scheduling employees for training is often problematic. If few employees are enrolled in a particular course, the cost per employee naturally increases. Waiting for more employees to be scheduled for the course means that some employees must wait for important training. One solution to some of these problems is network-enabled training. We prefer this term to distance training because it distinguishes online learning from correspondence and CD-ROM courses.

Many organizations offer training over the Internet or other networks using digital media. Typically, these courses utilize streaming media technologies to enable students to view and hear instructors, much as they would in a face-to-face course. Sometimes these courses are produced especially for network delivery. In other cases, videos of instructors delivering face-to-face training are encoded for streaming media delivery. In either case, organizations can build libraries of these courses and employees requiring the training can access the courses from virtually any location with a connection to the network, which eliminates travel costs. In addition, the training can be delivered in a just-in-time fashion, since it is not necessary to fill a class with students. Once the course is encoded in the correct format and made available, costs are essentially the same whether one or fifty students take the course at a time.

Sometimes network-enabled training is available through third parties. One example of this is the software company Oracle. Through its Oracle Learning Network, Oracle offers courses in a variety of formats, including RealMedia-based streaming media. Because of the relatively low costs of delivering network-enabled courses, Oracle is able to offer subscriptions at a reasonable price. Currently a one-year subscription is U.S.$1,195. Volume discounts are available for organizations. On the surface, this may seem like a considerable sum, but for the ability to access training for an entire year, the price seems reasonable to us. Oracle does not advertise these network-enabled courses as replacements for its face-to-face certification courses. Rather, the network-enabled courses are intended to provide just-in-time training on various Oracle technologies.

Many universities and colleges are making use of digital media to deliver network-enabled education. For example, the University of Central Florida delivered Web-based courses to more than thirty-five hundred students in a single semester in 2001. The total enrollment was about thirty-four thousand students. While the sophistication of the digital media content varies from course to course, many courses make use of streaming media to deliver lectures, speeches, and videos to students. Universities are very interested in learning how to best utilize network-enabled education due to the significant cost savings that are possible. These savings are illustrated by the introductory management information systems course that must be taken by all students in the College of Business at Central Florida. A single faculty member coordinates and delivers this network-enabled course to more than one thousand students a term. The only other personnel requirements are a handful of graduate teaching assistants. Compared with face-to-face courses with a student/faculty ratio of about 100 to 1, the network-enabled course is very cost effective. Of course, the question of quality still must be answered. Current research is unclear as to whether network-enabled, distant courses are as effective as face-to-face courses. Our take is that the answer is sometimes yes and sometimes no—it depends on the nature of the course, the students, and the instructor. Regardless, we expect to see the use of network-enabled education and training become even more widespread in the future.

Audio Content Distribution

Another e-business application for digital media comes from the distribution of audio content over communication networks. One interesting example of this is Audible.com, which distributes audio versions of books, newspapers, lectures, and other materials over the Internet. What makes this example interesting is how well suited the product is for distribution over a network. Once an audio book, for example, has been produced, most of the remaining costs pertain to packaging and distribution. In a traditional arrangement, the content must be copied onto cassettes or compact discs, packaged, then physically distributed to stores. All of this production and distribution is quite costly. Audible bypasses most of these costs by distributing the product (the audio content) over the Internet. Of course, there are costs involved for servers, technical staff, and so on, but each individual unit costs very little to distribute.

Another interesting feature of Audible's business model is the subscription. Audible offers subscriptions for a fixed monthly fee. Depending on the particular subscription, subscribers can access a certain number of audio books. Currently, U.S.$15.95 per month entitles a subscriber to download two audio books per month. This is an attractive price to many potential customers, since a standard compact disc-based, unabridged audio book typically costs about U.S.$30.

Audible uses a number of audio formats that can be replayed using RealPlayer, Windows Media Player, and a number of portable devices, such as MP3 players and handheld computers. Audible has even made MP3 players available at discounted prices to encourage potential customers to purchase subscriptions. Currently, almost all of the content available through Audible is produced by other companies—Audible is basically a retailer. We are certain that publishing houses are watching Audible with great interest. In the future we may see publishers bypass retailers and sell digital content directly to end customers. Already some music publishers are distributing their content electronically. For example, Sony Music Publishing currently makes a limited number of music tracks available for download for a fee. More of this will occur in the future as digital audio technologies improve and as more consumers get broadband Internet access.

Internet Radio and Television

One of our favorite applications of digital media technologies is Internet-based radio and television. Your authors are frequent listeners to music and other audio content that is delivered over the Internet. For example, one of the authors regularly listens to WMNF, which is a community-owned radio station based in Florida. We also occasionally listen to music from different radio stations around the world. Unlike traditional radio broadcasting, the physical location of the station's transmitter is of little consequence with network-delivered radio. The listener and the transmitter can literally be located on opposite sides of the globe. Some stations are available live, some stations make only archives available, and many offer both. Quite a few syndicated shows are also available over the Internet. As far as we know, all of these stations and shows use some sort of streaming technology, rather than using a download approach.

By using the Internet, radio stations can significantly increase their reach, which in turn can increase advertising rates for commercial stations and donations for nonprofit stations. Currently, advertising rates are largely unaffected by Internet listeners, but this situation will change as better tracking methods become available. (Advertising rates are based on numbers of listeners. Measuring listeners online is difficult at present.) Even though our discussion is focused on traditional radio stations that also broadcast over the Internet, there are many Internet-only "radio" stations. Internet-based television is currently limited. This is primarily due to bandwidth limitations. It is likely that Internet-based television broadcasts will become more popular as bandwidth improves.

So far, our goal for the material in this chapter has been to help you gain an understanding of content-related technologies and their applications. Clearly, these technologies have a major impact on e-business. However, when applying these or other e-business technologies, the topic of usability must be considered. Otherwise, potential users may choose to reject the use of e-business technologies. In the following section, we provide an overview of usability.

USABILITY

Extensive research indicates that the usability of any technology impacts its subsequent use. Simply put, the more usable a technology is, the more it will be used. In this section, we discuss issues related to usability in the context of e-business systems. We begin the section with a short exercise, and then proceed to a discussion of the definition of usability and why the concept is important to e-business. Next, we describe the nature of user/technology interaction. We follow this with a discussion of usability principles and how to achieve high usability. We conclude the section by providing an overview of usability testing.

Before diving into our discussion of usability, let us try a short exercise. On a sheet of scratch paper, write "Why Usability Is Important." That is the end of the exercise (we told you it was short). What does this have to do with usability? The answer is simple; the pencil or pen you used is an example of a highly usable technology. When you wrote on the paper using your pen or pencil, the chances are good that you gave the tools involved (the writing instrument and the paper) no conscious thought at all (unless your pen ran out of ink or your lead broke). When you are in class taking notes, you do not think about your pencil. Your total concentration is on the content of the class (hopefully). The use of the pencil consumes none of your conscious mental capacity. We like to think that achieving the usability of a pencil is the ultimate goal of computer systems, including e-business systems. You have reached the ultimate in usability when your users give no more thought to your e-business systems than you do to your pencil.

What is usability? According to usability guru Jakob Nielsen (1999), usability is a combination of several factors that, in combination, affect the experience users have with a system. These factors are described below.

- *Ease of learning*—The degree to which a user can learn how to properly interact with a system in order to achieve goals impacts usability. Ease of learning is a result of the length of time it takes to learn a system and the amount of effort that must be put into learning.

- *Efficiency of use*—Efficiency of use refers to how quickly an experienced user can accomplish tasks, once a system has been learned.

- *Memorability*—The degree to which a user who has previously interacted with a system can recall how to use the system. The more memorable the system is, the less likely it is that a user will have to "relearn" the system.

- *Error frequency and severity*—Error frequency refers to how many errors a user makes when interacting with a system. Error severity concerns the consequences of an error, as well as how easy it is for a user to recover from an error.

- *Subjective satisfaction*—Basically, subjective satisfaction is how well users like using the system. There are several dimensions that make up satisfaction, including perceptions of quality, ease of use, and likeability.

Now that you have an idea of what usability is, it is time to discuss why usability is so important. To answer this question, we refer to some statistics from Forrester Research (National Cancer Institute 2002). Poor usability costs money. Forrester reports that 50 percent of potential sales are lost when Web site visitors cannot find what they are looking for. In addition, 40 percent of visitors would not return to a site if their experiences on their first visits were negative. Taking a look at the factors that make up usability points to other potential costs of low usability. Difficulty in learning the information structure of an intranet translates into employees taking too long to become efficient in using the intranet. If the intranet is not memorable, employees may have to relearn how to locate information on the intranet, which of course results in lost time. More frequent and/or severe errors waste time and frustrate users. Finally, when users are less satisfied, they may be less likely to use the intranet. Of course, any benefits of the intranet are lost if employees are so dissatisfied that they refuse to use the system.

In order to better understand the impact of usability, we can look at the Technology Acceptance Model (TAM), which was developed by Fred Davis (see the Further Readings section for a reference). TAM is a widely researched, generally accepted theory based on theories that seek to explain human behavior. Basically, TAM says that two factors—ease of use and usefulness—impact users' attitudes toward using a technology, which impacts whether or not the users intend to and ultimately use a system. Figure 9-16 is a graphical representation of TAM. Arrows indicate the direction of impact. You may recall our discussion in Chapter 3 of perceived innovation characteristics and how they impact use. To a degree, TAM is another way to look at factors that influence use.

In TAM, perceived usefulness is the degree to which the use of a technology would help the user in the performance of some task. Perceived ease of use is the degree to which the use of a system is perceived to be free from effort. To a degree, TAM illustrates a cost-benefit view of technology acceptance; how well users accept a technology is dependent (in part) on how hard it will be to use (cost) and what they will gain from its use (benefit). This is only part of the picture, however. Both usefulness and ease of use impact a user's attitude toward using a system. The more useful and easier to use a system is, the more

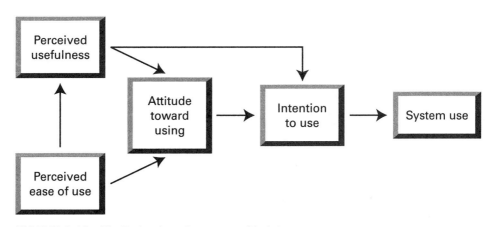

FIGURE 9-16 The Technology Acceptance Model

SOURCE: F.D. Davis, R.P. Bagozzi, and P.R. Warshaw, "User Acceptance of Computer Technology: A Comparison of Two Theoretical Models," *Management Science* 35 (8): 982–1003.

positive the user's attitude toward using the system. This attitude, in turn, impacts the user's intention to use the system. As the diagram shows, the user's perception of the usefulness of a system also affects intention to use. As you might imagine, intention to use influences subsequent actual use of a system. Although there is not a one-to-one correlation between intention and action, research shows that the correlation is typically quite high.

As you can see in Figure 9-16, ease of use not only impacts attitude toward a technology, it also impacts perceived usefulness. So, making an e-business system easier to use has a doubly important impact on subsequent use. The bottom line is that addressing ease of use (which is one aspect of usability) is critical to ensuring that users will accept and use your e-business system. Although TAM has its critics, in general the model has received support from empirical research. Of course, there are many other factors that also impact use, such as those discussed in Chapter 3. However TAM provides a useful framework for examining whether potential users will accept a system. As you develop and evaluate e-business systems, you would be well-advised to keep TAM in mind.

Another key to understanding usability is gaining some knowledge of how people interact with computers in general. In the next section, we provide an overview of one theory of human-computer interaction.

How Users Interact with Computers

Research into human-computer interaction (HCI) has produced many models of how users interact with computers. Keep in mind that although the theories and ideas we discuss here were not specifically developed for e-business systems, good design is good design. If you want to be able to design usable e-business systems or to evaluate the usability of e-business systems, you must gain an understanding of usability in general.

One popular theory comes from usability expert Don Norman's book *The Psychology of Everyday Things* (1988). Norman specified seven stages of action that users go through when using a system. These are described below.

1. *Forming the goal*—The first stage of action is the formation of what the user wishes to achieve through the interaction with the system. In other words, what does the user want to happen? Goals are often stated vaguely. For example, your goal might be to check out books on usability.

2. *Forming the intention to act*—The intention to act is more specific than the goal, but the intention flows from the goal. The intentions are specific "statements" of what must be done to satisfy the goal. Using our example, your intention could be to visit Amazon.com and search for books on usability.

3. *Specifying the action*—The next stage is for the user to plan a precise sequence of actions that can be used to carry out the intention. For example, your sequence (assuming you are already online and have your browser running) might be to enter the URL for Amazon.com, find the search box, choose the "Books" category, enter the word "usability," and so on.

4. *Executing the action*—This is where you actually do something; you put the action sequence developed in the last stage into action. In Norman's terms, this is where you actually interact with the world. This is the last stage in what Norman calls stages of execution. These first stages build up to the actual interaction with the system. The next three stages are called the stages

of evaluation; the user perceives the state of the system and interprets this state in terms of the ultimate goal.

5. *Perceiving the system state*—In this stage, the user perceives what has happened as a result of the actions executed. In terms of our example, you see the Web page that results from your search actions.

6. *Interpreting the system state*—This stage is where the user attempts to make some sense of the perceptions. Using our example, you notice Norman's book, *The Design of Everyday Things,* on the search results. The title of the book is underlined and is in blue text. You interpret this to mean that you can click on the title of the book in order to find out more about it.

7. *Evaluating the outcome*—Once the system state is interpreted, the user evaluates the results in terms of what was desired (the goal). Did your search result in you locating books on usability? Often, this evaluation results in the formation of a new, revised goal. For example, your new goal may be to learn more about *The Design of Everyday Things.* This goal then represents the beginning of a new cycle through the seven stages.

In terms of this model, there are two "gulfs" where things can go wrong. The **gulf of execution** is a mismatch between the intentions of the user and the actions that are allowed by the system. In other words, the user can perform actions that will not support the intentions. The **gulf of evaluation** exists when there is a mismatch between what the system represents and what the user expects. Put differently, the system may present something unexpected.

One way the stages of action can be used is to anticipate user errors by looking at where things can go wrong. Below we discuss four areas in which user failures can occur. In general, better interface design or increased experience with the system can help avoid the last three (although it is possible that system design can help in terms of the first, also).

- *Users can form an inadequate goal.* It is possible that the user can simply start out with the wrong goal in mind. Of course, when this happens, the ultimate outcome is not going to be satisfactory. Initially, you might think that there is not much that the system can do if the user has an inadequate goal to start with. Keep in mind that the stages often occur in cycles. While the system may not be able to prevent a user from forming an inadequate goal initially, it may be possible for the system to provide feedback that helps the user revise the original goal into one that is more appropriate.

- *Users do not find the correct interface object.* Poor design may lead to the user not being able to find the interface object that will enable execution of an action. Once, when one of the authors was teaching a continuing education class on Microsoft Office, one of the students was having trouble locating the "Save" toolbar button. The author walked over to the student and pointed to the disc icon on her screen. She immediately said, "Oh, you mean the TV set." The student knew what she wanted to do; she simply had trouble finding the right interface object for executing the action. As an aside, do not think that this student was stupid. She was very bright. However, in her experience, the icon looked like a television set, not a floppy disc. As a result, she did not associate the icon with the desired action. (The icon really does resemble an old console television set, in our opinion.)

- *Users do not know how to specify or execute a desired action.* Recently, one of the authors was filling out a Web-based survey for a professional organization. After spending about ten minutes completing the survey, the author was ready to submit it. Unfortunately, there was no "submit" button at the end of the form. (This is the standard way to allow users to submit an online form for processing.) The author tried hitting the "enter" key. Nothing happened. After searching for a few moments for a way to submit the form, the author gave up. The responses were never sent for processing and the author was left with an unfavorable impression of the organization (especially since it was an organization devoted to computing!). This example illustrates how a user can be prevented from accomplishing a goal simply because she does not know how to specify the action.

- *Users can receive inappropriate or misleading feedback.* An example of this comes from the search features of some e-business applications. Sometimes, when you attempt a search for a particular item, no matching items are found. You have all probably encountered this situation. If the search facility simply erases your search parameters from the search text box you may not realize why this has occurred. Better feedback comes from a message such as "no matching items found," which leaves little doubt about what has happened.

Usability in Network-Enabled Systems

Now let us get more specific in terms of the type of system. In the following section, we discuss a number of usability principles that pertain directly to network-enabled e-business systems (primarily Web-based systems).

Plan the System

Before designing any e-business system, it is important to engage in some planning. In this context, we are referring to planning for usability rather than more general project planning. When planning an e-business system, it is critical to understand the purpose of the system. On the surface, this seems obvious. Unfortunately, this understanding is often difficult to gain. For example, there may be multiple purposes. An organization may want to use an e-business system to reach more customers, lower order processing costs, and improve its image all at the same time. It is important to identify and interact with the various stakeholders when planning any system. This includes the potential users. Designers must understand who these users will be. In addition, it is important to know why these users will use the system. Understanding why you are developing the system, who its users will be, and why those users will interact with the system enables you to establish specific objectives for the system.

Collect Data from Potential Users

Creating usable systems requires collecting data from users. When collecting data, your main goals are to understand the users' needs and the nature of the users. User surveys, interviews, and focus groups will help you gain knowledge of your users. This understanding will help you design a system that not only meets the users' needs, but that also matches the nature of your users.

Use Page Flow to Match Task Flow

Think of how you might find and purchase a product, such as a shirt, online. You go to the merchant's site, then locate the area of the Web site for shirts. You then browse pictures of the shirts until you find one you like, you check to make sure it is available in your size, then "put" the shirt in your shopping cart and either continue shopping or check out. This is very similar to the process you would follow when buying a shirt in a traditional store. The merchant has arranged pages to match the flow of the task. Departments (such as men's clothing) are listed on the merchant's home page. Particular items are shown on the department pages. Pages devoted to particular items, such as your shirt, provide information about the product, such as the sizes available. The product page allows you to place the item in your cart, and the cart page includes a link to checking out.

Build an Efficient Navigational Structure

There is a widely held belief that users will abandon a task if it takes more than three clicks to find what they are looking for. While this is not an absolute truth, it is a good rule of thumb. Most users will give up if your navigational structure makes it too hard to find what they are looking for. By providing users with a well thought out navigational structure, you increase usability by making it easier for users to carry out tasks. One approach to achieving the three-click goal is to have many links on each page. However, this may violate an even better established principle—seven plus or minus ($\pm$) two. Research indicates that most people have trouble dealing with more than a certain number of items at a time. That "certain number" varies, but most studies peg it between five and nine (7 ± 2). So, any screen that contains more than nine options (such as links) may be troublesome for users. This is a bit of an oversimplification, however. It is possible to create zones on a page that in effect "chunk" choices into smaller sets, which helps users deal with the complexity. It may sound like an impossible task to achieve the three-click goal for an e-business site that offers thousands of items. However, relatively large sets of choices can be organized so that we do not violate the 7 ± 2 or three-click rules. For example, we may have different zones on a Web page that are perceptually separate to the user. Each of these zones organizes choices into "chunks." As long as there are not too many of these chunks, users can typically handle the complexity.

Make Controls Understandable

Cute icons or site maps often confuse users rather than help them. It is important to keep in mind that many different types of people with different backgrounds and experience levels may use your system. Remember the TV set icon story? Just because a control is obvious to you does not mean that it will be to your users. For example, it is a common practice to use a company's logo as a link to its home page. Experienced users may find this natural and understandable. However, less adept users may spend considerable time looking for a home page link. Something as simple as adding the words "Home Page" below the logo or ".com" to the logo can help the situation.

Replicate for Consistency

Users like consistency. Consistent designs help users apply what they have learned in one part of a system to other parts of the system. Think about most Windows software.

(By the way, we could use the Mac operating system as an example, also.) The interfaces for many Windows-based programs are remarkably similar. Most use a "pull-down" menu. Many have "File" and "Edit" as their first two menu choices. This consistency helps users learn the interface. You can help users of your e-business systems by striving for the same sort of consistency.

Collect, Create, or Revise Content

When collecting, creating, or revising the content of an e-business system, you should think in terms of how useful and understandable the content is. In addition, it is important to understand the difference between reading content online and offline. Long passages of unbroken text may, in some cases, be fine for offline reading, but when reading text online, breaking up text into smaller chunks is more usable. In addition, the use of headings can help readers quickly make sense of the flow of the content. In addition, the headings help readers locate the portion of the content they seek. (This is true of both online and offline reading.) Bulleted lists and tables can also be used effectively to help with online reading. It is important, however, to design tables with online reading in mind. For example, long tables (more than a single screen) may be better broken into multiple tables. At the very least, column headings should be repeated for each screen.

Use Iterative Usability Testing during Design

You should not wait until the very end of your development process to test for usability. Performing interim tests along the way helps you refine your system as it is designed. This prevents you from going too far with a design that exhibits poor usability. In addition, through usability testing, you gain additional knowledge of your users. The goal of these tests is to determine what will help and what will impede users in accomplishing tasks. Iterative usability testing consists of developing prototypes based on your current knowledge. Then, task scenarios are created. These scenarios are designed to have users perform tasks patterned after those they will perform with the real site. The users perform these tasks during the usability tests. Observations, surveys, and follow-up interviews are used to assess the usability of the system. Once these data are collected and analyzed, the system's design is modified accordingly. New prototypes are developed and additional testing is performed. This cycle is repeated until the desired level of usability is achieved.

Understand the Limits of the Technology (Compatibility)

It is important for designers of e-business systems to understand the technology their users will use when interacting with the e-business system. If you are designing an intranet-based system, you may have the luxury of knowing that all users will employ the same Web browser and that they will all have high-speed network connections. This consistency allows you to make design choices that optimize for the hardware and software of your internal users. However, it is more likely that your systems will need to be accessible to users running many different configurations. For example, an online merchant must make its systems accessible to potential customers running older browsers over dial-up connections. You should also be aware that some versions of popular Web-based programming languages do not operate on older Web browsers. Understanding these differences leads to a need to test under different technology sets. If your usability tests are run only under the ideal conditions of up-to-date software and high-speed connections, you may be quite surprised when real-world users shun your system because of its poor usability.

Know User Tolerances

It is important for e-business system designers to understand what users are and are not willing to put up with. For example, a commonly held rule-of-thumb is that the maximum time users are willing to wait for a page to download is ten seconds. While we are not convinced that this is an absolute truth, it is important to consider such matters. Reusing graphic elements on a page reduces download time because the reused elements can load from a disk cache. In general, users do not like to scroll excessively. This means that it is important for system designers to design screens in a manner that avoids the necessity for excessive scrolling. Any horizontal (side-to-side) scrolling tends to be irritating to most users. Understanding these and other user tolerances helps you design more usable systems. You can learn more about user tolerances through reading existing research and through your own usability tests.

Use Multimedia and Animation Sparingly

When used properly, multimedia can enhance the usability of an e-business system. However, when overused, multimedia can greatly reduce usability. When considering the use of multimedia or animation, keep in mind that the attractiveness must be offset by some benefit. We often run across Web sites that use animation for no apparent reason other than to show that the site designer knows how to do animation. In our opinion, there is little need for animation on most e-business sites. Others might argue that the animation attracts visitors and adds to the visual interest of the site. Multimedia, however, can be used to great benefit for some types of e-business applications. For example, online training can be significantly enhanced by the presence of multimedia. On the other hand, many users find the popular Flash-based multimedia introductory pages to be irritating, especially when there is no visible means of skipping the introduction. When using multimedia, it is very important to keep the technology of your potential users in mind. In many cases, it is useful to offer nonmultimedia options to those with lower-end technology.

Monitor Your Site Once It Is "Live"

The designer's job with respect to usability is not over when the e-business system is up and running. This is especially true with network-enabled e-business systems that employ Web sites. No matter how extensive your usability testing is, there is no way that you can test with the full range of environments and users present in the real world. As a result, it is important to monitor the site once it is live. For example, you should examine usage logs that indicate which pages within the site attract visitors and which ones drive them away. Identifying pages from which many users leave your site may provide insight into usability issues. Are there some common elements of these pages that may lower usability? If so, what can you do to correct the situation?

As you have learned from reading this section, usability is a complex topic with many different aspects. However, there is a large payoff from efforts to improve usability. In a nutshell, e-business systems with poor usability are likely to be ignored by users who have a choice whether or not to use the system. Even when users have no choice, poor usability can lead to lower efficiency and effectiveness for organizations.

SUMMARY

We started the chapter with a discussion of technologies related to text-based content. Although these technologies seem less exotic than those related to other forms of content, the fact is that most of the content in e-business systems is text-based. So, it is important to have an understanding of these technologies.

Next, we covered technologies related to image-based content. We discussed file formats, such as GIF, JGP, and PNG, and the advantages and disadvantages of each format. The chapter also provided an overview of some software tools used to create, edit, and manage images.

From images, the chapter moved to network-enabled digital audio and video—topics that have much in common. This section of the chapter discussed a number of digital media architectures, including the associated file formats. There was also a discussion of some of the choices that need to be made and the trade-offs associated with these choices. For example, digital audio files can be made smaller through compression, but a price is paid in terms of sound quality. A discussion of some business uses for network-enabled digital media was also provided.

Finally, the important topic of usability was considered. We defined usability and explained its importance. Also, this section looked at how users interact with systems and examined some areas in which user-based failures can occur. The section concluded with a discussion of some actions that e-business systems developers can take to address usability.

KEY TERMS

banner ad
bitmap image
codec
color depth
comma-delimited
    format

frame rate
frame size
gulf of evaluation
gulf of execution
image
lossless compression

lossy compression
metafile
MPEG-4
multicast
network-enabled audio
portal

raster image
rich text format (RTF)
skin
streaming ad
streaming media
vector image

REVIEW QUESTIONS

1. How does the level of technology used by a potential e-business system's users impact decisions related to content?

2. List and briefly describe four formats related to text-based content.

3. Compare and contrast raster (bitmap) and vector image formats.

4. Identify and describe the three most popular raster image formats. List the advantages and disadvantages of each.

5. Compare and contrast download and streaming network-enabled digital audio. Describe a situation in which each would be appropriate.

6. List and describe three popular digital audio formats.

7. List and describe the five steps for producing and distributing digital video.

8. Identify and describe three factors that impact the quality of digital video.

9. What is multicasting? How can multicasting impact the delivery of network-enabled digital media?

10. Describe how network-enabled digital media travels from the server to the desktop.

11. Discuss in detail three business uses for digital media. Provide specific examples to support your discussion.

12. What is usability? What factors combine to determine usability?

13. Briefly describe the Technology Acceptance Model (TAM). How can understanding TAM help you understand the impacts of usability?

14. List and describe Norman's seven stages of action that users go through when interacting with a system.

15. What is the gulf of execution? What is the gulf of evaluation?

16. Identify and describe four areas in which user failures can occur.

17. List and discuss five principles for attaining high usability in e-business systems.

EXERCISES

1. Pick a business model from Chapter 2 (such as the electronic merchant model). Discuss at least three reasons why content is important to organizations using that e-business model. Use concrete examples in your discussion.

2. For each situation below, choose the most appropriate format for text-based content. Justify each of your choices.

(a) The documents are highly formatted. You want users to be able to edit the documents. All users have access to WordPerfect.

(b) The documents are highly formatted. You do want users to be able to edit the documents. Not all users have access to the same word processing software.

(c) The documents are highly formatted. You do *not* want users to be able to edit the documents.

3. For each situation below, choose the most appropriate image format. Justify each of your choices.

(a) You want to post digital photographs on the Web. These photos do not have sharp "edges."

(b) You want to add your company's logo to a Web site. The software you are using to create the logo has all of the appropriate copyrights in place.

(c) You want to add your company's logo to a Web site. The software you are using to create the logo *does not have* all of the appropriate copyrights in place.

HANDS-ON PROJECTS

1. Find sites that mix free and subscription-only content. (Hint: You might try searching for "subscription" in your favorite search engine.) What content technologies do they use? How do they entice visitors to the free site to become subscribers?

2. Visit the Moreover Web site (http://w.moreover.com /webmaster/). Sign up for Moreover's content providing service. Add content from Moreover to a Web site that you have created. How did you decide which content would be appropriate for your Web site? Discuss how having content that is updated daily might increase traffic to your site. Search the Web and find two examples of organizations that use changing text-based content to attract visitors. Discuss each of these in terms of how well you think their content choices attract visitors.

3. Use the Systran service to translate a page from your personal Web page. (Choose a language that you speak or that a friend speaks.) How well did Systran translate the page? Discuss the importance of providing local-language content for e-business Web sites.

4. Visit the World Wide Web Consortium's Web PNG test site (http://www.w3.org/Graphics/PNG/Inline-img.html) to determine if your Web browser fully supports the Portable Network Graphics (PNG) format. Discuss why the PNG format was developed. Compare and contrast PNG with the GIF and JPG formats. Be sure to include the advantages and disadvantages of each format.

5. Locate and download three photographs and three logos from the Web. What formats were used for each image? For each kind of image, discuss the appropriateness of the image format choice.

6. Visit the CD Now Web site or another site as directed by your professor. Locate a CD from an artist you like. Listen to the samples of at least three tracks. For each track, listen to both the RealAudio and Windows Media formats. Which format did you prefer? Why?

7. Visit the Yahoo! Movie Web site. Find a movie trailer or short that is available in at least two different formats. View the movie in at least two different formats. Which format did you prefer? Why?

8. Locate a radio station that broadcasts live or archived shows over the Internet. Spend at least ten minutes listening to the station. What audio format did the station use? Discuss your listening experience. Your discussion should include the type of connection you used (e.g., dial-up) and your assessment of sound quality versus that of a CD and that of a traditional radio broadcast. Did the audio "skip" while you were listening? Adjust the playback buffer of the client software (such as RealPlayer). If skipping was a problem, increase the buffer. If skipping was not a problem, decrease the buffer. Listen to the station again. Were there any differences in performance from the first time you listened? Discuss the purpose of the playback buffer and why adjusting the buffer impacts performance.

9. Search the Web until you find one particularly good site and one particularly poor site in terms of usability. Compare and contrast the sites in terms of usability. What characteristics or features made each site highly usable or unusable? Be sure to use the usability information from the chapter to organize your discussion.

DISCUSSION POINTS

1. Describe a situation in which the content of a Web site lead you to return to that site. Discuss how the content made you want to return. Comment on the nature of the content (text, images, etc.), the quality of the content, and the content's organization.

2. Describe a situation in which the content of a Web site lead you to abandon the site with no intention of returning. Discuss why the content made you not want to return. Comment on the nature of the content (text,

images, etc.), the quality of the content, and the content's organization.

3. Describe a situation in which poor usability leads you to abandon the use of an e-business Web site. In what ways was the Web site's usability poor? Cite specific examples of poor usability that led you to abandon the site.

4. Visit two online merchants assigned by your Professor. Discuss each in terms of usability. Pay particular attention to how well the design of the site matches task flow.

RELATED WEB SITES

Amazon: http://www.amazon.com

Apple's Quick Time: http://www.apple.com/QuickTime /specifications.html

Audible.com: http://www.audible.com

CD Now: http://www.cdnow.com/

Flicker Free: http://www.flickerfree.com/vf.html

Google: http://www.google.com

Jasc software: http://www.jasc.com/

Microsoft Visio: http://www.microsoft.com/office/visio/

Moreover Technologies: http://www.moreover.com

RealMoney.com: http://www.thestreet.com/realmoney/

Rush Limbaugh: http://www.rushlimbaugh.com

SoftLab-nsk: http://www.softlab-nsk.com/index.html

Syntrillium Software Corporation: http://www.syntrillium.com/cooledit/

Systran: http://www.systransoft.com/

TheStreet.com: http://www.thestreet.com

Ticketmaster: http://www.ticketmaster.com

Wall Street Journal: http://www.WSJ.com

Winamp software: http://www.winamp.com/

WMNF radio: http://www.wmnf.org

WUMB radio: http://www.wumb.org

FURTHER READINGS

Content Management

HAKOS, J. *Content Management for Dynamic Web Delivery.* New York: John Wiley and Sons, 2002.

Language Translation

Browse Translation Software page. Translation.net, http://www .translation net/trans.html

Image File Formats

AutoCAD 2000 DXF Reference page. Autodesk, http://www.autodesk .com/techpubs/autocad/acad2000/dxf/.dxf_format.htm.

CompuServe Corporation. "Graphics Interchange Format Version 89a (specification)." RadZone.com, http://www.radzone .org/tutorials/gif89a.txt.

libmng (multiple-image network graphics) page. Triple-T, http: //www.3-t.com/libmng/.

LZW Patent and Software Information page. Unisys Corporation, http://www.unisys.com/unisys/lzw/.

PNG (Portable Network Graphics) page. World Wide Web Consortium, 14 February 1995: http://www.w3.org/Graphics /PNG/.

Audio and Video

BEGGS, JOSH, DYLAN THEDE, AND RICHARD KOMAN. *Designing Web Audio.* Sebastopol, CA: O'Reilly & Associates, 2001.

DAVIS PAN. 1995A Tutorial on MPEG/Audio Compression. *IEEE Multimedia* 2(2): 60–74.

International Organisation for Standardisation. "Overview of the MPEG-4 Standard." Document ISO/IEC JTC1/SC29/WG11 N4668, March 2002. Available at http://mpeg.telecomitalialab.com/standards/mpeg-4/mpeg-4.htm.

Multicast Streaming—An Introduction page. Microsoft Corporation. 13 July 2001: http://www.microsoft.com/ntserver /techresources/streaming/multiwp.asp.

Synchronized Multimedia page. World Wide Web Consortium, http://www.w3.org/AudioVideo/.

REFERENCES

ConsumerMarketingBiz. 2001. Streaming ads beat traditional banners on click throughs, conversions and cost per acquisition. MarketingSherpa, 13 February 2001: http://www.consumermarketingbiz.com/sample.cfm?contentID=1443.

National Cancer Institute. 2002. Usability.gov Web site. Accessed July 11, 2002: http://www.usability.gov/basics/index.html #importance

NIELSEN, JAKOB. 1999. *Designing web usability: The practice of simplicity.* Indianapolis, IN: New Riders Publishing.

NORMAN, DONALD. 1988. *The psychology of everyday things.* New York: HarperCollins.

PASTORE, MICHAEL. 2001. High speed access to pass dial-up in 2005. Internet.com, 22 January 2001: http://cyberatlas .internet.com/markets/broadband/article/0,,10099 _567101,00.html#table.

CHAPTER 10

PRIVACY AND SECURITY IN E-BUSINESS

CHAPTER OBJECTIVES

After reading and completing this chapter, you should be able to:

- Understand the differences between security and privacy
- Identify threats to privacy
- Identify and discuss different technologies and procedures related to privacy in the e-business context
- Identify and discuss security threats in an e-business context
- Understand the differences between preventive, corrective, and detective controls, and between logical and physical security
- Identify and discuss different technologies and procedures related to security in the e-business context
- Discuss security in the context of mobile commerce
- Develop an e-business privacy policy and statement
- Develop an e-business security plan
- Identify a number of security and privacy-focused organizations

---

Opening Case: DoubleClick, Inc.

It all started with a corporate merger in 1999, like many other companies today. DoubleClick, an Internet network advertising company, announced that it was merging with Abacus Direct Corporation, a leading provider of specialized consumer data. DoubleClick provides Internet network advertising and collects anonymous information on online purchasing and browsing habits through cookies (Anstead 2000). In other words, it can collect data on which sites consumers visit, called **clickstream** data, even without the knowledge of the consumers. Other information collected includes users' organization names and sizes, the operating systems of their computers, their preferred browsers, e-mail addresses, and more. As a result, when users click on certain links indicating their interests, appropriate online ads are sent to the pages they are browsing. At the end of 1999, DoubleClick posted ads for more than eighteen hundred companies sending billions of advertisements to consumers. Abacus Direct specializes in collecting and analyzing consumer data for direct marketing. It has a database of eighty-eight million buyer profiles collected by fifteen hundred direct marketers and online retailers, representing more than three billion transactions (Punch 2000). The information contained in the database includes transaction information, as well as information about geographical location, demographics, lifestyle, and behaviors of consumers. And of course, it also includes names, addresses, and phone numbers.

The companies announced that after the merger they would combine the data gathered by DoubleClick, which included anonymous purchasing habits, with personally identifiable information from the Abacus Direct databases. This led to a public uproar. Privacy advocates started filing lawsuits against DoubleClick, followed by the U.S. Federal Trade Commission and a number of state attorneys-general. What privacy advocates and consumers feared was that the companies would be cross-referencing real offline consumer data with online purchasing habits information collected with or without consumers' knowledge. Since they had not given permission to the companies to do so, many consumers thought this was a major violation of their right to privacy. In response to the issues being raised publicly, DoubleClick temporarily stopped their plans to merge the two databases in March 2000, created a new position of chief privacy officer, and established a privacy advisory board. They then hired well-known attorneys and privacy-related public figures for these positions.

In your opinion, were the consumers right to fear the DoubleClick/Abacus merger? Why, or why not? Where do companies like Abacus collect the offline data? What other potential privacy problems can you envision with the growth of the Internet and electronic business? Who or what should protect the privacy of consumers in their dealings with e-businesses? In January 2002, DoubleClick finally announced that it had decided to stop its Web tracking service (Krill 2002).

INTRODUCTION AND DEFINITIONS

Security versus Privacy

Security and **privacy** are said to be two of the biggest concerns regarding electronic business. In reality, both are major concerns for any computerized environment, including businesses, governments, and individuals. Before we can discuss in depth the issues of security and privacy, we need to clearly understand the differences between the two concepts since they are often used interchangeably, even though they are very different. There is a lack of agreement among academicians and practitioners on the extent to which privacy and security issues are conceptually distinct. Some writers use global terms such as **"safeguard assurances"** to represent both privacy and security concerns.

Privacy

Privacy of data can be thought of as the confidentiality of the data collected by businesses or governments about the individuals using their services. We could therefore define privacy as *the ability to manage information about oneself.* Since it is the willingness of consumers to share information over the Internet that allows transactions to be made, the consumers' control over how and what information is shared is the essence of privacy on the Internet.

Security

A **security threat** is defined as a "circumstance, condition, or event with the potential to cause economic hardship to data or network resources in the form of destruction, disclosure, modification of data, denial of service, and/or fraud, waste, and abuse" (Kalakota and Whinston 1996). Security, then, is the protection against these threats. Under this definition, threats can be attacks on network and data transactions or unauthorized access by means of false or defective **authentication.** In considering consumer transactions, it is important to acknowledge that consumer information has value. As such, economic hardship can include damages to privacy (loss of information), as well as theft, (for example, theft of credit information).

In other words, security relates to controlling one's environment for protection of data (Hoffman et al. 1999). Consumers, in the context of security, could be concerned with sharing information online because they fear hackers stealing their information. Privacy refers to controlling the secondary use of information. Consumers, in the context of privacy, could be concerned that once the information is freely submitted to a Web site, there is diminished or nonexistent control over whether and/or how there is further sharing of that information with third parties.

PRIVACY THREATS

The Web is not as anonymous as most people think. Whenever a Web page is browsed, the computer requesting the Web page (the Web surfer's computer) must provide an IP address to the server hosting the Web page, otherwise the server would not know where to send the Web page that is being requested. When the browser contains other personal information, such as an e-mail address, that information is often provided to the server as well. The server can then log all of this information for all visitors to its Web sites. Servers can also track which Web pages each user views. This is called clickstream data, and is the type of data that DoubleClick, in the opening case, was collecting. These elements of data collection, usage tracking, and the sharing of information with third parties are some of the major privacy threats on the Internet.

Data Collection

Collection of data about individuals has always invoked issues of privacy. However, online technology increases the concerns, as it allows for faster and easier storage of more data. It also allows for easier manipulation of that data and cross-referencing at unbelievable speeds (Punch 2000). In addition, in the online world, data collection can occur without the knowledge of the individual.

Faster and Easier Data Collection

Information about consumers was collected before the advent of the Web. Warranty registration cards, for example, were used to glean consumer information. The difference today is that the collection of data can be done faster and easier (and without individuals' knowledge). Current technology allows easy loading of data from forms on Web sites directly into databases. For companies, this is a major advantage, since the data are loaded immediately (faster) and accurately (no transcribing errors and no problems dealing with unreadable writing). Data are also easier to collect since tools have been developed, such as **cookies** (described later in the chapter), for collecting the information from the users, even information average users do not know (such as their IP addresses).

Cross-Referencing (Aggregation)

As you saw in the opening case, one of the biggest public outcries concerning online privacy happened following the merger of DoubleClick and Abacus Direct. Consumers feared that the companies would be cross-referencing real offline consumer data with online purchasing habits (collected with or without their knowledge). This is also called **triangulation** (Melillo 1999). There is also the potential for cross-referencing online data with other online data (between several Web entrepreneurs, for example), which raises other concerns for privacy advocates (Melillo 1999). One example is U.S. Bancorp, which in 1999 rented its customer information to other companies, in conflict with its privacy statement. It settled a legal case, but in doing so stated that it was following "industry-wide practice[s]" (Protecting your financial privacy 2000).

Hidden Data Collection

After the issue of cross-referencing data between online and offline databases, collection of data without consent is the biggest issue privacy advocates are raising with Web sites. Contrary to the "old days" of warranty card registration, data can be collected about individuals without their permission or active participation. As users customize their Web browsers with personal information, they may not realize that this information can be accessed by Web sites they visit and then stored in the Web site's back-end databases or on the users' own machines for later use. Usually this is accomplished by means of cookies.

Usage Tracking

Clickstream data is the term given to data that tracks user surfing habits online. The data can identify the best paths between an ad and an actual online purchase, for example. Since the user's computer sends its IP address to servers as the user browses the Web, it is possible for tracking software to know where the user goes before accessing the current page, where he goes after this site, how often the user comes back to this site, and when the user actually makes purchases from the site. Thorough analysis of this data can then give marketers an indication of successful and unsuccessful online ads, referring sites, and other information on the preferences of each user. Customized ads can also be delivered to the consumer's screen as he is browsing the pages. Interestingly, probably no one would agree to be followed like that in his or her buying decision process in a physical retail store. Imagine someone walking with you and observing you as you stroll through a Wal-Mart and look at various products!

Information Sharing

One of the issues that consumers are quite aware of in today's online world is that companies share and/or sell information about their consumers. Some Web sites offer the opportunity to consumers to **opt-out** of receiving "affiliated or other partner company" offers for products and services. But it becomes the consumer's responsibility to make sure the proper boxes are checked…when the option is offered! So, why then do consumers provide information to Web sites, knowing that they are at risk of having their information not only stored but also shared with other companies? Because in e-business, privacy concerns are often outweighed by the advantages for consumers and businesses. For example, data collection allows personalization and customization of the consumer's interaction with the e-businesses, and allows a more efficient allocation of business resources to meet the needs and desires of the consumer. As a result, consumers often agree to give personal information on the Web if it means they can get better service, convenience, or benefits on that particular Web site. When you go to your favorite shopping Web site, don't you like to see that they remember your size, preferences, or type of preferred accessories? Of course! And, they can even remember your credit card number, saving you laborious typing. But in doing so, they *know* that information about you. It is to your convenience, but even more to theirs.

Privacy Concerns in E-business

Privacy is a major issue for consumers on the Internet. A *Business Week*/Harris poll of 999 consumers in 1998 revealed that privacy was the biggest obstacle preventing them from using Web sites, above the issues of cost, ease of use, and unsolicited marketing (Green, Yang, and Judge 1998). In an IBM multinational consumer privacy survey in 1999 (Harris Interactive 1999), 80 percent of the U.S. respondents felt that they had "lost all control over how personal information is collected and used by companies." 78 percent had refused to give information because they thought it was inappropriate in the circumstance, and 54 percent had decided not to purchase a product because of a concern over the use of their information collected in the transaction. Specifically, 72 percent of U.S. respondents were worried about the collection of information over the Internet. Another study by Forrester Research supports these findings, showing that two-thirds of consumers are worried about protecting personal information online (Branscum 2000). Finally, a recent survey of consumer attitudes toward privacy reported by the Pew Internet & American Life Project (2000) reveals that 66 percent of respondents believe that online tracking should be outlawed, and 81 percent support rules for online information gathering. An impressive 86 percent believe that businesses should ask before collecting information about them **(opt-in).**

TECHNOLOGIES AND SOLUTIONS FOR PRIVACY

Cookies

We have discussed several times already in this chapter the use of cookies and how they can be a threat to privacy. First, it should be noted that cookies are part of the problem with privacy, not the solution. In the mid-1990s, companies wanted to be capable of customizing the shopping experiences of consumers by being able to retain information while a consumer browsed a company's Web pages. The designers of Netscape created text files called cookies as the solution. What are cookies?

A cookie is a text file that is stored on the user's (Web surfer's) hard disk. During a connection, information is sent to the computer's hard disk by the HTTP protocol

E-BUSINESS IN PRACTICE

Opting-out

Strategies for offering opting out options to consumers vary substantially from one organization to the next. In late 2001, for example, banks were required to send notices to their customers about what information they were collecting and how they were sharing it. Customers who did not want the bank to share information with its affiliates had to send written requests to their banks to that effect. Otherwise, information could be shared. The banks also provided Web pages where opting-out requests could be sent. Another common approach for opting-out with e-businesses is to indicate it at the checkout screen by un-checking boxes that indicate the desire to receive promotional or special offers from the company and/or its affiliates. In all cases, opting-out requires that the consumer take the action of requesting that her information not be shared. Privacy advocates are pushing for opting-in options instead, through which consumers would by default be opted out and would have to take action to let companies use their information (for some incentives, for example).

(recall this protocol from Chapter 4), together with a range of Uniform Resource Locators (URLs) for which it is relevant. When the user accesses one of these URLs (within the range) again, the browser transmits all of the information retained in the cookie for those Web sites to the server that the user is currently browsing. Any item used to personalize your experience on the Web uses a set of cookies. Depending on the browser used, the cookies are stored in one or several files. The default location for storing cookies on Windows systems is C:\Windows\Cookies, although it may be somewhere else on your computer. The cookie contains the main user identification and the set of URLs it applies to, and then it can contain anything the server (company) decides to put in! This can include user-selected preferences, IP numbers, personal user-provided information, shopping cart contents, last contact with the company, how much has been bought so far, and so on.

As previously discussed, cookies can be valuable in personalizing the shopping experience of the consumer. The only issue is that the amount and type of information that can be stored in them is almost limitless, creating major threats to privacy. Fortunately, there are a number of applications that have been developed in recent years to manage cookies. These applications read the cookie folder and present the user with the information that is collected. The user can then decide which cookies to keep and which cookies to delete. Table 10-1 lists a few of those cookie management tools.

Cookies are used extensively by e-businesses. In 1999, a survey of 361 Web sites, entitled the Georgetown Internet Privacy Policy Survey (Culnan 2000), revealed that 92.8 percent

Table 10-1 Cookie Management Tools

Name	Description	Creator
Cookie Crusher	Cookie manager	The Limit Software
Cookie Cruncher	Freeware cookie manager	Rendering Better Avenues Software
Cookie Pal	Cookie manager	Kookaburra Software
VacPack	General cleaner with cookie manager	Privacy Software Corporation
Window Washer	General cleaner with cookie manager	Webroot Software

of these sites collected at least one type of personal identifying information (name, e-mail address, or postal address). Of the Web sites, 56.8 percent collected at least one type of demographic information, such as gender, geographic location (zip code), or user preferences. And finally, 56.2 percent of the Web sites collected both types of information (personal identifying and demographic information).

Decision Point

An e-business must decide how it will handle consumer data as well as data about its business partners. The following questions should be answered for both consumers and partners.

- What information do we *need* to collect about them (consumers/partners)?
- What information do we *want* to collect about them?
- Given those, what information *should* we collect about them?
- How will we collect information?
  - Will we use cookies?
  - Will we only collect information when they voluntarily fill out forms?
- Should we include a privacy statement on our Web pages?
- What information about the above decisions will we include in our privacy statement?

Privacy Statement or Policy

One way that consumers have to be knowledgeable about the possible consequences of dealing with a Web merchant (if not protect themselves) is the **privacy policy** or **statement.** This statement should discuss the privacy policy of the Web merchant regarding the data collected and their subsequent use. It should be easily accessible through a link clearly visible on the first page (home page) of the merchant's Web site. Some companies show this link at the bottom of their home page, in small type, while others show it at the top of their home page. However, many Web sites do not even have privacy policies. In the 1999 Georgetown survey discussed previously, only 65.9 percent of the 361 Web sites polled had a privacy disclosure. **Trust seals,** discussed next, and government regulations are two forces pushing for more and better privacy disclosures on Web sites. Trust seals promote privacy in the form of self-regulation by industry, while government regulation takes the form of legislation, forcing companies into better privacy practices.

Trust Seals

One way that companies have tried to reassure consumers about transacting with them online has been the use of Web site seals. The idea is that some company or organization develops a Web seal program with a logo that participants can affix on their Web sites if they follow certain rules. These seals are then supposed to instill consumer confidence in the Web site. Examples of these seals include the Better Business Bureau online (BBBOnLine), AICPA WebTrust, and TRUSTe (Figure 10-1). A number of other

E-BUSINESS IN PRACTICE

Privacy Policy from REI.com

The following states REI policy regarding the privacy rights of visitors to this website. We respect your right to privacy and your desire for a secure online shopping experience.

This is a website of REI (Recreational Equipment Inc.)

Our postal address is:

6750 South 228th Street
Kent, WA 98032-4803

We can be reached via e-mail at service@rei.com or by telephone at 1-800-426-4840 (within the USA and Canada), or 1-253-891-2500 outside the USA.

Information We Collect and How It's Used

Domain Names

When a visitor comes to our website, our web server recognizes only the visitor's domain name, but not the e-mail address. This means that we can track visits to our site, while visitors remain anonymous.

Cookies

Cookies are pieces of data your web browser stores on your hard drive. We use cookies so we can recognize you when you pay a repeat visit to our website. Cookies let us personalize your shopping experience based on your preferences.

Most browsers accept cookies. However, if you wish, you can usually set them to refuse cookies. If you set your browser to refuse cookies, you will not be able to submit an order online. REI.com does not use cookies to gather any personal information.

Aggregate Information

We collect aggregate information on visits made to our pages. This information helps us improve the content of our site. We also track which websites refer visitors to REI.com.

Other Information We Collect

When you purchase a product on REI.com, we ask you for the following information: name, address, phone number, e-mail address and credit card. This information is used to process and follow up on your order. All information we collect from you is stored in a secure database.

REI also collects e-mail addresses voluntarily provided to us for subscriptions to Gearmail, Hot Values and/or Bargain Sleuth. We sometimes use list-serve e-mails to notify customers about updates and special features on our website.

About Children

For their protection, we ask that children do not submit information to us without the consent of a parent or guardian.

Secure Shopping

We use Verisign as our SSL (Secure Socket Layer) digital certificate provider, providing our customers the strongest certificate services available. Your credit card information is encrypted while traveling the Internet.

Disclosure of Information Policy

We never make your e-mail address available to any other company or organization without your permission.

If you supply us with your postal address, you may receive periodic mailings from REI with information on new products and services or upcoming events. If you do not wish to receive such mailings, please let us know by sending an e-mail, calling or writing us at the above address.

If you have supplied us with your postal address, we may share your name and address with companies we believe may interest you. If you prefer not to receive such mailings from other companies, please let us know by sending an e-mail, calling or writing us at the above address.

Need to Make a Change?

If you would like to change any of your transactional information in our database please feel free to contact us. You'll find our e-mail address, phone number and address at the top of this page.

REI co-op members may also specify mailing preferences by visiting the Mailing Options page on our website.

SOURCE: REI.com Privacy Policy page, REI, http://www.rei.com/reihtml/privacy.html. © Recreational Equipment, Inc. 2001.

FIGURE 10-1 Some Internet Trust Seals

SOURCE: © TRUSTe. Used with permission.

The BBBOnLine Privacy seal is a trademark of the Council of Better Business Bureaus, Inc.

seals exist on the Internet. For example, there is the VeriSign program, which is mostly for security through encryption and authentication products (these products will be discussed later in the chapter), or the International Computer Security Association's (ICSA) seal. Meeting privacy standards is only one requirement for some of the trust seal programs. Table 10-2 compares some of the requirements for businesses that want to display three of the trust seals previously presented. They are also described in more depth below.

The AICPA WebTrust seal program was specifically started to address consumer concerns about privacy and security on the Internet. It focuses on disclosure of not only what information is collected and how it will be used, but also on business practices of the company. It requires a thorough examination of the Web site by a certified public accountant or a chartered accountant.

BBBOnLine, a subsidiary of the well-established Better Business Bureau, administers the BBBOnLine seal, which is a private, nonprofit organization that promotes ethical business standards and voluntary self-regulation. While it promotes the idea that companies using this seal are good citizens, the program does not specifically address privacy and security online. It does require, however, that the company be in business for at least one year before being eligible to receive the seal.

TRUSTe is also administered by a nonprofit organization. It focuses on promoting online privacy. The role of the seal on a company's Web site is to reassure consumers that the company follows the set of self-regulating rules established by TRUSTe for the collection and use of private and personal information.

Table 10-2 Comparison of Some Web Site Seals

	AICPA WebTrust	**BBBOnLine**	**TRUSTe**
Fee?	■ Yes (high)	■ Yes (low)	■ Yes (low)
Policies	■ Web site must be examined thoroughly before seal can be affixed	■ Web site must follow BBB advertising ethics and policies	■ Web site must agree to site compliance reviews
Disclosures required	■ Yes; Business practices, transaction integrity, and information protection must be disclosed	■ No	■ Yes; Easily understandable and easy to find privacy statement
Consumer redress	■ Options for redress must be disclosed	■ Promptly handle consumer complaints ■ Agree to binding arbitration ■ Mechanisms for complaints provided	■ Promptly handle consumer complaints ■ Mechanisms for complaints provided

Decision Point

Once an e-business has made decisions regarding what practices it will follow with respect to the privacy of its consumers and partners, it needs to promote the fact that it follows such practices. Two ways to do this are having a strong written privacy policy available online and applying for trust seals. Some questions that can help guide management in doing this include:

- What should be included in our privacy policy?
- Where should our privacy policy be located?
- On which pages of our Web site do we want to have links to our privacy policy?
- Should we apply for trust seals? Which ones?
- How many trust seals should we use?

Government Regulations

Various government agencies have been active in the development of the Internet privacy policies or principles. For example, the U.S. Federal Trade Commission's (FTC) standard for privacy on the Internet requires that notice be properly given (having a clear privacy statement indicating what information is collected and how it will be used), choices be offered (to opt-out of personal information being shared or used), access be offered (to review the personal information and correct it if there are errors), and appropriate security (protection of the personal information) be provided as elements of a desirable privacy policy. Recent public outcries regarding online privacy have accelerated governments' involvement. In some areas of the world, there are laws protecting the privacy of citizens. For example, the European Union has strict online privacy laws that Web site operators must follow.

Privacy on the Internet is not a new issue. In 1986, the U.S. government enacted the Electronic Communication Privacy Act (ECPA) to protect access and disclosure to certain electronic communication content. In 1993, the government established the Information Infrastructure Task Force to lead the development of the National Information Infrastructure (NII). One of its task forces, the Privacy Working Group, prepared the report "Privacy and the National Information Infrastructure: Principles for Providing and Using Personal Information" (1995).

The task force recommended that the proposed principles for privacy apply to both public and commercial uses of private information. It defined information privacy as requiring respect for individual privacy, disallowing improper alteration or destruction of information, and ensuring that the information held is accurate, timely, complete, and relevant. The task force also recommended principles for providers and users of information. For providers of information (for example a consumer shopping on the Web), the principles include:

- Awareness—Individuals have a personal responsibility to obtain information about which data are collected and how they will be used.
- Empowerment—Individuals should have a way to access, correct, and technically control their information, and to be anonymous in certain cases.

■ Redress—Individuals should take action when harm occurs.

Principles for users of information (for example, companies that collect consumer data) include:

■ Impact assessment—Users of information should evaluate the impact on information providers of using their information.

■ Only reasonably necessary—Users should only use information that is necessary.

■ Notice—Users should provide information on why information is collected, what information is collected, which protections are offered, what consequences could result, and what redresses are available to the providers of information.

■ Security—Users of information should provide security measures to protect the data.

■ Limited use—Users of information should limit their use to the level of the individuals' understanding of that use.

■ Education—Users of information should provide education for providers of information and the public in general regarding privacy and collection of data.

Since then, there have been several reports and studies by various governments and agencies worldwide emphasizing the importance of protecting consumer privacy and security of data in the online world. Interestingly, while the U.S. government wants to protect the privacy of its citizens, it also creates its own privacy worries for citizens by eavesdropping on network transmissions. A program originally called Carnivore, now called DCS1000, is an e-mail sniffing software that captures data packets passing through Internet service providers (ISPs). To install the box that runs the Carnivore software at an ISP's site, FBI agents must first obtain a warrant, similar to obtaining a warrant for a wiretap. The software then monitors all transmissions coming from or going to a specific IP address they are targeting. Privacy advocates worry, however, that other e-mail messages could be randomly monitored once the software has been installed at an ISP. Legislation passed in the summer of 2001 requires the federal government to reveal how many times law enforcement used DCS1000, the workings of the approval process to use it, and whether it allowed gathering of any unauthorized information (Bowman 2001).

SECURITY THREATS

Most people think of illegal access to files and personal data when they think of security. However, security is much broader. It includes dealing with natural disasters, such as earthquakes and fires, as well as dealing with any threats to computerized systems, such as **viruses** or hackers.

Security has always been a chief concern of organizations. However, it seems that lately we hear more and more about security issues. Why is that? As nations and corporations have increased the reach of their telecommunication networks, increased the availability of systems, and provided access to far more people, they have increased the opportunities for security breaches. At the same time, they have become more and more dependent on computers and networks for day-to-day business operations, as well as for personal dealings. Today, several companies exist solely for the purpose of disseminating information online, and they obviously would not exist without the existence of computer systems. Think of Yahoo! or eBay. They would not exist without computers and networks. If the networks are down, because of technical failures or malicious hackers, the companies lose money—a lot of money. Banks are now conducting most of their transactions using online networks. If its network is down, a bank can lose millions and millions of U.S. dollars, euros, or other currency—*per day!* In addition, security breaches do not just cause monetary losses, they can also cause loss of customer trust, which in turn may result in loss of future business with current and potential customers.

What makes the Internet different from previous technologies with respect to security? Why do we suddenly feel threatened in our security and privacy with this network? In reality, giving your credit card number to a store over your cordless phone may be less secure than sending it over the Internet. So why don't we worry about it? Because we rarely hear about phone hackers. Accessing telephone transmissions provides one set of consumer data at a time, and it is not worth the effort. And the challenge of "breaking the codes" is not there. In the case of the Internet, however, there has been a proliferation of hackers whose focus is on breaking codes and accessing private and confidential information. By breaking into just one main commercial server, a hacker can access the financial and personal information of several thousand individuals at the same time. Since these stories are then publicized widely, everyone has been made aware of security threats on the Internet.

There are a large number of security threats to businesses and other organizations in the online environment. There are active threats (modification to the data or systems) and passive threats (monitoring or scanning information). In the case of passive threats, information can be released, used for fraudulent purposes, or analyzed for patterns. Another way to classify security threats is to divide them into three categories: denial of service, unauthorized access, and theft and fraud. **Denial of service** threats are those that render a system inoperative or limit its capability to operate. **Unauthorized access** threats are individuals accessing systems and/or data illegally. Theft and fraud threats are similar to those present in the offline world.

Denial of Service

Denial of service can result from disruptions, natural disasters, or malicious acts. Disruptions occur because of equipment or software failures (a router failure, for instance) or human errors (a construction crew cuts a network cable, for instance). They can reduce the capacity of the computer systems or network services, or completely stop operations. They are not typically the result of security breaches, though. There are exceptions to this, of course. For example, vandalism can occur, such as a disgruntled employee reformatting a server's main drive or starting a fire in the organization's computer room. These are threats that companies take very seriously.

Most of the time, disasters are not caused by individuals or systems. They tend to be natural events, such as earthquakes, tornadoes, hurricanes, or fires, which can completely destroy systems.

Finally, but not least, malicious acts perpetrated by individuals can result in denial of service. These acts are categorized as denial of service attacks, and their purpose is destruction, shutdown, or degradation of a system. We will discuss two primary types of denial of service attacks: **spamming** and viruses.

Spamming or E-mail Bombing

The term "spamming" has several meanings. The first is the sending of e-mails to many individuals at once. A second use of the term refers to sending unsolicited commercial e-mail to individuals. This is not necessarily harmful, but it is annoying. However, spamming has another definition—a hacker targeting one individual computer or network, and sending thousands of messages to it. This is a major security threat because it will fill the target's mailboxes and flood communication ports and memory buffers, effectively blocking legitimate messages from entering the mailbox or system. This is also called **e-mail bombing** when the messages being sent are e-mail messages. Other spamming attacks use control messages, such as synchronization (SYN) messages.

When a hacker uses an innocent third party to multiply the messages being sent to the intended target, such as a university server, this is called **smurfing.** To do this, hackers place software agents on the innocent third party's computer. These programs will then help them launch their attacks when they decide to strike. In early 2000, Yahoo!, eBay, Buy.com, Amazon.com, E*TRADE, and CNN.com were all targets of denial of service attacks. Smurfing allowed millions of packets to be sent to their servers. These attacks are also called **distributed denial of service attacks (DDOS),** because a number of computers are used for the attacks (the attacks are distributed among many "innocent" servers). Hackers typically select particular servers because they do not have firewalls or other protection from outside access. This happens very often with university research computers, which tend to be powerful, but not as protected as business computers (Radcliff 2001).

Why would anyone perform such malicious acts? Some may be disgruntled employees. Others may attack a given target for political reasons, for example, protesting a company's stand on some issue. A group of hackers, calling themselves the Cult of the Dead Cow, promotes hacking into systems as a way to serve human rights. They call their actions "hactivism," finding hidden, obscure, and important information. Their focus is on finding information that, if revealed, will advance human causes. However, denial of service attacks by hackers are very damaging to companies, mostly from an economic point of view. Any downtime in the computer systems or networks can mean lost sales and lost revenues for companies, or major losses in productivity if employees cannot perform their normal duties.

Viruses, Worms, and Trojan Horses

It was 1987; an e-mail message showing a nice Christmas tree appeared on a computer. It was during the Christmas season and the *christma.exe* file didn't look suspicious, until the person receiving it noticed that the system was resending the message to all of the fifteen hundred names in his address book. That's when the file wished him a Merry Christmas and disappeared, but not without leaving the employee slightly panicked. A few minutes later all employees were warned by security personnel to unplug their modems, but it was too late. This virus had infiltrated the internal communication network at the Thomas J. Watson laboratory of the IBM Corporation in New York, blocking all communication for almost twenty-four hours. This was one of the first major worldwide "outbreaks" of a computer virus. Since then, viruses have been a nightmare for all information technology security managers, and numerous users worldwide.

Viruses are computer programs designed to perform unwanted events. Some cause minor harm, such as sending undesirable messages. Others are very destructive, deleting all files on a computer or creating so much traffic on a network that it crashes and cannot be used by its customary users. Viruses have become major problems for all types of organizations and for individuals who get them on their home computers. According to an article by Lee Dembart in the *International Herald Tribune* entitled, "Anti-Virus Update: Makers of Protective Software Try to Get Ahead of Scofflaws" (16 April 2001), there are as many as five hundred new computer viruses released every month. The article estimated that the "love bug" virus that infected numerous organizations worldwide in 2000 may have infected as many as forty-five million computers and done U.S.$6.7 billion worth of damage. In 1999, the Melissa virus also caused worldwide problems. In 2001, it was the Anna Kournikova virus.

Viruses attach themselves to programs or files, which, when loaded or executed, allow the virus to spread and cause damage. **Worms** are special viruses that spread using direct Internet connections, and **Trojan horses** are spread by being disguised as legitimate software and tricking users into running the program. They travel to other computers most often by e-mail. An example of a worm is the program called Adore, which scans the Internet for Linux machines. There are four well-known vulnerabilities in a standard Linux software installation that the program looks for. If it finds a host with one of those vulnerabilities, it installs a copy of itself and creates a back door to give the hacker access to the system. This happens because many administrators do not "plug" the holes that exist in the software when it is shipped or downloaded, either because they do not know of the holes or they don't have time to take care of this "maintenance" task. A problem with Trojans is that users can be infected just by browsing the Web if malicious ActiveX controls are present on Web sites they visit. The Trojan horse would even get through a firewall (discussed later in the chapter) because the user is a legitimate user of the organization's system. Trojan horses have therefore become major concerns for organizations. In a 2001 survey, *Information Security* magazine reported that 90 percent of 2,545 respondents indicated that they had been hit by worms, viruses, or Trojans during the previous year (Costello 2001).

Viruses, being software programs, have particular bit patterns that can be recognized, which is how virus detection software knows your computer has contracted a virus. Some common virus types include:

- **Parasitic virus**—This virus attaches itself to files and replicates itself when the files have been loaded. It is the most common type of virus.

- **Boot sector virus**—This virus is loaded on a floppy disk and gets into the computer when the disk is loaded.

- **Stealth virus**—This is a more advanced virus that changes its own bit pattern to become undetectable by virus scanners.

- **Polymorphic virus**—This virus changes itself every time it infects a computer. By mutating this way, the virus is more difficult to detect.

- **Macro virus**—This virus affects macro applications (such as those found in word processors and spreadsheets) when the macros are executed.

There are also **virus hoaxes** on the Internet. These are not viruses, but false virus alerts being sent and resent by individuals. Their consequences include either substantial unnecessary network traffic, or unwanted actions by users (for example, telling users that certain files must be deleted to avoid the virus). Usually, hoaxes are propagated by unsophisticated users who panic at the idea that they might have caught a virus.

One way that companies have tried to deal with potential denial-of-service attacks is by sharing the data and processing loads between several servers. In particular, this can be applied to Web servers, allowing multiple copies of a Web site to operate on several servers on the Internet. If one of these servers becomes a target for a denial-of-service attack, the Web site could continue to operate from its other servers.

Unauthorized Access

Unauthorized access is a serious security threat for organizations. It refers to illegal access to systems, applications, or data. One of the biggest worries for organizations is theft of data, including customer information, trade secrets, or other important information regarding the organization, its business partners, or employees.

The most colorful image of unauthorized access is the lone marginal hacker who tries to access an organization's data files to do something good for the world or to prove he can. The reality, however, is that unauthorized access is often perpetrated by insiders with enough knowledge to get into the systems and obtain important information, such as credit card numbers. Some incidences of unauthorized access are more difficult to identify because they are passive, such as listening to communications in the hopes of finding trade secrets or scoops. However, **passive unauthorized access** should not be taken lightly, as it can cause much damage in the long run. Imagine a hacker that eavesdrops on transmissions communicating password information. She now has "legitimate" access information to the company's computer systems. **Active unauthorized access** involves modifying the system or data being hacked. For example, numbers or values can be changed (to create fraudulent transfers of money, for instance). Another active threat, classified as a **message stream modification** threat, is when the intent of the communication is changed. In this case, a hacker could change communications to abort or delay negotiations on an important contract, for example.

If a hacker actually assumes someone else's identity online, he is said to be **masquerading** or **spoofing.** Spoofing is the term used to refer to sending a message that appears to be from someone else. Basic spoofing in an e-mail message can be done by simply changing the information in the "From" line to reflect the name of the person the hacker wants to impersonate. However, this is not very sophisticated and the hacker can be easily caught. More advanced spoofing is done at the IP level; the message's source IP address is changed to look like another address. This is done by manipulating the information in the data packet, particularly the address fields, to change the source and/or destination address to make it look like a legitimate third party's address. Spoofing IP addresses is frequently done by hackers launching spamming denial of service attacks.

There is also software that can be used to access data illegally. Downloadable **sniffers** exist on the Internet for this purpose. The software is first installed on a user's station. If this personal computer has access to the organizations' intranet or has any open connection on the Internet, the user can run the software to monitor transmissions, capturing unauthorized data of interest.

Software and Operating Systems' Security Holes

All operating systems have security holes. It usually takes very little time after the release of a new operating system or a new version of an existing operating system for somebody to identify the security holes. Fixes are then developed as quickly as possible and made available to users via download on the software developers' Web pages. Unfortunately, many users and even security managers do not pay attention to these holes, or are not made aware of them. Security holes are not always as easy to fix as downloading a patch, however. It is actually one of the main responsibilities of e-business managers to keep up with the multitude of patches that have been applied, and must be applied, to their systems, which can be very time consuming.

Theft and Fraud

Theft and fraud are two major security threats that affect companies. We have already discussed theft of data via unauthorized access. When these data are used and/or modified, fraud can occur. Illegal transfers of money or individuals taking advantage of holes in security systems to generate checks to themselves are frequent occurrences of this type of fraud.

Companies also have to deal with theft of software and hardware. Typically, theft of software occurs when employees copy legitimate software installed on their companies' servers to bring home or to give to someone else. These copies do not carry licenses and are therefore illegal copies. This is a major concern for organizations, and many have started to perform audits of installed software. The best control for this problem, though, is user education. Most employees do not see a problem with copying software this way, although it is illegal. They need to be educated on this issue. Other companies have taken more stringent methods of dealing with this issue by installing network computers. Recall from Chapter 6 that network computers are stripped down personal computers with no floppy disk drives and less storage because the servers perform most of the work in this environment (thin client approach).

Theft of hardware is a major issue today because computers have become smaller and more portable. Laptop theft is considered a top security issue for information technology managers. The advent of handheld devices, such as the Palm Pilot, makes theft of computer hardware an even bigger problem. Besides the hardware itself, companies fear that the data contained in these devices are easily accessible to whoever has stolen the equipment, since most of them have little or no protection in case of theft. To a lesser extent, companies also have to deal with theft of mice, keyboards, monitors, power surge bars, and so on.

Summary of Security Threats

Before a manager can evaluate security measures and come up with a proper security plan, she must identify all of the threats to security that her organization faces. We have presented some of the most common security threats in this section. There are, however, other threats to security that can occur without malicious intent. For example, errors in programming or data entry can cause serious damage to some systems. Another issue that companies have to deal with that often falls on the security personnel, although it has little to do with security, is the tendency of employees to abuse their access to the Internet. Companies worry that employees will spend hours performing non-work-related tasks on the Web, checking on their stocks, their favorite sports teams, or their vacation plans. Table 10-3 summarizes some of the security threats described in this section.

Which of the security threats are the most common? Several surveys are conducted each year to identify the main sources of security breaches. Figure 10-2 presents the results of a July 2001 survey on computer attacks and misuse. Not surprisingly, viruses are the number one issue, followed by employee abuse of Internet access and laptop

Table 10-3 Summary of Security Threats

Maliciously Intended	Accidental
■ Theft of hardware	■ Disasters
■ Theft of software (illegal copying)	■ Equipment failure/unavailability
■ Unauthorized access to data (theft), systems, applications	■ Software bugs
■ Vandalism	■ Errors and omissions in data entry
■ Fraud, extortion	■ Lost messages
■ Viruses, worms, Trojan horses	
■ Denial of service	

theft. This reinforces the notion that very often security breaches are committed by individuals inside the organization. The survey of 538 security professionals in U.S. corporations published by the Computer Security Institute and the FBI's Computer Intrusion Squad on the risks of doing e-business also reveals that 64 percent of the responding companies had been victims of some form of unauthorized access, while 11 percent of the companies said they didn't know if they had. Some of the quantifiable losses (only 35 percent could quantify the value of the financial losses due to the security breaches)

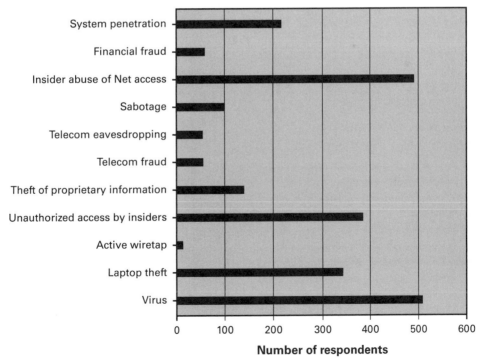

FIGURE 10-2 Computer Security Institute/FBI 2001 Survey of Security Threats

SOURCE: Computer Security Institute, "2001 Computer Crime and Security Survey," http://www.gocsi.com/forms/fbi/pdf.html.

include U.S.$151.2 million from theft of proprietary information and U.S.$92.9 million from fraud. The total projected losses for 2001 were U.S.$377.8 million, a major increase from the U.S.$265.6 million lost in 2000.

Security threats and concerns are similar worldwide. For example, a survey of security directors in Asian corporations revealed that their top ten security issues were similar to those of their U.S. counterparts (see Table 10-4). There are, however, some threats that U.S. corporations rarely consider as top priority, while managers in other areas of the world must take them into consideration. Political unrest and regional instability are two examples. Other examples of unique threats include natural disasters in areas prone to those, or civil unrest in other areas, all of which can cause business interruptions.

▶ Decision Point

A company needs to regularly assess all of the security threats it faces. Some of the following questions might help management identify the e-business' greatest security threats.

- ▪ Are we subject to disasters (flooding, earthquakes, hurricanes, etc.)?
- ▪ Are we subject to unauthorized access from employees? Outsiders?
- ▪ Are we subject to internal virus attacks? External virus attacks?
- ▪ Are we subject to denial of service attacks?
- ▪ Are we at risk of internal fraud and theft? External?
- ▪ Are we at risk of equipment failures, software bugs, user errors, or omissions?
- ▪ Is our operating software properly "patched" for security?

SECURITY TECHNOLOGIES AND SOLUTIONS

Table 10-4 Top Security Issues for Asia-Pacific Region Security Directors in Rank Order

- ▪ Internet/intranet security
- ▪ Business interruption/disaster recovery
- ▪ Kickbacks
- ▪ Insurance fraud
- ▪ Business espionage/trade secrets theft
- ▪ Inadequate security guarding services
- ▪ Intellectual property/piracy/counterfeiting
- ▪ Political unrest/regional instability
- ▪ Employee selection/screening concerns
- ▪ Illegal sales commissions
- ▪ General employee theft
- ▪ Embezzlement

SOURCE: "The Threat from the Net," *Asian Business* 36 (11): 34.

Preventive, Corrective, and Detective Controls

Once security threats are identified, it is possible to establish security measures or controls to deal with those threats. Security controls can be categorized as preventive, detective, or corrective. **Preventive controls** are intended to stop or limit the security breach/problem from happening. Examples include virus scan programs that alert users of viruses in files before they are opened, and requiring users to have IDs and passwords to access an organization's systems. **Detective controls** are meant to find or discover security threats or problems. Examples include **audit logs,** which are used to track individuals using a system; software programs that can scan for unexpected actions to detect potential hackers; and **virus check programs,** which can be used to scan diskettes before they are used. **Corrective controls** are used to correct a security issue or problem. An example is recovery software that is used to "remember" where the user was when the network shut down, and reinstate the user to the same application, hopefully having saved most of the user's data. Another example is, yet again, the virus check program, which can be used to fix or delete a virus from a file.

Disaster Recovery

As discussed early in the chapter, security refers not only to protecting resources from crimes, but also protecting them from disasters and destruction. These events can include floods, tornadoes, someone spilling coffee on the main server while it is running, and so on. While it is beyond the scope of this book to discuss disaster recovery procedures in depth, it is important to consider a **disaster recovery** plan as part of an e-business security plan (discussed at the end of the chapter). It should be noted that, as with pretty much every aspect of an e-business, a disaster recovery package can be outsourced to a specialized firm.

The most important feature of a recovery plan is redundancy. It is the absolute key to recovery. The following list identifies redundant equipment that can be used to protect against loss of data or information.

- *Fault-tolerant systems*—These are systems in which several processors run the same operations concurrently. Should one computer fail, everything keeps running on the other computer. All transactions, data, and processing is done on both systems at the same time. These dual systems are found within the same physical box.

- *Mirrored disks*—This involves duplicating storage disks. Every piece of data is written in two (or more) places at the same time, and is modified concurrently. This means that every action taken on every piece of data is reflected on multiple sets of data. An example of this is the RAID technology discussed in Chapter 6.

- *Disk duplexing*—This involves using two or more disk controllers. Disk controllers manage access to disk storage devices.

- *Multiple lines*—When a connection is required between two buildings or sites, multiple lines can be leased, even if the capacity of one would be sufficient for the data transfers. If one line fails, data transfers are moved onto one of the functioning lines.

- *Different networks*—When communication is crucial, it can be important not to rely on only one type of network. For example, a company can lease a high-speed line (T-1) between its two remote offices, but lease a satellite link in case the line breaks (e.g., a worker cuts all cables leaving the building during road construction in front of the building).

- *Additional devices*—Redundancy can be applied to all devices in the network, including routers, hubs, backup devices, communication controllers, etc.

- *Uninterrupted power supply (UPS)*—One of the key resources needed to run a computer network is electricity. Companies with critical networks must ensure that they continue running in the event of power failures. In this case, the use of a UPS unit is necessary. UPS units were discussed in Chapter 6.

Finally, redundancy must also exist in data for recovery from certain types of disasters to be possible. This is accomplished through backups. Complete backups of all systems and files should be run periodically. **Incremental backups** that contain only changed information since the last full backup should be done daily or even more often for some types of electronic businesses. If the type of data collected is very important and has a long life (for example, contract information), the backups should be stored in off-site secure locations.

Decision Point

An e-business' management must evaluate the preparedness of the business for handling disasters. Some of the questions that may help them evaluate their preparedness include:

- Do we have redundant equipment for key equipment?
- Do we have redundancy in our key software systems?
- Do we have redundant data in the form of backups?
- Do we have a backup site to go to in case of a disaster?
- Are our employees ready to handle a disaster (have they been trained to deal with a disaster and informed of the disaster recovery plan)?

Physical Access Control

Access to data, applications, or systems can be controlled physically or logically. This section will deal with **physical access controls.** When a hacker wants to access a company's system, there are basically three points of access: accessing a computer from within the organization (physical access), dialing into one of the organization's servers (logical access), or remotely accessing the organization's network (logical access). One of the most obvious means of securing data and systems is to lock computer systems away. Large organizations have mainframe or server rooms well protected by security systems. These systems include magnetic cards or other forms of identity control (such as fingerprinting) for entry into the room. The room is typically located in a less disaster-prone area (no windows, not in a basement, etc.), has temperature control, may have surveillance cameras, and has halon fire suppression systems (to prevent substantial damage to the equipment in case of a fire). Simple policies should also be established to protect the equipment from unintentional disasters, such as coffee spills on a main server.

A second level of physical security, besides access to the room or building, is actual locks on computers. This becomes especially important since, as previously discussed, theft is one of the most prominent security crimes today. Laptops, for example, are very easy to steal. So are computer disks with sensitive data. Locking away disks and computer equipment is often the only effective means of controlling access to them. This is common at universities, which should lock the doors to their computer laboratories, as well as lock the computers themselves, to prevent theft of valuable equipment.

Finally, an aspect of physical security that is rarely considered by newcomers in the security game is the selection of personnel. As discussed in the security threats section of this chapter, insider theft and fraud is one of the biggest security issues for corporations today. Ensuring that only proper personnel have access to main computer systems, networks, and data is an important security feature. Companies should run background checks on such personnel. In addition, these employees have to be educated about the security risks to the company so that they will not let others into secure facilities without authorization. A 2000 survey by PriceWaterhouseCoopers revealed that companies consider on-site contractors a major threat to security.

Computers locked inside an organization are easier to control physically than networks or computer systems outside the organization. Network components (bridges, routers, terminals, etc.) are the hardest to protect, although some controls exist (by shutting down target components when appropriate, for example). Eavesdropping over physical cables can be easily done if the cables are coaxial or twisted pair (made out of copper). Fiber optic cables are harder to access.

When outside computers are allowed to dial into the organization's servers, there is a great risk of intruders being able to access the company's systems and data. One physical control for dial-in systems is the use of **call-back modems.** These modems are programmed so that, when a user with proper authorization dials into the computer system, the modem will hang up after authorization verification and call the user back at a predetermined phone number. For example, if your university has such a system and a student tries to access your account information (the student has obtained your user ID and password), the modem will hang up and call your home computer before any applications can be accessed. So, unless this student also has access to your home computer in your home, your data are secure. There are several variations of this type of hardware available today (with magnetic cards used with the dialing-in computer to verify the identity of the caller, for example). We will discuss several other means of limiting logical access to systems, such as user profiles and firewalls, in our discussion of logical security.

Logical Access Controls

Controlling access to data and systems requires that individuals be differentiated from one another, and that only authorized individuals gain access. There are three levels of security controls that are available to control identification of authorized individuals: possession, knowledge, and trait. Using these, user profiles can be created to control unauthorized access to systems and data.

- ■ Possession refers to an individual owning a form of identification. For example, your driver's license is a form of identification; so are your student ID card and your passport. While there is a picture of the individual on most identity cards, it is fairly easy to borrow someone's identification card, making this the lowest level of security available. For example, if a student uses his friend's student ID card to borrow a book at the library and these two students have similar physical traits, the librarian may not notice that the picture does not match the person, and allow the book to be borrowed by the wrong student.

- ■ Knowledge means that the security control requires knowledge on the part of the individual. This is the case if you need, for example, a user identification number and a password to enter a computerized system. This provides better security than the first level. Ideally, combining levels one and two, such as requiring the use of a personal identification number (PIN) with an ATM card, provides even more security. Only the individual should know his PIN.

- The third level of security is physical traits; a particular trait, such as a fingerprint or a retinal pattern, is used to control access to physical spaces, data, or systems. This is part of biometrics, which will be described in more depth later in the chapter.

User Profiles

The most common form of controlling unauthorized access is the **user profile.** Users are assigned profiles that consist of a user identification, a password, and a set of privileges. The user identification (ID) is either selected by the user or assigned by the organization responsible for storing and protecting the information. Identification could also be verified by physical traits (see **biometrics** below). The user must state her identification and the related password or personal identification number (PIN) to enter the system. In many cases, only certain privileges are given to various users, and these privileges define the type of access that each user has. For example, database administrators can define the view for each type of user. **Views** are images of the actual data in the database that can be restricted to include only certain fields, and they usually do not allow users to modify the actual data.

While the password is the most common form of unauthorized access control, it is also a very weak control. Because users tend to have too many passwords, they often use words or numbers that are easy to remember, or they write them down. These passwords can then easily be "found" by the wrong people. For example, users often use the names of their pets, family members, dates (birthday), or important numbers (SSN), or use keyboard patterns (e.g., QWERTY or ZXCV) for passwords. Very often employees write their passwords on sticky notes placed just above their desks, or on sheets of paper taped to the inside of their desk drawers. Even computer specialists are not immune to using unsafe passwords. For example, several years ago, the most popular passwords among network specialists were "god" and "king."

To increase the level of security provided by user IDs and passwords, security managers can force users to change their passwords regularly (e.g., monthly, quarterly, etc.). They may also prevent users from using words found in the dictionary, or restrict the minimum and maximum size of passwords. The best passwords today contain a mix of uppercase letters, lower case letters, and numbers. Finally, security managers may also limit the number of attempts a user can make to enter a system (with the wrong password) before "freezing" that user account. Security managers can also configure users' systems to log off automatically after some time of inactivity on the system. One way to increase security beyond user profiles is to force users to use a smart card in addition to a password. Educating users on how to select passwords and how to handle them is also very important. Password-cracking tools that verify if users have strong passwords exist on the Internet.

Biometrics

Biometrics offer a higher level of security than possession (e.g., licenses) and knowledge (e.g., PIN) because they require the use of a physical trait. Biometrics are technologies that use human features to recognize individuals and grant them access. Fingerprinting is a low-cost example of biometric technology. Other biometrics include facial recognition (faceprints), iris and retina recognition (eyeprints), hand recognition, signature recognition, thermal imaging, and voice recognition (voiceprints). Obviously, some of these methods are more expensive than others, and some of them are more secure than others. Table 10-5 shows a comparison of these various biometric approaches.

Table 10-5 Comparison of Some Biometric Technologies

Biometric Approach	Cost for one Computer	Advantages	Disadvantages
Facial recognition	Low	■ Easy ■ Fast ■ One of least expensive biometric technologies	■ Lighting in image can affect authentication ■ People can change ■ Can be spoofed
Fingerprints	Very low	■ Inexpensive ■ Very secure	■ Cuts and dirt can mar images
Hand recognition	Medium	■ Very small storage requirements ■ Intuitive operation	■ Slow ■ Less accurate than fingerprints
Iris/retina recognition	High	■ Extremely difficult to fool	■ Intrusive and inconvenient
Signature recognition	Lowest	■ Inexpensive	■ Can be affected by physical or emotional condition
Thermal imaging	Extremely high	■ Extremely difficult to fool	■ Requires expensive infrared cameras
Voice recognition	Very low	■ Inexpensive ■ Good for remote access	■ Slow ■ Can be affected by physical or emotional condition

SOURCE: Adapted from K. Philips, "Biometric Identification Looms on Landscape of Network Log-ins," *PC Week* 14 (13): 99.

Fingerprinting has been used for a long time by law enforcement agencies in identifying criminals. Today, fingerprinting can be used on desktop computers, with proper scanners and software, to restrict access to the computers. Facial recognition requires equipment that takes a digital image of all of the features of the face of an individual and software that matches the image to stored "authorized" images. Retina scans use a similar technology, taking a digitized image of the retina of the eye. A better security measure is iris scanning because it has been shown that the iris is unique among all individuals. The iris is the colored portion of the eye. Again, software is used to match an image of an iris with "authorized" images. Hand recognition takes a digital image of the entire hand, instead of just the fingerprints. It can be done using palm scanning, or by matching the geometry of the hand. Signature recognition compares the signature of an individual with the stored version of the individual's signature. This can involve not only the letters and style of the signature, but also the pressure points—how much an individual pushes on the pen when she writes her name. Thermal imaging is much more complex, and requires infrared cameras that take thermal images of the body. You have seen these in science fiction movies a lot. It is very expensive. Finally, voice recognition uses equipment and software that will digitize an individual's voice as it is recorded and compare this with stored voiceprints. If the match is close enough, access is granted. Other biometrics include matching earprints. For example, England has a large database of earprints because no two ears are said to be the same.

Biometrics, like other security measures, work even better when they are combined with other controls. For example, fingerprint matching (physical trait) could be used in lieu of an ATM card, which can be lost or stolen, and with a password or PIN (knowledge). And why not ask for the ATM card and the fingerprints and the password for maximum security?

Firewalls

Firewalls have become a very popular security feature in organizations with Internet access. A **firewall** is a computer or a router that controls access in and out of the internal computer network of an organization by controlling access to its resources and systems. The term *firewall* was borrowed from the construction industry. A firewall, which is constructed with fire-resistant material, is used to protect a building from fire. If a fire breaks out in one section of a building, it won't spread to other sections if firewalls are used. Firewalls extend user profile security by controlling internal versus external access to an organization's data, applications, and systems. There are several types of firewalls, which vary in how they control access into and out of the organization. In a simplified explanation, the firewall reads the control information of the messages that are attempting to enter and/or leave the company's internal network, and decides whether those messages are allowed in and/or out of the organization's walls (Figure 10-3). These messages can be e-mail messages, requests for Web pages, file transfers, or other network traffic.

A **packet-level firewall,** also called a network-level firewall, searches the source and destination addresses in data **packets.** Packets are small units of data that flow through networks, allowing for the transmission of messages. If the source address of the packet is from an "acceptable" computer, the firewall will let the message through, assuming that the destination address is also a valid internal address. Because packets are small units of data, and numerous packets are needed to send a complete message, firewalls do not "read" the messages that are coming in. They just check to see which packets are allowed to come in. This can work both ways, preventing internal users from accessing external Internet sites as well. Of course, when spoofing, the address can be made to seem acceptable, and some firewalls will let hackers into the internal computer system without realizing it.

An **application-level firewall** requires users to log into the firewall before they can access applications inside the organization (from outside). The communication is then

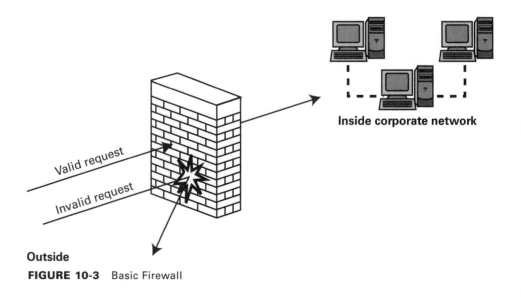

Inside corporate network

Valid request

Invalid request

Outside

FIGURE 10-3 Basic Firewall

performed between the firewall and the inside network. Application-level firewalls can also limit the types of applications allowed into the corporate network. For example, a company may decide that all File Transfer Protocols (FTP) and telnet applications should be denied access.

One type of application-level firewall is a **proxy server** (Figure 10-4). Transmissions from the outside world are sent to the proxy server, not the internal network, and all communications with the internal network are handled from the proxy server. The proxy server creates an application that will get the requested information from the internal network, without the external transaction actually going inside the network itself. This way the information cannot be manipulated or changed by the outside transaction. It is just transported and copied by the proxy for the outside transaction.

The proxy server can also create false IP addresses for its internal network so that external stations do not know the real IP addresses of stations on the internal network. When something is sent to the proxy server, it finds the proper internal address and then forwards the message to that address. This function is also called **network address translation,** and is available on most firewalls commercially available today.

Application-level firewalls are more complex to install and manage, but provide a much higher level of security than packet-level firewalls. One disadvantage of these servers, however, is that they slow down communication, since a proxy must be created for each transaction request. It should also be noted that firewalls would not protect an organization's system from a virus, if, for example, it is attached to a message with appropriate destination and source addresses. An example of a software-based firewall is Symantec's Enterprise Firewall, and an example of a hardware-based firewall is Cisco's PIX 535 Firewall.

Firewalls are also classified as static or dynamic. A **static firewall** has predetermined ways of dealing with transmission requests. A **default-permit static firewall** allows all traffic through except traffic that is explicitly marked to be blocked by the network administrator. A **default-deny static firewall** lets only allowed traffic through and refuses, by default, all other traffic requests into and out of the organization. It is, of course, much more secure than a default-permit firewall, since only a set of predetermined addresses and applications can be used to transmit into and out of

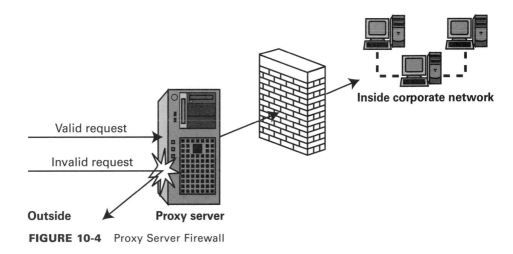

FIGURE 10-4 Proxy Server Firewall

the organization. It is less flexible, though, since a valid request from someone who happens to be using another computer that does not have an IP address that falls within the acceptable range would not be allowed in. Figure 10-5 shows a subset of a table of permissions on a firewall.

If the rules in Figure 10-5 are the only ones in the organization, who can do what? The computers on the 182.29.89.0 network are allowed to use the Web server of the organization (http). The users of the 182.29.0.0 network, however, would not be allowed to transfer files into the organization (ftp), but would be allowed to access the Web. Finally, users of the 182.29.22.1 network can use the telnet application, transfer files, access the Web server, and send e-mails (smtp) to anyone in the organization. The "Universe" keyword represents any IP address, internal or external to the organization.

A **dynamic firewall** manages the requests as they occur, deciding on both denials and permissions as they arrive. It requires much more management, but is also much more flexible.

An **internal firewall** is a firewall used inside an organization, between departments or divisions. A company may wish to protect data access even within its corporate walls. For example, there is no need for the sales force to know the payroll information for the whole company. The internal firewall can also add another layer of protection by stopping widespread hacking if a hacker accesses one part of the company's network.

A **personal firewall** is a firewall installed on a given personal computer. This can be a computer inside a corporation that has an external firewall, for added protection, or a home computer that is constantly connected to the Internet. Recall from Chapter 5 that some home computers can be "always connected" to the Internet using Digital Subscriber Lines (DSL) or cable modem connections. When a computer is always connected to the Internet, it has a greater chance of becoming a target for a hacker. So personal firewalls are a good option for home or home office computers. In addition to protecting the computer from outsider attacks and warning of arrival of malicious files, the personal firewall can offer privacy features, such as specifying how much information to give out to Web sites, blocking ads when browsing the Web, and providing parental control of the Web sites children can access on the home computer. Examples of personal firewalls available today include Symantec's Norton Internet Security and Zone Labs' ZoneAlarm.

It is important to realize that while firewalls are great security tools, they are not an answer for all security threats. Here are some of the security threats that a firewall won't eliminate: hackers can still exploit an unsecured modem connected to a desktop computer to access the inside network; disgruntled employees can still copy sensitive information and bring it outside of the company; and sensitive data loaded on an unsecured laptop, PDA, or cellular phone can still be lost at the airport.

Allow/Deny	Source IP Range	Destination IP Range	Protocols
Allow	182.29.89.0	182.118.10.9	http
Deny	182.29.0.0	182.118.10.9	ftp
Allow	182.29.22.1	"Universe"	telnet, ftp, http, smtp

FIGURE 10-5   Subset of a Permissions Table for a Firewall

Detecting Unauthorized Access

Since it is almost impossible for organizations, especially large ones, to totally prevent access to the organization, the next most important thing a company can do with respect to security is to detect that someone did indeed access the systems or data illegally. Unfortunately, many times, someone may access data without the company knowing about it. Two ways to detect such activities are audit logs and **entrapment servers.**

Audit Logs

Logs can be created for every user that signs into a system, all applications that are being used, any problems that are encountered with the systems, and all kinds of other activities that are performed on the computer systems and networks. Companies can use those logs to detect fraudulent activity. How can they do that? Software programs can be written to monitor all transactions on the system and look for anything out of the ordinary. Examples of "out of the ordinary" transactions include too many accesses, too many files downloaded, too many attempts to access certain applications from a given user ID, or too many login attempts. All of these may indicate the presence of an intruder. Numerous firewalls use audit logs as intrusion detection devices. The logs can be monitored in real time, or not. Some firewalls have automated responses to intrusion attempt patterns detected in real-time audit logs. For example, such automated responses can include launching tracking software, blocking access to the suspicious IP addresses, or shutting down certain operations. Logs are called *event-oriented* when they log system, application, or user events, or *keystroke-oriented* when they monitor and log every keystroke made.

Entrapment Server

Another, more recent method of detecting intruders is the use of an entrapment server, or what some call *honeypots.* An entrapment server comprises software and network equipment used to attract hackers to a secure lockbox, instead of letting them connect into the actual corporate network. The idea is that hackers will attempt to break into a server to gather company information. The entrapment server is designed to look genuine and provide interesting, but false, information that will attract hackers. Using sophisticated tracking software programs on the entrapment server, the company is able to detect and often identify the would-be hackers.

Since most networks and servers have vulnerabilities and configuration errors that a hacker can exploit, it is likely that a company may have inadvertently forgotten to fix one of these vulnerabilities, offering an easy entry point into its network. Leaving this back door open, but including a tripwire behind it, can allow a security manager to know when an intruder attempts entry into the server and to track the intruder. Some entrapment servers are hardware-based, while others use software emulation. Hardware for entrapment servers can include servers, switches, or routers. They are partially disabled, but made attractive. They serve no other purpose internally, but sit inside the network to look genuine. Some companies have even created networks of honeypots to further confuse hackers. Entrapment servers use programs that mimic real operating systems with vulnerabilities and advanced tracking software.

E-BUSINESS IN PRACTICE

Are You Protected?

Do you think that your computer is well protected? Why not put it to the test? A few Web sites offer security tests for your computer. One such site is offered by Steve Gibson of Gibson Research Corporation (grc.com). The site, called Shields UP!, allows you to test the firewall and security features on your computer. You can probe your communication ports to see how easy it is to access your information, and what information is provided. If you run these tests on your home computer with and without a firewall installed, you will see major differences.

SOURCE: Reprinted with permission of Gibson Research Corporation, Shields UP! page, https://grc.com/x/ne.dll ?bh0bkyd2.

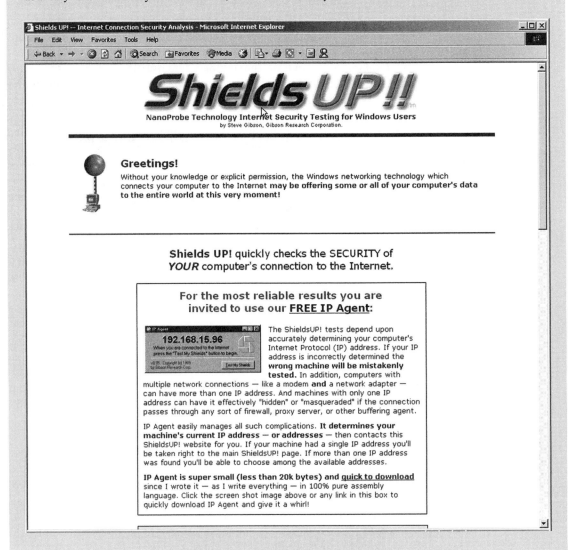

E-BUSINESS IN PRACTICE

Essential Components for a Good Honeypot

The essential requirements for a good entrapment server include the following items.

- The server must look and behave as if it was a real one.
- The existence of the entrapment server should not be disclosed at any point.
- The entrapment server should be partially disabled so hackers can't take it over.
- The entrapment server should have its own firewall protection so that it can't be used to compromise the internal network if it becomes compromised.

- The server should be on a network that is untouched by normal traffic.
- The server should have silent alarms to indicate all traffic going in and out of the server.
- The server should log all activities when an intrusion is sensed.

SOURCE: M. Schwartz, "To Trap a Thief," *Computerworld* (2 April 2001): http://www.computerworld.com/securitytopics/security/story/0,10801,59072,00.html.

Decision Point

One of the key security measures that an e-business can implement is access control, securing access to important systems and data. Some of the key questions that help an e-business identify whether the proper tools are being used for access control include:

- Are our rooms and equipment properly physically secured?
- Are our key security personnel properly screened? What about other personnel?
- Are our authentication schemes appropriate?
- Do we use authentication through possession? Knowledge? Physical traits?
- Are our user ID and password controls severe enough and monitored?
- Do we have firewalls? What types?
- Can we detect intruders if they gain access to our data or systems?
- Do we use audit logs? Do we monitor them?
- Should we use an entrapment server?

Rendering Data Unreadable: Encryption

It is unreasonable to assume that one can prevent all access to data and systems. One way to provide additional protection for the important data of an e-business, such as customer information, is **encryption.** A simple explanation of encryption is the application of a mathematical algorithm to a message or information that scrambles that message or information to make it unreadable. A broader term, for the use of encryption as a security measure, is cryptography. **Cryptography** is the "study of creating and using encryption and decryption techniques" (White 2001, 404).

Encryption Concepts

The whole purpose of encryption is to render data unreadable. This is performed with the use of keys. The **encryption key** makes the data unreadable. The **decryption key** allows the unreadable text to be converted into its original form. The readable message is called **plaintext.** The unreadable message is called **ciphertext.** Figure 10-6 shows the sequence of events in simple encryption.

The algorithms used to encrypt and decrypt the plaintext are called **ciphers.** They vary from the very simple to the very complex. The cipher is binary code, and is contained in the key. A very simple cipher, for purposes of example, is presented below. In this cipher, the letters of the alphabet are "coded" as one letter above their value.

```
Plaintext: a b c d e f g h I j k l m n o p q r s t u v w
x y z
Ciphertext: b c d e f g h I j k l m n o p q r s t u v w x
y z a
```

In this case, the words

```
computer lab closed
```

would be encoded as

```
dpnqtufs mbc dmptfe
```

Note that the actual encoded sentence would be dpnqtufsmbcdmptfe, with no spaces between the words, in order to make the patterns more difficult to view. This, of course, is a very simple key, which would be easy to guess with minimal effort.

Key Length

The strength of an encryption technique is a direct function of the length of the key. This is usually expressed in the number of bits the key has. The larger the size of the key, the more secure the encryption. This is because larger keys are harder to break. The reason for this is that there are more combinations of bits (a key) possible, and therefore it takes more time and effort to find the right combination. This would be the same concept as a combination lock that has fifty numbers and a combination of five numbers versus a thirty-number lock with only a three-number combination. The smaller encryption keys used to be 40 bits long. Today, keys in use commercially include 56-, 64-, and 128-bit lengths. In a code-breaking contest, it took less than twenty-three hours to break a 56-bit key using a specially built code-cracking computer and a network of one hundred thousand personal computers across the world (Greenstein and Feinman 2000). It is estimated that a 64-bit key can be broken in thirty-three to thirty-four days, while a 128-bit key would take more than two thousand years. Understandably, a 128-bit key is therefore much more secure.

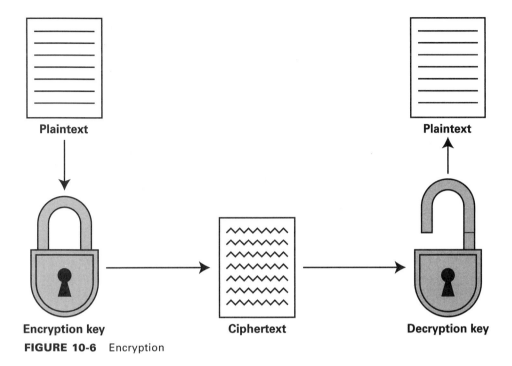

FIGURE 10-6 Encryption

Asymmetric Cryptography

It is important to realize that in Figure 10-6 the encryption and decryption keys can be either the same key or different keys, depending on the type of encryption a company uses. In **asymmetric encryption,** two keys are used. The public key is used to encrypt messages. It is sent to anyone with whom a person wishes to exchange encrypted messages. Using the person's public key, anyone can send her encrypted messages. This recipient will then use her private key to decrypt those messages. Therefore, the public key and the private key are linked, but only the recipient knows her private key's **passphrase.** The passphrase is a sentence entered by the user when she first creates a key. It is used by the system to generate the private and public keys, referred to as a **key pair.** If this person then wants to send her friend an encrypted message in return, she needs to have that friend's public key. This is also called public key cryptography, because two different keys are used in the process, and one of them can be shared with anyone (public). Individuals can even publish their public keys on key servers; however, the keys can also be transferred by e-mail or on a computer disk, making their distribution very simple.

A popular public key encryption tool is PGP (Pretty Good Privacy). Developed by Phillip Zimmermann, it is offered on the Internet for the residents of some countries as a freeware program (no commercial usage). It is available for U.S. and Canadian residents from the Massachusetts Institute of Technology (MIT), or for residents of some other countries at the International PGP site (see the Related Web Sites section at the end of the chapter for more information). There are also utilities that provide interfaces ("plug-ins") to mail packages, such as Eudora or Microsoft Exchange. They are available from the various PGP download sites or from the Web sites of the developers of those e-mail packages. The "plug-ins" make PGP very easy to use since they integrate PGP with the e-mail packages. In this case, the user writes the e-mail message, clicks on the PGP menu on the e-mail package's toolbar, and clicks on "encrypt message." The user is then presented with his keyring, which contains all of the public keys he has available on his system, and must decide which public key to use for the encryption. While it is used most often for e-mail messages, PGP can also be used for encrypting files, folders, and hard drives. As MIT puts it, "PGP is a high-security cryptographic software application that allows people to exchange messages with both privacy and authentication," and "enables you to encrypt files stored on your computer" (MIT 2002).

Symmetric Cryptography

In **symmetric** or **secret key encryption,** one key is used for both encrypting and decrypting data. In this case, individuals have to be very careful with whom they share their encryption keys because these individuals or companies will also be able to decrypt their messages. Since the same key is used to encrypt and decrypt messages, business partners only need to exchange one key to be able to send each other encrypted messages. The problem, however, is how to distribute the key. If the key is sent in an e-mail message it can be intercepted, thereby reducing the efficacy of that key in the future. It can also be distributed on a floppy disk, in which case better security is achieved by exchanging the disk face-to-face.

A well-known symmetric encryption technique is **DES (Data Encryption Standard),** created by IBM Corporation. It is widely used in business. While it is based on a 56-bit key (less secure), the strength of DES is a result of the multiple levels of encryption used. Some companies use two levels: the plaintext is encoded, then split into 32-bit blocks, then encoded again using another private key. Two keys must be maintained and "known" by the business partners. **Triple encryption** is even more secure. Three levels of encryption, with three private keys, are performed. The problem is that more levels of encryption mean more processing time and delays, something e-businesses do not like when conducting their transactions. A newer, stronger standard, the **Advanced Encryption Standard (AES)** proposed by the National Institute for Standards and Technology (NIST), supports 128-, 192-, and 256-bit keys.

There are also private efforts for encryption standards, such as RC2, RC4, and RC5 by RSA Data Security. Another well-known secret key encryption protocol is **Kerberos.** It is designed to work on client/server networks, and provides authentication of identity of users or servers, in addition to encryption. The concept of authentication requires a digital signature. We will discuss digital signatures and digital certificates in the next chapter, when we will also cover the two encryption protocols most used on the Web for electronic business: SET (Secure Electronic Transaction) and SSL (Secure Sockets Layer). Secure Sockets Layer (SSL) technology is present in most modern Internet browsers, and encrypts information so that it is difficult to view the information without the authorized key. Secure Electronic Transaction (SET) is another encryption technology that additionally uses a certificate authority to apply the key for decryption. The use of a combination of these technologies greatly decreases the opportunity for unauthorized access to information passed over the Internet. Finally, it should be noted that other encryption techniques and protocols exist, and that newer protocols are constantly being developed and tested, as security is a major issue in today's computerized environments. Most of these are well beyond the scope of this text.

In concluding our discussion of encryption, it should be noted that encryption can be used for more than transmission of data. It can be used to protect data within an organization. You could even encrypt your data on your personal computer so that no one could access it without the proper key. Encryption is therefore a tool for both security and privacy. When conducting e-business transactions and sending credit card information online, encryption can protect the user from theft of information that can lead to fraud. When encryption is used to protect messages between friends or to protect files that only certain people should see, it provides privacy to the users. One issue with commercial use of consumer information is that, while transmission of transaction data is secured through encryption, many companies then store all of these data in their databases without encrypting them. The main reasons for this? It requires more storage space to store encrypted data, and more processing is necessary to access the data (because it needs to be decrypted).

Virus Protection

Recall from an earlier section of this chapter that viruses are consistently ranked as one of the most frequent security threats in organizations. It is not surprising then that virus protection has become a major business in itself. Companies specializing in computer security have developed antivirus software programs that, when loaded, can check all of the files on a computer periodically and remove viruses that are found. If the antivirus software is set to scan other applications, it can also detect viruses that are stored in e-mails and files as they are opened, before any damage is done. For this to work, though, the virus has to be one of the known viruses for which there is a recognizable bit pattern or recognizable behavior. This is why virus software must be updated regularly. During an update to a virus check program, the most recent bit patterns (viruses) identified are downloaded and stored in the antivirus program's database. The most popular virus protection programs today include Symantec's Norton AntiVirus, McAfee's VirusScan, and Computer Associates's InoculateIT.

The problem with most antivirus software is that the software is primarily reactive. It cannot typically detect a new type of virus, but it can detect existing viruses, or ones that look similar to an old virus archived in the software's database or virus log. Once a new virus is identified, it usually takes less than twenty-four hours for the specialists to decode it and find a protection for it. Symantec had as many as fifty-five thousand viruses in its database as of early 2001, but new viruses appear constantly (as many as five hundred per month). This is because viruses are easier to write than ever. Numerous tools for writing viruses are available for download on the Web! The twenty-year-old who created the Anna Kournikova virus wrote it from a downloadable virus-writing kit.

Newer virus protection tools, called **behavioral-based protection tools,** are now being offered. These tools look for suspicious behaviors in programs. They can, for example, isolate all files downloaded from the Internet and observe them for any malicious behavior or suspicious actions. Some examples of these software tools include InDefense's Achilles'Shield, Aladdin Knowledge Systems' eSafe Desktop, and Pelican Security's SafeTnet.

Even with virus protection software, one of the best ways to protect your computer from catching viruses is to be very careful about opening executable files in electronic messages. Another good idea is to scan all floppy disks before they are loaded on your computer. Sometimes e-mail messages seem to come from someone you know, but the person who sent the file may not even know it has been sent. This is frequent with certain viruses, which, if successful in infecting a person's computer, will send themselves to everyone in the user's address book. Avoid opening attachments to electronic mails unless a person specifically tells you that there is an attachment and what the purpose of the file is, and it is a person that you know and expect an attachment from. The same can be said of diskettes. Do not use someone's floppy disk unless you scan it first with an updated virus check program.

Decision Point

In addition to the decisions previously discussed, management of an e-business must look into the following security controls.

- Should we use encryption for our data transfers? What type?
- Should we use encryption for storing key data? What type?
- Do we have appropriate virus protection software?
- How often is it updated? Who is responsible for that?
- How often are computers scanned for viruses?
- Are patches installed to prevent viruses from attacking our systems?

Wireless Security for M-commerce

Recall from Chapter 5 that m-commerce is a fast growing segment of the e-business environment. You may also recall from the discussion of wireless technologies that they are more susceptible to security breaches. Why? Because anything that travels over the airwaves is much easier to intercept than transmissions over cables (while some cables are very easy to break into, you have to have physical access to the cable). So what kind of security is available for those of us who want to use our smart phones to conduct Web-based transactions? First and foremost, it should be noted that digital signals offer better protection than analog signals. Why? Because they provide better encryption. Yes, encryption is still the best protection for data that travel over wireless networks. Several companies have developed public-key encryption software for handheld devices. For example, Certicom offers software called Trustpoint, which enables secure wireless transactions by requiring a digital certificate and encryption. In simple terms, both parties to the transaction must be authenticated before they are allowed to pass sensitive data back and forth. This authentication information is handled by a program on the server that communicates with the client program on the handheld devices.

Another issue with wireless connections is that some hackers use them to enter into companies' data networks. In other words, wireless networks are used as entry points into wired corporate networks. One solution to this security threat is to add firewalls to the wireless gateways, but this may reduce the overall performance for communications to and from individuals on the wireless network. Finally, while we think of security for wireless e-commerce as protecting transactions, we should also consider security for the wireless devices themselves. In particular, laptop computer theft is a problem for corporations because of the loss of the equipment itself and the loss of the data that are stored on it.

One way to deter laptop computer theft is to use specially-designed locks that can tie the computer to a table or chair. These become inconvenient, though, when the user has to move the laptop fairly often. Given that laptops have become prominent in the business world, a lot of research is being done on newer technologies to protect laptops and the data stored on them. Combining logical and physical security measures is the wave of the future for m-commerce security, and e-commerce in general. The Caveo anti-theft device presented in the E-business in Practice box is one example of a combination of logical and physical security measures.

Summary of Security Measures

Table 10-6 summarizes the security measures discussed in this section. We should mention that security alone does not guarantee secured electronic-business. The people, procedures, and practices in place will be equally important. We will discuss some of these in the managerial issues section at the end of the chapter.

In concluding our discussion of security technologies, the question of which technology to choose remains. Or rather, which technology should be deployed first and which technologies should be deployed together? As previously stated, the best security is to include a combination of logical and physical security measures.

MANAGERIAL ISSUES

Privacy and security are very important concerns of e-business managers today. Developing policies and plans to address them is but a first step in the direction of handling these important issues. In this section we discuss privacy and security policies, and then present some organizations dealing with security and privacy.

Table 10-6   Summary of Security Measures and Controls

Security Type	Physical Security Measures	Logical Security Measures
Handling disasters, disruptions, and destruction	■ Redundancy in hardware, software, and data (backups)	■ User education ■ Disaster recovery plan
Controlling access	■ Locking computers and rooms ■ Putting floppy disks and data backups in vaults ■ Surveillance cameras ■ Call-back modems	■ User profiles ■ Biometrics ■ Firewalls ■ User education
Detecting unauthorized access		■ Audit logs ■ Entrapment server
Rendering data unreadable		■ Encryption
Virus protection		■ Antivirus software ■ User education
Wireless security	■ Computer locks ■ Motion detectors	■ Encryption ■ User education

Developing an E-business Privacy Policy and Statement

In the section on privacy in this chapter, we discussed the importance of a clear, concise, easily accessible privacy policy on an e-business' Web site. What should such a policy include? How do you develop a good privacy statement? These are important questions for managers, and we will discuss them in this section.

First and foremost, it is important to state that laws vary significantly among countries worldwide with respect to protection of citizens' privacy. For example, at the time of the writing of this text, there are few federal laws in the United States forcing Web sites to protect the privacy of online users. The only two laws deal with the financial/banking industry, in which opt-out information must be provided to consumers, and a law protecting the privacy of children. This is why many consumers fear Web-based shopping. But the European Union has adopted privacy laws. In the European Union, Web site operators must apply the following rules:

- Provide clear and conspicuous notice about the collection and use of personal information and the choices users have regarding limiting the disclosure of this information.

- Offer a choice regarding the collection and disclosure of users' personal data. This includes "opting out" for non-sensitive data (telling the companies they do not want it collected/shared) and "opting in" for sensitive data (explicitly telling the companies they can collect/use the data).

- Assure users that any transfer of their data will be subject to the same controls.

- Assure users that their data will be subjected to security measures protecting them from loss, misuse, unauthorized access or disclosure, alteration, or destruction.

- Assure users that the integrity and accuracy of their data will be maintained.

- Provide users with access to their information derived from nonpublic records, and give them the ability to correct or amend any inaccurate data.

- Assure users that there will be enforcement of the principles, and offer them recourse if the principles are not followed.

E-BUSINESS IN PRACTICE

New Technologies for M-commerce Security

Caveo Technology, LLC has developed a new antitheft device that attaches to a laptop to provide security by using a motion-sensor memory, a sound producing unit, a micro-controller, two levels of passwords for access, and a motion password. The motion-sensor memory is used to remember user-selected parameters, such as a regular geographical work area. When the system is armed and the laptop is carried outside of that area, the system will sound an alarm that will increase in strength as the laptop is moved further away from its area. The data is protected by a sixteen-digit password that goes into effect at the same time as the alarm, and also by encryption of all the files, with keys stored on the anti-theft device, not on the laptop itself. There is also a four-digit password to arm the system, and a motion password that is activated when the computer is moved into a certain position (for example, being held vertically). The system remains on even when the computer is turned off.

While privacy statements are not required by law for those Web sites maintained by U.S. operators, the government has been very active in trying to enforce privacy principles. The Federal Trade Commission (FTC) has threatened to adopt similar laws to those of the European Union. Federal agencies are forced to be good examples for other organizations regarding the protection of citizens' privacy rights. As previously discussed, the U.S. government has issued memorandums to all agencies requiring them to follow certain privacy principles, such as not using cookies when inappropriate and disclosing proper privacy statements. The information provided to agencies also includes why the standards were established, allowable exceptions, when the standards should be implemented, and a general discussion of privacy issues.

Content of a Privacy Statement

The guidelines for U.S. federal agencies only suggest the topics that should be included in a good privacy statement or notice. When an e-business implements a Web site, how should the manager in charge of security and privacy design the company's statement? First, of course, the company must decide on which policies it intends to follow regarding the collection of consumer data. These decisions should be seriously considered and checked for any legal implications. The manager must then write the actual statement, have it approved by the company's management (and probably the company's legal department or law firm), and then post it on the Web site. The content of the statement will vary from company to company. Some of the basic elements that should be included in a privacy policy (Online privacy policy 2001) are:

- A statement about the company's commitment to privacy
- A description of the personal information that is collected and whether it will be disclosed or shared
- A statement suggesting that the company is not responsible for related companies' (such as advertisers, partners, etc.) privacy and data collection practices
- A statement describing how third party advertising companies linked to the company's Web site may collect information on their own, but suggesting that the company does not share personal information with them
- A description of information collected when users fill out forms on the company's Web site or answer company surveys, and a description of how users can opt out of receiving company information
- An explanation of how the company is not responsible for information shared by users on bulletin boards or discussion forums linked to the company's Web site
- An explanation of how IP addresses are handled—whether they are collected, for what purposes, and how they can or will be used
- A description of how the company uses cookies, and how users can elect to refuse cookies in their browsers
- A statement regarding the company's strong security measures
- A statement regarding whether services are suitable for children below the age of eighteen or not
- A description of the opt-out procedures

- A statement informing users about how to have the company correct or delete their personal information

- A statement to the effect that the company can amend its privacy policy as needed and where changes will be posted

- Contact information

- A statement suggesting that users agree to the terms and conditions of the privacy statement when using the company's Web site

Writing Your Own Privacy Statement

When a company wants to design its own privacy statement, the manager in charge has to be careful to include all policies to which the company wishes to adhere, and to include these in clear, concise language. To promote the use of privacy statements, several online tools have been developed to automatically generate or test privacy statements. For example, Microsoft has a privacy statement generator at www.microsoft.com/privacy/wizard/, and the IBM corporation has its own at www.alphaworks.ibm.com/tech/p3peditor.

Security in E-business

Security is obviously an issue for information technology managers and professionals. With the advent of electronic business and increased use of the Internet, security has become a frequent headline in the business press. We have discussed numerous threats and technologies to improve security. It is surprising, though, that many managers fear security threats, but lack a good understanding of the risks and controls related to various security technologies. Fred Langa (2000) highlighted this issue in a Winmag.com article in which he discussed four myths associated with online security.

- *Myth 1: "I'm not on a network, so my PC is safe."* Individuals may not understand that when connecting to the Internet, they are connecting to a network. The threat is even more present for those who have home computers or home office computers always connected to the Internet, either through cable modems or Digital Subscriber Line (DSL) connections. Langa predicts that there will be at least a few hackers trying to break into those computers every day.

- *Myth 2: "I just use a dial-up connection, so my PC is safe."* It is true that when using a dial-up connection, individuals are assigned a different IP address each time they connect, and that makes it harder to find the computer than it would be if it had a static address. However, with tools allowing hackers to scan tens of thousands of IP addresses per hour, computers on dial-up connections, especially for individuals who stay connected for long periods of time, are also at risk of being hacked.

- *Myth 3: "I use an antivirus application, so my PC is safe."* Antivirus software can protect a computer from viruses, but may not protect it from newer, just-released viruses. In addition, antivirus software will offer no protection against hackers trying to access data and applications on a system, or trying to crash a system.

- *Myth 4: "I use a firewall, so my PC is safe."* Firewalls do provide added security, but they won't provide protection against viruses, protection against some illegal access to data, or protection for an otherwise unsecured computer, such as a computer with a direct modem connection. In addition, if the firewall goes down, there is no protection.

So, if all tools do not protect computers and networks properly, what is a manager to do? Since not one technique will provide complete protection, combining logical and physical security measures, including several of each, is probably the best way to protect computers and networks. In addition, information technology managers should stay abreast of all new technological developments regarding security. This includes knowing about all updates available for their software environments. This is particularly important for patches that fix security holes in software applications and operating systems.

Developing an E-business Security Plan

All organizations, electronic or traditional, should have well-designed security policies. There is a major difference between security policies and the privacy policies described in the previous section: security policies tend to be for internal use, while privacy policies provide guidelines for internal use, but are disseminated to consumers. In other words, it is good practice to have a sound privacy policy and to let consumers know what the company's policy is. It is, however, not a good practice to share a company's security policy with external entities unless they have a need to know.

Security policies describe *what* the general security guidelines are for an organization. Security procedures, on the other hand, are specific statements describing *how* to implement the security policies. An example of a security policy is "All users must change their passwords every three months." A related security procedure would include what steps should be taken to change user passwords. For example, one procedure could be an automated system that forces users to change their passwords, lists actions if users do not change their passwords, and reacts to unacceptable passwords (such as words in the dictionary). Both security policies and procedures should be part of a security plan. The security plan is a comprehensive document containing the security threats that a company faces and all of the controls in place to address those threats.

Development of a Security Plan

Because a security plan is a very comprehensive document, its creation typically requires the involvement of key information technology personnel, as well as end users and management. The plan is developed by following a number of steps.

Step One: Assess Risks to the Company's Computing Environments   All of the threats discussed in this chapter should be considered in this phase, including natural disasters and human errors. It is also important to realize that there are a large number of computing environments, even within one organization, and that none of them should be ignored. Examples of computing environments to consider include external Web site, intranet, communication circuits, servers, client computers, mobile devices, software, and people. The list of computing environments should then be checked for risks of natural disasters (e.g., floods, fire), breakage (e.g., power loss, failures), or malicious attacks (e.g., viruses, intruders, eavesdropping).

In order to assess the weaknesses of, and threats to, the systems and networks, the company must collect data on system usage, events, and other activities. One way to assess certain risks is to conduct controlled security breaches. For example, the term "white hat" hackers is used to refer to individuals who are hired to try to break into systems (as opposed to "black hat" hackers, who have malicious intentions). Once the risks have been assessed, they should be ranked from most critical to least critical.

Step Two: Develop a Security Plan   As previously discussed, the security plan will be composed of policies and procedures. The policies will cover all aspects of access to the organization's systems and networks. Who has the right to access what services? How is that established? What are the exceptions? What systems are in place to protect against each threat? The company's security plan will also discuss the disaster recovery plan, the use of surveillance cameras, halon fire systems, user access, user authentication rules, virus checking software, and so on. Simply stated, all of the security controls available and in use in the organization should be included in the security plan, together with a description of which security threat they are eliminating.

Many security experts believe that the best security is offered when many automated enforcement mechanisms are established. These mechanisms provide automatic responses to security events and are created to detect, identify, and stop intruders before damage can be done. A mechanism could include simple steps, such as disabling a user's account automatically after a number of failed logon attempts, or intricate steps, such as identifying intruders on an entrapment server.

Step Three: Evaluate the Security Plan   A good plan needs to be tested and reevaluated periodically. There are several ways to test a security plan. One is to have "drills" during which security breaches are created. Companies often use drills to test their disaster recovery plan. A disaster is imagined, and everyone must follow the recovery plan as if the disaster actually did occur. Metrics are measured, such as how long it takes to get back online or how long it takes to resume normal business operations. The same drills can be conducted for security breaches. Other evaluations are done on the efficacy of the security measures. For example, a company might want to test whether the policy requiring an update of the virus check program every month is working. Do the users comply with the requirements? Why? Why not? What can be done to improve their responsiveness? One of the most important aspects of the evaluation of the security plan is constant monitoring of the security controls. Examples of this can include checking the effectiveness of the firewalls, checking accuracy of data, or even checking the actions of disgruntled employees. Finally, the security plan should be reevaluated regularly since computing environments tend to change at a fairly rapid pace in today's organizations.

Security Plan Considerations

Before creating a security plan and the related policies, the company must consider the level of security it requires. The more elaborate the required security features, the higher the cost and the more stringent the requirements on the users of the systems. The most secure firewalls are usually commercially-available systems with powerful and complex equipment and software. Their maintenance is also complex. Companies must have the resources and skills to manage this equipment. Users may also wish for less stringent security. If a company has several traveling employees who cannot access the systems from remote sites because of security features, and if this prevents them from doing their job efficiently, the company has to consider the overall impact that the security controls have on those employees. The company

E-BUSINESS IN PRACTICE

Top Ten Security Mistakes

In an article discussing computer security, Alan Horowitz describes how people are far more careful with their personal security (by locking doors, cars, and houses and using security devices) than they are with the security of their computers. He suggests a list of the top ten security errors that individuals—and even information technology professionals—commit with respect to computers. According to Horowitz, some of them include "pretty dumb behavior" by some individuals.

1. *The not-so-subtle sticky note*—These self-stick sheets of paper are often used to inscribe passwords, and are frequently posted right on top of the computer. The vice-president of information systems for one company admits that 15 to 20 percent of his users regularly do this!

2. *We know better than you*—Sometimes users think they know more than security managers, and turn off security features used by the company. Horowitz gives the example of people turning off their antivirus software.

3. *Leaving the computer on while unattended*—Numerous individuals leave their machines turned on without password protection. Anyone walking by can access all of an individual's files without even the effort of having to break into the computer!

4. *Opening e-mail attachments*—After our discussion of viruses, all of you should know that opening attachments from people you don't know, or even people you do know, presents a high security risk. Yet it seems that a lot of users open all e-mail attachments without thinking about it, even when they have been warned about the potential risks of doing so.

5. *Poor password selection*—Horowitz reports on an experiment in which NASA experts broke 60 percent of the passwords of the top twenty engineers of a company within thirty minutes. This is because people use obvious words or numbers as passwords. Remember our previous discussion about passwords. Using a combination of letters and numbers for a password,

with no particular significance, always provides better security.

6. *Loose lips sink ships*—This security mistake refers to people talking about security features, such as how they select their passwords, in public places. Anyone can hear and use the information for hacking into the person's account.

7. *Laptops have legs*—While individuals are careful with their laptops in public places, they often leave their laptops unattended and unsecured in their offices with the door open. It is easy for someone to walk by, take a laptop, and leave without anyone noticing.

8. *Poorly enforced security policies*—Information technology professionals may develop a very good security plan, but they need to enforce it if it's going to provide the needed security.

9. *Failing to consider the staff*—Recall from the statistics presented earlier in the chapter that one of the greatest security threats is from inside the organization, because of disgruntled employees who may cause serious damage, for example. Horowitz suggests that information technology departments should monitor all incidents, and have the technological capability to track the source of various problems that occur.

10. *Being slow to update*—Being slow to update security information can open doors for hackers to attack the company. For example, even though software vendors produce service packs to "plug" security holes in their systems, some companies wait too long before installing them.

SOURCE: A. S. Horowitz, "Top 10 Security Mistakes," *Computerworld* (9 July 2001): http://www.computerworld.com/securitytopics/security/story/0,10801,61986,00.html.

should also consider its own commitment to security. If users are unwilling to follow the procedures, the best security systems may be less than perfect.

In the previous section, we discussed the importance of periodically evaluating the security plan. What makes a good plan? What features do you look for in a good security plan? Following is a list of some of the features that are important to consider when evaluating a security plan (Fitzgerald and Dennis 1999).

- The security controls should be as simple as possible.
- It is always preferable to prevent a security breach than to detect and correct it.
- There must be a balance between the security and usability so that the security controls provide just enough security, but do not prevent users from being able to perform their tasks. In a perfect world everything would be secure, but who could get their job done?
- Security controls performed by computers are more reliable than those requiring human intervention.
- Security controls should apply to everyone in the organization.
- Security controls should include clear specifications of responsibilities.
- Security controls should be failure-safe, using some of the components presented in the disaster recovery discussion, for example. If they fail, the networks and systems should default to a condition in which everyone is denied access.
- Security controls should be well documented, but not available to everyone.
- A security policy should have clear goals and objectives.
- A security policy should have not only policies, but also enforcement procedures.
- Personnel roles should be clearly established in a security plan.

Security Jobs

This chapter should have made clear to everyone that security is a very serious concern for organizations. It has become such an issue that many companies look for individuals with security skills to complement their regular skill set. This is even more prominent in consulting companies, information technology companies, and government agencies. A recent survey by the journal *Computerworld* (2000) shows that companies are willing to pay a premium on the salary of information technology professionals when they have certain security skills. Figure 10-7 shows some of the kinds of premiums companies are willing to pay for various skills. Interestingly, while many companies worry about outside contractors in terms of security, others actually outsource their information security to managed security service providers (MSSP).

Security- and Privacy-Focused Organizations

Security and privacy are key concerns of technology managers, even more so when electronic business is involved. A number of organizations exist or have recently been developed for the purpose of dealing with these two issues. Tables 10-7 and 10-8 contain samples of these organizations.

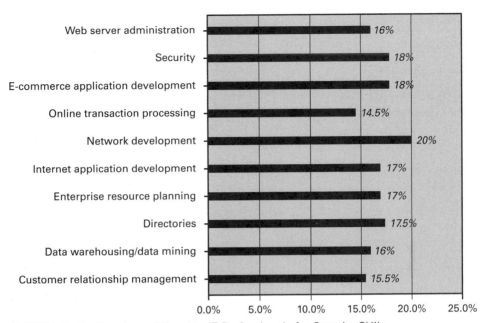

FIGURE 10-7 Premiums Offered to IT Professionals for Security Skills

SOURCE: *Computerworld's* 2000 Top Dollars for Top Skills, http://www.computerworld.com/news/2000/story/0,11280,54583,00.html.

CLOSING CASE: FIRSTGOV.GOV

FirstGov.gov is the first true portal service created for the United States Government (http://firstgov.gov/). A portal provides integration services with access organized by topics (instead of agencies). When individuals wish to obtain information on a particular topic, the information may be pulled from several different agencies or government branches, and yet appear as one source to the user. Another example of a portal for e-government integration is Singapore's eCitizen Centre.

FirstGov.gov advertises itself as "Your First Click to the U.S. Government." Its privacy link is highly visible on its navigation bar at the top of the page, right next to the main page link. The privacy policy is very clear: "We will collect no personal information about you when you visit our website unless you choose to provide that information." While the statement is easily understandable by all constituents, further explanations under the section "Information Collected and Stored Automatically" include details of what is collected automatically when individuals just browse through the Web pages or download information. They state that: "this information does not identify you personally." Yet, the list of information automatically collected includes:

- The Internet domain (e.g., vt.edu) and the IP address of the computer used to browse the page
- The type of browser and operating system used
- The date and time of the access to the site
- The page visited
- The address of the referring page

Table 10-7 Some Privacy-related Organizations

Organization	Description
American Civil Liberties Union	National civil liberties organization founded in 1920; conducts extensive litigation on constitutional issues, including privacy and free speech
Coalition Against Unsolicited Commercial Email (CAUCE)	Volunteer, entirely Web-based organization created by Netizens to advocate a legislative solution to the problem of UCE (spam); in 1997, proposed an amendment to the federal statute that outlaws junk "faxes" (47 USC 227) that would also prohibit junk e-mail; has remained a preeminent voice in the anti-spam community
Cypherpunks	Informal group that develops technological solutions to protect privacy, including writing cryptography and other programs, setting up anonymous remailers, and discussing political and technical issues
Electronic Frontier Foundation	Formed in 1990 to maintain and enhance intellectual freedom, privacy, and other values of civil liberties and democracy in networked communications; publishes newsletters, Internet guidebooks, and other documents; provides mailing lists and other online forums; hosts a large electronic document archive
Electronic Privacy Information Center	U.S. organization established in 1994 to focus public attention on emerging privacy issues relating to the National Information Infrastructure, such as the Clipper Chip, the Digital Telephony proposal, medical records privacy, and the sale of consumer data; conducts litigation, sponsors conferences, produces reports, publishes the EPIC Alert, and leads campaigns on privacy issues
Global Internet Liberty Campaign	International coalition of forty privacy, free speech, and human rights groups dedicated to fighting international threats to privacy and free speech on the Internet
Online Privacy Alliance (OPA)	A coalition of more than ninety organizations, including corporations and associations, that promote self-regulation of online consumer privacy
Privacy Coalition	Nonpartisan coalition of consumer, civil liberties, educational, family, library, labor, and technology organizations in support of legislation that effectively protects personal privacy
Privacy International	International human rights group based in London, England, with members in more than forty countries; led campaigns against national ID cards, video surveillance, and other privacy violations in numerous countries; sponsors yearly international conferences on privacy issues
Privacy Rights Clearinghouse	California-based organization formed in 1992; has produced many fact sheets and an annual report, and maintains a toll free hotline to provide advice to consumers about their rights
Privacy Council	Coalition of U.S. privacy groups and individuals who deal with privacy issues in the United States; monitors legislation and activities of government agencies; works with other privacy groups
U.S. Public Interest Research Group (PIRG)	Nonprofit, nonpartisan consumer and environmental watchdog group; advocates for better consumer privacy laws, preventing identity theft, and correcting credit reports

SOURCE: EPIC Online Guide to Privacy Resources page, Electronic Privacy Information Center, 6 May 2002: http://www.epic.org/privacy/privacy_resources_faq.html.

This information is collected "to help us make the site more useful to visitors—to learn about the number of visitors to our site and the types of technology our visitors use. We do not track or record information about individuals and their visits." Do you think the privacy statement is consistent with the practices of the Web site? Which information is or is not identifiable on the Internet?

Table 10-8 Some Security Related Organizations

Organization	Description
Alliance for Internet Security (AIS)	Initiated by ICSA.net to mobilize concerned organizations against the threat of distributed denial of service (DDoS) attacks
Center for Security Policy	A nonprofit, nonpartisan organization that wishes to stimulate and inform national and international debates about all aspects of security policy of the United States
Computer Emergency Response Team Coordination Center (CERT/CC)	Hosted at Carnegie Mellon University; for a fee, companies can get advanced warnings of Internet security threats; the center also offers education, training, and help in the development of best practices in security
Computer Security Institute (CSI)	Organization dedicated to serving and training information, computer, and network security professional; sponsors security conferences and exhibitions; also publishes surveys and reports on topics such as computer crime and information security program assessment
International Information Systems Security Certifications Consortium	Offers the well-known CISSP security certification for designers of security policies and procedures
IT Information Sharing and Analysis Center (IT-ISAC)	An organization formed originally by nineteen technology corporations to share information about denial-of-service attacks and software vulnerability in general; by keeping a database of shared information, they hope to be able to solve security problems
National Information Assurance Partnership (NIAP)	Developed by U.S. National Institute of Standard and Technology (NIST) and NSA in 1998 to "promote the development and use of evaluated, security-enhanced information technology (IT) products"; Some of its initiatives include independent testing labs for security-enhanced IT products and the promotion of security requirements specifications
National Security Agency (NSA)	U.S. federal agency that coordinates, directs, and performs activities to protect U.S. information systems and produce foreign intelligence information; it is the cryptography agency for the United States
TruSecure	An organization for information security, including infowar, firewalls, reliability, ethics, and privacy issues, plus defense against viruses, Trojan horses, and other malicious code attacks

Recall from Chapter 4 that an IP address is static if it is permanently assigned to a computer on a network (connected to the Internet). When a Web site obtains IP address information and domain information, it can track the computers that are browsing the Web site, but may not know personal information, such as name or address, if this information is not provided by (configured in) the browser. Do you believe that the IP address, coupled with domain information, is identifiable information? Should FirstGov.gov be more careful in their statements about information not being identifiable? While the government may make no attempt to trace the individual Web surfers to their site, do they have the means to do so with the information collected? What do you recommend they do?

SUMMARY

Security and privacy are two key factors that can have tremendous impact on the growth of electronic business. This chapter starts with a discussion of the differences between privacy and security. Privacy is the confidentiality of the data collected by businesses or governments about the individuals using their services, and the ability of individuals to manage information about themselves. Security is the protection against security threats, which are circumstances, conditions, or events with the potential to cause economic hardship by affecting data or network resources.

Threats to privacy on the Internet occur because technology allows collection of huge amounts of data faster and easier than ever, and data collection can even occur without the knowledge of individuals, through the use of cookies. Cookies are text files stored on the user's hard disk that contain information sent by the servers that have been accessed online. They do allow for personalization of Web sites, but can also collect information the user may not wish to have stored. Privacy is also threatened by the tracking of consumer usage by Web sites. Clickstream data is the term given to data that tracks user surfing habits online. Finally, privacy is threatened when individuals' data is shared by companies with other companies without the explicit approval of the individuals.

The privacy statement or notice should be easily accessible on an e-business' Web site, and should describe the privacy policy of the Web merchant regarding the data collected and its subsequent use. It is used to reassure the consumer, just like trust seals do. A trust seal on a company's Web site indicates that the company adheres to a set of policies and practices established by the organization that manages the seal program. Several seal programs require that participants follow strict privacy policies. Some popular seal programs include Better Business Bureau online (BBBOnLine), AICPA WebTrust, and TRUSTe. Finally, some governments have established laws to protect the privacy of consumers, while others are promoting self-regulation efforts.

Security threats can be classified as unauthorized access, denial of service, or theft and fraud. Denial of service threats render systems inoperative or limit their capability to operate. They occur through disruptions, natural disasters, or malicious acts. Disruptions include equipment or software failure or human errors. Natural disasters include earthquakes, tornadoes, hurricanes, or fires. Malicious acts include spamming and viruses. Spamming, or e-mail bombing, is the hacker practice of sending thousands of messages to a computer or network in order to fill its communication ports or memory buffers and render the system inoperative. When an innocent third party computer is used to multiply the messages sent, the practice is called smurfing. Viruses are computer programs designed to perform unwanted events. There are various types of viruses. Worms are special viruses that spread using direct Internet connections, while Trojan

horses spread by looking like legitimate software and tricking the user into running the program.

Unauthorized access threats occur when individuals access systems and/or data illegally. If the hacker takes someone else's identity to do this, he is said to be masquerading, or spoofing. Theft can be of data, software, or hardware. Theft is often a problem with the company's own employees. When stolen data is used and/or modified, fraud can occur.

Security controls can be categorized as preventive, detective, or corrective. Preventive controls stop or limit the security threat from happening. Detective controls find or discover security threats. Corrective controls correct a security issue. Security controls include disaster recovery for dealing with natural disasters and destruction. A disaster recovery plan requires redundancy in data, software, and hardware. Access to data, applications, or systems can be controlled physically or logically. Physical access controls include equipment locks, room access control systems, network personnel selection, and callback modems.

Logical access controls can exist at three levels: possession, knowledge, and trait. Possession means owning a form of identification. Knowledge means requiring individuals to know a piece of information for access. Trait involves using a physical trait for access, which is also known as biometrics. Logical access controls include user profiles, biometrics, and firewalls. User profiles are assigned to users, and consist of a user identification, a password, and a set of privileges. Biometrics is the set of technologies that use human features to recognize individuals and grant them access. Firewalls are systems used to control access between two networks, usually preventing unauthorized outsiders from accessing a company's intranet. There are several types of firewalls that vary in how they control access. Detecting unauthorized access can be performed with audit logs or entrapment servers. Entrapment servers comprise software and network equipment used to attract hackers into secure lockboxes that track them, instead of letting them connect into the actual corporate network.

Another security control is encryption or cryptography. It is the application of a mathematical algorithm to a message or information in order to scramble it and make it unreadable. The original message is called plaintext. The encrypted message is called ciphertext. The algorithm is contained in encryption and decryption keys. Asymmetric encryption requires that the encryption key be different than the decryption key (called a key pair), while in symmetric encryption both keys are the same. The length of the key is an important determinant of the level of security of the encryption technique. Virus protection is usually performed with antivirus software. User education is also very important. Security for m-commerce includes locks and special devices to prevent laptop theft, and encryption to protect the data.

Managerial issues discussed include the development of a privacy policy and statement for an e-business, as well as the development of a security plan, including security policies and procedures.

KEY TERMS

active unauthorized
   access
Advanced Encryption
   Standard (AES)
application-level firewall
asymmetric encryption
audit logs
authentication
behavioral-based
   protection tools
biometrics
boot sector virus
call-back modems
ciphers
ciphertext
clickstream
cookies
corrective controls
cryptography
decryption key
default-deny static
   firewall

default-permit static
   firewall
denial of service
DES (Data Encryption
   Standard)
detective controls
disaster recovery
distributed denial of
   service attacks
   (DDOS)
dynamic firewall
e-mail bombing
encryption key
encryption
entrapment server
firewall
incremental backups
internal firewall
Kerberos
key pair
macro virus
masquerading

message stream
   modification
network address
   translation
opt-in
opt-out
packet-level firewall
packets
parasitic virus
passive unauthorized
   access
passphrase
personal firewall
physical access controls
plaintext
polymorphic virus
preventive controls
privacy
privacy policy
   (statement)
proxy server
safeguard assurances

security
security threat
smurfing
sniffer
spamming
spoofing
static firewall
stealth virus
symmetric (secret key)
   encryption
triangulation
triple encryption
Trojan horses
trust seals
unauthorized access
user profile
views
virus check program
virus hoaxes
viruses
worms

REVIEW QUESTIONS

1. What is privacy?

2. What is security?

3. How do security and privacy differ? How are they similar?

4. Explain cross-referencing of data and why it is a privacy threat.

5. List three privacy threats.

6. What is clickstream data?

7. What is a cookie (in the e-business context)?

8. Explain the purposes, good and bad, of cookies.

9. What is a trust seal?

10. Name three major trust seals for e-business.

11. Explain the concepts of awareness, empowerment, and redress in the Principles for Privacy set forth by the U.S. government.

12. What is the Carnivore or DCS1000 program?

13. What is a denial of service attack?

14. List three types of events that can lead to denial of service.

15. Explain how spamming is performed and what the potential results are.

16. What is smurfing?

17. What is a virus?

18. Explain the relationship between viruses, worms, and Trojan horses.

19. What is a parasitic virus? A boot sector virus? A stealth virus?

20. What other types of viruses exist?

21. Explain the difference between active and passive unauthorized access.

22. What is message stream modification?

23. What is spoofing?

24. What company resources are subject to theft?

25. Define preventive security controls and provide two examples.

26. Define detective security controls and provide two examples.

27. Define corrective security controls and provide two examples.

28. What is the purpose of a disaster recovery plan?

29. List five resources for which redundancy can be recommended.

30. Explain what mirrored disks are.

31. What are fault-tolerant systems?

32. Provide three examples of physical access controls.

33. Provide three examples of logical access controls.

34. What is a callback modem?

35. What are the three levels of user identification for controlling access?

36. What should a user profile determine?

37. Define the term biometrics.

38. Provide at least five examples of biometric systems.

39. What is a firewall?

40. What is the difference between an application-level and a packet-level firewall?

41. Explain what an internal firewall is and what a personal firewall is?

42. Explain the differences between a static and a dynamic firewall.

43. List two ways to detect unauthorized access into a company's systems.

44. List important features of a good entrapment server.

45. What is cryptography?

46. What is encryption?

47. What is ciphertext? What is a cipher?

48. What is plaintext?

49. What is asymmetric encryption?

50. What is symmetric encryption?

51. What is public key cryptography?

52. Which key is used to decrypt a message in public key cryptography?

53. Why is the length of the key important in cryptography?

54. What is the best protection against viruses? What is another protection method?

55. What is a "behavior-based" virus protection tool?

56. List the primary security issues for m-commerce.

57. What are the main components of a privacy statement or notice?

58. How are security policies and privacy policies different?

59. What is a security plan? How does it differ from security policies?

60. What are security procedures?

EXERCISES

1. A Web-based company revealed that a hacker successfully accessed the personal information of five hundred of their consumers. Is this a threat to privacy or security for the consumers? Explain.

2. A company collects clickstream data and personally identifiable data. Provide at least five examples of the type of information the company has been collecting.

3. Explain the differences between "opting in" and "opting out" for data collection, and provide an example of each.

4. You are browsing a Web site for travel information. You record your favorite destinations so that alerts on spe-cial deals can be sent to you. Explain what transfers of information occur between the server and your personal computer while a cookie is being setup for this Web site.

5. Give examples of five types of data that could be stored in a cookie set up by your university when you browse the main student pages.

6. For the following denial of service events, state whether they represent a disaster, disruption, or malicious act. For each, propose two potential security controls.

(a) An employee clicks on an attachment that starts the spread of a new virus inside the company.

(b) A tornado hits the town where the central server is located.

(c) An employee starts a fire in the wiring closet.

(d) A hacker sends thousands of e-mail messages to the company's employees using the executive vice-president's e-mail account.

(e) An employee catches a worm while surfing the Internet.

(f) The network operator spills his soda on the main storage device for the server.

(g) The same network operator also spills coffee on the backup tape drive.

7. A friend sends you a new program called joke.txt.vbs as an e-mail attachment. Should you open the file? What will likely happen if you do? Would this be classified as a virus, worm, or Trojan horse? Explain.

8. What does a virus look like? How do experts know when a new virus exists? What can they do about it?

9. For the following examples, identify the type of virus:

(a) An attachment is sent to you that, when opened, will delete all files on your hard drive and then send itself to all users in your address book.

(b) The same virus described in part a, but when it sends itself, it modifies its code slightly.

(c) A virus that starts changing word processing files into templates; it only works when the particular word processor it affects is used.

(d) A virus that your computer catches after you have loaded the files given to you by a good friend on a floppy disk.

(e) A virus that deletes all of your files on the twentieth of the month, but that has been transferred to your computer without your knowledge when you browsed a malicious Web site.

10. For each of the following security threats, suggest one preventive, one detective, and one corrective security control.

(a) A parasitic virus is affecting the company's intranet.

(b) A hacker accesses consumer data on the company's Web site to commit fraud.

(c) A disgruntled employee steals trade secrets from the company's computers.

(d) A construction worker breaks the data communication and electrical cables coming into the company's building.

11. A Web-based company wants to protect its consumers' data collected from online transactions. Propose two logical access controls and two physical access controls that the company can use. Which is the most important?

12. Propose a security measure for a customer banking system that would require possession, knowledge, and physical traits.

13. Which of the biometric systems is the most secure? Why? Which is the least secure? Why?

14. List at least three security threats that a firewall will not protect a company against. Explain why.

15. A company has installed a software system that monitors logon attempts by its users. The software has just detected that a user has attempted to logon to the system five times in the last thirty minutes. Propose an automated response that can be designed into the system. What other measures do you think the company should consider?

16. Break the following code (hint: what are these three words?) 6-13-6-4-21-19-16-15-10-4-3-22-20-10-15-6-20-20-21-6-4-9-15-16-13-16-8-10-6-20. How hard was it? How did you do it? Can you design a better algorithm? What would be included in the algorithm to make it harder to crack?

17. A friend wants to send you encrypted messages. She asks you to send her both your public and private keys. What should your response be? Why? What should you send her? How will you send it? Does it matter?

18. List the main advantages of symmetric encryption over asymmetric encryption. List the main disadvantages.

19. Explain what happens when you request your antivirus software to scan your hard drive.

20. A new Web-based company is asked to provide a privacy notice by some of its customers. What steps should the company undertake to get this notice produced, and who in the company should be involved at each step?

HANDS-ON PROJECTS

1. Download the PGP software from the Massachusetts Institute of Technology's Web site and install it on your computer. Exchange encrypted e-mail messages with your classmates, and encrypt files on your hard drive.

2. Think of a small e-business that you could start with a couple of your classmates. Use one of the privacy notice generators described in the chapter to create a privacy statement for this small e-business.

3. Using the same e-business idea in problem two, develop a security policy covering both the company's employees and its customers.

4. Test the vulnerability of your personal computer using tools described in this chapter (and available on the Internet). Then search the Web for personal firewalls, select one, and install it on your computer. Test the vulnerabilities of your system again and compare the results. How much did the firewall improve your computer's security?

5. Investigate the type of firewalls used at your school or work place. What categories of firewalls are they from? Who has the responsibility for managing the firewall? What functions do the various firewalls perform?

6. Prepare a disaster recovery plan for your university. Make sure you identify all of the disaster-related threats. What is the most likely natural disaster that can occur in your school's area?

7. Pick five Web sites and rank their privacy policies from best to worst. Which has the best policy? Why? Which has the worst policy? Why? What criteria did you use for the ranking?

8. Visit five Web sites. Identify which trust seals are in use at each one. Are there any features that characterize the Web sites that show particular seals? Which seal program seems to apply more to Web sites that use good privacy practices?

9. Find three examples of Web sites where you would provide personal information and discuss the reasons why you would. Then find three examples of Web site where you would not want to provide personal information and discuss why.

10. The network administrator has decided to reevaluate an organization's security plan. You are in charge of designing a new policy for the use of passwords. Describe it.

11. Search the Web for commercially available firewalls. Prepare a comparison chart for three of them, comparing functions, costs, requirements, and reliability.

DISCUSSION POINTS

1. "When a company has to choose between privacy and security, security is the more important feature to have." Debate this statement with your classmates.

2. "Biometric security systems invade individuals' privacy and rights." Discuss this statement with your classmates.

RELATED WEB SITES

Aladdin Knowledge Systems: www.ealaddin.com

Caveo Technology: www.caveo.com

Certicom: www.certicom.com

Cisco Systems: www.cisco.com

Computer Associates International: www.cai.com

InDefense: www.indefense.com

McAfee.com: store.mcafee.com

MIT Distribution Center for PGP (Pretty Good Privacy): web.mit.edu/network/pgp.html

Pelican Security: www.pelicansecurity.com

Singapore's eCitizen Centre: www.ecitizen.gov.sg

Symantec: www.symantec.com

The International PGP Home Page: www.pgpi.com/

Zone Labs: www.zonelabs.com

FURTHER READINGS

Cookie Central home page. Cookie Central. http://www.cook-iecentral.com.

COSTELLO, S. "Hacking for a Better World." *PC World.com* (16 July 2001). http://www.pcworld.com/news/article/0,aid ,55223,00.asp.

COX, J. "Certicom Unveils Wireless Security Software." *Computerworld* (20 February 2001): http://www.computer-world.com/securitytopics/security/story/0,10801,57881,00 .html.

FirstGov home page. http://firstgov.gov/.

HARRISON, A. "Privacy Protection Tools Gain Support at Confab." *Computerworld* 33 (15): 6.

HILLER, J. S., and FRANCE BÉLANGER. "Privacy Strategies for Electronic Government." In *E-Government 2001,* edited by

M.A. Abramson and G.E. Means. New York: Rowman & Littlefield Publishers, 2001.

KAY, R. "Blowing the Whistle on Laptop Theft." *Computerworld* (2 April 2001): http://www.computerworld.com/security-topics/security/story/0,10801,59091,00.html.

LINVINGSTON, B. "New Program Stops Windows 2000/NT/98 Security Weaknesses and Trojans for Free." *Infoworld.com* (4 February 2000): http://www.infoworld.com/articles/op/xml/00/02/07/000207oplivingston.xml.

McCLURE, S., and J. SCAMBRAY. "Survey Points Out that Lack of Training is First Barrier to Improved Network Security." *InfoWorld* 22 (42): 107.

MERRICK, B. "Seven Steps to Beef Up IT Security." *Credit Union Magazine* 67 (4): 13.

NIAP labs to test security-enhanced IT products page. NIAP. http://niap.nist.gov/article1.html.

PANKO, R. R. *Business Data Communications*. Upper Saddle River, NJ: Prentice-Hall, 1997.

Persistent client state HTTP cookies page. Netscape support documentation. http://www.netscape.com/newsref/std/cookie_spec.html.

"Security Statistics." *Computerworld* (9 July 2001): http://www.computerworld.com/securitytopics/security/story/0,10801,62002,00.html.

VERTON, D. "Cybercrime Costs On the Rise in U.S." *Computerworld* (19 March 2001) :http://www.computerworld.com/securitytopics /security/story/0,10801,58737,00.html.

REFERENCES

BOWMAN, L.M. 2001. House pulls carnivore into the light. *ZDNet News* (23 July 2001): http://zdnet.com.com/2100-1106-270406.html.

BRANSCUM, D. 2000. Guarding on-line privacy. *Newsweek* 135 (23): 77–78.

COSTELLO, S. 2001. Code red worm inches along. *InfoWorld* 23 (32): 18.

CULNAN, M. 2000. Georgetown internet privacy policy study. McDonough School of Business, Georgetown University. http://www.msb.edu/faculty/culnanm/gippshome.html.

FITZGERALD, J., and A. DENNIS. 1999. *Business data communications and networking.* New York: John Wiley & Sons.

GREEN, H., C. YANG, and P.C. JUDGE. 1998. A little privacy, please. *Business Week* 3569: 98–99.

GREENSTEIN, M., and T. M. FEINMAN. 2000. *Electronic commerce: Security, risk management, and control.* Boston: Irwin McGraw-Hill.

Harris Interactive. 1999. IBM multi-national consumer privacy survey. Study commissioned by IBM Global Services, October 1999. Available at http://www-1.ibm.com/services/files/privacy_survey_oct991.pdf.

HOFFMAN, D., T.P. NOVAK, and M. PERALTA. 1999. Building consumer trust online. *Communications of the ACM* 42 (4): 80–85.

KALAKOTA, R., and WHINSTON, A. B. 1996. *Frontiers of electronic commerce.* Reading, Mass.: Addison-Wesley.

KRILL, PAUL. 2002. DoubleClick discontinues Web tracking service. *InfoWorld,* 9 January 2002: http://www.infoworld.com/articles/hn/xml/02/01/09/020109hndouble.xml.

LANGA, F. 2000. Four myths of online security. *Winmag.com* (14 February): http://content.techweb.com/winmag/columns/explorer/2000/04.htm.

MELILLO, W. 1999, Private lives? *Adweek* 40 (45): IQ22–IQ28.

MIT Distribution Center for PGP page. 2002. Massachusetts Institute of Technology. Accessed 30 May 2002: http://web.mit.edu/network/pgp.html.

Online privacy policy. 2001. *Intellectual Property & Technology Law Journal* 13 (1): 10–12.

Pew Internet and American Life Project. 2000. Trust and Privacy Online: *Why Americans Want to Rewrite the Rules,* available at: http://www.pewinternet.org/reports/toc.asp?Report=19.

Privacy Working Group of the National Information Infrastructure Task Force. 1995. *Privacy and the National Information Infrastructure: Principles for Providing and Using Personal Information.* 6 June 1995. Available at http://nsi.org/Library/Comm/niiprivp.htm.

Protecting your financial privacy: your finances are less secure than you think. But the web can help you fight back. 2000. *Money* (1 June): 161.

PUNCH, L. 2000. Big brother goes online. *Credit Card Management* 13 (3): 22–32.

RADCLIFF, D. 2001. University computers remain hacker havens. *Computerworld* (12 February 2001): http://www.computerworld.com/securitytopics/security/story/0,10801,57605,00.html.

WHITE, CURT M. 2001. *Data communications and computer networks: A business user's approach.* Cambridge, MA: Course Technology.

CHAPTER 11

ELECTRONIC PAYMENT SYSTEMS IN E-BUSINESS

LEARNING OBJECTIVES

After reading and completing this chapter, you should be able to:

- Explain the concepts of electronic cash and electronic checks
- Explain the concept of micropayments
- Discuss the various uses of cards for payments, including credit cards, prepaid cards, magnetic cards, and smart cards
- Explain the role of digital certificates
- Explain the role of digital signatures
- Understand the SET and SSL encryption technologies
- Discuss various managerial issues related to the use of electronic payment systems

Opening Case: paysafecard.com

Electronic business, especially Web-based e-business, cannot grow without the availability of appropriate **electronic payment methods.** We will discuss a number of electronic payment methods in this chapter, although credit cards continue to be the most used form of payment on the Internet. For each method, there are advantages and drawbacks. A newcomer in this market is the **scratch card.** The idea is simple—customers buy scratch cards that are worth a prepaid amount of money. The customer then scratches off a protective film covering a sixteen-digit personal identification number (PIN). These numbers can then be used for Internet payments. One of the companies that offers these cards is paysafecard.com (Werkarten AG), which originated in Austria (see Figure 11-1).

The paysafe cards are sold with a prepaid amount of €25, €50, and €100 (approximately U.S.$24, U.S.$49, and U.S.$97 at time of printing) by a number of distributors, including electronic equipment retailers, gas stations, and post offices. There are two types of cards: blue and red. The blue cards are sold to adults, while the red cards are sold to minors under the age of eighteen. Some Web sites accept only blue cards (e.g., gambling and erotic sites), while others (the rest) accept both blue and red cards. Because the cards contain PINs without identification, they are almost the same as cash, at least in terms of anonymity. Web sites that accept the paysafecard display the paysafecard logo on their sites. When a customer

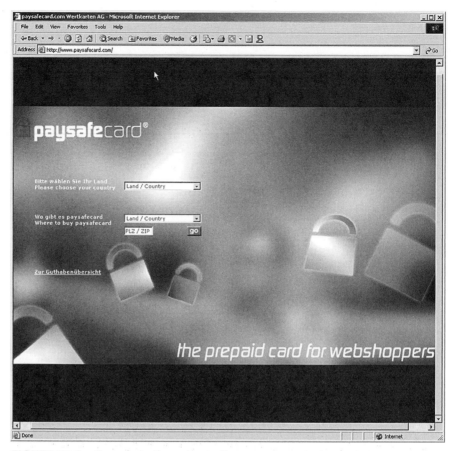

FIGURE 11-1 Paysafecard.com Home Page

SOURCE: paysafecard home page, paysafecard.com, http://www.paysafecard.com/. Used with permission.

proceeds to checkout on a retail Web site using the paysafecard logo, he is redirected to the paysafecard server site. At this point, there is a check to make sure that the card contains sufficient value to pay for the goods or services being bought. When the customer gets to the paysafecard site, he must enter the PIN from the card and, optionally, a passphrase to confirm payment. To make use of the passphrase option, which adds security, customers simply go to paysafecard.com and link their PINs to specific passphrases prior to using the cards. Once the payment is approved, the customer is redirected to the Web shop, which is notified at the same time that the payment is being made to its account. While one payment may use up to 10 cards (€1,000 or U.S.$350, approximately), other payments can be as small as one cent, allowing **micropayments** (very small payments). All transmissions are encrypted using SSL, which we will discuss later in the chapter.

There is no charge to consumers for using paysafecard.com. However, a consumer must use the total amount on the card within two years of the first use of the card, or three years after the production date visible on the outside of the card. After that, the amount on the card is reduced at a rate of €2 per month (approximately U.S.$2 per month). If customers change their passphrases, however, they can prolong the initial two-year period.

Paysafecard.com has announced its intention to support **person-to-person payments** in the future. Person-to-person payments occur when two consumers transact directly with one another, for example on the eBay.com auction site. The cards also offer customers the peace of mind of knowing that their maximum liability in case of theft or fraud is the value of the card. This solution for electronic payment is particularly attractive to young consumers, who have money but no credit cards or bank accounts of their own.

Who pays for the services? The Web merchants pay approximately 5 percent of the transaction costs for tangible goods, and 10 to 15 percent for downloadable goods, with high costs for erotic products and low costs for scientific information, for example. While these costs are higher than credit card costs for the Web merchants, the merchants benefit from the use of these cards in many ways. First, paysafecard.com provides technical support for the merchant's payment Web page. Also, the use of prepaid amounts and the possibility for micropayments allows firms to access new customers who may otherwise not be able to make purchases online. Another advantage is the payment guarantee for the merchant. Paysafecard.com suggests that their cards are very well accepted in Austria. They have started the service in Germany, and a similar service has been announced in Denmark (Webcard).

There are several advantages to the use of scratch cards, including the following.

- The consumer does not need a bank or credit card account.
- It is possible to make anonymous payments.
- There is no need to transfer personal financial data to use the card.
- There is no need for the consumer to possess special technology.
- There is limited need for special technology for the merchant (just the redirection of consumers to the paysafecard.com Web site).
- The payment method is familiar to many users, such as those who use it for mobile telephony.
- Micropayments are possible.
- The method can be used on a range of different platforms.

Do you think that scratch cards offer a good electronic payment method for e-businesses? Do you think that their use will gain popularity in the United States? Australia? Other countries in the world? What are the main disadvantages of using scratch cards? Can you think of other uses for scratch cards besides Web payments?

INTRODUCTION

The term "e-commerce" includes the word "commerce," a word that signifies that economic transactions are being conducted. The basic requirements for conducting commerce over the Internet are fairly simple: a virtual storefront, the ability to accept payment, a fulfillment process to handle shipping and tracking, and customer support. This chapter deals with one element at the core of business transactions: accepting payment. There are numerous forms of electronic payment methods that e-businesses and traditional businesses can consider. This chapter will describe these various payment alternatives. We will also discuss issues related to electronic payment methods, such as security.

Traditional versus Electronic Payment Methods

Traditional payment methods include cash, checks, credit cards, and debit cards. Electronic payment methods include new technologies, such as **electronic cash,** as well as variations on existing payment methods, such as **electronic checks.** Other electronic payment methods include credit cards and accounts and prepaid cards and accounts. These forms of payment may employ **smart card** or magnetic card technologies. Obviously, the two payment methods are not mutually exclusive (credit card payments are both traditional and electronic), but electronic payment methods use electronic means to convey the value of money. Early traditional payment methods included barter and cash. Before money was created, barter was the method of payment for goods and services. Goods and services were exchanged when there was overproduction, or an excess supply, of one good. Cash in the form of silver coined money was used in the seventh century B.C. in Greece as a unit of exchange, and it quickly spread to other empires. Over the centuries, money took different forms. Eventually, checks and money orders appeared in the late 1800s. A check is a written order to a financial institution to pay money to the bearer of the check from the account of the signer. If the check is a cashier's check, the amount has already been paid to the institution, and the money will be taken from the institution's own account. A money order functions similarly, with the amount already paid by the signer to the financial or other institution.

While credit has existed for a long time, through various accounts maintained by the creditor for each person that owed him money, the use of credit cards is far more recent. Credit cards can be used instead of cash or checks to pay for goods and services. These plastic rectangular cards were originally issued by oil companies and large retailers. Eventually, banks followed and formed organizations to operate as clearinghouses for credit card transactions. The two largest organizations today are Visa and MasterCard. Finally, debit cards recently appeared as a new form of traditional and electronic payment. Debit cards look similar to credit cards, but the bank accounts of the holders are directly debited (money is deducted from the accounts) when transactions occur.

For electronic business transactions, however, it would be quite difficult and insecure to use coins, checks, or even debit cards for payments. Therefore, a number of electronic payment methods have been developed. These methods include electronic cash, electronic checks, credit cards and accounts, and prepaid cards and accounts.

▶ *Decision Point*

An e-business must decide prior to establishing the company's Web site which method it will accept for payment of goods and services by its customers or business partners. The owner or management of the e-business must answer the following questions.

- Will we accept traditional payment methods, such as cash or paper checks?
- Will we accept electronic payment methods, such as credit cards, prepaid cards, electronic cash, or electronic checks?
- Should we accept a combination of both traditional and electronic payment methods?

ELECTRONIC PAYMENT METHODS

Electronic Cash

Electronic cash is a method of payment in which a unique number or identifier is associated with a given amount of money. It is also called **digital cash, e-cash,** or **cybercash.** It was developed as an alternative method to credit cards for purchases made over the Internet. Some definitions of electronic cash are much broader, describing it as any form of "prepaid, stored value that can be used for electronic purchases" (Greenstein and Feinman 2000, 320). This would then include prepaid cards, including smart and magnetic cards. The use of electronic cash requires the consumer to acquire an account number or identifier, and then "electronically" deposit money to this account. When making purchases online, this number is then used for payment. The first company to promote electronic cash in the United States was DigiCash, which went bankrupt in 1998. There are a few e-cash companies still in operation in the United States, such as EcashServices.com. Other digital cash service providers, such as CyberCash, have diversified into other electronic payment services (CyberCash was recently acquired by VeriSign, and we discuss this case in more depth in the discussion problems at the end of the chapter).

In recent years, e-cash has suffered from a lack of acceptance in the e-business world, with very few payments made with e-cash for e-commerce transactions. As previously stated, the first company to promote electronic cash in the United States, DigiCash, went bankrupt soon after it convinced only one bank to try e-cash. Many say that the downfall of digital cash is due to the fact that consumers have to download **digital wallets** to really make use of e-cash (we discuss digital wallets later in this chapter), and they simply did not want to have to do that. Furthermore, as more online consumers were less technologically savvy, there was even less interest in using e-cash. Yet, there is still a place for electronic cash as an electronic payment method, as exemplified by the success it has had in Europe and Japan, where this method of payment is widely accepted.

Reward System

Another form of electronic cash that has evolved over the last few years is the point system. It is used extensively in consumer reward systems. In reward systems, consumers are given electronic dollars for purchasing from Web merchants participating in the program. The electronic dollars can then be spent at any of the program affiliates. Customers can also be rewarded for viewing ads, participating in surveys, or linking to Web sites. Some companies also allow the electronic cash or points to be converted into real cash and deposited into the consumer's bank account. A number of such companies exist, including GoldPoints.com, MyPoints.com, and ipoints.co.uk.

Micropayments

Electronic cash payments that range from a few cents to U.S.$10 are called micropayments. For a while, the e-business industry thought that micropayments would fuel the growth of Internet shopping. The thinking behind this business model was that items selling for less than U.S.$10 on the Web should sell more than more expensive items (which would sell more in traditional stores). Micropayments would then be the payment method of choice for these transactions. Some Web-based companies created products specifically designed to enable micropayments. Trivnet Ltd. is one such company (see Figure 11-2). However, recent data show that few items cost less than U.S.$10 on the Web, and that consumers prefer credit cards for electronic payment. Because it is not economical to accept credit cards for micropayments, other methods (described later in the chapter) have been developed for online payments for low-cost purchases. Yet, micropayments will remain as a viable alternative electronic payment method on the Web.

E-mail Payments

Both electronic cash and credit card payments can be sent by e-mail. Person-to-person systems, for example, can use e-mail to handle transaction payments between consumers. Examples of person-to-person transactions can be found in online auctions, such as eBay. For e-mail payments, an account is opened with a company specializing in person-to-person payments, such as Bank One's eMoneyMail or Western Union's MoneyZap. Many similar services are available on the Internet. The process is quite simple. The payer sends an e-mail stating who the payee is, what amount is to be paid, and where the money is to come from (credit card or bank account). The payee receives a notification that the payment is available. She logs into

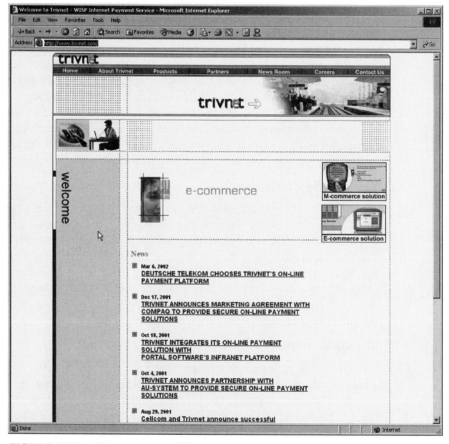

FIGURE 11-2 Micropayments: Trivnet

SOURCE: Trivnet home page, Trivnet Ltd., http://www.trivnet.com/homepage.asp. Used with permission.

the payment service's system and transfers the received amount into her bank account electronically. Different services perform the money transfers in a variety of ways. Some require both the payer and payee to log onto their systems, while others work with mostly electronic mail. Of course, the service providers charge a transaction fee for these services.

Electronic Checks

An electronic check is the same thing as a paper check, except that it is electronic, or online. Also known as an **e-check,** an electronic check is an instruction to a financial institution to pay a given amount to the payee. It therefore contains the same information you would see on a paper check, such as the routing information, account number, check number, and amount of payment. Electronic checks are used extensively in business-to-business transactions for which companies do not need to have a paper check. All payments are made electronically between the buyer's bank and the seller's bank. The main advantage of electronic checks is that they are substantially less expensive to process than paper checks. For example, a paper check can cost U.S.$0.75 to U.S.$3 to process, while an electronic check costs about 50 cents. As with all electronic payment methods, however, consumers may be worried that electronic checks are not as secure as paper checks when the information is sent over unsecured networks. Using the encryption technologies described in the previous chapter can help address some of these concerns.

When an electronic check is sent to a payee, the information can be sent to a third party check-clearing service (a clearinghouse), or directly to the financial institutions involved. If all parties are set up for electronic transactions, the financial institution of the payer will send an electronic transfer of funds to the financial institution of the payee, which will then credit the payee's account. If the payee does not accept electronic checks, the financial institution will probably produce a regular paper check for that payee. E-businesses wishing to use electronic checks can acquire software to produce and manage electronic checks, or can use a third party electronic check service provider to handle all of their e-check processing needs, which is usually a more costly but less troublesome approach. Such companies include PayByCheck, OnLine Check Systems, EZ Check Guarantee, CyberSource, and many others.

Electronic checks can also be used at regular brick-and-mortar stores. The person who wants to use such a check at the store would fill out a Web-based form at the checkout counter. This form authorizes electronic payment and provides the information previously listed (account number, bank routing number, check number, payee information, and payment amount). This information is then sent to an approval agency and a check clearinghouse, just as it would be for normal paper checks.

Prepaid Cards and Accounts

Prepaid cards and accounts represent a new breed of traditional and electronic payment methods that has grown in popularity in recent years. The principle is that cards are preloaded with specific amounts of money, which can then be spent online or in brick-and-mortar stores. Prepaid accounts can also be set up with online retailers for use on those retailers' sites only. This is appealing for consumers who do not have access to credit cards, choose not to have credit cards, or want control over their expenses. A new version of the prepaid card that is gaining attention in Europe is the scratch card. Cards are preloaded with amounts of money and are sold in wrapped packages. Once the package is opened, there is a film that is scratched off, revealing a 16-digit PIN (personal identification number), similar to scratching lottery tickets to discover prizes. The opening case, paysafecard.com, presented one example of such a scratch card.

Credit Cards and Accounts

Credit cards and credit accounts can be used both as traditional payment methods for transactions conducted with brick-and-mortar organizations, and as electronic payment methods for transactions with online merchants. Credit cards are the preferred method for online payments. In 2000, as many as 95 percent of online purchases were handled with credit cards (Napier et al. 2001). Some of the reasons why credit cards are the preferred online payment method include easy access to credit cards and convenience, since credit cards can be used for both online and offline purchases. For e-businesses, credit cards can be costly, but since consumers want to use them, there is little choice regarding accepting credit cards or not.

Companies using Visa, MasterCard, or another credit card system must pay a fee to the clearinghouse based on the total value of the transactions performed by their customers. This is usually a percentage of sales. It is important to realize that the fees charged can also be affected by certain high-risk factors, factors that tend to be even more present in an e-business environment. Two of these high-risk factors include:

- *Lack of presence of cardholder*—When a consumer acquires a good or service with her credit card in a traditional brick-and-mortar environment, the consumer signs the card, and her signature can be verified by the clerk for conformity with the signature on the back of the card. When the consumer performs a phone or Web-based transaction, however, she does not sign the receipt. These transactions are therefore considered higher risk, and, consequently, the fee for card use charged by the clearinghouse can be higher as well.

- *High-risk products or services*—Certain types of products or services are considered higher risk than others. If an e-business is involved with one of these types of products, the companies issuing credit cards may charge higher fees to protect themselves from the risk that the money will never be collected from the card user.

There are a few other issues with the use of credit cards for online purchases. One of them is security, which we will discuss in the next section. Another problem is privacy. Because consumers' purchasing habits can be tracked through the use of their credit cards, several privacy advocacy groups warn that extensive use of credit cards online leaves a trace or profile of purchases for each user. Another issue, as previously discussed, is that it is not cost efficient to accept credit cards for purchases of less than U.S.$10.

Card Technologies

Credit cards and prepaid cards typically use one of two technologies: magnetic cards or smart cards. We briefly review these technologies here, without going into the details of the technical fabrication of the cards.

Magnetic Cards

Magnetic cards have existed for several decades, and could therefore be considered a traditional payment method. However, because data are encoded magnetically, magnetic cards are a viable payment solution for some electronic business applications. Data is encoded and stored on the magnetic strips usually found on the back of the cards. Three basic technologies are used: **online strip, offline strip,** and **smart-card hybrid.** The online magnetic strip card is the simplest. Information to be accessed by a particular system is stored on the magnetic strip. Online magnetic strips are used, for example, for credit cards, debit cards, library cards, and other identification cards. The information is read from the card but nothing is written onto the card by the systems that are accessing the information. Offline magnetic strip cards store information, but also allow this information to be interpreted and modified by the systems that access it. For example, prepaid calling cards are interpreted by phone systems to calculate how much money is remaining on the cards. As the money is being used, new information about the remaining balance is computed and stored on the card itself. Hybrid cards use magnetic strips combined with smart card technology.

Magnetic cards suffer from a few major disadvantages, which have led to the development of smart cards. First, the strips are vulnerable to damage because they are on the exterior of the cards. For example, a card that comes into contact with a magnet (like the small ones used in many wallets) can be erased. Another vulnerability is scratches on the surface of the magnetic strip, which can render the card unreadable. Finally, it should be noted that security could be an issue with such cards because the information is easily readable with a card reader. If the information is not encrypted, then anyone with such a reader can access the stored information.

Smart Cards

Smart cards evolved from magnetic strip cards. Instead of encoding and storing data using a magnetic strip, a computer chip is included on the card itself. Smart cards are the same size as magnetic cards, but they can be used to store a much larger quantity of financial or nonfinancial data, such as bank account information, electronic cash, medical history, or network access identification. Like magnetic cards, smart cards can be used online and offline.

There are actually two types of smart cards available: **memory smart cards** and **intelligent smart cards.** Memory smart cards are used mainly to store information, just as magnetic strip cards are. They usually contain less information and have fewer processing capabilities than intelligent smart cards. However, they are less expensive to produce. Intelligent smart cards contain not only storage capabilities, but also microprocessors that can be used for processing information and making programmed decisions. Of course, they can be used for a large number of applications, but they cost more to produce than memory smart cards. Merchants who want to accept smart cards must have smart card readers, which can represent additional costs beyond what they already pay to accept credit cards.

Smart cards provide numerous advantages over magnetic cards. First, they can store a lot more data: at least 100 times the amount that can be stored on magnetic cards. They are also less vulnerable to external damage, since the data is stored internally (on the chips). Therefore, scratches and demagnetization are nonexistent problems. However, smart cards, just like magnetic cards, are not totally secure, as any appropriately equipped person can read the information. Yet, when the use of passwords is required for access to the information, smart cards provide some security, at least more than carrying cash.

Smart cards are very popular in some areas of the world. They are used, for example, as telephone cards for pay phones throughout Europe. They can also store money for use at a number of different locations. One example is the Mondex card, which can be loaded with money from multiple currencies, used for payments at participating merchants, used in public telephones, and reloaded electronically via the phone or the Internet. The card also supports micropayments (as small as three cents). It is used extensively in Europe and Asia. Several universities have also started using smart cards on their campuses. One of the authors works for Virginia Tech, where all students and faculty use identification cards that are smart cards. However, the IDs can also be used for payment at the university's many restaurants, cafeterias, and bookstores. It can also be used at numerous stores throughout the town where the university is located. For e-business, consumers could use smart card readers connected to their personal computers to transfer money electronically from their bank accounts to their smart cards. They can then use the cards for offline purchases or online purchases (via the card readers).

The advantages of using smart cards are numerous. First, the money is available immediately—what you have is what you get. They can be reloaded easily and remotely. They are as light as credit cards, and the amount that can be lost is limited to the amount stored. The disadvantages of the cards, however, are also important. First, the card can be stolen and there is no way to recover the amount loaded on the card, just as if cash was lost. The cards also require special equipment if they are to be used on the Internet with one's personal computer, which adds to consumers' costs.

Other Electronic Payment Methods

The electronic payment methods discussed so far in this chapter are all useful for business-to-consumer electronic commerce. As a matter of fact, B2C e-business offers far more online payment options than business-to-business commerce does (Frook 2000). While several of these methods are also employed for B2B transactions, they are mostly used when small businesses are involved. Large companies doing business together electronically tend to use Electronic Data Interchange (EDI) systems to send each other bills and notices of payments. The payments are made using electronic fund transfers (EFT) between banks. These payments through EFT represent a large portion of all electronic payments made in e-business. Refer to Chapter 6 for our discussion of EDI and its supporting infrastructures. The B2B market is very important for electronic payment processing providers, since, as of December 2000, only 14 percent of business transactions were conducted electronically, including those using EDI and EFT (Frook 2000). Therefore, there is a large potential market for electronic payment processing providers. These providers will continue to seek new tools because B2B companies are demanding new methods of payment in order to avoid credit card transactions, which cost, on average, 2.5 percent of the transaction amounts. Conversely, an EFT transaction costs approximately U.S.\$1, no matter how large the transaction is.

Other standards and technologies exist for electronic payments around the world. Actually, the fact that there are numerous nonstandardized local and national payment methods worldwide can be a barrier to cross-border electronic trade over the Internet. An example can be taken from methods used in the Netherlands. Three popular electronic payment methods there include Bibit and TWYP. Bibit offers two payment packages; one uses one currency only and the other allows multiple currencies with numerous additional options. It is in operation in the Netherlands, Germany, France, and Belgium, and is trying to penetrate the U.S. market. TWYP (The Way You Pay) is similar to Bibit, but uses only one currency. Numerous other standards and products exist throughout the world. Unfortunately there is not one universal standard for electronic payment, but this will become more and more important for global electronic commerce.

What fees exist for the use of various e-payment methods? A lot of them, and they depend on a variety of factors, including the type of e-payment method, the risks associated with it, and the volume of transactions each merchant makes. Table 11-1 provides sample fees for some of the e-payment methods discussed in this chapter. Note that in addition to the fees presented in the table, there are often equipment fees, software fees, hosting fees, access fees, and other special fees of all kinds. Often, these fees become substantial. For example, an e-business has to pay fees to its bank for its accounts, acquire a credit card machine or pay a credit card processing provider, and pay the credit card transaction fees in order to accept credit card payments.

Table 11-1 Sample Fees (February 2002) for Some E-payment Methods

Method	Example	Cost to Merchant (U.S.$)	Cost to Consumer (U.S.$)
E-cash	EcashServices.com	$2 per transaction + 6.5–8.5% processing fee (on net revenues) + 10% 6-month rolling reserve **or** 10–15% of net revenues for single sale accounts **or** 15% for adult paysites + rolling reserve (10%)	■ No cost to use ■ Cash deposited in account from credit card can be counted as advance (interest charged from day of transfer at credit card rate)
E-check	PayByCheck	2–5% of transaction value + Software or hosting service	■ Banking fees for checking account ■ Banking fee for electronic billing accounts (approx. $0 to $10 per month)
	Intell-A-Check	$0.15 to $1.00 per transaction 2–2.5% for credit check (e.g., Telecheck, Equifax)	■ Banking fees for checking account ■ Banking fee for electronic billing accounts (approx. $0 to $10 per month)
Credit card	Visa, MasterCard, etc.	2–6% of transaction value (average 2.5%) + Equipment, software, and/or hosting service	■ Annual fee ($0 to $150) + Interest (for incomplete monthly payments) at high interest rates
Scratch card	paysafecard	5% of transaction cost (tangible goods) **or** 10–15% of transaction cost (downloadable goods)	■ None (card acquisition at face value, but face value diminishes or is lost after time period elapses)

▶ *Decision Point*

Now that we have discussed various electronic payment methods, it is time for the e-business' management to decide which method(s) of payment the company will accept. The e-business owners or managers must answer the following questions.

- How many electronic payment methods do we want to accept?
- Do we want to accept e-cash?
- Will we have to accept micropayments?
- Do we want to accept e-checks?
- Will we allow the use of credit accounts?
- Will we allow the use of prepaid accounts?
- Can we accept prepaid cards?
- Do we accept credit card payments?
- Which credit cards should we accept?
- Will we accept smart cards?

ELECTRONIC PAYMENT SECURITY TECHNOLOGIES

In the previous section, we presented various electronic payment methods. The choice of the appropriate method depends on a variety of factors, including the size of the business, the type of business, the types of customers, and the types of products and services. In addition, no matter which method is selected, security has to be considered, since it is one of the major issues associated with electronic transfers of funds. In the previous chapter, we discussed several security threats and controls in e-business. We will not go over those details again, but we will expand the discussion of security as it applies particularly to electronic payment methods.

The basic security feature used for exchange of credit card information online is encryption. We discussed cryptography and its functioning in the previous chapter. There are two standards for encryption and security that particularly apply to electronic payments: SET and SSL. **Secure Sockets Layer (SSL)** provides server-side encryption and authentication for electronic payments (and other types of Internet communications). **Secure Electronic Transaction (SET)** provides secure data transmissions, specifically for electronic payments, via encryption and authentication. This section provides a more in-depth discussion of these two standards. But first, we review the topic of authentication and expand it to include the use of **digital signatures** and **digital certificates.**

Authentication

In the previous chapter, we discussed authentication as one of the security measures most used by businesses. For e-business transactions, authentication can be performed through user names and passwords, physical access controls, or biometrics. In e-business, security must go both ways—the user identity needs be verified so the merchant knows it is dealing with a legitimate user, and the merchant identity must be verified so the user knows the merchant is legitimate. Digital signatures and digital certificates play important roles in this process.

Digital Signatures

In traditional payment methods, a signature is often the legal proof that the consumer did indeed agree to the payment. For example, a paper check has to be signed to be valid, and a credit card receipt must be signed when a customer pays the bill at a restaurant or in a shop. In the electronic world, however, it is difficult to sign a document that is not printed anywhere. That's where digital signatures come into play. A digital signature is a unique code attached to an electronically transmitted message that identifies the sender. This unique code, called a hash, is generated through the encryption techniques discussed in the previous chapter. Digital signatures use public key cryptography to generate a number (the hash or message digest) based on the document that is being sent. The document and the hash are therefore closely linked. If either the document or the generated number is altered, they will not match and it will not be possible to open the document. The hash is very secure because once it is generated, it is encrypted using the user's private key. Only the user's public key can then be used to decrypt the hash. The decrypted hash and the hash generated by the user's public key are then compared at the receiving end, and if they match, the user did indeed "sign" this document. Since in theory, only the sender has access to the private key, only he or she can sign a document with it. Many governments now recognize digital signatures as legally binding.

Digital Certificates

A digital certificate is an electronic document that verifies the sender or receiver's identity, similar to a passport or driver's license. A number of different data can be stored in a certificate, including name, serial number, a copy of the entity's public key, a digital signature, and expiration date for the certificate. For e-businesses, obtaining digital certificates reassures others that they are legitimate entities. This reassurance is possible because certificate, or certifying, authorities issue digital certificates. A **certificate authority (CA)** is a trusted third-party organization, usually a commercial enterprise, that guarantees the identity of the persons or organizations involved in the online transactions. A certificate authority can also be specialized software, such as encryption software, that issues digital certificates for users. Examples of well-known certifying authorities include VeriSign, Thawte, AT&T, and Uptime. Lists of digital certificates recognized by a browser are listed in the "Internet options" on a user's computer (for the Windows operating system). Figure 11-3 shows an example of a digital certificate.

There are different types and classes of digital certificates. Certificates that serve as verification of a Web server's identity (you are indeed dealing with a valid merchant) are called **site certificates.** When users want to prove their identity, they may make use of a **personal certificate.** The certifying authorities themselves have certificates called **certifying authority certificates.** Finally, the certificates generated by software publishers for their software products are called **software publisher certificates.** Different certifying authorities ask for different proofs of identity before issuing certificates. The required documentation can also vary according to the level of assurance of identity provided by the certificate. VeriSign, for example, issues four classes of certificates. Class 1 certificates offer lower authentication of identity (e-mail address verification), while class 4 certificates offer the maximum level of identity assurance (someone must apply in person or provide notarized credentials before obtaining the certificate). Thawte has two server classes and three personal classes of digital certificates.

FIGURE 11-3 A Digital Certificate

When a Web browser is installed on a computer, it usually comes "equipped" with a number of well-known certifying authority certificates preinstalled. This allows the browser to communicate with them securely to request certificates for various sites the user visits. These preinstalled certifying authorities are called **root CAs.** They can authorize other CAs to sign certificates. This creates a **certificate chain.** E-businesses, of course, must apply for and receive digital certificates before consumers can deal with them using this authentication tool. The application process is fairly straightforward, and is available on the Web sites of all CAs. In order to select a certifying authority, the e-business must consider which browser its users will typically have (browsers do not support all of the same root CAs). Another consideration in this choice is the fee the e-business has to pay to the CA for the certificate, and the requirements of the CA.

Certificates expire after a given amount of time has elapsed. This is useful when public keys stored on certificates expire, or when identifying information changes. In addition, if a key is compromised, forcing the expiration of the certificate provides greater security. A **certificate revocation list** contains the certificates that were revoked for one of those reasons.

Secure Sockets Layer (SSL)

Secure Sockets Layer (SSL) was one of the earliest security protocols used on the Internet. SSL is a protocol designed to provide a secure connection between the sender and receiver of information. SSL has several components designed to provide data encryption, message integrity, and user authentication. In e-business, SSL can be used to secure the transmission of credit card information online. When using SSL, the online entry form that contains fields for credit card information (and for other personal information) is stored on a secure server. You can tell it is on such a server when the URL starts with *https://* instead of just *http://,* indicating that the SSL protocol is being used for the transmission. As the browser reads an SSL supported form, it also usually shows a lock or key icon at the bottom of the screen. The information provided by the user on the form is then encrypted before being transmitted. Major players in B2C e-business, such as Amazon.com and Travelocity.com, use SSL for conducting their transactions with customers.

Functioning of SSL

A consumer browses the Web site of an e-business and decides to acquire one of the company's products. The consumer adds the item to her shopping cart. When she is ready to check out, she hits the checkout button, which brings her into the payment form. She knows she has a secure connection between her browser and the server because the lock icon at the bottom of the screen is closed, rather than open. How is this secure connection established? Figure 11-4 shows a simplified example of how the browser and server exchange information to create a secure transmission channel. When the consumer hits "pay," "submit," "checkout," or a similar button, the server returns not only a form to the user's browser, but also a certificate that contains the server's public key (recall our discussion of public keys in the previous chapter) and a number of preferred cryptographic algorithms. The user's browser then selects one of the algorithms and generates a public key and a key pair for the user. It then encrypts the user's secret key with the server's public key. This information is then sent to the server, which can, using its private key, decrypt the user's key. With the browser and server having a secret key, secure transmissions can now be made between the two. When the user has finished filling in the information and sends it to the server, everything that is exchanged between the browser and the server is encrypted and therefore secure. The encryption can be done using nonproprietary keys, such as the Rivest, Shamir, Adelamn (RSA) public-key standard or the private-key Data Encryption Standard (DES). In other words, SSL uses a combination of symmetric and asymmetric encryption to provide transmission security.

The secure channel provided by SSL between the sender and the receiver has three basic properties (E-commerce 101: SSL 2001):

- The channel is private. Once the channel is secured through encryption, it is dedicated to the actual transaction.

- The channel is authenticated. Using digital certificates and signatures, the server endpoint is always authenticated, while the client endpoint might use digital signatures as well.

- The channel is reliable. There is an integrity check designed into the protocol to ensure that the message received accurately reflects the message sent.

In summary, SSL provides a secure connection between the sender and the receiver. This section really just provided an overview of the SSL protocol, which is much more

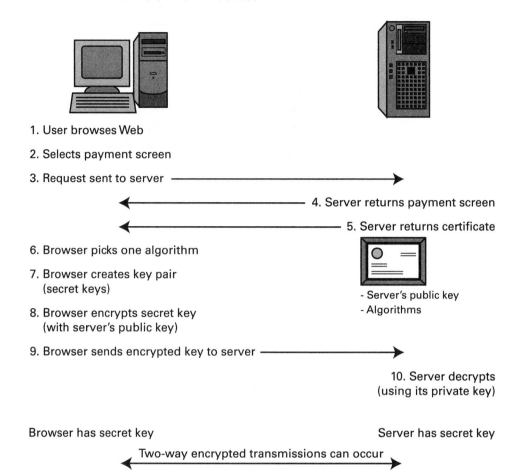

1. User browses Web

2. Selects payment screen

3. Request sent to server ————————————————→

←———————————————— 4. Server returns payment screen

←———————————————— 5. Server returns certificate

6. Browser picks one algorithm

7. Browser creates key pair
(secret keys)

- Server's public key
- Algorithms

8. Browser encrypts secret key
(with server's public key)

9. Browser sends encrypted key to server ————————→

10. Server decrypts
(using its private key)

Browser has secret key   Server has secret key

←——————— Two-way encrypted transmissions can occur ———————→

Note: Server may also request a certificate from the client (browser)

FIGURE 11-4   Establishing a Secure Connection with SSL

complete and complex than described here. It is important to remember that SSL is not a payment method but a security protocol. While we could have discussed it in the previous chapter, SSL was presented here because it was the first tool that really emerged as a way to protect the transmission of payment information online. The new contender for online payment security is SET, which we discuss next.

Secure Electronic Transaction (SET)

Secure Electronic Transaction (SET) is another security protocol, but it is specifically designed for handling encrypted electronic payments online. It was created in 1996 as a result of a unique partnership between Visa and MasterCard, with collaboration by IBM, Microsoft, Netscape, and other information technology-related companies. SET specifications were published in 1997 as an open standard, which allows all companies developing related applications to use this protocol and make their products work together successfully. SET uses digital certificates to authenticate the identity of all participants in the transaction.

There are three participants in the SET model: the consumer or cardholder, the merchant or seller, and the payment gateway or clearinghouse (which processes payment information), in addition to the certificate authority (which issues certificates and verifies their authenticity). Figure 11-5 presents a very simplified example of how the SET protocol works.

The process described in Figure 11-5 requires that every participant be authenticated with the use of certificates. The example is overly simplified and more steps are actually included in the process. For example, in reality the merchant requests a payment when the goods are shipped. The payment authorization described in step six is only a validation of the consumers' credit.

SET specifications include requirements for confidentiality of information (encryption); payment data integrity (through hash functions); authentication of merchants, cardholders, and payment clearinghouses (certificates); and interoperability with other protocols. SET functions similarly to SSL, and uses the DES for secret-key encryption and the RSA standard for public-key encryption. SET uses dual signatures. This means that two messages are generated, one for the consumer and one for the merchant (similar to creating two hashes or message digests, as described in the SSL protocol section). These messages are then combined into the **dual signature** message digest, which is directly linked to the two documents. When the information is decrypted and compared to the generated hashes, any "tampering" of the information on either side of the transaction would result in a nonmatch, and, therefore, an aborted transaction. There are two signatures because one message is for the merchant (order information) and one is for the bank (payment information). The bank's message is encrypted with its public key found in the certificate. As such, the merchant does not access customer credit information, just the order information. The bank itself has no access to the ordering information, which is encrypted with the merchant's public key.

Comparison of SET and SSL

Both SET and SSL are important security tools for electronic payments. They are both critical for the growth of Web-based e-business. They both use encryption as the key method for ensuring the confidentiality of the transmissions. There are, however, some differences between the two protocols. In terms of ease of implementation, SSL is the easiest to implement, requiring only the acquisition of a digital certificate from a certificate authority, and software to support SSL on the Web server. SSL has already been built into most major Web servers and browsers. SET requires implementation of point-of-sale client software. The protocols also differ in their use of digital certificates. SET mandates the use of digital certificates tied to financial institutions for both buyers and sellers. SSL, on the other hand, only requires sellers to have a digital certificate. Buyers may have one also. The SET protocol also includes methods to track individual merchandise and transaction totals, and to track merchant credit policies. The biggest difference, though, is that SET is designed to handle electronic payments specifically, while SSL is a general purpose Internet security protocol. SET includes credit card verification procedures, and, most importantly, separates order information from payment information so that merchants never actually see consumers' credit information, but just receive the payments from the payment gateway.

While overall it might be too early to talk of the "best" protocol for securing payment over the otherwise unsecured Internet, SET seems to offer greater capabilities. Yet, since certificates must be issued for all cardholders and merchants, and since dual signatures are used, SET requires more extended infrastructures and processing capabilities, and is therefore more costly to implement. Some suggest that SSL has already taken a large part of the market and

PRIOR TO TRANSACTION

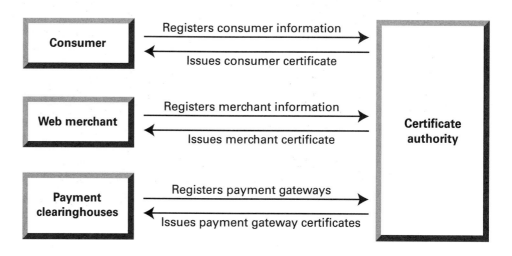

TRANSACTION

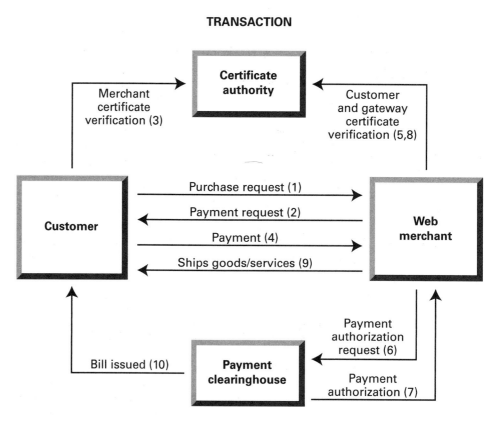

FIGURE 11-5 A Simplified Example of SET Credit Card Process

is solidly established as the secure protocol for credit card transactions. However, given its backing by the major credit card companies, SET is a major contender in the e-business environment. Table 11-2 summarizes some of the key differences between SSL and SET.

Digital Wallet

A digital wallet, also know as an **electronic wallet** or **e-wallet,** is software that encrypts payment information and stores it in a file. The e-wallet can be stored on the client side (the consumer's personal computer), or on the server side (the e-business' server). For the consumer, a digital wallet simplifies the online checkout process once products have been selected for purchase. A simple click inserts the e-wallet information into the payment forms on the merchant's Web site. A number of e-wallet applications are available on the Web, usually for free or minimal fees. Examples of e-wallet applications include SAFLINK's Jotter (even has a biometric e-wallet), Microsoft's Passport, and QWallet.com's Q*Wallet. Numerous banks and companies have now developed their own e-wallets, such as AT&T's e-wallet or MasterCard's e-wallet. Opponents of electronic wallet technology warn that there are serious privacy and security issues with the use of e-wallets. They urge individuals not to store personal financial information on their personal computers, let alone on someone else's server. They argue that these servers become attractive targets for hackers who seek access to a large number of consumers' data simultaneously.

Decision Point

Now that the e-business has decided to accept credit card payments on their Web site, since credit cards are the most common medium for Web-based payments, the company's management or owner must decide which security protocol the company will support on its Web site. The following questions address this decision point.

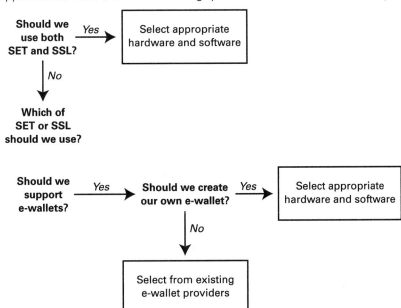

Table 11-2 An Overview of SSL and SET

	SSL	SET
Uses RSA public-key cryptography	✓	✓
Uses DES for private key encryption	✓	✓
Uses digital signatures	✓	✓ (dual)
Digital certificate required for merchant	✓	✓
Digital certificate required for buyer		✓
Ease of implementation (already built-in)	✓	
Protects consumer's credit information from merchant		✓

MANAGERIAL ISSUES

Selecting an E-payment Method

As we have seen in the chapter, there are numerous electronic payment methods available to e-businesses. Which method is best? Of course, it depends on the type and size of the e-business. For a small startup e-business, the appropriate methods will have to be relatively less expensive to implement, while providing flexibility for the company's consumers. For example, a firm selling to young consumers will have to keep in mind that they probably will not have access to credit cards, so the firm should consider pre-paid cards and accounts or electronic checks as payment methods. For a large click-and-mortar company, a host of methods can be appropriate. As a matter of fact, these companies tend to offer numerous options to their consumers or clients. Table 11-3 presents a summary of the electronic payment methods discussed in this chapter, with some of their characteristics.

When looking at Table 11-3, it becomes evident that making a decision about which electronic payment method is most appropriate for one's e-business is not an easy task. Obviously, a company selling mostly to youths is more limited in its options. The type of product sold can also impact the methods used. For example, products targeted to senior citizens will typically attract less computer-savvy users, and therefore ease of use of the payment method becomes one of the most important considerations. In this case, supporting traditional payment methods may be required. Other companies that have low cost products that require micropayments must focus on electronic cash or on portable prepaid or scratch cards. If their typical users are not computer savvy, then having to download digital wallets for e-cash may render this solution less appealing. Table 11-3 also shows that in addition to considerations of size and type of business, type of consumer, and types of products and services, other elements that should be considered in selecting an electronic payment method include (Shaw 1999):

1. Providing security against fraudulent activity
2. Being cost effective for low-value transactions
3. Being protective of the privacy of the users
4. Being convenient for Web purchasing

Outsourcing Payment Processing

With the growth of e-commerce, a number of companies have developed services supporting business functions needed by a small e-business. For example, United Parcel Services offers outsourcing for all shipping and delivery functions for an e-business. There are a number of providers of payment processing services. Some providers allow a small e-business to outsource its payment processing functions without the need to establish an account with Visa or MasterCard, or acquire expensive payment processing software. Firms specializing in payment processing perform these services for a number of small firms. There is a monthly fee for the service. For the user, however, it can be fairly transparent. As the transaction is being processed, the card data is sent to the payment processing service provider, who will check and obtain payment authorization and process the payment. There are literally hundreds of such service providers on the Internet. A search for the words "merchant account" in a good search engine will provide such a list. Figure 11-6 presents an example of one merchant account service called AMS (Advanced Merchant Service).

Decision Point

After evaluating electronic payment methods, the e-business must decide whether to acquire software for processing the payments in-house, or outsource the payment processing for the selected methods. Some questions that can help the owner or management of the e-business make this decision include:

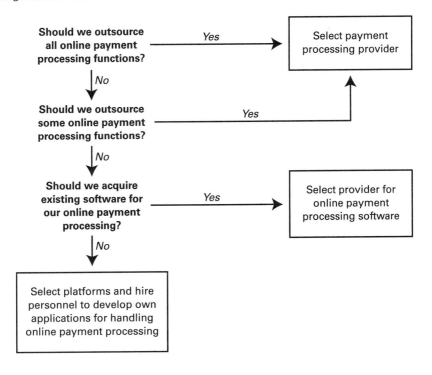

Table 11-3 Comparison of E-payment Methods

Payment Method	Characteristics for E-business				Characteristics for Consumer	
	Type of Consumer	Setup Costs	Security Provided	Low-Value Transaction Support	Web Purchase Convenience	Privacy (Anonymity)
Credit cards	Adult Company	Medium to very high	Low to medium	No	Yes	Low to medium
Prepaid cards and accounts	Youth Adult	Low to medium	High	Yes	No	High
E-checks	Adult Company	Medium to high	Low to medium	No	Yes	Low
E-cash	Adult Youth	Medium	Low to medium	Yes	Yes	Medium to high
Scratch cards	Adult Youth	Low to medium	High	Yes	No	High

Online Fraud

One of the main advantages of doing business over the Internet is universal access. Companies can tap into a very broad market, sometimes worldwide. Unfortunately, universal access is also a cause for concern for anyone involved in conducting transactions over the Internet. All kinds of individuals worldwide have access to companies' servers, and some may use this access for fraudulent activities. Online fraud over the Internet is twelve times higher than for traditional brick-and-mortar transactions (Litan 2000). In a Gartner Group survey, as many as 1.15 percent of all online transactions were fraudulent. Since credit card companies consider e-businesses more risky because there are no signatures to compare at purchase time, the electronic retailers tend to absorb these losses, in addition to paying higher fees for the use of the credit card clearinghouses' services. One way that credit card companies propose to protect themselves on the Web is the use of **disposable credit card numbers.** A number is generated for each transaction and becomes invalid after that transaction. Other restrictions can be placed on these disposable numbers, limiting the risk of fraud for both the user and the e-business. Some downsides of disposable credit card numbers include the fact that they cannot be used in an e-wallet; they cannot be used for transactions that are repeated regularly, such as monthly payments; and they cannot be used for guaranteed payments, such as those made for automobile rentals and hotel reservations.

CLOSING CASE: CYBERGOLD, INC. AND MYPOINTS.COM

As we discussed in this chapter, there are many different electronic payment methods used today. One of these alternative methods of payment for online transactions is electronic

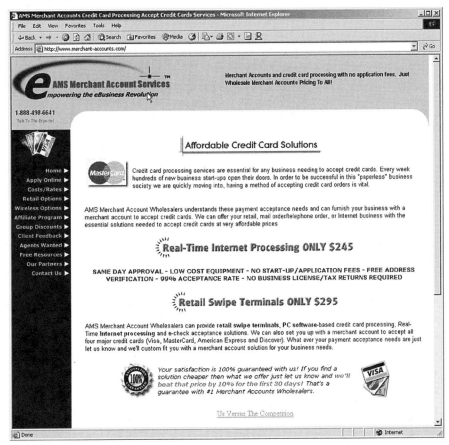

FIGURE 11-6   Payment Outsourcing Example: Advanced Merchant Services (AMS)

Source: Advanced Merchant Services home page, Advanced Merchant Services, http://www.merchant-accounts.com/. Used with permission.

cash, or e-cash, and we outlined its advantages and disadvantages. This case presents a particular type of e-cash that is focused on reward systems. Established in 1996, Cybergold was a direct marketing firm that introduced a new system in March 1999 that offered consumers credits for readings ads, answering marketing surveys, and registering at Web sites. Consumers could then use their "incentive" money to acquire online contents, such as downloadable music, news articles, or software. Consumers could also convert money taken from their credit cards to "incentive" money if they needed more for their purchases. The consumers could also use the rewards by converting them into dollars to be deposited in a credit card or bank account, or by donating their rewards to a number of nonprofit organizations participating in the Cybergold program. Cybergold signed up a number of electronic retailers and partners to participate in the program.

A number of other companies offered reward systems online. The earliest company in this market, beenz, is now out of business. Others have included iPoints and

Webrewards. In April 2001, MyPoints.com announced the acquisition of Cybergold for U.S.$167.3 million. At that point Cybergold had signed up more than nine million users, who were offered the opportunity to transfer to MyPoints.

MyPoints.com is also a direct marketing company that offers rewards to consumers who respond to targeted ads through e-mail and Web sites. Consumers can also earn points by reading marketing e-mail, filling out surveys, visiting Web sites, making referrals to friends, taking advantage of trial offers, and shopping at partner sites. MyPoints.com's database before the acquisition of Cybergold contained six million consumers who had agreed to receive such ads. Consumers can join for free. The points they accumulate can be redeemed at participating retailers. In October 2000, MyPoints.com launched a new service (ValuPage by MyPoints) that enabled its customers to earn even more rewards by printing coupon promotions from its Web site and using them in purchases at supermarkets in the United States.

While an electronic payment method is a crucial element of e-business, how do online reward systems help promote e-business? The reward systems cannot serve as payments unless the users can acquire goods or services from participating merchants, and only if consumers would otherwise have paid for these goods and services. Why do you think companies participate in the MyPoints and Cybergold programs? Why do users participate in the programs? Was the acquisition of Cybergold a good strategy on the part of MyPoints.com? What is your prediction for the long-term potential of survival for MyPoints.com? What should they do next to ensure their survival? Is the use of reward-based electronic cash going to grow as an e-business payment method?

SUMMARY

This chapter discusses one of the key elements of electronic commerce: accepting payment. It starts by comparing traditional payment methods and electronic payment methods. Electronic payment methods use newer technologies to provide electronic means of storing or representing the value of money. These electronic payment methods include electronic cash, electronic checks, credit cards and accounts (including smart and magnetic cards), and prepaid cards and accounts.

Electronic cash is a method of payment in which a unique number or identifier is associated with a given amount of money. It is not as popular as credit cards as a form of electronic payment. One variation is reward or point systems, which offer customers electronic cash for purchasing goods or services at participating affiliates, viewing ads, participating in surveys, or registering on Web sites. Another variation is to send such payments by e-mail. Micropayments are payments of very small amounts, typically less than ten dollars (U.S.), and for which e-cash might be a more appropriate payment method than credit cards.

An electronic check is an instruction to a financial institution to pay a given amount to a payee. These instructions include routing information, account number, check number, and amount to be paid. Prepaid cards and accounts are another electronic payment method; cards or accounts are preloaded with specific amounts of money that can be spent online or in brick-and-mortar stores.

Credit cards are the most used form of electronic payment for online stores. Two factors make the use of credit cards more costly for online merchants than traditional merchants: lack of presence of the cardholder, and therefore no physical signature and verification, and high-risk products or services, which applies to a number of e-businesses. Two technologies are used for credit cards and prepaid cards: magnetic strip cards and smart cards. On magnetic strip cards, data is encoded magnetically and stored on the strips typically found on the back of the cards. There are three basic technologies for these types of cards: online strip, offline strip, and smart-card hybrid. Smart cards store data using computer chips included on the cards. There are two types of smart cards: memory smart cards and intelligent smart cards.

Two tools used for authentication in e-business, and therefore for security, are digital signatures and digital certificates. A digital signature is a unique code attached to an electronically transmitted message that identifies the sender. A digital certificate is an electronic document that verifies the sender's identity, similar to a passport or driver's license. A certificate authority is a trusted third party organization that issues digital certificates and guarantees the identity of the sender.

The two most common encryption protocols for secure transactions on the Internet are SET and SSL. Secure Sockets Layer (SSL) was one of the earliest security protocols used on the Internet, and is designed to provide a secure connection between the sender and receiver of information through data encryption and user authentication. Secure Electronic Transaction (SET) is another protocol, specifically designed for sending encrypted electronic payments online. It is an open standard that utilizes digital certificates to authenticate the identity of all participants in the transaction,

including the buyer, the merchant, and the payment gateway or clearinghouse. Payment information can be stored in a digital wallet. A digital wallet, or e-wallet, is software that encrypts payment information and stores it in a file that can reside on the client side (the consumer's personal computer) or on the server side (the e-business' server).

There are other electronic payment methods, such as electronic funds transfer (EFT) for companies involved in B2B e-commerce. There are also different technologies for payment methods worldwide, such as Bibit and TWYP, which are used in the Netherlands.

Managerial issues discussed in this chapter include how to select an electronic payment method for an e-business, whether to outsource payment processing, and recognizing the problems for an e-business related to online fraud. Some of the considerations for selecting an electronic payment method include: security of the solution against fraudulent activity, cost effectiveness of the solution for low-value transactions, solution's protection of the privacy of the users, and convenience of the solution for Web purchasing.

KEY TERMS

certificate authority (CA)
certificate chain
certificate revocation list
certifying authority certificates
cybercash
digital cash
digital certificate
digital signature
digital wallet
disposable credit card numbers
dual signature

electronic cash (e-cash)
electronic check (e-check)
electronic payment methods
electronic wallet (e-wallet)
intelligent smart cards
magnetic cards
memory smart cards
micropayments
offline strip
online strip
personal certificate

person-to-person payments
root CAs
scratch card
Secure Sockets Layer (SSL)
Secure Electronic Transaction
 (SET)
site certificates
smart card
smart-card hybrid
software publisher certificates

REVIEW QUESTIONS

1. Identify three traditional payment methods.

2. What is a check?

3. Identify the main two clearinghouses for credit card payment in function today.

4. What is electronic cash?

5. How do reward e-cash systems make money?

6. What is a micropayment?

7. What payment methods can be used by e-mail to transfer money?

8. What is an electronic check?

9. What is the main advantage of electronic checks over traditional paper checks?

10. What information needs to be sent on an electronic check for payment to occur?

11. What are the two factors that can make credit card costs for e-businesses higher than for traditional businesses?

12. Which is the preferred method for online payment for B2C transactions?

13. Which is the preferred method for online payment for B2B transactions?

14. How are prepaid cards used for e-business?

15. What two technologies are used for prepaid and credit cards?

16. How do magnetic strip cards store information?

17. What are the different types of magnetic strip cards?

18. What is a smart card?

19. What are the different types of smart cards?

20. List some advantages of using smart cards for e-business.

21. What is authentication?

22. What is a digital signature?

23. What technologies are used for digital signatures?

24. What is a dual signature?

25. What is a hash? How is it generated?

26. What is a digital certificate?

27. Who issues digital certificates?

28. What are the two main protocols for security of Web-based transactions?

29. Explain how SSL works.

30. How can you tell when an SSL server is being used?

31. Explain how SET works.

32. Who created SET?

33. What does SET mean?

34. Name two main differences between SET and SSL.

35. What is a digital wallet?

36. What is one of the main issues with the use of digital wallets?

37. List four criteria that should be considered in the selection of an electronic payment method.

38. When should outsourcing be considered for electronic payment processing?

39. Why are e-businesses more subject to online fraud than traditional businesses?

40. How do disposable credit cards work?

EXERCISES

1. For each of the following short descriptions, pick one (and only one) electronic payment method. Justify your answer.

(a) A Web-based store selling camping gear

(b) A Web-based store selling chewing gum products from around the world

(c) A company operating an online job search facility

(d) An "everything for a dollar" online store

(e) A software vendor selling downloadable products

(f) An integrated shopping mall representing fifty stores

2. You are a consultant in a small firm specializing in e-business. Your firm has just received a contract for developing a payment strategy for a small bookstore that has an Internet café. You need to design payment methods for the customers' purchases of books and magazines at the store, coffee and related products at the café, use of the Internet terminals, use of the photocopy machines, and for customers who want to buy books from the bookstore's Web site. Suggest two payment methods for each type of purchase, and highlight the pros and cons of each. Make an overall recommendation integrating all of the services and payment methods.

3. Person-to-person payments are those in which individual consumers transfer money between themselves. The eBay auction site is an example of where such payments are used. Rank all payment methods discussed in the chapter with respect to their appropriateness for person-to-person payments.

4. Provide several potential reasons why it can cost up to six times more to process a paper check instead of an electronic check for e-businesses.

5. You work as the technology guru for a small e-business. Your boss has been told that he should use SSL for payment security. He asks you to explain to him how SSL works in simple terms. You need to show him what happens on the customer's client machine and on his server.

6. Can you send an encrypted message without using a digital signature? Can you send a digital signature without encrypting a message? Discuss in both cases the reasons for doing this and the potential impacts on security.

7. Which protocol requires that all parties to the transaction have digital certificates?

8. The four considerations for selecting an electronic payment method listed in the chapter include security against fraudulent activity, cost effectiveness for low-value transactions, protection of the privacy of the users, and convenience for Web purchasing. Identify at least two other important criteria that an e-business would consider and rank all methods on those two criteria.

9. Give an example of an e-business that would be better off outsourcing payment processing, and give an example of a company that would be better off not outsourcing payment processing.

10. You are working for a small e-business that sells electronic books from a Web site. Identify all risks of fraud the company is facing and suggest at least one solution to address those risks.

HANDS-ON PROJECTS

1. Use the PGP software that we discussed in the previous chapter (http://web.mit.edu/network/pgp.html) and send a message using a digital signature to one of your classmates. What did he receive? How did he know a digital signature was used? Send an encrypted message together with a digital signature. What is different?

2. Go on the Internet and look for the Web sites of all the companies mentioned in this chapter. Which ones are still in business? Which ones are not? Discuss potential reasons why they may still be/not be in business.

3. Visit five Web sites of your choice and identify whether they use SSL or SET for electronic payment security. Report your findings to the class. Discuss which types of companies seem to favor each protocol.

4. One of the early traditional payment systems in existence was bartering. Develop an electronic barter system that can be used for e-business. Who should control it? How are values assigned? Why would anyone participate in the system?

FURTHER READINGS

BRUNO, M. "Downward Spiral for CyberCash." *USBanker* 111 (4) 20.

E-Commerce 101: SET Basics page. iPier.com. Retrieved September 2001: http://www.ipier.com/ecom101/SET-basic.html.

E-Commerce 101: SET vs. SSLpage. iPier.com. Retrieved September 2001: http://www.ipier.com/ecom101/set-ssl.html.

KUYKENDALL, L. 1999. "The Online Challengers." *Credit Card Management* 12 (8): 78–83.

LARSEN, A. K. "Virtual Cash Gets Real." *Information Week* 736 (31 May 1999): 46–58.

LELIEVELDT, SIMON. "Solving the Standardisation Problem of Internet-payments: The Case of Bibit, TWYP and SmartAxis." *ePSO-Newsletter* 6 (March 2001): http://epso.jrc.es/newsletter/vol06/5.html.

MITCHELL, L. 2000. "Payment-processing Gateways Expedite Cybershopping." *Infoworld* 22 (46) 68–72.

MOLTZEN, E. "Cash Blast." *Computer Reseller News* 901 (3 July 2000): 234–238.

"MyPoints.com Enters $6.5 Billion Coupon Industry." *Direct Marketing* 63 (6): 10.

"MyPoints.com Inc. to Buy Cybergold Inc. for 31.57 Times Revenue." *Weekly Corporate Growth Report* Issue 1089 (24 April 2000): 10715.

RADER, MICHAEL. "Scratch cards: Here to Stay?" *ePSO-Newsletter* 6 (March 2001): http://epso.jrc.es/newsletter/vol06/3.html.

SINT, PETER P. "E-money Solution from Austria: Paysafecard.com," *ePSO-Newsletter* 6 (March 2001): http://epso.jrc.es/newsletter/vol06/4.html.

STALLINGS, W. *Network Security Essentials: Applications and Standards.* Upper Saddle River, NJ: Prentice-Hall, 2000.

STEIN, L. D. *Web Security: A Step-by-Step Reference Guide.* Boston: Addison-Wesley, 1998.

REFERENCES

E-commerce 101: SSL page. 2002. iPier.com. http://www.ipier.com/ecom101/ssl.html.

FROOK, J.A. 2000. Payment providers battle for B-to-B. *B to B* 85 (21): 4.

GREENSTEIN, M., and T. M. FEINMAN. 2000. *Electronic commerce: Security, risk management, and control.* Boston: Irwin McGraw-Hill.

LITAN, AVIVAH. 2000. "E-Tailers Squeezed by Higher Credit Card Fraud and Rates," Gartner Group (28 July 2000): http://www3.gartner.com/Init.

NAPIER, H.A., P.J. JUDD, O.N. RIVERS, and S.W. WAGNER. 2001. *Creating a winning e-business.* Boston: Course Technology.

SHAW, M. J. 1999. Electronic commerce: Review of critical research issues. *Information Systems Frontiers* 1 (1): 95–106.

CHAPTER 12

ELECTRONIC BUSINESS ARCHITECTURE

LEARNING OBJECTIVES

After reading and completing this chapter, you should be able to:

- Define the term "architecture" as it applies to e-business
- Identify and describe the layers of a typical e-business architecture
- Identify and describe the components included in each layer of a typical e-business architecture
- Discuss the advantages of global e-business
- Discuss the challenges of global e-business
- Discuss guidelines for successful global e-business
- Discuss technologies and applications that will help shape the future of e-business
- Describe the concepts of ubiquitous computing as they apply to e-business
- Name and describe technology-oriented and non-technology-oriented jobs in e-business

Opening Case: Selecting an Architecture

In February 2002, the Georgia Technology Authority (GTA) announced that it had selected Sun Microsystems to design a Web services portal for the government of the state of Georgia. In a GTA press release dated 25 February 2002, Larry Singer, the chief information officer for the state of Georgia, was quoted as saying that the project represents "one of the most sophisticated software architectures in the world." (An architecture is a blueprint for delivering applications and information.) Sun won the project over a number of strong rivals (including Microsoft and IBM), in part because its solution is based on industry standards rather than proprietary products. Sun's Open Net Environment (Sun ONE) serves as the basis for the solution offered to Georgia. A major advantage of Sun's solution was the fact that Sun ONE can easily integrate with existing and future systems, as long as those systems are standards-based. This allows considerable flexibility when choosing systems in the future. Any system that uses the open standards supported by Sun ONE can be integrated with the portal.

The development of an architecture is the key to ensuring that the various systems used by an organization fit together into an organized whole. Without a guiding architecture, an organization runs the risk of having a hodge-podge of systems that are unable to easily interact with one another. The lack of a guiding architecture is one reason so many organizations have "islands of automation" with systems that are unable to share information. By developing a solid, well-designed architecture, the GTA establishes guidelines that can be used for adding systems in the future. For example, one of the first applications to be integrated with the portal is drivers license renewal. The GTA can use the architecture to guide the specifications for the new system. For example, extensible markup language (XML) is one of the standards included in the architecture. So, the license renewal system must be capable of using XML. This ensures that the license-renewal system is able to interact with other systems that follow the architecture. For example, when a driver uses the system to renew his license, the system can use XML to communicate with a law enforcement system to see if the driver has any outstanding warrants. As long as both systems follow the architecture, such interactions are relatively easy to implement.

Georgia's development of a Web-based portal for governmental services is an example of the growing trend toward the use of e-business technologies by governments. This is known as **electronic government** or **digital government.** Just as e-business technologies allow businesses to improve the efficiency and effectiveness of interactions with customers, so can governments use the technologies to improve interactions with their citizens.

A portal, by definition, provides users with a single point from which to access various resources, such as information and services. The Georgia portal is an example of an enterprise portal, which is organized around the operations of a particular organization. Enterprise portals must balance the needs of internal users with those of external users, such as customers and suppliers. The Georgia portal is no exception to this. In fact, a government portal must serve several different types of internal and external users. Internal users include workers from many different agencies, as well as legislators and other office holders. External users include individual citizens, organizations operating in the state, external governmental agencies (such as cities, counties, and the federal government), and suppliers of goods and services. Each of these groups of users has vastly different needs and preferences. Designing an e-government portal that works well for all users is a complex job. Georgia has made a solid first step by grounding the portal with a well-designed, flexible architecture.

INTRODUCTION

What is an **electronic business (e-business) architecture?** To understand the answer to this question, it is helpful to first understand what the term "architecture" means in the context of information technology. An architecture is simply a guiding framework, or blueprint for delivering the applications and information required by an organization. Applegate, McFarlan, and McKinney (1996) have identified several elements that should be included in an IT architecture:

- Technical computing platform
- Information management platform

- Communications platform
- Structures and controls that dictate IT use
- Applications that utilize the platforms

An e-business architecture is similar, but its focus is on e-business applications. A major function of an architecture is to define how the various components of the environment fit together, as was illustrated in the opening case. Today, most large organizations have an IT architecture in place. This architecture helps guide IT decisions. Consider how a construction blueprint (which is an architectural plan) guides a house builder. If the builder wants to order the doors for the house, the blueprint specifies how many and what types of doors are required. When the blueprint was developed, the house designer, the architect, made sure that the front door specified would match the front windows. By simply following the blueprint, the builder can be sure that every element of the home fits together properly. The same sort of idea is behind the use of an e-commerce architecture. Suppose an organization wants to make digital videos of product demonstrations available to potential customers through a Web site. The choice of a digital media server is guided by the e-business architecture. The person making this choice consults the architecture to make sure that the selected digital media server will fit with other components of the overall e-business environment.

We have several goals for this chapter. First, we introduce the concept of an e-business architecture. Then, we discuss a number of software and hardware components that might be part of an e-business architecture. Another goal of this chapter is to provide you with an overview of some issues related to global e-business. We also discuss a handful of trends that may help shape the future of e-business. The chapter concludes with a brief overview of some e-business-related jobs.

BUILDING AN E-BUSINESS ARCHITECTURE

As discussed earlier, an e-business architecture is a blueprint that is used to guide the delivery of applications and data related to an organization's e-business activities. There are many different ways to express an e-business architecture. Large IT vendors, such as IBM, Microsoft, and Sun Microsystems, have developed their own ways to illustrate an architecture. We take a relatively simple approach to expressing an architecture by breaking it down into three layers: information, applications, and infrastructure. This view is shown graphically in Figure 12-1.

The **information layer** consists of guidelines that direct information creation, distribution, and access for an organization. Issues such as information modeling, standardization, control, and ownership are included in this layer. While the information layer is quite important, we concentrate most of our discussion on the other layers. The **applications layer** describes the environment in which applications will operate, as well as the applications that will implement the business logic required by the organization. Web applications, such as Web servers and content management systems, are also included in the applications layer. In this chapter, we discuss various components of the applications layer. The **infrastructure layer** describes the hardware, networks, and operating systems that serve as the foundation for e-business. Components of the e-business infrastructure

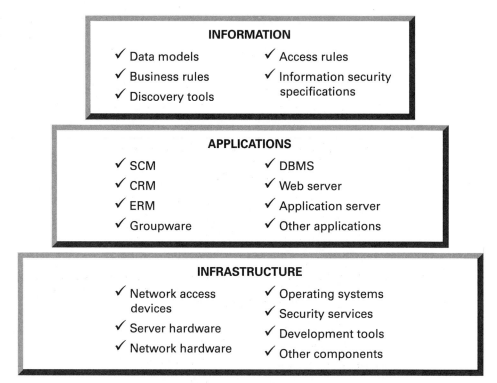

FIGURE 12-1 E-business Architecture

are also discussed in this chapter. As you read through this section, keep in mind that it is almost impossible to offer complete lists of all possible components of each layer. Our goal is to describe some of the most commonly used components, which should be enough to give you a good idea of what each layer is all about.

Information Layer

The information layer in an e-business architecture represents the organization of the data used in e-business applications. Individual data models for each application area are included, as are connections between these models. Data-oriented business rules are also specified in this layer. The information layer also contains specifications for various data warehouses and data marts associated with e-business. Information discovery tools, such as data mining software, data retrieval software, and search technologies, are also specified in the information layer. Information security specifications are also part of this layer.

Applications Layer

There are many different elements that compose the applications layer of an e-business architecture. To improve understanding, we divide our discussion of the applications layer into two categories: business applications and Web applications.

Business applications include the software that is used to implement the business logic of the organization. We have discussed a number of these in various chapters throughout this book. Examples of business applications include:

- Supply-chain management systems—These systems are used to manage the activities and organizations involved in producing a final product or service.

- Customer relationship management systems—Customer relationship management systems help organizations organize and utilize information about customers in order to improve customer satisfaction, while at the same time maximizing profits.

- Enterprise resource management systems—These systems help an organization connect various aspects of its operations by replacing separate, disconnected software applications with a single multi-mode application.

- Groupware—Groupware helps facilitate communication and information sharing among members of a work group. Types of groupware include messaging systems, shared calendars, shared discussion databases, and document management.

- Electronic storefront software—Electronic storefront software may include facilities such as shopping cart systems, wish lists, and product recommendation systems. Some of these systems also integrate shipping management and other order fulfillment capabilities.

- Electronic catalog software—Software in this category helps organizations put their product catalogs online. Typically, these systems make it easier to build and manage an online product catalog and include features such as database import, product categorization, and product searching.

- E-mail client software—E-mail client software allows users to send, receive, and manage e-mail messages. Related software allows users to manage e-mail marketing campaigns.

- Database management systems—Database management systems, which are sometimes included in the infrastructure layer, help organizations create, maintain, and provide access to data. Database management systems shield users and application programs from many of the details of data management.

- Workflow management software—Workflow management software helps organizations cope with the tasks and procedural steps required to complete the steps in business processes. Typically, workflow management systems are concerned with the flow of documents throughout a process.

Previously, we also discussed many technologies that fall into the Web applications category, including most of the servers we covered in earlier chapters. The Web application category includes:

- Web server software—Web servers store and deliver Web pages to users through the use of the HyperText Transfer Protocol. Web servers are discussed in detail in Chapter 6.

- Application server software—This is software that manages communication between Web browser client software and the back-end applications and databases. It allows communication between the Web-based front-end and back-end applications and databases. Typically, application servers are associated with transaction-oriented applications.

- Other server software—Electronic mail server software is responsible for handling electronic mail-related tasks on a network. Multimedia servers are used to distribute various types of digital media files, such as digital audio, video, and still images. Groupware server software handles tasks associated with the operation of groupware applications, such as Lotus Notes and Microsoft Exchange. There are also a number of other types of server software that might be part of the application layer, including chat and fax server software.

- Content management software—Managing all of the content available through an organization's e-business systems is an extremely difficult, complex task. Content management software helps organizations manage the process of creating, tracking, and deploying content.

Of course, any particular organization may have additional components included in its applications layer. However, we hope those described here are sufficient to give you an idea of what is typically included in the applications layer.

Infrastructure Layer

Components included in the infrastructure layer provide the foundation for the other elements of the e-business architecture. The infrastructure includes components that can be placed in several categories, including hardware platforms, operating systems, security services, and development tools. We discuss each of these in turn.

Hardware Platforms

The hardware platforms category can be further divided into computing hardware and network hardware. Computing hardware includes:

- Network access devices—Workstations consist of personal computers and other access devices, such as terminals, personal digital assistants, network-enabled kiosks, and mobile access devices. As new access technologies continue to evolve, organizations must ensure that their architectures are flexible enough to accommodate newer access devices.

- Server hardware—The server software described earlier must run on a computer that is equipped to accommodate the operations of the server software. For smaller e-business systems, standard personal computers may be suitable for these tasks. However, larger e-business systems commonly require specialized computers to act as servers. Often, these server computers can utilize multiple processors and are expandable to incorporate large primary and secondary storage capacities. Sometimes they do not look at all like normal personal computers; they may be rack-mounted, and many do not include a display device, such as a monitor.

- Mainframe computers—As noted in Chapter 8, many organizations have existing legacy systems that must be incorporated into e-business systems. These legacy applications typically operate on mainframe computers. Because of this, an e-business architecture may need to accommodate mainframe computers. In addition, even some newly developed software is developed to take advantage of the tremendous processing capabilities of mainframe computers.

Network hardware includes:

- Switches—Switches send data between different servers within a network.
- Routers—Routers connect different networks and enable packet transmission among the connected networks. These devices are able to analyze network traffic and adapt to current conditions in order to determine the best path for a packet to follow from one point to another.
- Load balancers—Most large organizations have many Web servers (often called a server farm). A load balancer is special software that helps evenly distribute inbound traffic across the servers in the server farm.
- Other network hardware—There are many other network hardware devices that might be included in an organization's infrastructure. A complete list is beyond the scope of this chapter. However, you may wish to refer to Chapter 6 for more information on telecommunications. There are also networking texts listed in the "Further Readings" section at the end of this chapter.

Operating Systems

Operating systems provide the basic interfaces and software environment for computing hardware platforms. In some cases, two different types of operating systems are required, one for basic operations and one for the network. The latter is called a network operating system or NOS. Many operating systems, such as Windows NT, Linux, and Mac OS, have network operating system features included as part of the basic operating system.

Security Services

As you know, security is a very important part of e-business. Protecting data from unauthorized access and accidental or intentional destruction or misuse is critical to a successful e-business environment. So, security services are an important component of an e-business architecture. Examples of security services include:

- Authentication—Authentication services establish the identity of a user before allowing access to various resources, such as applications. Network operating systems typically provide some authentication services. However, many organizations are using additional authentication services to provide a higher level of security.
- Encryption—Encryption services scramble data into an unusable form, and then allows the intended recipient to unscramble the data, returning the data to its original form. Encrypting the data prevents those who intercept the data in transit from being able to use it. A large organization may have thousands of "keys" (used to encrypt and decrypt data) to manage. Managing these keys is often a major problem.

- Firewalls—Firewalls are an important security component of an e-business architecture. A firewall is a system that acts as a barrier between an organization's internal networks and the outside world. Firewalls can be implemented in hardware, software, or a combination of both. A firewall can screen both incoming and outgoing traffic to determine if it should be allowed to pass through, into, or out of the system.

- Disaster recovery systems/services—For many organizations, losing the services provided by e-business systems, even for a short time, leads to serious negative consequences. Disaster recovery systems and services allow organizations to continue operating when some sort of disaster strikes. Simple disaster recovery systems may only entail backing up data remotely, while elaborate systems may run parallel, duplicate systems at different locations.

- Backup and recovery systems—An e-business architecture should also include components for routine data backup and recovery. There are many automated backup systems available. Backing up data for a large e-business system is a complex, but necessary, operation.

Development Tools

Developing e-business applications requires a number of different types of tools. The infrastructure layer of an e-business architecture should include the following development tools.

- Application development tools—Application development tools include (but are not limited to) programming languages, software development methodologies, code generators, component libraries, and form and report generators.

- Multimedia development tools—Multimedia development tools are used to create and edit various types of multimedia files, such as digital audio, video, and still images.

- Web page development tools—Web page development tools help designers create and manage Web pages. Common functions include hyperlink creation and management, page verification, and page layout. In addition, some tools in this category provide components that allow designers to quickly add advanced functions, such as site searching.

- Modeling tools—Various models, such as entity relationship models, and data-flow diagrams, may need to be created as part of the development of various e-business applications. Modeling tools help in this development.

- Document development tools—E-business systems commonly include huge volumes of many different kinds of documents. All of these documents must be created and maintained. An e-business architecture should include tools that help in the development of these documents. One example of a tool in this category is Adobe Acrobat.

- Testing environment tools—One often-overlooked component of an e-business architecture is the testing environment. Thoroughly testing any system is a key to delivering highly reliable systems. A testing environment should include testing tools, and test case generation methods, as well as test executing, monitoring, and reporting facilities.

Other Components

There are some other components of the infrastructure that do not fit well into the categories discussed previously. These include:

- Directory services—Directory services are basically electronic "phone books" for a network. These services provide access to a repository of information about the various users and resources available on a network.

- Network management—Network management systems help network administrators perform various network management tasks. These tasks include, but are not limited to, fault management, configuration management, performance management, security management, and providing statistics on network usage.

There are many different ways to express an e-business architecture. Regardless of the components included in the architecture, or the format used to illustrate the architecture, the point to remember is that the architecture provides a blueprint that can be used to guide future e-business-oriented decisions.

A related type of architecture is being discussed widely in the popular press. Many technology vendors have developed network-services architectures. These architectures are software-oriented, which differs from the e-business architecture presented in this section. The E-business in Practice box provides a discussion of two competing network-services architectures.

A GLOBAL VIEW OF E-BUSINESS

One of the most exciting aspects of e-business is the prospect of facilitating global business. Many businesses and governments view the application of e-business technologies as a way to extend into new markets worldwide. However, conducting e-business globally is not an easy task. There are a number of challenges that exist, and many points at which a global e-business project can go wrong. In this section, we discuss the advantages of, challenges to, and guidelines for conducting e-business globally.

While the United States once dominated e-business, other nations are gaining rapidly. CyberAtlas, a Web portal for online statistics, cited a Jupiter Research report that concluded that by 2005, only 25 percent of the world's Internet users would reside in the United States (Pastore 2001). The trend is expected to continue. Interestingly, the same report stated that only one-third of U.S. businesses were targeting global markets. As the global diffusion of e-business technologies continues, businesses that do not take advantage of global markets will miss out on an increasingly important opportunity.

Advantages of Global E-business

There are many advantages to global e-business. One of the most obvious is the ability to reach new markets. Gaining access to customers outside of a business' home area

E-BUSINESS IN PRACTICE

Dueling Architectures

A number of technology vendors are pushing proprietary architectures for enabling network services. Microsoft, Sun Microsystems, IBM, Hewlett-Packard, and Oracle are all putting serious effort into marketing network-services architectures. Although these architectures are certainly related to e-business, they are typically more narrowly focused than the e-business architecture we presented in this chapter. The focus of most of these architectures is on building and running network-enabled applications. The offerings from Sun and Microsoft seem to be attracting the most interest at the moment.

The Microsoft .NET platform is composed of the following elements (*Microsoft .NET Framework— Technical Overview* 2001):

- Programming model for the development of XML-based Web services
- XML services set
- Server software, including SQL Server, Windows 2000, Exchange Server, and others
- Software for client computers, including Windows XP
- Various related software development tools, including programming languages such as Visual Basic and C#.

Microsoft .NET is highly proprietary; Microsoft is and will continue to be the only vendor able to provide a complete .NET development environment. Microsoft has total control over the core technologies included in the architecture. The platform is interoperable in the sense that different programming languages can be used to develop various system components. In fact, a single component can be developed using different languages for different parts of the component (Vawter and Roman 2001).

In contrast to the proprietary nature of .NET, Sun's Open Net Environment (ONE) is much more standards-based. Recall that the Georgia Technology Authority viewed this as a major advantage. The architecture specifies components for creating, assembling, and deploying network services. The architecture's core is the Java programming language, which was developed by Sun. However, the architecture uses standards, such as Simple Object Access Protocol (SOAP), Universal Description, Discovery, and Integration (UDDI), and Electronic Business Extensible Markup Language (ebXML), to enable connections between various systems. The use of standards is a key advantage of ONE. Even though Sun specifies certain proprietary products for components of the ONE architecture (such as Sun's iPlanet Web server and Solaris operating system), if another vendor develops products superior to Sun's, as long as the new products comply with the standards included in the ONE architecture, organizations can replace Sun's products with those of Sun's competitors.

Regardless of which, if any, of the various architectures becomes dominant, organizations face a complex challenge when choosing a network-services architecture. The battle will be interesting to watch. See Vawter and Roman (2001) for an interesting comparison of the Sun and Microsoft architectures.

was often too difficult and expensive to justify. Now, however, the global nature of the Internet makes accessing foreign markets much easier. Consider the example of mailed advertisements. Using physical mail, reaching potential customers on another continent is prohibitively expensive. International mailings are much more expensive than domestic mailings. However, using e-mail for advertising eliminates the cost difference; sending an e-mail from the United States to New Zealand costs no more than sending a message within the United States. Of course, international shipping may still be cost prohibitive for some products.

A related, but less obvious, advantage is the ability to offer services globally. In the past, global trade primarily involved goods, such as produce, electronics, and automobiles (Iyer, Taube, and Raquet 2002). Traditionally, services were difficult to provide globally. While this is still true for many services (for example, plumbing or lawn maintenance), it is now possible to provide a variety of services globally. For example, educational services are now more feasible to distribute globally. E-business technologies allow students and instructors to be located in different parts of the world. As universities face greater pressure to become more efficient, the ability to inexpensively reach global markets is attractive. Soon, a student wishing to attend a remote university will no longer be forced to physically relocate in order to gain an education.

So far, our discussion of the advantages of e-business has focused on connections between businesses and their customers. However, global e-business may also help organizations improve their internal operations. One example comes from software development. Tandem Services Corporation uses global software development teams. Work flows around the world according to the working time in various locations. European team members write the initial code, and then send it to the United States, where the code is tested. Then the code moves to Japan, where errors uncovered by the U.S. team members are corrected. The code then moves back to Europe to begin another cycle. This arrangement is made possible by e-business technologies. Through their application, Tandem is able to engage in 24-hour development, which significantly speeds the completion of a software development project (Boudreau et al. 1998). Work on other types of projects can proceed similarly, making many types of work more efficient.

New, global partnerships among organizations in different countries are also facilitated by e-business technologies. These "virtual" organizations can help organizations improve their competitiveness. Flexible, global partnerships allow organizations to integrate capabilities to pursue worldwide opportunities. These virtual organizations are less bound by the limitations of time and geography, which enhances competitiveness. E-business technologies, such as groupware, e-mail, and Electronic Data Interchange, help enable global virtual organizations (Boudreau et al. 1998).

Global e-business may also help boost innovation (Iyer, Taube, and Raquet 2002). Through the use of e-business technologies, such as global networks, knowledge sharing across national boundaries is facilitated. Ideas can flow back and forth across countries without impediment. This free sharing of ideas and knowledge often leads to increased innovation.

Finally, e-business technologies may help some organizations create and maintain global supply chains. Using international suppliers is not new; organizations have been using suppliers outside their home countries for many years. However, using network-enabled supply-chain management systems may make the use of global suppliers more efficient and effective, making their use economically viable where it was previously infeasible.

As you can see, there are many advantages to global e-business. The ones discussed here are summarized in Table 12-1. However, there are a number of challenges that must be overcome in order to find global e-business success. These are discussed in the following section.

Table 12-1   Advantages of Global E-business

- Ability to reach new markets with products *and* services
- More efficient cross-national operations
- Facilitation of global virtual partnerships
- Global knowledge sharing boosts innovation
- More effective maintenance of cross-national supply chains

Global E-business Challenges

Organizations wishing to take advantage of global e-business face a number of difficult challenges. Some of these were discussed in Chapter 3 as barriers to e-business. In this section, we provide an overview of some of the more important challenges facing global e-business.

A number of legal challenges face global e-business organizations. Three hurdles seem to receive the most attention: taxation, privacy, and product laws. Even within some countries (such as the United States), how to tax e-business sales is a point of much debate. With global e-business, the problem is even more complex. Determining which governments are entitled to tax a global e-business transaction is problematic. Should the originating country receive the tax, or should the country where the final product delivery occurs charge the tax? What if the transaction server is located in a third country; should that country be entitled to charge any taxes? International tariffs are already a contentious issue. As global e-business continues, we expect the debate to intensify.

As discussed at length in Chapter 3, privacy laws differ widely from country to country. The United States has more of a self-regulation policy on privacy. The European Union, however, has much more stringent laws regarding consumer privacy. Organizations engaging in global e-business must contend with these differences. Refer to Chapter 3 for more information on this issue.

The final legal challenge we discuss here concerns various products that are legal in one country, but are banned in others. For example, neo-Nazi material that is banned in Germany and other countries is protected by free speech laws in the United States. Likewise, adult content that is legal in some countries may be illegal in more conservative nations. Concern over product legality extends to online content; Web site content that is allowed in one country may be banned in another. For example, there are interesting examples of differences in allowable forms of advertising. Several forms of advertising that are commonplace in the United States are banned in other countries. Child-oriented advertising is banned in Denmark, as is comparative advertising in Germany, while English-language advertising is banned in France (Iyer, Taube, and Raquet 2002). Managing content in a way that avoids legal problems, while still taking advantage of revenue opportunities, can be a major challenge for global e-business organizations.

Cultural and language differences across nations also represent a challenge to global e-business. A detailed discussion of this topic is provided in Chapter 3, so only a summary is offered here. Different cultures have different values and norms. Engaging in global e-business successfully requires dealing with these differences. There are also national differences in normal business practices. Something as simple as whether the normal practice is to quote prices with or without applicable taxes can cause confusion. Many American businesses quote prices without applicable taxes (airlines are an exception), while those in New Zealand, for example, often list prices that include the GST. Handling differences in currency can also be a problem. Currency exchange rates fluctuate constantly, which makes accurate pricing in multiple currencies difficult. At the very least, organizations must be sure to note in what currency prices are being quoted. This is a particular problem when using dollars. Is the company using U.S. dollars, Australian dollars, New Zealand dollars, Canadian dollars, Hong Kong dollars, or some other currency called "dollar?"

More subtle problems can also arise from ignorance of cultural differences. Many consumers outside the United States may find American advertising to be overly aggressive. In contrast, Americans may find some European advertisements to be more "racy" than is the American norm. An advertisement showing a partially clad female might be viewed as offensive in conservative Islamic countries. Successful global e-business requires paying strict attention to differences in culture across countries, which is easy to say, but difficult to do.

The final challenge we discuss concerns differences in e-business readiness across countries. The technology infrastructure and many other factors determine the e-business environment for a country. According to a study by the *Economist* Intelligence Unit and Pyramid Research, the United States is the most e-business-ready country in the world, followed by Australia, the United Kingdom, and Canada. Most of the thirty most e-business-ready countries are in North America, Western Europe, and Asia. Only one South American country (Chile) and no African countries appeared in the top thirty (Economist Intelligence Unit 2001). Engaging in e-business in countries that lack the proper infrastructure is often a difficult proposition.

The global e-business challenges discussed in this section are summarized in Table 12-2. Despite the many challenges, global e-business can be rewarding when done successfully. In the next section, we provide guidelines that may help organizations successfully engage in global e-business.

Guidelines for Global E-business

While engaging in global e-business is daunting, there are a number of steps an organization can take to increase its chances of success. In this section, we briefly discuss guidelines for using e-business globally. The guidelines presented here are compiled from various sources (Bulman and Gutierrez 1999; Federal Trade Commission 2001; The global business 2001; Iyer, Taube, and Raquet 2002), coupled with the authors' experiences.

Table 12-2 Challenges of Global E-business

- Complexity of cross-border taxation
- Differences in privacy regulations
- Differences in allowable products
- Cultural differences
- Language differences
- Differences in e-business readiness

- Plan carefully. Success in global e-business requires careful planning, not just of the global e-business efforts, but also in the broader context of strategic planning. Global e-business plans should align with those of the organization as a whole, otherwise even a successful global e-business project may not help the organization. Alignment helps in several areas. One of the most important is in choosing candidate countries. In order to be successful overall, the countries targeted in a global e-business project must fit with the overall plans of the organization. Important synergies may be available when directing global efforts in several business areas at the same target countries.

- Consider conditions in the target countries. At least four categories of local conditions should be considered when choosing target countries. First, understanding the legal environments of the target countries is important. Complying with local laws in the target countries is not the only consideration. Organizations should also consider protections afforded by local laws. For example, enforcement of intellectual property rights varies across countries. Some strictly enforce copyright laws, for example, while others do little or nothing to protect copyright holders. Second, organizations must consider the market sizes in and market readiness of the target countries. The size of the potential market in a target country must be large enough to justify the costs associated with creating and maintaining an e-business presence. The readiness of the market for the particular products or services to be offered must also be considered. Even if a potential market is quite large, if the market is not ready for the offered product or service, the revenue may be insufficient to make the e-business effort worthwhile. Organizations engaging in global e-business should also take the local business practices of the target countries into account. Business practices vary from country to country. For example, marketing practices that are common in some countries may be frowned upon in others. Ignoring this can lead to confusion or, in some cases, inadvertent illegal activities. For example, in some countries it is acceptable to engage government officials in consulting arrangements in order to gain access. In other countries, this is considered bribery and is illegal. Finally, the e-business readiness of the target country must be taken into account. Even if other factors indicate that a country is suitable, if the country is not sufficiently ready for e-business, success may be difficult to find.

- Consider and plan for logistics. Conducting global e-business is not simply a matter of making goods and services available through a Web site (Iyer, Taube, and Raquet, 2002). Organizations must be able to put logistical systems in place that allow for suitable order fulfillment. Delivering domestic orders is typically much easier than handling international orders. Not only are the distances greater, but companies must also comply with import/export laws. Organizations that underestimate the difficulties of international order fulfillment may find global e-business success elusive.

- Use fair, clear business practices. As we have discussed elsewhere, the level of trust customers place in a business has an impact on e-business success. This may be even more important when doing business globally. It is important that organizations engaging in global e-business use fair business practices. Taking unfair advantage of consumers may offer short-term benefits, but this is likely to be offset by long-term damage to the reputation of the organization. It is also important to clearly indicate what practices are used by the business. Otherwise, an honest miscommunication can result in dissatisfied customers and a damaged reputation. Two areas are particularly important. First, clearly describe all product and service offerings; include clear, detailed descriptions and product options. Second, organizations must be clear regarding transaction terms, conditions, and costs. For example, be clear about the currency used for prices and whether or not the customer will incur any additional costs for shipping or taxes, for example.

■ Follow both domestic and foreign laws. It is critical that organizations undertaking global e-business comply with both domestic and foreign laws. It is not enough to simply follow domestic laws. Successful global e-business requires detailed knowledge of and compliance with the laws of all countries in which e-business is conducted. It is easy to unintentionally violate foreign laws. For example, recall that France requires that advertising be in French. Ignorance of this law could easily cause problems for a global organization.

■ Consider a foreign partner. Global e-business can be simplified considerably by forging an alliance with a foreign partner located in the target country. A well-chosen partner can offer detailed knowledge of the conditions and market in the target country. The partner may also be able to help with logistical problems. While engaging a foreign partner has benefits, there are some dangers. First, organizations should be sure to only partner with reputable firms. Partners with questionable business practices or shaky financial situations may spell disaster. Second, arrangements with foreign partners should be clearly specified in advance. Otherwise, honest misunderstandings may lead to considerable difficulties.

It is likely that the trend toward more global e-business will continue for the foreseeable future. It is also likely that e-business will continue to evolve. Just as the mainframe-based EDI systems that exemplified e-business a decade ago gave way to Web-based e-business, so will new technologies lead to a shift in e-business in the future. In the next section, we discuss a number of trends that we feel will help shape the future of e-business.

THE FUTURE OF E-BUSINESS

What is the future of e-business? The first observation we make is that e-business is here to stay. We believe that the use of network-enabled technologies by organizations will continue to expand. The dot-com boom may be over, but as the dust clears we are seeing an increasing number of organizations making e-business central to their operations. This trend is likely to continue, until e-business becomes as ingrained in organizational life as the personal computer.

One aspect of e-business that we believe will continue is the rapid development of new e-business-related technologies and applications. When investigating innovations, we urge caution. When the hype around an emerging technology reaches a certain point, some will claim that the technology is the holy grail of e-business; life as we know it will change drastically because of the technology. We saw this happen with the emergence of Web-based e-business. While we believe that e-business is here to stay, and that it is having and will continue to have significant impact on how organizations and individuals interact, there is little doubt that the phenomenon was over-hyped. This was followed by a period in which some pundits claimed that the e-business boom was *all* hype and no substance. In our opinion, this thinking is just as wrong as those who over-hyped e-business. There is a lesson to be learned; the truth is generally somewhere in the middle. In our many years of involvement with information technology, we have seen the same sort of thing happen over and over. A technology emerges and its impact is vastly overestimated. Then the technology cools off, and it is declared dead. The actual impact of the technology is almost always somewhere between these two extremes. We encourage you to remember this as you observe the emergence of new technologies.

In this section, we investigate some technologies and applications that we feel will help shape the future of e-business. We discuss two technologies and three applications that we believe will become increasingly important in the future. Of course, any such prognostications are risky; we really do not know what is going to happen. All we can do is look at the signs and use our knowledge and experience to make an educated guess. Keep in mind that this text is being written in the late spring of 2002. Do not judge us too harshly if we are proved wrong in our predictions; predicting the future is fun, but risky.

Wireless Communications

The ability to connect to a network, such as the Internet, without any physical, wired connection may help shape the future of e-business. Currently, there is considerable speculation surrounding wireless communication and e-business. The term "mobile business" or m-business is being used to describe the application of wireless communications for business purposes. There are many applications being used and developed that use wireless communication. For example, an increasing number of people are using personal digital assistants (PDAs) or Web-enabled cellular telephones to access e-mail. Many schools are beginning to install wireless networks in classrooms and computer labs. Recently, a student in one of the authors' classes used a notebook computer with a wireless network card to access class notes over the Web while in class. What made this so interesting was that the class was taught in a standard classroom, not a lab. The classroom had an instructor's station equipped with a computer and projection system. The station also had both wireless and standard network connections to allow the connection of a notebook computer. The student took advantage of the wireless connection, which was not being used by the instructor.

There are many other applications for wireless computing. Consumer-oriented examples include receiving traffic updates while on the road, interactive games, and travel and entertainment booking. There are also work-related applications, such as sales force automation (see Chapter 8), calendaring, and time and expense reporting. Some applications are used for both personal and work purposes, including e-mail and instant messaging.

Currently, m-commerce does not seem to have a "killer application" to spur its use. Killer applications are applications that are so useful to such a large number of people and organizations that the desire to have the killer application leads people to acquire all the technologies necessary to use the application. A good example is the spreadsheet and the personal computer (PC). When the first PC spreadsheet (Visicalc) was introduced, financial analysts and accountants found the capabilities of the application to be so desirable that many used their own funds to purchase a personal computer just so they could use the spreadsheet software. (This was not a trivial expense. In those days, you could easily spend several thousand dollars on a PC.) Some experts believe that the Web was the killer application for the Internet. Many people have purchased PCs and pay for Internet access just so they can surf the Web. Of course, they may later discover the benefits of related technologies, such as e-mail and digital media. So, we predict that m-commerce will not live up to its promise until a killer application emerges. What will that killer application be? Only time will tell; we certainly do not know. However, we do think that monitoring the development of m-commerce is worth the effort.

Broadband

The move to broadband network access is an ongoing trend that we feel will have a major impact on the future of e-business. Consumers are flocking to broadband network access technologies, such as cable and digital subscriber lines. According to a Nielsen//NetRatings 20 May 2002 press release, the number of U.S. homes using broadband connections grew from 15.9 million in April 2001 to more than 25 million in April 2002. Although this is a large increase, a large percentage of homes still use dial-up access. So, broadband is expected to experience significant growth.

Broadband access is exciting because of the e-business applications it enables. For example, listening to a Web-based music broadcast is a much more pleasant experience with a broadband connection than it is with a dial-up connection. Digital video almost requires the use of broadband. Applications such as video on demand are simply not practical without the fast data transfer speeds of broadband connections. Broadband connections are also "always on," which makes communication applications, such as instant messaging, more rewarding.

E-business applications that make use of digital media are also more practical with broadband connections. For example, e-learning that makes use of digital video and desktop video conferencing, two applications that almost require high bandwidth, is thought to be more effective than e-learning that does not use these technologies. Internet-based telephony (making voice telephone calls over the Internet) is an emerging application that requires broadband to be effective. Even applications that do not require broadband are often more effective when high bandwidth is available. For example, viewing image-laden online product catalogs may require long waits when using a dial-up connection. The same catalog downloads much more rapidly when using a broadband connection.

As the number of broadband users increases, we believe that new, currently unknown applications that take advantage of high bandwidth will emerge. These applications may lead to a new wave of e-business.

So far, our discussion of the future of e-business has focused on underlying technologies rather than specific applications. Now we turn attention to applications of e-business technologies that we feel will become increasingly important in the coming years.

Ubiquitous Computing

Ubiquitous computing, along with being one of our favorite terms, also has the potential to be an important development in e-business, especially when combined with wireless communications. Experts are beginning to talk about "transparent commerce" and **"ubiquitous commerce"** (u-commerce). What does this mean? First, let's consider the term "ubiquitous," which basically means seeming to be everywhere at once. In terms of IT, **ubiquitous computing** is touted as the next wave in computing (following the mainframe and the personal computer). The basic idea is that computers will be everywhere and touch almost all aspects of our lives. However, we will barely be aware of their presence. To a degree, we are already living this way. Your automobile has multiple computers, your digital cable box is a computer (some of them even have USB ports), and most office telephones are actually computers. There are many other examples of computers that sit in the background, doing their jobs without getting in the way.

This idea has been extended to e-business; u-commerce occurs in the background automatically, without any effort on the part of the customer. For example, if you have a toll pass installed in your car, you can pay expressway tolls automatically by simply driving through a special lane. With some newer systems, you do not even have to slow down. Soon a wearable computer or some other portable device will enable you to carry out all sorts of commerce without much thought on your part. Rather than fumbling for change at a parking meter or vending machine, you may simply pass a mobile device (such as a cellular phone) over a spot on the meter or machine, and payment will be made electronically. Although still in its very early stages, we think that the u-commerce that results from the convergence of wireless communication and ubiquitous computing will soon be a part of everyday life.

E-government

Governments world-wide are making more use of e-business technologies to make their operations more efficient and communications more effective. We saw an example of this in the opening case. The use of network-enabled technologies in government goes by a number of terms, including e-government, digital government, and government-to-constituent e-business. (These terms are basically interchangeable.) As the use of the Internet and other networks continues to spread, we expect that e-government will continue to develop. In a few years, it would not be surprising to find that, for many citizens, interacting with governments using networks will be the norm rather than a novelty.

E-government applies e-business technologies to three broad areas: internal and interagency operations, service delivery, and communication with citizens. Many governments are following the lead of nongovernmental organizations and applying e-business technologies to help improve the efficiency and effectiveness of internal operations. One area of particular interest is improving operations and communication that occurs among various governmental agencies. As is the case with many large organizations, some governments have a difficult time coordinating efforts across various subunits. For example, it is critical that the school board stay informed of new housing developments approved by the planning department. Otherwise school construction and expansion projects may not align with shifts in population locations.

Governments are also using e-business technologies to improve service delivery to their constituents. More popular services being offered through the Internet include tax filings, vehicle registrations, and license applications. Making fully executable services available is one of the most challenging of e-government applications, in part because of the necessity for secure payment. A more commonly available e-business application is the distribution of forms and other documents. Most governments engaged in e-government make various publications available through Web sites. Recall that earlier in this book we discussed how the U.S. Internal Revenue Service provides a large number of forms and other documents through an extensive Web site.

Many governmental agencies are making extensive use of e-mail, both for internal communication and communication with constituents. Some citizens prefer e-mail communication to long waits on the telephone or the seemingly endless rounds of telephone tag that often accompany communicating with governmental officials. Some governments are making use of online complaint forms to better handle citizen concerns. Frequently asked question (FAQ) sites also help improve communication by eliminating the need to contact the government for answers to common questions. Citizens can search the FAQ site and often locate the answer to a question without ever having to pick up the telephone or send an e-mail message.

Following the 2000 U.S. elections, much attention is being given to electronic voting. There are good arguments for and against e-voting. Regardless of which side is more correct, the idea of network-enabled voting is intriguing. Proponents of e-voting claim that it will improve participation and accuracy, as well as ease the tabulation process. Opponents are concerned about security, privacy, and the impact of access inequities.

The fact that some have better access to technology than others is a general concern for e-government. Although it seems clear that the proper application of e-business technologies can make it easier for some citizens to access services, it is also clear that there are many who lack the necessary technology and/or technological literacy to make use of e-government. Recall that we discussed this issue in depth in Chapter 3.

E-learning

The final trend we discuss is **electronic learning (e-learning),** which is also known as technology-mediated distance learning. As we have pointed out several times in this book, network technologies have had an impact on education. While distance education has existed for many years in the form of correspondence courses, the advent of the Internet and Web have changed the face of distance learning. This is reflected by the emergence of the term "e-learning" to specifically indicate the use of network technologies for the delivery of education and training that occurs at a distance.

The obvious advantage of e-learning for students is the ability to take courses from almost any location and, in many cases, at any time. This is particularly important for working students and those who find it impractical to travel to campus. Working students who must travel often find e-learning an attractive way to pursue advanced degrees. Universities also find e-learning to have advantages, mainly through efficiency and extended reach. When done well, using e-learning allows a faculty member to handle more students than is practical for face-to-face courses. In addition, universities are able to attract a wider range of students than is possible with traditional, face-to-face education. Many professors are using the Internet and Web to improve traditional courses. Providing tutorials, class notes, study guides, and the like through a Web site offers students easy access to supplemental material. Innovative faculty are also using e-mail, chat, and instant messaging to improve their availability to students.

E-learning extends beyond universities. High schools are also using e-learning technologies to improve their services. These schools use e-learning as a cost-effective way to expand their course offerings, particularly in the areas of college preparation and advanced placement.

Organizations other than schools are also using e-learning. Many view e-learning as an effective way to provide training to employees. This not only improves the skill sets of employees, but may also help improve employee retention. Some organizations are simply consumers of e-learning. These organizations make courses developed and managed by others available to their employees. Other organizations have staff that design and develop custom e-learning courses that are tailored to the needs of the organization. Many organizations recognize that e-learning represents a potential profit center. They develop courses and then make them available for a fee to outsiders. Companies that sell complex products, such as computer software, often find that using e-learning to expand training offerings has a double benefit. Revenue is generated through course fees, but more importantly, the easy availability of training makes their products more attractive. For example, Oracle Corporation offers a large number of courses through the Oracle University. There are several delivery options, including instructor-led and self-paced online courses. Oracle also offers a subscription service that allows subscribers to take an unlimited number of electronically delivered courses for an annual fee (U.S.$399 in 2002).

Other kinds of organizations are also using e-learning to "pull-through" sales of other products. A good example of this is Barnes & Noble University. The University offers short courses in a variety of subjects, ranging from Basic Dog Training to Java Programming. There is no charge for these classes. Barnes and Noble makes money by selling books to accompany the courses. Many courses have both required books and "materials for further exploration," which are related books that are not specifically used in the course. This strategy has been successfully used in the offline world by companies such as home improvement stores that offer free classes in various home improvement topics.

Regardless of the level of education being discussed, it is clear that e-learning is having a significant impact. We expect that this trend will continue and that the impact of e-learning will only increase.

We can only guess at where e-business will go in the future. However it progresses, many people performing an astonishing variety of jobs will be involved. In the next section, we provide an overview of some of the jobs that exist in e-business.

JOBS IN THE E-BUSINESS WORLD

As you have seen throughout this book, e-business involves many activities that utilize a variety of technologies. So, it is probably not surprising to you that there are a wide variety of jobs that go along with e-business activities. In this section, we provide descriptions of a few employment possibilities for those interested in e-business. Keep in mind that regardless of what your interests may be, there is likely to be an e-business-related job that matches those interests. Do not think that the list of jobs provided here is complete; building such a list is virtually impossible. To see how extensive the "e-business" label is, go to an employment Web site (such as Hotjobs.com or Monster.com) and search for jobs that include "e-business" or "e-commerce." You will discover an amazing variety of positions.

To organize the list, we divide the positions into "More Technical Jobs" and "Less Technical Jobs." While placement in the categories is not arbitrary, there are a number of positions that could arguably be placed in either category. So, we suggest that you not spend time deciding whether a particular job should be placed in a particular category.

As the labels imply, all of the jobs listed here involve some technical knowledge, but some are more technology-oriented than others. It is important for you to realize that even if your job is relatively nontechnical, knowledge of e-business technologies can still be an advantage. For example, a human resource specialist that has a good understanding of e-business technologies has an advantage over someone without such knowledge.

More Technical Jobs

The positions in this category, in some cases, precede the emergence of e-business. Some have existed since the early days of data processing. However, for many organizations, the jobs have migrated to involve e-business applications. So, you may know someone who is a database designer, for example, who does not have anything to do with e-business. Do not take this as evidence that *no* database designers work in e-business. Below are some examples of technically-oriented e-business jobs.

- Database designer—Database designers are responsible for analyzing organizations' e-business data needs, then creating logical and physical designs that meet those needs. Data modeling is a large part of a database designer's job. In the context of data warehousing, database designers are sometimes called data architects. Since databases are a fundamental part of many e-business systems, database designers are important to e-business.

- Database administrator—A database administrator (DBA) is responsible for the operation of an organization's databases. DBAs handle a variety of tasks, including database creation, backup and recovery, performance tuning, database security, and data access. Becoming a DBA typically requires extensive knowledge of a particular database management system, such as Oracle, SQL Server, or DB2.

- Programmer—As you know, application programs are a key element of e-business systems. Someone must create and maintain these programs. So, e-business systems require programmers with skills in many different languages, such as Java, ASP, Perl, C++, among many others. In addition, back-office systems may be developed in older languages, such as COBOL and C. Remember that back-office systems are often critical components in an e-business system. Performing maintenance programming is often an entry point into a technical e-business career.

- Systems analyst—Systems analysts work with users and existing documents to determine system requirements, and then create the specifications for the system. In some cases, systems analysts are also responsible for system testing. Some of the tasks performed by systems analysts are problem definition, requirements determination, and process modeling. E-business systems require systems analysis, just as all other systems do. So systems analysts are important in the e-business world. If you are interested in learning more about what systems analysts do, we suggest that you consult one of the systems analysis texts included in the Further Readings section of this chapter.

- Consultant—Consultants are outside experts in an area in which an organization lacks sufficient expertise. Sometimes an organization does not have any employees with the expertise required to solve a problem, while in other cases, the organization needs more people with expertise in an area than it currently employs. Consultants work on both long-term and short-term projects. It is not unusual for a consultant to have an engagement with a company for over a year. It is also common for a consultant to work with an organization for only one or two days. In some cases, consultants are independent, while in others, they work for a consulting firm, such as Booz Allen Hamilton, or PricewaterhouseCoopers. Both technical and nontechnical consultants work in e-business.

- Application specialist—There are many applications in the e-business environment, many of which we have discussed throughout this book. Often, applications are purchased rather than developed within the organization. However, for large organizations in particular, purchased applications must be customized to fit the organization's needs. As a result, many organizations employ experts in specific applications. For example, in the late 1990s, those with expertise in ERP applications (such as those sold by SAP, PeopleSoft, and Oracle) were in very high demand. Some time later, experts in CRM applications became highly sought after. We expect that application specialists will continue to be in demand, although the particular applications will change over time.

- Network administrators—Network administrators design networks and keep them running smoothly. Typically, a network administrator has expertise in a particular network operating system. Network administrators are responsible for many tasks, including performance tuning, installing new hardware and software, assigning proper access rights to users, and troubleshooting and correcting network problems.

- Technical support—There are many different types of technical support specialists working in e-business environments. Some work on help desks that provide assistance to users who have problems or questions. Others work with the workstations on employees' desks, installing new hardware and software, updating software, and troubleshooting and correcting problems. Being a good technical support specialist requires a combination of technical expertise and interpersonal skills. Most of the people a technical support specialist comes into contact with are having problems; they are often frustrated and stressed. Having a calm, confident, but understanding approach can overcome the frustration of the user, which can help solve the problem more quickly. Many people enter the technical side of the e-business world through technical support positions.

■ Business analyst—Business analysts analyze business processes in order to determine ways e-business technologies can be applied in order to improve the processes. (Note that the term "business analyst" is also used to describe a variety of positions unrelated to e-business.) Business analysts are also responsible for properly communicating requirements to other teams involved in e-business, such as the systems development team. The business analyst's job is similar to that of a systems analyst. The two differ in that systems analysts typically work with systems within their own organizations, while business analysts usually work as consultants on external systems. Of course, this is not universally true.

■ Security specialist—Opening up an organization's networks to external parties, such as customers and suppliers, has great benefit, as we have discussed throughout this book. However, providing network access to the outside world brings the increased possibility of security breaches. Most large organizations involved in e-business now employ specialists in network security. These individuals are responsible for ensuring the safety of the organization's networks. This is a challenging job that requires constant learning. Hackers are quite adept at coming up with new ways to infiltrate network defenses. New versions of software have different security "holes" that must be plugged. Security specialists must work hard to stay one step ahead of the hackers.

■ Webmaster—A Webmaster is responsible for maintaining one or more Web sites for an organization, often including running the site's Web server software. For smaller organizations, a Webmaster may also develop software for the Web site. Maintaining the Web site requires adding new content and refreshing existing content to keep it up to date. A successful Webmaster must have a combination of technical and graphic design skills. Users not only expect a Web site to "work," they also expect Web pages to be visually appealing.

■ Web developer—Web developers are similar to programmers, but they focus on languages that are more Web-oriented, such as Perl, ASP, or Java. Some Web developers may specialize in Web development environments, such as ColdFusion.

Of course, there are many other technically-oriented jobs in the e-business world. Visit any e-business organization's Web site and you are likely to see openings for many jobs not listed above. Some are quite creatively named, such as "Interaction Designer," and "Spam Cop" (spam is unwanted e-mail). In any case, we hope that the jobs listed above give you a taste of the variety of technical jobs available in e-business.

Less Technical Jobs

While any e-business job involves technology to some degree, many are not as technology-oriented as those previously described. Individuals who are not interested in the "ones and zeros" of the technology may find a happy home in e-business through one of the less technical jobs listed in this section.

- Project manager—Many e-business projects are very large and complicated. Successfully completing these projects requires skillfully coordinating the efforts of dozens of people working on different, interdependent aspects of the projects. Project managers are responsible for keeping the project running smoothly. For large e-business projects, this is a daunting task. Project managers must have an understanding of the various parts of a project and must also have expert knowledge of project management techniques, such as PERT and CPM. They must also have "people" skills to overcome the inevitable conflicts that arise in the course of a project.

- Graphic designer—Web pages must be well designed, which requires someone with knowledge of graphic design. You have probably visited more than one Web site that was simply ugly. The typefaces used did not fit with each other, the colors were jarring, and logos and other graphic elements were poorly designed. It is likely that the site did not have the benefit of a knowledgeable graphic designer. Graphic designers are also required to create the various graphics included as part of a Web site. Sometimes logos and other graphics that look fine on paper do not translate well to computer screens. In such cases, having a graphic designer with knowledge of computer graphic design is valuable. In the context of e-business, graphic designers typically create graphics and layouts using computerized tools. In addition, they may be specialists in a particular area of network-enabled graphics, such as Flash animation.

- Technical sales—There are many different types of sales and marketing positions that involve e-business. Companies offering network services, Web hosting, various types of e-business software, training, and myriad other products and services all employ salespeople. In fact, both of the authors of this book spent some time working in technical sales. These positions are often the most lucrative e-business jobs, although they are typically high stress positions. Individuals who have technical knowledge, but prefer interpersonal contact may want to look into a career in technical sales. Few people have the necessary combination of skills to be successful in this area. Those who do can find a career in technical sales to be quite rewarding.

- Training specialist—Many e-business systems require training for those in the organization who will be using the systems. For example, in 2002, the University of Central Florida rolled out an implementation of an e-business system to allow many academic and human resource functions to be performed using e-business technologies. Faculty and staff were offered a variety of opportunities to take training in various aspects of the system. The training continued for many months. Conducting this sort of training requires individuals who have knowledge of the technology, as well as training skills. Most organizations offering e-business products and services employ training specialists. This is another good choice for individuals with an interest in e-business, but a preference for dealing with people rather than machines. Of course, building a successful career as an e-business trainer requires the ability to both understand the various technologies and communicate that knowledge to others.

- Product specialist—Product specialists concentrate on the marketing and development of a particular e-business product. For example, an e-business services provider might have one product specialist in charge of e-commerce hosting services for small businesses and a different product specialist responsible for marketing domain name registration services. Typical duties of a product specialist include defining and prioritizing product enhancements, developing business and functional requirements, and building partnerships in support of the product. Product specialists must have solid knowledge of marketing and management principles, as well as sufficient technical knowledge to understand the product.

- Procurement specialist—Procurement specialists are responsible for purchasing goods and/or services required by an organization. Today, many procurement specialists are very involved with e-business technologies. For example, procurement specialists make extensive use of supply-chain management systems.

- Database marketer—Many organizations have compiled huge volumes of data through various operational e-business systems. Recall that data warehousing efforts are often directed at making use of this data. A database marketing specialist analyzes this data in order to more appropriately develop and market products and services. For example, a database marketer may use customer segmentation methods to identify groups of customers that behave in similar ways. Special offerings can then be tailored to various customer segments. Success as a database marketer requires knowledge of marketing, statistical analysis, and database technologies.

- Online advertising specialist—The trend toward online advertising has led to the need for advertising professionals that specialize in online advertising. While there are similarities between traditional and online advertising, there are also many differences. Advances in Web programming leads to new online advertising methods. An online advertising specialist must stay informed about these advancements in order to develop and utilize proper online advertising techniques.

Of course there are numerous other less-technical jobs that involve e-business; in fact there are too many to list here. If you are not overly technically inclined, but still want to be involved in e-business, we encourage you to investigate how your areas of career interest interact with the e-business world.

SUMMARY

This chapter covered four topics: e-business architectures, global e-business, the future of e-business, and jobs in e-business. In the IT context, architectures are blueprints that help guide organizations in the delivery of applications and data related to e-business. While there are many different ways to express an e-business architecture, this chapter provided an example of a typical e-business architecture that includes three layers. The information layer is made up of components that guide the creation, distribution, and access of data. The applications layer describes the operating environment for application software. The hardware, networks, and operating systems that make up the e-business infrastructure are described in the infrastructure layer.

E-business can help organizations extend their operations and reach markets across the world. There are a number of potential advantages to be gained from global e-business, including access to new markets, improved internal operations, the facilitation of global virtual partnerships, improved innovation, and the enabling of global supply chains. However, there are a number of challenges to global e-business, including the complexity of taxation, differences in privacy and product laws, cultural and language differences, and differences in e-business readiness. This chapter also presented a number of guidelines that may help organizations find success in their global e-business efforts.

None of us has a crystal ball with which to accurately predict the future of e-business. However, we feel that there are some technologies and e-business applications that are likely to help shape this future. Advances in wireless communication technologies, and the increased use of broadband network access may impact the future of e-business. The chapter also discussed applications of e-business technologies that we expect to become increasingly important in the future. Ubiquitous computing, coupled with wireless communication, may lead to the emergence of ubiquitous commerce, which occurs almost without the user's notice. E-government is playing a bigger role in the operations of many governments. It is also having an impact on how governments deliver services to and communicate with individuals and organizations. E-learning is changing the way people gain access to education and training. Schools and other kinds of organizations are using e-business technologies to improve the efficiency of education and training. In addition, students of all kinds are using e-learning to take advantage of learning opportunities that were previously impractical.

There are many different types of jobs related to e-business. This chapter provided descriptions of many of these. More technically-oriented jobs discussed included database designer, systems analyst, programmer, and network administrator. A number of less technical jobs were also described, including project manager, sales, training specialist, and graphic designer.

KEY TERMS

applications layer	electronic government	electronic learning	infrastructure layer
e-business architecture	(e-government)	(e-learning)	ubiquitous commerce
digital government		information layer	ubiquitous computing

REVIEW QUESTIONS

1. What is an e-business architecture?

2. What benefits are there to establishing an e-business architecture?

3. Identify and briefly describe the layers included in the e-business architecture described in this chapter.

4. Identify and briefly describe five components included in the application layer of an e-business architecture.

5. Identify and briefly describe five hardware components included in the infrastructure layer of an e-business architecture.

6. Identify and briefly describe five software components included in the infrastructure layer of an e-business architecture.

7. List three advantages of global e-business.

8. List three challenges to global e-business.

9. What is ubiquitous computing?

10. How do students who use e-learning benefit?

11. How do universities benefit from e-learning?

12. Identify three ways in which governments are using e-business technologies.

13. Briefly describe five more technology-oriented jobs in e-business.

14. Briefly describe five less-technology-oriented jobs in e-business.

EXERCISES

1. Locate and interview someone engaged in e-business. Briefly describe the person's job. What are the person's responsibilities? What skills are important in the performance of the job? Comment on whether or not you would enjoy the job.

2. Pick a non-technology course you are taking or have taken in the past year. Describe three ways in which e-business technologies could have been applied to improve the delivery of the course. Be clear as to how the application might have improved the course.

3. Pick a course that you are taking or have taken in the last year. Do you feel that this course is suitable for e-learning? Justify your answer.

HANDS-ON PROJECTS

1. Search the Web (or some other source) and locate a detailed description for the IT or e-business architecture of an organization. Describe the organization of the architecture (such as the layers in the architecture described in the chapter).

2. Pretend that you are a manager for a bookseller (or some other business assigned by your instructor). Pick two foreign countries and investigate their e-business readiness. Compare the two countries in terms of e-business readiness. Be sure to consider the legal and technological environments, as well as market size.

3. Find an area where e-voting is being considered. Describe what is being done by the government to investigate e-voting. What advantages of and challenges to e-voting has the government discovered?

4. Identify two emerging technologies or applications (other than those discussed in the chapter) that you think will have a major impact on e-business in the future. Describe each and discuss how you expect each one to impact e-business.

5. Go to an employment Web site (such as Hotjobs.com or Monster.com) and search for jobs that include e-commerce or e-business in their description. List and describe at least five jobs that were included in your results. Comment on the variety of jobs you found.

6. Search for available positions in at least two technical and two nontechnical jobs described in this chapter. What required skills are listed for each of the jobs? What kinds of organizations (size, industry, etc.) have the available positions? What salary ranges are given for each job type?

DISCUSSION POINTS

1. Discuss why an organization needs an e-business architecture.

2. Contrast Microsoft .NET and Sun ONE. Identify the advantages and disadvantages of each.

3. Describe how a business should go about selecting countries to target with global e-business efforts. What factors should they consider? Why?

4. Discuss at least three e-business applications of wireless communication (other than those discussed in the chapter). For each application, describe the application and discuss its benefits to organizations and individuals.

5. Which of the jobs described in the chapter most appeals to you? Discuss the aspects of the job that make it appealing to you.

RELATED WEB SITES

HotJobs.com: www.hotjobs.com

Monster.com: www.monster.com

FURTHER READINGS

BÉLANGER, FRANCE, and DIANE JORDAN. *Evaluation and Implementation of Distance Learning: Technologies, Tools and Techniques.* Hershey, PA: Idea Group Publishing, 2000.

DENNIS, ALAN, and BARBARA WIXOM-HALEY. *Systems Analysis and Design.* New York: John Wiley & Sons, 1999.

MARAKAS, GEORGE. *Systems Analysis and Design: An Active Approach.* Upper Saddle River, NJ: Prentice-Hall, 2000.

DENNIS, ALAN. *Networking in the Internet Age.* New York: John Wiley & Sons, 2002.

FITZGERALD, JERRY, and ALAN DENNIS. *Business Data Communications and Networking,* New York: John Wiley & Sons, 2001.

REFERENCES

APPLEGATE, L., F.W. MCFARLAN, and J. MCKENNEY. 1996. *Corporate information systems management: The issues facing senior executives.* 4th ed. Chicago: Richard D. Irwin.

BOUDREAU, M.C., K. LOCH, D. ROBEY, and D. STRAUB. 1998. Going global: Using information technology to advance the competitiveness of the virtual transnational organization. *Academy of Management Executive* 12 (4): 120–128.

BULMAN, R., and J. GUTIÉRREZ. 1999. Practical strategies for global e-commerce. *E-business Advisor* (June): https://secure.advisor.com/Articles.nsf/aid/BULMR01.

Economist Intelligence Unit. 2001. The Economist Intelligence Unit/Pyramid Research e-readiness rankings. ebusinessforum.com (8 May 2001): http://www.ebusinessforum.com/index.asp?layout=rich_story&doc_id=367.

Federal Trade Commission. 2001. E-commerce guidelines for selling internationally. GigaLaw.com (February): http://www.gigalaw.com/articles/2001-all/ftc-2001-02-all.html.

IYER, L., L. TAUBE, and J. RAQUET. 2002. Global e-commerce: Rationale, digital divide, and strategies to bridge the divide.

Journal of Information Technology Management 5 (1): 43–68.

Microsoft .NET Framework—Technical Overview. 2001. Microsoft Corporation. Available at http://www.gotdotnet.com/team/framework/DotNet%20Framework%20Technical%20Overview%20v3.doc.

PASTORE, MICHAEL. 2001. Global Internet population moves away from US. CyberAtlas (11 January 2001): http://cyberatlas.internet.com/big_picture/geographics/article/0,1323,5911_558061,00.html.

The global business: Just a point and click away? 2001. *International Business Advisor* (23 May): https://secure.advisor.com/Articles.nsf/aid/SMITT242.

VAWTER, C., and E. ROMAN. 2001. J2EE vs. Microsoft .NET: A comparison of building XML-based Web services. TheServerSide.com (June 2001): http://www.theserverside.com/resources/article.jsp?l=J2EE-vs-DOTNET.

GLOSSARY

2.5G networks Interim networks before 3G (third generation) networks are available

3G networks Third generation wireless networks that offer broadband transmission with speeds of up to 2 Mbps, allowing high-speed wireless access to the Internet

A

access points Entry points into a switched network

ACID properties Four properties (atomicity, consistency, isolation, and durability) that are required for "well-behaved" transactions

activating element HTML element where the action will be triggered

active documents A document that performs functions (in contrast to static HTML files)

Active Server Pages (ASP) A scripting language developed by Microsoft

active unauthorized access Involves modifying the system or data being hacked

address resolution Process by which a computer requests the address of another computer from the DNS server

addressing Function of a network protocol that determines the addresses of computers on the network

Advanced Encryption Standard (AES) A newer, stronger encryption standard proposed by the National Institute for Standards and Technology (NIST) supporting 128-, 192-, and 256-bit keys

Advanced Peer-to-Peer Networking (APPN) Network protocol that allows computers to communicate together

AMPS (Advanced Mobile Phone Service) First cellular technology standard that used analog signals

analog circuits (voice-grade circuits) Regular phone (voice) types of lines

animated gifs Images that move

anonymous FTP FTP environment where files are loaded on public sites

ANSI ASC X12 standard North American standard for EDI transactions

applets Java programs in executable form

application server Server where applications used by the organization are stored for access by various clients or other servers

application-level firewall Requires users to log into the firewall before they can access applications inside the organization (from outside)

applications layer A layer of an e-business architecture that describes the operating environment for application software

Archie A search index for locating files available on public FTP servers

ASCII A standard that is a plain text file format

asymmetric digital subscriber lines (ADSL) DSL network where upload and download speeds are different

asymmetric encryption Uses two keys: a public key for encrypting and a private key for decrypting

asymmetrical When downloading and uploading speeds are different

ATM A packet-switched network that supports various speeds that a company can negotiate

atomicity Property of a transaction that states that if a transaction does not occur in its entirety, it should not occur at all

audit logs Software programs that can scan for unexpected actions to detect potential hackers

authentication Process by which the identity of a transacting party is verified

automatic teller machines (ATMs) Special purpose terminals that provide twenty-four–hour banking services to consumers

available bit rate ATM rate where the provider guarantees a minimum capacity and will support bursts when it has available capacity to do so

B

backbone Underlying network for communication between user sites

back-end technologies Technologies that provide the support for business processes and which consumers are not in direct interaction with

back-office Systems and operations that exist behind the scene and are not typically interacted with directly by customers or other trading partners

banner ad An advertisement, typically rectangular in shape, placed at the top, bottom, or sides of a Web site

bar code readers Devices used to read bar codes on products

basic rate ISDN (ISDN-BRI) ISDN that offers two channels at 64 Kbps (called B channels) and one 16 Kbps channel (called the D channel) for control information

behavioral-based protection tools Antivirus software that look for suspicious behaviors in programs

biometrics Technologies that use human features to recognize individuals and grant them access

BISDN or broadband ISDN Allows multiple channels of communication on the one medium at varying speeds (instead of at fixed speeds like 64 Kbps)

bitmap image A representation of an image consisting of rows and columns of "dots"

Bluetooth Standard for wireless communications between computers, cell phones, printers, scanners, and other devices

boot sector virus A virus that is loaded on a floppy disk and gets into the computer when the disk is loaded

bootstrap protocol (bootp) Protocol that assigns IP addresses dynamically

buffer Additional space kept in main memory to hold data and programs temporarily

bulletin boards *See* electronic boards

business model How a company generates revenue; includes descriptions of the basic architecture of the business, the potential benefits to the entities involved, and sources of revenues

C

cable modems Technology that allows individuals to connect to the Internet using cable television connections

call-back modems Modems that are programmed so that, when a user with proper authorization dials into the computer system, the modem will hang up after authorization verification and call the user back at a predetermined phone number

capacity planning Process by which the memory and processing capabilities required to run the e-business are estimated

cartridge A backup system that makes use of magnetic tapes

cascading style sheets (CSS) Multiple style sheets in the same document that build on each other

CD burners Devices used to engrave data on CD-ROMs or optical disks

CDMA (code division multiple access) A cellular communication standard

CD-ROMs Compact disk read-only memory that can store a large number of files

certificate authority (CA) A trusted third-party organization, usually a commercial enterprise, that guarantees the identity of the persons or organizations involved in online transactions

certificate chain When certificate authorities authorize other CAs to sign certificates

certificate revocation list Contains the certificates that were revoked

certifying authority certificates Certificates for certifying authorities

channel conflict When two or more channels for an organization's products or services destructively compete with one another

chat facility Similar to Internet Relay Chats

ciphers Algorithms used to encrypt and decrypt the plaintext

ciphertext Unreadable encrypted message

circuit An end-to-end connection between two computers

circuit-switched A network in which circuits are established and all packets of a message follow the same circuit to destination

class library Java library of objects already written

classes Compiled Java programs

clickstream Data that tracks user surfing habits online

client A process that requests services from server processes

client/server architecture A computer architecture in which processes are divided into two tiers; client processes are responsible for presentation (including the user interface) and making requests from server processes, which respond to those requests

codec Abbreviation of compressor/decompressor; technology used to compress and decompress multimedia files

color depth A measure of color quality; color depth is usually expressed in bits, such as 8-bit or 16-bit

column The smallest named unit of data in a table; also called a field

comma-delimited format Data file in which separate data fields are separated by commas

committed information rate (CIR) Frame relay rate that provides a guaranteed speed provided on the circuit

Common Management Interface Protocol (CMIP) An international standard for network management

Common Messaging Calls (CMC) Standard for interconnectivity of mail packages, similar to X.400, but simpler

communication server Handles all communication-specific tasks for the internal network

compatibility The degree to which the use of an innovation fits with existing values, beliefs, experiences, and needs

compiler Takes the program written in text and turns it into machine code

complexity The degree to which an innovation is perceived to be relatively difficult to use and understand

Compressed Serial Line Internet Protocol (CSLIP) Communication protocol used to establish a remote connection

consistency Property of a transaction that states that if a transaction starts with the database in a consistent state, the database should be in a consistent state at the end of the transaction; if the transaction fails, the database should be returned to the starting state

constant bit rate ATM rate where the provider guarantees a transmission rate and makes sure that users do not exceed that rate

container tags Tags that surround content

converter Program that takes existing documents and converts them into HTML

cookies Text file that is stored on the user's (Web surfer's) hard disk

corrective controls Used to correct a security issue or problem

crash protection software Performs crash stalling, which fixes a problem or closes all applications properly when an application signals that it is about to crash to the operating system

cryptography The study of creating and using encryption and decryption techniques

customer relationship management Tools (including methods, software, and hardware) that help organizations manage relationships with their customers in an organized manner

cybercash Another term for electronic cash

D

D-AMPS (digital AMPS) A cellular communication standard

data bursts Peaks of network traffic that occur at certain points in time, which are above the regular rate of traffic agreed to and/or generated by the user

data cleansing Process of improving the quality of operational data by removing errors and inconsistencies; cleansing is performed before loading data into a data warehouse

data compression Reduces the total number of bits used to represent a set of data items using a compression algorithm

data compression algorithms Used to reduce the amount of data being transmitted by compressing them

data integrity When the data in the database are consistent, accurate, and valid

data migration Taking data from source systems and loading them into the data warehouse

data mining Process of extracting previously unknown information, typically in the form of patterns and associations, from large databases

data warehouse A subject-oriented, time-variant, integrated set of databases organized to support decision making

data warehousing The process of extracting organizational value from information resources through the use of data warehouses

data Facts that exist in the user environment

database management system (DBMS) Software that is used to create, maintain, and utilize databases

database server Server on which a database is installed to store customer and business information

database Organized collection of logically related data that is used by the systems of an organization

decryption key Key used to convert the unreadable text into its original form

dedicated circuit networks Network that provides permanent connections between two locations

deep link A hypertext link to a Web page other than the site's home page

default-deny static firewall Lets only allowed traffic through and refuses, by default, all other traffic requests into and out of the organization

default-permit static firewall Allows all traffic through except traffic that is explicitly marked to be blocked by the network administrator

denial of service Threats that render a system inoperative or limit its capability to operate

DES (Data Encryption Standard) A well-known symmetric encryption technique created by IBM Corporation

desktop teleconferencing Application on a personal computer that allows individuals at several remote locations to use a software package to connect to each other and communicate in real-time

detective controls Controls meant to find or discover security threats or problems

dial-up connection Connections for which users use a phone line and a modem with communication software to connect to the Internet

digital camera Also called Web camera; allows a site to send a video image of people, events, or things in real-time

digital cash Another term for electronic cash

digital certificate An electronic document that verifies the sender's or receiver's identity

digital government *See* electronic government

digital signature A unique code attached to an electronically transmitted message that identifies the sender

digital subscriber lines (DSL) Telecommunication network that uses existing twisted-pair cables that are wired to most people's homes for high-speed digital links

digital wallet software that encrypts payment information and stores it in a file

digitized when voice signals are converted to digital signals

disaster recovery Procedures and tools to recover systems affected by disasters and destruction

discussion groups *See* electronic boards

disintermediation Process of eliminating intermediaries ("middlemen") from the supply chain

display attributes Tags that indicate how the text is to be displayed

disposable credit card numbers A credit card number that is generated for a single transaction and becomes invalid after that transaction

distributed computing A computing architecture in which computing tasks are spread across multiple computers

distributed denial of service attacks (DDOS) When a number of computers are used for the attacks (the attacks are distributed among many "innocent" servers)

DNS servers Translate Internet addresses from names to numbers

Document Object Model (DOM) Structure that gives object properties to a document loaded in the browser

Document Type Definitions (DTDs) External definition of the document structure, including information about the data or content of the Web pages

downstream communication Communication from the provider to the user's home

dual processor A server that has two processors

dual signature In the SET protocol, this requires a signature for the information sent to the merchant (order information) and the information sent to the bank (payment information)

durability Property of a transaction that states that changes made to the database resulting from a completed transaction should persist, even if later hardware or software failures occur

dynamic firewall Manages the requests as they occur, deciding on both denials and permissions as they arrive

Dynamic Host Control Protocol (DHCP) Protocol that assigns IP addresses dynamically

Dynamic HTML (DHTML) Markup language that makes use of HTML, together with JavaScript and style sheets, to add dynamism to HTML pages

E

E/T/L process Process of *extracting* data from operational databases, *transforming* those data into a form suitable for decision support, and *loading* those data into a data warehouse

e-business architecture A blueprint that helps guide organizations in the delivery of applications and data related to e-business

e-carriers A dedicated digital circuit line available in Europe

EDIFACT European standard for EDI transactions

electronic boards Location where newsgroup users read and post messages; also called bulletin boards or discussion groups

electronic business (e-business) The use of electronic communications networks to allow organizations to send and receive information; the term e-business is often used interchangeably with e-commerce, however, it is generally accepted that e-business is more encompassing in that it includes communications internal to an organization

electronic business XML (ebXML) XML standard for global e-commerce computer-to-computer information exchange

electronic cash (e-cash) Method of payment in which a unique number or identifier is associated with a given amount of money

electronic check (e-check) Similar to a paper check, except that it is electronic, or online

electronic commerce (e-commerce) Any form of economic activity conducted via electronic connections; typically, e-commerce refers to interactions between an organization and its trading partners

Electronic Data Interchange (EDI) Direct computer-to-computer exchange of information between companies using a standard format

electronic government (e-government) The use of network-enabled technologies by governments; also known as digital government

electronic learning (e-learning) Education and training that occurs at a distance through the use of electronic networks

electronic payment methods Methods of payment that make use of digital tools and can be used for online purchasing

electronic wallet (e-wallet) See digital wallet

e-mail bombing A spamming attack that uses e-mail messages

embedded style sheets Style sheets defined in the beginning section of an HTML document

empty tags Tags that do not surround any content

encryption key Key used to make the data unreadable

encryption Application of a mathematical algorithm to a message or information that scrambles that message or information to make it unreadable

entrapment server Software and network equipment used to attract hackers to a secure lockbox, instead of letting them connect into the actual corporate network; also called a honeypot

ethernet A popular Local Area Network (LAN) architecture

event Action taken by a user (mouse movement or keyboard use) recognized by the JavaScript software

Extensible Markup Language (XML) New markup language that provides a way to structure documents, and also give meanings to the elements that are in the document

Extensible Style Sheet (XSL) XML-based language that details how XML documents will be formatted

extranets Use of Internet technologies to create networks that connect trading partners

F

fat client Computing approach where the client handles most of the application logic

fault-tolerant systems Systems that have duplicated processors and peripherals to ensure that any breakdown will not stop operations

field The smallest named unit of data in a table; also called a column

file server Central location where information is stored and accessed by multiple clients

File Transfer Protocol (FTP) Allows users to move files back and forth between nodes on the network

firewall A computer or router that controls access into and out of the internal computer network of an organization by controlling access to its resources and systems

foreign key One or more columns in a table that match the primary keys of related tables

frame rate The number of frames per second a video file displays; the standard frame rate for movies is about twenty-four frames per second

frame relay A second-generation packet-switched network

frame size The amount of screen space (in pixels) that the video takes up; sometimes called window size

FTP server Server that provides file transfer services

G

gateway services Perform connections from inside the organization to the outside world

gateway Computer that isolates a local area network from the rest of its networking environment

gopher A tool for browsing through Internet resources via a menu-based interface

graphical user interface (GUI) A method of interacting with a system by which the user chooses pictorial representations of desired actions rather than typing commands

groupware Computer-based technology designed to facilitate the work of groups. Common groupware functions include discussion databases, shared calendars, and chat systems

GSM (global system for mobile communication) a cellular communication standard

gulf of evaluation A mismatch between what the system represents and what the user expects

gulf of execution A mismatch between the intentions of the user and the actions that are allowed by the system

H

HDSL (high rate DSL) a high speed DSL network

heterogeneous system Systems that involve hardware and software from various vendors, typically running on multiple operating systems

HomeRF A wireless network that uses an unregulated radio frequency for data transmission

honeypot See entrapment server

hopping frequencies Frequencies of communication (in Hertz) on a Bluetooth network

HTML assistant A program that translates a user's application file into an HTML file

HTML editor Applications used specifically for writing HTML documents

HTTP server Server that provides Web hosting services

hub Box containing a high-speed medium that allows all the computers connected to it to communicate together

hyperlinks Links in HTML files that allow users to move to other documents directly

HyperText Markup Language (HTML) Main markup language used to develop Web pages

Hypertext Transport Protocol (HTTP) Protocol that governs the interaction between browsers and Web servers

hypertext A presentation format that allows users to view some information and to expand the information when needed by clicking on words that are identified as hyperlinks to other documents

I

image Synonym for graphics

i-mode Wireless protocol being used in the Japanese and European markets

incremental backups Contain only changed information since the last full backup

information layer A layer of an e-business' architecture that includes components that guide the creation, distribution, and access of data

information Data that have been processed in some meaningful way

infrared A wireless transmission technology

infrastructure layer The hardware, networks, and operating systems that compose the e-business infrastructure

inheritance Subclasses inherit all of the properties and methods included in the classes above them

inline style Style attribute placed within the tag itself in the body of the document

intellectual property rights Rights associated with creative works, including copyrights, patents, and trademarks

intelligent smart cards Smart cards that contain not only storage capabilities, but also microprocessors that can be used for processing information and making programmed decisions

internal firewall Firewall used inside an organization, between departments or divisions

Internet Engineering Task Force Organization responsible for discussing operational and technical problems and standards for the Internet

Internet Mail Access Protocol (IMAP) Standard similar to POP, which also allows users to leave their mail messages on the server after having read them instead of having all of them transferred to the client computer

Internet phones Phones used for Internet telephony applications

Internet protocol (IP) address Address for computers on the Internet composed of four numbers separated by periods, such as 128.173.171.37

Internet Relay Chat (IRC) Multi-user chat application that allows individuals to communicate synchronously using the Internet as the communication backbone

Internet service provider Organization that provides access to the Internet to consumers

Internet Society (ISOC) Organization that attempts to establish standards for the Internet

Internet telephony See Voice over IP (VoIP)

Internet A global network of networks utilizing the TCP/IP protocol

Internet2 Consortium of over 170 universities that, in conjunction with business and government partners, are working on the development of a higher speed network

Internetwork Packet Exchange/Sequenced Packet Exchange (IPX/SPX) Network protocol developed by Xerox corporation

interoperability Ability of systems running in different operating environments to communicate and work together

interpreted language Language in which programs are compiled when they are run

interpreter Interprets machine code

intranet A network that utilized Internet and Web protocols, but is located inside the organization and is intended for use exclusively by organizational members

intranets Use of Internet technology for internal networks, often protected by a firewall

IPv6 (version 6) Addressing scheme that expands the IP address size from the current 32 bits to 128 bits

IrDA (Infrared Data Association) An organization devoted to wireless infrared data transmissions

ISDN (integrated services digital network) An all-digital network that uses twisted-pair copper cables wired to the homes of consumers and to businesses

isolation Property of a transaction that states that changes to the database from a transaction should be hidden from all other transactions until the transaction is complete

J

Java binary file Program that the browser can run locally

Java An object-oriented programming language

Javac Java compiler

JavaScript Scripting language developed by Netscape to add dynamism to Web (HTML) pages

K

Kerberos Encryption protocol designed to work on client/server networks, and provide authentication of identity of users or servers, in addition to encryption

key pair Combination of generated private and public keys

kiosks Special purpose terminals connected directly to an application

L

legacy system Information system based on older technologies

linked style sheets Separate file containing the style sheet linked into the HTML document using a LINK tag

listservs Mailing lists used by individuals with similar interests to share information and create discussion groups

load balancing Balancing the computing loads between various servers

local area network (LAN) Provides direct connections between personal computers, and sometimes hosts, in a limited geographic area (usually less than five kilometers)

local loop Telecommunication sub-network for individuals residing close together

local multipoint distribution services (LMDS) A wireless transmission technology

logical schema A structure used to show the tables that make up a database, the columns included in each table, and the relationships among the tables

loop statements Statements written for actions that are performed until a given condition is met

lossless compression Compression technology that does not result in degradation of the quality of the original multimedia file

lossy compression Compression technology that results in degradation of the quality of the original multimedia file

M

macro virus Affects macro applications (such as those found in word processors and spreadsheets) when the macros are executed

magnetic cards Cards on which data are magnetically stored on the strips usually found on the back of the cards

magnetic tapes A plastic ribbon covered with a metal oxide coating used to store the data

magneto-optical drives Storage devices that use lasers and reflected light to sense data values

mail server Dedicated to handling all electronic mail for the organization

main memory Another term for RAM

mainframes Larger computers offering the capability to run multiple applications and support information processing for multiple users, but in even greater numbers

markup language Language used to add information to the text to format and structure it, and describe how it is to be used

masquerading Another term for spoofing or pretending to be someone else

maximum allowable rate (MAR) Frame relay rate that provides the maximum speed that the network can try to provide if it has the available capacity

memory smart cards Smart cards used mainly to store information with few processing capabilities

message stream modification When the intent of the communication is changed

metadata Data that defines or describes other data

metafile A set of commands that can be used to display an image or other form of multimedia

metaphor The use of a familiar context to facilitate a user's understanding when interacting with a system; a common example is the desktop metaphor used by the Windows and Macintosh operating systems

methods An element in a Java program where behaviors are programmed

microcomputers Typically single-user computers

micropayments Very small payments

middleware Software that allows otherwise incompatible software to operate together

minicomputers Multiple-user computers that can run multiple applications simultaneously

mirroring When some of the drives are used to store files, while the other drives are used as backup

mobile commerce (m-commerce) Concept that users can conduct business transactions wherever they are using a wireless network

MPEG-4 An international standard for network-enabled digital video

multicast Transmission of a single message to a group of recipients

multicasting Allows multiple computers with the same multicast address to receive the same message sent to that one address.

multiplexing Capability of including several communication channels on one medium

Multi-purpose Internet Mail Extensions (MIME) Set of specifications for sending attachments with e-mail messages

multitasking When an operating system can keep two or more programs running at the same time

N

narrowband ISDN Another term for basic and primary rate ISDN

network address translation When a proxy server translates an external address into the proper internal address and then forwards the message to that address

network computer Toned down computer that has no directly attached secondary storage capacity

Network File Service (NFS) Provides built-in functions to support file server services in UNIX systems

network interface card (NIC) LAN card installed in the computer to allow it to be connected to the LAN

network management Set of functions performed to manage telecommunication networks

network operating systems (NOS) Fairly complex program that can be used to manage internal resources (like a server operating system), as well as the resources on a local area network

network printers Printers connected on a network and available to all users on the network

network protocol Rules used by clients and servers to communicate on the vast Internet network

newsgroups Applications that allow users to read and post messages to various electronic boards on the Internet

nodes Computer systems that make up a network

normal forms Rules that govern the structure of tables in a relational database

n-tier architecture A computer architecture based on more than three tiers

O

object programming Programming methods that make use of objects, which can contain both data and behaviors

object An entity that is used in object programming and that can contain both data and behaviors

offline strip Magnetic cards that store information on the strips but also allow this information to be interpreted and modified by the systems that access it

online strip Magnetic card where information to be accessed by a particular system is stored on the magnetic strip

open source When source code of Linux is available to everyone

operating system Manages the internal resources of a computer system

optical carrier (OC) Speed ratings for SONET networks

optical disk Device similar to the CD-ROM, but programmable

opt-in Feature that requires businesses to ask consumers before collecting information about them

opt-out Feature allowing consumers to indicate their desire not to receive "affiliated or other partner company" offers for products and services

P

packet assembly and disassembly A VAN service where data packets (chunks of data transmitted) are assembled or disassembled to be sent over certain network types

packetized When voice signals are split down into packets

packet-level firewall Also called a network-level firewall; controls access by looking at the source and destination addresses in data packets

packets Small units of data that flow through networks, allowing for the transmission of messages

packet-switched network A network where messages are broken down into packets, which are sent over the network to a final destination, but may not follow the same route

paging systems A wireless transmission technology

parasitic virus Attaches itself to files and replicates itself when the files have been loaded

parked devices Inactive devices on a Bluetooth network

passive unauthorized access No action is taken but the hacker eavesdrops on transmissions communicating password information

passphrase Sentence entered by the user when she first creates a key

PDC (personal digital communication) A cellular communication standard

peer-to-peer (P2P) Networking that allows users to locate and download files residing on other users' computers rather than on a traditional server

peripherals Auxiliary equipment that connects to a computer

Perl/CGI Server-side programming language used often for forms processing on Web sites

personal area network (PAN) Wireless network connecting a computer to its peripheral devices or other computers

personal certificate Certificate that allows users to prove their identity

personal communication services (PCS) Name to represent digital cellular networks

personal digital assistants (PDAs) Electronic agendas that also allow users to send e-mail or access the Web through wireless connections

personal firewall Firewall installed on a personal computer

person-to-person payments Payments when two consumers transact directly with one another

person-to-person trading E-business model where consumers transact with other consumers directly

physical access controls Ways to control physical access to systems and data

piconet Basic Bluetooth network structure formed by a master device and one or more slave devices

pixels Known as picture elements, represent single points on an image or display

plaintext Readable message in its original form

platform independent Can run on different types of computing environments

plug-ins Software components that can be added to existing application software

point of presence (POP) An access point into a network

point-of-sale devices Computers specially designed to operate at the place where sales are recorded

point-to-point connection Direct connection from one point to the other, where no intermediary nodes or lines are connected in between

point-to-point protocol (PPP) Communication protocol used to establish a remote connection

polymorphic virus Changes itself every time it infects a computer, making it more difficult to detect

portability (platform independence) Can run on different types of computing environments

post office protocol (POP) Standard that allows users to prepare their mail ahead of time, reply to mail, and connect only for the time it takes to upload and download incoming and outgoing mail

preventive controls Controls intended to stop or limit the security breach/problem from happening

primary key One or more columns used to uniquely identify a particular record in table

primary rate interface ISDN (ISDN-PRI) ISDN that provides twenty-four to thirty channels at 64 Kbps each (resulting in speeds of up to 1.544 Mbps or 2.048 Mbps)

print server Print server services allow multiple users access to high-end printers

privacy policy or statement Statement that discusses the privacy policy of the Web merchant regarding the data collected and their subsequent use

privacy Confidentiality of the data collected by businesses or governments about the individuals using their services

program File written with a programming language by a programmer

programming language Tool is used to write programs or applets that perform functions over and above formatting and displaying text

protocol conversion A VAN service where transmissions can be converted from one protocol to another

protocol Set of rules that govern communication; common examples include TCP/IP and the hypertext transfer protocol (http)

proxy server Application-level firewall where transmissions from the outside world are sent to the proxy server, not the internal network, and all communications with the internal network are handled from the proxy server

push technology Technologies that allow a merchant to send information to subscribers instead of waiting for them to request information from their Web site

R

RADSL (rate adaptive DSL) A DSL network with flexible rate structures

RAID (Redundant Arrays of Independent Disks) A technology that provides access to multiple hard drives simultaneously, allowing the controller to store parts of files on each of the drives

RAM (random access memory) Internal memory that allows a system to run multiple applications at the same time

raster image A representation of an image consisting of rows and columns of "dots"; also known as bitmap image

record Collection of one or more fields that refer to the same occurrence of an entity included in a database

referential integrity A constraint in relational databases that states that a foreign key value must match the value of a primary key in a related table or be null

relational database A database made up of one or more logically related tables (also called relations); these tables consist of rows and columns of data

relative advantage The degree to which an innovation is perceived to be better than its predecessor

remote logins Allows users to connect to other computers on the Internet from their local system

remote server Server system located in a remote location from the user or system

reusability Ability of software code to be re-used in other programs

rich text format (RTF) A standard used to specify the formatting of text files

root CAs Certifying authorities' certificates preinstalled in software

root server system Higher level DNS server systems allowing computers to find addresses on systems outside of their domain so that the Internet can operate properly

routers Systems that interconnect networks together

routines Chunks of codes that perform specific functions

routing Function that determines the best route for the information to get to the intended receiving computer

runtime environment Environment that is used to run Java programs

S

Safe Harbor Privacy Principles A set of seven principles designed to streamline ways for organizations (particularly U.S.-based) to comply with the European Commission's Directive on data privacy

safeguard assurances Global term to represent both privacy and security concerns

scalability The increase or decrease of a company's speed requirements as needed

scanner Device used to input images and text from a paper format to an electronic format

scatternet Two overlapping Bluetooth piconets

scratch card Cards worth a prepaid amount of money that a customer can access after scratching off a protective film covering a personal identification number (PIN)

scripting languages Languages used to add functionality and interactivity to electronic business Web pages, but which are interpreted directly by browsers and therefore do not need separate compilers

scripts Programs written using scripting languages

Secure Electronic Transaction (SET) Security protocol that provides secure data transmissions specifically for electronic payments, via encryption and authentication

Secure Sockets Layer (SSL) Security protocol that provides server-side encryption and authentication for electronic payments (and other types of Internet communications)

security threat "Circumstance, condition, or event with the potential to cause economic hardship to data or network resources in the form of destruction, disclosure, modification of data, denial of service, and/or fraud, waste, and abuse"

security Protection against security threats

server clustering Process by which server farms are put together

server failover Transferring load from one server to another server in case of a failure

server farms Concept of tying together servers to distribute software loads and better manage server failures

server A process that responds to requests from client processes or other server processes in a multi-tier architecture

server-side scripting Programs written so that actions are taken on the server instead of by the browser on the client

servlets Programs written in Java that run on the servers

set–top boxes Connection box used to provide Internet access using a television and the services of an Internet service provider (ISP)

Simple Mail Transfer Protocol (SMTP) The Internet mail standard

Simple Network Management Protocol (SNMP) The Internet network management protocol

site certificates Certificates that serve as verification of a Web server's identity

skin Customization of the user interface of software; commonly used for media player software and games

smart card Cards that encode and store data using a computer chip included on the card itself

smart phones Combine a cellular telephone, a PDA, and access to the Internet

smart-card hybrid Cards that use magnetic strips combined with smart card technology

SMTP server Server that provides an Internet mail server

smurfing When a hacker uses an innocent third party to multiply the messages being sent to the intended target

sniffer Software that monitors transmissions, capturing unauthorized data of interest

socket Combination of IP address and port number (e.g. 128.173.175.49:80)

software publisher certificates Certificates generated by software publishers for their software products

SONET (synchronous optical network High-speed digital wide area network that uses fiber optic lines

spamming Sending emails to many individuals at once; sending unsolicited commercial email to individuals; or targeting one individual computer or network and sending thousands of messages to it

speed translating A VAN service where differences in speed between a merchant and their trading partner are properly adjusted

spoofing Sending a message that appears to be from someone else

spread spectrum radio A wireless transmission technology

Standard Generalized Markup Language (SGML) Complex and comprehensive markup language from which HTML and XML are derived

static firewall Has predetermined ways of dealing with transmission requests

stealth virus More advanced virus that changes its own bit pattern to become undetectable by virus scanners

store-and-forward messaging A VAN service where messages are kept on the server until downloaded by the user

storyboards Paper-based layouts that show what the various pages of a Web site are, what their content is, and how they are related

streaming ad Online advertisements that utilize streaming media

streaming audio Protocol that allows the real-time download of audio signals on the Internet

streaming media Network-delivered digital media (video or sound) that begins playing before the entire file is transmitted

structured programming Programming methods where programs are broken up in chunks of code called routines that are called from other routines or subroutines

Structured Query Language (SQL) A standard language used to create, maintain, and retrieve data in relational databases

style sheets Define the display properties of the Web pages

subnet mask Indicates computers that are part of the same subnet

subnets Smaller networks that, when connected, make up an organization's network

supercomputers Tend to be used to compute large numbers of mathematical compilations as quickly as possible

supply chain management Management of the processes and relationships involved in transforming raw materials or products into the delivery of finished goods to the customer

switched networks Networks that allow the company to send data back and forth between multiple locations without the need to establish direct connections between those locations

switching equipment Equipment that allows an e-business to build its own telecommunications network

symmetric (secret key) encryption Only one key is used for both encrypting and decrypting data

Synchronous Digital Hierarchy (SDH) International version of SONET

systems development life cycle Structured series of phases used in developing information systems

Systems Network Architecture (SNA) Network protocol developed by IBM

T

table A data structure consisting of rows and columns of data; each row of data represents a record that is made up of logically related columns of data

tag An HTML code

target element Resulting HTML element after an action

T-carriers A dedicated digital circuit line available in North America; also called digital service lines

TDCC A lesser-known standard for EDI transactions

TDMA (time division multiple access) A cellular communication standard

telecommuting The use of telecommunication technologies to work outside traditional work locations

teleconferencing Application that allows individuals at several remote locations to use a software package to connect to each other and communicate in real-time

text messaging Phone technology that allows users to receive and read written messages

thin client Computing approach where the servers handle most of the application logic

thin servers Pre-configured network "appliances" dedicated to a single network function

three-tier architecture A computer architecture where processes are divided into three tiers: client, business logic (i.e., application), and database

Token-Ring A popular Local Area Network (LAN) architecture

transaction terminals Computers designed for special purposes

transaction A set of operations associated with some event (such as an order); these operations must either all complete or none of them should complete

Transmission Control Protocol/Internet Protocol (TCP/IP) A network protocol originally developed by the military as a data communications standard and upon which the Internet is based; TCP/IP is available for most operating systems

triangulation Cross-referencing real offline consumer data with online purchasing habits (collected with or without their knowledge)

triple encryption Three levels of encryption, with three private keys, are performed

Trojan horses Viruses spread by being disguised as legitimate software and tricking users into running the program

trust seals A logo of a company or organization that Web merchants can affix on their Web sites if they follow certain rules. They are supposed to instill consumer confidence in the Web site

U

ubiquitous commerce The application of ubiquitous computing technologies and concepts to commerce

ubiquitous computing The concept that computers will become so pervasive in everyday life that most interactions with computers will take place without any notice by the user

unauthorized access Threats where individuals access systems and/or data illegally

Uniform Resource Locators (URLs) Addresses on the Internet used by the protocols to locate the resources

uninterrupted power supply (UPS) Provides electricity when the main power supply is shut down

unspecified bit rate ATM rate where the provider does not guarantee a specific rate and will transmit all it can within its available capacity

upstream communication Communication from the user's home to the service provider

usability Combination of factors, such as navigation, shopping carts, etc., that, in combination, affect the experience users have with a system

USB (Universal Serial Bus) An interface port available on most modern computers

User Datagram Protocol (UDP) Network protocol used on the Internet

user profile Users are assigned profiles that consist of a user identification, a password, and a set of privileges

V

validators Applications that check HTML code

value added networks Wide area networks provided by common carriers or Internet systems providers that provide not only the underlying wide area network, but also additional services

variable bit rate ATM rate where the provider and the company agree on a normal usage rate and a faster burst rate for unexpected high volume transfers

VBScript Scripting language developed by Microsoft for Internet Explorer

VDSL (very high speed DSL) A very high speed DSL network that uses fiber optic cables

vector image Images that are defined through mathematical statements or commands that define lines and shapes

Veronica Tool to analyze the menus of several Gopher servers and index them

vertical XML vocabularies XML standards developed for given industries

views Images of the actual data in the database that can be restricted to include only certain fields, and they usually do not allow users to modify the actual data

virtual home environment Network where a roaming user will have access to the same services he has at home or in the office

virtual organization A network of organizations or individuals that come together on a temporary basis, but appear to outsiders as a single organization; members of the organization use information technologies to communicate and coordinate their actions

virtual port A port that can be accessed by users on a network, for example to print to a printer located on another station

virtual private network (VPN) Connection over a public network that a company uses for internal purposes

Virtual Reality Modeling Language (VRML) Language to create file format for sharing 3D environments on the Web

virtual store Online store such as Amazon.com

virus check program Can be used to scan diskettes or disks for viruses

virus hoaxes Not viruses, but false virus alerts being sent and resent by individuals

viruses Computer programs designed to perform unwanted events

Voice over IP (VoIP) Allows individuals to have "phone" conversations over the Internet and intranets using the TCP/IP protocol

W

WAIS (Wide Area Information Service) Service that allows users to search databases of text available on the Internet

WAP proxy server Server that accesses the requested Web server and scans the server for WML (Wireless Markup Language) pages

Web master Individual in charge of managing an organization's Web environment

Web server Hardware and software system where an e-business' Web site is hosted

Web3D Consortium Organization overseeing changes to Web 3D environment standards

WebTV A television that can also be used to browse the Internet for a monthly fee

wide area network (WAN) Network of computers that spans a large geographic area

WiFi Wireless Ethernet LAN standard (also known as 802.11b)

WINS A lesser-known standard for EDI transactions

Wireless Application Protocol (WAP) Protocol that allows operators, manufacturers, and application providers to handle the differences between each wireless service provider

wireless LANs Local Area Networks that use wireless networks for transmissions

Wireless Markup Language (WML) Markup language used to create Web pages for micro-browsers

Wireless Transport Layer Security (WTLS) Security protocol built into the WAP protocol

World Wide Web (Web) A hypermedia-based system for browsing the Internet; a system of Internet servers that house specially formatted documents that generally utilize the hypertext markup language; note that although the Web operates over the Internet, the Web and the Internet are *not* the same thing

Worlds Files created with VRML

worms Special viruses that spread using direct Internet connections

X

X.400 Standard for interconnectivity of mail packages

X3D (Extensible 3D) A new language for 3D environments proposed to replace VRML

Z

ZIP disks External or internal storage device that contains 100 or 250 MB of data on a disk

INDEX